The Source Book for Higher Education

THE SOURCE BOOK FOR HIGHER EDUCATION

A Critical Guide to Literature and Information
on Access to Higher Education

by Warren W. Willingham

in association with Elsie P. Begle, Richard I. Ferrin,
Judith M. Gray, Katherine Kelemen, and James C. Stam

College Entrance Examination Board · New York · 1973

The College Entrance Examination Board is a nonprofit
membership organization that provides tests and other
educational services for students, schools, and colleges. The
membership is composed of more than 2,000 colleges, schools,
school systems, and education associations. Representatives
of the members serve on committees that consider the Board's
programs and participate in the determination of its policies
and activities.

Copies of this book may be ordered from
Publications Order Office, College Entrance Examination Board,
Box 592, Princeton, New Jersey 08540. The price is $15.

Editorial inquiries concerning this book should be directed to
Editorial Office, College Entrance Examination Board,
888 Seventh Avenue, New York, New York 10019.

Publication of this volume has been made possible by a grant from the Exxon Education Foundation.

Contents

Contents

II. *The System*

III. *The Students*

V. *Sources of Information*

Foreword

THIS book is the last and culminating product of the College Board's Access Research Office that was directed by Warren W. Willingham. It is perhaps the most important work by Willingham and his associates of this period from the standpoint of working practitioners and others needing to orient themselves to literature and information on access to higher education.

Since World War II access to higher education has been a pressing issue of public policy in the United States. Judicial and legislative breakthroughs during the postwar years with respect to the rights of minorities helped accelerate the movement toward widening access to higher education. Now that the lush expansion of the 1950s and 1960s appears to be over, the task of more precisely defining and applying access policies for the 1970s becomes an even more difficult but urgent undertaking.

The formulation of rational public policy requires a conceptualization of the situation and the drawing together of information that is pertinent. This is what this source book has attempted to do, and in Willingham's taxonomy we have for the first time a comprehensive structure for examining the whole access process.

The references and annotations in this volume are not intended to be exhaustive. Rather, they have been selected because they represent basic information relevant to the topic. For this reason, the book should be highly useful for all who are concerned with the question of access to higher education for the next 10 to 15 years. The College Entrance Examination Board is gratified to be able to make *The Source Book for Higher Education* available to its membership and all others concerned with the question of access to higher education. We expect it to be an outstanding contribution to the literature relating to this important subject.

ALBERT G. SIMS
Vice President, Programs
College Entrance Examination Board

Preface

THE broad field of "access to higher education" includes all the factors that influence young people's aspirations for higher education; the social and financial barriers to education; and those aspects of the whole process that determine whether educational opportunity is real and worthwhile. In both theory and fact the process of access to higher education affects virtually all age groups from young adulthood on, all types of college-level education, and all the administrative procedures and planning that govern the entire process and shape its character.

There are several reasons why a guide to the literature on the access process is needed. The first and most obvious is the overriding importance of higher educational access. To the student, the question of access usually involves an important break in his life, and is a primary opportunity for the development of personal aspirations and interests. To the institution, the access process is a principal means of establishing its role and identity. To the broader society, the process is one of the important ways in which individual opportunity is provided and human talent is used. In sum, access to higher education has critical social significance from educational, political, and economic standpoints.

Another consideration leading to the development of this volume comes from the need to understand the access process as an integrated whole, even though in reality it is made up of many parts, often uncoordinated and compartmentalized. Thus Lindquist did an extensive and important study demonstrating little if any practical advantage to adjusting high school grades according to high school origin to aid in the prediction of student performance in college (462). These findings and similar results of other investigators are well-known among measurement specialists but evidently not among admissions officers, who continue to adjust grades of students who come from certain high schools. Similarly, McConnell described the hierarchical system of higher education that has a critical bearing upon access and has been adopted by many states (660). His book is regarded as a classic among educators but is not part of the literature of most researchers working on other aspects of the access question. Many similar examples could be cited. When we refer to such national goals as the effective use of talent or the availability of universal educational opportunity beyond the secondary school, we implicitly treat access as if it were an integrated process. To be sure, there are interdisciplinary efforts, particularly in such relatively new fields as long-range educational planning and computer-assisted guidance. In the main, however, most professionals associated with various aspects of the higher educational access process do not consciously identify it as a separate field. Consequently there is a special need for bibliographic efforts to integrate this interdisciplinary activity.

A third problem is that most people have more to read than they can handle. The proliferation of excessive trivial information is an increasingly serious problem in all disciplines. In this instance the problem is more serious since the access process involves so many different disciplines and professions. Keeping up with the important ideas in one's own field is harrying enough without having to cope with strange journals and unfamiliar reports. Secondary guides to information are almost a necessity if busy professionals are to maintain an informed perspective on fields functionally related to their own. The problem is well stated by Hefferlin and Phillips in their book on information problems in academic administration: "According to the college administrators we have questioned, their first and most common unmet need regarding educational literature is for better information materials—that is, for reference guides to the literature and in particular for abstracts of what is important . . ." (639).

A useful guide to information must select, organize, and describe the most important items from a much larger literature. These are essentially the objectives of this source book; they can be stated a bit more specifically as follows.

A primary objective in the development of this volume was the creation of a conceptual framework to deal with the field of higher educational access. This was done partly in order to clarify the social and educational dynamics of the total process, and also to enable the construction of a broader view of the interrelationships among the various disciplines and professions that play an important role. This objective is largely met by the taxonomy that determines the organization of this book. (Explanation of the taxonomy begins on page 11. The full structure of the taxonomy is shown on pages 12–13 and also on the end papers of this book.) Introductions to the various sections of annotations describe the nature of the work, types of problems and people involved in each area, and also relationships among the major areas.

Articles and other publications relevant to some aspect of access to higher education easily number more than 1,000 a month. Much of this material has limited significance, but the mass camouflages the gems. Critical items appear in a variety of sources including newsletters, special reports, government documents, books, and journals. Under normal circumstances no one person can possibly cope with this literature unless it is his specific job to do so. Thus another objective of this source book is to identify the most critical literature published over the previous decade or so.

A third objective is to provide a secondary reference to sources of information concerning all aspects of access to higher education; this function, then, is not to answer the reader's question, but to direct him to primary sources that might do so. This is accomplished partly by the annotations of literature in sections 1 through 11 and by the subject index. In addition, considerable effort has been directed to describing different types of agents and sources of information that play an important role in the access process. This is done by the annotations in sections 12 through 15, which provide a secondary reference to a wide variety of material and sources that are complementary to the published literature.

Development of This Guide

Some details of the evolution of this guide help to explain its nature. The development of the taxonomy and the selection of items for inclusion took place over a period of three years. The selection process suggested possible changes for the taxonomy, and work on the taxonomy revealed poorly covered areas and the need for additional relevant literature.

In the process of item selection, a large number of journals, newsletters, and specialized bibliographies published during the 1960s were searched, with emphasis given to the last half of the decade. Some 50 specialists reviewed preliminary bibliographies in their fields and made many valuable suggestions for additional items. Items were selected for various reasons. This source book includes influential theories and ideas; important research findings; innovative methods of dealing with problems; and reports of prominent commissions, professional committees, and other groups. It also includes reports of major projects and the bench-mark data they frequently generate; bibliographies and special reviews of literature; and sometimes reports that simply represent the best available discussion of an important problem.

There were a few areas in which it was difficult to find high-quality publications; however, in most areas the items selected represent only a small fraction of the articles, books, and reports published in the past decade or so. Consequently, in most sections of this volume, many additional items could well have been included. Space limitations often allowed the inclusion of no more than a few illustrative publications, particularly standard works with good bibliographies.

In preparing the annotations the main intent was to give the reader an understanding of what each publication is about and why it is important in relation to the access process. The annotations are evaluative in the sense that the publications referred to have been selected from a large group. Specific evaluative comments in the annotations are intended to assist the reader in appreciating the special value or limitations of a publication rather than to offer critical commentary upon its internal consistency or validity. All annotations were written in the voice of the annotator, and every effort consistent with style was made to clarify the attribution of comments to the original author or the annotator. A few items were judged to be of such importance in two or more areas that they were listed more than once. In most cases, however, such situations were handled with cross references.

The annotations in sections 12 and 13 are generally nonevaluative. These annotations simply describe the program or organization, particularly with respect to those activities especially related to the access process. All the annotations in these sections were reviewed by an informed representative of the program or organization concerned.

The material in this source book will not date quickly. Most of the critical literature will be as basic and important five years from now as it is at the time of this writing. Agencies and other sources of information described in sections 12–15 are permanent organizations that do their own updating as necessary. Selected journals, catalogs, and other publications were checked routinely up to the spring of 1971. Some items published later in 1971 were added, but it was not possible to cover that time period systematically. Most incidental information such as addresses, dates of new editions, etc., was brought up-to-date in the spring of 1971. Prices were included for all publications where the information was readily available. The primary reference was *Books in Print, 1970*. There is an inherent ambiguity about the pricing of minor items. Often small pamphlets that appear free are not, and on the other hand sometimes minimal prices are placed on essentially free items in order to control volume requests. These facts should be kept in mind when ordering such items.

WARREN W. WILLINGHAM

Acknowledgments

WHEN this project was started in early 1968, a primary goal was the documentation of the process of "access to higher education" as a complex socioeducational activity that involves the interests and competencies of many disciplines and professions. Such diverse areas as educational administration, phychometrics, guidance, economics, and demography are involved. From the beginning it was clear that the identification of critical literature and sources of information in these fields would require the help of many people. That assumption turned out to be even more true than could have been suspected originally. Literally hundreds of colleagues made valuable contributions to this work either through reviewing material or by suggesting additional useful information for inclusion. It is a pleasure to express appreciation for that help.

Some 200 representatives of various agencies and organizations took the time to review listings, and many made valuable corrections and additions. A number of people were kind enough to review portions of this work at various times during its development, particularly with respect to what items should be included. Their critical attention was invaluable in providing the sound judgment that only competent professional specialization can provide. These individuals include: Walter Adams, Jack N. Arbolino, Alexander W. Astin, Leonard L. Baird, Stanley L. Bowers, George L. Brandon, Lowell A. Burkett, Albert L. Clary, J. Douglas Conner, K. Patricia Cross, J. A. Davis, Richard A. Dershimer, Douglas D. Dillenbeck, John M. Duggan, Henry S. Dyer, John K. Folger, William Gaul, Edmund J. Gleazer Jr., Lyman A. Glenny, Robert H. Glover, W. Lee Hansen, John R. Hills, John L. Holland, John I. Kirkpatrick, Carole A. Leland, Winton H. Manning, Harvey Marron, S. V. Martorana, Robert T. Merritt, Jack Morse, Leo A. Munday, James E. Nelson, Robert C. Nichols, C. Robert Pace, Ernest G. Palola, Richard Pearson, Richard E. Peterson, Lois D. Rice, Edward Sanders, Alexander G. Sidar Jr., Ann Z. Smith, Robert E. Stoltz, Jose A. Toro, James W. Trent, John R. Valley, William D. Van Dusen, and Marjorie Wheat.

Many useful critical comments and suggestions were received from Joshua A. Fishman, Dorothy M. Knoell, Sam A. McCandless, Lewis B.

Preface Mayhew, and Albert G. Sims. Substantial portions of the manuscript were also reviewed critically by Ben F. Cameron Jr., S. A. Kendrick, B. Alden Thresher, and David V. Tiedeman. The interest and help of these good friends and colleagues were of immense value and greatly appreciated.

Those who are most directly responsible for this volume are the members of the College Board staff who worked in the Access Research Office from 1968 through 1972. They were an unusual group of people who brought unusual talent to the task, plus aggressive pride and singular dedication. Those five listed alphabetically on the title page — Elsie P. Begle, Richard I. Ferrin, Judith M. Gray, Katherine Kelemen, and James C. Stam — made such substantial contributions that they share authorship. Each wrote a large number of annotations and assumed responsibility for important phases of the bibliographic work and information retrieval. In particular James Stam and Richard Ferrin worked on sections 1–11 and 12–15, respectively, in the early part of the project. Later Elsie Begle and Judith Gray worked on those sections. Katherine Kelemen free-lanced in various sections and prepared the initial draft of the subject index. The senior author was responsible for the development of the taxonomy, selection of items for inclusion, the final form of all annotations, and all introductory narrative.

Other staff deserve special mention and expression of gratitude. Donna Kofnovec, Carroll Cotten, and Jan Wezelman wrote some annotations and offered other valuable assistance. Nancy Galvin, Margaret Taylor, and Carol Bain provided secretarial skill at the beginning, middle, and end of the project, and Nancy Lambert offered administrative assistance and coordination throughout this work. Jane Porter is due special recognition for important contributions to all aspects of the bibliographic work and final editing.

All of those connected with this project express their appreciation to the publications staff of the College Board, especially to Agnes Creagh and Marcia Van Meter, who followed the project throughout its life and made valuable suggestions that improved the final volume. We also give warmhearted thanks to the Stanford University library and its staff who provided much help in tracking down information.

W.W.W.

How to Use This Book

EVERY reader has a somewhat different interest in using a book of this sort, but any reader can approach this volume in basically the same manner. The following steps suggest a quick way to familiarize oneself with the contents.

1. Examine fairly carefully the taxonomy that appears on the end papers and on pages 12–13. Look over each section to see what topics are included, and note unusual areas that might not immediately be associated with this field. Note also the overall organization of the framework and how the topics are grouped together. Familiarity with the taxonomy will be a great help in using this source book since the section numbers shown in the taxonomy appear in the side headings of the text pages with corresponding information.

2. Turn to a section of interest (among the first eleven) and read the introduction to that section. It gives a brief indication of the content of the annotations found in the section; describes the scope of the literature, the major problems included, the people and organizations involved, and why

that section is important in relation to the larger concept of the access process.

---

3. Scan some annotations in the section in order to get an impression of how the items are described. Pick a few that are familiar and a few that are not.

---

4. After browsing a bit, pick one or two terms that have special importance in that particular section and find them in the subject index. For example, in section 3 on college admissions you might check "open admissions" or "admission of disadvantaged students." Checking such terms in the subject index will reveal cross references to other sections that contain information relevant to the topic. The subject index is useful not only for locating information on specialized topics; it can also help tie together work from different disciplines.

These four steps should give the general reader a sufficiently clear idea of what this volume contains and how to use it. Readers who have a direct professional interest in the access process may also wish to look at additional sections more carefully. Parts IV and V describe some 400 organizations, programs, and sources of information that play an important role in the access process. These are all dynamic agents. Not only do they influence the access process, they actually are the access process as it operates through the schools and colleges. Familiarity with the role of these various agents can help in understanding the interdisciplinary complexity of the access process.

The overview of the access process which begins on page 1 describes the theoretical rationale for the taxonomy and for the organization of this volume. It will be of interest primarily to those readers who are concerned with the broad question of the role of access to higher education in modern American society, and the particular functions it serves. The discussion is philosophical rather than practical, but it touches on many issues concerning national policy and professional responsibility.

Access to Higher Education
— *An Overview*

FOR many decades transition to college has involved a variety of problems associated with curriculum continuity, selection of applicants, and the procedures whereby students are admitted. After World War II as considerably larger numbers of students began to attend college additional problems gained prominence. As the nation became more concerned with effective utilization of talent, increasing attention was given to procedures that would serve that end. These included the development and expansion of testing programs, guidance services, and programs of student financial aid. Recently the question of access to college has become tangled with social issues such as equality of opportunity, the purposes of higher education, and the relevance of its programs to students and to society.

The nature of these concerns has tended to change progressively from problems associated with institutional administration to problems involving individual students and finally to problems of broad social concern. These additional layers of problems over the years have combined with traditional problems of college admissions to define a more general educational and social process. "Access to higher education" is a convenient phrase for describing this process. It has the semantic value of implying a variety of important problems generally connected with college entrance, but not necessarily included under the term college admissions; a process that involves educational, financial, social, and even political questions. How then is access to higher education to be conceived? What is the relevant literature and how is it organized? What are the major problems? What professions and disciplines are involved in what ways, and to what extent do they coordinate their work?

One purpose of this volume is to develop a conceptual framework that will be useful in considering such questions. We are not concerned here with the philosophical rationale of the present educational system, with how efficiently it operates, or with what effect. The objective is rather to develop a comprehensive view of the access process and to describe the relevant information in an organized manner. This introduction examines the nature of access to higher education by outlining its important characteristics, considering the social functions it performs, and describing a taxonomy that provides the conceptual framework for the remainder of this guide.

Critical Characteristics of the Access Process

Recent Changes. The higher education access process has undergone major change within the past decade. In a recent analysis of these changes (688), the senior author concluded that "extensive federal funding has supported a quantum leap in the rate of college attendance. The civil rights movement and the student rebellion have brought into serious question the academic values that underlie restrictive admissions and discipline-oriented curriculums. Accelerating public expectation now demands that equal opportunity for relevant education beyond high school be a right not a privilege. The assumption of public responsibility in order to meet these public interests is reflected in the rapid development of state planning and coordination. Greatly expanded research and technology are becoming an integral part of the whole process of planning and monitoring access to higher education." Thus, access to higher education has undergone fundamental changes that have transformed the process from a scholastic to a societal issue. The consequences of these changes are far reaching but as yet incompletely described and little understood.

Social Role. Higher education serves many roles in society. Access to higher education is only somewhat more narrowly conceived. It is primarily a social mechanism for the effective development of human resources. Since higher education is closely connected with economic and social opportunity, a very important, though perhaps secondary role of the access process is the distribution of privilege. Obviously, there are other means whereby society accomplishes these objectives. Nonetheless, this view of the access process largely accounts for its mounting importance and public interest. It seems obvious that a college's admissions policies and practices profoundly affect and reflect what that institution is. With less immediate and certain impact, perhaps, but by the same principles, the conditions of access to higher education affect and reflect the conditions and values of the surrounding society.

Institutions Involved. There is in most people's minds a distinction between "college" (or higher education) and other forms of postsecondary or nontraditional schooling beyond high school. When the context suggests a distinction between higher education and other forms of postsecondary education, we take the former to mean that group of recognized universities, four-year colleges, and two-year colleges listed in the United States Office of Education's "Opening Fall Enrollment" (1426). The broader term includes a variety of proprietary institutions, vocational schools, and such nontraditional modes of postsecondary education as military programs, adult education, correspondence courses, etc.

It is important to state, however, that the general concept of access to higher education is not restricted to formal, recognized colleges. A conception of educational opportunity beyond high school that is at all consistent with current social expectations and needs must encompass a fairly catholic view of college-level work regardless of its particular institutional form. Consequently, we have specified institutional form where it seems helpful to do so; otherwise the term "higher education" is used here in generic form and refers to any type of college-level schooling.

Time Factors. The time characteristics of access to higher education are considerably broader than those normally associated with college admissions. First, the access process refers to a period that extends from at least junior high school through the later adult years. Formative attitudes and decisions in those earlier years have an important bearing on the access possibilities that are later considered. Furthermore, the accelerating pace of technological change has led to the widely-held assumption that extensive retraining and adult education will characterize all advanced societies within the next 25 years.

It is partly for this reason that access to higher education cannot be considered a one-time affair. Many students delay college entry after high school; some migrate from one college to another; increasing numbers transfer from junior to senior or undergraduate to graduate institutions; many others drop in and out of school at personal or financial convenience; and most individuals can be expected to enter some form of adult education at some time. It is probably an unusual 18-year-old who cannot expect to seek access to some form of postsecondary education on at least several occasions.

Disparate Interests. It is important to recognize that the dynamics of access to higher education are often different from the standpoints of the individual, the institution, and society. The individual is naturally interested in his own welfare and personal development. The institution must look after its tradition and its continued well-being. Needless to say, the interests of the individual and the institution are not always completely compatible. The

3

report of the Commission on Tests (354) placed special emphasis on the need to achieve a better balance between the interests of the individual and the institution in the admissions process. The report of the Commission on Human Resources and Advanced Education (509) stressed the societal interest in access to higher education and proposed national mechanisms for monitoring certain aspects of the process and protecting the public interest.

Disparate Problems. Access to higher education is not one problem but many very different problems. In addition to the two million first-time students who enter colleges annually, other millions seek access to various forms of postsecondary education under widely varying conditions. These include the very able girl seeking admission to the "right" northeastern college; the Mexican American youth using higher education as an exit from the constraints of the barrio; and the middle-aged professional mastering a new technology. These illustrations involve radically different problems—social, personal, financial, and educational. They illustrate the diverse complexities of the access process, and the fact that any one individual is likely to be sensitive to only a few of the problems involved.

Participants. Access to higher education is an active, constantly changing process that involves programs and organizations by the thousands and professionals by the tens of thousands. There is also a bewildering variety of procedures and processes that sometimes vary for good purpose but often reflect idle confusion. Various publications describe different parts of the process, but they themselves are too diverse and numerous to give an integrated view. All of these "participants"—professions, programs, organizations, procedures, sources of information—interact constantly and affect one another. So, a major problem in understanding access to higher education is to know what participants do what.

Ultimate Relevance. Access implies a great deal more than entrance. If entrance procedures and policies are useful and fair to the individual and to society, then it is shortsighted and improper to think of access as a momentary event unrelated to what follows. The programs to which an individual gains access must have various forms of relevance—personal, social, educational, and economic. Consequently, an adequate theoretical foundation for planning and evaluating the access process must include not only the background of the student and the conditions of entrance, but also the nature of the learning experience and its relation to student aspiration and the objectives of higher education.

The characteristics described in the preceding paragraphs are helpful in conceiving the bounds and general nature of access to higher education, but there is another characteristic that is perhaps even more important, the fact that the access process represents a discontinuity. This particular quality requires special attention.

Access as a Discontinuity

In simplest terms, the word access implies a change from one situation to another. Access to an educational program is a discontinuity because it carries the assumption that the individual will somehow be different—presumably for a substantial period of time if not permanently. That discontinuity requires that the individual accept a commitment, evaluate its implications, and adjust to a new situation. The adjustments may be quite minor, or they may involve a major change of life style. But the critical fact is that access (particularly, successful access) necessarily involves a discontinuity in habitual patterns. There are two types of discontinuities to consider.

As a first instance, the access process bridges a natural discontinuity; it may appear in several guises. From the individual's standpoint, there is a natural discontinuity of major importance between adolescence and adult life. There are also a variety of educational breaks between institutional forms. The most obvious illustration is the movement of a student from school to college—two educational institutions often operating under different forms of governance and enjoying minimal communication. Other educational discontinuities that are becoming increasingly common are progression from two-year to four-year to graduate institutions; transfer among colleges; and credit recognition and articulation among different types of educational institutions.

In a broader context, another natural and repeated discontinuity is that occasioned by successive waves of young people who must be acculturated into existing institutions and social roles. Similarly, the professions must be continuously replenished with new pools of appropriately trained young adults. With these types of natural discontinuity, the main interest is to bridge the gap, maintain continuity, and minimize access shock. To a considerable extent, traditional procedures in guidance and admissions are designed to do just that. They represent a scholastic interpretation of access to higher education.

A second and very different form of access discontinuity is one that is intentionally created in order to alleviate an individual or social need. A good example is the expansion of educational opportunity for the minority/poor; a very different illustration of much smaller magnitude is the retraining of aerospace engineers for work on environmental problems. That is, access to an educational program is designed to create beneficial discontinuities and thereby provide new opportunities or the means to adapt to new conditions.

These purposive discontinuities are especially associated with a societal interpretation of access to higher education. The major examples are almost all relatively recent, and they differ radically from the natural discontinuities described above. But whether discontinuities are natural or created, the central purpose of the access process is to make those discontinuities as socially

5

constructive as possible. Access to higher education is a constructive discontinuity to the extent that it provides the individual with a proper balance of stability and opportunity, maintains institutional tradition and also adaptability, and supports social progress as well as equality.

It is the educational program itself rather than access to higher education that is associated with opportunity, beneficial outcome, etc. Of course, this is true, so why the special significance of the discontinuity? One principal reason is that these discontinuities are moments of choice and commitment. Once an individual makes the decision to enter a program, he tends to be caught up in a natural sequence of events and affiliations and there is a narrowing of acceptable alternatives. Consequently, the conditions of the choice are especially important because those conditions (physical environment, social milieu, character and difficulty of the program, possible economic benefit, other feasible alternatives, etc.) determine the decision and much that follows.

Another reason that access discontinuities are increasingly important is the simple fact that they are increasingly numerous. This is partly due to the much larger proportion of the population affected than was true even a generation ago. An equally important consideration is the fact that young adults are now likely to face multiple access discontinuities throughout adult life.

There is ample indication that society is attaching far more importance to these discontinuities than was previously true. The massive development of the guidance profession since the late 1950s is one sign. Another is the keen public interest in barriers to higher education. There is also the rapid development of statewide coordinating mechanisms that place emphasis on monitoring educational opportunity. Furthermore, many professional groups including psychologists, economists, and sociologists are now especially interested in the dynamics of the access process and how it affects society.

These developments illustrate the diverse character and impact of access to higher education. It is a singularly complex social mechanism for supporting or creating constructive discontinuities. These discontinuities are reflected in several very different functions.

Major Functions of the Access Process

It is by now fashionable to note that higher education is overly blessed with diverse goals and objectives. Of course, these include important goals not especially related to the access process, e.g., community-service functions, the generation of knowledge, and higher education's role as an intellectual resource for the nation. But the access process does serve functions that are critically related to some of the most important objectives of higher education. The process is better understood by a brief examination of those functions.

Table I illustrates 10 major functions of access to higher education. The first 5 functions, listed in the first column, tend to maintain continuity. As indicated earlier, they are especially associated with a traditional scholastic interpretation of access to higher education. The remaining 5 functions, listed in the second column, are more often associated with intentional efforts to create beneficial discontinuity. Such interventions typically stem from attempts to alleviate a specific social problem and therefore reflect a newer, societal purpose and interpretation of the access process.

Table I. Major Functions of Access to Higher Education

Level of Application	Functions That Maintain Continuity	Functions That Create Beneficial Discontinuity
Individual	1. Support career development	6. Provide individual opportunity
	2. Support social roles	7. Provide retraining
Institutional	3. Maintain institutional integrity	8. Diversify programs and institutions
National	4. Transmit culture	9. Release social pressure
	5. Develop professions	10. Channel human resources

1. *Support Career Development.* As already noted, much of the present guidance/admissions structure is intended to help students develop and maintain a commitment to a career goal. With increasing complexity, flexibility, and change in the occupational structure, this form of continuity has become especially difficult to maintain. A common assumption is that computer system will play a central role in clarifying options and identifying next steps in career development. A closely related problem that is more directly concerned with education is the need to maintain curriculum continuity from one program or institutional form to another. This is one of the classic functions of the admissions process that now receives far too little attention.

2. *Support Social Roles.* Access to an educational program provides one means whereby individuals maintain and continue social roles. These include religious commitments, particular life styles, personal interests, and perhaps even family traditions, though the latter seem rapidly diminishing. This is basically a stabilizing function. An important objective is to maintain

flexible access to the special interest programs and institutions that permit and support continuity of diverse social roles and commitments. The private colleges now under financial siege are vitally important in serving this function.

3. *Maintain Institutional Integrity.* One of the principal means whereby an institution can create continuity of role and function is through careful definition and execution of its admissions policy. The principle applies to public as well as private institutions, though in very different ways. The public institution must fulfill its primary responsibilities in the face of political pressure, momentary diversions, and insufficient funds. In ostensibly open-door institutions or systems, there are inevitable decisions regarding what students to serve in what manner with limited resources. These decisions are frequently converted from admissions decisions to more subtle and less obvious administrative decisions. Examples include the choice of programs to be supported and decisions regarding sites for new campuses, both of which can affect access as much as admissions policy does.

The private institution faces a constant dilemma. Compared to the public institution, it is more likely to have a tradition and special function to maintain. But the private college enrolls students only so long as it remains attractive and appears responsive to current interests. The added need to attract a seemingly diminishing group of applicants who have the personal and intellectual characteristics to maintain the institution's role and the financial means to insure its existence makes the problem even more difficult.

4. *Transmit Culture.* Even though colleges are usually no longer expected to serve as surrogate parents, they still carry out a vital socialization process for the most educated and generally most influential element in the nation. Much is written and perhaps now seldom read about the value of a liberal education. The principle remains the same even though the semantics vary or attract less attention. There is an intellectual and social tradition that must be maintained across the discontinuity of successive generations of emerging young adults. As religion and the family reduce in salience, higher education remains one of the few social institutions to carry out this function.

5. *Develop Professions.* Similarly, there is a body of knowledge and tradition that is represented in the various professions. The access process that feeds successive generations into the training programs for these professions serves to maintain national continuity. In recent years, economic factors and public attitudes have created serious problems of supply and demand in certain professions. This has been due in part to fluctuations in national priorities, but also to a poorly developed understanding of manpower aspects of the access process.

6. *Provide Individual Opportunity.* The most dramatic development in college admissions since the influx of World War II veterans has been the de-

velopment of new programs for minority/poverty students. Some are special programs within an institution; others characterize an institution's entire operation. In either case, the conscious objective is to create a beneficial discontinuity for the student—to change his life style or to create new avenues to cultural respect, social mobility, and economic security.

Closely associated with this developing function has been an explosive debate over the extent to which higher institutions should divert their energies to this objective and the extent to which its pursuit endangers other more traditional goals. The debate has gone under the name of "open admissions." This societal objective goes far beyond the traditional function of supporting career development (item 1 above). It often involves basic changes in the style and purpose of an institution.

7. *Provide Retraining.* In recent years it has become recognized that formal continuing education will likely become a fact of adult life. This is partly because of accelerating change in society and the need for individuals to learn new skills throughout their lifetimes. It is also because an educated, affluent society also creates its own continuous demand for intellectual stimulation and retraining. Access to educational programs provides a structured and premeditated discontinuity whereby individuals are able to learn new skills as necessary, utilize their talents continuously, and combat the obsolescence and boredom that paradoxically permeate modern life.

8. *Diversify Programs and Institutions.* As the complement of the third function above, the admissions process is one of the most direct and effective means of altering an institution. In recent years this has been discovered somewhat inadvertently by many colleges. Nonetheless, relatively few institutions have taken bold and imaginative steps in recruiting students who by their very presence can create beneficial discontinuity in the institution. The obvious and frequent exception is the substantial number of colleges that have recruited significant numbers of minority students.

9. *Release Social Pressure.* The entire system of postsecondary education stands as a national resource for mitigating various types of social pressures. When educational opportunity for the individual becomes institutionalized into massive national programs, the purpose is to create a socially beneficial discontinuity. There were minor examples of this prior to World War II, but the GI Bill was the first major manifestation. Educational opportunity programs of the 1960s are, of course, another major effort to alleviate some of the more pressing problems of discrimination and restricted opportunity through large-scale access programs.

10. *Channel Human Resources.* There are various instances in which it is important to redirect national resources. There are needs to develop new technologies, to accomplish specific goals, to change national priorities, or to alleviate economic or manpower problems. Any of these may represent a

fairly substantial national discontinuity. While there are different means of handling such problems, massive channeling of human resources is often an important and even necessary step. Whether the rechanneling occurs among employed persons or younger students, governed access to appropriate educational programs is a principal means of bridging the desired discontinuity.

It is obvious that the country has been fascinated with functions 6 through 10, the societal functions, in recent years, and that higher education has taken giant strides in that direction. It would be a gross oversimplification, however, to imply that this is the only significant shift in the access process or that this shift is uniformly supported and inevitable. There is, for example, also a well-recognized shift of power to students that is in some senses incompatible with the societal functions; and there is a great deal of popular and academic resistance to further development of these societal objectives. Some of this resistance is quite well founded. Whether the current view of access to higher education (as here described) is a reliable indicator of a continuing trend is difficult to say.

Perhaps it is better to ask how much the country is willing to spend for educational objectives that may be effective for equalization of social opportunity but probably are not optimally efficient in national economic terms. How much are voters willing to spend for education as a social investment instead of such reasonable alternatives as the alleviation of urban blight and poverty or the improvement of health care and the environment? There are in fact various signs that emphasis on societal access functions are losing some momentum. It is commonly agreed that higher education does not have the unquestioned support from the general population that it once enjoyed. Young adults show increasing interest in alternatives to college such as public service or other types of training programs.

More serious, however, is the realization that the financial resources to support massive public expenditures in higher education are not limitless. Momentary concerns over inadequate legislative appropriations are constant and in addition the overall picture of economic growth does not lead to unbounded optimism that the economy can support all legitimate and worthy aspirations. Significant social programs cost significant amounts of money that have to come either from increments in national income or from reductions in other expenditures. It is worth noting that some economic indicators give little reason for assuming that larger amounts of new money will soon be available. For example, one important index is spendable income (take-home pay) of workers on nonfarm payrolls. That figure was actually lower in 1971 than in 1965 (*Monthly Labor Review,* March, 1971, p. 105).

But whether or not the country's ideas and actions concerning the process of access to higher education continue to move toward societal values, there have already been such substantial changes that turning back is not at all a feasible possibility. Consequently, a new interdisciplinary field has evolved and continues to do so. The taxonomy described on the following pages suggests the shape of the field and the literature involved.

The Taxonomy for *The Source Book*
for Higher Education

THE discussion in the preceding introduction gives the rationale for the view of access to higher education presented in this volume. It is a broad view because the process is complex and the literature bearing on it is unusually diverse. Up to now we have spoken of characteristics and functions but little of content. The taxonomy presented in the following pages provides a conceptual framework for the content and organization of this source book.

In simplest terms, access to higher education is a set of processes whereby students enter educational programs. At the same time, these programs satisfy the needs of individuals, institutions, and the nation. The general character of this social mechanism is suggested by the critical characteristics and major functions already outlined. Perhaps the main interest in the access process is the extent to which these major functions are accomplished in a manner that is fair, efficient, and effective. When the problem is viewed in this manner a variety of topics that are useful in describing and evaluating access to higher education are suggested. These include:

• The various procedures, programs, and processes that govern the flow of students; these range from early influences on educational aspirations to the evaluation and logical conclusion of the access process. It is important to understand theory as well as practice, the connection between the two, and how various aspects of the access process are related to each other. These subjects are treated in Part I: *Access Processes.*

• The organization and coordination of the educational system and how its programs are planned and evaluated; the means for monitoring access and implementing decisions in the public interest is an especially critical aspect. These subjects are dealt with in Part II: *The System.*

• The special characteristics and needs of students; how students are distributed through the educational system and the barriers they face are central problems. The meaning of equal opportunity and how it affects special groups of students is the major philosophical issue. Part III: *The Students* is concerned with these topics.

• The organizations and programs involved, the professional relationships,

THE TAXONOMY
for *The Source Book for Higher Education*

I. *Access Processes*

1. STUDENT GUIDANCE	2. FINANCING EDUCATION	3. ADMISSIONS
THEORY		
1.1 Career Development	2.1 Economics of Higher Education	3.1 National Policy
1.2 Vocational Interest	2.2 Financing Methods	3.2 Institutional Policy
1.3 The Decision Process		
PRACTICE		
1.4 Guidance Procedures	2.3 Administration of Financial Aid	3.3 Recruitment and Selection
1.5 Research and Technology	2.4 College Costs	3.4 Administration of Admissions
1.6 Guides and Directories	2.5 Financial Aid Sources	3.5 Transfer Admissions
1.7 Career Information Sources		

III. *The Students*

9. DISTRIBUTION OF TALENT	10. EDUCATIONAL OPPORTUNITY	11. SELECTED STUDENT GROUPS
9.1 The Nature of Ability	10.1 Discrimination and Equality	11.1 Student Activists
9.2 Student Characteristics	10.2 Equity in Selection	11.2 Talented Students
9.3 Motives to Attend College	10.3 Opportunity Programs	11.3 Women Students
9.4 Who Goes to College?		11.4 Black Students
9.5 Social Mobility		11.5 Other Minority/Poverty Students

II. *The System*

EDUCATIONAL [PR]OCESS	5. EDUCATIONAL EVALUATION	6. MANPOWER UTILIZATION	7. ORGANIZATION & ADMINISTRATION	8. STRUCTURE OF THE SYSTEM
[Cu]rriculum	5.1 Social Context	6.1 Manpower Resources	7.1 History and Philosophy	8.1 Secondary Education
	5.2 Educational Context	6.2 Educational Resources	7.2 National Goals	8.2 Vocational Education
			7.3 Current Issues	8.3 College Environments
			7.4 Governance and Planning	8.4 Community Colleges
[Co]urse Placement	5.3 Testing and Evaluation	6.3 Education and Work	7.5 Management Information	8.5 Senior Institutions
[In]struction	5.4 Institutional Research	6.4 Occupational Structure	7.6 System Coordination	8.6 Negro Colleges
[Inn]ovation	5.5 Prediction	6.5 Transition to Work	7.7 System Planning Studies	8.7 Continuing Education
	5.6 Follow-up and Dropout Studies		7.8 Master Plans	8.8 International Education
				8.9 Urban Education

[IV]. *Access Agents*   V. *Sources of Information*

[12.]ORGANIZA-[TI]ONS	13. PROGRAMS	14. PERIODICALS	15. SPECIAL RESOURCES
[12.]1 [As]sociations	13.1 Financial Aid	14.1 Journals	15.1 Data Sources
[12.]2 [Ag]encies	13.2 Testing	14.2 Newsletters	15.2 Information Centers
[12.]3 [Fo]undations	13.3 Guidance and Admissions Systems	14.3 Report Series	15.3 General References
[12.]4 [Re]search Centers	13.4 Special Admissions	14.4 Statistical Series	15.4 Publication Catalogs
[12.]5 [Co]ordinating Boards	13.5 Talent Search	14.5 Proceedings and Yearbooks	15.5 Biographical Directories
[12.]6 [Spe]cial Commissions	13.6 Nontraditional Learning		
	13.7 Federal Legislation		

and the types of information available—all of which have an important bearing on the access process, how it is perceived, and how it is governed. Discussions of these subjects are found in Part IV: *Access Agents* and Part V: *Sources of Information*.

The taxonomy that appears on pages 12–13 (and also on the end papers) was developed partly on a deductive and partly on an inductive basis. That is, the foregoing considerations influenced the structure of the taxonomy and the choice of items; at the same time, the taxonomy reflects the literature available. The evolution of the taxonomy and the selection of items for inclusion proceeded hand in hand over a period of three years. The collection of new items suggested many revisions in the taxonomy; the taxonomy revealed poorly covered areas and occasioned additional searching for relevant literature. The taxonomy started with 15 categories; after three major revisions, it ended with 85 categories. Each major division, section, and subsection is clearly shown in the taxonomy. The placement of each part and its relationship to the whole can be seen both from its location in the taxonomy and its numerical order. The development of an understanding of the taxonomy and the interrelationships it illustrates is essential for the effective use of this source book.

I. *Access Processes*

SECTION 1: STUDENT GUIDANCE

Guidance is a large and diverse profession. Those specialties most directly concerned with access to higher education are educational guidance in the secondary school, vocational guidance in schools and other agencies, and guidance of students in college. Material in this guide places primary emphasis on college guidance in the secondary school.

Guidance serves a critical function in maintaining personal and career continuity and also in facilitating new aspiration. Its role is vital because alternatives open to individuals become increasingly difficult for them to understand as society becomes more and more complex. The development of self-concept and understanding of the relationship of education and career to adult life is itself an educational process. The guidance function represents the formal means for helping individuals learn about the access process.

1.1 — *CAREER DEVELOPMENT*. Most of the theoretical work of quality in student guidance has been concerned with the general process of career decision-making. There has been relatively little theory and research dealing strictly with educational guidance; personal guidance is another vast field, but that literature has largely come from psychiatrists and psychologists operating outside the educational system.

Career development represents a special body of theory and research that has only recently developed in this general field of the career-decision process. Even classic references are less than a decade old. Most of the literature is concerned with theory construction and reports of longitudinal studies. Much of this work has been done by counseling psychologists. Holland and Whitney (8) provide a recent review and bibliography.

Important problems in career development include the developmental aspect of career planning, how to educate people for career decisions (5), the relation of the self-concept to career choice (10), and the nature of career satisfaction (12). Some of the most valuable and necessary data related to career development come only from comprehensive longitudinal studies over a period of time. Regrettably, these are rare and extremely difficult to execute.

Theory and research in guidance is generally well coordinated with practice in the same field. There is a well-recognized gap between good practice and what is common in many schools, but the problem seems to be caused more by training and manpower deficits than by isolation of theorists and practitioners. Many of the leading theorists are also leaders in the guidance profession. Possibly because theoretical work in this area is relatively new, there seems to be little success as yet in coordinating guidance theory with theory in other fields such as manpower utilization and curriculum.

1 AMERICAN PERSONNEL AND GUIDANCE ASSOCIATION, National Vocational Guidance Association. *A report of the invitational conference on implementing career development theory and research through the curriculum.* Wash., D. C.: NVGA, 1966, 194 pp. (Mimeographed)

The 1966 National Vocational Guidance Association Conference convened to discuss the urgent necessity of translating the research and theory of guidance into practice. The strikingly readable papers in this volume, all background information for or a result of the conference, cover such topics as strategies for curriculum change, the meaning of work in an age of affluence, work and the productive personality, and the guidance counselor in the "plausible future."

Among the conclusions reached are: (1) Interdisciplinary communication about vocational development must be improved. (2) Our value system is closely tied to the meaning of work, and as machines do more and more of the routine tasks, man's satisfaction must come from service to his fellow man. (3) Tiedeman's structural conceptualization of age, developmental stages, and counselor functions will be useful in guidance theory and practice. (4) Study of various curricular programs is needed to reveal their respective strengths and weaknesses in relation to vocational guidance. (5) Counselors must be trained to discern more efficiently the worker's perceptions of his job, his attitudes, and the relationship between his job and his way of life.

2 ASTIN, HELEN S. Career development during the high school years. *Journal of Counseling Psychology*, 1967, vol. 14, pp. 94-98.

This study attempted to identify the personal characteristics of the ninth-grade student that tend to predict his vocational choice at the twelfth-grade level, and to identify the secondary school characteristics that affect expressed career choice at the time of graduation. The sample for the study consisted of 650 males from the Project TALENT data bank who had originally been tested in 1960. The students' measured interests and expressed career choice at the ninth-grade level were the best predictors of career outcomes at the twelfth-grade level. The discriminating power of the test battery was improved somewhat by adding selected environmental characteristics of the high schools attended by the subjects.

3 BERDIE, RALPH F. Personality changes from high school entrance to college matriculation. *Journal of Counseling Psychology,* 1968, vol. 15, pp. 376-380.

The author administered the Minnesota Counseling Inventory to a group of 259 students in order to determine the nature of personality changes during secondary school. In most respects, mean score changes indicated psychological maturation during this period. Whereas there was a significant relationship between self-ratings of personality at the beginning and end of this time span (correlations clustered about .50), considerable variations did occur through time.

4 BERDIE, RALPH F., PILAPIL, BONIFACIO, AND IM, IN JAE. Entrance correlates of university satisfaction. *American Educational Research Journal,* 1970, vol. 7, pp. 251-266.

The goal of this study was to investigate relationships between satisfaction with college, personality characteristics and aptitude measured prior to entrance, and success and progress in college. A questionnaire based on the College Satisfaction Index was administered to 300 graduating students from six colleges of the University of Minnesota. It included student ratings of satisfaction with curriculum, instructors, social life, faculty advising, cultural development, health service, residence, and college in general.

A correlational analysis of the above items found satisfaction in one area relatively independent of satisfaction in other areas. Results indicated that these students were mildly satisfied with the college experience. Students were highly satisfied with cultural development but reported low satisfaction with faculty advising and professional counseling. Findings indicated positive correlations between satisfaction, student characteristic data, and progress in college. The authors conclude that the most significant determinant of satisfaction is the prior history and personality of the student, followed by facility in obtaining the degree and the experiences and services offered by the college. The authors also suggest satisfaction with high school experience as a predictor of college satisfaction.

5 BOOCOCK, SARANE S. The life career game. *Personnel and Guidance Journal,* 1967, vol. 46, pp. 328-334.

This paper reports results of field testing of a simulated game in which adolescent players make critical career decisions for a fictitious student and receive "feedback" on the consequences. The purpose of the game is to increase students' understanding of the interrelations between decisions regarding occupation, education and family life, and the factors affecting success and satisfaction in these areas. The author conducted field testing of the game using control groups of nonparticipating students and collected questionnaire and interview data from both groups. Evaluation of the results indicated intense interest and involvement among players. The game influenced attitudes towards individual vocational possibilities. Girls who played the game became more aware than did nonplayers of career opportunities outside the home. The game also provided factual information about educational and vocational opportunities and guided students to sources containing such information. The authors suggest the inclusion of the game in guidance programs and curricular areas such as social studies and home economics. They conclude the game might best be used as a basis for a "work unit" involving vocational testing, supplementary reading or films, and more detailed role playing.

6 GINZBERG, ELI, AND HERMA, JOHN L. *Talent and performance.* New York: Columbia University Press, 1964, 265 pp. $5.

In an attempt to investigate the extent to which talented individuals fulfill their promise in later life, the authors surveyed 433 men who had been awarded fellowships for graduate or professional study at Columbia University between 1944 and 1950. The authors give a brief profile of their group. All were on the two highest rungs of the occupational ladder, either in professional or technical work or in managerial positions; 7 in 10 had earned their doctorates. More than half were employed by a college, university, or professional school. Other topics include patterns of career development, measures of success, value orientations, work satisfactions, self-realization, life styles, and performance potential. In the final chapter on the conservation of talent the authors discuss the impact of three elements on career development: (1) the current educational and guidance structure, (2) the influence of specific work environments, and (3) certain broad social policies such as compulsory military service and the pattern of social expectations. The study provides a comprehensive though somewhat dated view of career development among very talented males.

7 GRIBBONS, WARREN D., AND LOHNES, PAUL R. *Emerging careers.* New York: Teachers College Press, Columbia University, 1968, 202 pp. $8.95.

The authors present a description and analysis of the career development of 111 boys and girls over a period of seven years—from the eighth grade until two years after high school. An instrument to measure a student's vocational maturity or "readiness for vocational planning" was developed, and this instrument was found to be valid in predicting the choice of a high school curriculum. The study tests current theories of career development and, by application of Markov chain analysis, explores new methods for statistical interpretation of longitudinal data. As such it represents one of the few serious attempts to study career development as an evolving process.

8 HOLLAND, JOHN L., AND WHITNEY, DOUGLAS R. Career development. *Review of Educational Research,* 1969, vol. 39, pp. 227-237.

This article reviews individual, comparative, and longitudinal research in the area of career development from April 1965 to July 1968. The authors charge that a typically narrow approach has brought no information explosion of "ideas worth having." This has limited research to "narrow experimentalism, indiscriminate statistical manipulations and timid theorizing." They call for a new problem-oriented, open-minded view of the study of career development.

9 OSIPOW, SAMUEL H. *Theories of career development.* New York: Appleton-Century-Crofts, 1968, 259 pp. $6.75.

This book has a dual focus, making it a useful overview of the field of career development and of the problems of developing models to categorize behavioral phenomena. It combines comparative analysis of four major approaches to the theory of career decision-making with interpretations of their potential practical value to counselors. The four approaches described in detail are: trait-factor theories, sociology and career choice, self-concept theory, and vocational and personality theories.

10 SUPER, DONALD E., STARISHEVSKY, REUBEN, MATLIN, NORMAN, AND JORDAAN, JEAN PIERRE. *Career development: Self-concept theory.* Research Monograph No. 4. New York: College Entrance Examination Board, 1963, 95 pp. $2.50.

This collection of five essays, one outgrowth of the longitudinal Career Pattern Study, examines the thesis that a person's concept of himself is reflected in the career he chooses. The first chapter deals with historical questions, the research literature, and the elements necessary to a self-concept theory of vocational choice; the second presents definitions of operational terms. The third chapter views occupational self-concept as the incorporation of a person's self-concept and his "dictionary" or understanding of various occupations. The fourth presents various approaches to exploratory behavior and seeks a basis for systematic theory building about this aspect of the developing self-concept. Finally, an examination of vocational development in adolescence and early adulthood shows that stages, tasks, and behaviors are identifiable and usable in assessing vocational maturity on three scales: (1) classifying according to life stage, (2) classifying within life stages, and (3) a longitudinal approach — "analyzing changes in maturity . . . throughout two or more adjacent sequential life stages." This monograph, and a companion by Tiedeman and O'Hara (12), represent two classics in the career development literature.

11 TENNYSON, W. WESLEY. Career development. *Review of Educational Research,* 1968, vol. 38, pp. 346-366.

Tennyson reviews the recent literature pertaining to vocational development and behavior and in each topical area points out specific gaps in current knowledge. This review came somewhat before and partly overlaps the one by Holland and Whitney (8), but it does contain more flavor of vocational education.

12 TIEDEMAN, DAVID V., AND O'HARA, ROBERT P. *Career development: Choice and adjustment.* Research Monograph No. 3. New York: College Entrance Examination Board, 1963, 108 pp.

This monograph explores the relationship between personality and career. The first two sections are essentially illustrative. Section I is an explanation of the "language" used for analysis of career development. Section II consists of four "cases" — interviews with a third grader, a ninth grader, an eleventh grader, and a college junior. Each case is followed by an analysis of such factors as structure of the interview, interests, self-evaluation, awareness resulting from past life experiences, vocational choice process, and interplay of personality and career development. Resulting generalizations note the importance of differentiation and integration processes (i.e., "making choices") at various stages. The final three sections, which are more technical, illuminate the interdependence of life situation and career and relate each of these to the process of choosing. Topics include: (1) differentiation and integration: the mechanisms of career development, (2) time and occupation: a frame for career development, and (3) observation and career: an assessment of, and some suggestions for, research. This monograph is one of a pair of classics (see 10) published by the College Board in the early 1960s.

1.2—VOCATIONAL INTEREST. These studies tend to be concerned with the psychometric development of instruments for measuring interest and goals or with censuslike surveys of vocational interest. Crites (17) has provided a recent summary and bibliography.

Aside from the technical problem of developing appropriate measurement instruments, the principal research interest in this area is better understanding of the vocational interests expressed by various types of individuals. This area is closely related to section 6.4, Occupational Structure, which includes studies of the characteristics of people who actually work in different fields.

Despite copious literature, much of the work in this area is theoretically superficial or especially concerned with normative data developed in connection with different programs or development of instruments. There has been relatively little work on the dynamics of interest changes, particularly as they relate to career changes. Much more needs to be learned about what types of interests are critical and how interests and goals influence satisfaction with a career.

13 ASTIN, ALEXANDER W., AND NICHOLS, ROBERT C. Life goals and vocational choice. *Journal of Applied Psychology*, 1964, vol. 48, pp. 50-58.

This study is an investigation of talented students' major "life goals" and the relationships between these goals and career choice. The authors constructed items describing goals in vocational, personal, and social areas and administered them to a sample of 5,495 high-aptitude college seniors. Responses were factored using separate random samples of 250 male and 250 female students. Finally, groups of students were compared to determine relevance of certain life goals for particular careers. Results indicated that high-aptitude students choosing different careers identify quite different goals. These goals exist prior to career choice and thus may determine both choice and future satisfaction. The implications of these findings point to possible errors in present selection of criteria for evaluating adult achievement. The authors suggest that criteria must be relevant to the students' actual goals in order to enhance prediction accuracy, especially *within* career groups.

14 BAIRD, LEONARD L. *The educational goals of college-bound youth.* ACT Research Report No. 19. Iowa City, Iowa: American College Testing Program, 1967, 27 pp.

A large group of students participating in the American College Testing Program were sorted into categories based upon their expressed goal in attending college (e.g., learn how to enjoy life, become a cultured person, secure vocational or professional training, etc.). Students expressing each goal were described on a variety of measures including ability, grades, nonacademic achievements, choice of major degree plans, and so forth. While the results are not necessarily very stable beyond the age at which the data were gathered, they do give useful impressions of the values of students prior to entering college.

15 CAMPBELL, DAVID P., AND HARMON, LENORE W. *Vocational interests of nonprofessional women.* (Project No. 6-1820) Wash., D. C.: Bureau of Research, U. S. Office of Education, 1968, 255 pp. (Mimeographed)

The purpose of this study was to describe the vocational interests of women in nonprofessional occupations. Completed questionnaires were received from more than 5,000 women in 17 occupations such as beautician, saleswoman, secretary, and dental assistant. Scales for the Strong Vocational Interest Blank were constructed for each of the seventeen occupations. The report contains a variety of useful information such as profiles on: (1) a job description checklist, (2) the basic demographic scales, and (3) occupational scales of the Strong Vocational Interest Blank.

16 CLARK, KENNETH E. *Vocational interests of nonprofessional men.* Minneapolis, Minn.: University of Minnesota Press, 1961, 129 pp. $4.25.

Clark describes in this book the development of the Minnesota Vocational Interest Inventory on the basis of responses from some 25,000 workers in skilled trades. Many individuals in the standardization group were Navy personnel, and this work includes a chapter on the use of occupational and homogeneous scoring keys for classifying men into occupations—a practical problem in the military. The instrument and the book provide a valuable complement to other interest measures that tend to be directed primarily to higher-level occupations.

17 CRITES, JOHN O. Interests, in Robert L. Ebel (Ed.), *Encyclopedia of educational research.* (4th ed.) New York: Macmillan, 1969, pp. 678-686.

This article provides a manageable but authoritative overview of interest measurement. Crites notes that most of what is known about measurement of interest is based upon findings of Strong's Vocational Interest Blank (SVIB), and to a lesser extent, Kuder's Preference Record (KPR). The empirical model of test construction, such as SVIB, have dominated the field so that conceptual theories have lagged behind. More specifically, interest inventories have been developed from a set of implicit assumptions about individual and group differences in specific likes and dislikes, which has seriously impeded the formulation of useful conceptual definitions. Research on the correlates of interests are here classified according to four types of variables: (1) stimulus — any physical incident, event, social circumstance; (2) organismic — some characteristic, property, or state of an organism, for example endocrine glands, physique, and heredity; (3) response — any observable change in behavior, such as movement or speech; and (4) theoretical — one of two kinds of abstractions: hypothetical constructs or intervening variables. Six fairly distinct approaches to the problem of explaining individual differences and developmental trends in interests can be identified and summarized by their central propositions: (1) interests are learned; (2) interests are adjustment modes; (3) interests are an aspect of personality; (4) interests are an expression of the self-concept; (5) interests are motives; and (6) interests are multiply determined.

18 DAVIS, JAMES A. *Great aspirations: The graduate school plans of America's college seniors.* Chicago: Aldine, 1964, 319 pp. $9.75.

The vocational focus of graduate education makes this study of the graduate school plans of college seniors a useful reference in the context of career choice and manpower planning. Of more than 30,000 graduating seniors who completed an extensive questionnaire in the spring of 1961, an overwhelming majority (77 percent) expected to enroll for advanced work at some future time. Although students expected to continue immediately in preparing for careers in law or medicine, delay was the norm rather than the exception, particularly in education and social work. The book contains many detailed statistical analyses dealing with career preferences and student attitudes toward graduate education.

19 HOLLAND, JOHN L. A theory-ridden, computerless, impersonal vocational guidance system. *Journal of Vocational Behavior,* 1971, vol. 1, pp. 167-176.

In this presidential address to the Division of Counseling Psychology of the American Psychological Association, Holland describes the development and use of an instrument entitled "Self-Directed Search for Educational and Vocational Planning," which he likes to call SDS. It is a self-instructional instrument which yields a three-letter code. In turn, this code routes the individual to a variety of occupational possibilities that tend to fit his interest and competencies. Such relatively simple schemes for self-evaluation are not uncommon, but it is unusual to find one based on an elaborate theory of vocational choice and a great deal of sophisticated research over a 10-year period. The instrument would seem to be well suited for group counseling.

20 NICHOLS, ROBERT C. Career decisions of very able students. *Science,* 1964, vol. 144, pp. 1315-1319.

This article examines the career choices and prospective major fields of National Merit semifinalists in order to determine what trends have occurred in various vocational areas. Available data on major field and career choice of semifinalists were coded into categories, and yearly percentages were plotted to indicate trends over time. In addition a sample of talented students also indicated their career choice and major field when they entered college and again at the time of graduation.

The author concludes that in general "talented male students appear to have shifted their interest from the physical sciences and engineering to the humanities and social sciences.... The same general trend appears to be true for females, but for them it is much less clear cut." The career of college teaching showed the largest net increase while careers in scientific research and engineering decreased by more than 50 percent for both sexes. Some possible explanations for these trends are tentatively suggested; however, the author hastens to add that "the factors determining the distribution of talent are not simple and many of the important influences remain unknown."

21 RICHARDS, JAMES M. JR. Life goals of American college freshmen. *Journal of Counseling Psychology,* 1966, vol. 13, pp. 12-20.

The purpose of this study was to determine a limited set of concepts that can adequately describe the life goals of most students. In samples of more than 12,000 college freshmen, 35 items pertaining to life goals were intercorrelated and factored. Seven resulting factors common to both sexes were designated: prestige, personal happiness, humanistic-cultural, religious, scientific, artistic, and hedonistic. These factors should be useful in developing career-counseling materials.

22 WATLEY, DONIVAN J., AND NICHOLS, ROBERT C. *Career decisions of talented youth: Trends over the past decade.* NMSC Research Reports, vol. 5, no. 1. Evanston, Ill.: National Merit Scholarship Corporation, 1969, 14 pp.

Since vocational decisions will partly determine the future supply of talent in various occupations, this study was undertaken to examine the career decisions of the nation's ablest young people over the past decade. In 1957 and each year since, finalists on the National Merit Test, just prior to entering college, have filled out forms indicating their career choices and probable majors. Year-by-year changes in the percentage of these students choosing each profession reveal certain trends. For example, interest in physical sciences has always been high, interest in business has shown a steady decline, and interest in humanities is on the rise. In the cases of engineering for men and teaching for women, where there have been strong campaigns to attract recruits, it is noted that student interest has not increased. This result and the fact that the real factors underlying trends in career decisions are largely unknown both frustrate manpower planning.

1.3—*THE DECISION PROCESS.* The research in this area tends to be closely related to that of the previous two sections; and the people, organizations, and journals tend to be similar. The emphasis here, however, is on the process of making decisions, and the literature is based on longitudinal studies of students' decisions and developed theories of decision-making. This area is closely related to section 9.3, which deals specifically with factors influencing students' motives to attend college.

Strangely enough this is a fairly new field, and there has been surprisingly little work on the nature of the decision process. One of the main initial problems has been to understand the relationships among interests, personal values, abilities, and career plans (25). Another problem given special attention by Holland (30) is stability and change in the decision process. A third major area of interest has been the development of procedures whereby guidance counselors can facilitate effective student decisions (see Katz, 34 and Gelatt, 28).

23 BAIRD, LEONARD L. The indecision scale: A reinterpretation. *Journal of Counseling Psychology,* 1968, vol. 15, pp. 174-179.

Holland and Nichols developed a so-called indecision scale (31) consisting of items that characterize those students who are undecided about their career interests. The author determined the relationship between this scale and a wide variety of other variables in two large samples of students. The high scorer on the indecision scale "seems to be blessed with many talents and the desire to use them." The author argues that more often than not a high score on this indecision scale may indicate "general effectiveness," and an inclination to be a generalist rather than to be tied down to a specific narrow career line.

24 BAIRD, LEONARD L. *Patterns of educational aspirations.* ACT Research Report No. 32. Iowa City, Iowa: American College Testing Program, 1969, 21 pp.

One of the most common problems in guidance is a wide discrepancy between educational/vocational aspiration and the reality of academic aptitude or financial resources. In this study the author identified groups of students exhibiting such discrepancies and examined their other characteristics. He concludes that degree aspirations seem to be relatively independent of the influence of academic ability or family income—both powerful restraining variables. Aspiration has some qualities of a "self-fulfilling prophecy" and can be considered an important predictor in its own right. Another major conclusion is that both academic and nonacademic accomplishments seem to have a pronounced impact on aspiration.

25 COOLEY, WILLIAM W. Interactions among interests, abilities, and career plans. *Journal of Applied Psychology Monograph,* 1967, vol. 51, no. 5, part 2, pp. 1-16.

Since guidance counselors often rely heavily on vocational interest inventories in counseling about careers, the assumption that such inventories are accurate predictors of postsecondary educational and career decisions deserves close examination. In 1960 as ninth graders and in 1963 as twelfth graders, 3,000 male and female students answered the TALENT interest inventory. They rated their reactions on a five-point scale to 205 items dealing with activities, specific occupations, and broad vocational areas. Analysis revealed "... interest inventories ... simultaneously (seem) to anticipate changes in abilities and plans and yet change themselves to become more consistent with previous abilities or new plans." In fact, students' own statements of their career plans proved to be a more accurate predictor than the entire inventory! The author feels that this is probably because vocational interest inventories are highly affected by the student's self-concept and knowledge of occupations. Therefore, as his self-concept matures, his expressed interests can change—even his abilities can change to reflect developed interests.

26 DAVIS, JAMES A. The campus as a frog pond: An application of the theory of relative deprivation to career decisions of college men. *American Journal of Sociology,* 1966, vol. 72, pp. 17-31.

The theory of "relative deprivation," a World War II psychiatric term, suggests a plausible explanation for undergraduates' decisions about graduate school. Students tend to rate themselves relative to their classmates in assessing their academic success; hence those ending up at the bottom of the heap in a highly selective college underestimate their chance of success in graduate school, regardless of their ability. The conclusion is that students have stronger feelings of success as "big frogs" in a small "campus frog pond." Data for this well-known study were based on a large national survey of seniors graduating in 1961.

27 DOUVAN, ELIZABETH, AND KAYE, CAROL. Motivational factors in college entrance, in Nevitt Sanford (Ed.), *The American college.* New York: John Wiley, 1963, pp. 199-224.

This chapter discusses the motives that guide adolescents toward college and some of the psychological forces that may affect decisions regarding higher education. The authors consider "what the image of college represents to youngsters in high school and to their parents, what adolescents seek in their departure for college." Finally, some attention is given to the process by which particular schools are chosen.

On the basis of a series of studies, the authors suggest that plans and concepts concerning college show sex-specific orientations. Boys tend to view college in terms of job preparation, whereas for girls college plans are not specifically tied to vocational goals. "Girls are absorbed much more in phantasy, particularly about boys and popularity, marriage and love." Boys tend to view college as a means to freedom more than girls do. Two basic motivational types are considered, the student who has serious intellectual and academic goals and the student who views college as a means for mobility. The choice of a school is discussed in terms of three variables: (1) the criteria by which schools are judged, (2) the individuals or agencies that influence the choice, and (3) the involvement of parents in the process. The paper provides a good introduction to the student decision process but is somewhat dated, as is anything written on student attitudes prior to about 1965.

28 GELATT, H. B. Decision-making: A conceptual frame of reference for counseling. *Journal of Counseling Psychology,* 1962, vol. 9, pp. 240-245.

In searching for a unitary, direction-providing framework for guidance counseling, Gelatt singles out "sequential decision-making." This frame of reference requires definition of objectives, collection and analysis of data, study of alternatives, and evaluation of results—in other words, a scientific approach. Rather than being restrictive or giving guidance a position of excess control, this framework would increase the student's "freedom of choice" because he would not have to make decisions on the basis of only haphazardly perceived alternatives evaluated with subjective bias.

Implications of adopting this framework include: (1) the necessity for collection and utilization of reliable empirical data, (2) the chance to develop the student's capacity for future decision-making, (3) the availability of a valuable tool in attacking the ever-present unrealistic expectations of both students and parents, (4) an early opportunity for the student to test his self-concept and so have the benefit of that test in making future educational and career decisions, (5) the specification of expected professional behavior on the part of counselors, and (6) the availability of a basis from which the theory and the practice of guidance can be evaluated.

29 HOLLAND, JOHN L. *The psychology of vocational choice.* Waltham, Mass.: Blaisdell, 1966, 132 pp. $2.50.

Holland suggests that "the choice of a vocation is an expression of personality. Vocational satisfaction, stability, and achievement depend on the congruency between one's personality and the environment (composed largely of other people) in which one works."

From this starting point he develops a theory of vocational choice based on the following assumptions: (1) People can be characterized according to their resemblance to one or more personality types. (2) Environments in which people live can be characterized by their resemblance to one or more model environments. (3) The pairing of persons and environments leads to predictable outcomes in such phenomena as vocational choice, vocational stability and achievement, personal stability, creative performance, and susceptibility to influence.

Both people and environments are categorized as one of six types—realistic, intellectual, social, conventional, enterprising, and artistic. By comparing a person's attributes with those of each of the model types, it is possible to obtain a personality "profile" with which to determine which type he resembles most. Similarly, each environment is dominated by a given type of personality and "thus the environment can be assessed in the same terms as we assess people individually." The author suggests that "if we know a person's personality pattern and the pattern of his environment, we can...forecast some of the outcomes of such a pairing."

30 HOLLAND, JOHN L. Explorations of a theory of vocational choice: VI. A longitudinal study using a sample of typical college students. *Journal of Applied Psychology*, 1968, vol. 52, no. 1, part 2, pp. 1-37.

In this detailed article the author's purpose was to test his theory of vocational choice against a sample of typical college students. In skeletal form the theory is: (1) each person belongs to one or more personality types, and the closer he is to a conceptual type, the more he will exhibit behavior associated with that type; (2) environments can also be characterized by their likeness to model environments; and (3) coupling of persons and environments results in several predictable outcomes including vocational choice, vocational stability and achievement, personal stability, creativity, and susceptibility to influence (see 29).

Two groups totaling 6,289 male and 6,143 female college students were each tested twice—one group in fall 1964 and in May 1965 as freshmen and the other group in May 1964 as freshmen and in May 1965 as sophomores. Using the Vocational Preference Inventory, students were classified as personality types—realistic, intellectual, social, conventional, enterprising, or artistic. (For women the categories were adjusted to eight: intellectual, social-intellectual, social-conventional, social-enterprising, social-artistic, conventional, enterprising, and artistic.) Vocational aspirations and several additional scales and inventories were administered.

From tests of concurrent and predictive relationships, the author interprets the results as generally supportive of the theory and suggests that demonstrated relationships between individuals and college environments might generalize to employee-organizational interactions (i.e., tenure, job satisfaction).

31 HOLLAND, JOHN L., AND NICHOLS, ROBERT C. The development and validation of an indecision scale: The natural history of a problem in basic research. *Journal of Counseling Psychology*, 1964, vol. 11, pp. 27-34.

The authors developed an indecision scale by empirically selecting items which differentiate students who are certain or uncertain regarding career interests. The scale was judged to have substantial construct validity because of its relationships with other variables including life goals and achievements. The scale seems reasonably stable over a one-year period. It is also related to creative performance, for the authors note the tendency for creative individuals to delay commitment to any single line of work. A somewhat different interpretation of the meaning is suggested by Baird (23) who regards the scale as a measure of "general effectiveness."

32 HOLLAND, JOHN L., AND NICHOLS, ROBERT C. Explorations of a theory of vocational choice: III. A longitudinal study of change in major field of study. *Personnel and Guidance Journal*, 1964, vol. 43, pp. 235-242.

This study tests certain aspects of the senior author's theory of vocational choice by examining characteristics of students who change majors after entering college. Results indicate that students remaining in a given field tend to have personal characteristics similar to the students in that field, while those changing fields are less similar.

33 HOLLAND, JOHN L., AND WHITNEY, DOUGLAS R. *Changes in vocational plans of college students: Orderly or random?* ACT Research Report No. 25. Iowa City, Iowa: American College Testing Program, 1969, 31 pp.

This study examined the hypothesis that occupational choices follow orderly patterns and can be predicted from earlier choices. When Holland's classification scheme was applied to successive occupational choices indicated by students, it was found that to varying degrees later choices were predictable from earlier ones. The report includes "occupational change maps" which are useful in understanding the pattern of changes in occupational decisions.

34 KATZ, MARTIN. *Decisions and values.* New York: College Entrance Examination Board, 1963, 67 pp. $2.

This excellent monograph defines "guidance" to mean "professional intervention in the choices an individual makes among the educational and occupational options our society allows him." Thus the emphasis is on "career" guidance which is, to a considerable extent, guidance for occupational choice. The author suggests that many vocationally oriented decisions are concentrated in the secondary school years and that two crucial choice-points fall in this period, one at the beginning and the other near the end of the high school years. The author reviews the state of occupational choice theory and its corollaries in guidance, and then considers more specifically a rationale for the nature of the guidance process, focusing on these two important choice-points.

35 KATZ, MARTIN. A model of guidance for career decision-making. *Vocational Guidance Quarterly,* 1966, vol. 15, pp. 2-10.

In this article the author describes a theoretical model of decision-making, perhaps the least studied and least understood aspect of the guidance process. The model attempts to incorporate the student's values explicitly into the decision-making process. It attempts to provide a vocabulary for discussing values, and also a means whereby they can be examined in the real world of necessary choices. The model is presented as a paradigm for development and research rather than an immediate aid to the practicing counselor.

36 KROLL, ARTHUR M., DINKLAGE, LILLIAN B., LEE, JENNIFER, MORLEY, EILEEN D., AND WILSON, EUGENE H. *Career development: Growth and crisis.* New York: John Wiley, 1970, 262 pp. $8.95.

Although the title of this work implies a general treatment of career development, the process of decision-making is the dominant theme. It includes useful discussions of such topics as models of decision-making, research on the teaching of decision-making, and individual coping styles. An especially interesting section is devoted to decision-making in the career crisis of losing a job.

37 SUPER, DONALD E. Consistency and wisdom of vocational preference as indices of vocational maturity in the ninth grade. *Journal of Educational Psychology,* 1961, vol. 52, pp. 35-43.

Consistency and realism of vocational goals are often used as an indication of the need for or effectiveness of counseling. This study explored the nature of consistency and realism among ninth-grade boys. The author concludes that ideas of the working world are too poorly formed at this grade level to lay great store in the relative level of consistency or realism.

38 THISTLETHWAITE, DONALD L., AND WHEELER, NORMAN. Effects of teacher and peer subcultures upon student aspiration. *Journal of Educational Psychology,* 1966, vol. 57, pp. 35-47.

Some 1,700 students at 140 colleges were questioned in this survey regarding their impressions of their own college's "environmental press" and the students' plans to seek advanced training. Holding precollege characteristics constant, the authors found that approximately one-third of the environmental variables were significantly related to educational aspiration in men, though none were significant in the case of women.

39 WERTS, CHARLES E. *Paternal influence on career choice.* NMSC Research Reports, vol. 3, no. 2. Evanston, Ill.: National Merit Scholarship Corporation, 1967, 19 pp. Also in *Journal of Counseling Psychology*, 1968, vol. 15, pp. 48–52.

In a study of 76,000 males entering 248 four-year colleges and universities in the fall of 1961, fathers' occupations were compared with sons' career choices in an attempt to determine whether occupational inheritance follows broad occupational types. Some acknowledged limitations of the study are: (1) the fact that college students from low socioeconomic backgrounds rarely plan careers in low socioeconomic occupations; (2) stated occupational plans do not necessarily indicate actual occupation; and (3) the reliability of the student's report of his father's occupation and his own anticipated career choice is unknown. The findings suggest that professional occupations in at least three broad areas, the physical sciences, the social sciences, and medicine, appear to be passed from father to son, and that "for the sons of professionals, the occupational groupings on the Strong Vocational Interest Blank are useful in describing broad types of 'inherited' occupations." Unfortunately the study does not add greatly to the understanding of social mobility because it is restricted largely to high-level professions. Nevertheless it is a good illustration of the effect of parental influence in the decision process.

40 WERTS, CHARLES E., AND WATLEY, DONIVAN J. A student's dilemma: Big fish-little pond or little fish-big pond. *Journal of Counseling Psychology*, 1969, vol. 16, pp. 14–19.

What effect does college selectivity have on the probability of a student's going on to advanced study? The theory of "relative deprivation" (Davis, 26) suggests that attendance at a highly selective college adversely affects motivation for graduate study because the student will obtain relatively poorer grades there, and this will lead to a lower self-evaluation of his capacity for graduate study. In evaluating his own ability, the student compares his grades with those of his classmates and seldom takes into consideration the academic ability differences between colleges.

On the other hand the "environmental press" theory (Thistlethwaite and Wheeler, 38) suggests that motivation for graduate study is increased at a highly selective institution because the environmental press favors graduate study. In this article the authors develop a means for testing the contrasting predictions of the two theories and offer some preliminary evidence that favors the relative deprivation theory.

1.4—*GUIDANCE PROCEDURES*. The literature in this section is primarily concerned with effective procedures, professional responsibility, and the training of guidance personnel. These are principally general texts and reports written by leaders in the field. Herr and Kramer (51) provide a good bibliography and comprehensive treatment of guidance for the college-bound student. Ginzberg (49) has prepared an incisive analysis of career guidance.

The secondary school counselor is necessarily somewhat isolated from the other professions represented in the six access processes of Part 1 because all the others work in colleges. There have been successful periodic efforts in a number of states to bring counselors together with college personnel. Most of this interaction has been with admissions officers, though financial aid officers, college counselors, and faculty are often included in such exchanges. Among national organizations, the College Entrance Examination Board is especially characterized by its efforts to represent both secondary school counselors and college personnel in dialogs concerning access problems.

The American Personnel and Guidance Association serves the professional interests of guidance counselors, and its eight divisions publish a variety of journals. The best known is *Personnel and Guidance Journal* (1341), which regularly includes a variety of articles concerning professional affairs and practice. Many school counselors are members of one or both of the APGA divisions, the National Vocational Guidance Association, and the American School Counselor Association. The quarterlies of these divisions — *The Vocational Guidance Quarterly* and *The School Counselor* — carry articles about school guidance, with considerable emphasis on practice.

Many individuals who are prominent in guidance research are active in the American Psychological Association (1106). Its *Journal of Counseling Psychology* (1324) is a principal source of articles.

There are a number of specialized newsletters, but *CAPS Capsule* (1351) is of special interest because it is published by the ERIC center most directly concerned with guidance information. (See section 13 for annotations of several types of programs closely related to guidance, and sections 2.4 and 2.5 for information concerning college costs and aid sources.)

41 BENTLEY, JOSEPH C., AND SALTER, STERLING. College freshmen view counselor help in college selection. *Personnel and Guidance Journal,* 1967, vol. 46, pp. 178-183.
   This article describes a survey of 270 college freshmen designed to explore the activities of high school counselors in college admissions. Results of the study indicated: (1) counselors are becoming increasingly important in influencing college choice; (2) counselors' assistance and suggestions are direct and active; (3) students expect counselors to provide detailed information of possible college choices and to recommend specific schools; and (4) students in some cases felt counseling was restrictive.

42 BLOOM, A. MARTIN. *Successful programs and practices for counseling the college-bound student.* Englewood Cliffs, N. J.: Prentice-Hall, 1969, 317 pp. $9.95.
   As the title implies, this volume is not a general text but rather a guidebook of practices and programs. It should be of value to the working counselor. Part I contains advice and information concerning a variety of procedures such as developing effective records, writing recommendations, and using national programs. Part II is perhaps the most interesting of the book. It contains descriptions of 10 programs for group guidance, selected from various parts of the country. Part III contains practical information on developing relationships with colleges. Part IV is a brief section on upgrading the counseling program.

43 COLLEGE ENTRANCE EXAMINATION BOARD. *From high school to college: Readings for counselors.* New York: College Entrance Examination Board, 1965, 86 pp. $2.25.

This publication includes papers presented at the Work Conference on Guidance for School-College Transition sponsored by the College Entrance Examination Board and the Department of Guidance and Student Personnel Administration of Teachers College, Columbia University. The purpose of the conference was to assist school counselors in understanding the scope and variety of higher education and the role of the counselor in school-college transition. Papers covered a range of useful topics including personality growth in college, noncollegiate programs of higher education, curriculum articulation, opportunities in higher education, and nonintellectual factors in college achievement. Though a bit dated, the publication provides very useful background reading for practicing counselors.

44 COLLEGE ENTRANCE EXAMINATION BOARD. *Preparing school counselors in educational guidance.* New York: College Entrance Examination Board, 1967, 146 pp. $2.50.

This publication includes the papers presented at an invitational conference on the preparation of school counselors sponsored by the College Board in 1966. The steering committee advocated that the conference should not attempt to produce detailed recommendations nor course syllabi for the preparation of counselors, but rather should address itself broadly to the consideration of needed improvements from theoretical, practical, and institutional perspectives. The papers cover a variety of topics, focusing on content in counselor education, problems and practices of the school counselor in educational guidance, and theoretical application to improve practices. The final paper in this volume includes an excellent summary and analysis of the conference, in both its formal and informal proceedings, by David Tiedeman.

45 CRAMER, STANLEY H. (ED.) *Pre-service and in-service preparation of school counselors for educational guidance.* Wash., D. C.: American Personnel and Guidance Association, 1970, 68 pp. $2.

This monograph provides recent data and valuable recommendations for more effective training in educational guidance and counseling. Part I presents findings of a four-state survey of the opinions of 1,100 school counselors regarding their own training; Part II discusses the content of precollege guidance and counseling as well as the techniques; Part III deals with noncollegiate post-high school educational guidance; Part IV offers a useful annotated bibliography of the field. This volume should be on every counselor's shelf.

46 CRAWFORD, PAUL. Counselor responsibility in investigating private vocational schools. *Vocational Guidance Quarterly,* 1969, vol. 17, pp. 173-177.

Crawford urges counselors to make renewed efforts to help students distinguish between legitimate private, profit-making vocational schools and fly-by-night "diploma mills." Now that students have more aid available from the National Vocational Student Loan Insurance Act of 1965, they are in need of much more help in evaluating private vocational opportunities. The specific guidelines Crawford sets for judging such institutions should be a source of great help to counselors.

47 DILLENBECK, DOUGLAS D. *Guidance services 1968-1973.* A Report to the Trustees of the College Entrance Examination Board. New York: College Entrance Examination Board, 1969, 24 pp.

This report proposes a comprehensive program of guidance services designed to enable individuals to make more fully informed decisions regarding postsecondary education. Although it has general applicability for all involved in guidance and counseling, it has specific programmatic implications for the College Board. The report proposes: (1) developing a more comprehensive information system on all higher institutions, (2) providing instruments to assist individuals in developing realistic self-concepts with respect to education, (3) helping individuals learn rational processes of educational decision-making, and (4) providing guidance materials intended for an individual's independent use. On the basis of these proposals, the author spells out recommended components of College Board programs aimed at both high school and junior high school populations. Several of the proposals have resulted in new programs including the Decision-Making Program (1238), the Educational Guidance Information System (1240), and the College Locator Service (1235).

48 GANNON, FREDERICK B. *The many faces of Kevin Michael Pullen: A guidance case study.* New York: College Entrance Examination Board, 1968, 43 pp. $1.25.

This case study traces an academic career using records and interviews with the subject and his high school counselor conducted 10 years after he entered secondary school. The method of study identifies major points of decision and emphasizes influences on and consequences of these decisions. The report includes background description of the subject and his environment, description of high school life, the process of college choice, and college career. Transcripts, test scores, college profiles, and recommendations are reproduced. Suggested study questions, a review of related publications, and commentary on the study by a counselor, an educator, and a guidance director are also included. The study should be useful for counselor education courses and in-service workshops.

49 GINZBERG, ELI. *Career guidance: Who needs it, who provides it, who can improve it.* New York: McGraw-Hill, 1971, 356 pp. $7.95.

In this unusually forthright book Ginzberg applies his experience in manpower and career development research to the field of career guidance in school, government, and industry. The book is based on a searching inquiry and contains fundamental criticisms of the guidance movement. He decries, for example, the way counselors are recruited and trained and how they spend their time. His recommendations include the following: (1) Educational and career guidance should be the primary commitment of the profession. (2) The education of guidance personnel must include more training in the dynamics of the labor market. (3) The requirement of teaching experience for the certification of school counselors should be rescinded. (4) Improved counselor performance should be sought through more emphasis on group techniques.

Ginzberg's analysis of shortcomings and his prescriptions to the profession are presented with sufficient candor to incite rebuttal on specific points, but the overall effect of this book should be highly beneficial. It ought to be read by anyone seriously interested in guidance.

50 HARDEE, MELVENE D. *The faculty in college counseling.* New York: McGraw-Hill, 1959, 391 pp. (Out of print)

In theory most agree that the college faculty should play the major role in the educational guidance of college students. In practice the ideal seldom seems to work well, and in recent years students have been inclined to comment upon that fact. This book by Hardee is perhaps the classic reference on faculty counseling. It covers theory as well as practice and includes a good deal of illustrative material.

51 HERR, EDWIN L., AND CRAMER, STANLEY H. *Guidance of the college bound: Problems, practices, perspectives.* New York: Appleton-Century-Crofts, 1968, 305 pp. $3.95.

The authors contend that guidance counselors have made a serious mistake in the past by focusing on techniques while excluding the basic ideas and perspectives that should direct their work. Guidance counselors need to know the rationale behind the counseling process. Accordingly, the authors include a representative overview of the growing body of theory and research concerning the transition from school to college.

The book examines the diversity of American higher education and the nature of the college experience. From this context, the application of guidance services is considered and an array of elements is presented that should provide guidance practitioners with a theoretical and practical base from which to construct guidance programs that will meet the needs of college-bound students. Appendixes include a bibliography of commercial, governmental, and professional publications relating to guidance for post-high school education, and also a listing of audiovisual materials for use in guiding college-bound students. It is a comprehensive and unusually good text and general reference for college guidance work.

52 HOPPOCK, ROBERT. *Occupational information: Where to get it and how to use it in counseling and in teaching.* (3rd ed.) New York: McGraw-Hill, 1967, 598 pp. $9.50.

This standard text is designed for the practical education of counselors, teachers, psychologists, administrators, and others involved in providing occupational guidance and information. Opening chapters identify the basic types of occupational information, show where this material may be obtained, and how it should be classified. Further chapters discuss basic theories of vocational choice and career development. Final chapters deal with the principles and methods of teaching occupations and describe a variety of ways in which occupational information may be presented. The book includes numerous sketches of actual practice in schools, government, and industry. The appendixes present demonstration group and case conferences, practice job interviews, and lesson plans for use in counselor education. The bibliography contains over 500 selected items.

53 KATZ, MARTIN R. Counseling—secondary schools, in Robert L. Ebel (Ed.), *Encyclopedia of educational research.* (4th ed.) New York: Macmillan, 1969, pp. 242-252.

This article is concerned primarily with counseling as opposed to a variety of other guidance functions sometimes loosely included under that heading. The author discusses the history and purpose of counseling, major theoretical approaches and processes, and means of evaluating counseling. The article provides an excellent brief overview and a good bibliography.

54 KRUMBOLTZ, JOHN D., AND THORESEN, CARL E. (EDS.) *Behavioral counseling: Cases and techniques.* New York: Holt, Rinehart and Winston, 1969, 515 pp. $7.95.

The authors call this a "cookbook" designed to provide counselors and psychologists with detailed descriptions of promising counseling techniques. The articles were written by practicing counselors and psychologists who have used these techniques, and case materials are included from elementary, secondary, college, and adult levels. Cases and techniques are described in sufficient detail to acquaint the interested counselor with new procedures, and editors' notes are scattered throughout the book to call attention to important points, issue warnings or cautions about possible dangers, and suggest needed research.

55 NATIONAL ASSOCIATION OF COLLEGE ADMISSIONS COUNSELORS. *Guiding the college-bound student.* Evanston, Ill.: NACAC, 27 pp. $1.

This unusual and useful publication is basically a checklist of topics of interest to counselors working with college-bound students. It is a relatively brief document containing a wide variety of information in telegraphic form. It includes such topics as: who goes to college, overview of higher education, role of high school guidance program, college admissions procedures, alternatives to college, adjustment to college, and so on. A number of publications are also listed by publisher. The report could be useful to counselors at any level of experience as a quick means of identifying topics for further exploration or aspects of guidance that deserve more attention in a particular program.

56 REISS, JEAN, AND FOX, MILDRED G. *Guiding the future college student.* Englewood Cliffs, N. J.: Prentice-Hall, 1968, 327 pp. $8.95.

The primary purpose of this book is to provide high school counselors with a comprehensive picture of their responsibilities and functional duties to their college-bound counselees. The authors describe specialized services, procedures, and activities that will prepare counselors to help students achieve the goals of choosing a college, gaining acceptance to that college, and, finally, finding academic and social success at the college level.

57 THORESEN, CARL E. (ISSUE ED.) Guidance and counseling. *Review of Educational Research,* 1969, vol. 39, pp. 127-281.

The authors review research efforts in guidance and counseling from the viewpoint of their relevance to theory and practice, and single out specific examples of relevant and dead-end avenues of inquiry.

58 TILLERY, DALE. Will the real guidance counselor please stand up? *College Board Review,* Winter 1969-70, no. 74, pp. 17-23.

This article is based on data from Project SCOPE—a six-year, four-state study of high school students and the decisions they make regarding work and college. The author provides an interesting contrast and comparison of the role of counselors and teachers in influencing and working with students on matters concerning their vocational/educational planning. Overall, students see counselors and teachers exhibiting very similar behavioral characteristics. The items students ranked first, second, and third as descriptive of both groups were: "likes people who are hard workers," "expects others to follow the rules," and "likes to help others." Among the few perceived differences was a tendency for teachers to be considered more stimulating and encouraging of new ideas, and counselors more prone to encourage others to confide in them. The details of these perceptions should be especially interesting to those who work directly with students.

59 TYLER, LEONA E. *The work of the counselor.* (3rd ed.) New York: Appleton-Century-Crofts, 1969, 274 pp. $7.

This well-established and respected text incorporates a broad view of educational, vocational, and personal counseling and places special emphasis on the processes whereby counselors exercise professional responsibility. The author has done an unusually careful job of relating research literature to counseling practice. The appendix contains some 500 references to research literature.

60 U. S. OFFICE OF EDUCATION, NATIONAL CENTER FOR EDUCATIONAL STATISTICS, AND AMERICAN ASSOCIATION OF COLLEGIATE REGISTRARS AND ADMISSIONS OFFICERS. *Definitions of student personnel terms in higher education.* Wash., D. C.: NCES, 1968, 60 pp.

This collection of definitions clarifies and standardizes the terminology used by registrars, admissions officers, and other student personnel officers dealing with student affairs. It is a well-organized and handy reference for newcomers to personnel work in colleges and for counselors in high schools.

1.5—RESEARCH AND TECHNOLOGY. There is great need for comparative studies on different guidance practices, but there is relatively little

controlled experimentation of high quality. While the references included
in this section make no attempt to give a complete representation of that
work, there are a few examples included and some practical guides for
carrying out research in operational guidance situations.

The current fascination and the most important technological development in the guidance field is without doubt the computer-based guidance
information system. Throughout the country, there are a number of projects
developing various computer applications to guidance practice. Some of
these are reviewed in 65. See section 13.3 for annotations of several such
systems.

61 ASSOCIATION FOR COUNSELOR EDUCATION AND SUPERVISION, EXPERIMENTAL
DESIGNS COMMITTEE. *Research guidelines for high school counselors.* New
York: College Entrance Examination Board, 1967, 114 pp. $2.

This volume resulted from a joint effort on the part of the Association for
Counselor Education Supervision and the College Entrance Examination
Board. It contains seven papers providing practical advice on such research
topics as prediction studies, evaluating counselor effectiveness, and follow-up
studies. A shortcoming of the volume is the fact that most of the contributions
are not self-sufficient and contain relatively few references to illustrate examples or more extended treatment of the topics. Nonetheless, the collection of
papers can be quite useful in broadening a counselor's view of his work. (Also
annotated in section 5.4.)

62 CAMPBELL, DAVID P. *The results of counseling: Twenty-five years later.* Philadelphia: W. B. Saunders, 1965, 205 pp. $6.

Attempting to determine whether counseling in college makes any difference
25 years later, Campbell engagingly tells the story of his research on some
1933-36 college freshmen. A group of these University of Minnesota students
who received counseling and a matched group that did not were tested and
compared one year following counseling. The counseling had been largely vocational and curriculum-oriented with strong emphasis on standardized tests.
These data were resurrected, and the 768 students were followed up a quarter
of a century later with an extensive questionnaire, an interview, and an administration of the Minnesota Scholastic Aptitude Test. The author reports that
the value of the counseling was confirmed, despite the fact that inferences of
causality are somewhat dubious when based on matched rather than randomly
assigned groups. The book is interesting and entertaining and offers useful
advice on how to locate individuals after many years.

63 DUGGAN, JOHN M. Field testing a central prediction service. *College Board
Review,* Winter 1963, no. 49, pp. 12-15.

Bloom and Peters (452) suggested that predictions of college success could
be improved by adjusting high school grades to take into account variations in
grading standards from school to school. This article describes an extensive
effort on the part of the College Board to determine whether it would be
feasible and useful to develop a centralized procedure for carrying out such
operations. A series of later studies indicated that the original idea was probably not feasible, but the activity described in this article did support the
development of a greatly expanded edition of *The College Handbook* (84) including new forms of predictive information.

64 FLANAGAN, JOHN C. The implications of Project TALENT and related research
for guidance. *Measurement and Evaluation in Guidance,* 1969, vol. 2, no. 2,
pp. 116-123.

The author reviews briefly some implications of Project TALENT that have led to Project PLAN (Program for Learning in Accordance with Needs), a computer-supported individualized education program. The central function of the program is guidance and individual planning of curriculum units. It provides information regarding status of individual development in intellectual, occupational, and social areas and stresses the developmental nature of aptitude and intelligence. The program is also designed to inform students of occupational possibilities and to direct them in assuming responsibility for setting and achieving goals through management of their educational and personal development. The author describes methods used in the program and discusses further contributions to curriculum, instruction, measurement and evaluation, and teacher development. (See also 1243.)

65 HAVENS, ROBERT I. (ISSUE ED.) Technology in guidance. *Personnel and Guidance Journal,* 1970, vol. 49, pp. 170-263.

This special issue is a collection of invited articles designed to interpret the potential of computers in the field of guidance. Written in nontechnical language by guidance experts who are also knowledgeable about computer technology, the papers present a valuable introduction. Information storage and retrieval processes are described as well as some educational and career information systems. Invasion of privacy is also discussed, and some suggestions are given for regulation of the release of information. The role of the counselor is described as that of "linker," one who can help information generators and systems designers understand the needs of users, and who can also assist students in using the systems. Counselors are warned to keep abreast of the new technologies if they wish to share in the decisions that are likely to affect guidance in the future.

66 HILLS, JOHN R. College expectancy tables for high school counselors. *Personnel and Guidance Journal,* 1964, vol. 42, pp. 479-483.

This article describes a simple form for dissemination of admissions research data. The author reviews disadvantages of other methods including regression equations, predicted grades, frequency distributions, average test scores, and multiple predictors. The method described involves the use of the standard multiple regression analysis to compute an "index number," a combination of College Board Scholastic Aptitude Test scores and high school average. This index is used to indicate proportion admitted as freshmen and probability of achieving various freshman averages. The advantages of the expectancy table are ease of computation, flexibility of the approach, elimination of average scores, and statement of results in probabilities. This system has been used in a pacesetting statewide program of counselor information in Georgia.

67 HOLLIS, JOSEPH W., AND HOLLIS, LUCILE U. *Personalizing information processes: Educational, occupational and personal-social.* New York: Macmillan, 1969, 461 pp. $8.95.

This book deals with counseling methods used to identify, assimilate, and integrate information for the most meaningful use of each individual. The first part of the book reviews historical and philosophical foundations of personalizing information. The authors apply communications principles to counseling and guidance, formulating a three-dimensional conceptual model including the person, the area of information, and the depth of information needed. Further sections deal with three main areas of information: educational, occupational, and personal-social. The authors stress the integration of the three areas pointing out that trained ability, potential, and willingness for continuing education are major determinants of occupational development. The book approaches counseling from a different point of view than most and should provide a stimulating sourcebook.

68 Katz, Martin R. Can computers make guidance decisions for students? *College Board Review*, Summer 1969, no. 72, pp. 13-17.

The author describes a System of Interactive Guidance and Information (1244) under development at Educational Testing Service. While it has been clear that computers can do a number of routine noncounseling tasks, the intent of this system is to go beyond mere storage and retrieval of data and help students in the process as well as the content of career decision-making. In this regard, the intent is to help students take responsibility for those decisions. One takes special hope from the fact that the author talks like a counselor, not a computer.

69 Krumboltz, John D. (Ed.) *Revolution in counseling: Implications of behavioral science.* Boston: Houghton Mifflin, 1966, 121 pp. $2.36.

This small volume reports the proceedings of a conference at Stanford University on new directions in counseling. It includes papers by John Krumboltz, Sidney Bijou, Edward Shoben, H. B. McDaniel, and Gilbert Wrenn. A major theme in the conference was the application of modern behavioral sciences in the counseling process. It includes interesting though perhaps controversial new theoretical approaches.

70 Loughary, John W., and Bowman, Calvert W. Guidance information systems. *The School Counselor*, 1970, vol. 18, pp. 43-48.

Guidance information systems are criticized as having improved little in the last 20 to 30 years because they have been developed without sufficient regard for the ways pupils use them. The authors suggest that some of the processes needed for an effective system should be allocated to librarians, teachers, educational psychologists, and research personnel. Counselors should serve only in the end processes of developing specifications for information systems, helping students use them, and planning guidance information programs. They conclude that the technology is waiting to be used, but that "the critical question is not how to build guidance information systems, but what information should be put in them, including what form it should take."

71 Loughary, John W., et al. *Man-machine systems in education.* New York: Harper & Row, 1966, 242 pp.

This nontechnical guidebook to the potentials of man-machine systems in education is directed to an important goal—to make computer technology a partner instead of an afterthought in educational planning. Defining man-machine systems as "a set of planned procedures in which human and machine capabilities are used in an integrated manner," the authors complain that too often educators attempt to use machines to achieve results that were planned independently of the machines. They have provided excellent descriptions of a wide range of educational applications including instruction, instructional management, school management, pupil personnel services, student appraisal, and counseling and guidance.

72 Minor, Frank J., Myers, Roger A., and Super, Donald E. An experimental computer-based educational and career exploration system. *Personnel and Guidance Journal*, 1969, vol. 47, pp. 564-569.

The authors describe their view of the proper and useful functions of a computer-based information system for guidance. They emphasize fallibility of both student and counselor in handling information and their inability to devote sufficient time to the enormous clerical task of integrating relevant information. It is these functions that are suggested as especially well suited for computer support.

73 Rosser, Donald S. What you should know about new computer-based college selection services. *National Schools*, 1969, vol. 84, no. 5, pp. 47-49.

This brief article provides a useful thumbnail description of some of the computerized college selection services available as of early 1969. It mentions some advantages of such systems but gives less attention to possible disadvantages and the very uneven quality of programs.

74 SUPER, DONALD E., ET AL. *Computer-assisted counseling.* New York: Teachers College Press, Columbia University, 1970, 133 pp. $4.50.

This volume presents a series of papers focusing on the use of computers in the counseling process. They explore the impact of computers on guidance and instruction and describe several computer systems now being used in the field. The final three papers examine some of the larger issues involved in computer-assisted counseling: the effects on counselor roles, the possibility of dehumanization, the educational and political implications of this innovation, and the present status of research.

75 TIEDEMAN, DAVID V. Comprehending epigenesis in decision-making development: The Information System for Vocational Decisions, in Donald E. Super, *Computer-assisted counseling.* New York: Teachers College Press, Columbia University, 1970, pp. 23-36.

This report describes a computer-based Information System for Vocational Decisions, which is designed to aid in decision-making throughout the lifetime of the user from kindergarten to retirement. The system includes data concerning occupation, education, military service, family, and personal characteristics. The major purpose of the project is to assemble a system that incorporates vocational education and development into liberal education. Such a computer program is to remain merely heuristic, not determining career, but educating for individual responsibility and choice. The program is not operational, but it stands as an early landmark of theoretical development. (See also 1242.)

76 U. S. OFFICE OF EDUCATION. *Computer-based vocational guidance systems.* Wash., D. C.: Government Printing Office, 1969, 168 pp. $1.25.

This volume includes papers presented at a symposium concerning the development of systems for vocational guidance. Part I presents theoretical considerations in developing such systems; Part II considers a variety of problems involved in implementation; and Part III summarizes 10 vocational guidance systems under development. The authors are quite knowledgeable, and the volume describes well the state of the art as of 1968.

1.6 – *GUIDES AND DIRECTORIES.* A critical type of reference material for the guidance of high school graduates is the guide to postsecondary educational opportunities. There are a large number of these guides, and they vary a great deal with respect to purpose, content, and quality. The guides and directories represent two fairly distinct varieties, but both are lumped together because some publications fall in the indistinguishable middle ground.

There are directories to different types of educational institutions, and then there are books on how to go about planning for college. Many of the directories are intended for student use and consequently include a good deal of the "how to" information. Often the most authoritative and comprehensive directories (*American Universities and Colleges,* 101, and *American Junior Colleges,* 89) are restricted to accredited institutions or certain types of colleges or specialized programs.

77 ASTIN, ALEXANDER W. *Who goes where to college?* Chicago: Science Research Associates, 1965, 125 pp. $5.50; paperback $3.25.

In 1961 the author conducted a study that led to an assessment of 1,015 four-year colleges and universities in terms of characteristics of entering freshmen and institutional environment. Although Astin cautioned readers not to use the report as another "how to pick your college" guide, he acknowledged that it does provide a source of unique and relatively objective information about colleges. Indexes for each college provide estimates of intellectualism, estheticism, status, pragmatism, masculinity, size, selectivity, and six orientations: realistic, scientific, social, conventional, enterprising, and artistic. The usefulness of these data is diminished to whatever extent the environments and characteristics of freshmen at institutions have changed in a decade. (Also annotated in section 8.3.)

78 BARRON'S EDUCATIONAL SERIES. *Barron's college profiles in-depth.* A series of 150 studies of individual colleges. Woodbury, N. Y.: Barron's Educational Series, 1967-70. $1.50 each.

Barron's College Profiles In-Depth provide students and parents a comprehensive analysis of 150 American colleges and universities. Each institution is described and frankly assessed in an illustrated booklet averaging 20 pages. The contents are more than a catalog rehash; they contain much useful information presented in a readable style. Some of the *Profiles* may be a bit dated and their usefulness thus reduced. Nevertheless, they are a valuable source of information on selected colleges.

79 BOWLES, FRANK H., PACE, C. ROBERT, AND STONE, JAMES C. *How to get into college.* (4th ed.) New York: E. P. Dutton, 1968, 160 pp. $4.95.

This guide uses a unique question-and-answer format to cover a variety of concerns expressed by students and parents as they prepare for college admissions. The 373 specific questions reportedly resemble those usually asked by students or their parents and, therefore, range from quite general to very specific. In addition to chapters on traditional subjects such as testing, college choice, and finance, the book provides interesting information on studying abroad and the relationship of college to military service. This fourth edition is evidence of the book's continuing popularity and usefulness.

80 BURCKEL, CHRISTIAN E. *The college blue book.* (13th ed.) New York: CCM Information Corporation, 1969, 10 vols., 4,594 pp. $99.

This 10-volume directory provides a variety of information on nearly 3,500 accredited and nonaccredited two- and four-year institutions throughout the country. The complete set is revised every three years, and some sections are updated annually. Designed primarily to benefit those involved directly in the college admissions process, the volumes also have general reference value and are no doubt found in many public and collegiate libraries. A possible weakness is the fact that some of the factual information is evidently included as received from colleges without critical editing of apparent inconsistencies.

81 CASS, JAMES, AND BIRNBAUM, MAX. *Comparative guide to American colleges.* (1970-71 ed.) New York: Harper & Row, 1969, 837 pp. $10; paperback $4.95.

Normally published every other year, this handbook provides narrative descriptions of all accredited four-year colleges in the nation. The length and extent of information in each exhibit depend both on an institution's input and on editorial assessment of an institution's quality and reputation. In addition to providing readable information on admissions requirements, academic environment, campus life, and costs, the authors have categorized each college according to a Selectivity Index. The guide is well organized and well researched.

Although its usefulness varies from one exhibit to another, it is one of the best college guides prepared especially for students and counselors.

82 CASS, JAMES, AND BIRNBAUM, MAX. *Comparative guide to two-year colleges and four-year specialized schools and programs.* New York: Harper & Row, 1969, 275 pp. $7.95; paperback $3.50.

This volume provides information both on two-year colleges and on selected baccalaureate programs in the visual, performing, and communication arts. It separates the two-year colleges into two groups—residential and nonresidential. Descriptions of the residential colleges are similar in style and content to *American Junior Colleges* (89), whereas those for nonresidential colleges are considerably abbreviated. Descriptions of the specialized schools and programs include not only admissions requirements and student expenses but also commentary on the nature of various programs. Available in paperback, this volume is particularly valuable for its extensive information on specialized programs and unique data on the percentages of students in two-year-college terminal and transfer programs. The authors have also prepared the well-known *Comparative Guide to American Colleges* (81).

83 CRONER, ULRICH H. E. (ED.) *American trade schools directory.* Queens Village, N. Y.: Croner Publications, 1971. $12.

The *American Trade Schools Directory* is a looseleaf guide to public and private trade, industrial, and vocational schools in the United States. It is designed for use by counselors and others called upon to give vocational guidance. Names and addresses are provided for 4,500 schools in more than 250 trades; they are classified by trades and by states and cities. The directory is kept up to date by monthly supplements.

84 DILLENBECK, DOUGLAS D., ET AL. (EDS.) *The college handbook.* (1969 ed.) New York: College Entrance Examination Board, 1969, 1,327 pp. (Out of print)

This *Handbook* contains extended and readable self-descriptions of more than 800 accredited colleges that are members of the College Board (1112). In addition to complete information on curriculums, admissions, college life, expenses, and financial aid, most colleges supplied tables that describe the College Board Scholastic Aptitude Test scores and high school grades of applicants for admission, enrolled freshmen, and aid applicants. By comparing his own data with the data in these tables, a student may gain a better understanding of his likelihood for success at a particular college. Much of this tabular information is unique to the *Handbook.* Both the content and format make this guide useful not only for students and counselors but also for other professionals concerned with access to higher education.

[*Editor's note:* The 1969 *Handbook* was superseded in the fall of 1972 by a new edition, edited by Douglas D. Dillenbeck and Sue Wetzel. The 1972 *Handbook* describes more than 2,000 nationally recognized two-year and four-year colleges and includes advice to students on planning for college and applying for admission; tables as described above; and a series of state maps showing locations of all colleges listed and described. In two volumes. $9.50.]

85 ESKOW, SEYMOUR. *Barron's guide to the two-year colleges.* Woodbury, N. Y.: Barron's Educational Series, 1967, 368 pp. $5.95; paperback $3.50.

This readable guide for students and parents was prepared by a community college president. It provides the usual factual information on admissions requirements and procedures, program offerings, and costs for each of 859 colleges; it also includes several chapters on such pertinent topics as "Why go to college?" and "How to study effectively." In addition, it lists all the two-year colleges in the country that offer various transfer and vocational programs, ranging from data processing to horticulture to stewardess training. A companion volume for four-year institutions is *Barron's Profiles of American Colleges* (87).

86 Federation of Regional Accrediting Commissions of Higher Education. *Accredited institutions of higher education, 1970-71.* Wash., D. C.: American Council on Education, 1970, 327 pp. $2.50.

This annual directory reports the accreditation and preaccreditation status of United States colleges and universities. Part I includes very brief descriptions of these institutions in one of three groups: those that are accredited, those that are recognized candidates, and those that are correspondents. Part II is a supplement to *American Universities and Colleges* (101) and *American Junior Colleges* (89) and includes lengthy descriptions of those institutions accredited since the most recent publication of these two directories. This directory is particularly valuable to registrars and others interested in the accreditation status of institutions.

87 Fine, Benjamin. *Barron's profiles of American colleges* (1971-72 ed.) Woodbury, N. Y.: Barron's Educational Series, 1970, 882 pp. $9.95; paperback, $4.95.

This annual directory of all accredited, four-year colleges and universities is prepared particularly for students. The lengthy descriptions of each institution are easy to read yet include most of the descriptive and statistical information students generally seek. Although basically factual, each exhibit is intended to portray the college's academic and social environment; the author is often successful. The directory also includes a listing in which colleges are grouped into seven categories on the basis of academic selectivity. *Barron's Guide to the Two-Year Colleges* (85) is also available.

88 Foster, J. F., and Craig, T. (Eds.) *Commonwealth universities yearbook.* (47th ed.) London: Association of Commonwealth Universities, 1970, 1,874 pp. Wash., D. C.: American Council on Education. $24.

This unusual annual publication is the standard guide to universities in the 30 nations within the British Commonwealth; it is also the handbook of the Association of Commonwealth Universities. This 1,800-page volume provides exhaustive descriptions of most universities in the Commonwealth, complete with admissions requirements and the names and teaching fields of all full- and part-time faculty. Taken together, this volume, the *International Handbook of Universities* (93), and *American Universities and Colleges* (101) provide a comprehensive directory to most of the universities in the world. The *Yearbook* is also annotated in 819.

89 Gleazer, Edmund J. Jr. (Ed.) *American junior colleges.* (7th ed.) Wash., D. C.: American Council on Education, 1967, 957 pp. $14.

As the two-year counterpart to *American Universities and Colleges* (101), this directory presents principal characteristics, offerings, and statistical information for all 751 recognized, nonprofit two-year colleges in the nation. In most cases the material included is not only comprehensive and factual but also gets across the unique aspects and particular environment of each institution. Published every four years, the directory also provides articles on junior college trends and occupational education. It is the standard reference of its type and is particularly useful to guidance counselors, researchers, and other professionals in the junior college field.

90 Harper, William A. (Ed.) *1970 junior college directory.* Wash., D. C.: American Association of Junior Colleges, 1970, 112 pp. $2.

This very concise annual directory lists characteristics, enrollment, and student expense information for all approved, nonprofit two-year colleges in the nation. Although it includes virtually the same colleges as those reported in

American Junior Colleges (89), it is less detailed and presents the data in statistical rather than narrative form. As such it provides the reader with considerable information for over 30 colleges on a single page. Another important virtue is the fact that it is the most current publication of its type; consequently, the directory is especially valuable to professionals in the junior college field. See section 2.4 for another annotation of this publication.

91 HAWES, GENE R. *New American guide to colleges.* (3rd ed.) New York: New American Library, 1966, 560 pp. $10; paperback 95 cents.

This guide provides statistical data on more than 3,600 accredited and non-accredited colleges. Institutions are grouped into 14 categories, including private, coeducational, liberal arts, and Bible-training colleges. The exhibits make considerable use of abbreviations and are compact though sometimes difficult to read. Although intended to serve students and counselors directly, the guide seems most useful for an initial screening of colleges or for research purposes. The age of the data limits its usefulness, but a new edition is scheduled for 1972.

92 HOY, JOHN C. *Choosing a college.* New York: Dell, 1967, 298 pp. 75 cents.

Choosing a College is a comprehensive, readable description of the admissions process. Basically a handbook for students, the book covers college admissions in lively, narrative form making liberal use of examples and anecdotes. Some of the issues discussed are: how colleges weigh test scores and high school records; the basic types of interviews the applicant may anticipate, including 37 specific leading questions he may be asked; what colleges look for in application autobiographies; and how students can evaluate a college community.

93 KEYES, H. M. R., AND AITKEN, D. J. *International handbook of universities and other institutions of higher education.* (4th ed.) Paris: International Association of Universities, 1968, 1,178 pp. $16.

This large and comprehensive volume is the authoritative reference for information about universities and other institutions of higher education throughout the world, excluding the British Commonwealth and the United States. Published every three years since 1959, this edition covers 104 countries and territories. Individual entries are presented alphabetically by country, and most include brief descriptions of academic offerings, history and structure, admissions requirements, degrees and diplomas offered, and the size of the faculty and student body. Being the only reference of its type in the English language, it is an indispensable source of information for international higher education. It is a companion volume to *American Universities and Colleges* (101) and *Commonwealth Universities Yearbook* (88).

94 LASS, ABRAHAM H., AND WILSON, EUGENE S. *The college student's handbook.* New York: David White, 1970, 201 pp. $2.65.

This comprehensive guide identifies and discusses the academic, financial, and social problems facing college students. It is extremely readable and unusually practical. Written specifically for college-bound high school students, the handbook gives information and advice on such topics as how to take notes, the wise use of freedom, drugs, and the risks of drug use. It is not primarily a book that tells students how to get into a college; it is more a description of what to expect and suggestions on what to do after arriving on campus. As such it is one of the best references available.

95 LOVEJOY, CLARENCE E. *Lovejoy's career and vocational school guide.* (3rd ed.) New York: Simon and Schuster, 1967, 176 pp. $3.95.

This guide provides an orientation to vocations not requiring traditional academic degrees. It gives brief background information on vocational training and includes numerous lists: career titles, armed services assignments that prepare for civilian careers, names and addresses of organizations supplying information about specific careers, apprenticeable careers, institutions offering training in different vocational fields, and capsule descriptions of 3,533 vocational schools.

96 LOVEJOY, CLARENCE E. *Lovejoy's prep school guide.* (3rd ed.) New York: Simon and Schuster, 1968, 240 pp. $5.95; paperback $3.95.
   Lovejoy's Prep School Guide is a reference book to over 2,300 American preparatory schools. The scope of information is uneven; some institutions are thoroughly described, others hardly at all. Schools are listed alphabetically by name and state, and accreditation status is indicated. A useful listing of church-controlled or church-related schools by denomination is also provided.

97 LOVEJOY, CLARENCE E. *Lovejoy's college guide.* (11th ed.) New York: Simon and Schuster, 1970, 447 pp. $7.50; paperback $3.95.
   This guide includes more than 3,200 American colleges and universities and is generally published biennially. While it provides extensive information on most well-known institutions, it often includes minimal information on smaller institutions or community colleges. The exhibits are organized to get across factual information rather than to provide interesting narrative. One useful feature of the guide is its listing of all the colleges offering programs in each of nearly 500 career fields. Companion volumes include *Lovejoy's Career and Vocational School Guide* (95) and *Lovejoy's Prep School Guide* (96). A monthly *Lovejoy's Guidance Digest* provides information on current developments in admissions, costs, accreditations, etc., and thus bridges the gap between revisions of the *Guide.*

98 MIDDLE STATES ASSOCIATION OF COLLEGES AND SECONDARY SCHOOLS. *Freshmen and transfer space availability survey.* New York: Middle States Association of Colleges and Secondary Schools, 1971.
   This useful monthly survey lists available space for freshmen and transfers at all member colleges. The openings are listed by sex and residential or commuter status. The booklet also lists the admissions officer and telephone number for each college.

99 PLANS FOR PROGRESS. *Directory of predominantly Negro colleges and universities in the United States of America.* Wash., D. C.: Government Printing Office, 1969, 85 pp. $1.
   This specialized directory provides selected information on 85 predominantly Negro four-year institutions located primarily in the Southeast. Its unique features include a listing of the administrative staff at each college and a listing of all degrees offered including how many students received each degree.

100 SARGENT, PORTER. *Handbook of private schools.* Boston: Porter Sargent, 1970, 1,506 pp. $14.
   The *Handbook of Private Schools* is based on an annual survey of about 1,000 independent schools in 49 states. General information for all institutions is given in abbreviated statistical form in addition to a short paragraph presenting unique characteristics of each school. More than one-third of the schools paid for inclusion in a supplementary illustrated section giving more information. A concise listing of additional schools not included in the descriptive sections and a directory of summer academic programs are also provided.

101 SINGLETARY, OTIS A. (ED.) *American universities and colleges.* (10th ed.) Wash., D. C.: American Council on Education, 1968, 1,782 pp. $22.
   This comprehensive directory is the standard reference for descriptions of all accredited four-year colleges and universities in the nation. Published every four years, this volume provides the most authoritative and detailed institutional information of any publication of its type. Data included range from descriptions of student life to departmental offerings, faculty size, and enumeration of sources

of income. In addition to institutional exhibits, the directory provides descriptions of various types of professional education and lists colleges offering training in each area. Essentially a straightforward factual publication, the directory is particularly valuable to guidance counselors and other professionals concerned with higher education.

102 STANFORD UNIVERSITY. *Approaching Stanford.* Stanford, Calif.: Stanford University, 1970, 141 pp. Free.

Colleges and universities are beginning to respond to the charge that college catalogs do not "tell it like it is." One of the most interesting responses is this bulletin prepared largely by Stanford students. Although intended as a handbook for freshmen, it is now sent to freshman applicants. It provides the same basic information that traditional catalogs do, but it does so from a student rather than an institutional frame of reference. Pages are embellished with interesting and pertinent student quotations and illustrations, and as Stanford's dean of admissions stated, it "yields far more insights into what it might be like to attend Stanford . . . than we would otherwise have been able to provide."

103 SULKIN, SIDNEY. *Complete planning for college.* New York: Harper & Row, 1968, 324 pp. $6.95.

This handbook presents considerably more factual information than the other how-to books in this section, yet its organization and style make it equally readable. The book goes beyond a general discussion of admissions problems to provide specific advice on choosing a college and preparing for college entrance. It includes a number of lists, among them a list of the most competitive colleges and a list of accredited colleges that frequently have openings for more freshmen. Because of its factual base and the number of references it gives to further sources of information on specific areas such as testing or financial aid, this guide is as useful to counselors as it is to students and parents.

104 TURNER, CORNELIUS P. (ED.) *A guide to the evaluation of educational experiences in the armed services.* Wash., D. C.: American Council on Education, 1968, 527 pp. $10.

This guide facilitates recognition of military educational experiences by colleges and universities. It lists and concisely describes all military educational programs and includes recommendations for collegiate credit developed by civilian educators on ACE's Commission on Accreditation of Service Experiences. The guide also describes two national testing programs, the Tests of General Educational Development (1227) and the College-Level Examination Program (1222), that provide adults with a method for evaluating their educational achievements. Since this is the only directory of its type, this publication is particularly important to collegiate registrars and admissions officers. The most recent previous edition was published in 1954, and this infrequent publication schedule has been a limitation to its usefulness. (Also annotated in section 8.7.)

105 UNITED NEGRO COLLEGE FUND. *Information for applicants to colleges in the United Negro College Fund.* New York: UNCF, 1968, 52 pp.

This pamphlet describes each UNCF college in two-page annotations, including programs of study, admissions requirements, expenses, and financial aid available. (See 1133 for an annotation of the United Negro College Fund.)

106 U. S. OFFICE OF EDUCATION, NATIONAL CENTER FOR EDUCATIONAL STATISTICS. *Education directory, 1970-71: Higher education.* Wash., D. C.: Government Printing Office, 1971, 515 pp. $3.75.

This annual directory lists virtually all the higher education institutions recognized by the U. S. Office of Education. In addition to information on location, control, program offerings, and accreditation status, each entry lists the name and title of each administrative officer. This is the only national directory with such information, and therefore it is particularly useful to professionals in the field who want to communicate directly with specific persons or offices. (Also annotated in section 15.5.)

1.7—CAREER INFORMATION SOURCES. As in the case of guides and directories, career-information sources tend to fall either into the category of advice manuals or annotated listings of career possibilities. Some of the latter are quite comprehensive and extremely useful (e.g., 109 and 117). Most of the guides and directories to educational opportunities are prepared under private auspices, whereas many of the major sources of career information tend to be developed by government agencies or professional groups.

107 ADAMS, CHARLES, AND KIMBALL, SAMARIA. *Career facts.* Reading, Mass.: Addison-Wesley, 1966, 299 pp. $4.

Career Facts presents information on more than 400 jobs and careers requiring education beyond the high school level and/or extensive experience. The guide is well organized and easy to use. In addition to giving general facts on specific careers, it is designed to provide an overview of careers available in major industries. Included for each career are job descriptions, training and other requirements, sources of information, and pay scales. The data are compiled mostly from United States Department of Labor materials. A companion volume, *Job Facts,* deals primarily with jobs immediately available to people with some high school education. Both books were sponsored by the research and development program of the National Association of Manufacturers.

108 CALIFORNIA DEPARTMENT OF HUMAN RESOURCES DEVELOPMENT. *Occupational guides.* Sacramento, Calif.: Research and Statistics Section, California Department of HRD.

Occupational Guides are single sheets or leaflets providing general job descriptions of 460 occupations. The information covers job duties, working conditions, employment outlook, salaries and hours, entrance requirements, promotions, and training requirements. About half the occupations are college oriented. This series is particularly useful for junior college vocational programs. California Department of Health Resources Development also publishes a series of *Occupational Profiles*—single volumes describing 70-80 occupations in a selected local area generally open to persons who have not gone beyond high school. These are available at local offices of the Department of HRD. Other states have various means of making available similar information through state employment offices, though these guides are probably more extensive than those available in most states.

109 HOPKE, WILLIAM E. (ED.) *The encyclopedia of careers and vocational guidance.* Vol. I. *Planning your career.* Vol. II. *Careers and occupations.* Garden City, N. Y.: Doubleday, 1967, 1,536 pp. $30.

This comprehensive, illustrated encyclopedia gives extensive information on jobs in all areas. Volume I contains chapters on guidance plus 71 articles describing major career areas written by authorities in the various fields. It also includes a useful bibliography. Volume II includes 220 articles covering over 650 specific jobs. Each article contains detailed information on the nature of the work, requirements, history, methods of entering, advancement, employment outlook, earnings, social and psychological factors, and sources of additional information.

110 KAUFFMAN, WARREN E. (ED.) *College placement annual, 1971*, Bethlehem, Pa.: College Placement Council, 1970, 640 pp, Free.

This guide is sponsored by the eight regional placement associations of the United States and Canada for the benefit of graduating seniors seeking employment. It includes a series of articles describing the current employment situation for college graduates and provides suggestions concerning employment interviews, preparing resumes, etc. The bulk of the publication consists of brief statements from 2,000 corporate and governmental employers describing the nature of each organization and the types of positions open. It is provided free to college seniors and alumni through their college placement offices. (Also annotated in section 6.5.)

111 LISTON, ROBERT A. *On the job training and where to get it*. New York: Julian Messner, 1967, 190 pp. $3.95.

This handy and informative little book was written for the career-seeking high school graduate. It describes many on-the-job training opportunities in such traditional fields as industrial production, building trades, retail sales, and service occupations as well as newly developing technological industries. Types of training are suggested by illustrations from specific firms such as Bell Telephone and IBM. The author includes advice on the practical aspects of choosing a field and a specific company.

112 SCIENCE RESEARCH ASSOCIATES. *SRA career information kit*. Chicago: SRA, 1970. $90 for series; some briefs available for 49 cents.

This kit is a series of 400 occupational briefs covering all major fields. The four-page briefs are printed on heavy durable paper for repeated use. Each describes for a single occupation: the duties generally performed, personal requirements, necessary education and training, earning and working conditions, advancement opportunities, and future employment outlook. Selected references and addresses of relevant organizations for obtaining further information are also provided. A list of titles is available.

113 TOY, HENRY JR. *Federal dollars for scholars*. Wash., D. C.: Nu-Toy, 1970. $4.20.

This especially valuable volume describes for students, parents, and counselors a large number of federal career-training programs that are available through such diverse agencies as the United States Army and the National Science Foundation. Eligibility requirements, application procedures, and support available are described for each program. Other sections provide an excellent description of military requirements, alternatives and opportunities, and a description of the executive branch of the government to give students an insight into the agencies with which they may need to deal. (Also annotated in section 2.5.)

114 U. S. AIR FORCE. *Let's go Air Force! A guide to Air Force opportunities*. Wash., D. C.: Government Printing Office, 1969, 28 pp. Free from recruiting centers.

This booklet explains career opportunities open to enlistees in the Air Force. It contains short descriptions of the many technical training courses offered by the Air Force in four categories: electronics, mechanical, general, and administrative. It is designed to give the prospective enlistee an initial idea of careers in such specialties as air-traffic control, radar repair, and medical technology. The pamphlet also discusses basic training, options for further education financed completely or partially by the service, and benefits—pay, vacation, retirement, and family security.

115 U. S. ARMY. *The secret of getting ahead*. Wash., D. C.: Government Printing Office, 1970, 39 pp. Free from recruiting centers.

This booklet provides the prospective enlistee an introduction to career opportunities in the Army. It describes the three major categories of Army training: (1) Army Service Schools, which are listed in the pamphlet and provide training for occupations ranging from aircraft electrician to offset press operator; (2) Army Career Groups, in which an enlistee selects a field rather than a specific classroom training course and then receives either on-the-job training or specific technical courses; and (3) Combat Arms, which allows a choice of the fighting branches—infantry, armor, or field artillery. Opportunities in Army Air Defense, medical training, the Special Forces, Army Intelligence, and the Army Band are also mentioned, in addition to Officer Candidate School and various benefits of Army life. Each recruiting center maintains a set of briefs on current specific courses available for review by the prospective enlistee. These briefs detail the work performed, qualifications, etc., for each career opportunity.

116 U. S. BUREAU OF LABOR STATISTICS. *Education and jobs: A series of pamphlets to guide young people to jobs that match different levels of education and training.* Wash., D. C.: Government Printing Office, 1968. $1 per kit or $57 per 100 kits.

This very useful set of five charts condenses the highlights of the *Occupational Outlook Handbook* (117). The charts are arranged by level of education required: (1) jobs for which a high school education is preferred, but not essential; (2) jobs for which a high school education is generally required; (3) jobs for which junior college, technical institute, or other specialized training is usually required; (4) jobs for which apprenticeship training is available; and (5) jobs for which a college education is usually required. For 700 occupations in 30 major industries, these brief charts summarize the number of people employed in that occupation in 1966, qualifications and training required, and employment opportunities and trends. (Also annotated in section 6.5.)

117 U. S. BUREAU OF LABOR STATISTICS. *Occupational outlook handbook: Employment information on occupations for use in guidance.* (1968-69 ed.) Wash., D.C.: Government Printing Office, 1968, 763 pp. $4.25.

Occupational Outlook Handbook is an extremely useful and authoritative source of career information. This widely used illustrated handbook gives the latest information on over 700 occupations. Included for each occupation is detailed information on the nature of the work, training requirements, earnings and working conditions, employment outlook, and sources of additional information. The handbook also contains brief overviews of the major occupational areas, introductory chapters on employment, population trends, and supplementary sources of occupational information. *Occupational Outlook Quarterly* (1339) presents the latest developments between biennial editions; *Occupational Outlook Reprint Series* provides over 100 reprints from the *Handbook*.

118 U. S. DEPARTMENT OF LABOR. *Job guide for young workers.* Wash., D. C.: Government Printing Office, 1969, 200 pp. $1.50.

Published annually by the U. S. Department of Labor, the *Job Guide for Young Workers* is an especially useful resource for career guidance particularly at the secondary level. Written for young people, the *Job Guide* provides occupational briefs discussing usual duties, job characteristics, qualifications, employment prospects, advancement opportunities, and application procedures for 150 jobs. Introductory material giving general career-guidance information is also provided.

119 U. S. DEPARTMENT OF LABOR, MANPOWER ADMINISTRATION. *Merchandising your job talents.* Wash., D. C.: Government Printing Office, 1969, 26 pp. 25 cents.

This pamphlet tells job seekers how to prepare a resume and how to write a letter of application and provides an illustration of each. It lists sources of job information, such as placement services and industrial unions, and comments on the most effective use of each. The pamphlet also explains how to prepare for job interviews and psychological tests.

120 U. S. DEPARTMENT OF LABOR, MANPOWER ADMINISTRATION. *Apprentice training: Sure way to a skilled craft*. Wash., D. C.: Government Printing Office, 1970, 8 pp. 15 cents.

This small pamphlet lists 79 occupations and the number of years of apprenticeship training required for each. It gives general pay scales for apprentices and journeymen and briefly describes apprenticeship benefits available to veterans. Addresses are listed for the 10 regional offices of the U. S. Department of Labor's Bureau of Apprenticeship and Training and the 35 nationwide Apprenticeship Information Centers. A student can also obtain information from his city's Urban League or the union representing individual trades.

121 U. S. NAVY. *Guidebook: Special Navy enlisted tours*. Wash., D. C.: Government Printing Office, 1969, 96 pp. Free from recruiting centers.

Since the educational structure of the Navy is more complex than that of the other Armed Forces, this publication first gives a general explanation of the various Navy technical training schools and on-the-job instruction programs. Then it presents a series of vocational training briefs describing individually the more than 60 major occupations in eight categories: deck; ordnance; electronics; administrative and clerical; engineering; construction; aviation; and medical, miscellaneous, and steward. For each occupation the booklet describes duties performed, training provided, qualifications, and related civilian jobs. It also discusses briefly the citizen's military obligation, the Naval Reserve, the advantages of Navy life, and how to enlist.

122 WHITFIELD, EDWIN A., AND HOOVER, RICHARD. *Guide to careers through vocational training*. San Diego: Robert R. Knapp, 1968, 312 pp. $5.95.

This especially useful and well-organized volume contains job descriptions for 145 careers requiring no more than two years of post-high school training. The occupations covered are divided into science, technical, outdoor, business, clerical, linguistic, esthetic, and service categories. In addition to descriptions, the guide provides information on requirements and qualifications, preparation and training, special entry requirements, employment outlook, and wages offered in the four major geographical regions. Each category concludes with a list of sources for further inquiry.

SECTION 2: FINANCING EDUCATION

Problems of financing education range across several quite different areas of interest. This access process includes academic theory concerning the economic value of education, programs to finance education, and the problems of dispersing the funds. It is a critical process for several reasons.

First, higher education has become accepted as a major route to economic development through effective utilization of human resources. Second, mass attendance in higher education and greatly increased unit costs have combined to make college a substantial financial commitment of the nation. Consequently, the allocation of resources and the means whereby the burden is distributed become matters of considerable public and political interest. Third, the financing process has become a major social issue because it bears heavily on equality of educational opportunity.

The major aspects of the financing process described in the following sections differ markedly with respect to the nature of the problems, the character of the literature, and the professionals involved. On that basis alone, it seems safe to conclude that communication between theory and practice in this area is quite limited. There are, in fact, some data that support that conclusion (185).

2.1 – *ECONOMICS OF HIGHER EDUCATION*. Much of the work concerned with the economics of higher education involves the construction of economic theory and analysis of the distribution of financial resources associated with the expenditure of funds for education. It is a relatively new field, and most of the significant work has been done since the mid-1950s. Blaug (125) has prepared an excellent bibliography for much of that period.

There are several prominent problems. One is the question of estimating the benefit from the investment in human capital (123 and 129 are classic references). Another favorite topic has been the estimation of economic returns to the individual from higher education (see 130). Recently there has been considerable interest in the question of who pays and who gains. A well-known study by Hansen and Weisbrod (132) provides a good example of the latter type of analysis.

Work in this area has been carried out primarily in the context of the academic discipline of economics. Most of the significant literature is in the form of books or special reports; journal articles tend to be scattered throughout the economic literature. The *Journal of Human Resources* (1328) is a new and especially useful source. The Organization for Economic Cooperation and Development (1138) has been active in recent years in sponsoring and publishing work in this area. Its journal, the *OECD Observer* (1340), is a good source of material on international data and comparative studies of the economics of education. In this country the Brookings Institution (1158) and the Committee for Economic Development (1166) are important centers of economic research that periodically publish work related to access to higher education.

123 BECKER, GARY S. *Human capital: A theoretical and empirical analysis, with special reference to education.* New York: Columbia University Press, for National Bureau of Economic Research, 1964, 187 pp. $5.50.

Interest in human capital investment has resulted from the realization that the growth of physical capital explains a limited part of the growth of income in most countries. Much circumstantial evidence testifies to the economic importance of human capital investment, especially in the form of education. In this highly regarded book, Becker presents a general theory of human capital and discusses the effect of various types of human capital investment on earnings, unemployment, etc. One type of such investment, formal education, is examined in detail. New estimates are given of the private and social rates of return during the last 25 years, including separate estimates for demographic groups at various ability levels.

The author concludes that an average college entrant may expect a 10 to 12 percent return per annum on investment. The rate is higher for urban, male, white graduates, and lower for rural, female, and nonwhite graduates, and for college dropouts. Even though college graduates are more able than high school graduates on the average, Becker argues that the earning differential between the two is due more to the college education than to the ability differential. The rapid growth in the number of high school and college graduates over the past two decades has not reduced their economic position, indicating that "educational attainments adjust to, as well as influence, the demands of the economic system."

124 BENSON, CHARLES S. (ED.) *Perspectives on the economics of education. Readings in school finance and business management.* Boston: Houghton Mifflin, 1963, 475 pp. $7.50.

This book of readings provides a broad perspective of the economics of higher education. It gives considerable attention to taxation and fiscal administration but also explores fundamental questions of the economic structure of public education, the effective use of resources in the educational establishment, and investigations of the economic returns from schooling.

125 BLAUG, MARK. *Economics of education: A selected annotated bibliography.* Oxford: Pergamon Press, 1966, 190 pp. $8.50.

In recent years the rapidly increasing interest in the economics of education has brought an acceleration in the literature relating to the topic. This annotated bibliography surveys research on the economics of education published in English, French, and German. A chronological listing has been used to demonstrate the development up to the end of 1965. One section contains a bibliography of bibliographies. It is an especially well-organized and annotated reference to the important literature in this area.

126 CHAMBERS, M. M. *Higher education: Who pays? Who gains?* Danville, Ill.: Interstate, 1968, 302 pp. $6.95.

The author calls his book a subjective essay dealing with comprehensive concepts applicable to the support of higher education in the United States during the final third of the twentieth century. Throughout the book one is reminded of the author's chief thesis—that American higher education should be largely tax supported and should be available, free of charge, to all who desire it and can profit from it.

127 COLLEGE ENTRANCE EXAMINATION BOARD. *The economics of higher education.* New York: College Entrance Examination Board, 1967, 89 pp. $2.

This publication includes 11 papers by prominent authors presented at the Third College Scholarship Service Colloquium on Financial Aid, held in May 1966. Topics include economic and pricing problems of higher education, the role of government in the financing of higher education, and various suggested alternative methods of educational financing. The volume provides a useful brief overview of many interrelated problems affecting the finance of higher education.

128 DENISON, EDWARD F. *The sources of economic growth in the United States and the alternatives before us.* New York: Committee for Economic Development, 1962, 297 pp.

In this classic study, the author identifies major sources of economic growth in the United States in the last 50 years and measures the quantitative importance of each source. In devising these measures, he attempts to offer a "menu of possible ways to affect the rate of growth that states, in quantitative terms, the probable effect of each alternative upon economic growth and its price tag." In measuring the effect of increased education of the labor force, Denison offers evidence attributing three-fifths of income differentials among males of the same age to formal education.

129 DENISON, EDWARD F. Education and growth, in Charles S. Benson (Ed.), *Perspectives on the economics of education: Readings in school finance and business management.* Boston: Houghton Mifflin, 1963, pp. 33-43.

This article by Denison provides a summary of the contribution of formal education to economic growth. It also includes an attempt to estimate the economic effects of raising the school-leaving age. This analysis along with some others undertaken by economists does not take adequately into account the indirect benefits of education. Nonetheless, it does quantify some aspects of investment in human capital.

130 HANOCH, GIORA. An economic analysis of earnings and schooling. *Journal of Human Resources,* 1967, vol. 2, pp. 310-329.

This study is an analysis of the economics of earnings, in relationship to age and level of schooling of a sample of 57,000 males drawn from the 1960 Census. The first section sets up earnings-age profiles, corresponding to schooling levels within racial and geographic subgroups. Internal rates of return are then derived and analyzed in terms of the demand function for investment in education. The author points out that the estimates refer to private rates of return and do not take into account social costs and benefits, or the establishment of a criterion for evaluating the social rate of return of additional schooling for a given group.

131 HANSEN, W. LEE. Economics of education, in Robert L. Ebel (Ed.), *Encyclopedia of educational research.* (4th ed.) New York: Macmillan, 1969, pp. 337-342.

This brief review of the economics of higher education is useful and readily available, though the bibliography is not so extensive or any more up-to-date than that provided in Woodhall's brief review (145).

132 HANSEN, W. LEE, AND WEISBROD, BURTON A. *Benefits, costs, and finance of public higher education.* Chicago: Markham, 1969, 114 pp. $5.95.

This analysis of the benefits and costs of public higher education in California, based on a study done for the California State Legislature in 1965, has important implications for educational finance. The study found that a four-year education at tax-supported public colleges and universities represented a substantial subsidy going disproportionately to those in relatively high income groups. The authors point out the paradox of a system where "those who benefit most from the public higher education system are, in general, those least in need of help in paying for what they receive." See Windham (143) for a generally similar result from a Florida study. See Pechman (138) for a counterargument.

133 HARRIS, SEYMOUR E. (ED.) *Economic aspects of higher education.* Paris: Organization for Economic Co-operation and Development, 1964, 246 pp. $3.75.

This volume, the first publication of the Study Group in the Economics of

Education of the OECD, contains background papers of the June 1962 meeting concerning education as a link to economic progress. Pooling the resources of economists, educators, and policy makers in the 20 countries represented by OECD, these comparative analyses of how problems in admissions, enrollments, and financing are handled in different administrative structures provide useful information for long-range planning.

134 MACHLUP, FRITZ. *The production and distribution of knowledge in the United States.* Princeton, N. J.: Princeton University Press, 1962, 416 pp. (Out of print)

This book is addressed to the general question of how knowledge is produced. The author systematically examines education, research and development, communication media, information machines, and information services. He analyzes each with respect to its use of resources, its productivity, and its contribution to the body of knowledge. The study is unusual in attempting to analyze the complementary roles of formal schooling and incidental education.

135 MILLER, JAMES L. JR. *State budgeting for higher education: The use of formulas and cost analysis.* Ann Arbor: Institute of Public Administration, University of Michigan, 1965, 228 pp. $3.50.

This study describes procedures as of 1963 in making formulas for budget requests and cost analysis used to work out appropriations to public higher education in California, Kentucky, Florida, Indiana, and Texas. The author summarizes the need for further investigation on such matters as the significance of measurement units, the effects on innovation and creativity, and the long-term accuracy of a formula as institutions grow and change. It is useful background reading for educators and officials concerned with the financing of public higher education.

136 MUSHKIN, SELMA J. (ED.) *Economics of higher education.* Wash., D. C.: Government Printing Office, 1962, 406 pp. $1.50.

This collection of papers by leading economists is intended as a "working tool" for those concerned with higher education as an investment for the development of human capital. Part I considers the increasing demand for higher education in relation to manpower needs. Further chapters outline the theory of human capital with special attention to education and economic growth and assess the sources of funding available to universities. The final chapter summarizes the present scope of research and suggests directions for future investigation. The volume is dated in many respects, but it still offers a useful view of many aspects of the economics of higher education.

137 ORGANIZATION FOR ECONOMIC CO-OPERATION AND DEVELOPMENT, STUDY GROUP IN THE ECONOMICS OF EDUCATION. *Financing of education for economic growth.* Paris: OECD, 1966, 429 pp. $7.

This volume contains the papers presented at the 1964 OECD Paris conference of the Study Group in the Economics of Education. The purpose of the conference was to investigate problems and to assess progress toward the educational goal for OECD countries—the expenditure of economic resources in proper relationship to the essential contributions of education to economic growth and social progress. One of the major concerns was to determine whether justified claims on economic resources can be met by existing tax and budget structures, and if not what educational priority systems should be established. In addition to treatments of general principles and problems, the papers include reports on the status of educational progress and spending in individual countries.

138 PECHMAN, JOSEPH A. The distributional effects of public higher education in California. *Journal of Human Resources,* 1970, vol. 5, pp. 361-370.

In this article the author takes issue with conclusions reached by Hansen and

Weisbrod (132) to the effect that the system of taxation and financing of higher education in the state of California act to redistribute income from the poor to the wealthy. Pechman argues for a different method of analysis that would supposedly reverse the conclusion. In a further comment in the following issue of the same journal, Hartman attempts to dismiss the methodological quibble and argues that the real problem is to broaden the social benefits of higher education and to eliminate inequality of opportunity.

139 RIBICH, THOMAS I. *Education and poverty.* Wash., D. C.: Brookings Institution, 1968, 163 pp. $5.50.

The conclusion of this study is that money spent on education does not provide commensurate payoffs in the war on poverty, judging by cost-benefit analysis of federal educational programs. Using the impact on personal income as a yardstick for gauging the success of educational spending, Ribich evaluates compensatory and vocational programs and across-the-board increases to school districts. He cautions that his conclusions should be considered tentative, pending further research. Even so, he warns, "One cannot assume complacently that any and all new educational expenditures yield returns far in excess of costs." Children who participated in Higher Horizons, the largest prototype compensatory program, did not change in capacity to learn—as measured by IQ, or in anticipated lengthening of educational careers; hence the author asserts that the extra $61 per pupil per year cost of the program did not accomplish commensurate gains. Arguing that "'the younger the better' is not an unassailable maxim," Ribich finds that older children benefited more in cost-benefit ratios than children in early grades and preschool programs. He recommends that they should participate equally in compensatory programs. His conclusion is that policy makers should take into account alternative use of funds in direct help to alleviate poverty, and that they "should search for an optimum mix between education and direct help."

140 SCHULTZ, THEODORE W. *The economic value of education.* New York: Columbia University Press, 1963, 92 pp. $3.

In this brief monograph commissioned by the Ford Foundation, Schultz succinctly reviews literature, identifies unanswered questions, and suggests research needed in the economics of education. Starting with the concept of investment in human capital as a key factor in economic growth, Schultz goes on to discuss the economic components and costs of education and to define educational economic value in terms of returns. The 200-item bibliography provides a useful reference to early work on the economics of higher education.

141 SCHULTZ, THEODORE W. Resources for higher education: An economist's view. *Journal of Political Economy,* 1968, vol. 76, pp. 327-347.

This article provides a perceptive and generally nontechnical review of the current status of the economics of higher education. The author outlines and discusses the following major propositions: Education is a form of human capital, and its main functions are discovering talent, instruction, and research. There are few, if any, gains in the measured productivity of teachers. Earnings forgone by students constitute over half of the real cost of higher education, and long-term projections of the demand for higher education are "beset with all manner of uncertainty." The central economic concept in financing should be the rate of return to investment. Finally, an important social condition is the fact that education changes the distribution of personal income.

The author cites a number of important advantages to the present organizational structure of higher education and goes on to specify some organizational changes that would "strengthen the tendency toward a more efficient allocation of resources." The article provides coherent and educational, if not easy, reading. It has the advantage of identifying strengths and weaknesses in current economic theory of higher education.

142 WEISBROD, BURTON A. Education and investment in human capital. *Journal of Political Economy,* Supplement, 1962, vol. 70, no. 5, part 2, pp. 106-123.

Most analyses of the economic returns from education have focused on earning capacity, but this paper suggests various ways by which society benefits from formal education. In addition to increased earning power, education provides the recipient with varied options, ranging from job opportunity to leisure and security, additional schooling, way of life, and adaptability options that can provide a hedge against technological displacement. Among the external beneficiaries of a person's education are: his future children who receive informal education in the home; his neighbors who benefit from the inculcation of acceptable social norms; taxpayers who are spared certain welfare, crime, and law enforcement costs; employers who benefit from the improved quality of the labor force; and society in general which benefits from the type of political, economic, and social system that widespread literacy makes possible.

143 WINDHAM, DOUGLAS M. *Education, equality and income redistribution: A study of public higher education.* Lexington, Mass.: D. C. Heath, 1970, 127 pp. $10.

This study is concerned with the financing of higher education in Florida and its relation to taxation and the redistribution of income. The author concludes that since the poor pay, in regressive taxes, for the educational benefits enjoyed by the well-to-do, "As a whole the lower income classes would be better off without a public system of higher education." This is similar to the conclusion reached by Hansen and Weisbrod (132), though those authors used a somewhat different method of analysis of public higher education in California. Pechman (138) suggests that the California system of taxation and financing of higher education may not actually be regressive. Although taxation in Florida may be a special case because of its constitutional prohibition against income taxes, the other policy revisions suggested by Windham can be extrapolated to apply to the general case of public higher education. They are: (1) increasing the contributions of the federal government, (2) reframing admissions policies to minimize "income bias" in distributing students attending college, (3) changing fee policies to direct tuition grants or to sliding scales according to family income, (4) changing the role of the black public university to endorse the principle of providing education for the disadvantaged at levels commensurate with their abilities and needs.

144 WITMER, DAVID R. Economic benefits of college education. *Review of Educational Research,* 1970, vol. 40, pp. 511-524.

This article summarizes and evaluates selected literature dealing with the economic benefits of higher education. Witmer traces the development of the theory of economic benefit and reviews early attitudes and pioneering studies. The bulk of the article covers contemporary attitudes and concepts with special attention to internal rate of return; studies concerning indirect, external, and social benefits; and methods using aptitude, motivation, and schooling as predictors of income.

145 WOODHALL, MAUREEN. The economics of education. *Review of Educational Research,* 1967, vol. 37, pp. 387-398.

This article provides a very readable brief review of the literature on the economics of education. Topics include: economic returns of education, investment in human capital, contribution of education to economic growth, educational planning, and cost-benefit analysis.

2.2 — *FINANCING METHODS*. It was during the 1960s that large amounts of state and federal funds were first appropriated for direct support of institutions and students. Section 13.7 includes annotations of the major federal legislation that has provided funds for student aid. Section 13.1 includes representative examples of different types of large aid programs.

The advent of large aid programs has occasioned a new and somewhat amorphous literature concerned with policy considerations and the development and evaluation of these programs. Much of the literature has come in the form of special reports from such agencies as the United States Office of Education, the College Entrance Examination Board, and the Carnegie Commission on Higher Education. The Southern Regional Education Board, Western Interstate Commission for Higher Education, and the Education Commission of the States (1178) also publish useful material. The best sources of current information regarding pending legislation and status of federal programs of financial support are the *Chronicle of Higher Education* (1355) and *Higher Education and National Affairs* (1373).

Part of this literature is concerned with the nature of aid programs and how they should be administered (for example, see Kirkpatrick, 160 and Johns, 159). In the late 1960s, there were a number of studies concerned with estimating various types of financial need: need of different types of students, need within various professions or institutions, and need for different purposes such as equalization of educational opportunity. There also has been considerable interest in estimating gross financial need of higher institutions (150) and developing comprehensive financial aid programs (172).

Since most of this work is recent, one should reserve judgment, but several shortcomings are worth noting. The actual results of alternative methods of financing higher education or providing aid to students are more often than not based on guesswork. Relatively little systematic research has been put to such questions. Too often the arguments for particular programs seem to be primarily economic and political rather than educational and social.

146 BECKER, ERNST. The financing of higher education: A review of historical trends and projections for 1975-76, in U. S. Office of Education, *Trends in postsecondary education.* Wash., D. C.: Government Printing Office, 1970, pp. 97-180.

In this chapter the authors review the costs and the sources of income for higher education from 1959 through 1967 and then attempt to project probable income and expenditures through 1976. Assumptions about the future are based largely on trends of the recent past, but the relative priority assigned to higher education poses a considerable uncertainty.

Several major trends are documented. Between 1959 and 1967 total institutional expenditures increased at a higher average rate than income in all types of institutions except the two-year public college. Tuitions and fees have been increasing at a rate considerably higher than that for personal disposable income. Federal funds are almost evenly distributed between public and private institutions, and federal aid to higher education has risen at higher rates than federal income. Voluntary support, with some minor exceptions, tends to make up a declining share of total institutional income, and endowment income represents only a small portion of institutional budgets for the large majority of colleges and universities. Public two-year colleges are the principal recipients of local support to higher education. Finally, an analysis of expenditure trends and cost factors indicates that overall expenditures would continue to rise even if enrollments were not to increase. The effects of inflation, the attempt to maintain or improve quality, and the need to broaden the range and depth of knowledge offered all imply more expensive education in the years ahead. The authors suggest that total institutional expenditures for 1975 might range from $36 billion to $39 billion.

147 BOWEN, HOWARD R. *The finance of higher education.* Berkeley, Calif.; Carnegie Commission on the Future of Higher Education, 1968, 36 pp. $1.

Innovative recommendations for the best way to pay the bills of higher education—both for students and institutions—are the substance of this report. For individual students, Bowen advocates a national system of minimal educational grants involving a means test supplemented by a national system of long-term loans without a means test. Such a policy would mean that the federal government would provide the funds, but the institution would administer them. This combination should enable every student to finish college without a heavy debt load. For institutions, Bowen feels the principle should be to allocate federal money to cover future increases in the cost of education, not to relieve present burdens. He proposes a specific formula for yearly cost-of-education grants to institutions tied to the number of students enrolled. His concluding chapter argues the case against tuition, calling it a regressive burden that falls most heavily on students least able to pay. Not only does he feel that tuition should be low or nonexistent at public institutions, he recommends unrestricted federal grants to help private institutions hold the tuition line to a moderate level. Otherwise, he sees the danger that they will become one-class institutions, serving only the affluent student.

148 BOYD, JOSEPH D. An examination of state efforts to remove financial barriers to postsecondary education, in U. S. Office of Education, *Trends in postsecondary education.* Wash., D. C.: Government Printing Office, 1970, pp. 57-68.

This chapter provides a convenient analysis and summary of comprehensive state programs of financial aid in the 19 states having such programs. The author also includes a brief review of general and categorical support of higher education by the states and an examination of the various philosophies of programs and evolving changes in purpose, both immediate and anticipated.

149 CARNEGIE COMMISSION ON HIGHER EDUCATION. *Federal aid to higher education: An essential investment in the nation's future.* Berkeley, Calif.: CCHE, 1968, 10 pp.

The urgency of the need for massive increases in federal aid to higher education is outlined in this brief policy statement. Presented for public consideration and discussion in advance of the Commission's full-scale report, it urges that federal aid be doubled in the immediate future—from $4 billion to $8 billion per year. The magnitude of these needs is judged to far exceed the resources of state, local, and private agencies. Top priority is assigned to the need to make financial provision for the one million students now kept out of college by financial barriers, and to provide training facilities for 60 percent more medical and PH.D. students. The Commission estimates that by 1975 an additional two million students will be ready for college: two new colleges per week would be needed to provide enough spaces.

150 CARNEGIE COMMISSION ON HIGHER EDUCATION. *Quality and equality: New levels of federal responsibility for higher education.* A Special Report and Recommendations by the Commission. New York: McGraw-Hill, 1968, 54 pp. $1. Supplement, 1970, 37 pp. $1.

The 1968 report is the first set of recommendations issued by the Commission on Higher Education established by the Carnegie Foundation for the Advancement of Teaching. It spells out national needs for higher education, both in goals and in dollars. The report focuses on 14 specific areas where massive federal aid is a major factor: student aid, expansion needs of institutions of higher education, graduate training of professional personnel, support for talented PH.D. candidates, university research, and new directions in curriculums. These proposals anticipate that the percentage of the gross national product spent for higher education will rise from two to three percent by 1976, reaching a total of nearly $13 billion. It is suggested that the federal share of funding should rise from 21 to 32 percent, the state share should drop from 27 to 17 percent, and the private share should remain at its present level of approximately 50 percent.

The 1970 supplement delayed the same total level of projected aid to 1979-1980 and made some changes in emphasis. The later report details the efforts that should be made in the areas that lagged behind in the 1960s. The Commission recommends a federal aid program for students that would incorporate a National Student Loan Bank. However, it cuts back, without explanation, projections for the number of new community colleges needed, from 500 in the 1968 report to 230-280 in the 1970 booklet.

151 CHEIT, EARL F. *The new depression in higher education: A study of financial conditions at 41 colleges and universities.* New York: McGraw-Hill, 1971, 169 pp. $5.95.

This well-publicized case study investigates the financial situation of a sample of the nation's colleges and universities. On the basis of interviews and investigation of financial records, Cheit classifies the institutions into three groups: those not in financial trouble, those headed for trouble, and those now in financial difficulty. The author's analysis seems especially timely because of his estimate that 7 out of 10 institutions fall into the latter two categories. He describes the financial operation of each group and analyzes in greater depth the cost components and income requirements for institutions in financial trouble. Cheit further examines the response of institutions to the financial crisis and outlines administration recommendations for necessary policy changes.

152 COLLEGE ENTRANCE EXAMINATION BOARD. *Crisis in student aid.* Proceedings of an invitational conference. Atlanta: Southern Regional Office, College Entrance Examination Board, 1970, 53 pp.

The report of this conference includes papers by Lyman Glenny, Herman Branson, and Steven Tonsor addressing the options that are open for states to bridge the gap between the costs of higher education and the financial resources of students. Recognizing that no one master plan will answer the needs of all states, the papers stress the common concern of accountability – the responsibility of state governments in the allocation of tax dollars for education. The points of view are divergent, the authors are highly regarded and outspoken, and the papers provide interesting reading.

153 COLLEGE ENTRANCE EXAMINATION BOARD. *Student financial aid and national purpose.* New York: College Entrance Examination Board, 1962, 103 pp. $2.50.

The first colloquium on financial aid held by the College Scholarship Service of the College Entrance Examination Board was in May 1962. The colloquium was directed by Byron S. Hollinshead and included a number of prominent speakers; this publication contains the 11 papers presented at that meeting. In his introduction Hollinshead sums up the "sense of the meeting" to the effect that a comprehensive national student aid program should be developed to remove all economic barriers to higher education. The papers that follow discuss various aspects of the scope and form of such a program.

154 COLLEGE ENTRANCE EXAMINATION BOARD. *Financing equal opportunity in higher education.* New York: College Entrance Examination Board, 1970, 44 pp. $1.

The urgency of a course of action that will translate equal opportunity into educational reality is the message of this colloquium, sponsored by the College Scholarship Service of the College Entrance Examination Board. Educational leaders and minority group participants at the colloquium, held at Scottsdale, Arizona, in November 1969 drew up a resolution urging that the College Scholarship Service appoint a panel of black, Chicano, Puerto Rican, and Indian members to formulate a "workable program for massive financial aid to higher education" appropriate to the needs of minority students. Some corollaries to this resolution were: (1) The level of commitment should be to achieve a proportion of minority/poverty students at least equal to the national distribution of minority/poverty populations. (2) Full-time professional lobbying, through the machinery of the National Association of Student Aid Administrators, should provide a strong voice in Washington for minority/poverty students. (3) Federal funds should be redirected. It was alleged that 80 percent of federal funds go for research and development, and many other funds are inefficiently allocated because of patchwork administrative policies.

155 FROOMKIN, JOSEPH. *Aspirations, enrollments and resources: The challenge to higher education in the seventies.* Planning Paper 69-1. Wash., D. C.: Office of Program Planning and Evaluation, U. S. Office of Education, 1969. (Mimeographed)

This report is not an official policy statement of the U. S. Office of Education, but it does attempt to estimate the federal resources that will be required for postsecondary education by 1976. Two levels of support are considered. Meeting minimum goals will require $1.5 billion for student support and another $2.0 billion for institutional support. A second budget "which is more likely to achieve equality of opportunity for the poor" will require $3.5 billion in student aid and an additional $4.5 billion for institutional support. These figures are substantially below those of the Carnegie Commission on Higher Education (150).

156 HANFORD, GEORGE H., AND NELSON, JAMES E. Federal student loan plans: The dangers are real. *College Board Review,* Spring 1970, no. 75, pp. 16-21.

The authors call attention to current forces urging the massive use of loans to students to pay the mounting cost of higher education. Despite the fact that "no other nation has given serious thought to reducing their public investment in higher education in the face of increasing demand," they maintain that the "loan-bank plan" has never been fully or seriously debated and discussed. The authors describe the main characteristics of the Educational Opportunity Bank and enumerate several potential problems. These include: (1) the questionable value of loans in improving equality of educational opportunity, (2) the influence loans might have in further undermining the precarious position of private colleges, and (3) the social problems that can be created by large numbers of women students approaching marriage with substantial negative dowries in the form of student loans. The authors feel that the potential problems in excessive reliance on loans are deeply disturbing and assert that it is imperative that "the subject be fully aired *before* it becomes an accomplished fact."

157 HANSEN, W. LEE. An examination of financial barriers to college attendance, in U. S. Office of Education, *Trends in postsecondary education.* Wash., D. C.: Government Printing Office, 1970, pp. 31-55.

This chapter examines the impact of financial barriers to college attendance and considers ways to offset them. The author reviews the current distribution of college enrollments and nonenrollments, the impact of family income and related factors on attendance, the costs of college attendance, and the availability of financial aid. He develops estimates of the total cost of attendance at different types of colleges, considers the estimated financial need and the total financial aid available, and, finally, offers some conclusions regarding desirable steps that might be taken. While a multitude of factors affect college attendance, the financial barriers are important and operate to prevent a number of qualified young people from attending college. Financial aid operates to offset these barriers; what seems to be called for are more selective policies, which by tying the "costs of college to financial need and setting commensurately higher charges for those who can pay, will produce added revenue that will help to promote greater equality of educational opportunity."

158 HARRIS, SEYMOUR E. *Higher education: Resources and finance.* New York: McGraw-Hill, 1962, 713 pp. $9.95.

This massive volume covers numerous aspects of the general problem of financing higher education. Major sections are devoted to pricing, scholarships, loans, government contributions, fund management, and cost and economics. The volume provides a very valuable reference and might well have been regarded as a definitive work at the time of publication, but higher education has changed greatly in 10 years, and the relatively slight attention in this volume to the implications of equality of educational opportunity attests to that fact. Moreover, the study stands in clear contrast to a greatly broadened conception of federal responsibility for comprehensive postsecondary education that developed in the mid-1960s.

159 JOHNS, KINGSTON, JR (STUDY DIRECTOR) *Studies of student financial aid programs and needs in Florida.* Vol. I. Tallahassee, Fla.: Florida Department of Education, 1970. (Multilithed)

This study was undertaken by the Southern Regional Office of the College Entrance Examination Board for the Florida Department of Education. The report comes in three sections: one presents an analysis and set of recommendations concerning the operation and administration of student aid programs in the state; a second section presents an analysis of the financial aid needs in the state of Florida and the current deficit between need and aid available; finally, a section outlines a procedural framework for the development of an optimal aid program for the state. The report provides an unusually comprehensive background document that can be used to develop priorities and design programs to meet local needs.

160 KIRKPATRICK, JOHN I. (STUDY DIRECTOR) *A study of federal student loan programs.* New York: College Entrance Examination Board, 1968. (Mimeographed)

The College Entrance Examination Board at the request of the United States Office of Education undertook this study of the six federally assisted student loan programs: (1) the National Defense Student Loan Program, (2) Guaranteed Loans under Higher Education Act of 1965, (3) Guaranteed Loans for Vocational Students, (4) Health Professions Student Loan Program, (5) Nursing Student Loan Program, and (6) Cuban Refugee Student Loan Program. The study called for gathering information and evaluating the organization and operation of these loan programs. The study was based on questionnaires, personal interviews, and seven one-day seminars held in various cities. Each of the six individual loan programs is discussed in detail together with several problems that affect the loan programs. These discussions lead to a series of specific recommendations for action. The report provides a detailed exposition of federal loan programs as of 1968. (See also 1203, 1204, 1293, 1294.)

161 KIRKPATRICK, JOHN I. Financing higher education: The role of the state. *College Board Review,* Spring 1971, no. 79, pp. 22-25.

This article provides a useful overview of recent trends in state funding of undergraduate higher education. It notes increases in tuition, taxes, scholarships, support of private institutions, and programs of full-cost tuition. The author anticipates that parents and students will share the costs of tuition with the state, on the basis of ability to pay. In addition, he foresees that the state will rely more on tuition and less on tax appropriations, will increase scholarship programs based on financial need, will increase aid to private schools, and will develop more general master plans.

162 NASH, GEORGE. Student financial aid, college and university, in Robert L. Ebel (Ed.), *Encyclopedia of educational research.* (4th ed.) New York: Macmillan, 1969, pp. 1339-1359.

This article provides a useful overview of student financial aid. It begins with a brief history of financial aid and then discusses the growth of federal and state programs for both undergraduate and graduate students. The article contains a fairly comprehensive review of the research literature on various aspects of financial aid and includes an extensive bibliography.

163 NORTH, WALTER M. *The relationship of aid to fee increases and enrollment growth.* Bloomington, Ind.: Midwest Association of Student Financial Aid Administrators, 1970, 60 pp. $1.50 to MASFAA members; $3.50 to nonmembers.

This report appraises the policy of increasing both enrollment and student fees as a means of alleviating financial problems. Since the increases compound the necessity of financial aid for more students, North concludes pessimistically that the policy "adds to the problems of institutional financing as much as it helps with the difficulties." He feels that it places the college in a vulnerable position since it must rely on aid programs controlled outside the institution. He recommends that institutions need to assess both good and bad effects of such a policy before setting it in motion.

164 ORWIG, M. D. (ED.) *Financing higher education: Alternatives for the federal government.* Iowa City, Iowa: American College Testing Program, 1971, 390 pp. $3.

This book includes 13 papers by well-known experts on the issues and strategies involved in financing undergraduate education. Part I discusses the economic and social background and includes papers on efficient allocation of resources, progress toward equality of educational opportunity, and a summary of related research. Part II examines opposing strategies for financing higher education, particularly full-cost pricing vs. free public education. Part III reviews the five programs most often suggested for increased participation of the federal government: the federal student loan bank, federal income tax credits, direct noncategorical institutional grants, and an "eclectic approach." Political implications for federal aid to higher education are discussed in Part IV.

165 PEARSON, RICHARD. *The opening door: A review of New York State's programs of financial aid for college students.* New York: College Entrance Examination Board, 1967, 89 pp.

In 1966 the College Board was invited to conduct a six-month study of the relationship between access to higher education and the operation of New York State's student financial aid programs. The first part of this report summarizes the major factors affecting access to higher education with specific attention to overall enrollment trends, national manpower needs, student opportunity, institutional trends, and trends in consumer expenditures for higher education. Turning to the current New York scene, the report reviews the present extensive programs of financial aid and then considers the changing patterns of college attendance in New York. Given the statewide goal of equal and open educational opportunity beyond high school for every qualified person regardless of race, creed, or national origin, the author makes a series of recommendations designed to reach this goal. In general they call for greatly expanded aid programs. One unusual feature is the recognition of forgone income (and related family expenses) as a legitimate expense of higher education that the state should pay for in accordance with need. This state study is unusually comprehensive both in background substance and scope of proposals.

166 PEARSON, RICHARD. Can colleges reclaim the nonstudent? Maybe — with hard cash. *College Board Review,* Winter 1967-68, no. 66, pp. 14-19.

Despite recent progress in removing barriers to higher education, the author contends that we have not made substantial gains in reaching nonstudents from the poverty population. He cites the College Scholarship Service estimate that one-fourth of all families in the United States lack the financial resources to meet any of the expenses of college, even at a low-cost commuting college. Pearson contends that loans and jobs will not overcome this barrier. What the poor student needs is grants or scholarships — hard cash to pay for his personal expenses, to supplement parental earnings, and to cover such direct college expenses as tuition and textbooks.

167 QUINDRY, KENNETH E. *State and local revenue potential 1969.* SREB Research Monograph No. 16. Atlanta, Ga.: Southern Regional Education Board, 1970, 88 pp. $2.25.

This report presents comparative data on state-by-state efforts to raise additional revenue for public services including higher education, and also analyzes future state and local revenue potential. Tables and charts provide information on the total tax picture in 1969 and 1970.

168 SANDERS, EDWARD, AND NELSON, JAMES. Financing of undergraduates, 1969-70. *Financial Aid News,* 1970, vol. 10, no. 2, pp. 3-5.

The annual college cost to undergraduate students and parents in 1969-70 was estimated at $10.5 billion; about 65 percent of this cost was borne by students and their families. This study sought to determine the resources used to meet the remaining 35 percent and particularly focused on the needs of the nearly one million students who could expect no financial assistance from their families. Using national summary data, the authors conclude that the four federal student aid programs (1200, 1202, 1203, 1204) fall far short of meeting the needs of currently enrolled students. Although other types of aid help to fill the gap, considerable deficits still exist for typical students with family incomes between $3,000 and $9,000. The authors state that $1.1 billion additional assistance (from summer earnings and increased aid funding) was necessary in 1969-70 and that this figure will swell as college costs rise faster than average incomes and as major increases in enrollments come from lower-income families.

169 SANDERS, EDWARD, AND PALMER, HANS. *The financial barrier to higher education in California.* Claremont, Calif.: Pomona College, 1965, 295 pp.

This thorough and well-organized report was prepared for the California State Scholarship Commission. Its purpose was to supply specific information to aid in budgetary decisions for 1965-66 and in general plans for the next decade. The following general conclusions are offered on the basis of extensive statistical data: (1) Freshman enrollment and part-time enrollment in California institutions of higher education are higher than the national average, but there is a very high attrition rate during the freshman and sophomore years. (2) A smaller percentage of those in the 20- to 24-year-old age group graduate from college than the average for the nation as a whole. (3) The number of students from very low-income families ($3,000 or less) is lower than the national average, and only a small number of the state scholarships go to these students. (4) "The increasing amount of part-time attendance, the extensive stretch out of the training period, and the increasing amount of borrowing are indications of the increased effort required by students presently enrolled."

Stressing the importance of the economic returns to society from higher education, the authors recommend an expansion in the scholarship funds for undergraduate education, particularly among those unable to attend without financial aid. The report provides a model of excellence for state studies of educational opportunity.

170 SHELL, KARL, FISHER, FRANKLIN M., FOLEY, DUNCAN K., AND FRIEDLAENDER, ANN F. The educational opportunity bank: An economic analysis of a contingent repayment loan program for higher education. *National Tax Journal,* 1968, vol. 21, pp. 2-45.

This report is a feasibility study of the August 1967 recommendation of the Panel on Educational Innovation for an Educational Opportunity Bank for student loans. The Panel proposed that the Bank borrow money at government rates to lend to students for their full expenses. Each student would then pledge a percentage of his annual gross income for a fixed number of years as repayment. The authors favorably compare the Educational Opportunity Bank with systems of federal scholarships, income tax credits, and deductions from parents' income. They conclude that the Bank would promote more economical use of the nation's resources and increase benefits for children of low-income families. Sections of the report deal with loan repayment by married women, estimates of size of the program, fiscal impact of the Bank on federal monetary policies, and suggestions for complementary grant programs for minority students.

171 U. S. CONGRESS, JOINT ECONOMIC COMMITTEE. *The economics and financing of higher education in the United States.* Wash., D. C.: Government Printing Office, 1969, 683 pp. $3.

This compendium of study papers was undertaken to provide a framework for debate of the major economic issues confronting higher education. Contributors include Alice Rivlin, Allan Cartter, Seymour Harris, Ralph W. Tyler, William Bowen, Clark Kerr, and others. The first chapters of the report present an overview of the structural relationship between economics and higher education, including the nature of efficiency and equity and the quality of output and costs of higher institutions. Further sections consider the outlook for higher education in the next decade in terms of projections of enrollment, staffing, labor market requirements, and private demand. Special attention is devoted to the private institution. The final chapter outlines the potentials for federal and nonfederal funding.

172 U. S. DEPARTMENT OF HEALTH, EDUCATION AND WELFARE. *Toward a longrange plan for federal financial support for higher education.* Wash., D. C.: Office of the Assistant Secretary for Planning and Evaluation, HEW, 1969, 73 pp. (Mimeographed)

This report was prepared under the direction of Alice M. Rivlin, HEW Assistant Secretary for Planning and Evaluation, in response to a presidential request; it is often called the Rivlin Report. After outlining the basic objectives of federal support for higher education, the report focuses on the present financial state of higher education both from the student viewpoint and from the institutional viewpoint. Major issues and alternative means of financial support are discussed, and recommendations are made for the expansion of existing federal aid programs, the consolidation and broadening in scope of categorical aid programs, and the creation of new programs to fill acknowledged voids. The report is particularly valuable because it summarizes briefly a number of national policy issues concerning the financing of higher education and includes data directly focused on these issues.

2.3 — ADMINISTRATION OF FINANCIAL AID.

The profession of student financial aid administration is quite young, and the associated literature is limited. Perhaps the closest thing to a general text on aid administration is the *Manual for Financial Aid Officers* published by the College Entrance Examination Board (176). One of the major research problems in the administration of financial aid is accountability. There have been some good studies of aid dispersal (e.g., 182) but surprisingly little research on the effects of aid either on a short- or a long-range basis.

There has also been relatively little systematic development of literature concerned with administrative procedures and professional development. Unfortunately, these understandable growing pains of the aid profession have made it difficult to coordinate professional activity with other groups serving closely related functions — especially student guidance.

During the first decade (1955-65) of the financial aid profession, its primary associational identification was the College Scholarship Service of the College Entrance Examination Board (1211). In recent years, regional associations of student financial aid administrators have been organized, and the umbrella National Association of Student Financial Aid Administrators (1122) initiated the first *Journal of Student Financial Aid* (1330) in the spring of 1971. Prior to that time *Financial Aid News* (1368) and the *College Board Review* (1315) were the primary periodicals publishing articles on the administration of student aid.

173 AMERICAN COLLEGE TESTING PROGRAM, *Handbook for financial aid officers.* Iowa City, Iowa: ACT, 1970, 61 pp.

This handbook is designed to provide a general framework for the administration of financial aid and instructions for the use of the ACT Student Need Analysis Service. It includes separate sections on administration of aid, need analysis, rationale of the ACT system, and how the program works.

174 CARTTER, ALLAN M. (CHAIRMAN) *New approaches to student financial aid: Report of the Panel on Student Financial Need Analysis.* New York: College Entrance Examination Board, 1971, 133 pp. $3.

The College Scholarship Service Panel on Student Financial Need Analysis was appointed to "review, within the current frame of reference of parental responsibility, the present CSS system and submit both evaluations of the present system and recommendations for changes which might make the system more definitive and comprehensive." The panel surveyed a number of problems: admissions and financial aid policies, financial aid attitudes, concerns of users and problems of special student populations, adequacy of the CSS need analysis system for low-income and minority students, technical changes to improve equity, and the packaging of financial aid.

The study suggested that students with the greatest financial need were most likely to be excluded from higher education because of insufficient aid. The panel recommended that "the institution's aid resources be utilized to the maximum benefit by limiting aid to the amount of need; and allocating funds so as to assure equal access to educational opportunity to students with the greatest need." Other recommendations included a national study of student and parent attitudes, encouragement of student participation in the financial aid process, an increase in the study of financial need at the graduate level, and changes in CSS procedures for determining need.

175 COLLEGE ENTRANCE EXAMINATION BOARD. *Student financial aid and institutional purpose.* New York: College Entrance Examination Board, 1963, 114 pp. $2.

These papers were prepared for the second colloquium on financial aid sponsored by the College Scholarship Service of the College Entrance Examination Board. A central theme is the need for coordinating the administration of financial aid programs with admissions as well as long-range financial and educational planning of the institution. Financial aid decisions are central to determining the kinds of students an institution wishes to help and the kind of college it wants to be. Such decisions are also increasingly complex, as package awards of grant, loan, and job reflect varying emphases on ability vs. need. Therefore, aid decisions are cited as the responsibility of a central, professional staff, functioning in close relationship with other administrative offices. More emphasis on institutional research is recommended for establishing systematic approaches to processing information on both institutional and individual resources.

176 COLLEGE ENTRANCE EXAMINATION BOARD. *Manual for financial aid officers.* New York: College Entrance Examination Board, 1970, 202 pp. $5.

This *Manual* was compiled by the College Scholarship Service of the College Entrance Examination Board in order to provide some assistance to financial aid officers in the operation of their programs. The constantly changing nature of financial aid and need analysis is reflected in the format of the *Manual*. It is bound in looseleaf form to allow insertion of supplementary materials and revisions. This *Manual* includes sections on the financial aid officer and his professional role, student aid programs, techniques in aid administration, special topics (e.g., foreign and graduate aid programs), and need analysis. The appendix includes sample cases, special data, and a selected bibliography. Through the past decade the *Manual* has represented the nearest equivalent to a general textbook on financial aid administration.

177 CRAWFORD, NORMAN C. JR. *Effects of offers of financial assistance on the college-going decisions of talented students with limited financial means.* NMSC Research Reports, vol. 3, no. 5. Evanston, Ill.: National Merit Scholarship Corporation, 1967, 21 pp.

A follow-up study of 1,545 Merit finalists of 1959 whose parents were unable to meet minimum contribution levels reflects the "talent loss" incurred by lack of financial aid. Students who enrolled without aid usually attended college under less than optimal conditions. They frequently commuted to low-cost colleges near home. One-third withdrew from college in the two-year period, while one-sixth of those with aid discontinued their studies. The report suggests that half of those who did not go to college would have enrolled had it been possible financially.

178 HAVEN, ELIZABETH W., AND SMITH, ROBERT E. *Financial aid to college students, 1963-64.* College Entrance Examination Board Research and Development Reports, no. 11. Princeton, N. J.: Educational Testing Service, 1965, 62 pp.

This survey examines institutionally administered financial aid awarded to full-time undergraduates in 1,221 colleges for the academic year 1963-64. The authors establish that the total sum included about $120 million in scholarships, $85 million in loans, and $45 million in jobs. They also describe the various forms of distribution of aid by geographic region, type of institution, type of student, amount and type of aid received, etc. This important study now serves primarily as a benchmark because the conditions of student financial aid changed so radically in the 1960s.

179 KATES, ROBERT J. JR. Financial aid, in Asa S. Knowles (Ed.), *Handbook of college and university administration.* Vol. II. *Academic.* New York: McGraw-Hill, 1970, sec. 7, pp. 151-171.

This chapter gives a useful overview of the organization and administration of financial aid programs. Individual sections concisely discuss aid principles, operational activities, data collection and reporting, and office responsibilities for program administration. Various forms of institutional and noninstitutional aid sources are briefly described.

180 NASH, GEORGE. The current status of financial aid administration. *National ACAC Journal,* 1968, vol. 13, no. 2, pp. 5-8.

Strengths and weaknesses in the occupational status of college financial aid administrators are discussed in this article based on studies supported by the College Entrance Examination Board. The findings indicated a sharp rise in the number of full-time aid directors at accredited four-year colleges and universities —from 36 to 59 percent in the one-year period between 1965 and 1966. The author concludes that the aid officer derives important job satisfaction from his expertise in administering complex federal aid programs, and from his guidance role in helping needy students. However, Nash feels that financial aid administration has not yet achieved "occupational maturity." He reports that aid directors are not knowledgeable about research on financial aid, nor does their influence carry sufficient weight in state and national legislation. He recommends that short-term institutes or some specialized academic courses would be helpful in professional training. (See 181 for a more detailed report.)

181 NASH, GEORGE, AND LAZARSFELD, PAUL F. *New administrator on campus: A study of the director of student financial aid.* New York: Bureau of Applied Social Research, Columbia University, 1968. (Mimeographed)

This extensive study of the financial aid profession includes much data concerning the background of the aid officer and the image of his profession. The social characteristics of the profession and its organization in higher education institutions is also examined in detail. The complete study is unpublished, but a summary of the main findings is given in 180 above. (See 185 for a more recent report on professional development of aid officers.)

182 SCHLEKAT, GEORGE A. Do financial aid programs have a social conscience? *College Board Review,* Fall 1968, no. 69, pp. 15-20.

How is socioeconomic background related to grants of financial aid to college students? To explore this question the author analyzed over 19,000 questionnaires returned by 1,000 colleges that had received completed Parents' Confidential Statements (a questionnaire made available by the College Scholarship Service of the College Entrance Examination Board) in support of aid applications. The questionnaire requested information about the college's decision to award or deny aid and the amount and type of aid offered on each of 16,000 randomly selected applications. The questionnaires were categorized into five social classes according to an index based on father's occupation and the amount and source of family income. Schlekat found that lower-class applicants were almost twice as likely to receive financial aid and in larger amounts than were upper-class applicants. However, this aid more often included loans and jobs, whereas the upper-class applicant was more likely to receive an outright grant. "The lower-class aid recipient was thus expected to mortgage his future more heavily and devote more free time in college to employment than the upper-class recipient, who was more likely to graduate with little or no indebtedness."

183 SIDAR, ALEXANDER G. JR. Where small-college financial aid programs go wrong. *College Board Review,* Fall 1966, no. 61, pp. 23-26.

This article combines ethical guidelines with practical advice for the small college struggling to operate a financial aid program with undertrained staff and inadequate resources. Sidar warns that college aid programs should operate from a concern for the best interest of the student. He argues that when the orientation centers on the interests of the college, dubious practices are likely to mar the administration of available funds. The most flagrant is to publish inaccurate total costs of attendance, but he sees other pitfalls: attaching strings of grade-point performance or repayment requirements to the awarding of aid, using aid as an "admissions come-on," or accepting questionable scholarship funds. He includes many helpful suggestions directed to the new or inexperienced aid officer.

184 VAN DUSEN, WILLIAM D., AND O'HEARNE, JOHN J. *A design for a model college financial aid office.* New York: College Entrance Examination Board, 1968, 49 pp. $1.

This report presents a model for administration of financial aid and describes accepted procedures in most institutions. The report is especially helpful for inexperienced aid officers. Specific suggestions include recommendations for a standardized set of definitions, practices, and principles within the aid profession, the centralization of student financial aid administration in one office in each institution, the use of a single application form for all types of financial aid, and an increase of direct communication between the director of admissions and the director of financial aid and students in secondary schools and junior colleges.

185 WILLINGHAM, WARREN W. *Professional development of financial aid officers.* Higher Education Surveys Report No. 2. New York: College Entrance Examination Board, 1970, 42 pp.

This survey was concerned with the level of professional development of financial aid officers, their training needs, and their attitudes concerning future development of the profession. Results were based on responses of aid directors from a representative group of 122 institutions in the West. The findings indicated a discrepancy between the training needs of aid officers and the extent of training currently received. One out of three aid officers was classified at a low level of professional development in the sense that they were involved in relatively few activities normally associated with a developed profession. The steps respondents most often recommended for furthering development of the aid profession were development of a code of ethical standards, additional workshops, state and regional associational meetings, and a journal devoted to financial aid.

2.4–COLLEGE COSTS. It is surprisingly difficult to find reliable, current information concerning tuition charges and other costs of college. It is often necessary to go to different sources, depending on one's purpose in seeking the information and the type of institution involved. Another problem is that these different sources are sometimes inconsistent in the way they define costs.

In seeking dependable information about a few specific institutions, there is no substitute for communicating with the individual college or examining its current literature. In screening a larger number of institutions with respect to cost, college directories can be quite helpful (see annotations of directories in section 1.6), but information contained in these sources is often one to four years old. Consequently, the data are inaccurate because of the steady increase in college costs. For research purposes or quick reference, there are several publications that provide a compact listing of college costs. There are four that tend to complement one another: 189, 190, 191, 192.

186 CARBONE, ROBERT F. *Resident or nonresident? Tuition classification in higher education in the states.* Report No. 18. Denver, Colo.: Education Commission of the States, 1970, 58 pp. $1.

This study of residency requirements at public institutions is based on a questionnaire sent to approximately 350 institutions and 40 boards of higher education. The study was directed to five specific questions: Who makes the rules? What are the minimum requirements? Who is exempt from nonresident tuition? What are the special features, if any? Is there an appeals procedure? The report summarizes data pertinent to these questions and includes a number of fairly specific recommendations for improved procedures for defining and administering residency policies. A particularly valuable aspect of the report is a state-by-state description of residency regulations.

187 CAVANAUGH, WILLIAM J. *Student expense budgets of colleges and universities for the 1969-70 academic year.* College Scholarship Service (College Entrance Examination Board) Technical Reports. Princeton, N. J.: Educational Testing Service, 1969, 62 pp. (Multilithed)

Each year the College Scholarship Service of the College Entrance Examination Board prepares a list of institutions that utilize the CSS need analysis service and return the necessary information in time for inclusion in the report. The listing of tuition and fees, resident and commuting budgets, and out-of-state charges includes a number of institutions not represented in the previous reference.

188 FERRIN, RICHARD I. *Student budgets and aid awarded in Southwestern colleges.* Higher Education Surveys Report No. 5. New York: College Entrance Examination Board, 1971, 40 pp.

A typical student attending a private college in the Southwest in 1970-71 had expenses of $2,900 a year, his counterpart in a public four-year college had expenses of $1,900, and his counterpart at a public two-year college had expenses of $1,600. Furthermore, according to this survey of financial aid officers in the Southwest, student aid met only 16 percent of the expenses of private college students, 10 percent of the expenses of public four-year college students, and 7.7 percent of the expenses of public two-year college students. The survey also indicated that, within each of the three types of institutions, colleges with high student budgets were no more likely to award large amounts of aid than were colleges with low student budgets. In addition to regional data, this report provides information on student budgets for both 1970-71 and 1971-72, as well as the various types of aid – grants, loans, and jobs – awarded for full- and part-time students in 1970-71.

189 HARPER, WILLIAM A. (ED.) *1970 junior college directory.* Wash., D. C.: American Association of Junior Colleges, 1970, 112 pp. $2.

This directory provides in compact form the charges for practically all two-year institutions in the country. Tuition is listed for in-district, out-of-district, and out-of-state students. Room and board expense is listed for those institutions with residential facilities. The directory is revised each year and includes in usable form other basic information such as enrollment, college address, affiliation, etc. (Also annotated in section 1.6.)

190 LIFE INSURANCE AGENCY MANAGEMENT ASSOCIATION. *1970-1971 college costs.* Hartford, Conn.: LIAMA, 1970, 48 pp.

This brief booklet contains tuition, fees, and total room and board costs for practically all accredited four-year institutions in the country. It is revised each year and is perhaps the most up-to-date source of information for this group of institutions.

191 PUGLIESE, ALFRED. Tuition, fees, deposits, and other charges, in Asa S. Knowles (Ed.), *Handbook of college and university administration.* Vol. I. *General.* New York: McGraw-Hill, 1970, sec. 8, pp. 13-26.

This chapter provides a comprehensive but brief review of the various financial charges of higher education institutions including tuition and fees for instruction, special fees, rental and charges for housing and food services, punitive charges, deposits and bonding fees, and charges for use of facilities.

192 U. S. OFFICE OF EDUCATION, NATIONAL CENTER FOR EDUCATIONAL STATISTICS. *Basic student charges.* Wash., D. C.: Government Printing Office, 1970, 8 pp.

This annual report may include student charges for as many as 95 percent of all colleges listed by the Office of Education in its report *Opening Fall Enrollment* (1426). It sometimes also includes some analysis of trends in costs for different types of institutions. Consequently, the publication is potentially very useful; unfortunately, irregular publication has sometimes limited the usefulness of the information.

2.5—FINANCIAL AID SOURCES. Sources of financial aid are quite numerous and diverse, and there are a variety of publications that describe them. Some are relatively brief and mostly offer useful advice (e.g., 196 and 201). Others provide listings of aid opportunities for the benefit of students. There are also reference publications that provide quite comprehensive listings (197).

193 AMERICAN LEGION EDUCATIONAL AND SCHOLARSHIP PROGRAM. *Need a lift? To educational opportunities, careers, loans, scholarships, employment!* (18th ed.) Indianapolis, Ind.: American Legion, 1969, 128 pp. Single copy 25 cents; 15 cents each for 100 copies or more.

Need a Lift? is an annually revised guide to sources of financial aid. While helpful to students, parents, and counselors in general, it is of special value to veterans and their dependents. This booklet provides the most detailed information available on special opportunities available to those who qualify for veterans' benefits. Included are: (1) a list of careers with the names and addresses of organizations supplying information about each; (2) detailed information describing scholarships and loans given by various organizations, foundations, states, and the federal government; and (3) annotations on sources of additional information.

194 CHRONICLE GUIDANCE PUBLICATIONS. *Student aid annual 1970-1971.* Moravia, N. Y.: CGP, 142 pp. $7.50.

Student Aid Annual is a guide to both undergraduate and graduate financial aid offered on a national or regional scope. Essential information is given on programs ranging from essay awards, loans, scholarships, grants, and work-study programs to postdoctoral fellowships. These programs are sponsored by approximately 575 diverse public and private organizations. Subject indexes facilitate finding programs suited to a student's interest and eligibility. The guide is revised annually. The *Student Aid Bulletin* is a series of educational guides put out by the same publisher. It gives similar but generally less detailed information on financial aid programs offered by state governments and by labor unions.

195 COLLEGE ENTRANCE EXAMINATION BOARD. *Financial planning for study in the United States: A guide for students from other countries.* New York: College Entrance Examination Board, 1970, 42 pp. Single copies free.

This booklet provides students from other countries with a realistic and detailed portrayal of the costs of higher education in the United States, the responsibilities they will be expected to assume in order to meet these costs, and the kinds of financial aid available to foreign students. A companion booklet *Entering Higher Education in the United States: A Guide for Students from Other Countries* (820) is also available. (See 815 for another annotation.)

196 COLLEGE ENTRANCE EXAMINATION BOARD. *Financing a college education: A guide for counselors.* New York: College Entrance Examination Board, 1970, 39 pp. (Out of print)

This booklet describes the various kinds of financial aid and their sources and how colleges and other agencies measure financial need and administer their aid funds. It describes the function of the College Scholarship Service (1211), an activity of the College Board, in analyzing financial need and provides examples of its operation. Also included is a list of colleges and agencies using the CSS Parents' Confidential Statement. A complimentary copy of this publication is supplied to all secondary schools annually.

[*Editor's note:* This booklet was superseded in 1972 by *Helping Students Meet College Costs,* a booklet designed for counselors and others involved in helping students and their parents apply for financial aid. A companion booklet to *Meeting College Costs* (see 201).]

197 COLLEGE OPPORTUNITIES. *Financial aid for undergraduate students 1970-71.* Cincinnati: CO, 1970, 1,500 pp. $37.50 postpaid.

This compendium gives both general information and detailed financial aid data on over 1,800 accredited institutions. For each college it includes a listing of scholarships and loans available; numbers, types, amounts, and restrictions of awards; and general application procedures. The directory also provides information on state and federal financial aid programs, non-school-administered financial aids, specialized aid associated with programs of study, other information sources, and articles with advice about higher education. Designed as a reference volume for counselors or libraries, the materials are presented in a way that enables students and parents to do most of the initial information gathering. A companion volume *Financial Aid for Graduate Students 1970-71* ($10) is also available.

198 FEINGOLD, S. NORMAN. *Scholarships, fellowships and loans.* Vol. IV. Cambridge, Mass.: Bellman, 1962, 368 pp. $10.

This is a comprehensive guide to student aid distributed independently of institutions of higher education. It provides detailed information on scholarships, fellowships, loans, and grants available to undergraduates and graduate students. In recent years the format has been changed to a subscription news service, which enables the publisher to keep the material updated on a quarterly basis. Entitled *Scholarships, Fellowships and Loans News Service,* it is available at a yearly subscription rate of $20.

199 GOLDSTEIN, GLORIA (ED.) *College bound: Directory of special programs and financial assistance for black and other minority group students.* White Plains, N. Y.: Urban League of Westchester, 1970, 140 pp. $2.75.

College Bound is designed to acquaint guidance counselors and students with some of the many college programs for minority groups or disadvantaged students. Information was obtained by means of questionnaire responses from 176 colleges. Annotations describe special programs, financial assistance, and admissions policies. Educational costs at the institutions are not mentioned, but each college lists a source for obtaining further information. A description of general aid programs for minority/disadvantaged students and a listing of organizations that help these students are also included.

200 KEESLAR, OREON. *A national catalog of financial aids for students entering college.* (4th ed.) Dubuque, Iowa: William C. Brown, 1969, 487 pp. $8.75.

This extensive catalog was written primarily for graduating high school seniors in a simple, easy-to-use style. It gives advice and valuable information on making a systematic search for financial assistance for college. It contains specific details on over 1,600 programs, including such information as eligibility and restrictions, value and basis of awards, application procedures and deadlines, and sources of further information. Also included is an index listing sources of financial aid according to special purposes and restrictions, advice on employment at college, information about testing programs, and a bibliography.

201 MARGOLIUS, SIDNEY. *A letter to parents: Financial aid for college.* New York: College Entrance Examination Board, 1970, 10 pp. (Out of print)

This booklet is published annually to help parents understand what is expected of them regarding financial support for their children's college expenses. It explains some of the important considerations in how financial aid is awarded today, gives general descriptions of the types and sources of aid available, and explains the function of the College Scholarship Service (1211) in determining need. Some two million free copies are distributed annually by the College Board.

[*Editor's note:* This booklet was superseded in 1972 by *Meeting College Costs,* a booklet for both students and parents explaining how to apply for aid in the right way at the right time and how much colleges might expect families to pay toward college costs. A companion booklet to *Helping Students Meet College Costs* (see 196).]

202 NATIONAL RESEARCH COUNCIL, OFFICE OF SCIENTIFIC PERSONNEL. *A selected list of major fellowship opportunities and aids to advanced education for United States citizens.* Wash., D. C.: National Academy of Sciences, 1968, 36 pp.

This small booklet gives concise descriptions of major undergraduate, graduate, and postdoctoral fellowship opportunities sponsored by various associations, foundations, and government agencies. Information is given on the number, amount, restrictions, and basis of awards, in addition to notes on application procedures and sources of further information. A similar list of fellowship opportunities for foreign nationals is also available from the Fellowship Office of the National Research Council.

203 PROIA, NICHOLAS C., AND DiGASPARI, VINCENT M. *Barron's handbook of junior and community college financial aid.* Woodbury, N. Y.: Barron's Educational Series, 1970, 704 pp. $6.95.

This handbook was prepared for students with financial need who are considering attendance at a two-year college. It consists primarily of data charts of financial aid information for each of over 800 two-year colleges. These charts contain information on the types of grants and loans available, the name of the financial aid director, and how to apply. The handbook also includes a useful glossary of educational and financial aid terms.

204 SULKIN, SIDNEY. How to pay for college, in Sidney Sulkin, *Complete planning for college.* New York: Harper & Row, 1968, pp. 227-252.

This 27-page chapter contains helpful information on how to pay for college, including advice on estimating costs, a variety of scholarship and loan programs, work-study programs, etc. (See 103 for an annotation of the entire book.)

205 TOY, HENRY JR. *Federal dollars for scholars.* Wash., D. C.: Nu-Toy, 1970. $4.20.

This volume describes the benefits provided by the federal government to individuals to assist them in furthering their education or training. It is written for students and for counselors and parents. The major portion of the book consists of descriptions of more than 300 financial aid programs administered by the federal government. Included for each is information on purpose, eligibility, application procedure, nature and amount of support, scope, authorizing legislation, and the federal agency that administers each program. Other sections provide an excellent description of military requirements, alternatives, and opportunities and a description of the executive branch of the government to give students an insight into the agencies with which they may need to deal. This publication is also annotated in section 1.7.

206 U. S. OFFICE OF ECONOMIC OPPORTUNITY. *Catalog of federal domestic assistance.* Wash., D. C.: OEO, 1969, 610 pp.

This large volume provides comprehensive listing and description of 581 domestic assistance programs and activities administered by 47 federal departments and agencies. It includes information on various forms of assistance available to state and local governments, public and private organizations and institutions, and individuals. The types of assistance described in the catalog include: financial aid in the form of grants, loans and advances, loan guarantees, and shared revenues; provision of federal facilities, direct construction, or goods and services; donation or provision of surplus property; technical assistance and counseling; statistical and other information services; and service activities of regulatory agencies.

The summary description for each program or activity provides specific and useful information about the program, its nature and purpose, its availability, its authorizing legislation, the administering agency, and where additional information may be found. The publication is unusually well organized and indexed for convenient use.

207 U. S. OFFICE OF EDUCATION. *Financial aid for higher education.* Wash., D.C.: Government Printing Office, 1969, 110 pp. $1.

This handbook is a well-written introduction to financial aid intended primarily for students; the tone is optimistic and encouraging. It provides easy-to-read, clear information on the nature and apportionment of financial aid, how it may be secured, and the federal programs designed to assist students. Also included are lists of other financial aid sources, college information sources, and colleges participating in the National Defense Loan, College Work-Study, and Educational Opportunity Grants programs.

208 U. S. SENATE, COMMITTEE ON LABOR AND PUBLIC WELFARE, SUBCOMMITTEE ON EDUCATION. *Federal and state student aid programs.* Wash., D. C.: Government Printing Office, 1970, 82 pp. 40 cents.

This booklet provides a compact and comprehensive survey of federal and state student aid programs for all levels of higher education, including professional and postdoctoral training. It was prepared for the Senate Subcommittee on Education by the Legislative Reference Service of the Library of Congress. Program descriptions include type or amount of assistance, eligibility and application procedures, and sources of further information. Federal programs are grouped by level of study and further subdivided by area of study. State programs are listed alphabetically by state. A brief, selected listing of other sources of information on colleges, career opportunities, and private programs of student financial aid is also provided. This booklet is a very useful and inexpensive document for students, parents, counselors, or anyone concerned with student financial aid.

SECTION 3: ADMISSIONS

Many portions of the conceptual framework described here could be justifiably included under college admissions because it is the pivotal and critical process. It seems preferable, however, to focus in this section on the entrance characteristics of college admissions and to utilize the taxonomy to illustrate the fact that the access process depends on a variety of logical and coordinated relationships among various processes and professions. Consequently, in this context the admissions process is somewhat narrowly defined to include the fundamental problems of defining the basis for admissions policy, recruiting and selecting candidates, and the massive job of administering the operation.

Naturally, these functions are related in one way or another to practically all offices and functions of the institution. It is worth emphasizing, however, that admissions is a primary instrument of institutional purpose. In the broader view admissions is the key process that affects the distribution of students within the system, the state, or the nation. In this sense it is also an instrument of manpower planning and such social objectives as the equalization of educational opportunity. Consequently, the coordination of admissions with other aspects of the access process is especially important.

In some respects that coordination works well; in others not so well. For example, admissions practice is especially sensitive and highly responsive to admissions theory because admissions theory and practice are quite well integrated with respect to the people involved and to administrative control. On the other hand the technology and procedures for directly relating admissions policy to institutional purpose are limited. The prediction model is useful in this connection but overworked and for many purposes irrelevant.

Similarly, admissions theory is frequently discussed in relation to manpower theory, the philosophy of educational opportunity, economic theory, etc. But these modes of social control and planning are, even in theory, still quite rudimentary. If governing boards are to act in the public interest in influencing access to higher education, it is supposedly through policy adjustment in admissions, financing, approval of new programs, etc. Such decisions are made daily but typically on intuitive or political grounds, partly for the simple reason that no more systematic methods have been developed for connecting admissions policies with other important considerations in access to higher education.

While there are a great many organizations and sources of information relevant to some aspect of access to higher education, those connected specifically with college admissions are relatively few. The major organizations are the College Entrance Examination Board (1112) which will celebrate in 1975 its 75th anniversary as an association of schools and colleges, the American College Testing Program (1101) which offers several services to a large number of institutions, and the American Association of Collegiate Registrars and Admission Officers (1096), which with the National Association of College Admissions Counselors (1119) constitute the major professional associations for admission officers.

The College Board Review (1315) is the periodical that probably comes closest to representing the variety of problems involved in access to higher education. The primary professional journals are *College and University* (1314) and the *National ACAC Journal* (1337). The corresponding newsletters for the two professional associations are the AACRAO *Newsletter* (1383) and the *National ACAC Newsletter* (1381). The primary news outlet concerning the American College Testing Program is *ACTivity* (1347).

3.1—*NATIONAL POLICY*. Issues concerning national admission policy are not always easy to distinguish from institutional policy. The literature in this section also tends to overlap in an important way with parts of section 7. Section 3.1 includes important essays on open admissions (216) and the general picture of admissions policy from a national standpoint. Thresher's small book on *College Admissions and the Public Interest* (222) is worth close reading, and Glazer's analysis (215) of meritocracy versus egalitarianism sets many difficult problems in clear perspective.

Section 7.1 includes several histories of college admissions and several papers that have philosophical significance. Section 7.2 contains much important material on national goals with respect to access to higher education. In particular it includes recent statements by the Carnegie Commission (574, 575) and various references on the move to universal higher education (e.g., 581).

Omissions in this literature are worth noting. Several writers have commented on the fact that many important aspects of the economy are constantly monitored (e.g., unemployment, gross national product, etc.), but there are few social indicators of man's welfare. Certainly, one would include in this category the need for indicators of the accessibility of higher education. Another matter of national policy that has gained some attention is the need for attractive alternatives to college. It is widely recognized that many students have little taste for academic work and would prefer socially acceptable alternatives to higher education. Aside from the Peace Corps and limited domestic service programs, little action has been taken in this area.

209 AGNEW, SPIRO T. Spiro T. Agnew on college admissions. *College Board Review,* Spring 1970, no. 75, pp. 12-15.

Open admissions policies dilute education with "bargain basement diplomas," Agnew charges in a hotly disputed speech delivered at a Republican fund-raising dinner. Using universities to achieve social goals, he says, "can only result in tragic losses to both universities and the nation," and "clutters our universities with unqualified students and pre-college-level courses." He considers the resulting mushroom growth of enrollment to be a major cause of campus inefficiency and unrest.

As an alternative, he proposes a commitment to equality of opportunity to be achieved by (1) "a perpetual talent search to find and advance every child of ability to the limit of his potential," and (2) upgrading compensatory education with more community colleges and special preparatory schools. This kind of commitment, he feels, will balance the scales and achieve equality but not dilution of opportunity. (See reactions in the following issues of *College Board Review*.)

210 ASTIN, ALEXANDER W. The challenge of open admissions: Folklore of selectivity. *Saturday Review,* 1969, vol. 52, no. 51, pp. 57-58, 69-70.

Astin charges that continued stress on high school grades and test scores in making decisions regarding college admissions has resulted in a woefully inadequate representation of black students among college freshmen. He suggests that purely meritocratic selection procedures based on test scores and grades are in basic conflict with the goal of furthering racial integration and are inappropriate for institutions of higher education. The admissions officer should function less like a "handicapper" trying to pick winners and should concentrate on funding those students who will benefit most from the particular educational program offered by the institution. This article is stimulating, though it bears a tenuous relationship to the research on which it is purportedly based.

211 BOWLES, FRANK H. *Admission to college: A perspective for the 1960s.* 57th Report of the President. New York: College Entrance Examination Board, 1960, 144 pp.

A survey of educators early in the 1960s showed this report to be one of the 10 most influential books in education at that time. It anticipates many of the admissions trends and problems of the following decade and provides a perceptive view of the development of the field.

212 BOWLES, FRANK. The democratization of education—a worldwide revolution. *College Board Review,* Fall 1969, no. 73, pp. 11-13.

Bowles interprets the revolution in education as a worldwide demand for democratization of educational opportunity that keeps pace with economic and social progress. Targets for the revolution in each country are its own particular kind of barriers to opportunity, whether financial, racial, academic, geographic, or social. His discerning observations on the impact of this revolution on the roles and responsibilities of universities make this an unusually significant reference. Bowles predicts that in coming decades society's demands that universities "assert and administer intellectual leadership" and also shoulder social responsibilities will result in universities' having more power than they would wish.

213 DYER, HENRY S. Admissions—college and university, in Robert L. Ebel (Ed.), *Encyclopedia of educational research.* (4th ed.) New York: Macmillan, 1969, pp. 24-43.

This excellent article provides one of the best overviews of college admissions in America. The author applies his wide experience to four basic areas. First, the nature and scope of college admissions is discussed. The author treats such topics as: (1) the initial transition from school to college, (2) admission by transfer, (3) admission to graduate and professional schools, (4) the role of associations, (5) the role of student financial aid, and (6) the nature of admissions research. Under the heading of demographic characteristics, the author discusses the flow of the American student population and suggests four factors that greatly affect it: (1) availability of higher education opportunities, (2) academic ability, (3) sex (the ratio of boys to girls among college entrants is approximately three to two), and (4) socioeconomic status.

The third general area of consideration is the choice of institutions by students. The author discusses various factors that affect this choice and then suggests three information sources designed to aid the student in making the choice: (1) descriptive handbooks, (2) prediction systems that help applicants assess their chances of doing satisfactory work at a particular college, and (3) procedures for measuring the "climate" of a college. The selection of students by institutions is the final area of discussion. The author covers such topics as: (1) admissions policies, (2) administrative organization of the admissions office, (3) the decision process, (4) the relevance of tests and measures, and (5) the admission of disadvantaged students.

214 FURNISS, W. TODD (ED.) *Higher education for everybody? Issues and implications.* Wash., D. C.: American Council on Education, 1971, 284 pp. $7.

Educational decision makers discuss the implications of universal higher education in these essays, prepared for the 1970 annual meeting of the American Council on Education. The underlying theme is the desirability and feasibility of revamping the whole structure of American higher education, now geared to serve an "out-of-date stereotype"—the full-time undergraduate at a four-year college. The redefining of student clienteles to include tremendously diverse age, ability, racial, and socioeconomic groups implies the need for diverse "production models" for institutions and programs. The participants also debate policies, priorities, and the division of responsibility for paying the costs of universal higher education.

215 GLAZER, NATHAN. Are academic standards obsolete? *Change,* 1970, vol. 2, no. 6, pp. 38-44.

This comprehensive and thoughtful article includes most of the main problems and considerations involved in the debate over meritocratic vs. egalitarian values in the admission of college students and the evaluation of their performance. The major issues include equal opportunity, fair distribution of privilege, social bias in evaluating competence and promise, certification versus education as a primary purpose of education, the narrow range of abilities now rewarded, the extent to which present academic outcomes help or harm society, and what society needs to survive. All these issues boil down to one question: "Can we maintain a society of some degree of peace, material comfort, humanity, without a means for rewarding it, without a ladder for those who have done best?"

216 HEALY, TIMOTHY S. The challenge of open admissions: Will Everyman destroy the university? *Saturday Review,* 1969, vol. 52, no. 51, pp. 54-69.

This article describes the controversial and highly publicized move to open admissions at The City University of New York (CUNY). To insure that CUNY's open door will not become a revolving door, the plan calls for a level of remedial and supportive services equal to the needs of the students. Ethnic integration of all colleges, student mobility among the various programs, and increased standards of academic excellence are all listed on the agenda of open admissions. In response to opposition voiced over the threat to academic standards, Healy argues that there are only two ways in which open admissions could downgrade standards: driving away the talented students, and forcing the faculty to lower their sights. In refuting these concerns, he points out that the university's moral commitment to meeting this urgent social need is "the demand, not the fear" of the bright students. They also benefit from exposure to superior teaching and the variety of learning and involvement that only a city university can offer. The second danger—that faculty may lower their standards "is also in no way an inevitable consequence." He describes the various levels and programs offered by CUNY and concludes that the job can be accomplished if the city and state will provide the necessary funds.

217 HILLS, JOHN R. Diversity and the effect of selective admissions. *Journal of Educational Measurement,* 1966, vol. 3, pp. 235-242.

The impact of selective admissions on the University System of Georgia was examined to determine whether there was a decrease of diversity in classes entering college in 1964, compared with classes of 1958 and 1960. Fears that selectivity narrows the band of admitted students and creates a homogeneity among colleges were not borne out; on the contrary, this was seen to be a period of increasing diversity of educational opportunity.

218 KAYSEN, CARL. Higher education: For whom? at whose cost?, in Educational Testing Service, *Proceedings of the 1970 Invitational Conference on Testing Problems.* Princeton, N.J.: ETS, 1971, pp. 114-126.

This provocative paper provided a foretaste of some subsequent recommendations of the Carnegie Commission on Higher Education, of which the author was a member. He argues that some of the more difficult problems of higher education are connected with its rapid and continued expansion at all levels. One must question whether such generalized expansion is defensible in the broadest social terms and whether the public will be willing to divert the necessary massive funds from competing social priorities. Kaysen proposes separation of basic college training from the broader research and service functions associated primarily with the university. In such basic training, students would earn a B.A. degree in three years. Present community colleges would serve this local, free, and open access function. Higher training would be characterized by selective admissions and substantial tuition.

219 MOYNIHAN, DANIEL P. On universal higher education. *Educational Record,* 1971, vol. 52, pp. 5-11.

Moynihan warns that untroubled progress toward universal higher education seems unlikely. He states that this progress has been impeded by rising discontent with mass education and the belief that the number of people who can benefit from traditional methods of higher education is limited. However, he places the bulk of the blame on the growing politicization of the academic world.

In Moynihan's view, "the issue is an adversary culture firmly entrenched in higher education." Since this culture holds values opposed to those of the majority of the American people, public support of universities decreases as politicization increases. The polarization between the universities and the larger society will lead to the point where "higher education will stand for the humiliation of traditional America" and universal higher education will have lost its prime motivating force.

220 PEARSON, RICHARD. Admission to college, in Earl J. McGrath (Ed.), *Universal higher education*. New York: McGraw-Hill, 1966, pp. 140-158.

Speaking from experience as president of the College Entrance Examination Board, the author outlines his views of the impact universal higher education will have on the admissions process. He delineates a different set of problems in each of three circumstances: highly selective admissions, moderately selective admissions, and transition to open-door institutions. Suggested solutions include expansion of guidance and testing at the junior high school level, improved articulation between secondary school and college, and means for providing flexible admission for students at a variety of ages and personal circumstances. This paper is part of a worthwhile collection presented at a symposium on universal higher education in 1964 (see 581).

221 SIMS, ALBERT G. On the university, admissions, and international education, in College Entrance Examination Board, *College admissions policies for the 1970s*. New York: College Entrance Examination Board, 1968, pp. 115-125.

This perceptive article is directed partly to international education, but it has much to say about admissions generally. The author suggests that the history of the university makes evident its natural and substantial involvement in contemporary society. Relevance to the needs of the community has become "greatly extended, overwhelmingly apparent, and utterly crucial." Recent history suggests that when new requirements arise for expanded university involvement, and the universities themselves do not respond adequately, the terms of their response will be determined by the external authority providing their upkeep. The author argues that the role and relevance of the university is, and must be, significantly shaped by and expressed through the institution's admissions policy.

222 THRESHER, B. ALDEN. *College admissions and the public interest*. New York: College Entrance Examination Board, 1966, 93 pp. $2.50.

In this important monograph Thresher focuses on the general problem of access from three levels: (1) the individual student, (2) the individual college, and (3) a systems view of the whole process. He explains the "great sorting process" as it now works and then discusses what it ought to be in terms of the public interest. The present "competitive free enterprise" recruiting system does not seem to be effecting advances in educational quality, and he feels the public habit of brand loyalty and pursuit of "status symbol" degrees have even retarded such achievement.

The study of admissions will merge into the study of higher education in its totality, he predicts, with expectations of three major changes. (1) We will educate for coping with a changing environment in a way that will help students cultivate the habit of learning and the appetite for it. (2) We will see richer varieties of institutions, with more attention to innovation and reform, and increased student awareness of different options open to him. As the primitive device of application-and-reply becomes unbearably clumsy, there needs to be redirection of students into various appropriate categories of further education. (3) The guidance process will be an integral part of education, and college teachers will devote more time to interaction with students. Thresher speaks with wisdom and authority; this book should be read by anyone seriously interested in access to higher education.

223 THRESHER, B. ALDEN. Admissions in perspective, in Asa S. Knowles (Ed.), *Handbook of college and university administration*. Vol. II. *Academic*. New York: McGraw-Hill, 1970, sec. 3, pp. 3-25.

The chapter provides an excellent overview of the process of access to higher education with special emphasis on the "great sorting" of students and implications of various admissions models from a national or public standpoint. This overview briefly summarizes many of the perceptive ideas recorded in an earlier book by Thresher (222).

224 VROMAN, CLYDE. Problems and issues confronting the admissions community, in College Entrance Examination Board, *College admissions policies for the 1970s*. New York: College Entrance Examination Board, 1968, pp. 1-8.

An elder statesman defines the task of the college admissions officer as formulating admissions policies that implement the goals of his institution and at the same time take cognizance of areas of broad concern to all institutions. Some of the developments that will have nationwide impact on higher education are: (1) Rapid growth in enrollments. By 1975-76 college enrollment is expected to show a 49 percent increase over enrollment in 1966-67. (2) Expansion of educational opportunity. The trend will be to open up higher education to cross sections of the population whose needs are not fulfilled by traditional programs, and whose talents are not measurable by traditional testing methods. (3) The expanding role of government. Federal involvement is seen by Vroman as largely financial but implies "the beginnings of external controls." The trend to statewide systems of higher education is seen to be of great significance to individual institutions.

225 WARD, F. CHAMPION. Higher education in the 70's: How strait the gate? *College Board Review,* Winter 1969-70, no. 74, pp. 11-13.

The author identifies three distinct areas in which crises are affecting educational institutions: (1) efficiency and support, (2) relevance and control, and (3) race and class. He suggests an approach to resolution of these crises involving a "greater variety of means to more clearly stated ends," urging schools to examine routines, explore options, and develop measures and standards of educational goals and methods. Thus variation in student characteristics might be reflected in multiple curriculums and role differentiation of professors. Carefully designed examinations testing level of knowledge, thought, and social perception could be administered at the beginning and end of the academic career to help define progress and goals.

226 WEST, ELMER D. Access to colleges and universities in the United States, in The International Study of University Admissions, *Access to higher education.* Vol. II. *National studies.* Paris: United Nations Educational, Scientific and Cultural Organization, and The International Association of Universities, 1965, pp. 593-644.

The stated goal for education in the United States is "the maximum development of every person to the limit of his ability." In the light of this goal, the author discusses the problem of access to higher education in America and evaluates the present admissions process. The first section discusses college preparation, the size of the potential admissions pool, the process of admissions, and the structure of higher education. The second section considers operations and problems, including the lack of standard admissions procedures, the lack of effective guidance programs, and the financial and other difficulties confronting foreign students. In his evaluation of the admissions process in the United States, West concludes that although "the goal has not been reached, and may never be, when it is evaluated against progress towards that goal, the results are overwhelmingly favorable."

3.2 – INSTITUTIONAL POLICY. This section includes a number of thoughtful articles that are relevant to the establishment of admissions policy on an individual campus. Much of this work is based on studies of the admissions process, and the authors are frequently individuals who have in some sense wed interests in admissions and research.

Three types of problems are worth special mention; each is quite important and has received too little attention. Webb (239) describes the side effects that can result from implementation of an admissions policy. In proposing an experimental approach to admissions problems, Manning (235) clarifies the critical connection between admissions policy and institutional purpose. Several writers (for example, see Fishman, 232) have discussed the importance of clearly established criteria connected directly to institutional objectives and also subject to reliable evaluation.

All these problems demonstrate the subtlety of admissions theory as it applies to the individual institution. Not only is such theory badly in need of further development, there is also a notable lack of technique whereby admissions officers can broaden their admissions policies and evaluate the results. Such techniques would require a way of establishing connections between multiple criteria and multiple methods of selecting and evaluating students. The formalization of institutional values would doubtless prove to be a problem — how many oboe players equal one good quarterback?

227 BAIRD, LEONARD L., AND RICHARDS, JAMES M. JR. *The effects of selecting college students by various kinds of high school achievement.* ACT Research Report No. 23. Iowa City, Iowa: American College Testing Program, 1968, 27 pp.

Previous research at American College Testing Program indicated that academic and nonacademic achievement are not highly related. This study illustrates the effect of various admissions strategies that emphasize academic or nonacademic factors. The authors suggest that too much emphasis on either is not appropriate for most colleges and argue for a combination of the two. While this brief report is oriented toward data, it does illustrate the diverse possible outcomes of different admissions philosophies.

228 CAMPBELL, DAVID P. The vocational interests of Dartmouth College freshmen: 1947-67. *Personnel and Guidance Journal,* 1969, vol. 47, pp. 521-530.

This study reports profiles of Dartmouth College students collected over a 20-year period that revealed that: (1) academic aptitude of the current student body at Dartmouth is mostly superior to that of its predecessors, and (2) the current Dartmouth students are increasingly oriented to biological, physical, and social sciences and substantially less interested in business, outdoor, and skilled trades occupations than their predecessors.

The implication is that by favoring students with high scholastic ability, Dartmouth has also been favoring students with scientific or cultural interests over those with a business orientation. The administration may choose to justify the current trend, or to develop a new policy. The author suggests that diversity of interests among a student population should be the goal and admissions committees should expand their ideas of excellence.

It is interesting to note that this phenomenon was discovered and much discussed by the selective colleges several years earlier and without the benefit of such selective data as here presented. One wonders how much earlier it might have been discovered by appropriate routine admissions research.

229 COLLEGE ENTRANCE EXAMINATION BOARD. *College admissions policies for the 1970s.* New York: College Entrance Examination Board, 1968, 175 pp. $3.

This publication contains the papers delivered at the Colloquium on College Admissions Policies held at Interlochen, Michigan, in June 1967. The conference, sponsored jointly by the College Board and the University of Michigan, brought together 80 professional admissions officers in order to lay a foundation of ideas, information, and perspectives relevant to planning for the decade ahead. The colloquium included prepared papers presented by nationally known authorities on topics of key importance to college admissions policies. Several of the papers are annotated separately (221, 224, 236, 259).

230 DAVIS, JUNIUS A. The criterion problem in college admissions research, in College Entrance Examination Board, *Research in higher education: Guide to institutional decisions.* New York: College Entrance Examination Board, 1965, pp. 25-34.

This article is concerned with the complicated problem of connecting admissions standards with outcome criteria. In a thoughtful discussion, the author makes clear that an institution must know what it is trying to do before it can truly justify the procedures whereby it selects its students.

231 DOERMANN, HUMPHREY. *Crosscurrents in college admissions.* New York: Teachers College Press, Columbia University, 1968, 166 pp. $7.95.

This widely quoted study captured the attention and the worries of many private colleges. It dramatized the fact that the number of students each year who test high in academic aptitude and who also come from families prosperous enough to pay the rising costs of private higher education is surprisingly limited even though the total college-bound pool is expanding.

Using family income and College Board Scholastic Aptitude Test scores as variables, Doermann makes an approximate projection of the size of different applicant pools that might be expected through 1975 as defined by different levels of financial and academic ability. These tables can aid colleges in estimating whether their candidate pools have been expanding or shrinking, and in considering the effect of specific changes in admissions standards, student fees, aid programs, etc. Private colleges must understand the student market from which they draw a large element of their financial support. These measures, even though rough, do give some valuable information and help to clarify the scope of the financial problem facing private colleges. "The Market for College Education" in *Educational Record,* 1968, vol. 49, pp. 49-60, summarizes much of the material in this book.

232 FISHMAN, JOSHUA A. Unsolved criterion problems in the selection of college students. *Harvard Educational Review,* 1958, vol. 28, pp. 340-349.

This unusually perceptive article was written before its time and is still well worth reading despite the convulsive changes in higher education over the past decade. In discussing the criteria against which the admissions process is evaluated, the author considers such critical variables as the time period to which the criteria refer, criteria of desirability vs. criteria of success, and criteria that can be predicted as opposed to those that cannot. In summing up, he speculates legitimately on the extent to which colleges should want to predict various criteria of success.

233 FISHMAN, JOSHUA A. Some social-psychological theory for selecting and guiding college students, in Nevitt Sanford (Ed.), *The American college*. New York: John Wiley, 1962, pp. 666-689.

Fishman presents some theoretical considerations bearing on college selection from the vantage point of social psychology. He notes that many colleges still use only intellective factors (high school grades and standardized measures of scholastic aptitude) in making selections. When these two measures have been combined the average multiple correlation with freshman grades has been about .55. Simply adding a personality test score to the usual predictors produces a gain in the correlation of less than .05 because these personality predictors usually correlate just as highly with high school grades and aptitude test scores as they do with the freshman average in college.

Improved prediction of college performance will not come so much from getting more comprehensive pictures of the student's personality, but rather by coming to grips with the "contingency factors" that intervene between the taking of measures in high school and the outcome in college. On the basis of assumptions concerning the presence of individual and institutional changes, Fishman suggests nine different strategies for studies in selection and guidance, eight of which include nonintellective factors. He recommends a temporary moratorium on prediction per se that would give more time to study the different ways in which students make use of varying college environments.

234 HEIST, PAUL, AND WEBSTER, HAROLD. Differential characteristics of student bodies—implications for selection and study of undergraduates, in Field Service Center, and Center for the Study of Higher Education, *Selection and educational differentiation*. Berkeley, Calif.: Field Service Center, and Center for the Study of Higher Education, University of California, 1960, pp. 91-106.

This well-known paper is one of the early discussions of the use of personality variables in student selection. Illustrative data are used to demonstrate the relationship between selection policies and the resulting intellectual climate on the campus. The authors recommend that greater consideration should be given to personality and motivational variables to broaden the diversity of student populations.

235 MANNING, WINTON H. Personal and institutional assessment: Alternatives to tests of scholastic aptitude and achievement in the admissions process, in College Entrance Examination Board, *Barriers to higher education*. New York: College Entrance Examination Board, 1971, pp. 81-99.

In this provocative paper the author cites two massive problems in improving the means whereby students and colleges select one another. First, there is the substantial logistical problem of developing new approaches, new instruments, and new programs to facilitate college admissions among a very large group of institutions only loosely federated. Second, a rational development of college admissions requires a better-founded means of selecting students who actually benefit more from one college than from another. This latter goal requires an explicit experimental approach. Manning's paper constitutes an eloquent statement for the need for such experimentation.

236 MILLETT, JOHN D. Clear institutional objectives essential to admissions function, in College Entrance Examination Board, *College admissions policies for the 1970s*. New York: College Entrance Examination Board, 1968, pp. 52-65.

In this paper presented at the 1967 Colloquium on College Admissions Policies, Millett suggests several areas in which colleges and universities need to clarify and articulate their objectives. The first major choice that faces an institution is whether it is going to be residential in character or urban in its orientation. Second, at the undergraduate level of instruction a choice must be made between general and professional education as the objective of the baccalaureate degree. Undergraduate institutions should clarify their objectives and should then relate their admissions policies to them. The third set of choices has to do with the attitude of the institution toward "in loco parentis." Colleges and universities should do more to define the behavioral standards they expect and should make these standards a part of their admissions process. Finally, the author views the act of admission as a kind of contract between student and institution and feels that both parties should be expected to fulfill their commitment in this contractual agreement. While many of Millett's observations bear close reading, this latter hope seems badly eroded by events since 1967.

237 STUDY OF EDUCATION AT STANFORD. *Report to the university.* Vol. IV. *Undergraduate admissions and financial aid.* Stanford, Calif.: Stanford University, 1968, 81 pp.

This forthright report provides a good example of an institutional self-study of admissions and financial aid. It sets three goals: (1) broadening the "all-around" stereotype of the Stanford student, (2) accepting the responsibility to increase opportunities for minority groups, and (3) providing sufficient financial aid to realize these aims. The report recommends that more "one-talent" students be drawn into the admissions pool. The feeling that they cannot measure up to the "Renaissance Man" stereotype often deters such students from entering the competition. Hence they need to be informed of categories of talent within which applicants will compete, indications of the percentage of acceptance from each category, and the necessary level of achievement for consideration. In carrying out the commitment to search for minority candidates, Stanford minority students should be sent out to recruit in high schools and junior colleges with heavy minority enrollments. Special consideration should be given to assessing these candidates in terms of already-enrolled minority students, rather than conventional yardsticks of achievement. Realizing that the key obstacle to accomplishing this goal is an inadequate financial budget, they conclude, "The only answer over the long run is money. Our recommendation is 'find it.' "

238 WALLACH, MICHAEL A., AND WING, CLIFF W. JR. *The talented student: A validation of the creativity-intelligence distinction.* New York: Holt, Rinehart and Winston, 1969, 131 pp. $3.95.

The basic argument of this provocative little book is that scholastic aptitude is a good predictor of scholastic achievement, but other measures are necessary to predict creative achievement outside the classroom. The reader is supposed to conclude that less weight should be placed on admissions tests – an undoubtedly correct conclusion but reached through dubious research methodology. Since the students in this study all scored in the top range on the College Board Scholastic Aptitude Test, one could hardly expect much variation in the performance of students with "high" and "low" scores. Bearing that important fact in mind, the book makes stimulating reading.

239 WEBB, SAM C. Changes in student personal qualities associated with change in intellectual abilities. *College and University,* 1966, vol. 41, pp. 280-298.

This study considers measurable changes in the personality characteristics of entering students that occur concomitantly with and because of student selection in terms of scholastic abilities. Four measures of scholastic ability and 34 measures of personality were available for analysis for five successive freshman classes of the liberal arts college of Emory University for 1958-62. During this period students were selected largely on the basis of a predicted first-year average, which was derived from a regression equation based on high school average and scores on the College Board Scholastic Aptitude Test.

The data show that there was, over the five-year period studied, significant gain in the scholastic ability of students admitted to Emory. There were also significant changes in the personality structure of admitted students. These include a decrease in dependency needs, emotional expressiveness, interest in pragmatic activities, and striving for grades. In addition, there was more openness of mind and an increase in intellectual interests and motivation. The author concludes that Emory students are becoming "more able to work at a higher level of abstraction and on a more independent and possibly more creative basis." The study is important because it demonstrates vividly one way in which admissions policy can have sweeping effects on the very nature of an institution.

3.3 — *RECRUITMENT AND SELECTION.* The admissions process includes a long schedule of intricate procedures that are worrisome to the professionals involved and baffling to the students. It is almost a national idiosyncrasy seemingly out of the control of individual colleges. As Hanford (248) has succinctly summarized, there are many problems, and they require many solutions. The literature of this section describes some of those procedures; it also includes some of the criticism.

It is important to note the scarcity of work on the selection process. One noteworthy study by Whitla (468) is found in section 5.5 on Prediction. In that section and the following one on Follow-up and Dropout Studies, there are many reports of research on problems closely related to admissions, but few that are concerned with the nature and effects of the selection process itself.

240 CAMPBELL, L. HOWARD, AND HAHN, WALTER. Readmission of former students after absence from the campus: Problems and opportunities. *College and University,* 1962, vol. 37, pp. 126-134.

This article reports results of a study of 538 students at the University of Utah who had been requested to take a leave of absence because of poor grades and later were readmitted. Results showed that the majority of students improved their academic performance after absence from school. In addition, those students involved in "activities of import" (i.e., responsible employment, military service, or marriage) improved significantly more than students reporting no such activities. The study thus makes a case for readmission of former students, though it does not include a control comparison of students remaining in the institution.

241 COLLEGE ENTRANCE EXAMINATION BOARD. *College admissions.* New York: College Entrance Examination Board, 1954-1963. Complete set, $24; individual copies, $3.

This is a series of reports of colloquiums on college admissions sponsored yearly from 1954 through 1963 by the College Entrance Examination Board. Begun as a "school for admissions officers," the colloquium perspective broadened to include many aspects of college and high school programs. Although some of the material is dated, many of the individual papers are lively and still quite relevant. Some of the papers are annotated separately. Together, they are the closest thing to a comprehensive text on college admissions anywhere available. (For a list of topics covered and colloquium chairmen, see 1434.)

242 COLLEGE ENTRANCE EXAMINATION BOARD. Students speak out about college admissions. *College Board Review,* Winter 1966-67, no. 62, pp. 22-26.

This article contains excerpts from a panel discussion at which six students were asked to discuss experiences in college selection and admission and to evaluate the available informational and planning services. Topics discussed include parental influence in college choice, weaknesses of guidance facilities, limitations of catalogs, uneven value of visits and interviews, importance of understanding the college environment, and use of college students as counselors. The narrative provides a brief but pointed catalog of student perceptions for admissions counselors who may be either too new or too "experienced" to see the other side of the coin.

243 COLLEGE ENTRANCE EXAMINATION BOARD. *Admissions and financial aid requirements and procedures at College Board member colleges: For students planning to enter college in the fall of 1972.* New York: College Entrance Examination Board, 1971, 140 pp. (Out of print)

This annual publication summarizes in tabular form the basic admissions procedures and test requirements of all College Board member colleges. It also supplies information on test and notification dates, financial aid statements required, etc. It is especially useful for students and high school counselors. Revised each spring, a complimentary copy is sent to the director of guidance at each secondary school that has had College Board Scholastic Aptitude Test candidates.

[*Editor's note:* This publication was discontinued in 1972. The 1972 edition of *The College Handbook* (84) lists comparable and more detailed information.]

244 COLLEGE ENTRANCE EXAMINATION BOARD, COMMITTEE ON ENTRANCE PROCEDURES. A statement of college admissions principles and procedures offered as guidelines for schools and colleges. *College Board Review,* Winter 1964-65, no. 55, pp. 10-12.

This statement of principles and procedures is based on two assumptions: (1) that each candidate should be given full and serious consideration, and (2) that procedural safeguards need to be established so that the interests of the individual candidate are not subordinated to institutional interests. Major sections deal with institutional self-interpretation, protection of candidate interest, confidentiality, and evaluation and improvement of admissions procedures. The statement also reviews specific responsibilities of colleges concerning the educational role of the admissions office, notification, and cooperation with secondary schools. Additional sections outline the informational role and educational responsibilities of the secondary school. This report should be on the required reading list of every new admissions officer.

245 CREAGER, JOHN A. Use of research results in matching students and colleges. *Journal of College Student Personnel,* 1968, vol. 9, pp. 312-319.

The author assumes that the main objective of matching students with colleges is to maximize output in terms of certain educational objectives. This output is a function of three factors: student input, college environment, and the interaction effects from a particular match between student and institution. Both student and institutions possess a great many characteristics that will affect outcomes, and this multiplicity of characteristics implies the need for complex prediction equations. Furthermore, the many different possible outcomes should be considered differently, according to the needs of the student.

This article presents a dream in which is visualized a large directory that is divided into two sections. The first section, to be used by the high school counselor, gives information on different types of students and indicate the probability of a wide range of outcomes at various types of institutions. The second section would be used by the college admissions officer who finds the page that best describes his own institution. From this page he determines which student profiles are preferable for certain specific outcomes. The article dramatizes the complexity of a humane and socially useful admissions process and makes clear how far we are from being able to assign students to colleges.

246 CROSSLAND, FRED E. Politics and policies in college admissions. *Phi Delta Kappan,* 1965, vol. 46, pp. 299-302.

The author argues that enrollment pressures have created a need for regional, perhaps national, cooperation in college admissions practice. The present system is described as chaotic, wasteful, and unfair. Crossland calls for a plan resembling the British Central Council on Admissions, which serves as a clearinghouse for the nation. Since this article appeared, there has been movement in several states toward central admissions systems.

247 EDUCATIONAL RECORDS BUREAU, COMMITTEE ON SCHOOL AND COLLEGE RELATIONS. *Admission to American colleges: Summary of policies and procedures.* New York: ERB, 1964, 10 pp.

This brief report is the sixth in a longitudinal series begun in 1929 to explore college admissions policies. It summarizes the findings of a questionnaire completed by 560 institutions in the summer of 1963. The four most important admissions criteria were reported to be: (1) transcript of grades, (2) recommendations from principal or counselor, (3) test scores, and (4) rank in class. Compared with an earlier survey, these results showed colleges weighting data on personal qualities more heavily now than in 1953. Test scores are used not only in admissions decisions, but also in placement. Colleges find letter grades important, but typically use no scale for equating grades from different secondary schools. (See 463 for a review of research indicating that such adjustments serve no useful purpose when admissions test scores are available.)

248 HANFORD, GEORGE H. A new Rx for our admissions ills. *College Board Review,* Fall 1965, no. 57, pp. 6-8.

Speaking from considerable experience with national, regional, and institutional admissions problems, the author suggests that there are not one but many different ills that plague the admissions process. He sees the need for a variety of solutions, many requiring cooperative effort among colleges and some perhaps needing centralized mechanisms. The article provides a concise but vivid picture of the complexity of present-day admissions procedures.

249 HILLS, JOHN R., GLADNEY, MARILYN B., AND KLOCK, JOSEPH A. Nine critical questions about selective college admissions. *Personnel and Guidance Journal,* 1967, vol. 45, pp. 640-647.

The authors list a series of questions about statistical prediction that commonly concern admissions officers. They cite a number of references and their own considerable research and offer general advice on each question (e.g., inclusion of nonacademic grades does not reduce the accuracy of a high school average). The article sticks fairly close to the mechanics of prediction but provides a useful summary well worth reading.

250 HOY, JOHN C. Admissions—student selection, evaluation of credentials, use of the predictive formula as an admissions tool, in Asa S. Knowles (Ed.), *Handbook of college and university administration.* Vol. II. *Academic.* New York: McGraw-Hill, 1970, sec. 3, pp. 74-81.

This chapter reviews a variety of topics concerning the selection of students. These include relations between the admissions office and the admissions committee, criteria for development of a candidate rating system, identification of special secondary school courses, equivalency diplomas, and credit for nontraditional course work. The author also suggests guidelines for obtaining health clearance and for handling special problems of disadvantaged and foreign students.

251 KINKEAD, KATHARINE T. *How an Ivy League college decides on admissions.* New York: W. W. Norton, 1961, 94 pp. $3.50.

After spending several months in the admissions office at Yale University, the author produced this largely anecdotal account of that university's admissions practices. First published in *The New Yorker,* the article elicited many letters from admissions directors of colleges and universities throughout the country which "seem to indicate that the general process used at New Haven is similar to that of most institutions today enjoying the painful blessings of being truly selective." The author notes with gratification that, in spite of a current trend toward judging college candidates from paper data that obscure the elements of personality, creativity, and individual talent, Yale's selection remains an individual and personal process. This brief book makes interesting reading for those on the outside wondering what goes on inside.

252 KNOELL, DOROTHY M. Are our colleges really accessible to the poor? *Junior College Journal,* 1968, vol. 39, pp. 1-11.

This article is dedicated to a humane and relevant admissions process. It identifies procedural hurdles that tend to discourage disadvantaged students from attending even open-door colleges. Rigid cutoff dates for application for admission, testing programs, or financial aid shut the door administratively to students who have little know-how and motivation. Complicated financial forms are often totally irrelevant to the basic economic situation of the very poor while college catalogs often fail to get across the necessary information. In addition, poor students lack the person-to-person guidance that middle-class students take for granted from their day-to-day contacts with other students.

Colleges are urged to "scrutinize their catalogues and consciences" to provide flexibility of deadlines and simplification of procedure and prose, to make use of "unconventional antennae" to find and inform potential students, and to provide effective financial aid for high-risk students.

253 SIMMONS, ADINE, MARTIN, WESLEY JR., AND JACKSON, ROBERT L. Students in recruiting and selection. *National ACAC Journal,* 1970, vol. 14, nos. 3-4, pp. 25-27.

This panel discussion from a meeting of the National ACAC provides some pros and cons regarding the use of students in recruiting and selection but does not include systematic evaluation of the practice or information documenting the extent to which it has grown.

254 STEWART, BLAIR, AND WISHART, PATRICIA. UCCA and SAM: A look at two very different single application methods. *College Board Review,* Spring 1971, no. 79, pp. 14-19.

This article discusses the purposes and problems involved in the operation of two central application systems: the Universities Central Council on Admissions (UCCA), a clearing and processing house for application for universities in Great Britain, and the Single Application Method (SAM), an admissions program serving 11 liberal arts colleges in the Midwest. Though the two systems are similar in their intent to reduce the burden of multiple applications for the student as well as the admissions staff, they do reflect differences between the two systems of higher education. Thus UCCA communicates directly with the applicant, reflecting the centralized nature of the British system, while SAM applicants communicate directly with the colleges. The operation of the two systems is reviewed in some detail, as is the Early Decision Plan of the College Entrance Examination Board.

255 TIEDEMAN, DAVID V. Can a machine admit an applicant to continuing education? *Measurement and Evaluation in Guidance,* 1969, vol. 2, pp. 69-81.

This article is not intended to answer the question posed by its title, but rather to examine new possibilities in college admissions that might be exposed by seriously considering the question. The author joins his prominent careers in psychometrics and guidance to construct a theoretical "admissions machine" that is intended not only to admit the student to education beyond secondary school, but also to educate him in self-awareness. In a response appearing in the same journal issue, Cronbach lauds the effort but questions whether a truly educative and mutually accommodative admissions process is possible as long as that process represents a competitive route to social status. (Several examples of operating information systems serving limited purposes in admissions and guidance are described in section 13.3.)

256 TRENT, JAMES W. A new look at recruitment policies. *College Board Review,* Winter, 1965-66, no. 58, pp. 7-11.

This article presents implications of a six-year longitudinal study of 10,000 graduating high school seniors. The author investigated factors relating to college attendance, attrition, students' expectations, and personal development in college. Findings indicated that socioeconomic status is the main determinant of college attendance and that persistence through graduation is influenced by family environment, academic motivation, and attitudinal disposition. Expectations regarding colleges were limited and often incorrect because of insufficient awareness of the student's own potential and the corresponding institutional characteristics. Students based choice of college primarily on proximity, peer popularity, and prestige. The author recommends that college recruitment be considered part of the educational process, coordinating the needs of society with the individual needs of the students. He suggests that innovations in recruitment such as "student mix," intermediary colleges, and cooperation between institutions would be effective in facilitating individual development.

257 WALTON, JEAN B., AND WHEATON, WILLIAM L. Student participation in the admissions program. *Journal of the National Association of Women Deans and Counselors,* 1967, vol. 30, pp. 115-119.

In 1951, Pomona College became one of the first institutions to establish student representation on the admissions committee. Thirty students who served on the committee were asked to evaluate the contributions of student membership. Their comments are thoughtfully written and point out the value of the practice not only as an improvement in the selection process but in the relationships among students, faculty, and administration on the campus.

258 WARD, LEWIS B. The interview as an assessment technique, in College Entrance Examination Board, *College admissions, 2.* New York: College Entrance Examination Board, 1955, pp. 62-71.

The author sees little value in the interview as a method of assessing candidates for admission to educational institutions, because of the difficulty of sorting out the personal reactions and prejudices of the interviewer. Written questionnaires have been found more likely to show evidence of validity when checked against later performance. However, if the interview is judged for its value in personalizing educational institutions and its effect on morale and expectations of candidates, then there is justification for its use. Ward also reports data from the doctoral thesis of S. A. Kendrick, which involved an experiment with and without the interview technique in judging candidates for the Harvard Graduate School of Business Administration. Those results cast doubt on the value of the interview for evaluative purposes.

259 WHITLA, DEAN K. Candidate overlap studies and other admissions research, in College Entrance Examination Board, *College admissions policies for the 1970s.* New York: College Entrance Examination Board, 1968, pp. 137-165.

In this report to the 1967 Colloquium on College Admissions Policies, Whitla describes his research on the nature and extent of candidate overlap. In order to bring a factual approach to the guessing game played by admissions officers in gauging the number of candidates who file multiple applications, this study pooled information on 78,000 applicants for 1966-67 admission at 43 participating colleges. Students who applied to highly selective colleges were found to make more multiple applications, but usually on a "horizontal" basis—to equally competitive colleges, rather than to colleges of differing styles and standards. The findings refute the theory that multiple applications usually come from those who can least afford it—financially or emotionally—for it is the students with high College Board Scholastic Aptitude Test scores and those from private schools who tend to file several applications. Whitla concludes that the study provides a rationale for establishing cooperative ventures in college admissions that should transcend geographical location.

3.4—*ADMINISTRATION OF ADMISSIONS.* Any process as complicated as college admissions requires a highly developed and complete array of administrative procedures. This section includes references to articles on office management, record keeping, public relations, etc. Section 13.3 contains additional information concerning computer applications in admissions work.

It is unfortunate that no individual or organization has assumed the responsibility for preparing a text on college admissions. Perhaps the nearest thing to a current text would be the section on admissions in Knowles's *Handbook of College and University Administration* (268). It includes fourteen chapters of uneven quality. Of all periodicals, *College and University* (1314) is most concerned with the administration of admissions.

260 AMERICAN ASSOCIATION OF COLLEGIATE REGISTRARS AND ADMISSIONS OFFICERS, COMMITTEE ON RECORDS MANAGEMENT AND TRANSCRIPT ADEQUACY. *A guide to an adequate permanent record and transcript.* Wash., D. C.: AACRAO, 1971, 22 pp. $2.

This useful handbook reviews policies and practices of academic record keeping and describes the essential items of the permanent record and transcript. It also includes sections on forged transcripts, transcripts for teacher certification needs, and release of student information.

261 AMERICAN ASSOCIATION OF COLLEGIATE REGISTRARS AND ADMISSIONS OFFICERS, AND NATIONAL ASSOCIATION OF SECONDARY-SCHOOL PRINCIPALS, JOINT COMMITTEE ON SCHOOL-COLLEGE RELATIONS. *Manual for the secondary-school record.* Wash., D. C.: NASSP, 1964, 23 pp.

This *Manual* contains guidelines for the construction and interpretation of the high school transcript and student description summary. Recommended forms are reproduced and directions for their use are provided. The detailed interpretation of the scales used in the description summary is especially helpful. It can hardly be said, however, that this document has persuaded all secondary schools to use a common transcript.

262 COUNCIL OF STUDENT PERSONNEL ASSOCIATIONS IN HIGHER EDUCATION, COMMISSION ON STUDENT RECORDS AND INFORMATION. Student records—their collection, use, and protection. *National ACAC Journal,* 1970, vol. 15, no. 3, pp. 27-28.

This article contains guidelines dealing with institutional responsibilities for maintaining student records. The commission recommends that each institution consult with faculty and students to formulate general policies. Further recommendations cover student inspection of records, staff access to files, composition and release of various types of records, nonconfidential material, and release of data for research purposes.

263 GARLAND, GILBERT C. Admissions—freshman class quota, in Asa S. Knowles (Ed.), *Handbook of college and university administration.* Vol. II. *Academic.* New York: McGraw-Hill, 1970, sec. 3, pp. 26-36.

This chapter discusses factors involved in predicting and controlling freshman-class size. The author stresses the maintenance of accurate statistics and includes samples of weekly admissions reports. Individual sections discuss the processing of transfer applications, projection of enrollment figures, deposits, and useful student forms.

264 GARLAND, GILBERT C., AND WILSON, EUGENE S. Admissions—public relations, in Asa S. Knowles (Ed.), *Handbook of college and university administration.* Vol. II. *Academic.* New York: McGraw-Hill, 1970, sec. 3, pp. 37-43.

This brief chapter provides practical information concerning techniques used by admissions counselors to present their institution to the public. These include informational literature, correspondence, personal visits, and promotional devices such as college open-house programs.

265 GLOVER, ROBERT H. *College Entrance Examination Board Cooperative Admissions Information System.* White Plains, N. Y.: IBM, 1967.

This useful document describes the operation of a computer-based admissions information system that can be used by institutions to operate and monitor their admissions program. The system described here by its author was one of the first fully successful programs. (See 1247 for additional information.)

266 HAUSER, JANE Z., AND LAZARSFELD, PAUL F. *The admissions officer in the American college: An occupation under change.* New York: College Entrance Examination Board, 1964, 100 pp. (Mimeographed)

This is the only detailed study available of the college admissions profession. From the results of a questionnaire sent to 1,200 colleges, the authors developed a typology of admissions officers: the specialist, the intermediate type, and the registrar. The specialist is designated by his institution as a full-time admissions officer. The intermediate type has only part-time admissions responsibilities, while the registrar is so designated by his institution. These classifications are considered to give a crude indication of the expectations that a college has about the activities of the admissions officer and the importance attached to the admissions function. The report discusses the relationship of this typology to various areas of impact, among them the characteristics of the college, personal characteristics of the individuals, the operation of the admissions office, attitudes and beliefs of the individual officers, and the social context of the admissions officer. The report includes considerable detail but is lacking in broad appraisal of the role of the admissions officer in American education.

267 HOY, JOHN C. The mechanics of admissions, in Asa S. Knowles (Ed.), *Handbook of college and university administration.* Vol. II. *Academic.* New York: McGraw-Hill, 1970, sec. 3, pp. 50-73.

The author provides practical information about the processing of applications for admissions. Individual sections discuss the use of data-processing equipment, the development and supervision of admissions procedures, security controls and confidentiality, and the organization of an admissions timetable. The chapter also includes a number of sample forms.

268 KNOWLES, ASA S. (ED.) Admissions, in Asa S. Knowles (Ed.), *Handbook of college and university administration.* Vol. II. *Academic.* New York: McGraw-Hill, 1970, sec. 3, 133 pp.

This entire section of the *Handbook* is one of the best sources for practical information dealing with the day-to-day administration of admissions offices. It includes 14 chapters written by practitioners in the field. They deal with a wide variety of admissions concerns, including freshman-class quota, public relations, internal relations, selection and recruitment, admissions in the junior college, and administration of the admissions office and staff. (Selected chapters are annotated separately in various places, particularly in this section on administration.)

269 NATIONAL ASSOCIATION OF COLLEGE ADMISSIONS COUNSELORS, COMMITTEE ON RESEARCH AND EXPERIMENTATION. A survey of budgetary and management practices among admissions officers in American colleges and universities. *National ACAC Journal,* 1969, vol. 14, no. 1, pp. 2-14.

This article reports results of a survey of 65 public and 216 independent colleges and universities. Data were collected in the following areas: total operating and admissions budget; salaries of admissions directors and other personnel; the number of freshmen who applied, were accepted, and matriculated; freshman aid and its apportionment; and budgets for travel, printing, and other administrative costs. Additional tables provide information on administrative responsibilities and authority.

270 PERRY, RICHARD R. Admissions department costs and budgeting, in Asa S. Knowles (Ed.), *Handbook of college and university administration.* Vol. II. *Academic.* New York: McGraw-Hill, 1970, sec. 3, pp. 112-122.

The author offers guidelines for efficient management of the admissions office budget. He deals with such topics as administrative salaries, travel costs, costs of promotional literature, on-campus conferences, mailing and office forms, income from application fees, budget development and approval, and fiscal accounting using a monthly flow chart. A sample summary budget form and budget-request form are included.

271 PERRY, RICHARD R. The office of admissions—role of the administrator, in Asa S. Knowles (Ed.), *Handbook of college and university administration.* Vol. II. *Academic.* New York: McGraw-Hill, 1970, sec. 3, pp. 99-111.

This useful chapter summarizes administrative operations in an admissions office. Topics include channels of authority and reporting, supervision of clerical and faculty efforts, recruitment of faculty personnel, professional qualifications of the admissions counselor, and in-service training techniques.

272 THOMPSON, RONALD B. *Projections of enrollments: Public and private colleges and universities 1970-1987.* Wash., D. C.: American Association of Collegiate Registrars and Admissions Officers, 1970, 56 pp.

This booklet presents enrollment projections for public and private higher education in each state through 1987. The projections are based on birth rates and do not take into account shifts in support for higher education or access rates. Nonetheless the data provide a useful point of departure for planning.

3.5 — *TRANSFER ADMISSIONS.* Transfer admissions is a topic of special interest because it involves special problems, and the feasibility of many state master plans depends on a smooth transfer process involving no gross inequities. Unfortunately, there has been extremely little work on transfer admissions.

Major problems include articulation between junior and senior institutions, maintenance of equitable standards, transfer shock among students, inadequate financial aid, and inadequate attention given the entering transfer student. These problems are well discussed in the most comprehensive study of transfer students, by Knoell and Medsker (277).

273 ASSOCIATION OF AMERICAN COLLEGES, AMERICAN ASSOCIATION OF JUNIOR COLLEGES, AND AMERICAN ASSOCIATION OF COLLEGIATE REGISTRARS AND ADMISSIONS OFFICERS, JOINT COMMITTEE ON JUNIOR AND SENIOR COLLEGES. *Guidelines for improving articulation between junior and senior colleges.* Wash., D. C.: American Council on Education, 1966, 17 pp. 25 cents.

The format for these guidelines is a discussion of issues and problems, followed by recommendations for action that will facilitate student transfer from junior to four-year college. Drawing on the Knoell-Medsker analysis of the characteristics and problems of transfer students (277), the committee also tested the guidelines in a series of conferences held in the 10 states participating in the study. The aim of the project was to define procedures that maintain the autonomy of the institution and at the same time protect the student from jurisdictional conflict. Basic areas covered are admissions, evaluation of transfer courses, curriculum planning, counseling, and articulation of programs. These guidelines are especially important for the successful operation of hierarchical systems of higher education (similar to that of California) now being developed by many states.

274 CLARY, ALBERT L. (ED.) *Report of credit given by educational institutions.* Wash., D. C.: American Association of Collegiate Registrars and Admissions Officers, 1970, 127 pp. $3.

This is the annual report of the acceptance of transfer credits for work done at colleges and universities. It is based on a voluntary exchange of information, with help from the National Commission on Accrediting. Credit policy is listed for each higher education institution in the country.

275 GOSSMAN, CHARLES S., NOBBE, CHARLES E., PATRICELLI, THERESA J., SCHMID, CALVIN F., AND STEAHR, THOMAS E. *Migration of college and university students in the United States.* Seattle, Wash.: University of Washington Press, 1968, 180 pp. $8.50.

This book is the primary reference on interstate migration of college students. Student migration is important to educational administrators and planners, for it bears directly on problems of cost, curriculums, enrollment distribution, educational policy, and institutional needs. This study is based on data authored by the United States Office of Education in the fall of 1963, when 760,543 degree-credit students out of a total national enrollment of 4,144,420 were attending institutions located outside their state of residence.

The authors consider different enrollment categories—undergraduate, graduate, and first-professional—in both public and private institutions and study the similarities and differences of migratory patterns of these groups of students on a state and regional basis. They also explore state and regional patterns of migration from a historical perspective and examine the four most recent periods for which the United States Office of Education has published data: 1938, 1949, 1958, and 1963. Two chapters deal with the social, economic, and demographic variables that influence student migration, with special emphasis on the distance factor. Statistics are weighted in a way that will help to develop a method for predicting the amount and direction of interstate college migration. A distinctive feature of this study is the utilization of well-constructed graphs, which present an accurate exposition in a minimum of space.

276 HILLS, JOHN R. Transfer shock: The academic performance of the junior college transfer. *Journal of Experimental Education,* 1965, vol. 33, pp. 201-215.

Reacting to the prevailing view that junior college transfers do as well at four-year institutions as do "native" students in the same fields, the author presents an analysis of the literature on the question. More than 20 studies on academic performance of junior college transfers are discussed. "Transfer shock" was found to be a pervasive occurrence; most junior college students who transferred to four-year institutions suffered an appreciable loss in their initial grade level. (See 277 for evidence of later recovery.) In 33 sets of data relevant to the question of whether junior college transfers or "native" students get better grades, 22 indicated that the natives performed better, 4 indicated that the junior college transfers performed better, and 7 indicated that they did equally well. Furthermore, there is strong evidence (19 out of 21 sets of data) that natives graduate sooner or in greater proportions than do junior college transfers. The author provides a valuable service in describing the nature of "transfer shock" but seems to go beyond his data in concluding that students planning a baccalaureate degree are better off starting in a four-year institution.

277 KNOELL, DOROTHY M., AND MEDSKER, LELAND L. *From junior to senior college: A national study of the transfer student.* Wash., D. C.: American Council on Education, 1965, 102 pp. $2.50.

This is the classic study of transfer from junior to senior college. It focuses on how well the transfer process works—both for the individual student and the two- and four-year institutions. The sample consisted of 7,243 junior college students who transferred in 1960 to four-year institutions in 10 states with very large junior college enrollments. The study was influential in developing an important set of transfer guidelines (273). In general, the authors see the junior college in a "melting pot" role in higher education, opening opportunities to those whose education would otherwise terminate at high school graduation. However, they deplore the attitude of the general public—one of undervaluing the junior college as "a kind of refuge for the 'cannots' and the 'havenots.' " As a result, the junior college has been slow to come into its own as a positive force. They also warn that the junior college transfer must accept grade-point drops as one of the realities of university life. The student transferring with a marginal grade point should be realistically counseled to seek a four-year institution where he has a reasonable chance for success.

278 MIDDLE STATES ASSOCIATION OF COLLEGES AND SECONDARY SCHOOLS. *The junior college transfer: Senior college admissions policies and procedures.* New York: MSACSS, 1968, 61 pp.

This useful booklet lists in chart form the transfer admissions policies and procedures of 212 senior colleges in the mid-Atlantic states. Information listed includes: name of admissions officer and transfer coordinator, application and notification dates, housing, tests required, financial aid, minimum grade-point average, and amount of transfer credit accepted.

An unusual and valuable aspect of this survey was the inclusion of four "transcripts" and accompanying course descriptions for prototype transfer students in liberal arts, business administration, science, and engineering. Each responding college indicated what credit would be awarded in each case.

279 WILLINGHAM, WARREN W., AND FINDIKYAN, NURHAN. *Patterns of admission for transfer students.* New York: College Entrance Examination Board, 1969, 47 pp. $1.

In recent years transfers to four-year institutions have increased at twice the rate of new freshmen. The expanding number of public junior colleges and the many state master plans that are based on a transfer model make the problems of the transfer student a crucial issue for American higher education. In this study the authors surveyed 146 representative, four-year colleges to determine what sort of students are transferring from where to where nationally and what factors seem to determine whether they are admitted. The data indicate that institutions vary widely in their attitudes and practices with respect to transfer students, and freshman admissions usually takes precedence over transfer admissions. The northeastern states appear to be the least hospitable to transfers, a condition that seems to be related to the relative lack of public higher education in some northeastern states.

The study reveals that financial aid is a definite problem for the transfer student. In large institutions only 1 transfer in 10 received any form of aid, and "in most cases present prospects for aid seem totally inadequate for the master plans that many states are trying to implement."

Nevertheless, the authors report some encouraging signs that institutions are trying to adapt to the needs of the transfer student. Large public institutions have absorbed much of the expanded movement of transfers. Junior college students appear to enjoy a favorable acceptance rate in most colleges. They suffered less credit loss than other transfers and were fairly well represented in all types of senior institutions.

280 WILSON, GAYLE C. The impact of transfer admissions in the next decade. *College and University,* 1970, vol. 45, pp. 266-272.

This brief article discusses changes in admissions policies necessary to accommodate the increasing number of transfer students from two-year colleges. It focuses on three major problems in transfer articulation: accreditation, evaluation, and communication. Wilson believes senior colleges should accept students from unaccredited schools as long as these schools are working toward accreditation and should inform transfer students of the exact number of transfer credits accepted prior to enrollment. The report also emphasizes the inclusion of more transfer information in catalogs and the importance of informing high school counselors of transfer admissions procedures.

SECTION 4: EDUCATIONAL PROCESS

In this context the educational process includes what to teach, how to teach it, and how to improve the value and effectiveness of the content. The importance of these topics to the access process is simply stated. An increasingly large and diverse group of students continuing education beyond high school have widely different needs, aspirations, circumstances, and capabilities. If access is to be useful, it must be relevant to those interests and characteristics. The educational process must also be fitted to different learning styles, to career opportunities currently available, and to those cognitive and social skills likely to be in continual demand in a changing society.

Perhaps the greatest problem is the fact that diverse student interests and needs cannot be served by traditional programs, but it is frequently traditional programs that are expected and desired. Putting it another way, those students not in the familiar mainstream of scholastic commitment need and often deserve two outcomes that are sometimes incompatible: an education relevant to their interests and character, and a formal credential that has social and economic value.

It will continue to be extremely difficult to balance these demands in a socially equitable manner that protects the strengths and reforms the weaknesses of higher institutions. As a consequence of these problems and their attendant political pressures, there has been intense interest in the theoretical and practical aspects of the relationship of curriculum to financing, admissions, manpower utilization, and educational opportunity. Over the long range, the resolution of these problems will likely settle into the bureaucratic intricacies of planning, management, and system coordination. That is why it is so important that the educational process be properly represented in the management systems and coordinating mechanisms now under energetic development (see sections 7.4 through 7.8).

There are innumerable organizations, associations, and journals concerned with curriculum and instruction in various subject areas. The American Association of University Professors (1099) and the American Association for Higher Education (1095) are two organizations with a broad interest in these matters. The *AAUP Bulletin* (1303) is a source of current information. The *Journal of Higher Education* (1327) is a well-known journal of opinion in general education that plans to put more emphasis on research-based articles. *Daedalus* (1317) and the *American Scholar* (1309) are other influential journals of high quality.

4.1 – *CURRICULUM*. Most of the literature concerning curriculum involves rational analysis, though periodically there are surveys of practices. Some researchers have contributed to this area, but the authors are largely prominent educators who have been active in curriculum development. The so-called Muscatine Report (298) from the University of California at Berkeley is highly regarded for its analysis of current problems of higher education.

There are three main problems covered by the literature in this area. The matter of curriculum relevance attracted much attention during the late 1960s. A monograph by Mayhew (296) provides a good summary, and a book by Axelrod et al. (281) is especially useful. Reform in specific subject-matter areas has been a major movement since the 1950s. The School Mathematics Study Group is a prominent example (282). Trends in curriculum change provide another focus of interest. Dressel and DeLisle have reported a recent survey (290).

281 AXELROD, JOSEPH, FREEDMAN, MERVIN B., HATCH, WINSLOW R., KATZ, JOSEPH, AND SANFORD, NEVITT. *Search for relevance.* San Francisco: Jossey-Bass, 1969, 244 pp. $7.75.

This volume addresses critical issues related to the "campus in crisis." It begins with a theory of student development from which important goals of education should derive and suggests that the curriculum is the chief avenue to the solution of campus problems. New curricular programs are described that are highly innovative. The characteristics of student activists and the causes of conflict and protest on the campus are discussed. Finally the impact of the college campus on the attitudes, values, and personality of the student is considered with special reference to recent research on this question.

282 BEGLE, EDWARD G. SMSG: The first decade. *The Mathematics Teacher,* 1968, vol. 61, pp. 239-245.

This is a summary of the work undertaken by the School Mathematics Study Group in its first 10 years as a national curriculum improvement project funded by the National Science Foundation. Joint efforts of university mathematicians and classroom teachers produced examples of textbooks considered to be both mathematically and pedagogically sound, ranging from elementary school arithmetic to calculus. In-service training programs were developed to help teachers to make effective use of the new materials. A National Longitudinal Study of Mathematical Abilities (NLSMA) was undertaken, not only to assess the effectiveness of SMSG materials but to learn more about the factors that underlie or affect the learning of mathematics. The project is an outstanding example of curricular reform in a single subject area.

283 BELL, DANIEL. *The reforming of general education: The Columbia College experience in its national setting.* New York: Columbia University Press, 1966, 320 pp. $7.50; paperback (Doubleday) $1.75.

Sociologist Bell writes prophetically that the most serious intellectual crisis of universities today is the confrontation between the "technocratic" emphasis on increasing specialization and the "apocalyptic" current of nihilism of the new radicals. This 1966 report to the Columbia faculty examines its general education program from the viewpoint of "reforming"—a continuing effort to adapt tradition to meet fresh circumstances. He discusses three areas of change that challenge the format of higher education. (1) the "exponential" growth of knowledge, (2) the impact of the federally funded research and development explosion on the research function of a university (see similar discussion by Clark Kerr in 765), and (3) the changes in secondary school education. The specific curriculum proposals he advocates for Columbia have obvious implications for curriculum planning in general; e.g., the abolition of freshman composition, extending music and fine arts courses in the humanities program, and a senior year devoted to "braking specialization" by applying disciplined knowledge to broad intellectual and policy questions.

284 BLOOM, BENJAMIN S. (ED.) *Taxonomy of educational objectives: The classification of educational goals. Handbook I: Cognitive domain.* New York: David McKay, 1956, 207 pp. $2.50.

This volume is a classic attempt to build a classification system (i.e., taxonomy) of educational goals. First formulated at an informal gathering of college examiners attending the 1948 American Psychological Association Convention, the system is intended for teachers, administrators, professional specialists, and researchers working with curriculum and evaluation problems. The book is designed to: (1) provide a common language for the exchange of information, (2) assist in setting new educational goals, (3) clarify what specific behaviors are emphasized by a particular set of educational plans, (4) aid in curriculum design, and (5) help in evaluating progress. A complete taxonomy would cover three domains—cognitive, affective, and psychomotor. This volume is concerned with the cognitive. (See 295 for the affective taxonomy.)

285 COLLEGE ENTRANCE EXAMINATION BOARD. *Freedom and discipline in English: Report of the Commission on English.* New York: College Entrance Examination Board, 1965, 190 pp. Clothbound, $2.75; paperback, $1.75.

The Commission on English was funded and administered by the College Board to encourage and facilitate improvement in curriculum, teacher training, and methods of classroom instruction. This final report of the Commission is an example of the curriculum reform undertaken in several important subject areas in the 1950s and 1960s.

286 COLLEGE ENTRANCE EXAMINATION BOARD. *The challenge of curricular change.* New York: College Entrance Examination Board, 1966, 181 pp. $2.75.

This volume reports the proceedings of a colloquium sponsored by the College Board and the National Association of Secondary-School Principals in 1965. It includes 17 brief articles by prominent educators who have been active in curriculum reform. The report is especially valuable in documenting the nature and extent of "explosive" curriculum reform in the decade prior to the colloquium. Much of this reform has been in certain subject areas, and the authors delineate resulting strengths and weaknesses at both the secondary and higher education levels. The colloquium came shortly before intense interest in comprehensive postsecondary educational opportunity, the special educational problems of minority youth, and student rebellion at the national level. The content of the papers tends to reflect that timing, though this fact does not reduce the value of an otherwise perceptive documentation of an extremely important period of educational change.

287 DENNIS, LAWRENCE E., AND KAUFFMAN, JOSEPH F. (EDS.) *The college and the student.* Wash., D. C.: American Council on Education, 1966, 292 pp. $6.

This volume includes a selection of papers from the 1965 annual meeting of the American Council on Education, which was devoted to problems of the college student. Though some papers are naturally a bit dated because events have moved so swiftly, nonetheless the collection contains a useful group of papers on curriculum by such noted educators as Mayhew, Hobbs, McKeachie, and Cosand.

288 DRESSEL, CAROL A., AND DRESSEL, PAUL L. Changing emphases in higher education. *College and University,* 1966, vol. 41, pp. 290-301.

In this brief article the authors analyze shifting emphases in higher education through comparison of a representative sample of institutional reports in five successive editions of *American Universities and Colleges* (101) during the period 1940-64. Special attention was devoted to the basic curriculum, international and other off-campus programs, individualization, instruction, and institutional cooperation. The results document increased opportunity for faculty research accompanied by decreased attention to curriculum and instruction. In addition, interinstitutional cooperation occurred primarily in the areas of graduate study and research. The authors suggest that changes in emphasis are often a result of current fads and proliferate through imitation.

289 DRESSEL, PAUL L. *College and university curriculum.* Berkeley, Calif.: McCutchan, 1968, 232 pp. $8.50.

The need for a coherent, cumulative approach to the total undergraduate experience is the central message of this book, addressed primarily to administrators and faculty charged with curriculum decisions. Dressel feels this concept could be brought to reality by replacing the departmental major with a program in which the student encounters "sustained contact" with at least two different disciplines. This should interweave depth knowledge with a problem-solving approach to a relevant current problem. It should include independent study, practical experience in summer jobs, individualized research or tutoring, work or study abroad. These are the components of the seven competencies that Dressel defines as the end result of an integrated educational experience. They include competency and versatility in job skills, ability and motivation for continuing self-education, skill in communicating with others, appreciation of value systems—the student's own as well as conflicting ones, and a commitment to become involved in society's problems. He sees the major institutional obstacles to this "larger vision" as: (1) isolation and overcompartmentalization, and (2) the faculty view of undergraduate instruction as less prestigious than research or graduate instruction.

290 Dressel, Paul L., and DeLisle, Frances H. *Undergraduate curriculum trends.* Wash., D. C.: American Council on Education, 1969, 83 pp. $2.

This concise but comprehensive report reviews changes in the undergraduate curriculum in a representative sample of 322 institutions during the period 1957-67. The authors review the historical background of curriculum development, examine specific changes in undergraduate requirements, review provisions for individualized instruction, and identify nine types of comprehensive programs including traditional and experimental curriculums. Major trends included expansion of individualized programs such as work-study, study abroad, community service, and independent study. The authors find reduced requirements in English, literature, philosophy, and religion, but increases in foreign-language and science specifications.

291 Foshay, Arthur W., and Beilin, Lois A. Curriculum, in Robert L. Ebel (Ed.), *Encyclopedia of educational research.* (4th ed.) New York: Macmillan, 1969, pp. 275-280.

This article is concerned primarily with curriculum theory in education generally. It provides a brief introduction to some of the major considerations and lines of thought that have dominated discussion of educational curriculum. This same volume includes several other useful articles concerned with various aspects of curriculum.

292 Hochman, William R. *The Council on Curriculum.* A report to the trustees of the College Entrance Examination Board. New York: College Entrance Examination Board, 1968, 26 pp.

This report proposes the establishment of a Council on Curriculum as an adjunct of the College Board. It describes the need for a national agency and identifies major issues relating to curriculum articulation between the eleventh and fourteenth grades. These include the relation between curriculum and values, the significance of the curriculum in determining college attendance, the relation between technical programs and general education, the introduction of new disciplines, and independent study in the lower grades. Further suggested areas for study included special curriculums for culturally different students, techniques for assessing achievement and for measuring creative potential, and the nature of curricular change.

293 Huff, Robert A., and Chandler, Marjorie O. *A taxonomy of instructional programs in higher education.* Wash., D. C.: Government Printing Office, 1970, 32 pp.

This report makes public the new uniform classification system of instructional programs to be used in Higher Education General Information Surveys (hegis), beginning in 1971-72. It was developed by the National Center for

Educational Statistics, the National Center for Educational Research and Development of the Office of Education, and the Western Interstate Commission on Higher Education for use in their Management Information Systems Program (WICHE-MIS). It is published far in advance of its first prospective use to give institutions time to standardize their records.

294 KATZ, JOSEPH, AND SANFORD, NEVITT. The curriculum in the perspective of the theory of personality development, in Nevitt Sanford (Ed.), *The American college.* New York: John Wiley, 1963, pp. 418-444.

The authors assert that the curriculum in United States colleges does not fulfill its potential in accomplishing what should be the prime goal of liberal education—the development of personality. Modes of presentation that are "antidevelopmental" are: (1) emphasis on the academic discipline, (2) emphasis on the right answer, (3) impersonality in the classroom, (4) abstractedness, (5) excessive orientation to method, (6) segmentation of presentation. Modes that encourage the development of student personality are: (1) objectivity, (2) intellectual mastery, (3) social experience of learning with others, (4) learning to think by way of hypothesis. Curriculum experiments hitherto have been tailored to fit a preconceived philosophy; once enacted, experimentation is over. What is needed, the authors say, is a curricular science—"a continuing process of theoretically guided experimentation and assessment of its results."

295 KRATHWOHL, DAVID R., BLOOM, BENJAMIN S., AND MASIA, BERTRAM B. *Taxonomy of educational objectives: The classification of educational goals. Handbook II: Affective domain.* New York: David McKay, 1964, 196 pp. $2.50.

The purpose of this work was to develop a taxonomy of educational objectives that would clarify the language, provide classifications of objectives, aid in the development of evaluation instruments, and contribute to the development of a learning theory. Volume I was devoted to the cognitive domain (284). This second volume is patterned after the first but deals with those affective educational objectives that emphasize feelings, interests, attitudes, values, appreciation, and adjustment. Part I includes a description of the nature of the affective domain and the classification structure pertaining to it. Also included in Part I are an analysis of the relation of the affective to the cognitive domain and a description of how the domain structure can be used to classify both objectives and test items. Part II contains a complete and detailed description of the categories and subcategories of the affective domain and gives illustrative objectives and test items for each category.

296 MAYHEW, LEWIS B. *Contemporary college students and the curriculum.* SREB Research Monograph No. 14. Atlanta, Ga.: Southern Regional Education Board, 1969, 86 pp.

Charging that orthodox curriculum and instruction are failing to meet the fundamental needs of college students, Mayhew sees a significant relationship between this failure and the increase in student unrest. Structural weaknesses in the institutions that contribute to this neglect are cited: (1) Faculty research interests dominate curriculum decisions. (2) The "publish or perish" doctrine encourages neglect of students and teaching. (3) The demand for professionally trained manpower has put concern for graduate education above that of undergraduates. (4) The admissions process has built unhealthy pressures to demonstrate aptitude in solid subjects at the expense of concern for total development of the individual. He argues for curriculum choices that do fulfill students' needs.

297 THOMPSON, MARY M., AND DRESSEL, PAUL L. A survey of independent study practices. *Educational Record,* 1970, vol. 51, pp. 392-395.

This brief article reports preliminary results of an investigation of the experience of 372 colleges with independent study. Survey findings indicated that independent study programs occur most frequently in small, private colleges, that the few evaluations that have been conducted point to low effectiveness of such programs, and that independent study was often only available to a limited number of students. From visits to some participating colleges the authors observed that major barriers to the development of independent study were: (1) faculty opposition, (2) student apathy, and (3) financial limitations. They conclude that for independent study to be widely effective, administrators, faculty, and students must regard the ability to work independently as a major goal of higher education.

298 UNIVERSITY OF CALIFORNIA, BERKELEY, ACADEMIC SENATE SELECT COMMITTEE ON EDUCATION. *Education at Berkeley.* Berkeley, Calif.: University of California, 1968, 252 pp. $1.95.

This well-known report resulted from the turmoil at Berkeley in 1964. The Muscatine Committee conducted a comprehensive study of the university, covering student characteristics, improvement of teaching, advising, orientation, grading, undergraduate requirements, graduate education, and the role of the teaching assistant. It drew up the framework for a Board of Educational Development, a faculty committee charged with determining policy and budgets for innovative curricular proposals. This influential study prompted similar investigations at other institutions. In addition to the complete text of the report, the book contains a minority report and the resulting action taken on the committee's recommendations.

299 WARREN, JONATHAN R. Changing students and constant curricula. *Educational Record,* 1970, vol. 51, pp. 182-187.

In this article Warren argues that present-day college programs are not responsive to the educational needs of the growing number of lower-class students. The system of "antiseptic" lectures, reading, and examinations is termed of little relevance for the practically inclined, vocationally oriented "new" students. He recommends fresh approaches that could combine "immediacy, direct involvement, and unfragmented time periods." These might also appeal to middle-class students who find the routine of college work unstimulating and irrelevant. Such changes need not supplant the traditional approach but would add valuable diversity of choice.

300 WILLINGHAM, WARREN W. The importance of relevance in expanding postsecondary education, in U. S. Office of Education, *Trends in postsecondary education.* Wash., D. C.: Government Printing Office, 1970, pp. 69-84.

This chapter analyzes four types of relevance resulting from the extent to which the basic functions of education serve the needs of individuals and society. Personal relevance is described as "the extent to which education provides equal opportunity for individuals to define their roles and responsibilities in society." Social relevance represents a marshaling of academic resources to carry out social commitments and relieve social pressures. Educational relevance involves helping students learn the modes of action necessary to fulfill adult responsibilities with success and satisfaction. Economic relevance is described as the development of socially useful modes of individual action—that is, "a reasonable fit between educational outcomes and occupational requirements and opportunities."

4.2—COURSE PLACEMENT. Access to an effective educational experience assumes that the student starts off in courses that are appropriate to his level of achievement. If this does not happen, the best designed curriculum is at least momentarily sabotaged. Course placement problems develop for several reasons. Entering freshmen come from widely different high schools. Transfer students come from diverse colleges. In both instances previous grades are not always a reliable indicator of what the student knows. Most colleges have very heterogeneous student bodies, and large institutions have an extreme variety of programs with diverse purposes. So there are many ways for an entering student to end up in an inappropriate course.

Correspondingly, there are many manifest placement problems. The more common instances include the following: awarding credit for a course, proper placement of a student in a sequence of courses, placement in an honors section designed for enrichment, placement of talented students in an accelerated course, and provision of alternate courses that may have different objectives or methods.

These placement problems are quite different but uniformly complex. The unfortunate aspect of course placement is the fact that on most campuses it is handled in a fairly casual manner. Placement usually is not recognized as a measurement problem. Part of the reason for that is the paucity of literature and technical development in this field. The Advanced Placement Program (1220) is the only national activity of its sort, and it is well documented (302). The classic psychometric development concerning the general problem of course placement was done by Cronbach and Gleser (307). Hills (309) has recently provided a very useful discussion of the placement problem at a somewhat more practical level.

301 BOWLER, ADELE S. (ED.) *College programs for high school students: Summer, 1971.* Hillsdale, N. J.: Directory Publishers, 1971, 233 pp. $7.

This directory describes in detail college programs open to high school students on campuses across the country. Calendar, costs, eligibility requirements, and the scope and content of the courses are listed.

302 CASSERLY, PATRICIA L. What college students say about Advanced Placement. Parts I and II. *College Board Review,* Fall 1968, no. 69, pp. 6-10, 28-34; Winter 1968-69, no. 70, pp. 18-22.

During 1966-67 the author asked over 400 college students who had taken courses under the College Board's Advanced Placement Program in high school to evaluate how participation in the program had affected their high school and college experiences. The majority of those interviewed were upperclassmen, because it was assumed that they could best evaluate the program in the light of their total educational experience. This unusually interesting pair of articles reports on their responses and includes many of their suggestions on improving the AP Program at both the high school and the college level.

Almost 70 percent of the students came to AP courses through tracking or homogeneous grouping of some sort. More than 90 percent of the students who prepared for the AP Examinations ranked AP courses as the most valuable in high school. Approximately 80 percent of the students felt their guidance counselors were either unfamiliar with the nature of the AP Program or ultra-conservative in their advice. In many cases colleges failed to make adequate provision for AP students, and this resulted in considerable discontent.

303 COLLEGE ENTRANCE EXAMINATION BOARD. *College Placement Tests: Score use and interpretation manual.* New York: College Entrance Examination Board, 1969, 20 pp.

College Placement Tests are institutionally administered Achievement Tests of the College Entrance Examination Board. This booklet describes how the tests can be used for placement purposes. It includes consideration of the objectives of a placement program, how to validate the tests locally, and practical use of scores for different types of placement needs.

304 COLLEGE ENTRANCE EXAMINATION BOARD. *College Advanced Placement policies, 1970.* New York: College Entrance Examination Board, 1970, 98 pp. $1.

This booklet, revised annually, lists the Advanced Placement Examination grades acceptable for college credit in more than 1,000 colleges and universities. It is an essential reference for students and counselors in schools offering AP courses.

305 COLLEGE ENTRANCE EXAMINATION BOARD. *Tests and services: College-Level Examination Program.* New York: College Entrance Examination Board, 1970, 15 pp.

This booklet describes the nature of the College-Level Examination Program (CLEP) and how colleges use the program to award credit by examination. This program serves a placement function for students who have acquired college-level achievement through some unusual means such as self-study, industrial programs, military training, etc.

306 COLLEGE ENTRANCE EXAMINATION BOARD, COMPARATIVE GUIDANCE AND PLACEMENT PROGRAM. *Interpretive manual for counselors, administrators, and faculty 1969-1970.* New York: College Entrance Examination Board, 1969, 108 pp.

Appropriate placement of students in initial mathematics and English courses is one purpose of the College Board's Comparative Guidance and Placement Program. This interpretive manual provides illustrative data and practical information on how colleges use this program.

307 CRONBACH, LEE J., AND GLESER, GOLDINE C. *Psychological tests and personnel decisions.* (2nd ed.) Urbana, Ill.: University of Illinois Press, 1965, 347 pp. $7.95; paperback $2.95.

This is the classic and most comprehensive treatment of the logic and psychometric characteristics of the placement problem. Originally published in 1957, this later edition includes some more recent papers and commentary. Hills (309) gives a more recent and less technical treatment of placement that utilizes the basic approach suggested by these authors.

308 FERRIN, RICHARD I., AND WILLINGHAM, WARREN W. *Practices of Southern institutions in recognizing college-level achievement.* Higher Education Surveys Report No. 3. New York: College Entrance Examination Board, 1970, 42 pp.

Colleges use a variety of mechanisms for recognizing college-level achievement and granting course exemption and college credit. This survey describes how these mechanisms are coordinated and the extent to which they are used. Results were based on responses from a representative group of 141 institutions in the South. Two-thirds of all institutions grant advanced standing through course exemption, though only one freshman in nine received such exemption in the fall of 1970. Departmental examinations, the College Board Advanced Placement Program, and United States Armed Forces Institute courses are the mechanisms most often accepted for advanced standing. While the colleges indicate a great deal of interest in practices that recognize a student's actual level of achievement at entry to college, the extent of such practices is still quite limited.

309 HILLS, JOHN R. Use of measurement in selection and placement, in Robert L. Thorndike (Ed.), *Educational measurement.* (2nd ed.) Wash., D. C.: American Council on Education, 1971, pp. 680-732.

This chapter provides the most comprehensive and generally useful summary of the use of tests in selection and placement that is currently available. The author describes different types of tests and other measures used in selection, different methods of selection, and the concept of utility and decision theory in such use. The section on placement is easily the best general discussion yet written from a practical educational standpoint. Hills describes a number of different types of placement problems and discusses placement strategies and unsolved problems in both theory and practice.

310 MELCHIOR, OLIVER W. Curriculum articulation between schools and colleges, in College Entrance Examination Board, *From high school to college: Readings for counselors.* New York: College Entrance Examination Board, 1965, pp. 37-44.

In this article, the author argues that innovation in secondary school and college curriculums must be coordinated to keep pace with changes in society. Such coordination could involve opportunities for professors and teachers to work together through fellowship and visiting programs. Melchior points out that increased curricular flexibility would include experience and learning in fine and applied arts, emphasis on quality rather than quantity of assignments, and direct concern with character development through discussion of change in value systems. He stresses the role of the guidance counselor in developing individualized instructional programs, in providing feedback to faculty, and in facilitating the school-college transition. The article gives little attention, however, to the practical problem of evaluating the extent of knowledge incoming freshmen have in various subject areas.

311 PETERSON, RICHARD E., AND CASSERLY, PATRICIA L. What's really happening in Advanced Placement? Parts I and II. *College Board Review,* Winter 1965-66, no. 58, pp. 12-18; Spring 1966, no. 59, pp. 16-22.

In the spring of 1964, Educational Testing Service researchers conducted over 500 personal interviews with faculty and administrators at 63 selected institutions across the country in order to determine what colleges were doing about granting credit or advanced placement or both to students who have taken the College Board's Advanced Placement Examinations. The authors report the results in this pair of articles. They conclude that actual policies are diverse; however, the vast majority of the colleges visited had policies that enabled granting of both credit and placement to candidates meeting locally defined standards of achievement. A majority of policies provided for the granting of automatic credit for AP Examination grades of 4 and 5. It was in relation to credit for grades of 3 that the widest policy disparity existed. In general the locus of policy making also varied, ranging from "unmitigated centralization" to "explicit decentralization." The majority of the faculty were poorly informed about the AP Program, and procedures for communicating with Advanced Placement candidates were often inadequate. The favorable impact of the Program is seen in the attitudes of faculty members, the general upgrading of curriculums, and the institution of special programs for able students.

312 RADCLIFFE, SHIRLEY A., AND HATCH, WINSLOW R. *Advanced standing.* New Dimensions in Higher Education No. 8, Wash., D. C.: Government Printing Office, 1961, 24 pp.

This monograph describes the operation of the Advanced Placement Program of the College Entrance Examination Board and other programs of individual colleges that provide able high school students with opportunities for college-level work. Some matters that need further research are suggested: (1) rationale for institutions' policies of granting advanced standing, (2) evaluative procedures for measuring the effectiveness of advanced standing, (3) effect on social adjustment of students, (4) effect on total academic program of the college, and (5) effect on the teaching-learning climate in both high school and college.

313 STONE, JAMES C. Articulation of educational units, in Robert L. Ebel (Ed.), *Encyclopedia of educational research.* (4th ed.) New York: Macmillan, 1969, pp. 86-90.

This brief article gives an historical overview of some of the problems in articulating educational programs across transition points such as junior high school to senior high school or secondary to higher education. The emphasis here is more upon curriculum, educational policy, and administrative organization rather than the practical problem of insuring continuity in the educational programs of individual students.

4.3 — INSTRUCTION. This literature is concerned with research, media development, systems approaches to instruction, and teaching techniques. The authors are largely psychologists, educators, and technologists. The four major problems are concerned with teaching methods, individualizing instruction, utilizing media, and training teachers.

The classic reference to research on teaching is edited by Gage (321). A recent monograph (318) summarizes results of research on different teaching methods and suggests that there is no stable superiority of one method over another. A very popular approach has been to individualize instruction through the development of behavioral objectives, striving for content mastery, and the use of tests that refer specifically to objectives rather than to relative performance of students in broad areas. A practical and operational description of this approach is provided in 324.

A burgeoning area of instructional technology is represented by the development of new media. These include: programmed learning, computer-assisted learning, visual aids, closed-circuit television, etc. (see 331). The more conventional problem and one that is often conceded to be *the* problem is the fact that college teachers are too often untrained and not especially interested in teaching. This is a large problem with little helpful literature, but there is a classic book on "teaching tips" now in its sixth edition (326).

314 ANDERSON, RICHARD C., FAUST, GERALD W., RODERICK, MARIANNE C., CUNNINGHAM, DONALD J., AND ANDRE, THOMAS (EDS.) *Current research on instruction.* Englewood Cliffs, N. J.: Prentice-Hall, 1969, 396 pp. $5.95.

This compendium of somewhat technical papers is intended for students of educational psychology. It summarizes and documents significant recent research in instruction and learning. Several papers discuss approaches to instructional research, instructional objectives, and evaluation. The authors include further sections dealing with specific techniques and variables. These include prompting and fading techniques, reinforcement and feedback, the student response in relation to programmed material, concept learning, and the organization and sequence of learning.

315 BEGGS, DAVID W. III, AND BUFFIE, EDWARD G. (EDS.) *Independent study: Bold new venture.* Bloomington, Ind.: Indiana University Press, 1965, 236 pp. $5.95.

This book deals with the nature and goals of independent study and presents methods and techniques for incorporating independent study into the schools. Though the authors focus on elementary and secondary schools, much of the material would be useful for those interested in increasing the use of independent study in colleges and universities. Chapters report successful experiences in independent programs at the University of Chicago Laboratory High School and at Lakeview High School in Decatur, Illinois, where team teachers supervised independent work. Further chapters present detailed models of practices and programs including flexible programming in senior high schools, a model of a complete program of independent work in the humanities, possible technological aids, in-service programs, and the role of faculty and administration in planning.

316 BRIGGS, LESLIE J., CAMPEAU, PEGGIE L., GAGNÉ, ROBERT M., AND MAY, MARK A. *Instructional media: A procedure for the design of multi-media instruction, a critical review of research, and suggestions for future research.* Pittsburgh, Pa.: American Institutes for Research, 1967, 176 pp. $4.50.

The primary focus of this book is the presentation of an analytical procedure for the selection of instructional media. The authors suggest that educational specialists direct this selection by a process involving definition of educational objectives in behavioral or content terms, identification of instructional events and stimuli required to obtain these objectives, and translation of these stimuli into the appropriate medium. The result of such a procedure would be the use of varied types of media, each suited to a specific dimension of the learning process. Additional chapters illustrate the use of the above technique in two elementary school courses. This volume has a practical orientation but is based on the most sophisticated academic, military, and industrial research of the past two decades.

317 DUBIN, ROBERT, AND HEDLEY, R. ALAN. *The medium may be related to the message.* Eugene, Ore.: Center for the Advanced Study of Educational Administration, University of Oregon, 1969, 114 pp. $2.

This monograph analyzes the research literature on the effectiveness of television as an educational medium. The introduction presents comparative data on the effectiveness of one- and two-way television teaching techniques and concludes that one-way television is superior to two-way techniques employing feedback. The authors suggest that administrators regard educational television as an innovation in technique rather than in educational policy. Further data detail the reaction of professors and students to this innovation and the problems each group faces in its adoption. Findings indicated that students exhibited little resistance to the new technique. Professors, on the other hand, often resisted the adoption of educational television on philosophical as well as practical bases. The authors conclude that the major impact of television in higher education would be an increase in research time for the professor.

318 DUBIN, ROBERT, AND TAVEGGIA, THOMAS C. *The teaching-learning paradox.* Eugene, Ore.: Center for the Advanced Study of Educational Administration, University of Oregon, 1968, 78 pp. $2.

The purpose of this monograph is to encourage new directions in research on comparative college teaching methods. Analysis of 100 comparative studies of different teaching methods punctures the assumption that there is any one method of teaching that produces better student performance on course examinations. Instead of rehashing dead-end theories, the authors suggest that researchers should look at fresh approaches to find out what is common to all the technologies of college teaching, and to develop models of the teaching-learning situation. The implication that teaching methods make no difference is important for educational administrators coping with large enrollments and spiraling costs. The study leaves open the question of whether there are beneficial ways of matching student and teaching method.

319 ERIC CLEARINGHOUSE ON HIGHER EDUCATION. *Preparing college teachers.* Compendium Series of Current Research, Programs and Proposals No. 2. Wash., D. C.: ERIC Clearinghouse, George Washington University, 1970, 22 pp.

A critical aspect of the potential effectiveness of instruction is the training and preparation of college teachers. This compendium includes 53 annotations, ranging from proposals to operating programs. A brief introductory summary outlines several recent major proposals concerning the preparation and credentialing of college teachers.

320 FINGER, FRANK W. *Professional problems: Preparation for a career in college teaching.* Report 1. Wash., D. C.: ERIC Clearinghouse on Higher Education, 1970, 8 pp.

In this brief article the author describes a successful seminar he has conducted at the University of Virginia to prepare college students for their roles as professors. The seminar is especially interesting in the face of recent controversy over the quality of college teaching. The article includes a list of suggested reading.

321 GAGE, N. L. Teaching methods, in Robert L. Ebel (Ed.), *Encyclopedia of educational research.* (4th ed.) New York: Macmillan, 1969, pp. 1446-1458.

As the author states, "The question of how to teach is perennial." This useful article deals not with specific advice on how to teach, or with research evidence regarding alternative teaching methods, but rather with the definition, history, and character of teaching methods. In particular it explores the relationship of teaching methods to curriculum and educational objectives. The major methods included are classroom discourse, the lecture method, the discussion method, and the discovery method.

322 GLASER, ROBERT (ED.) *Teaching machines and programed learning.* Vol. 2. *Data and directions.* Wash., D. C.: National Education Association, 1965, 831 pp. $11.50.

This volume had its beginnings at a three-day National Education Association symposium on research in programmed instruction. Its purpose is to help coordinate efforts of behavioral scientists, subject-matter scholars, and educators in further developing this field. The authors are among the most prominent in this field. The first section presents perspectives on past and present use of technology in education. The second section covers technology and subject matter, including such topics as programming in mathematics and logic, programmed learning of a second language, and programmed instruction in English. The final papers examine the role of schools, industry, and government agencies in implementing programmed instruction.

323 HATCH, WINSLOW R., AND RICHARDS, ALICE L. *Approach to independent study.* New Dimensions in Higher Education No. 13. Wash., D. C.: Government Printing Office, 1965, 73 pp. 30 cents.

Ten educators from various types of institutions explore the concept of independent study, and describe specific programs. In general the authors conclude that independent study does produce some benefits in terms of intellectual independence and improved inquiry skills; however, content mastery seems not to differ greatly from traditional methods.

324 JOHNSON, STUART R., AND JOHNSON, RITA B. *Developing individualized in-structional material.* New York: Westinghouse Learning Corporation, 1970, 108 pp. $3.75.

This volume practices what it preaches. In self-instructional format, the authors describe how college teachers can move from their present instructional techniques to a self-instructional system that allows each student to proceed at his own pace. In each section of this manual, the authors declare their behavioral objectives and end with a criterion-referenced test so that the reader can determine whether he has met those objectives. This report is noteworthy because it represents a successful operating program in which college teachers are being trained to organize their course and instructional methods around new theoretical approaches that have gained much favor in recent years. This publication serves as basic source material for a junior college instructional program developed in 1970 at the National Laboratory for Higher Education (1458).

325 LEE, CALVIN B. T. (ED.) *Improving college teaching.* Wash., D. C.: American Council on Education, 1967, 407 pp. $6.

This book is a distillation of some of the best thinking of the academic profession on the state of college teaching and how to improve it. The essays grew out of the background papers, addresses, and ensuing commentaries presented at the 1966 ACE annual meeting, which is described as a "stock-taking" of the quality of college teaching. Several essays are devoted to a reexamination of the academic community and the loyalty conflicts confronting the academic man, particularly in the teaching vs. research dilemma. Other essays and commentaries are addressed to some of the factors felt to be deterrents to improving standards of teaching: the use of inexperienced teaching assistants, rigid curriculums, the academic recognition and reward system, and expanding student enrollments.

326 MCKEACHIE, WILBERT J. *Teaching tips: A guidebook for the beginning college teacher.* (6th ed.) Lexington, Mass.: D. C. Heath, 1969, 280 pp. $3.95.

These hints on teaching by an experienced psychology professor are guided by three assumptions: (1) Education should make optimum use of the democratic philosophy; students as well as teachers should contribute. (2) Students are adults. (3) The teacher can be wrong occasionally. The topics discussed include course preparation, traditional and innovative methods of teaching, examinations and grading, discipline, class size, counseling, ethics, motivation, evaluation and research on teaching, and student ratings of faculty. The fact that this book is in its sixth edition should provide sufficient evidence that it is well done and very useful.

327 MCKEACHIE, WILBERT J. *Research on college teaching: A review.* Report 6, Wash., D. C.: ERIC Clearinghouse on Higher Education, 1970, 18 pp.

This helpful paper summarizes research on college teaching from 1924 to 1970 and examines such issues as class size, teaching methods, independent study, and the new media. The report concludes with a recommendation that college teachers develop a "repertoire of skills" in order to maximize the learning potential of each individual student. The paper also includes a selected bibliography of some 150 items.

328 MILTON, OHMER, AND SHOBEN, EDWARD J. JR. (EDS.) *Learning and the professors.* Athens, Ohio: Ohio University Press, 1968, 216 pp. $6; paperback $2.95.

This book of essays addresses the need to jar faculty members into discussion of new instructional philosophies, in the face of mounting college enrollments, the knowledge explosion, and the "radical character of social change." The editors selected articles they hoped would challenge conservative academic tradition and would suggest innovative concepts of the "central task of learning." The contributions are provocative and should provide a useful focus for faculty discussion of the basic institutional problems underlying effective instruction.

329 MORRIS, WILLIAM H. (ED.) *Effective college teaching: The quest for relevance.* Wash., D. C.: American Council on Education, 1970, 162 pp. $3.50.

This book contains selected chapters from a larger study of teaching conducted by the Joint Committee on College Teaching, administered by the American Association for Higher Education. Stanford Ericksen deals with instructional matters, learning theory, technological teaching aids, evaluation, and examinations. Lewis Mayhew discusses the complexity of the teacher's relationships to extrainstitutional organizations, and Harold Hodgkinson describes systems of campus governance in relation to the participation of new faculty members. Other chapters deal with teaching in the disciplines of humanities, science, mathematics, social sciences, and psychology. This book is especially useful for the young faculty member, though all members of the academic profession would undoubtedly profit from this refresher course on the disciplines and the complexity of the modern university.

330 SAETTLER, PAUL. *A history of instructional technology.* New York: McGraw-Hill, 1968, 399 pp. $9.50.

In this history of instructional technology, the author distinguishes between the physical science concept of various media as instructional aids, and the behavioral science concept which emphasizes differences between individual learners and selection of instructional content. The histories of the two are integrated through the volume, though the latter approach has only come into prominence in recent years. The discussion of current usages of instructional media covers museums, radio, films, and television; it also includes a case history of the effect of military and industrial interest in instructional technology during World War II.

331 THORNTON, JAMES W. JR., AND BROWN, JAMES W. (EDS.) *New media and college teaching.* Wash., D. C.: National Education Association, 1968, $8.50; paperback $7.

This publication provides many illustrations of the use of new media technology in higher education. In 1966 some 1,400 institutions were invited to submit information about media innovations. This volume contains articles by 114 of the responding professors, and annotations of several hundred others. Chapters cover the use of instructional television, films, listening laboratories, programmed instruction, mediated self-instruction, computer-assisted instruction, telephone applications to instruction, simulation systems, and management of media services. The editors conclude that ". . . machines in themselves are the least important aspect of technology, and . . . the primary concern must be *new relationships between men and machines* to accomplish clearly thought-out objectives."

332 TWYFORD, LORAN C. JR. Educational communications media, in Robert L. Ebel (Ed.), *Encyclopedia of educational research.* (4th ed.) New York: Macmillan, 1969, pp. 367-380.

The author provides a fairly comprehensive though brief description of various aspects of educational media. A useful bibliography is included.

333 WITTICH, WALTER A., AND SCHULLER, CHARLES F. *Audiovisual materials: Their nature and use.* (4th ed.) New York: Harper & Row, 1967, 554 pp. $12.50.

This handbook provides a useful reference to a wide variety of media aids to instruction; it is unusually well illustrated and includes numerous references to materials, research, and sources of information.

4.4 — *INNOVATION*. Increasing pressure on higher education has greatly heightened interest in the change process. The literature carries ample exhortation and polemics. More than a few writers have noted that change in higher education doesn't come easily. The validity of this generalization seems supported by the fact that much innovation appears trivial, and that which is not is found in a limited number of institutions. The literature directed specifically to "innovation" seems seldom concerned with the educational program. This may merely be the semantic result of curriculum change being called reform (section 4.1) or compensatory (section 10.3). The literature in this particular section tends to be concerned with institutional forms and educational methods. There is also increasing interest in the process of change itself (for example, see 339 and 341).

334 ALTMAN, ROBERT A. *The upper division college.* San Francisco: Jossey-Bass, 1970, 202 pp. $7.75.

This book studies the upper division college as the "logical capstone" to the junior college. It traces the ties of such contemporary institutions with historical efforts to restructure the four-year baccalaureate institution, and discusses the problems that some of these new colleges have encountered. Chief among the difficulties are the inability to offer lower-division courses and the inadequacy of enrollments. He suggests that the upper-division college needs to work in tandem with junior colleges to provide satisfying opportunities for their graduates. Other educational planners see this institution as a potentially important ingredient in state master plans, which include heavy reliance on two-year colleges.

335 BASKIN, SAMUEL (ED.) *Higher education: Some newer developments.* New York: McGraw-Hill, 1965, 342 pp. $7.50.

This collection of essays is oriented toward evaluating innovations in four-year undergraduate institutions. It covers the background, format, advantages and disadvantages, and possibilities for broader applications of such developments as independent study, study abroad, use of new media and technology, off-campus experience, programs for the superior student, year-round use of facilities, the community as a learning resource, programs for the improvement of college teaching and administration, and others. It also describes some newly created colleges as well as some new programs at established institutions. The book was sponsored by the Association for Higher Education as a compendium of new programs already in use and new ideas of teaching and learning.

336 BRICK, MICHAEL, AND MCGRATH, EARL J. *Innovation in liberal arts colleges.* New York: Teachers College Press, Columbia University, 1969, 173 pp. $3.95.

This book documents many specific innovations under way at four-year colleges. Institutions that had reported some involvement in new practices on an HEW Survey for the *Education Directory* of 1965-66 were followed up in this study. New approaches to curriculum were interdisciplinary courses, honors programs, freshman seminars, independent study, non-Western study, study abroad, and community service projects. The instructional experiments centered on the use of television, teaching machines, language laboratories, programmed instruction, learning resource centers, interinstitutional cooperation, dormitories as learning centers, comprehensive examinations, and innovative grading procedures. Trends involving students were new admissions policies, advanced placement, and student participation in faculty evaluation and hiring. Other institutions reported they were engaged in reorganizing and restructuring the college itself. The authors conclude that the trend has been to replace the old idea of "coverage" with "learning to learn" or exposure to representative ideas, constructs, and experiences. The volume provides very useful documentation of practices and includes many interesting ideas.

337 GAFF, JERRY G., ET AL. *The cluster college.* San Francisco: Jossey-Bass, 1970, 249 pp. $8.50.

This volume takes a comprehensive view of the strengths and weaknesses of cluster colleges. Initial chapters describe the typical hallmarks of such colleges — nongrading, independent study, core curriculums, and unique living and learning arrangements. Succeeding chapters deal with student concerns about the value of a degree from a nontraditional college, particularly as preparation for graduate school, faculty insecurity in the "publish or perish" job market, and the college's tendency to resist further innovation after the initial honeymoon. In spite of the problems, the author makes the case that cluster colleges do provide tentative solutions to some pressing needs. They facilitate adequate recognition for teaching skill, opportunities for broad cross-disciplinary study, student involvement as a member of the educational community, and raising educational policy to the forefront of faculty concerns.

338 HALLAM, KENNETH J. (ED.) *Innovations in higher education.* Proceedings of the Towson Conference on Curricular and Instructional Innovation. Baltimore, Md.: Towson State College, 1966, 131 pp.

This five-day conference afforded representatives from state colleges the opportunity to become informed about new trends in curriculum and instruction. The papers in this book of proceedings describe innovations in curriculum, teacher education, the use of instructional media, and educational research, as well as discussion of policy and philosophy for change.

339 HEFFERLIN, JB LON. *Dynamics of academic reform.* San Francisco: Jossey-Bass, 1969, 240 pp. $8.50.

This book provides a great deal of insight into the process of organizational change. Hefferlin documents his major thesis — that "continuous adaptability" is essential to the vitality and effectiveness of any college or university — both from an historical perspective, and from the findings of the Study of Institutional Vitality, conducted by the Teachers College Institute for Higher Education. In analyzing the historically persistent difficulties of accomplishing institutional change in higher education, he delineates three factors that determine the boundaries of change: the resources available, the advocates of the change, and the openness of the system.

The 1966-67 Study of Institutional Vitality examined curricular changes in more than 100 universities over a five-year period; it sought to single out the factors that stimulate, develop, and sustain reform, and to explore the reasons why "some institutions seem to maintain a spirit of experimentation and change . . . while others . . . seem to stay in an educational rut." Hefferlin defines the major correlates of an innovative institution as a market for new ideas, development of new models rather than imitations, circulation of ideas, and the help of marginal members such as trustees and consultants. He concludes that the organizational style most conducive to innovation is one in which initiative is not permanently centralized, where high status is assigned on the basis of expertise, and where positions of status shift according to different tasks rather than in rotation.

340 HENDERSON, ALGO D. *The innovative spirit.* San Francisco: Jossey-Bass, 1970, 308 pp. $8.50.

This book presents both the philosophical rationale and a platform of specific recommendations for restructuring higher education to achieve social change. The author, a distinguished educator and retired president of Antioch College, sees validity in student charges that colleges and universities are materialistically oriented, resistant to change, and run by boards of trustees who are more knowledgeable about finance than education. He urges sweeping changes in the curriculum and focus of undergraduate education, community colleges, medical and professional education, and institutional governance.

Some specific proposals are: (1) Replacement of the business-inherited board of trustees concept with that of group participation that would draw faculty, students, and college administrators into policy making. (2) Urban-related undergraduate college systems that adapt the community college concept of serving the needs of the individual community. He recommends programs (similar to Antioch's work-study plan) that focus on solving problems (environmental, health, etc.) rather than on subject matter. (3) Overhauling medical and professional training to emphasize flexibility in requirements, effective use of new technology — computers, TV, etc., and service orientation as an educational goal.

341 HIRSCH, WERNER Z., ET AL. *Inventing education for the future.* San Francisco: Chandler, 1967, 353 pp. $7.95.

This volume has a systems analysis approach to the evaluation of educational innovation. It grew out of a seminar sponsored by the Institute of Government and Public Affairs, University of California at Los Angeles, to draw together educators and engineers, mathematicians, psychologists, and economists. Among the innovations discussed are computer-assisted education, simulation and gaming, and the Operations Analysis Program of the United States Office of Education.

342 HOLTZMAN, WAYNE W. (ED.) *Computer-assisted instruction, testing, and guidance.* New York: Harper & Row, 1970, 402 pp. $10.

This book deals with the progress, problems, and issues of computer-assisted teaching, testing, and counseling. The individual chapters were prepared for a joint conference organized by the Social Science Research Council and the College Entrance Examination Board. They combine the perspectives of computer specialists with those of educators, psychologists, and counselors. Holtzman describes the major uses that computers will have in education: business administrative services, educational management and library file systems, research tools, and computer-managed and computer-assisted instruction. Many of the chapters are highly technical, but the general discussions of the social and psychological implications of the computer in the classroom are of special importance and value.

343 JOHNSON, B. LAMAR. *Islands of innovation expanding: Changes in the community college.* Beverly Hills, Calif.: Glencoe, 1969, 352 pp. $5.95.

This volume is based on a 200-institution survey of innovations in junior colleges, conducted in 1967-68. The most widely used innovations were found to be cooperative work-study programs, programmed instruction, television and other technological aids, games and other simulation in teaching, developmental teaching, students as teachers, and independent study. The author also discusses aids and obstacles to innovation, and makes some projections and recommendations for the future. The volume represents a great deal of work. It is an impressive testament to the imagination and energy of many junior college faculties.

344 LADD, DWIGHT. *Change in educational policy: Self-studies in selected colleges and universities.* New York: McGraw-Hill, 1970, 231 pp. $6.95.

During the 1960s many institutions undertook self-studies in order to understand the problems besetting them and to seek possible solutions. The Carnegie Commission on Higher Education sponsored this study of 11 such reports

(Berkeley, University of New Hampshire, University of Toronto, Swarthmore, Wesleyan, Michigan State, Duke, Brown, Stanford, Columbia College, and University of California at Los Angeles). It includes detailed discussion of the types of recommendations made and the feasibility of real change in higher institutions. The book provides an interesting examination of this formal method of encouraging innovation.

345 MARTIN, WARREN BRYAN. *Conformity: Standards and change in higher education.* San Francisco: Jossey-Bass, 1969, 288 pp. $8.50.

The concept of diversity in higher education has long been considered a hallmark of the American system; institutions of every conceivable size and orientation offer a wide variety of curricular programs and experiences. The author states, however, that recent developments in higher education, particularly student unrest, have challenged the lack of substantive diversity in educational goals and values. In this study the institutional character of eight institutions, each involved in recent innovation, was examined to determine whether the structures and forms of higher education are paralleled by differing value orientations. After comparing the educational philosophies, the standards of excellence, and innovative processes of each institution, the author concludes that "American higher education has been characterized by conformity where diversity is needed," and that all goals and philosophies are dictated by one value: professionalism. The author is specific as to which group is responsible—"Faculty, not administrators or students, are the most zealous guardians of the conventional criteria to which all interest groups are obligated." Martin stresses that holistic planning and a commitment to educational philosophies rather than professional standards will be necessary to develop diversity at the value level.

346 NASATIR, DAVID. Resistance to innovation in American education, in Werner Z. Hirsch et al., *Inventing education for the future.* San Francisco: Chandler, 1967, pp. 295-305.

This essay discusses the attributes of educational institutions that tend to inhibit innovation. The first of these he terms "traditional morality"—the veneration of established routines and customs. Second, schools generally do not have enough leeway in financial resources to provide teachers and administrators with much opportunity for experiments. Third, Nasatir argues that many of the goals of education are deliberately ambiguous because they are based on conflicting values. Finally, he points out that innovations that tend to remove from parental control those decisions which foster social mobility, or universalize the education received by all children, will meet with resistance from the more privileged and powerful elements in our society. Thus, the educational innovator must consider not only the organizational dynamics of the system but also the value implications of his proposals.

347 SPURR, STEPHEN H. *Academic degree structures: Innovative approaches.* New York: McGraw-Hill, 1970, 213 pp. $6.95.

The need to redesign the academic-degree structure to achieve a simple and flexible system is the theme of this book. Because the crucial importance of degree requirements filters down into all areas of planning for higher education, the Carnegie Commission on Higher Education commissioned this study of degree certification. The author investigated the background and development of degree policies, and interviewed a number of prominent American and European educators. In the present structure he sees the master's and doctor's programs as unsuccessful. The master's degree is appraised as a stockpiling of additional undergraduate credits, ending as a "consolation prize." The PH.D. program is criticized as "notoriously inefficient in both dragout of time and dropout of students" and has been impervious to change, despite a barrage of suggestions in recent years. The inordinate length and rigidity of the M.D. requirement and the second-class status of the ED.D. degree are also discussed. In contrast, the bachelor's degree is rated successful because of its flexibility and the "variety of doors it opens." The broad umbrella aspect of the bachelor's degree provides a pattern for remaking the overall degree structure to create a "fluid and interconnecting system" that offers maximum opportunities for students to develop their potential. The author concludes with a discussion of how this concept could work out in the six established levels of certification—associate, bachelor, master, intermediate graduate, doctoral, and postdoctoral.

348 STICKLER, W. HUGH (ED.) *Experimental colleges: Their role in American higher education.* Tallahassee, Fla.: Florida State University, 1964, 185 pp. $3.50.

This volume documents experiments in higher education that are now well-known and influential. Included are brief but incisive reports of the history, organization, and experience of representative experimental institutions such as Antioch, Stephens, Parsons, New College, Santa Cruz, and Monteith. Further chapters discuss educational innovation at Michigan State, the University of the Pacific's cluster colleges, curricular change at Florida Presbyterian, and the role of industry in planning and development of the University of Michigan at Dearborn.

SECTION 5: EDUCATIONAL EVALUATION

Evaluation plays a central role for two good reasons. First, all the major access processes involve a heavy element of evaluation. The nature of those evaluation measures and how they are used is necessarily of vital social importance. Second, evaluation of the outcome of the access process has special importance for the student; his academic record and his credential have a heavy bearing upon his future alternatives.

Evaluation is an inseparable component of admissions in selective institutions. To a considerable extent, guidance is a process of evaluating alternatives. Administration of financial aid is typically based on an evaluation of need. The educational process goes hand-in-hand with concurrent evaluation of achievement. And the more general processes of educational planning, manpower utilization, and equalization of opportunity are all based on different forms of systematic evaluation.

These applications of evaluation vary considerably with respect to the type of techniques involved and the sophistication of their development. The underlying theory is fairly elaborate in guidance and education, but less so in other areas. Practice (as opposed to theory) is typically fairly rudimentary and common sense in all applications—and this is probably to the general good. The integration of theory and practice is probably more effective within this evaluation process than in the case of any other access process; evaluation theory and evaluation practice are basically the same profession.

In addition to the two major admissions testing organizations— College Entrance Examination Board (1112) and American College Testing Program (1101)—there are several agencies that play an especially important role in educational evaluation. Educational Testing Service (1115) is the major agency of its kind in the country. It not only administers a number of major testing programs but carries on an unusually extensive program of activities in educational research and evaluation. Other agencies with important research and evaluation functions include American Council on Education (1156), Center for the Study of Evaluation (1164), the National Laboratory for Higher Education (1172), and the Center for Research and Development in Higher Education (1161).

The major professional organization in educational research and evaluation is American Educational Research Association (1104). Its major periodical, *American Educational Research Journal* (1306), is an important source of material in this area. The Association for Institutional Research (1109) is another professional group that has become quite active in recent years. The *College Board Review* (1315) is an especially frequent source of nontechnical articles on different aspects of evaluation that are particularly pertinent to the access process.

There are a number of programs, organizations, and periodicals that focus more specifically on educational testing. The National Council on Measurement in Education (1127) is especially concerned with measurement applications in the classroom. Section 13.2 describes a number of national testing programs that are involved with the access process. Periodicals that emphasize applied educational measurement include the *Journal of Educational Measurement* (1325), *Measurement and Evaluation in Guidance* (1335), *Evaluation Comment* (1367), and *Measurement in Education* (1377).

5.1—SOCIAL CONTEXT. Virtually all the literature in this area is theoretical. It includes essays, analyses, and recommendations—some precipitous but many balanced and thoughtful.

There are several major issues. One revolves around the present and future functions of testing and research. A major publication especially focusing on the functions of testing with respect to access to higher education is the final report of the College Entrance Examination Board's Commission on Tests (354). Another important issue in the social context of evaluation is the attitude toward the strengths and weaknesses of tests. There was a flurry of this literature in the 1960s. Various points of view are represented in the references included in this section. Another important issue of recent interest is that of individual privacy. Westin (369) has prepared a comprehensive treatment covering various aspects of privacy including testing and research.

349 AMERICAN PSYCHOLOGICAL ASSOCIATION. Testing and public policy. *American Psychologist,* 1965, vol. 20, pp. 857-993.

Because of the barrage of criticism leveled at psychological testing and selection procedures climaxing in Congressional hearings in 1965, the American Psychological Association devoted this entire issue to informing its membership about the controversies. It contains condensed versions of testimony before the Senate Subcommittee on Constitutional Rights, and the House Subcommittee on Invasion of Privacy. Michael Amrine, public relations adviser for the APA and guest editor for this issue, comments on the background and current status of the criticisms, and some nonpsychologists present their interpretation of the problems involved.

350 ASTIN, ALEXANDER W., AND BORUCH, ROBERT F. A "link" system for assuring confidentiality of research data in longitudinal studies. *American Educational Research Journal,* 1970, vol. 7, pp. 615-624.

This article describes an ingenious method for protecting the anonymity of respondents in large-scale surveys. The system involves storing critical identifying information at a computer center in a foreign country. The agreements under which such information is stored prevent accidental or purposive invasion of privacy under almost any foreseeable circumstances, including a court subpoena. This system was developed in connection with the Cooperative Institutional Research Program of the American Council on Education and is also described in *ACE Research Reports,* vol. 5, no. 3, 1970.

351 BRIM, ORVILLE G. JR., GLASS, DAVID C., NEULINGER, JOHN, AND FIRESTONE, IRA J. *American beliefs and attitudes about intelligence.* New York: Russell Sage Foundation, 1969, 291 pp. $7.75.

The results of this research reveal a pattern of general ignorance and misinformation about intelligence and its measurement. Ten thousand high school students were questioned in 1968 on the following topics: their own experience with tests, beliefs about accuracy and importance of testing, self-estimates of intelligence, interest in receiving test scores, and their feelings about ability grouping and the use of test scores in decision-making. School policies of keeping scores confidential are blamed for the ignorance and inequities in knowledge about the individual's own intelligence. Although the rationale for this practice is that it prevents possible damage to the student's self-esteem, the authors consider it "shocking and astonishing to find so little solid social research about the consequences of feedback of information about abilities." They recommend development of uniform procedures for score reporting but caution that school personnel charged with this responsibility should be better educated about the pitfalls of test interpretation as well as their own possible biases.

A national educational program is recommended to achieve better understanding of the predictive importance of test scores and flexibility in use of ability classifications. Students from families with low educational backgrounds tend to regard test scores as infallible and need help in developing a more realistic perspective. They feel that children from culturally deprived families should be given sufficient exposure to test taking starting in early school years so that they are not handicapped by procedural unfamiliarity. The authors' general view is that testing can be an opportunity to rectify mistakes in class or career allocation, but too rigid interpretations can create more dead-end mistakes.

352 CHAUNCEY, HENRY, AND HILTON, THOMAS L. Are aptitude tests valid for the highly able? *Science,* 1965, vol. 148, pp. 1297-1304.

This article summarizes recent studies dealing with the validity of aptitude tests for students of high ability. Various arguments against the adequacy of tests with the very talented are reviewed, and relevant evidence is cited. The authors conclude that aptitude tests can reliably discriminate among able students and are valid predictors of future performance.

353 CHRIST-JANER, ARLAND F. The College Board at 70: Priorities for the future. *College Board Review,* Winter 1970-71, no. 78, pp. 14-19.

As recently installed president of the College Entrance Examination Board, the author provides perceptive comments on the status of both higher education and the College Board. He considers the implications of the report of the Commission on Tests, the establishment of a new Committee on Student Economics, revisions needed in traditional programs of the Board, and growing interest in the extramural baccalaureate degree.

354 COLLEGE ENTRANCE EXAMINATION BOARD. *Report of the Commission on Tests.* Vol. I. *Righting the balance.* Vol. II. *Briefs.* New York: College Entrance Examination Board, 1970, Vol. I, 118 pp. $2; Vol. II, 194 pp. $3.

The Commission on Tests was appointed by the College Board and charged with reviewing the Board's testing functions in American education and recommending possibilities for fundamental changes in tests and their use. The Commission recommended that the Board should modify and improve its testing programs in order to serve three functions: (1) a distributive function by contributing to comprehensive and sensitive descriptions of students and colleges; (2) a credentialing function by certifying demonstrable educational attainment whether or not acquired by attendance in school or college; and (3) an educative function by instructing students both in subject-matter areas and in skills and methods of making decisions.

The Commission placed considerable stress on the principle of symmetry in college choice—that is, students as well as colleges should be provided with useful information relevant to the selections they make. The Commission advanced various suggestions regarding new directions for College Board tests. These dealt with different approaches to the assessment of abilities of minority students, a broadened view of the college admissions process of the future, and the role of modern technology in providing better services to students and colleges.

355 CRONBACH, LEE, AND SUPPES, PATRICK (EDS.) *Research for tomorrow's schools: Disciplined inquiry for education.* New York: Macmillan, 281 pp. $3.95.

This report of the Committee on Educational Research of the National Academy of Education charts new bases for future educational research and scholarship. It examines the historical background and discusses the current status of educational research in order to bring perspective to the direction of the future. It makes some searching criticisms of the United States Office of Education for the "paperwork blizzard" that hampers national mobilization to remedy social problems through education, and for its "communications gap" with the scholarly community, particularly in panels reviewing research proposals. An important contribution of the study is its discussion of the distinctions between conclusion-oriented research and decision-oriented research—both of which are needed in highest quality, but under very different circumstances.

356 EBEL, ROBERT L. The social consequences of educational testing. *College Board Review,* Winter 1964, no. 52, pp. 10-14.

This article discusses the criticism that educational testing may lead to predetermined social status, a narrow definition of ability, an increase in the influence of testers over the educational system, and undue emphasis on mechanistic decision-making. Ebel concludes that educators should deal with these possible dangers by regarding aptitude tests as a means to increase achievement rather than a determination of fixed intelligence, by offering a greater variety of tests, and by using tests to facilitate rather than impose decision-making. In addition, Ebel believes that educators should communicate more openly with the public concerning test scores and methods. See 351 for a similar viewpoint.

357 FINDIKYAN, NURHAN, MANNING, WINTON H., AND PASANELLA, A. K. *Bibliography of test criticism.* New York: College Entrance Examination Board, 1967. $2.90; Microfiche, 65 cents. (Available from ERIC, ED 039 395)

This annotated bibliography is a fairly comprehensive compendium of the more important criticisms of standardized testing that appeared prior to 1967. It was prepared in conjunction with hearings held by the Commission on Tests (354).

358 FISHMAN, JOSHUA A., AND CLIFFORD, PAUL I. What can mass-testing do for-and-to the pursuit of excellence in American education. *Harvard Educational Review,* 1964, no. 34, pp. 63-79.

The authors suggest that much of the criticism of testing may be misplaced. Thus, they feel that the mechanization of education that so many fear is not so much attributable to tests as to the pursuit of the standard mind and the standard man. "We need not scrape and bow to mass-testing, but neither should we make it the whipping boy for our serious educational shortcomings and disappointments." They further suggest that those who lead us away from a serious analysis of educational goals into a consideration of testing procedures are hardly doing us a favor.

359 FRIEDENBERG, EDGAR Z. The real functions of educational testing. *Change,* 1970, vol. 2, no. 1, pp. 43-47.

In this brief article Friedenberg, a well-known "radical" educator and member of the Commission on Tests, criticizes educational testing as an "inherently conservative function" that services the existing social structure. The testing process, he continues, "usually cannot muster the imagination or sponsorship to search out and legitimate new conceptions of excellence which threaten the hegemony of existing elites." He argues that the technology of testing *could,* however, serve "humane goals in a more humane society," because it is technically capable of helping people find out what purposes might be realistic for them in view of their actual characteristics. In discussing how this philosophy relates to minority group charges of test bias, he says "the inherent bias of the present system is to determine the entire life of a student on the display of a narrow range of cognitive behavior."

360 GOSLIN, DAVID A. What's wrong with tests and testing. *College Board Review,* Fall 1967, no. 65, part I, pp. 12-18; Winter 1967-68, no. 66, part II, pp. 33-37.

In this pair of articles Goslin points out that proper consideration of criticisms of testing must take into account the type of test involved, the use to which it is put, and the relevance of the test to such usage. He notes that tests often discriminate among groups of people so as to reveal social and educational differences – and thus they are doing the job they are designed to do. A more serious problem, he asserts, is the rigid misuse of tests in evaluating candidates for programs, institutions, or jobs. With respect to broad social implications, the author's main concerns lie with overuse of tests, which may in turn result in undesirable homogenization in certain situations, invasion of privacy in others, or a generally mechanistic manner of dealing with individuals.

361 HOFFMANN, BANESH. *The tyranny of testing.* New York: Crowell-Collier, 1962, 223 pp. $3.95; paperback 95 cents.

The entrenched power of the testing "tyranny" over student careers is sharply censured in this book, one of the best-known criticisms of testing. Hoffman campaigns most strenuously against the proliferation of easy-to-score multiple-choice tests at the expense of subjective essay tests which are difficult to mass administer and evaluate. The multiple-choice test rewards the "superficially brilliant, quick-reading student" who perceives the answer wanted, and penalizes the "creative, intellectually honest" student. He concludes that since testing programs carry such intimidating weight, the whole field should be reviewed by an independent committee of intellectual leaders who can bring fresh vision to their usage. (See 354 for the report of the Commission on Tests which held hearings on such criticisms.)

362 LAUWERYS, JOSEPH A., AND SCANLON, DAVID G. (EDS.) *Examinations: World year book of education 1969.* New York: Harcourt, Brace & World, 1969, 404 pp. $12.95.

This *Year Book* presents a comparative analysis of the way in which examinations are devised, administered, and assessed in different countries. It also examines the effects of examination systems on the education process as well as the larger society. Individual sections trace the evolution and development, aims, theories, and techniques of examinations. Further sections evaluate the validity of tests in current use and investigate the effects of examinations on teachers, students, and educational objectives. Three sections are devoted to national studies. The first reviews organization and administration of examinations in various countries, the second deals with examinations as selection instruments, and the third evaluates the socioeconomic effect of examinations in highly industrialized and developing countries.

363 MANNING, WINTON H. Affidavit, in Civil action no. EC 70-51-5, Bernice Armstead et al., plaintiffs, vs. Starkville Municipal Separate School District et al., defendants. U. S. District Court for the Northern District of Mississippi, Eastern Division, August 13, 1970. (Unpublished affidavit available from Educational Testing Service)

In Starkville, Mississippi, a district ruling required all teachers to qualify for their jobs by achieving a certain score on the Graduate Record Examination. As one result relatively few blacks could qualify for teaching positions in the public schools. In this detailed and thorough court affidavit the author explains why the ruling is arbitrary, unfair, and not supported by proper scientific and professional supporting evidence. The essence of the argument lies in the fact that the GRE was not developed to select teachers, and there is no evidence of its validity for that purpose. The discussion is especially valuable in relating technical aspects of educational measurement to social implications of testing applications.

364 MESSICK, SAMUEL, AND ANDERSON, SCARVIA. Educational testing, individual development, and social responsibility. *CounselingPsychologist,* 1970, vol. 2, no. 2, pp. 80-88.

This article is written in response to a call by the Association of Black Psychologists for "an immediate moratorium on all testing of black people until more equitable tests are available." The authors make the important clarification that controversy concerning the adequacy of tests involves two issues — one deals with the question of whether a test is any good; the other deals with the question of whether a test should be utilized for a specific purpose. The first question is scientific; the second is ethical and social. The authors examine various aspects of these questions including the critical social consequences of not testing. The result is a very informative discussion of the issues involved and a reasoned defense of continued use of appropriate testing for members of minority groups.

365 OFFICE OF SCIENCE AND TECHNOLOGY, EXECUTIVE OFFICE OF THE PRESIDENT. *Privacy and behavioral research.* Wash., D. C.: Government Printing Office, 1967, 30 pp. 15 cents.

This final report of the Presidential Committee on Privacy and Behavioral Research considers the propriety of certain procedures in behavioral research which may endanger individual privacy. The panel chose to emphasize flexibility in determining professional responsibility. The report places the responsibility for safeguarding privacy and for determining how that protection shall be afforded upon the individual researcher and his institution rather than upon uniform federal restraints. The panel assumes a definite position in disfavor of detailed review with respect to protection of privacy of proposals volunteered to government agencies. The major import of the report seems clear — this distinguished group strongly prefers decentralized responsibility. The implied responsibility for procedural and ethical guidelines, therefore, rests with professional associations and their leadership.

366 SIMS, ALBERT G. The case of the Student Descriptive Questionnaire. *College Board Review,* Fall 1971, no. 80, pp. 13-20.

In 1971-72 the College Board introduced a Student Descriptive Questionnaire (SDQ) to its Admissions Testing Program. The questionnaire elicits a variety of information concerning students' background, achievements, and interests. The purpose of the questionnaire is to provide students with more information useful in selecting a college and to provide colleges with more information about applicants than would otherwise be possible.

The introduction of this questionnaire caused serious concern in a number of colleges on several grounds. Perhaps the main worry on the part of some member institutions was the fear that a significant proportion of potential candidates might not apply after receiving information that might cause them to question the appropriateness of a given college. This article gives a case history of the introduction of the questionnaire. It is an excellent example of a legitimate conflict between student and institutional interests.

367 TURNBULL, WILLIAM W. How can we make testing more relevant? *College Board Review,* Spring 1968, no. 67, pp. 5-10.

The author, president of Educational Testing Service, notes that since the end of World War II both the college-going population and the educational programs offered college students have changed dramatically. He comments, "The day when an array of traditional academic measures was an adequate yardstick has vanished forever." He urges that examination programs undergo changes of equal scope so that they match the diversity of students and programs. Turnbull suggests three possible stages in the future development of testing programs:

(1) for the immediate future, a "multiplex program" which will extend the recent trend toward a diversity of tests and broaden still further the range of aptitude, interests, and varieties of attainment measured; (2) next, a "school-based program" with a reduction of emphasis on external examinations and increased reliance on the record compiled by the student in his own school; (3) finally, a "student-based program" in which each student is presented with the individual questions most pertinent to his past preparation and to his responses to test questions earlier in the sequence. Such tests would require the aid of a computer and would provide the individual student with the best opportunity to display his own talent and accomplishment, without wasting time on tasks either well below or well beyond his level of development ability.

368 U. S. OFFICE OF EDUCATION, NATIONAL CENTER FOR EDUCATIONAL RESEARCH AND DEVELOPMENT. *Educational research and development in the United States.* Wash., D. C.: Government Printing Office, 1970, 200 pp.

This volume explores the development, present status, and possible lines of future growth of educational research and development in the United States. It is a useful document for understanding the relationship of educational research to policy and practice. Individual chapters cover such topics as the organization of educational research, its management and financing, the substance of this research, and its impact on policy and practice.

369 WESTIN, ALAN F. *Privacy and freedom.* New York: Atheneum, 1967, 487 pp. $12.50.

In this book Westin investigates the effects on the individual of such privacy-invasion devices as surveillance mechanisms, subliminal suggestion, lie detectors, and personality tests. He begins with a theoretical basis for the concept of privacy, describes the various techniques, and surveys public reaction to establish changing norms of privacy. The author also reviews the legal aspects of privacy and suggests specific measures to protect privacy in the future. Westin argues that control of surveillance technology must be developed by a balance of private forces (such as scientific counter-devices), professional standards, intraorganizational restraints, and moral consciousness with governmental action. The latter should include legislative restraints, executive action, and judicial review.

5.2—*EDUCATIONAL CONTEXT.* This area consists mainly of theoretical research on the outcome of the student's experience in college. It was an especially provocative and rich area of research throughout the 1960s. It consists largely of surveys, longitudinal studies, and statistical analyses, primarily based on work by research psychologists.

There are three closely related problems. One special concern has been the development of the student as an individual. One of the most highly praised studies of student development has been that of Katz and associates (384). Student development is commonly assumed to be closely related to the question of how the college affects the student. There have been hundreds of studies on this general question all summarized unusually well by Feldman and Newcomb (382). A slightly different question is whether different colleges have differential effects. Astin (375) has been a leading investigator on this problem and has succeeded in questioning much conventional wisdom.

370 ASTIN, ALEXANDER W. Influences on the student's motivation to seek advanced training: Another look. *Journal of Educational Psychology,* 1962, vol. 53, pp. 303-309.

In the early 1960s several prominent researchers maintained a widely read running argument in the literature on the methodology and conclusions of research concerning the effect of faculty influence and college environments on student aspirations to seek the PH.D. This article is a good example; it cast doubt on earlier research indicating that the faculty "press" affects student level of aspiration. Other examples can be found in the same journal in the same period.

371 ASTIN, ALEXANDER W. "Productivity" of undergraduate institutions. *Science,* 1962, vol. 136, pp. 129-135.

In this article Astin provides a summary of his work to date on the relationship between college characteristics and "PH.D. productivity." His general conclusion is that Eastern men's colleges and universities were significantly underproductive while public and coeducational private institutions were overproductive. The author suggests, however, that the data give reason to question whether PH.D. productivity is a sensitive measure of the effectiveness of undergraduate institutions. Despite the pioneer character of this line of well-known work, PH.D. productivity must be recognized as a narrow view of a college's output.

372 ASTIN, ALEXANDER W. Differential college effects on the motivation of talented students to obtain the PH.D. *Journal of Educational Psychology,* 1963, vol. 54, pp. 63-71.

A variation of the input-output design was used in this study of college effect upon student aspiration. Data were collected on some 6,500 high aptitude students. Certain characteristics of colleges were associated with a higher or lower percentage of college seniors aspiring to PH.D. study than would be expected on the basis of those students' characteristics as freshmen. Even though entering freshmen at Northeastern men's colleges had a slightly higher rate of PH.D. aspiration than entering students at coeducational liberal arts colleges, the actual rate of graduating seniors in the coeducational colleges expressing this goal was considerably higher (59 vs. 34 percent).

These same liberal arts colleges, the author notes, tend to combine several of the college characteristics that are positively related to PH.D. aspiration: small student bodies with about equal numbers of males and females, and relatively low "conventional orientations." These results confirm some earlier findings but dramatize the subtle and complex ways in which colleges affect students. The study also shows that methodological problems are critical and exceedingly difficult.

373 ASTIN, ALEXANDER W. Effects of different college environments on the vocational choices of high aptitude students. *Journal of Counseling Psychology,* 1965, vol. 12, no. 1, pp. 28-34.

The relationship of various college characteristics to career plans of some 3,500 very able boys was examined in a four-year study in 73 institutions. Even after accounting for the fact that a student often chooses his type of college because of its orientation to his type of occupational choice, it was still found that the career choice tends to grow closer to the dominant career choice of the college environment. Astin speculates that although the mechanism for this effect could be very complex, it could also be a simple learning phenomenon, in which the dominant forces in the college environment "selectively reinforce behavior which conforms to the 'party line.' "

374 ASTIN, ALEXANDER W. A program of research on student development. *Journal of College Student Personnel,* 1968, vol. 9, pp. 299-307.

This article describes the American Council on Education's program of longitudinal research aimed at assessing the impact of different college environments on student development. Among the principal objectives of the research program are: (1) to improve techniques for measuring differences in college environments; (2) to determine how these environmental variables affect the performance of the student; (3) to make data files available to other researchers. This research program involves annual surveys of a large group of freshmen at a representative group of colleges, systematic follow-up questionnaires, and special studies of current issues. A useful routine output of the program is the production of the annual norms of the characteristics of entering freshmen.

375 ASTIN, ALEXANDER W. Undergraduate achievement and institutional "excellence." *Science,* 1968, vol. 161, pp. 661-668.

This article is based on an extensive study reported by Astin and Panos (377). It focuses on the frequent assumption that intellectual achievement of the undergraduate student is favorably affected by traditional forms of institutional excellence. The author presents evidence that the student's achievement in social science, humanities, and natural science is not facilitated either by the intellectual level of his classmates or the financial resources of his institution. He contends that these analyses suggest that it would be wise to reexamine traditional notions of institutional excellence. (See 390 for contrary evidence.)

376 ASTIN, ALEXANDER W. Measuring student outputs in higher education, in Ben Lawrence, George Weathersby, and Virginia W. Patterson (Eds.), *The outputs of higher education: Their identification, measurement, and evaluation.* Boulder, Colo.: Western Interstate Commission for Higher Education, 1970, pp. 75-83.

Astin suggests that student outputs must be viewed in relation to the total system and considered as part of a three-component model that also includes student inputs and the college environment. Attempts to measure student output must be varied and broad in order to take into account the variations in values and objectives of different students. He describes a taxonomy of student output measures that is based on the type of outcome (cognitive vs. affective), the type of data (psychological vs. sociological), and the temporal aspects of the measure (short-term vs. long-term).

377 ASTIN, ALEXANDER W., AND PANOS, ROBERT J. *The educational and vocational development of college students.* Wash., D. C.: American Council on Education, 1969, 211 pp. $6.

In the fall of 1961 Astin initiated a longitudinal research study with an assessment of all entering freshmen at 248 colleges and universities. Data gathered from the original sample of 127,000 freshmen were analyzed in *Who Goes Where to College?* (731). This study followed up 36,000 of the original sample four years after matriculation. In order to assess the impact of institutional diversity, particular attention was given to institutional characteristics and educational practices that bear on a student's educational progress and career plans. Comparative analysis of these data with the earlier studies revealed that academic accomplishment and career choice depended more on the student's characteristics and plans at the point of college entry than on his choice of an undergraduate institution. The authors conclude, "The implication here is not that his choice of a college is an unimportant fact, but rather that the college environment is of relatively little importance in determining the outcomes considered in this study." Moreover, the student's scholastic achievement did not seem to be enhanced by attending an affluent institution with relatively high concentrations of able students. The authors are a bit too prone to assume causal relationships in explaining their findings, but the analysis is quite sophisticated in comparison with most studies of the effect of education. The book is interesting as well as important.

378 CHICKERING, ARTHUR W. *Education and identity.* San Francisco: Jossey-Bass, 1969, 367 pp. $9.50.

With the goal of translating research findings on student development into action, Chickering describes ways of shifting the focus in higher education from concern for the disciplines to concern for persons. He defines seven major areas of student development—competence, emotions, autonomy, identity, interpersonal relationships, purpose, and integrity—and discusses what kinds of action can be taken to foster progress in these dimensions in six elements of college environments—clarity and consistency of objectives; institutional size; curriculum, teaching, and evaluation; residence hall arrangements; faculty and administration; and friends, groups, and student culture. His suggestions are based on two principles: (1) Education starts with the learner and builds increased differentiation and integration, in contrast to training, which starts with the task and conforms the learner to it. (2) The impact of an experience is significantly influenced by the characteristics of the person who encounters it—a principle which should enter into policy decisions on admissions, grading, residences, and discipline. The book makes interesting reading and contains many useful ideas, but it is sparse in reference to the vast literature available on the subject. There is frequent reliance on anecdotal evidence and exposition.

379 COMMITTEE ON THE STUDENT IN HIGHER EDUCATION. *The student in higher education.* New Haven, Conn.: Hazen Foundation, 1968, 66 pp.

Based on the premise that "the college years see the conversion of idealism into cynicism," this report calls for major qualitative changes in higher education that can reverse the trend toward "giantism and dehumanization." They recommend wide experimentation with developmental education, a philosophy that views the freshman year as an orientation to learning rather than the first year of academic instruction. The committee feels that, "The spin-off school . . . associated with the multiversity" is the most effective instrument for innovation and reform. The report also calls for a new kind of faculty, committed to aiding the emotional development of students, wide democratization of rule making on campus, integration of education with volunteer service, and increased flexibility for time requirements in colleges.

380 DAVIS, JAMES A. *Undergraduate career decisions.* Chicago: Aldine, 1965, 307 pp. $7.50.

This is the second volume reporting on findings from the National Opinion Research Center (NORC) study of the career plans and aspirations of a national sample of June 1961 college graduates. The first volume, *Great Aspirations* (18), is concerned primarily with graduate study plans while this report focuses on the shifts in occupational preferences that take place during the undergraduate years. The author concludes that the changes that occur during the four college years amount to relatively minor modifications and that "on the whole, the students come out oriented to the jobs they chose as freshmen." Changes do occur, but they often appear to be "a continuation of trends that began before entry into college."

381 FELDMAN, KENNETH A. *Research strategies in studying college impact.* ACT Research Report No. 34. Iowa City, Iowa: American College Testing Program, 1970, 35 pp.

This report is based partly on a paper prepared for a seminar on college effects sponsored by ACT. The author presents a broad overview of research on the impact of college on students. He outlines the theories and methods underlying such research and discusses the difficulties in defining and measuring "impact." The report is carefully documented and includes a useful bibliography.

382 FELDMAN, KENNETH A., AND NEWCOMB, THEODORE M. *The impact of college on students.* Vol. I. *An analysis of four decades of research.* Vol. II. *Summary tables.* San Francisco: Jossey-Bass, 1969, Vol. I, 474 pp.; Vol. II, 171 pp. $15 set.

This monumental two-volume work is the final report of a study commissioned by the Carnegie Foundation for the Advancement of Teaching. Forty years of research were reviewed and analyzed in an attempt to assess the evidence concerning the influence of American colleges on their students. The first volume presents the text of the analysis; the second volume includes short summaries of selected studies, tables, and data on which the authors base their generalizations. Among their general conclusions are the following: (1) Freshman-to-senior changes in several characteristics, particularly those showing openness to change, occur with considerable uniformity in most American colleges and universities. (2) College faculties appear to have little campus-wide impact on students, although individual faculty members are often influential. (3) Small residential colleges more frequently provide the best conditions for faculty impact on students. (4) College impacts are conditioned by a student's background and personality; however, the college experience can often strengthen existing values or attitudes that might otherwise have been weakened or reversed. (5) Attitudes held on leaving college tend to persist thereafter, often as a consequence of living in environments supportive of these attitudes.

383 HEATH, DOUGLAS H. *Growing up in college.* San Francisco: Jossey-Bass, 1968, 326 pp. $9.50.

In this book Heath presents a theoretical model of the maturing process of the healthy adult. The model involves various hypotheses of mature growth and was developed from a combination of the biological, psychoanalytic, psychosocial, and mental health theories of personality growth. He examines the adequacy of the theory by his study of the development of selected groups of students and alumni at Haverford College. In relating the model of maturing to the goals of a liberal education, he postulates three conditions that define a "powerful liberally educating environment: the educability of its students, its communal educative conditions, and the coherence of its purposes and means." He notes with dismay that changes now occurring "dilute the power of a college to educate liberally" just when it is most needed. He blames this dilution on the move to "universitize" the college and to supplant the development of mature values with training in narrow intellectual specialties. This study emphasizes the case history approach and seems useful primarily for the insights it may facilitate rather than documented conclusions.

384 KATZ, JOSEPH, ET AL. *No time for youth.* San Francisco: Jossey-Bass, 1968, 463 pp. $10.

This highly praised report is based on a study of 3,500 freshmen entering Berkeley and Stanford. Some 200 of these students were randomly selected for intensive interviews held several times a year during the subsequent four years. The book begins with a section on how students change during their college years and includes two detailed case studies. A section on the curriculum and careers describes and documents the "profound differences in the way students learn, their motivations for learning, and the interplay of choice and coercion in their career decisions." The problems of student life are considered in a third section, and individual chapters deal with drinking, student activism, and students who seek psychiatric help. The final section offers recommendations for policy and philosophy based on the premise that the individual development of the student is the chief purpose of educational institutions and this fact demands "radical changes in the curriculum, in the role of the teacher, and in the life of the student in and out of the classroom."

385 LEHMANN, IRVIN J. Changes in critical thinking, attitudes, and values from freshman to senior years. *Journal of Educational Psychology,* 1963, vol. 54, pp. 305-315.

In order to measure changes in the critical thinking ability, attitudes, and values of college students over a four-year period, a battery of instruments was administered to 1,000 Michigan State University students as freshmen and again as seniors. Among the significant changes reported were: (1) a decrease in stereotyped beliefs and resistance to new ideas, (2) an increase in tolerance and independence, (3) an improvement in critical thinking, (4) an increased interest in political and social issues. The greatest changes took place during the first two years of college. In the absence of a noncollege control group, the changes cannot necessarily be related directly to the college experience, and the authors point to evidence that much of the influence is due to nonacademic experiences.

386 NEWCOMB, THEODORE M., AND WILSON, EVERETT K. (EDS.) *College peer groups: Problems and prospects for research.* Chicago: Aldine, 1966, 301 pp. $8.95.

This collection of essays by prominent writers examines how peer-group influences reinforce or contradict college and faculty goals particularly with respect to student development. Different chapters concentrate on specific research problems in which the various authors are experts. The first section deals with the framework in which peer groups operate—i.e., types of student culture, conditions under which peer groups are most influential, etc. The second topic concerns problems of empirical inquiry. David Riesman concludes the final section on problems and prospects in the study of college peer groups with a warning that "research on peer groups must confront the possibility . . . that loyalty to the ideal of individualistic academic excellence, favored in general by faculty members, may be at odds with loyalty to the group, to the college, or to any larger entity."

387 NICHOLS, ROBERT C. Effects of various college characteristics on student aptitude test scores. *Journal of Educational Psychology,* 1964, vol. 55, pp. 45-54.

In this study of the relationship between college characteristics and scores on the Graduate Record Examination, precollege characteristics of the students were controlled statistically. On the basis of a sample of 356 students attending 91 colleges, the author concludes that differential effects of colleges are relatively small compared to differences among freshman classes that existed at the time the students entered higher education. There was in general a tendency for some colleges to enhance verbal aptitude of students at the expense of quantitative aptitude (or vice versa).

388 NICHOLS, ROBERT C. Personality change and the college. *American Educational Research Journal,* 1967, vol. 4, pp. 173-190.

This longitudinal study of the effect of college on personality change involved 636 National Merit finalists. Personality and interest inventories were administered prior to college entrance and again just before graduation. The author concludes that ". . . the major portion of the differences observed between college graduates can be attributed to events which happened before the students entered college. Of the changes which occur during the college years the proportion attributable to the gross characteristics of the college is relatively small." The changes that were attributable to college characteristics were: at affluent institutions extraversion increased in both sexes; at realistically oriented colleges (engineering, agriculture) anxiety increased in both sexes; business emphasis was associated with increases in masculinity in girls; and at Catholic colleges dominance decreased in boys.

389 PLANT, WALTER T., AND TELFORD, CHARLES W. Changes in personality for groups completing different amounts of college over two years. *Genetic Psychology Monographs,* 1966, vol. 74, pp. 3-36.

This study of personality and attitude change during the college years was based on students applying to six California public junior colleges. Approximately 50 percent response was obtained in retesting subjects after a two-year period. Whereas various personality changes were noted, these changes were little different for students who had attended college through the two-year period and those who had not. The authors suggest that many changes attributed by others to the collegiate experience may be no more than developmental changes under way in young persons whether or not they attend college.

390 ROCK, DONALD A., CENTRA, JOHN A., AND LINN, ROBERT L. Relationships between college characteristics and student achievement. *American Educational Research Journal,* 1970, vol. 7, no. 1, pp. 109-121.

This study is based on some 6,800 students from 95 colleges and an advanced method of data analysis. It provides clear evidence of a relationship between academic quality and student achievement. Although the level of achievement at individual colleges is heavily dependent upon the aptitude of entering freshmen, the results of this study do indicate that colleges with relatively high income per student and with a higher proportion of faculty with a doctorate turn out upperclassmen with higher performances on the Graduate Record Examination (GRE).

391 SANFORD, NEVITT. *Where colleges fail.* San Francisco: Jossey-Bass, 1968, 228 pp. $7.50.

Sanford's main thesis in this book is that the primary aim of education should be the individual development of the student, and to that end a *total* educational environment must embody a theory of personality "that restores the student to his rightful place at the center of the college's activities." From this starting point he discusses various aspects of student development, including personality, social responsibility, motivation for academic achievement, education for creativity, the use of alcohol, and the integration of sexuality in personality. He also discusses how some particular environmental factors influence student development, among them student peer culture, teaching, and the size of the institution. In generalizing his thesis he argues that "universities or colleges that make student development their primary aim can find ways to integrate their activities and thus serve society and students at the same time." Like most of Sanford's writing, this essay is frequently wise and always eloquent.

392 SKAGER, RODNEY, HOLLAND, JOHN L., AND BRASKAMP, LARRY A. *Changes in self-rating and life goals among students at colleges with different characteristics.* ACT Research Report No. 14. Iowa City, Iowa: American College Testing Program, 1966, 24 pp.

This longitudinal study is addressed to the question of whether there are consistent differences among colleges in the nature of student personality change and to relate these personality changes to such institutional characteristics as size, expenditure, and type of environment. The measures of personality are self-ratings of scholarship, expressiveness, popularity, practical-mindedness, sensitivity to the needs of others, and intellectual self-confidence. Ratings were obtained on the following goals: becoming accomplished in one of the performing arts, becoming influential in public affairs, making a theoretical contribution to science, following a formal religious code, and being well read. The survey was administered in a limited sample of institutions, and the analysis did not include the statistical controls other authors favor (388, 377). The authors do cite numerous effects that are often consistent with those of other studies, and they hold that institutional differences may have more bearing on personality changes than is sometimes concluded.

393 TRENT, JAMES W., AND MEDSKER, LELAND L. *Beyond high school.* San Francisco: Jossey-Bass, 1968, 333 pp. $10.

In this important study of some 10,000 high school graduates from 16 communities the authors compare two groups—those who were admitted to college and those who went directly to work. The two basic questions considered are: (1) why some young people go to college while others do not, and (2) what happens to members of both groups throughout the four years following high school. It was hypothesized that personality development would be most evident among those who completed college and least evident among those who did not enter.

Basic data were collected through 10 attitudinal scales from the Omnibus Personality Inventory, a student questionnaire, and interview schedules.

A host of conclusions are suggested, including the following: (1) Both ability and social status are associated with college attendance; however, of these two positively related factors, social status is the more important. (509 reports an opposite result.) (2) Parental encouragement and academic motivation are important factors in distinguishing those who go to college and those who do not. (3) The availability of a college was highly related to the rate of college entrance, but not to the rate of completion. (4) Persistence in college is largely dependent on three factors: perceived importance of the degree, an early decision to attend college, and parental encouragement. (5) Personality development takes place most among college persisters and least among those with neither college nor employment experience. (6) It appears that college may provide the opportunity for growth rather than consciously fostering it, and that students change to about the same degree regardless of the type of college attended.

394 WALLACE, WALTER L. *Student culture: Social structure and continuity in a liberal arts college.* Chicago: Aldine, 1966, 236 pp. $8.50.

This study concentrated on a small, midwestern, coeducational, liberal arts college to determine the impact of informal social structures on first-year students—their academic values, achievement, and aspirations. Questionnaires were administered to all freshmen three times during the year—their second day on campus, seven weeks later, and the following April. Upperclassmen and faculty were also studied. Analysis included an ingenious method of examining peer attitudes and how they interact. The most startling discovery was the finding that most academic attitude change among the freshmen occurred within the first seven weeks of their college experience. The data also showed that the socialization of freshmen derived primarily from nonfreshmen and faculty members rather than from peers. Faculty members relied for influence on sanctions and on personal relationships, whereas the student system relied largely on group influence and the rewards of social integration.

395 WERTS, CHARLES E. Career changes in college. *Sociology of Education,* 1967, vol. 40, pp. 90-95.

This effort to discover factors relevant to career plan changes during college involved some 30,000 male freshmen at 248 colleges, polled twice—at college entry, and again the following summer. The study is based on research by Davis (380) and, in general, confirmed his results by showing a trend toward social homogeneity. Students who switched career preferences chose occupational categories in which students were more like themselves in terms of social class and academic ability. Students originally aiming for the same occupation that their fathers had chosen were less likely to switch than other students with that occupational choice.

396 WERTS, CHARLES E., AND WATLEY, DONIVAN J. *Analyzing college effects: Correlation vs. regression.* NMSC Research Reports, 1969, Vol. 5, No. 2. Evanston, Ill.: National Merit Scholarship Corporation, 15 pp.
    This technical paper considers the strengths and weaknesses of two input-output models commonly used in studying college effects. The authors use four models to illustrate the advantages of partial regression coefficients in a causal framework as opposed to the computation of expected output by controlling student input.

5.3 — *TESTING AND EVALUATION.* This section is concerned with applications of measurement practice in the evaluation of individual student performance. The material included here ranges from essays and descriptive material to informational documents and research reports. The references are largely nontechnical or at least presume little technical background. Almost all the work in this area is produced by psychologists. The problems tend to fall into one of three categories.

First, there is a body of material concerning the use of tests in education. These include general texts, various types of useful manuals, and reference materials. It also includes special publications connected with programs of the College Entrance Examination Board and American College Testing Program — their interpretation, characteristics, and uses.

A second portion of this literature deals with the evaluation of student achievement in higher education. This includes grading practices, faculty values in evaluation, and various types of noncognitive evaluation. It is a surprising area in several respects. Measurement specialists have tended to focus on measurement theory or on formal standardized tests rather than the measurement process as it operates in thousands of classrooms. And since most faculty members assume they know all there is to know about grading, there is extremely little development in this area.

A good example is the fact that there is almost no literature on the relationship of student evaluation to systems of academic standing in higher education (see 417 and 426 for exceptions). Even though formal academic regulations have a crucial bearing on educational attainment and the access process in general, educators have tended to tackle the whole problem in the spirit of alchemy.

There is a third set of references in this area that have to do with special testing problems. These include personality tests, tests of nonacademic accomplishment, writing ability, etc. — simply a potpourri of items that have some special bearing on access to higher education.

397 AIKEN, LEWIS R. JR. The grading behavior of a college faculty. *Educational and Psychological Measurement,* 1963, vol. 23, pp. 319-322.
    This article documents a finding noted informally on many college campuses. The average grade assigned to incoming freshmen does not necessarily reflect the ability level of those freshmen as it changes from year to year. In this ex-

ample the predicted freshman grade average moved up progressively with increasing selectivity of the institution while the actual freshman average remained essentially constant over a three-year period. The author notes the tendency of the teaching faculty to regard grades as based on some absolute scale and suggests that ample evidence to the contrary should be periodically exposed.

398 AMERICAN PSYCHOLOGICAL ASSOCIATION, AMERICAN EDUCATIONAL RESEARCH ASSOCIATION, AND NATIONAL COUNCIL ON MEASUREMENT IN EDUCATION. *Standards for educational and psychological tests and manuals.* Wash., D. C.: APA, 1966, 40 pp.

This booklet is a revision of an earlier document published in 1955. It states the professional standards for test development as prepared by a joint committee of the major organizations concerned with educational and psychological measurement. These standards form the appropriate basis for evaluation of tests.

399 ANASTASI, ANNE (ED.) *Testing problems in perspective.* Wash., D. C.: American Council on Education, 1966, 671 pp. $10.

This volume provides an unusually valuable book of readings on educational and psychological measurement. The papers were selected to commemorate the first 25 years of the Invitational Conference on Testing Problems. The authors include many of the best-known names in psychometrics. Topics range from theoretical to practical concerns, and from professional problems to broad social issues.

400 ANGOFF, WILLIAM H. (ED.) *The College Board Admissions Testing Program: A technical report on research and development activities relating to the Scholastic Aptitude Test and Achievement Tests.* New York: College Entrance Examination Board, 1971, 181 pp. $5.

This sizable volume is a comprehensive technical manual for the major testing program of the College Board. It describes in considerable detail the technical aspects of what has been undoubtedly the nation's single most complex and massive educational testing program of the past 35 years. Separate chapters are devoted to the history of the Admissions Testing Program, the Scholastic Aptitude Test, the Achievement Tests, descriptive statistics of the program, and predictive validity of the tests. A final chapter is devoted to special studies of such topics as coaching, practice, fatigue, new item types, the English essay, and test bias.

401 BLOOM, BENJAMIN S., HASTINGS, J. THOMAS, AND MADAUS, GEORGE F. *Handbook on formative and summative evaluation of student learning.* New York: McGraw-Hill, 1971, 923 pp. $11.95.

This comprehensive analysis of evaluation techniques is intended as a handbook for teachers and students in teacher-training programs. The first part provides a framework for general evaluation problems and discusses evaluation in relation to mastery of specific learning levels, evaluation used for instructional decisions, techniques for evaluating cognitive and affective objectives, and improvements in techniques through the use of cooperative teacher-specialist teams. The second section examines evaluation in the major subject fields and levels of education and illustrates specific learning objectives and testing techniques in each area. The volume is a basic reference and major contribution because of its scope and special emphasis on nontraditional methods of testing specific outcomes of education.

402 BUROS, OSCAR K. (ED.) *The sixth mental measurements yearbook.* Highland Park, N. J.: Gryphon Press, 1965, 1,713 pp. $35.

For many years this volume has been the standard reference on psychological and educational tests in print. It is privately published but consists of objective reviews of tests by hundreds of measurement experts. Virtually all commonly used published tests are included.

403 CHAUNCEY, HENRY, AND DOBBIN, JOHN E. *Testing: Its place in education today.* New York: Harper & Row, 1963, 223 pp. $4.95.

This book presents an overview of current testing developments and their use in education. It is intended to provide teachers, interested school-board members, and parents with a broad picture of what the testing in schools and colleges is all about. Among the topics discussed are: the history of testing; tests of learning ability and achievement; how to select a good test; tests as tools in teaching, selection, and admissions; and helping students to do their best. The authors give practical answers to many questions and include helpful examples from various tests.

404 COLLEGE ENTRANCE EXAMINATION BOARD. A statement on personality testing. *College Board Review,* Fall 1963, no. 51, pp. 11-13.

This statement approved by the College Board trustees came in response to considerable interest among admissions officers in the use of personality tests for selective admissions. This statement discourages such use and cites the following considerations: (1) Personality scales should be examined with respect to the kind of communication they make to the secondary schools and to the public. (2) Use of personality tests raises serious and complex ethical and moral problems. (3) Personality tests involve sensitive problems of faking and coaching. (4) Personality tests seem unlikely to improve predictive power substantially, and there is reason to doubt that such an objective is appropriate. (5) Much research remains to be done on the way in which personality tests might be used.

405 COLLEGE ENTRANCE EXAMINATION BOARD. *Effects of coaching on Scholastic Aptitude Test scores.* New York: College Entrance Examination Board, 1968, 28 pp.

This booklet reports the conclusion of College Board trustees that coaching does not improve scores on the Board's Scholastic Aptitude Test in significant degree. In seven studies, four sponsored by the Board, and three carried out independently, changes were too small to have any effect on admissions decisions. The studies were undertaken in the light of frequently expressed concerns of parents and schools about the effectiveness of cram-course techniques. The Board views the Scholastic Aptitude Test as "a measure of abilities that seem to grow slowly and stubbornly, profoundly influenced by conditions at home and at school, but not responding to hasty attempts to relive a young lifetime."

406 COLLEGE ENTRANCE EXAMINATION BOARD. *College Board score reports: A guide for counselors and admissions officers.* New York: College Entrance Examination Board, 1970, 36 pp.

This booklet explains how to interpret student scores on the Preliminary Scholastic Aptitude Test, the Scholastic Aptitude Test, and the Achievement Tests. It contains charts showing percentile ranks of various groups of students and includes information particularly valuable to guidance counselors and admissions officers. It is routinely sent to guidance directors in secondary schools.

407 CURETON, LOUISE W. The history of grading practices. *Measurement in Education,* 1971, vol. 2, no. 4, 8 pp.

This very readable report gives a brief but informative account of how classroom grading practices evolved. It includes a wealth of historical references, and it documents the initiation of some grading methods, scales, and ideas. Numerous anecdotes and quotes make it a joy to read.

408 DAVIS, JUNIUS A. What college teachers value in students. *College Board Review*, Spring 1965, no. 56, pp. 15-18.

In this extensive study of student evaluation, the faculty of eight selected institutions were asked to observe a sample of students for a term and to rate them on many traits. Sixteen basic factors, falling into five groups, were found necessary to explain the variance in ratings: (1) intellectual qualities—academic performance, intellectual curiosity, creativity; (2) characteristic approach to work—habitual orientation to tasks, achievement motivation, open-mindedness; (3) character traits—probity, likableness or cooperativeness, altruism; (4) peer relationships and social style—extroversion, popularity or leadership, social maturity, conformity; and (5) personal adjustment—freedom from anxiety, self-insight, freedom from status-centeredness. Statistical analysis revealed which components of these characterizations were associated with high scores on the Scholastic Aptitude Test, good grades, and high general desirability ratings. Those correlated with high SAT scores were academic performance, intellectual curiosity, and creativity. Good grades correlated with intellectual curiosity, achievement motivation, creativity, and habitual orientation to tasks. Desirability was related to cooperativeness, probity, open-mindedness, altruism, self-insight, and social maturity. This report is particularly valuable in suggesting different values that might be applied to evaluating students and also in exposing some of the problems inherent in such use.

409 DRESSEL, PAUL L. Evaluation of the environment, the process, and the results of higher education, in Asa S. Knowles (Ed.), *Handbook of college and university administration*. Vol. II. *Academic*. New York: McGraw-Hill, 1970, sec. 2, pp. 53-80.

This chapter provides a very useful overview of methods for evaluation of the major phases of the operation of a higher education institution. Individual sections discuss selection, classification, and placement of students; evaluation of instruction, faculty, and administration; internal and external institutional appraisal; and use of evaluation results. The author also briefly deals with the question of continuous vs. periodic self-evaluation. The major weakness of this limited treatment is the fact that it covers a very broad field with very few references to assist the reader further.

410 DRESSEL, PAUL L., AND MAYHEW, LEWIS B. *General education: Exploration in evaluation*. Wash., D. C.: American Council on Education, 1957, 302 pp. (Out of print)

This volume is the final report of the Cooperative Study of Evaluation in General Education sponsored by the American Council on Education. It represents a landmark cooperative effort to examine the rationale and objectives of evaluation in several subject areas. The book is an invaluable source of information concerning the philosophical and practical problems in evaluation. The committees concluded that the abilities that make up critical thinking are the most important outcomes of general education, and in the final chapter the authors explore the possibility of critical thinking as a unifying concept of general education.

411 DRESSEL, PAUL L., ET AL. *Evaluation in higher education*. Boston: Houghton Mifflin, 1961, 480 pp. $8.50.

The process of evaluation takes many forms in colleges and universities. This classic book discusses basic principles, concepts, procedures, and resources in the various areas of evaluation. The nature and role of evaluation, problems of defining educational objectives, and the relation of evaluation to the learning process are covered in the opening chapters. Specific problems in testing and evaluation in the four broad areas of social sciences, natural sciences, humanities, and communications are singled out for discussion. Other chapters treat the problems of grades and comprehensive examinations, the role of evaluation in student selection and placement, evaluation of instruction, state and regional needs and problems, and institutional self-evaluation.

412 EBEL, ROBERT L. Measurement in education, in Robert L. Ebel (Ed.), *Encyclopedia of educational research.* (4th ed.) New York: Macmillan, 1969, pp. 777-785.

This brief article provides numerous references and an introduction to the general topic of measurement in education. It includes sections on the history of educational measurement, the measurement literature, the nature of the measurement process, attitudes toward educational measurement, and major testing programs and services. The same reference includes a number of other relevant articles.

413 EDUCATIONAL TESTING SERVICE. *Multiple-choice questions: A close look.* Princeton, N. J.: ETS, 1963, 43 pp. Free.

This booklet analyzes a representative sample of multiple-choice questions in major areas of the curriculum. Each question is followed by a statistical analysis of responses, and by a discussion of the process used in formulating the question and choosing the correct response. The purpose is to dispel the myth that multiple-choice questions are superficial and require little thought or insight. At the very least the reader is afforded an understandable exposition of the complex process of test construction by the organization that has undoubtedly developed more tests than anyone else.

414 EDUCATIONAL TESTING SERVICE. *Tests and measurement kit.* Princeton, N. J.: ETS, 1970. Free.

This kit of materials was prepared for use by instructors of tests and measurement classes, but it provides a variety of useful materials for anyone interested in practical aspects of testing. Among the items included are the following brief booklets: (1) *Short Cut Statistics for Teacher-Made Tests;* (2) *Selecting an Achievement Test: Principles and Procedures;* (3) *Making the Classroom Test: A Guide for Teachers;* (4) *ETS Builds a Test;* (5) *Selected References in Educational Measurement;* (6) *Multiple-Choice Questions: A Close Look;* and (7) *Testing Programs, Special Services, Instructional Activities at Educational Testing Service.*

415 FINDLEY, WARREN G. (ISSUE ED.) Educational and psychological testing. *Review of Educational Research,* 1968, vol. 38, no. 1, 110 pp.

This issue of the journal is devoted entirely to testing problems. Separate chapters deal with educational and psychological development of different age groups and special populations. Additional chapters are concerned with methodology, external testing programs, and the relation of testing to the evaluation of curriculum development. Each provides a brief review of recent literature.

416 GODSHALK, FRED I., SWINEFORD, FRANCES, AND COFFMAN, WILLIAM E. *The measurement of writing ability.* Research Monograph No. 6. New York: College Entrance Examination Board, 1966, 84 pp. $2.50.

This monograph reports what is probably the most thorough research ever undertaken on the measurement of writing ability. It supports the assumption that colleges can accept scores on the College Board's English Composition Test as valid indices of candidates' ability to write. Data obtained from testing of 646 students by the use of essays, objective tests, and interlinear exercises justify the following generalizations: (1) The reliability of essay scores is primarily a function of the number of different essays and the number of different readings included. (2) When objective questions specifically designed to measure writing skills are evaluated against a reliable criterion of writing skills, they prove to be highly valid. (3) The most efficient predictor of a reliable direct measure of writing ability is one that includes essay questions or interlinear exercises in combination with objective questions.

417 HUMPHREYS, LLOYD G. The fleeting nature of the prediction of college academic success. *Journal of Educational Psychology,* 1968, vol. 59, pp. 375-380.

The author presents data that illustrate the relatively low correlations between college grade averages from year to year. With some alarm he relates these findings to the system of academic standing and probation and suggests various possible interpretations. This article (with 426) represents one of the few published examinations of the generally confused and chaotic system of evaluation and secondary selection (attrition) of students that occurs on most campuses after students are enrolled.

418 KENDRICK, S. A. The personality testing tangle. *College Board Review,* Fall 1964, no. 54, pp. 26-30.

Faced with an impending tide of students in the mid-1960s, most admissions officers in the country were ready to be persuaded that personality tests provided a convenient way to screen excess, unmotivated, uncongenial, or confused applicants. In a typically readable article the author examines the premise and clarifies some of the questions and problems that need to be solved before admissions officers can feel comfortable in using personality tests now available.

419 MANNING, THURSTON E. Academic policies and standards, in Asa S. Knowles (Ed.), *Handbook of college and university administration.* Vol. II. *Academic.* New York: McGraw-Hill, 1970, sec. 2, pp. 3-14.

This chapter provides practical information on formulation and administration of academic policy. Individual sections discuss the roles of the governing boards, faculty, administration, students, and extrainstitutional influences in determining academic policy and the delegation of authority. Further sections offer policy suggestions for course requirements for earned and advanced degrees, approval of new courses, graduation with honors, grade requirements for admission and graduation, transfer credits, and credit for work-study and other nontraditional programs. The author's treatment provides a useful context for considering the many aspects of academic policy. A serious weakness is the lack of any systematic consideration of the relation of academic standards to evaluation of academic achievement of students.

420 MESSICK, SAMUEL. Personality measurement and college performance, in Educational Testing Service, *Proceedings of the 1963 Invitational Conference on Testing Problems.* Princeton, N. J.: ETS, 1964, pp. 110-129.

Messick discusses the potential contributions of personality measurement to the prediction of college performance from two viewpoints — scientific value and ethical justifications. He applies scientific criteria of reliability and construct validity to three kinds of measures of personality: (1) factorial inventories, (2) empirically derived inventories, and (3) rational inventories. Although he finds that none of the measures available so far meets psychometric standards, he is optimistic that rapid advances in technology and supporting research in this area may bring a breakthrough in the near future. Scientific reliability would then raise the question in earnest of what ethical considerations justify the choice of any particular test. He concludes with the warning that "selection on any given personality variables might lead to conformity pressures toward the stereotype implied by the selected characteristics."

421 RICHARDS, JAMES M. JR., HOLLAND, JOHN L., AND LUTZ, SANDRA W. *The assessment of student accomplishment in college.* ACT Research Report No. 11. Iowa City, Iowa: American College Testing Program, 1966, 13 pp.

This developmental work was undertaken to provide additional measures of student accomplishment in college. A questionnaire on nonacademic accomplishments was administered in 1965 to almost 10,000 college students from diverse institutions. It covered 12 areas: leadership, social participation, art, social service, science, business, humanities, religious service, music, writing, social science, and speech and drama. Self-reported grade averages supplied data on academic accomplishment. Analysis of the scales indicated that correlations between nonacademic accomplishment and grades were generally low. The nonacademic scales were judged to have validity as socially relevant measures that could be used in assessing the relationship between college and adult achievement.

422 STANLEY, JULIAN C. *Measurement in today's schools.* (4th ed.) Englewood Cliffs, N. J.: Prentice-Hall, 1964, 414 pp. $9.50.

This fourth edition of a widely used text provides a comprehensive introduction to educational measurement. The author assumes no prior preparation but covers the technical and practical aspects of test development, use, and interpretation. The treatment is based on a broad view of measurement and includes much material on the practical aspects of measurement in the school situation.

423 THORNDIKE, ROBERT L. Marks and marking systems, in Robert L. Ebel (Ed.), *Encyclopedia of educational research.* (4th ed.) New York: Macmillan, 1969, pp. 759-766.

In this brief article the author provides numerous insights into the practical, social, and political aspects of grading students. He provides nontechnical advice based on thorough understanding of the technical problems involved. It is worthwhile reading for any teacher or educational administrator.

424 THORNDIKE, ROBERT L. (ED.) *Educational measurement.* (2nd ed.) Wash., D. C.: American Council on Education, 1971, 768 pp. $15.

Since its first publication in 1951, this comprehensive volume has been regarded as one of the leading reference works in the theory and techniques of educational measurement. In this completely rewritten second edition, papers by 23 authorities deal with recent developments in the field, including the impact of technology, conceptual shifts in testing theory, and social and political issues raised by increasing use of tests. Part I discusses test design, construction, administration, and processing. Part II deals with special types of tests, such as performance evaluation and essay examinations. Part III examines measurement theory, and Part IV focuses on the application of tests to educational problems.

425 WARREN, JONATHAN R. *College grading practices: An overview.* Report 9. Wash., D. C.: ERIC Clearinghouse on Higher Education, 1971, 29 pp.

This comprehensive review of the literature argues that the purpose of grading should be to make it "an educational tool that accurately reflects the many dimensions of student performance." The author suggests that the widespread controversy over grading has a superficial ways-and-means focus that fails to recognize the fundamental issues: the influence of grades on the total educational process, their role in selection and admissions, their value as incentives to learning, and the relationship of grades to the social and institutional structure. He summarizes reports of technical issues, and suggests possible new approaches to grading.

426 WILLINGHAM, WARREN W. Erroneous assumptions in predicting college grades. *Journal of Counseling Psychology*, 1963, vol. 10, pp. 389-394.

Whereas there have been thousands of prediction studies concerned with the evaluation of applicants for admission, there has been extremely little research concerned with the evaluation of the academic performance of college students in relation to the system of academic standing employed by the institution. Though this latter system receives very little attention, it has a pronounced effect on educational attainment and the utilization of talent. This article is based on a longitudinal analysis of the grades of 799 college students in one institution. It starts with three accepted assumptions that were intimately related to the system of academic standing and educational guidance at this particular institution. All three are proved false, and the implication is that colleges should give more attention to the measurement characteristics of their systems of grading and academic standing.

427 WOMER, FRANK B. Test use, in Robert L. Ebel (Ed.), *Encyclopedia of educational research*. (4th ed.) New York: Macmillan, 1969, pp. 1461-1469.

This article provides a brief but comprehensive overview of various aspects of test use. The author cites important considerations and especially valuable references in the following areas: development of testing programs, test administration, test scoring, test use and interpretation, and test norms. The article includes a bibliography on testing practice.

5.4—INSTITUTIONAL RESEARCH. The literature included in section 5.4 is concerned largely with discussions of institutional research and the methods involved rather than substantive results. There are several rather different types of work in this field. Perhaps the most common is the research on students. This includes studies of admission, attrition, student development, attitudes and values, the grading system, etc. A closely related area is research on instruction or teaching effectiveness.

A third type of institutional research is related to the management function. Many studies are concerned with space utilization, personnel policies, salary administration, campus planning, and related topics. A fourth area of interest that is closely connected with management studies is the development of information systems. These usually involve formal systems models and computer applications. Examples of this type of work are summarized in section 7.5, Management Information, and section 13.3, Guidance and Admissions Systems.

428 ASSOCIATION FOR COUNSELOR EDUCATION AND SUPERVISION, EXPERIMENTAL DESIGNS COMMITTEE. *Research guidelines for high school counselors.* New York: College Entrance Examination Board, 1967, 114 pp. $2.

This publication is intended to encourage research interest among high school counselors. It offers a great deal of practical advice on such topics as studying students' attitudes, the follow-up study, evaluating counseling effectiveness, prediction studies, etc. It might have been more useful had the authors been more liberal with citations of additional sources of information and reference materials. Nonetheless, the papers do provide a useful introduction to a variety of research topics. (Also annotated in section 1.5.)

429 BARNES, FRED P. *Research for the practitioner in education.* Wash., D. C.: National Association of Elementary School Principals, National Education Association, 1964, 141 pp. $5.

This volume is designed to aid the individual who may be interested in research but has relatively little technical background. It emphasizes various aspects of the research process such as development of hypotheses, sampling problems, statistical probability, data analysis, statistical tests, and reporting results. It is an attractive and well-organized document but provides the reader with relatively little help in finding additional material on research methods.

430 College Entrance Examination Board. *Research in higher education: Guide to institutional decisions.* New York: College Entrance Examination Board, 1965, 66 pp. $2.

The papers at the Invitational Conference on Educational Research were presented by an unusually able and thoughtful group of researchers. They provide a variety of complementary views of the nature and the utility of research on higher education.

431 Cook, Desmond L. *Program evaluation and review technique: Applications in education.* Cooperative Research Monograph No. 17. Wash., D. C.: Government Printing Office, 1966, 100 pp.

In the late 1950s the Navy Department Special Projects Office developed a new method for managing large complex tasks. It became known as the Program Evaluation and Review Technique to which the acronym PERT has been applied. PERT involves identifying all the individual steps involved in a complex task and specifying the timing and scheduling characteristics of each. One important result is the production of a network that describes the timing and interrelationships of all activities. PERT has become an invaluable tool in managing large research projects. It can also be a very useful tool in planning more limited operations that involve close timing.

432 Duggan, John M. Researchable problems in college admission. *National ACAC Journal,* Summer 1961, pp. 5-9.

New admissions officers will find this article especially valuable, and most experienced directors of admissions will probably also find it well worth reading. It is not a "how to" article on research but rather a series of imaginative questions and thoughtful commentary on the sorts of problems that an admissions office can and should pursue from a research standpoint. These range from very simple matters of summarizing available information to more complicated questions that probably require expert consultation.

433 Dyer, Henry S. Shirtsleeves research for deans and counselors. *Journal of the National Association of Women Deans and Counselors,* 1960, vol. 24, pp. 48-54.

The author offers wise and entertaining advice on some useful types of research activity that can be practiced by educational administrators without benefit of extensive statistical or technical training. The emphasis is on practical educational problems.

434 Dyer, Henry S. Can institutional research lead to a science of institutions? *Educational Record,* 1966, vol. 47, pp. 452-466.

Institutional researchers seem frequently in search of their proper identity and role in higher education, but few authors have approached the philosophy of institutional research with the insight and scholarship exhibited in this article. Dyer considers the role of measurement and experimentation in developing a true science of institutional research. He concludes that such a science is feasible but that it must be so organized that it deals with real problems of institutions while at the same time endeavoring to fit those problems into generalizable solutions. Institutional researchers must develop better measures and more sophistication about how to conduct genuine experiments. The author might have put more emphasis on what appears to be the controlling factor on many campuses: whether or not the administration actually wants any institutional research to come about.

435 Eckert, Ruth E., and Keller, Robert J. (Eds.) *A university looks at its program.* Minneapolis, Minn.: University of Minnesota Press, 1954, 223 pp. $4.

This book describes one of the earliest systematic programs of institutional research. The 23 studies reported here are representative of the continuing research the University of Minnesota conducts on its own programs and policies.

Some of the topics covered are: the undergraduate program, specialized and graduate programs, follow-ups of Minnesota PH.D.s, enrollment trends, faculty promotion policies and practices, and student ratings of college teaching.

436 GAGE, N. L. (ED.) *Handbook of research on teaching.* New York: Rand McNally, 1963, 1218 pp. $15.
  This handbook is a standard reference in its field. It contains 23 chapters by outstanding authorities on theory, methodology, and subject areas of teaching. Many of the chapters are fairly technical and intended for an audience of researchers rather than practitioners.

437 HOYT, DONALD P., AND MUNDAY, LEO A. *Your college freshmen.* (1968-69 ed.) Iowa City, Iowa: ACT Research and Development Division, American College Testing Program, 1968, 249 pp. $3.
  The main purpose of this volume is to help institutional researchers and other college administrators to understand and use effectively the data provided by the various ACT research services. These individual services are described in detail, and additional useful chapters are concerned with presenting research findings to others, special research topics, and a number of bibliographies relevant to potential uses of the research service. Other sections include national norms for certain aspects of the ACT assessment and a variety of special technical notes.

438 KOILE, EARL A., HARREN, VINCENT A., AND DRAEGER, CAROLYN. Higher education programs. *Review of Educational Research,* 1966, vol. 36, pp. 233-255.
  This article covers a variety of institutional research published from 1963 to 1966 related to students in higher education. Thumbnail reviews report work in such areas as needs and press, campus environments, student subcultures and college goals, programs, student organizations, women students, married students, discipline, etc. The reviewers see a research gap in admissions, financial aid, and student affairs. They feel this may be because program officers "are likely to be practitioners who have neither the time nor the resources to plan and execute complex research." The authors suggest that this gap calls for administrative and financial support and collaboration of social scientists.

439 LINN, ROBERT L., DAVIS, JUNIUS A., AND CROSS, K. PATRICIA. *A guide to research design: Institutional research program for higher education.* Princeton, N. J.: Educational Testing Service, 1965, 53 pp. $2.50.
  College and university staffs will find this guideline to institutional research valuable in planning and carrying out research strategies for their own institutions. It focuses on the human resources of the institution, with particular emphasis on the study of the student, and also on problems of general relevance to the institution. One chapter interprets the potential uses of specific instruments such as the College and University Environment Scales (CUES), College Student Questionnaire (CSQ), and tests of academic achievement. Another chapter discusses methodological considerations — sampling, longitudinal studies, and problems of interpreting results.

440 LINS, L. J. *Methodology of enrollment projections for colleges and universities.* Wash., D. C.: American Association of Collegiate Registrars and Admissions Officers, 1960, 67 pp.
  This publication presents techniques for the development of estimates of future enrollment levels and for effective presentation of these estimates. The author believes that national projections of enrollment are not the best source for such estimates, which should be based on conditions peculiar to the institution. Four basic topics are discussed: (1) long-range projections of enrollment, (2) enrollment projection techniques, (3) short-range estimates of enrollment, and (4) data presentations. The author gives an example of projecting enrollments for one institution.

441 MORISHIMA, JAMES K. (ED.) *An annotated bibliography of institutional research 1969-70.* Auburn, Ala.: Association for Institutional Research, 1970, 63 pp. (Mimeographed)

This bibliography is distributed annually by the Association for Institutional Research (1109) to its membership and other interested persons. It is compiled from abstracts submitted by AIR members. Some 250 institutional research projects are cited, briefly described, and organized under 10 subject headings.

442 OPPENHEIM, ABRAHAM N. *Questionnaire design and attitude measurement.* New York: Basic Books, 1966, 298 pp. $6.95.

This practical handbook outlines step-by-step procedures for the design of questionnaires of various types. The author summarizes and evaluates major findings related to the topic and provides examples from commercial and academic research. Specific chapters discuss problems of design, question wording, checklists, rating scales, and inventories. Following chapters deal with attitude statements and scaling methods, projective techniques, and the quantification of data. Each chapter is followed by a short annotated bibliography.

443 ROUECHE, JOHN E., AND BOGGS, JOHN R. *Junior college institutional research: The state of the art.* Wash., D. C.: American Association of Junior Colleges, 1968, 66 pp. $2.

This report is based on a survey of institutional research in 70 junior colleges. It provides numerous examples of studies in individual colleges and summary statistics on the nature of institutional research activities in junior colleges. Among the authors' conclusions is the conviction that an essential ingredient in a successful institutional research program is a clear commitment on the part of the institution's president.

444 SAUPE, JOE L. *Memo to a newcomer to the field of institutional research.* Berkeley, Calif.: Association for Institutional Research, 1967, 16 pp. (Mimeographed)

This pamphlet gives a brief orientation to the field of institutional research and answers several specific questions of interest to any newcomer in the field. It identifies the major institutional research offices, academic centers for the study of higher education, regional and national organizations and agencies, and professional organizations. In addition, the memo includes a briefly annotated bibliography on institutional research.

445 SAUPE, JOE L., AND MONTGOMERY, JAMES R. *The nature and role of institutional research . . . Memo to a college or university.* Berkeley, Calif.: Association for Institutional Research, 1970, 18 pp. (Mimeographed)

This brief memorandum is useful in acquainting college administrators with the nature and purpose of institutional research. It outlines a number of functions institutional research can serve on the campus and states 10 essential requirements for an effective program of institutional research.

446 STECKLEIN, JOHN E. Institutional research, in Asa S. Knowles (Ed.), *Handbook of college and university administration.* Vol. I. *General.* New York: McGraw-Hill, 1970, sec. 4, pp. 123-135.

The author provides practical information on the establishment and operation of offices of institutional research. Individual sections discuss the functions of institutional research as an evaluational unit, the organization and administration of institutional research offices, operational fields for research, staffing, and suggested reading.

447 VAN NESS, ROBERT G. *Principles of punched card data processing.* (3rd. ed.) Elmhurst, Ill.: Business Press, 1962, 321 pp. $10.85.

Despite the rapid move to electronic computers for data processing, punched-card equipment is still widely used for administrative and research purposes.

"Slow" punched-card methods will likely continue to be a mainstay of many limited data-processing operations because of their relatively low cost, flexibility, and simplicity. This successful book provides a comprehensive introduction to the use of punched-card methods. It is an especially useful reference for anyone unfamiliar with these methods but moving into a position that depends on their use or service.

448 WRIGHT, PATRICIA S. (ED.) *Institutional research and communication in higher education.* 10th Annual Forum. Berkeley, Calif.: Association for Institutional Research, 1970, 279 pp. $6.

The 83 papers presented in this book cover many aspects of the forum theme: the responsibility of the institutional researcher to communicate with the important constituents of higher education relevant information on current problems of education. Papers are grouped by general topic (communication of policy, long-range planning, management information systems), as well as by specific areas of concern (communicating with state agencies, administrative units, instructional units, students, etc.). Proceedings of annual forums for the years 1966 through 1969 are: 1966—*Research on Academic Input;* 1967—*The Instructional Process and Institutional Research;* 1968—*Institutional Research and Academic Outcomes;* and 1969—*The Challenge and Response of Institutional Research.* Copies of these earlier reports can be obtained at $6 each from the Office of Institutional Research, Claremont University Center, Claremont, California 91711.

5.5—PREDICTION. Too often prediction is perceived rather narrowly as a means of estimating what sort of freshman average an applicant is likely to earn. Prediction is actually a formal methodology for dealing with various types of alternative decisions in student guidance, college admissions, the educational process, and evaluation in general.

The references cited here include descriptions of various types of prediction problems and the techniques involved. They also include some key references on problems that have generated much interest in recent years—such issues as the use of grade adjustments to improve prediction, biographical information as a predictor, and prediction of nonacademic performance. A good general treatment of the prediction model is found in 309.

449 ANASTASI, ANNE, MEADE, MARTIN J., AND SCHNEIDERS, ALEXANDER A. *The validation of a biographical inventory as a predictor of college success.* Research Monograph No. 1. New York: College Entrance Examination Board, 1960, 81 pp. $2.50.

This careful study examined the validity of the biographical inventory as a predictor of nonintellective measures of success in college. A variety of college records and ratings were used to choose from each of two Fordham College classes 50 students considered positive, 50 average, and 50 negative in relation to the kind of person the college aimed to develop. Correlations between the "success" standing and the score on the biographical inventory revealed that the inventory was a better predictor than other achievement, personality, interest, and aptitude tests. The study is important as an exploration of nonintellectual criteria of college success. It also provided an early demonstration of the feasibility of predicting criteria other than grades.

450 BAIRD, LEONARD L. Factors in the continuance of accomplishment from high school to college. *Measurement and Evaluation in Guidance,* 1969, vol. 2, pp. 5-18.

Addressing the question of why some students with outstanding records of high school achievement continue to perform in college while others do not, this study examines the personal characteristics of achievers and nonachievers in high school and college. A variety of assessment devices was used in following up a sample of students who had participated in the American College Survey in 1964-65. The author finds little likelihood that high school nonachievers reverse the pattern in college, but, he points out, "Apparently one of the effects of college is to turn high school achievers into college nonachievers." He describes the best predictors of continuing achievement as: (1) prior achievement, (2) self-ratings, and (3) life goals relevant to fields of achievement. He concludes that the high school achiever who is also successful in college is distinguished by "his life goals, a broad range of relevant experiences and skills, and a self-concept that is a manifestation of his interest, capacity, and persistence in his area."

451 BAIRD, LEONARD L. Prediction of accomplishment in college: A study of achievement. *Journal of Counseling Psychology,* 1969, vol. 16, pp. 246-253.

In this study the author examines what sorts of variables are useful in predicting accomplishment in specific activities at a later date. On the basis of this and other studies, he concludes that the best predictors are past achievements in the same area, but the student's self-rating of his competency and life goals also gives good indications of future achievement. Many types of college achievement can be usefully predicted by the most simple and most direct questions concerning prior activities. The author suggests that more attention should be concentrated on the development of reliable measures of goals and self-description rather than attempting to develop new scales of "some universal creative mind."

452 BLOOM, BENJAMIN S., AND PETERS, FRANK R. *The use of academic prediction scales for counseling and selecting college entrants.* New York: Free Press, 1961, 145 pp. $6.50.

The authors examine various methods by which available data may be used for improved prediction of academic achievement in college. Three types of evidence have been widely used in predicting college achievement—high school grades, aptitude test scores, and achievement test scores. Of these three, high school grades have been found to be the best single type of evidence from which to predict; however, institutional variation in grading standards presents a problem. The authors maintain that by using adjustment and scaling techniques, institutional differences can be taken into account, and correlations between high school and college grades "reach the level of +.70 to +.80 in contrast with the usual level of about +.50."

This result was discounted by other authors, and subsequent research demonstrated that such adjustments make little if any difference in predictive accuracy when grades are combined with an aptitude test score. See 462, 463, 469.

453 COLLEGE ENTRANCE EXAMINATION BOARD. *A staff aid for the interpretation and implementation of validity studies.* New York: College Entrance Examination Board, 1969, 50 pp. (Mimeographed)

The technical aspects of prediction are well covered in this report. It assumes no special background and provides a brief introduction to statistical concepts. The report is designed for use with the College Board Validity Study Service (1221). A companion document, *Designing Validity Studies and Collecting Data,* is also available free of charge from the College Board.

454 FINGER, JOHN A., AND SCHLESSER, GEORGE E. Academic performance of public and private school students. *Journal of Educational Psychology,* 1963, vol. 54, pp. 118-122.

Several studies have substantiated the fact that, as a group, public school students receive higher grades in college than do private school students. Several reasons have been suggested to account for this difference. In this study the authors hypothesized that private school students do less well because they are lower in scholastic aptitude and motivation.

The study sample consisted of 313 Colgate University students; 97 had attended private schools and 216 public schools. Grades were regressed for the verbal and mathematical sections of the College Board Scholastic Aptitude Test (SAT-V and SAT-M); the Ohio State Psychological Examination (OSPE); and the Personal Values Inventory (PVI). The group means did not differ significantly. Thus, the authors contend that when the two groups are equated for both motivation and academic aptitude, most if not all of the difference between them is accounted for. Other studies have not included any measure of motivation (here represented by the Personal Values Inventory), and it is frequently assumed that superior motivation results in superior grades of public school graduates.

455 FISHMAN, JOSHUA A., AND PASANELLA, ANN K. College admission-selection studies. *Review of Educational Research,* 1960, vol. 30, pp. 298-310.

This article is one of the basic references on the technology of college admissions. Pointing to the 580 studies of admission to college and selection of applicants done in 1949-1959, the authors rate this topic as the most intensively explored topic in educational psychology in that decade. Noteworthy studies using both intellective and nonintellective predictors are discussed by the authors, and they suggest that the true potential of nonintellective predictors will not be realized until a solid theoretical foundation is laid and nonintellective criteria are outlined for researchers to aim at. The authors conclude with the hope that a new influx of intellectual forces in this area will help to anchor admissions procedures, with a philosophy of education at one end and social science theory and methods at the other. In this way consideration of the educational-societal goals upon which admissions should rest will catch up with mass testing and operational routinization. Whereas routine prediction studies have indeed diminished greatly since this article was written, it can hardly be said that systematic methods and philosophy of education have filled the vacuum in the crises of open admissions.

456 FREEBERG, NORMAN E. The Biographical Information Blank as a predictor of student achievement: A review. *Psychological Reports,* 1967, vol. 20, pp. 911-925.

During the 1960s the Biographical Information Blank became the subject of considerable interest in various types of student research. This article provides a good summary of the literature of one aspect of that interest—potential improvement in the prediction of college achievement. The author discusses the literature as it relates to four types of college achievement: grades, creative achievement, persistence in school, and vocational or curriculum choice. Among his conclusions the author notes that there is still considerable controversy surrounding the notion of using biographical information for predictions that might routinely support administrative decisions such as selective admissions.

457 HILLS, JOHN R. Prediction of college grades for all public colleges of a state. *Journal of Educational Measurement,* 1964, vol. 1, pp. 155-159.

The data reported in this comprehensive state study support the generalization that first-year college grades can be predicted with useful accuracy using only high school averages and test scores. Data were collected from all publicly supported institutions of higher education in the state of Georgia for the years 1958 through 1962. Thus 19 different public institutions yielded 175 sets of data involving 27,961 different students. Using high school grades as the only predictor, correlations with first-year college grades were found to average 0.55. Adding College Board Scholastic Aptitude Test scores produced multiple correlations that averaged about 0.65. The mean level of the correlations remained quite stable from year to year.

458 HOLLAND, JOHN L., AND ASTIN, ALEXANDER W. The prediction of the academic, artistic, scientific, and social achievement of undergraduates of superior scholastic aptitude. *Journal of Educational Psychology,* 1962, vol. 53, pp. 132-143.

The authors used high school background information to predict undergraduate achievement in academic, artistic, scientific, and social areas for four samples of high-aptitude students. The criteria of college achievement were grades and checklists of unusual accomplishments such as publications, prizes, or awards. Predictors included aptitude, personality measures, originality, interest, and other background information. The authors concluded from the analysis that achievers in these various areas resemble stereotypes of the scientist, artist, leader, and academic achiever.

459 HOLLAND, JOHN L., AND NICHOLS, ROBERT C. Prediction of academic and extracurricular achievement in college. *Journal of Educational Psychology,* 1964, vol. 55, pp. 55-65.

This study was somewhat similar to an earlier effort to predict extracurricular achievement in college (458), but in this research the authors put special emphasis on Potential Achievement Scales based on common activities in high school. The results indicated that past behavior is the best predictor of future behavior; that is, special types of accomplishment in college can be predicted with reasonable accuracy by prior evidence of similar accomplishment in secondary school. This research was a forerunner of some of the more significant developmental work subsequently undertaken by Holland at the American College Testing Program.

460 HORST, PAUL. The differential prediction of success in various college course areas. *College and University,* 1956, vol. 31, pp. 456-471.

During World War II psychologists developed effective methods of predicting differential success in different types of military training. The mathematical and the programmatic development of differential prediction is particularly attributable to Paul Horst, who implemented a differential prediction system at the University of Washington. This article provides a comprehensive nontechnical description of differential prediction as it applies to college admissions and guidance. While differential prediction is theoretically of considerable importance in student guidance, it has not been successfully implemented to the extent informed observers initially expected. The reason for this is probably that most college curriculums are fairly similar in the sense that they require similar student abilities. Consequently, differential prediction of success in different areas is often not sufficiently effective to warrant the effort.

461 LAVIN, DAVID E. *The prediction of academic performance: A theoretical analysis and review of research.* New York: Russell Sage Foundation, 1965, 182 pp. $6.50.

This reference is included because it is the only book available on academic prediction that is not highly technical—but the reader should beware. The book was written from a sociological perspective and omits any reference to some of the most significant developments in prediction from 1955 to 1965.

462 LINDQUIST, E. F. An evaluation of a technique for scaling high school grades to improve prediction of college success. *Educational and Psychological Measurement,* 1963, vol. 23, pp. 623-646.

In this study conducted by the American College Testing Program, several forms of analysis were utilized in an attempt to ascertain a practical method of scaling a large number of schools and colleges in order to adjust high school grades to make them better predictors of college grades. Records of a sample of 9,364 students attending 31 different colleges were examined. Two methods of scaling grades were used. "Method A" consisted of scaling the grades for each high school with reference to all colleges collectively. "Method B" involved first scaling the college grades with reference to high school grades in general, and then scaling the high school grades with reference to the scaled college grades. The study showed a very small improvement in predictive ability as a result of such internal scaling, and it was concluded that "the internal method of scaling is not a promising way of improving the prediction of college grades." See 452, 463, and 469 for related articles.

463 LINN, ROBERT L. *Grade adjustments for prediction of academic performance: A review.* College Entrance Examination Board Research and Development Reports, no. 18. Princeton, N. J.: Educational Testing Service, 1965. 27 pp.

High school grades or class rank has generally been considered to be the best single predictor of college grades; however, wide variations exist among secondary schools regarding their students, curriculums, and grading standards. Several techniques for making grade adjustments have been developed, and these are reviewed and evaluated on the basis of the empirical results that accrued from the application of these techniques. The author concludes that "the improvement in predictive validity due to the use of adjusted grades as compared to unadjusted grades has generally been discouragingly small. The slight improvement that has been found for zero-order correlations has usually disappeared for multiple correlations which include standardized test scores as predictors." It is recommended that a minimum requirement for future research on the question should be "the inclusion of multiple correlation results involving a standardized test variable." See 452, 462, and 469 for related articles.

464 MICHAEL, WILLIAM B. Prediction, in Robert L. Ebel (Ed.), *Encyclopedia of educational research.* (4th ed.) New York: Macmillan, 1969, pp. 982-992.

This article presents a good general overview of the principles and procedures of prediction. The author discusses such topics as types of prediction problems, guiding principles in the development of prediction devices, statistical methods, expectancy tables, and procedures for prediction of multiple criterion measures. In each area the reader is referred to several basic works that provide comprehensive discussions of the topic. This article is nontechnical in format but assumes some familiarity with statistical techniques.

465 RICHARDS, JAMES M. JR., HOLLAND, JOHN L., AND LUTZ, SANDRA W. Prediction of student accomplishment in college. *Journal of Educational Psychology,* 1967, vol. 58, pp. 343-355.

This important study involved the prediction of accomplishment in college from different types of student achievement in high school. It included over 9,000 students who participated in the American College Survey just prior to entering college. Follow-up data were obtained in 1965—for some students it was the end of freshman, for others the end of sophomore year. Instruments for prediction were American College Testing Program scores, high school grades, and six scales assessing nonacademic high school accomplishment. The criterion for achievement in the follow-up inventory included college grades, 12 scales measuring accomplishment outside the classroom, and one scale measuring academic accomplishment. Correlations of the data revealed that: (1) academic and nonacademic accomplishment can be usefully predicted; and (2) nonacademic accomplishment is largely independent of academic potential or success. These conclusions are the same as those for previous similar studies, but they have added importance because they are based on students with a broad range of academic potential.

466 SCHRADER, W. B. The predictive validity of College Board admissions tests, in William H. Angoff (Ed.), *The College Board Admissions Testing Program*. New York: College Entrance Examination Board, 1971, pp. 117-145.

This chapter provides a useful introduction to the practical aspects of predicting college grades. It covers such topics as the design of conventional or special purpose validity studies, the development of appropriate criteria, and the interpretation of results. There is also included considerable documentation of the validity of the Scholastic Aptitude Test and the Achievement Tests of the College Board Admissions Testing Program. Various tables summarize a large number of studies pertaining to the validity of the SAT, incremental validity added by inclusion of the Achievement Tests, and validity of the Achievement Tests against grades in relevant courses.

467 THORNDIKE, ROBERT L. *The concepts of over- and under-achievement*. New York: Teachers College Press, Columbia University, 1963, 79 pp. $3.25.

Over- and underachievement are actually failures in accurate prediction of achievement. The consequent research problems involve developing more accurate measures or methods of raising the level of achievement. Data are frequently imperfect because of: (1) errors of measurement; (2) heterogeneity of achievement (for example, an A at Harvard is not the same as an A at "Podunk College"); (3) limited scope—no predictor can include *all* the determinants of a behavioral outcome; and (4) modification of personal factors by intervening events such as the death of a parent. The author describes in simple language the basic types of research problems involving over- and underachievement and suggests useful ways of approaching those problems through systematic research.

468 WHITLA, DEAN K. Evaluation of decision making: A study of college admissions, in Dean K. Whitla (Ed.), *Handbook of measurement and assessment in behavioral sciences*. Menlo Park, Calif.: Addison-Wesley, 1968, pp. 456-490.

Admission to Harvard is a painstaking process for all concerned. It is also supported by an unusually elaborate and sophisticated system of information and predictions. In a somewhat technical but illuminating paper, Whitla describes prediction technology at Harvard and, incidentally, at its best.

469 WILLINGHAM, WARREN W. Adjusting college prediction on the basis of academic origins, in Martin Katz (Ed.), *The twentieth yearbook of the National Council on Measurement in Education*. East Lansing, Mich.: NCME, 1963, pp. 1-6.

It has often been assumed that the prediction of college grades can be improved by adjusting the high school average on the basis of the high school origin. Bloom and Peters (452) fanned this assumption. This article reports on the first systematic study in which several spurious sources of enhanced predictions were simultaneously controlled after such grade adjustments had been made. The results indicated that grade adjustments serve no useful purpose when predictions are based on high school achievement plus a standardized aptitude test. See 462 for a more extensive study and 463 for a subsequent summary of related research.

470 WILLINGHAM, WARREN W. The interpretation of relative achievement. *American Educational Research Journal*, 1964, vol. 1, pp. 101-112.

471

─────────

5.6
Follow-up
and Dropout
Studies

The comparison of relative achievement on two measures is perhaps the most common form of psychometric interpretation. A prevalent form of such interpretation is the so-called over- or underachievement which results from comparing a performance measure and some type of aptitude measure. Most research on this topic amounts to a distorted form of the multivariate prediction problem. This article outlines the logical and statistical properties of two forms of relative achievement. The author maintains that valid interpretation and effective educational treatment are dependent upon certain types of empirical research that are largely nonexistent. Several necessary conditions for the evaluation of relative achievement are outlined and described with illustrative cases.

471 WILLINGHAM, WARREN W. The application blank as a predictive instrument. *College and University*, 1965, vol. 40, pp. 271-281.

While there are innumerable studies concerned with the prediction of academic success in college, relatively few have systematically examined information routinely available on the college application blank. The results of this study indicated that such information, properly coded and summed into a single score, can predict freshman grade-point averages with about the same accuracy as high school grades. This type of information did add significantly to the predictive efficiency of either the College Board Scholastic Aptitude Test score or high school grade record taken alone, but relatively little when the two were combined. The same sort of analysis was not particularly successful in predicting which students would drop out of college. Whereas the study seems reasonably straightforward as far as it goes, the author gives relatively little attention to the social and ethical problems involved when this type of personal information is used as a partial basis for administrative decisions in selective admissions.

5.6—*FOLLOW-UP AND DROPOUT STUDIES*. There have probably been thousands of studies concerned with the conditions under which students leave college. Much of this literature is trivial and repetitious, but the problem is especially important because it represents a significant type of criterion in the access process. Student achievement in traditional academic terms (grades) is an insufficient criterion of the outcome of access to higher education for obvious reasons. Some students with excellent grades drop out, and of those who complete educational programs many have negative reactions to the experience.

Some of the most interesting literature on this general question has been anecdotal reports in the popular press. One reason that there has been relatively little systematic, high-quality research on the experiences and impressions of students after they leave educational institutions is the fact that this type of study requires a longitudinal analysis over time that is unusually difficult from a logistical standpoint and surprisingly expensive. A more subtle reason is the fact that there is no immediate administrative necessity for this type of research.

The studies included here are highly selected. Most fall into one of three categories. There is the necessary social bookkeeping that produces estimates of the extent of dropping out and so forth. There is also the literature concerned with the causes and consequences of student withdrawal. Finally, there are those follow-up studies intended to evaluate the nature and effect of the educational process (e.g., 480).

472 BAYER, ALAN E. The college drop-out: Factors affecting senior college completion. *Sociology of Education*, 1968, vol. 41, pp. 305-316.

This extensive analysis based on a follow-up of 8,567 Project TALENT students indicates that only about one-fourth of the variance in dropping out vs. completing senior college can be associated with aptitude and background factors. The inclusion of 38 such variables in a multiple regression equation illustrated again the difficulty of predicting college attrition with any great degree of accuracy. Aptitude measures and marriage and family variables emerged as primary predictors of college progress, and it is suggested that "relatively high multivariate probability predictions of college completion might prove possible if there were specification of various subgroups within the dropout group — such as dropping out due to financial reasons, to poor academic performance, or to marriage and parenthood — as well as further specification of the type of college attended."

473 ECKLAND, BRUCE K. College dropouts who came back. *Harvard Educational Review*, 1964, vol. 34, pp. 402-420.

This exceptionally careful 1962 dropout study was based on male students who had entered the University of Illinois in 1952. Data were obtained from university records, from a mail questionnaire to the former students, which yielded 94 percent response, and from 104 colleges and universities that supplied the records of transfer and graduation elsewhere. It was found that 50.3 percent of the sample dropped out of college for a time before graduation. Of these dropouts, 70.2 percent returned sometime during the 10 years following matriculation, and of those who came back, 54.9 percent went on to graduate during the 10-year period. Counting those students still working toward the degree, and allowing for nonrespondents, Eckland predicts that a probable 70.8 percent will eventually attain degrees. He concludes that the 10-year rate of graduation found in this study "may be considered a conservative estimate of the rate for a very large segment of the American male population." While this conclusion may be too optimistic, the study did dramatize the errors in the attrition estimates that resulted from not taking into account long-range persistence and transferring to second or third colleges.

474 ECKLAND, BRUCE K. Social class and college graduation: Some misconceptions corrected. *American Journal of Sociology*, 1964, vol. 70, pp. 36-50.

The author summarizes a number of earlier studies, most of which indicate little or no relationship between socioeconomic level and persistence in college. Data given in this article, from a large state university, do indicate such a relationship, and Eckland attributes the effect to cultural aspects of class rather than economic factors.

475 FLORIDA COMMUNITY JUNIOR COLLEGE INTER-INSTITUTIONAL RESEARCH COUNCIL. *Where are they now? A follow-up study of first time in college freshmen in Florida's community junior colleges in Fall 1966.* Tallahassee, Fla.: Institute of Higher Education, University of Florida, 1969, 55 pp. (Mimeographed)

This 1969 follow-up study of students who had entered Florida community junior colleges in fall 1966 undertakes to determine their educational progress and to find out how they valued their college experience. Students gave a very positive rating to their experience in junior college. However, the report cites difficulties in interpreting some of the data because of ambiguous wording of some of the questions. The report concludes by urging the establishment of a state-wide student information system that would provide uniform and easily retrievable data on students in the Florida community college system—a system regarded as one of the most highly developed in the nation. With such an information system, follow-up studies "could provide insights of a scope and depth that are not at present possible."

476 HOYT, DONALD P. *The relationship between college grades and adult achievement. A review of the literature.* ACT Research Report No. 7. Iowa City, Iowa: American College Testing Service, 1965, 57 pp.

This discussion of the "meaning of grades" reviews 46 studies relating college grades to postcollege achievement, both in vocational prestige and nonvocational accomplishments. Although the author observes a need for methodological refinement in this area of research, he does conclude that from the evidence available so far, college grades have at best only a small correlation with adult success. Since Hoyt views college grades as "falling far short as comprehensive measures of professional promise," he calls reliance on grades an "indefensible policy" for admission to graduate and professional schools. He proposes as an alternative policy the use of a "profile of student growth and development" that would identify students with great potential for professional contributions.

447 IFFERT, ROBERT E. *Retention and withdrawal of college students.* Wash., D. C.: Government Printing Office, 1957, 177 pp. 65 cents.

Concern over the "educational mortality rate of capable students" led to this survey of the extent and character of retention, transfer, and withdrawal of approximately 13,600 students who matriculated in higher education institutions in fall 1950. The author estimates that, according to the results of this sample, slightly less than 40 percent of a freshman class will remain and graduate four years later; another 20 percent will graduate later either from the first or a transfer institution. He also sees the first year of college as the most critical dropout period, since almost as many drop out during the freshman year as leave during the next three years. He also points to the effect of selective admissions in comparing the persistence of students attending public institutions with those attending private, non-church-related institutions; almost half the students who matriculate at a private institution finish in four years, but only one-third of those who enter a public institution earn a degree in four consecutive years. However, the survey coincided with the country's involvement in the Korean War, which meant that military service was a major factor in dropout figures. Despite some methodological flaws, this is without doubt the classic empirical study of college attrition.

478 IFFERT, ROBERT E., AND CLARKE, BETTY S. *College applicants, entrants, dropouts.* Wash., D. C.: Government Printing Office, 1965, 88 pp. 35 cents.

This monograph reports a follow-up of the senior author's classic study of college dropouts (477). Individual studies were undertaken on 20 campuses; the design and interpretation of findings were coordinated by the authors. The institutional studies gave special attention to multiple applications, "no-show" students who are admitted but do not enroll, and sources of funds for defraying college expenses. The study generated some potentially useful information, but there was a somewhat unusual selection of colleges (practically all east of the Mississippi). Also, the fact that the data were somewhat dated by the time of publication limits the value of the findings.

479 KNOELL, DOROTHY M. A critical review of research on the college dropout, in Lawrence A. Pervin, Louis E. Reik, and Willard Dalrymple (Eds.), *The college dropout and the utilization of talent.* Princeton, N. J.: Princeton University Press, 1966, pp. 63-81.

This chapter has special value for its forthright diagnosis of weaknesses in current research on student attrition, and its proposal for a new focus in future studies. The author points to "some questionable assumptions" that blur the findings of recent research, particularly the reliance on the stability of gross attrition rates over an extended time period, and the taking-for-granted that every student has both the ability and motivation to complete a baccalaureate program. She also would declare a moratorium on "autopsy studies" that use case history approaches in favor of a "many-pronged" attack on attrition as a part of the general study of the flow of students in higher education. Her program would start with a new national census study, accompanied by research on special aspects of the problem: the long-term effects of failure, "sporadic attenders," follow-up studies on student mobility among institutions, college environmental press, and junior college attendance patterns.

480 MARKS, EDMOND. Student perceptions of college persistence, and their intellective, personality and performance correlates. *Journal of Educational Psychology,* 1967, vol. 58, pp. 210-221.

This study surveyed some 300 randomly selected freshmen entering Pennsylvania State University in 1965. It is the first in a series of studies of student expectancies planned to continue through and beyond college to include job attitudes. This technically sophisticated study approaches college dropouts as "the behavioral outcome of a decisional process" where the students specify the perceptions, cognitions, and stimuli relevant to that decision. Marks notes that the students arrived at college with certain well-formed perceptions, adding "If you want to know whether a student is a potential college dropout, a good starting place is simply to ask him." They emphasized that the important factors were: (1) academic and work skills, (2) motivation, and (3) adjustment or coping behavior. Their own expectancies regarding withdrawal were related to their level of aspiration, fear of failure, and parental attitude. Of particular importance is the role of parents; in comparing the group who showed high probability of becoming dropouts with the low probability group, Marks found the likely dropouts much more concerned about satisfying the expectations of their parents. Three times as many students in the probable dropout group withdrew in the course of the three terms as did students in the low probable group.

481 NICHOLS, ROBERT C., AND ASTIN, ALEXANDER W. Progress of the Merit Scholar: An eight year follow-up. *Personnel and Guidance Journal,* 1966, vol. 44, pp. 673-681.

To find out what achievements can be expected from high-talent National Merit Scholars, a follow-up study was done in 1964 of the 3,106 students who had been awarded Merit Scholarships in the first four years of the program (1956-59). The overwhelming majority had finished college, and of those with B.A.s, 87 percent of the men and 69 percent of the women were enrolled in graduate school. In addition many more had plans for eventual graduate study. Fields of graduate study chosen by men were more likely to be mathematics, physical sciences, humanities, or medicine than education, theology, or dentistry; women were more likely to be studying law or biological sciences. Over half of the men and one-third of the women planned to obtain a PH.D. Career choices as of 1964 compared with those given at the time of the scholarship award showed a decline in plans to go into scientific research and engineering, initially the most popular fields. Two-thirds of the men and three-fourths of the women reported they had made major changes in career plans during college.

482 NICHOLSON, EVERARD. *Success and admission criteria for potentially successful risks.* Providence, R. I.: Project under grant from the Ford Foundation, Brown University, 1970, 248 pp. (Mimeographed)

This massive study of so-called risk students was based on males entering Brown University in the early 1950s and late 1960s. The study gained a good deal of attention because of its general conclusions that risk students admitted to Brown did well on several success criteria. The findings of the study were undermined, however, by unusually liberal definitions of "risk"—a student with a College Board Scholastic Aptitude Test verbal score below 620 for example.

483 O'CONNOR, THOMAS J. *Follow-up studies in junior colleges.* Wash., D. C.: American Association of Junior Colleges, 1965, 75 pp. $1.50.

This useful report is intended to encourage the sorts of follow-up studies that can help two-year colleges improve their programs and services. It includes general discussion of a wide variety of study topics and their possible usefulness. The author gives more attention to general suggestions than to methodology, but he does devote one section to follow-up procedures. An especially valuable aspect of the report is the inclusion of a number of follow-up forms and questionnaires in the appendix.

484 PANOS, ROBERT J., AND ASTIN, ALEXANDER W. *Attrition among college students.* ACE Research Reports, vol. 2, no. 4. Wash., D. C.: American Council on Education, 1967, 10 pp. Also in *American Educational Research Journal,* 1968, vol. 5, pp. 57-72.

This 1965 longitudinal study followed up 36,000 students four years after their college matriculation in 1961. Those who did not complete four years of college came from lower socioeconomic backgrounds, had lower high school grade records, and had lower levels of educational aspiration. The findings suggest that students are more likely to complete four years if they attend colleges with favorable student-peer relationships, a high degree of student participation in college activities, permissive administrative policies, and a high level of concern for the individual student.

485 PERRONE, PHILIP A., AND LINS, L. JOSEPH. *Post-secondary activities of Spring 1968 high school seniors.* Madison, Wis.: Wisconsin Coordinating Council for Higher Education, 1970, 76 pp. (Mimeographed)

This follow-up of 1968 graduating high school seniors was conducted to determine their actual educational and vocational choices as compared to preferences determined in an earlier survey (see 683). The report presents and analyzes data concerning the general activities of three groups of graduates between 1968 and 1970: those who anticipated continued education but did not enroll, those who attended institutions of higher education as planned, and those who entered institutions but later withdrew or transferred. Finally, the report examines the relationship of high school performance and family background variables to post-high school activities.

486 PERVIN, LAWRENCE A., REIK, LOUIS E., AND DALRYMPLE, WILLARD (EDS.) *The college dropout and the utilization of talent.* Princeton, N. J.: Princeton University Press, 1966, 260 pp. $6.50.

The phenomenon of college dropouts, particularly from prestige institutions, became a matter of such social concern in the early 1960s that Princeton University called a special conference in 1964. This book includes the discussions of participants, who sought to probe the causes and effects and suggest some solutions. Their interpretations represent a wide range of concerns—psychiatric, academic, and outcomes in later life. They examine the complicated personal and institutional factors that influence the student's decision to leave college, and investigate family attitudes, personality traits that contribute to the student's difficulties, the effectiveness of psychiatric treatment, and decisions on readmission. Many of the contributions have a clinical orientation that makes the book's contents interesting reading but difficult to generalize. One chapter (479) presents a critical review of research literature on the dropout.

487 SCHREIBER, DANIEL. Dropout—causes and consequences, in Robert L. Ebel (Ed.), *Encyclopedia of educational research.* (4th ed.) New York: Macmillan, 1969, pp. 308-316.

This article focuses on the high school dropout. It provides a useful national picture of the educational and employment problems associated with attrition at the secondary level. Special attention is devoted to the characteristics of students who leave school.

488 SPADY, WILLIAM G. Dropouts from higher education: An interdisciplinary review and synthesis. *Interchange,* 1970, vol. 1, pp. 64-85.

In this first of a pair of articles, the author undertakes a review of prior significant work on college dropouts. On the basis of a methodological critique and theoretical analysis, he concludes that a much broader interdisciplinary approach is necessary to understand the phenomena involved. He presents a sociological model in which both the academic and the social systems of the university are included as frameworks from which the dropout process must be examined. See 489 for an empirical test of the model.

489 SPADY, WILLIAM G. Dropouts from higher education: Toward an empirical model. *Interchange,* 1971, vol. 2, no. 3, pp. 38-62.

In this empirical test of a model reported earlier (488), the author uses data based on 683 freshmen at the University of Chicago, to broaden understanding of the dropout process. Multiple regression analysis is used to assess the independent contribution of such factors as family and previous educational background, academic potential, grade performance, social integration, etc. The author concludes that personal and social development play an important role, but formal academic performance is clearly the dominant factor in accounting for attrition.

490 SPAETH, JOE L., AND GREELEY, ANDREW M. *Recent alumni and higher education: A survey of college graduates.* New York: McGraw-Hill, 1970, 199 pp. $6.95.

This follow-up study of the class of 1961 is intended to determine what college graduates think of their education and how it might be improved. The authors report a variety of interesting findings including their general conclusion that alumni see the main function of college as cognitive and personal development. They further suggest that the payoff for a student in graduating from one of the elite institutions is not as great as most people seem to think.

491 SUMMERSKILL, JOHN. Dropouts from college, in Nevitt Sanford (Ed.), *The American college.* New York: John Wiley, 1962, pp. 627-657.

This well-known chapter presents a fairly comprehensive summary of the existing research literature on college attrition in the early 1960s. Two basic areas are considered—the rate of attrition and factors associated with it. The variation in the rate of attrition reported in 35 studies ranged from 12 percent to 82 percent. On the average, Summerskill reports that American colleges and universities lose approximately half their students in the four years after matriculation. Some 40 percent of college students graduate on schedule, while an additional 20 percent also eventually graduate.

492 VOCATIONS FOR SOCIAL CHANGE. *Vocations for social change: May-June 1970.* Canyon, Calif.: VSC, 1970, 64 pp.

This fascinating newsletter is a potpourri of articles, news items, and especially job listings directed to the individual seeking alternative life styles that allow "personal creativity and collective action against injustice." Put out by Vocations for Social Change—a clearinghouse for information pertaining to institutional change—it seeks to share information on job opportunities that do not perpetuate "de-humanized life styles and ecological and psychological disasters" of basic existing institutions. It is addressed to social dropouts of all varieties.

493 WENRICH, J. WILLIAM, HANIGAN, JANE, AND PFLUG, RAYMOND. *Keeping dropouts in: Retention of students identified as high probability dropouts.* San Mateo, Calif.: College of San Mateo, 1971, 28 pp. (Multilithed)
    This study is interesting not so much because of its results (which are not especially clear cut), but because it represents an all-too-rare institutional effort to examine systematically the effectiveness of special programs. Results indicated that potential dropouts who used learning-center counseling were more successful in course work and had a lower dropout rate than a matched group of students who were not involved in the learning center.

SECTION 6: MANPOWER UTILIZATION

Students utilize higher education in many different ways—for individual advancement, cultural enrichment, personal gratification, etc. There is not much evident interest among educators in identifying and evaluating most types of educational outcomes. But in the past two decades, there has been growing interest and an increasing amount of work on the ways in which higher education facilitates effective use of manpower. This field includes the theoretical connection between human and educational resources and the practical problem of preparing a person for a job.

The importance of manpower utilization as an access process lies in the fact that it represents a highly specific form of payoff—to the individual and to society. Higher education has by now ceased to provide its own reason for being. The public has assumed that higher education serves an effective and vital function in hard economic terms, but recently the concept of accountability has put such assumptions to test.

Consequently, effective manpower utilization plays a central role in maintaining a liberal public view of the access process. There are several reasons why this is so. First, and perhaps most obvious, higher education is becoming increasingly expensive in relation to competing worthwhile uses for public and personal funds. Second, modern industrial society feeds on educated manpower, and some social institution has to provide it. Third, advancing technology requires adaptive education and skill development, not simply training for specific jobs. And finally, it is increasingly recognized that educational opportunity is not synonymous with economic opportunity, and the latter is probably the ultimate interest of most people.

In theory, manpower utilization should be coordinated with admissions, guidance, and financing of higher education. It should also be based on effective communication between curriculum planners and manpower specialists. This is all good theory, but those relationships are not well worked out, and practical implications have received even less attention.

6.1 – *MANPOWER RESOURCES*. Work in this area is as diverse as the topic itself. It includes theory, statistical reports, various types of forecasts, and numerous reports of governmental or quasipublic bodies. The individuals involved are largely manpower specialists, sociologists, demographers, and public officials. A good general reference is available in a softcover book edited by Mangum (499).

Of the many problems in this area, three are particularly important. Accurate anticipation of future manpower needs is a vital, but relatively new, field of interest (see 498). The current manpower situation is perhaps the problem of greatest public interest. A key document is the annual manpower report of the President (503). There is also recognition of a need for other more humanistic forms of social reporting (502). And finally, there is continued interest in more effective utilization of manpower resources (see 495). The United States Department of Labor is the central agency concerned with human resources. Internationally, the Organization for Economic Cooperation and Development (1138) is a leading organization in this field. Two journals of special significance are the *OECD Observer* (1340) and the *Journal of Human Resources* (1328).

494 BAYER, ALAN E. The effect of international interchange of high-level manpower on the United States. *Social Forces,* 1968, vol. 4, pp. 465-477.

In this report the author has gathered and summarized information supporting the general assumption that the United States incurs short-run losses in educational costs but long-run gains in the international movement of trained manpower. While the proportionate contribution of foreign manpower to the United States is relatively small, the author holds that the consequences of manpower losses to other nations is largely unknown. He cites the need for more precise information, though such advice may now be too late to abate the international anxiety that already attends the well-known "brain drain."

495 DAVID, HENRY. *Manpower policies for a democratic society: The final statement of the National Manpower Council.* New York: Columbia University Press, 1965, 121 pp. $3.75.

This is the final report in a series of 11 volumes resulting from the work of the National Manpower Council at Columbia University. This relatively short, nontechnical book summarizes some general conclusions and values of the Council based on more than 10 years of study. It outlines the serious national manpower problems that intertwine questions of race, family, social class, education, mobility, and the role of work in society.

496 INTERAGENCY COMMITTEE ON MANPOWER RESEARCH. *Manpower research: Inventory for fiscal years 1966 and 1967*. Wash., D. C.: Government Printing Office, 1968, 261 pp. $2.75.

This volume contains a number of abstracts of manpower research compiled under the auspices of a committee representing several agencies of the federal government. The reproduction leaves something to be desired, but the inclusion of several indexes (subject, institution, contract number, etc.) provides a useful framework for understanding the variety and scope of federally sponsored manpower research.

497 LECHT, LEONARD A. *Goals, priorities, and dollars: The next decade*. New York: Free Press, 1966, 365 pp. $2.95.

Partly in response to the shock of Sputnik, President Eisenhower appointed a Commission on National Goals. That Commission recommended goals (see 576) in a number of important areas but did not attempt to evaluate their feasibility, compatibility, or cost. This study was undertaken by the National Planning Association in order to examine carefully the budgetary implications of such a comprehensive statement of national goals. Each section is necessarily limited, but the overview dramatizes the fact that all good causes have good competition for dollars.

498 LECHT, LEONARD A. *Manpower needs for national goals in the 1970's*. New York: Praeger, 1969, 183 pp. $7.50.

This book examines the manpower and educational implications of pursuing national goals in 16 critical areas such as health, urban development, and ecology. It is the second major study undertaken by the National Planning Association's Center for Priority Analysis; the first study (497) focused on the financial priority decisions necessary to translate into action the Eisenhower Commission goals (576). The author concludes that attempts to implement these goals could create a substantial shortage of educated manpower in the 1970s. However, this outcome is not inevitable, he acknowledges, since pursuit of national goals is selective. He also foresees some important social consequences of an expanding labor market: a breakdown of racial discrimination in employment, new job opportunities for young people and women, better housing, better medical care, etc.

499 MANGUM, GARTH L. (ED.) *The manpower revolution: Its policy consequences*. Garden City, N. Y.: Doubleday, 1965, 580 pp. $2.45.

This book is a condensation of expert testimony given at hearings of the Senate Subcommittee on Employment and Manpower held in 1963-64 with Senator Joseph S. Clark as chairman. The committee explored the dimensions of the "manpower revolution"—the impact of technology on the kind of labor force needed in the American economy. Witnesses testified on a wide range of subjects dealing with problems of keeping the rapidly expanding labor force trained or retrained with skills needed in a rapidly changing technology. Recommendations of the subcommittee majority urge a comprehensive employment and manpower policy in place of the "piecemeal, crisis-by-crisis" approach.

500 NATIONAL ACADEMY OF SCIENCES, COMMITTEE ON UTILIZATION OF SCIENTIFIC AND ENGINEERING MANPOWER. *Toward better utilization of scientific and engineering talent: A program for action*. Wash., D. C.: NAS, 1964, 183 pp.

Concern that the national asset of engineering and scientific talent should be put to optimum use led to this 1964 study sponsored by the National Academy of Sciences. At the time it was written, the study was addressed to the dislocation caused by the switchover to space technology; it has, however, special relevance in the early 1970s when unemployment of engineers and scientists stands at unusual levels. Recommendations are addressed to three sectors: the federal government, industry, and colleges and universities. It is emphasized that the government plays a massive role in deploying scientific and engineering manpower and therefore must assume a new order of responsibility to prevent the squandering of talent. This responsibility includes assessing in advance the impact of its decisions to undertake new projects or discontinue old ones; such decisions affect not only the scientific talent pool but also the civilian economy. The report also calls for a new dimension in managerial ability and leadership. Universities are urged to take the lead in updating engineering and science education, as well as research on the educational process. The report is well organized and summarized for quick reading.

501 U.S. BUREAU OF LABOR STATISTICS. *Counselor's guide to manpower information: An annotated bibliography of government publications.* Wash., D. C.: Government Printing Office, 1968, 101 pp. $1.

This selected bibliography includes material from national, state, and local manpower agencies published between 1962 and 1968. Categories include basic references, occupational and industry manpower literature, education, finance and placement material, and literature dealing with special issues and special groups in the labor force such as migrants, minority groups, and women. Further sections describe sources of statistics and list directories, catalogs, and bibliographies. The appendixes provide information on ordering government publications, addresses of federal agencies, a cumulative index of the *Occupational Outlook Quarterly* (1339), and selected periodicals.

502 U.S. DEPARTMENT OF HEALTH, EDUCATION AND WELFARE. *Toward a social report.* Wash., D. C.: Government Printing Office, 1969, 198 pp. $1.

This report presents recommendations from a distinguished group of social scientists who were asked to advise HEW on developing yardsticks for charting social progress. They compare the abundance of comprehensive indicators of the economic health of the nation with the lack of measures of the quality of American life. Social areas most in need of systematic and periodic pulse-taking are discussed, including conditions of the nation's physical environment, national health care, crime and public safety, as well as others of greater concern, perhaps, to the individual than the gross national product and other economic problems of the country.

503 U.S. DEPARTMENT OF LABOR. *Manpower report of the President: A report on manpower requirements, resources, utilization, and training.* Wash., D. C.: Government Printing Office, 1970, 329 pp. $2.50.

This report is one outcome of the Manpower Development and Training Act of 1962, which required that an annual review of manpower requirements, resources, utilization, and training be submitted to Congress. It presents a general assessment of manpower policy and its relation to economic policy in solving unemployment problems. It also reviews trends in employment and resulting new manpower programs. Special sections deal with critical problems of equal opportunity, the relationships between employment and poverty, income maintenance and work incentives, and the changes in supply and demand in the professions. This annual volume is a very useful source of primary manpower statistics and provides a status report on current unemployment problems.

504 U.S. DEPARTMENT OF LABOR. *U.S. manpower in the 1970's: Opportunity and challenge.* Wash., D. C.: Government Printing Office, 1970, 28 pp. 55 cents.

Skillful use of graphics makes for easy assimilation of these statistics on labor-force trends for the 1970s. The major trend expected is the increase in the number of young adults in the labor market—the 25- to 34-year olds—who will also be "markedly better educated" than their counterparts of a decade ago. Blacks will enter the decade with a "larger but still lagging share in the American economy." Despite their occupational gains in the last decade, blacks still have an unemployment rate twice that of whites, a proportion that has not changed from 1960 to 1968. However, black college graduates are gaining parity rapidly, and by 1980 their number in the labor force is projected to approach one million.

6.2 – EDUCATIONAL RESOURCES. Many of the same people and organizations are concerned with this area as with the previous one, but the emphasis here is on the utilization of the educational system for effective development of human resources. Some of the work is theoretical; much is empirical. It is mostly concerned with planning educational systems and programs in relation to projected manpower needs. Three examples illustrate major problems in this area.

The supply and demand of college-trained personnel is a broad problem of continuous concern. One of the most significant books on this problem (and other aspects of access to higher education as well) is the report of the Commission on Human Resources and Advanced Education (509). An unusually interesting and surprisingly difficult problem is that of anticipating the need for educational resources on the basis of manpower needs (514). Another important problem to which economists have made valuable contributions in the last decade is the relationship between education, manpower development, and economic growth. Harbison and Meyers (512) wrote a highly praised book on this problem.

505 ANDERSON, C. ARNOLD. The adaptation of education to a mobile society. *Journal of Human Resources,* 1967, vol. 2, pp. 221-253.

"We can do it and we can do it without forgoing flexibility" is the attitude. Anderson takes in this paper addressing the problem of channeling the manpower supply into appropriate occupations. In discussing the educational system, he is an ardent opponent of early specialization, homogeneous student bodies, and the mania for increasing the "efficiency" of our schools. Drawing several comparisons between the United States and other countries, he concludes that there are advantages to having wide variation in ability among the members of a vocation.

He feels that basing a master plan for education on manpower-need projections would be unwise because the validity of projections has never been proven; because they do not allow for the use of middle-level skills and thus do not allow for the best use of top men; and because estimators or requirements seldom understand that in many cases there would be a larger supply of a given kind of worker if men were merely better matched to their jobs. Concern over shortages in manpower is seen to be largely unwarranted, because the flexible processes for career choice have proven adaptable to reorientation as demanded by changes in the economy.

506 COMMISSION ON HUMAN RESOURCES AND ADVANCED EDUCATION. Proceedings of the symposium on manpower theory. *Journal of Human Resources,* 1967, vol. 2, no. 2, pp. 140-253.

This symposium provides a useful overview of manpower theory from the different vantage points of sociology, education, and economics. The participants are especially knowledgeable and often take differing views. See 505, 507, 511, 513 for annotations of individual articles.

507 FOLGER, JOHN K. The balance between supply and demand for college graduates. *Journal of Human Resources,* 1967, vol. 2, pp. 143-175.

This article forecasts how projected trends of sharply increased numbers of college-trained workers will balance with the supply of jobs over the next two decades. For graduates with a bachelor's degree, who normally are in greatest demand for teaching jobs in elementary and secondary schools, adjustments can be worked out to accommodate a current situation. In contrast, the shortage of research opportunities for the increased number of PH.D. graduates will take long-range planning to head off an imbalance predicted for 1975. Folger suggests that adjustments can be made at the graduate school level, either in raising admissions standards, or in diverting students from a research-oriented program to one of teaching or professional service.

508 FOLGER, JOHN K. Social change and educational planning: A selective summary, in Stanley Elam and William P. McLure (Eds.), *Educational requirements for the 1970's: An interdisciplinary approach.* New York: Praeger, 1967, pp. 246-259.

In this review Folger highlights several implications of the papers presented at a symposium on future educational requirements sponsored by Phi Delta Kappa. He cites the need for fundamental changes in curriculum and teaching methods and the need for attention to new concepts in the field of organizational behavior. He expects that the problem of educating the disadvantaged will require a great deal of the educator's attention in the coming decade. Technological changes will produce an increase in the number of occupations requiring advanced levels of education, and Folger argues that a sizable expansion in higher education will be required to meet the manpower needs implicit in our national goals.

He feels it is likely that the implementation of needed changes will be left to local administrators as long as that approach works; however, when local initiative produces little progress, the federal government will probably assume a more active role. The rapid rate of change in our society demands that educational agencies make wider use of available information and respond more rapidly to new research concepts.

509 FOLGER, JOHN K., ASTIN, HELEN S., AND BAYER, ALAN E. *Human resources and higher education.* New York: Russell Sage Foundation, 1970, 475 pp. $17.50.

This final report of the Commission on Human Resources and Advanced Education is probably the most comprehensive treatment of human resources to date; it is, however, restricted largely to a traditional interpretation of high-level talent and to professions mostly associated with graduate or professional baccalaureate programs. The initial and concluding portions of the volume include ample recognition of the necessity for manpower theory and programs to embrace a broad spectrum of occupations, types of talent, problems of special groups, and diverse bases for developing and evaluating manpower policies; the detailed studies constituting the bulk of the volume seem more conventional. Nonetheless, many of these individual chapters are very significant contributions to the literature in their own right. Chapter 5, for example, describes an extremely valuable analysis of the flow of students through the educational system; it is the most comprehensive anywhere available.

In its overview of the report, the Commission summarizes a number of implications of this work. Perhaps the most significant relate to the role of the federal government in formulating manpower policy and its effect on the manner in which human resources are utilized and nourished. The Commission argues that "There is no point in asking whether public action is needed. Public action is constantly being taken." They conclude that manpower matters urgently need continuing research; higher education needs more stable federal support; and the time has come for a permanent, national body to represent the public interest and to review and appraise policies of human resources utilization.

510 GINZBERG, ELI. *Human resources: The wealth of a nation.* New York: Simon and Schuster, 1958, 153 pp. (Out of print)

Ginzberg was quite prominent in the early development of the concept of human resources. As director of staff studies for the National Manpower Council at Columbia University, he was involved in much of the post-World War II discussion and research on problems of utilization of human potential. This book is based on that work and is intended for general readers. Aside from its trailblazing character, it also makes interesting reading.

511 HANSEN, W. LEE. The economics of scientific and engineering manpower. *Journal of Human Resources,* 1967, vol. 2, pp. 191-215.

In discussing the validity of widespread anxiety over manpower shortages in science and engineering, Hansen views the problem from the economist's concern for efficiency in allocating resources. He argues that the informational and prescriptive approaches to research should be discarded in favor of an analytical approach—the only hope of bringing fresh insight to the problem. Since he finds no evidence to substantiate the fear that progress has been impeded by shortages of adequately trained scientists and engineers, he concludes that much of this uneasiness is "misplaced." Subsequent events proved him correct in assuming that there was no continuing problem of manpower shortages.

512 HARBISON, FREDERICK, AND MYERS, CHARLES A. *Education, manpower and economic growth.* New York: McGraw-Hill, 1964, 229 pp. $8.95.

This well-known and influential book analyzes economic and social development from the perspective of human resources. It outlines a generalized concept of human resource development with suggestions for action. Countries are grouped into four levels: underdeveloped, partially developed, semiadvanced, and advanced. Each group is analyzed separately with respect to characteristics, problems, and strategies for resource development. The book joins theory and practice, scholarship and politics, facts and fertile imagination. It is necessary reading for educational, manpower, and economic planners.

513 HOLLAND, JOHN L. Current psychological theories of occupational choice and their implications for national planning. *Journal of Human Resources,* 1967, vol. 2, pp. 176-190.

Holland examines two questions concerning the contributions that current theory and knowledge about occupational choice make to manpower planning: How can we manipulate distributions of students and adults in their choice of vocation? How can we increase *everyone's* educational aspiration and eventual vocational attainment?

The author cites some theories and facts about occupational choice, then offers practical recommendations such as: alternatives to traditional vocational counseling; recovering such overlooked sources of talent as women, handicapped persons, and those from rural or depressed regions; and a broader definition of the goals of manpower planning that would include concern for mental health. The thread running through all these suggestions is that it would be wiser to be concerned with the encouragement of talent rather than with the manipulation of it according to some notion of an ideal distribution.

514 HOLLISTER, ROBINSON. *A technical evaluation of the first stage of the Mediterranean Regional Project.* Paris: Organization for Economic Co-operation and Development, 1967, 188 pp. $2.50.

The Mediterranean Regional Project was a joint program undertaken by six countries in southern Europe (Greece, Italy, Portugal, Spain, Turkey, Yugoslavia) to prepare for their respective governments an assessment of their educational needs up to 1975 and to arrive at detailed plans and financial estimates for meeting these needs. The project represents a major attempt by these countries to assess the implications of economic and social objectives on the size and distribution of requirements for education.

This volume is a critique of the methods used in the project forecasts. It is not just a description of what was done but rather a careful examination of the methodological problems involved and of the theory on which the forecasting methods were based. Included in the conclusions are suggestions for several improvements in the methodology. An important conclusion is the fact that educational planning is especially difficult because the educational requirements of specific manpower needs are hard to identify reliably.

515 ORGANIZATION FOR ECONOMIC CO-OPERATION AND DEVELOPMENT. *Higher education and the demand for scientific manpower in the United States.* Paris: OECD, 1963, 102 pp. $1.

The Organization for Economic Co-operation and Development assists member countries in evaluating the twin problems of maximizing the value of human resources and meeting manpower needs. This volume is one of a series of reviews of policies concerning science and education within individual countries. A small team of experts visited the United States for intensive discussions with government officials, university administrators, faculty, and students, and members of other institutions connected with American higher education.

The initial report, Part I of this volume, covers such areas as supply and demand for scientific manpower, structure of higher education in the United States, resources for the expansion of the educational system, supply of teachers in higher education, the quality of teaching, the effect of federal funding on higher education, and educational help to underdeveloped countries. This report raised questions for discussion at a "confrontation meeting" held at OECD headquarters in Paris and attended by the examining team, a delegation from the United States, and delegates from the other member countries. Comments that received special consideration at that meeting, included in Part II, range from the hazards and advantages of federal financing of higher education to the effects of increased emphasis on scientific research, and the American experience with almost universal secondary education and the probability of universal higher education. The report has unusual value in providing some sense of outside perspective.

516 ORGANIZATION FOR ECONOMIC CO-OPERATION AND DEVELOPMENT. *The Mediterranean Regional Project: An experiment in planning by six countries.* Country Reports. Paris: OECD, 1965, 39 pp. 80 cents.

This cooperative study reviews the educational systems of six countries — Greece, Italy, Portugal, Spain, Turkey, Yugoslavia — for the purpose of increasing their contributions to economic growth and social advancement. The central finding is the need for more scientific and technical personnel, particularly at middle levels. Suggestions for meeting this need are: (1) curriculum changes in the secondary schools, (2) upgrading social prestige of terminal secondary technical education, (3) increasing the supply of teachers by raising salaries and opening up opportunities for nonuniversity graduates who are qualified to teach technical subjects, and (4) economizing in the use of teachers by using new teaching aids and shortening the length of studies found to be excessive. This report has much carry-over for those charged with technical education in United States high schools; it also represents an unusual attempt to join educational planning and manpower requirements at the international level. See 514 for a technical evaluation.

517 UNITED NATIONS EDUCATIONAL, SCIENTIFIC AND CULTURAL ORGANIZATION, INTERNATIONAL INSTITUTE FOR EDUCATIONAL PLANNING. *Manpower aspects of educational planning.* Paris: Unesco, 1968, 265 pp. $3.50.

This book reports the proceedings of a conference held at the International Institute for Educational Planning in Paris. The papers were directed to three main themes: employment opportunities for the educated, the role of education in rural and agricultural development, and the implementation of educational and manpower plans. The international context and the reporting of considerable verbal exchange among the participants add interest and value to this volume.

518 WOLFLE, DAEL (DIRECTOR) *America's resources of specialized talent. Report of the Commission on Human Resources and Advanced Training.* New York: Harper & Brothers, 1954, 332 pp. (Out of print)

This classic report pulled together a sizable body of data on the country's resources of talent and its development and utilization as it existed in the early 1950s. It discusses college graduation trends, occupational distribution of graduates, supply and demand in specialized fields, characteristics of students entering specific fields, and the utilization of educated specialists, and it makes suggestions for improving the overall situation. Many of the suggestions are still of significance and value today, and many had real impact on policy and practices in the late 1950s and early 1960s. For example, the report concluded that specialization would continue to increase and that this increase would be largely dependent on college graduates. Better utilization of talent and the educated population was seen to be both necessary and possible. An excess of college graduates was not anticipated to be a national problem; however, the need for more and better educational and vocational guidance was stressed. See 509 for a recent report of a reinstated commission some 15 years later.

6.3—EDUCATION AND WORK. The relationship between a particular educational program and the requirements of the job for which that program supposedly trains students is naturally a critical part of the whole process of manpower utilization. There is actually surprisingly little systematic work in this field that would pass for theory or research, though there is a good deal of descriptive literature.

In a somewhat overwritten but interesting report, Berg (519) broaches the fundamental question of the extent to which education is actually related to occupational requirements in a useful way. His conclusions are largely pessimistic. There are various mechanisms for improving the relevance of occupational and professional training in educational institutions. These include the advisory committee (521), professional accreditation (522), and follow-up studies by the institution (528). Cooperative education (520) is a well-established formal means of enhancing the relationship between education and work. New Careers (531) is a new programmatic approach that has gained much attention.

Organizations that are especially active with respect to the relation of education to work are the American Vocational Association (1108), the American Association of Junior Colleges (1097), and the National Commission on Accrediting (1126). Publications of these organizations are good sources of information, as is the *New Human Services Newsletter* (1382) of the New Careers Development Center.

519 BERG, IVAR. *Education and jobs: The great training robbery.* New York: Praeger, 1970, 200 pp. $7.50.

This volume challenges the common assumption of employers, economists, and educators that improved levels of education lead to improved job performance. In relating educational level to the specific problems that plague employers – high turnover, low productivity, and worker dissatisfaction – the author finds "over-education" an important cause of all three. The author uses a wide variety of data and cites many studies in exploring the relationship between education and performance. Among the suppositions he holds to be invalid are: (1) that advances in technology require better educated workers; (2) that education is a "screening device" to single out workers who can fit in harmoniously, make use of opportunities, and have greater potential for advance to better paid and more responsible positions. Education, he asserts, is not an "unqualified good." The crucial employment issue is not increasing the educational level of the labor force, but increasing the demand for labor. The style and substance of this book are tipped off by its title. It will attract attention and no doubt will have beneficial influence on many opinions. It is, however, more journalistic than it need be and less constructive than it ought to be.

520 BROWN, ROBERT L. *Cooperative education.* Wash., D. C.: American Association of Junior Colleges, 1971, 32 pp. $2.

This report of a national advisory committee presents guidelines for establishment of cooperative programs in occupational education. Individual sections discuss advantages of association with outside employers, present models of cooperative programs in various professions, outline employer responsibilities, and review important factors of organization and staffing. Additional sections discuss program implementation and problems of coordination, dropouts, matching students with jobs, and securing the participation of employers. The booklet also lists sources of additional information and cooperative nondegree programs.

521 BURKETT, LOWELL A. *The advisory committee and vocational education.* Wash., D. C.: American Vocational Association, 1969, 52 pp. $1.25.

This report sets guidelines for establishing an effective advisory committee to work with the vocational education staff at the community level. Emphasizing the importance of making it clear that legislative and administrative matters are not within the province of such a committee, the author lists the specific kinds of functions that are most useful. These include occupational surveys that provide the school with up-to-date figures on local job needs and report on the job performance of the school's graduates, verification of course content to insure that the training is realistic and appropriate to the community needs, and support for proposed legislation. (See also 530.)

522 DICKEY, FRANK G. *The 1970s: Time for assessment in accreditation.* Annual report of the executive director of the National Commission on Accrediting. Wash., D. C.: NCA, 1970, 12 pp. 25 cents.

The major item under discussion in this brief essay is the need for upgrading the voluntary system of accrediting in the face of increasing influence of the federal government. A national study is proposed that would address the major issues in accrediting: the proliferation of accrediting in the professions, the charge that accreditation impedes innovation, the growing pressures for the state-agency approach, the growing importance of vocational-technical education, and the demand for accountability in education. The annual report of the NCA for 1969 summarizes the 20-year history of the Commission.

523 EBERLY, DONALD J. Service experience and educational growth. *Educational Record*, 1968, vol. 49, pp. 197-205.

Eberly defines a "service curriculum" as one that merges the community's need for service, the students' desire for personal commitment and social involvement, and the faculty's recognition of the academic value of such programs. He describes four programs already in operation: (1) Harvard-Radcliffe —Education for Action; (2) California State, Los Angeles—Educational Participation in Communities; (3) Franconia College—Outreach; (4) Southern Regional Education Board—Resource Development Internship Program. Financial and accreditation problems are seen as the major hurdle. Credit for such experiences, which provide opportunities for growth in maturity, self-confidence, and discretion in career choice, are equated with credit given for general education requirements or basic requirements for a degree. The author concludes by listing some sequential guidelines for institutions considering developing this type of program.

524 FOLGER, JOHN K., AND NAM, CHARLES B. Trends in education in relation to the occupational structure. *Sociology of Education*, 1964, vol. 38, pp. 19-33.

This article is an analysis of the relation between educational attainment and occupational level with special attention to the problems of educational supply and demand. The authors use census data for the male population to investigate increasing educational attainment in the labor force and find a declining association between education and occupation. They interpret the rising educational level within specific occupations as the prime factor in increasing attainment. For this reason they stress the inadequacy of the supply-demand construct as an interpretation of educational attainment.

525 HENDERSON, JOHN T. *Program planning with surveys in occupational education.* Wash., D. C.: American Association of Junior Colleges, 1970, 26 pp. $2. (Mimeographed)

This useful handbook provides specific information on the use of surveys for the planning and development of occupational curriculums in junior colleges. Sections outline methods and techniques for organizing and conducting surveys and include information on budgeting, staffing, and the use of consultants. Other chapters deal with problems in manpower requirement studies, methods for evaluating the enrollment potential, and suggestions for effective evaluation and implementation of survey results. A reference table and bibliography are included.

526 INSTITUTE FOR LOCAL SELF GOVERNMENT. *Community college programs for public service occupations.* Berkeley, Calif.: ILSG, 1969, 160 pp. $3.

This report supplies guidelines for focusing community college vocational-technical programs on a previously unmined field of job opportunities — staffing of local governments. The institute surveyed approximately 85 percent of California community colleges and over 30 local government agencies. Among the specific job areas for which the report correlates curriculum guidelines with job specifications are inspection services, civil engineering, accounting, library services, recreation, planning, and government supervision and management. This is a good illustration of one method of making community education relevant to student and societal needs.

527 KATZ, JOSEPH, KORN, HAROLD A., LELAND, CAROLE A., AND LEVIN, MAX M. *Class, character, and career.* Stanford, Calif.: Institute for the Study of Human Problems, Stanford University, 1968, 219 pp. (Multilithed)

This research report investigates the occupational decision process in two very different groups of college students. Descriptive data were gathered through questionnaires, personality inventories, and vocational tests administered to samples of the undergraduate student bodies at Stanford University and San Jose City College, a two-year institution. Chapters of the report deal with the impact of socioeconomic class on personal needs and career selection, the social psychology of career choice and implications for manpower policy, and career choice and autonomy in college women. The study documents sharp differences in psychological need between the two social classes represented in the sample. The study of career choice among women identified contradictions in the educational and social environment inhibiting women in their "autonomy strivings." The authors' recommendations include an increase in the number of women on college faculties, educational programs dealing with the status of women, and curricular changes instituted to prepare women for careers.

528 LITTLE, J. KENNETH. *Review and synthesis of research on the placement and follow-up of vocational education students.* Columbus, Ohio: Center for Research and Leadership Development in Vocational and Technical Education, Ohio State University, 1970, 48 pp.

This publication reports on recent follow-up studies of graduates of vocational-technical education programs. Three basic types of studies are reviewed: (1) administrative reports, which describe the occupational status of graduates of specific programs; (2) comparative studies, which compare graduates of differing types of programs; and (3) cost-benefit studies, which attempt to determine the economic effectiveness of programs. The author decries the paucity of well-executed research in this area but concludes that "despite the inadequacies and deficiencies of the follow-up studies, findings seem to contribute a refrain. The vocational-technical education programs are serving important parts of our population in ways that these people would not be helped without them . . . and, although the findings are contradictory, the preponderance of evidence is that vocational education programs are probably worth their cost."

529 NATIONAL COMMISSION ON ACCREDITING. *Procedures of accrediting education in the professions.* Wash., D. C.: NCA, 1967-70, $4.

This series of brief reports describes the accrediting procedures used and criteria developed by national organizations in specific professions. They cover some 30 fields such as art, chemistry, nursing, and law. Each report describes eligibility, team visits, appeal procedures, and costs.

530 RIENDEAU, ALBERT J. *The role of the advisory committee in occupational education in the junior college.* Wash., D. C.: American Association of Junior Colleges, 1967, 75 pp. $1.50.

This monograph presents a detailed description of the role of the advisory committee in occupational education in the junior college. The author stresses the need for advice of outside industry personnel in the development of vocationally oriented programs. Chapters deal with the structure, function, and organization of advisory committees. Further sections outline procedures for conducting committee meetings, implementing recommendations, and evaluating effectiveness. Samples of letters of invitation, appointment, and appreciation are reproduced in the Appendix along with examples of agendas, minutes, and committee handbooks. (See also 521.)

531 RIESSMAN, FRANK, AND POPPER, HERMINE I. *Up from poverty.* New York: Harper & Row, 1968, 332 pp. $7.95.

This book provides guidelines for using the "New Careers" concept that has gained much attention in the war on poverty. In place of locking the poor into compensatory or "plantation" programs, the New Careers goal is to open up opportunities for useful work, combined with education-as-you-go. "Jobs first, diplomas later" means the individual combines an immediate job with a related educational program and planned advancement—the "ladder of skills" approach. The social sectors where manpower needs far exceed the numbers of trained professionals provide excellent opportunities for the use of gradually trained auxiliary personnel. In public service areas such as social work, school systems, health services, and police and correction departments, New Careers has introduced a different and provocative approach to coordinating education and work. The authors report that one difficulty has arisen from the reluctance of some professional groups and unions to support such programs. Fearful of a mass influx of untrained workers into their field, they "dig in behind barriers of professionalism and credentialism." Of course, this is exactly what the approach is intended to alleviate. Some particular programs are described in detail, making this a useful handbook for administrators.

532 VENN, GRANT. *Man, education, and work: Postsecondary vocational and technical education.* Wash., D. C.: American Council on Education, 1964, 184 pp. $1.50.

This well-known report is concerned with the impact of modern technology on American education. The author was commissioned by the American Council on Education to examine the current relationship of education to work and the responsibilities of higher education in those occupational areas that are not well served by traditional academic disciplines. Venn traces the impact of the technological revolution and states well the urgent need for effective vocational education. He goes on to outline beneficial developments in secondary education, in business and other noneducational enterprises, and in federal legislative support. The report concludes with a series of strong recommendations for the development of vocational education to meet national needs, promote individual development, and improve equality of social opportunity.

533 WILSON, JAMES W., AND LYONS, EDWARD H. *Work-study college programs: Appraisal and report of the study of cooperative education.* New York: Harper, 1961, 240 pp. (Out of print)

This book includes the complete report of the Committee of the Study of Cooperative Education chaired by Ralph W. Tyler. This study was the first comprehensive investigation of the purposes, values, processes, and results of work-study programs. The investigators selected a representative sample of institutions with and without cooperative work-study programs, then collected and compared data from students, faculty, administrators, and outside agencies. The authors interpret the findings in support of claimed values of cooperative programs: close interrelation of theory and practice resulting in increased student motivation; students exhibiting greater sense of responsibility and maturity and improved skill in interpersonal relations; faculty reporting greater communication with business and other professions; colleges realizing more efficient utilization of facilities. The authors present recommendations for improving and extending cooperative programs. They suggest designing programs to serve the needs of the individual college, increasing the involvement of faculty in planning, and improving the relationship between the college and the outside employers. It is also recommended that cooperative programs be extended throughout the professions, in liberal arts colleges, and with special attention to women's education. The appendixes, presenting the basic data of the study in complete detail, are especially valuable.

534 WOOLDRIDGE, ROY L. Cooperative education, in Asa S. Knowles (Ed.), *Handbook of college and university administration.* Vol. II. *Academic.* New York: McGraw-Hill, 1970, sec. 2, pp. 223-233.

This chapter provides practical information on the administration of programs integrating classroom and outside work experience. Individual sections discuss problems of administrative and faculty acceptance, calendar design, funding, and staffing. Further sections describe the functions of a planning committee, necessary policy decisions, hiring and training of a program coordinator, and contacts with employers.

535 YOUNG, ANNE M. Employment of school-age youth. *Monthly Labor Review,* 1970, vol. 93, no. 9, pp. 4-11.

This Special Labor Force Report presents an analysis of trends in youth employment in the last decade. Findings indicate an increase in the labor-force participation of secondary and college students and a simultaneous increase in school attendance at both levels. The author discusses changes in occupational distribution among students and nonstudents and reports that students hold a greater proportion of white-collar jobs. Unemployment rates were high for students, though periods of unemployment were relatively short. The high rate reflects students' limited experience and availability and the unstructured school-to-work pattern. This is the eleventh of an annual series of similar reports based on the October Current Population Survey of the Census Bureau.

6.4—*OCCUPATIONAL STRUCTURE.* An understanding of the relationship of education to work requires some appreciation of the structure of occupations. Studies in this area tend to be descriptive and highly empirical. They include surveys of attitudes and vocational behavior (e.g., occupational mobility) and general texts on the nature of the occupational structure.

The standard reference in the field is the *Dictionary of Occupational Titles* (546), and Blau and Duncan (537) have recently prepared a useful text. The prestige of different occupations has been a matter of considerable interest because of its obvious bearing on questions concerning social mobility. Closely related to prestige and structure is the question of what sort of people go into different occupations. In this sense the literature of this area is closely related to that of section 1.2.

Organizations of particular importance with respect to the problems of occupational structure and also the following section on transition to work are the United States Bureau of Labor Statistics (1447) and the United States Employment Service, both agencies of the Department of Labor. The Department of Labor prepares the most useful publications in this area, including the *Monthly Labor Review* (1336), the *Occupational Outlook Quarterly* (1339), and the *Handbook of Labor Statistics* (1411). Valuable data are also available from census publications, particularly the *Current Population Reports* (1418).

536 BEREITER, CARL, AND FREEDMAN, MERVIN B. Fields of study and the people in them, in Nevitt Sanford (Ed.), *The American College.* New York: Wiley, 1963, pp. 563-596.

This chapter is based largely on the authors' work in connection with the Vassar studies—one of the first and most systematic efforts to understand student development through the college years. This particular report provides a good narrative discussion of the dynamics through which individuals with varying interests and personalities become attracted to different fields.

537 BLAU, PETER M., AND DUNCAN, OTIS DUDLEY. *The American occupational structure.* New York: John Wiley, 1967, 520 pp. $14.95.

This volume presents an analysis of the American occupational structure and the factors that influence social mobility. It is assumed that "the hierarchy of prestige strata and the hierarchy of economic classes have their roots in the occupational structure." The study is based on a body of empirical data collected from a representative sample of over 20,000 American males between the ages of 20 and 64. The authors do not attempt to build a general theory of stratification; however, they do seek to place their research findings into a theoretical framework and suggest theoretical interpretations for them. The book begins with a discussion of the structure of relations among occupational groupings and their changes through time, continues with an analysis of the processes of occupational achievement and mobility that find expression in this structure, and then presents a theoretical model of these processes. The authors examine the effects of influences such as race, region of birth, migration, number and position of siblings, family emphasis on education, and the relationship between marriage and occupational attainment. The book provides a useful overview of the working world and complements the theoretical work in career development undertaken primarily by psychologists in the guidance context.

538 CRITES, JOHN O. *Vocational psychology.* New York: McGraw-Hill, 1969, 704 pp. $13.50.

In 1956 Anne Roe wrote a book similar to this one on the psychology of vocations—as she said, because no one had written such a book. This volume by Crites, written slightly more than a decade later, amply illustrates the considerable amount of research in this area during the intervening period. It is an ambitious and comprehensive volume which includes a description and history of vocational psychology, theory and research on vocational choice, and a major section on the dynamics of vocational adjustment. It is a well-organized and carefully researched book including well over 1,000 references.

539 DUNCAN, OTIS DUDLEY. The trend of occupational mobility in the United States. *American Sociological Review,* 1965, vol. 30, pp. 491-498.

This study of inter- and intragenerational mobility compares data for 1962 with that for corresponding age groups from one, two, and three decades earlier. In general, the recent data indicate more upward mobility into salaried, professional, and technical positions and less downward mobility into blue-collar and farm occupations than was true in earlier decades. Thus, the data give no cause for concern that the American occupational structure is providing fewer opportunities. The author warns, on the other hand, that movement off farms may be a major factor in inducing upward mobility, and there may be no clear counterpart in a future era when few persons originate on farms.

540 HODGE, ROBERT W., SIEGEL, PAUL M., AND ROSSI, PETER H. Occupational prestige in the United States, 1925-63. *American Journal of Sociology,* 1964, vol. 70, pp. 286-302.

This paper reports changes in occupational prestige during the last four decades. In 1963 the authors conducted a replication of the 1947 National Opinion Research Corporation (NORC) study of prestige for 90 adult occupations. They found little evidence of major change in prestige and, correlating these findings with earlier studies, concluded that the structure of occupational prestige has been relatively stable since 1925. Certain occupations did exhibit increases in prestige, notably scientists and artisans, while culturally and politically oriented positions decreased. The authors conclude that a stable system of occupational prestige "provides a necessary foundation to which individuals may anchor their careers."

541 HOLLAND, JOHN L., VIERNSTEIN, MARY COWAN, KUO, HAO-MEI, KARWEIT, NANCY L., AND BLUM, ZAHAVA D. *A psychological classification of occupations.* Report No. 90. Baltimore, Md.: Center for the Study of Social Organization of Schools, Johns Hopkins University, 1970, 47 pp. (Mimeographed)

This report classifies 431 common occupations which the authors estimate constitute about 95 percent of the United States labor force. The main classes (realistic, investigative, artistic, social, enterprising, conventional) are based on Holland's theory of occupational choice and include a number of subclasses organized according to the number of years of education required. The classification scheme should prove useful in vocational counseling, particularly if it is a part of a larger effort to educate the student regarding the nature of work in relation to his own interests and competencies.

542 LITTLE, J. KENNETH. *The occupations of non-college youth. American Educational Research Journal,* 1967, vol. 4, pp. 147-153.

This study reports on the occupational attainments of Wisconsin high school graduates seven years after their 1957 graduation. Forty percent had no further schooling; 16 percent attended a vocational or trade school; of the 43 percent who attended college, more than one-third failed to graduate. About half of all three groups were found to be in middle-level occupations. The author concludes that the occupational advantage of education was the extent to which college attendance enabled students to escape low-prestige occupations. The attainment of high-prestige occupations was found to be associated with a complex of psychocultural factors, such as above average scholastic aptitude and achievement, upper socioeconomic status, and father's occupational and educational background. It was also found that high school performance did not have a high relationship to the level of occupational attainment, and even among college-going students, the low achievers often attained occupations equivalent to their higher-ranking classmates.

543 REISS, ALBERT J. JR., DUNCAN, OTIS DUDLEY, HATT, PAUL K., AND NORTH, CECIL C. *Occupations and social status.* New York: Free Press, 1961, 305 pp. $7.50.

In 1947 the National Opinion Research Center collected data that became a standard reference in estimating the prestige of occupations. This book presents a detailed analysis of the ratings and how they were made. It has general interest as a social document but primary value as a research tool.

544 ROE, ANNE. *The psychology of occupations.* New York: John Wiley, 1956, 340 pp. $9.95.

This classic book provided one of the first systematic analyses of occupations and how they differ. With this work the author dramatizes the importance of compatible career choice in contributing to the satisfaction and total psychology of the adult life.

545 STEWART, NAOMI. AGCT scores of army personnel grouped by occupation. *Occupations,* 1947, vol. 26, pp. 5-41.

An interesting outcome of the massive testing of Army enlisted men in World War II was the development of average intelligence-test scores for men following various lines of work in civilian life. This article is based on more than 80,000 cases and includes 227 occupations. The data have many shortcomings (e.g., they are out of date, based on whites only, exclude higher-level occupations) but remain a useful rough index of human resources in conjunction with data supplied by Dael Wolfle in *America's Resources of Specialized Talent* (518).

546 U.S. EMPLOYMENT SERVICE. *Dictionary of occupational titles.* (3rd ed.) Vol. I. *Definitions of titles.* Vol. II. *Occupational classification and industry index.* Wash., D. C.: Government Printing Office, 1965, Vol. I, 809 pp. Vol. II, 656 pp.

This standard reference work was the first source to provide a standard job terminology and a means of classifying occupations according to the elements involved in their performance. Annotations of each occupation include duties and skills involved, equipment and material used, and working conditions under which they are performed. Volume I contains an alphabetical listing of 21,741 job definitions known by 35,550 titles. Volume II consists of 12 sections that further categorize the various occupational divisions and groups by titles, codes, worker traits, industry designations, etc.

547 ZYTOWSKI, DONALD G. (ED.) *Vocational behavior: Readings in theory and research.* New York: Holt, Rinehart and Winston, 1968, 486 pp. $7.95.

This collection of papers offers a useful and comprehensive overview of recent theory and research in the field of vocational behavior. Emphasizing articles published since 1957, the editor has drawn from industrial and personal psychology and also sociology and social psychology. The collection begins with material on the nature and meaning of work, considers next the structure and perceptual qualities of work, and then examines such factors as maturation, choice, satisfaction, and adjustment. The developmental character of vocational behavior is presented, and the differing theories of occupational determinants are given along with evidence for each. In the choice of papers and excerpts the editor attempts to demonstrate "that vocational role determinants are also the determinants of satisfaction and performance."

6.5—TRANSITION TO WORK. This section is concerned with the employment of students at the completion of postsecondary educational programs. In that sense it is a corollary to section 1.4, which involves the placement of high school graduates in jobs or postsecondary education. The literature in this area is largely concerned with one of two problems: supply and demand in various academic fields and the logistical problem of matching graduates with jobs. The former is largely social bookkeeping; the latter is associated with the college placement function.

The placement office is by now quite active on most college campuses, and the placement officer represents for this process the nearest parallel to those practitioners associated with other access processes previously discussed. The College Placement Council (1113) is the official organization for this group, and it publishes various relevant material including the *College Placement Annual* (552) and the *Journal of College Placement* (1322), which are standard references in this field.

Career information and guidance for college graduates is not highly developed. Many of the better developed placement offices continue to serve their alumni after the initial job placement, but there are relatively few means for maintaining and supporting career development for the more highly educated portion of the occupational structure. Professional associations do fill this gap but only in a minor and disorganized manner. All in all, there seems relatively little coordination between higher education and subsequent career development or systematic continuing education—the final rung of the access ladder is left somewhat dangling. Of course, the ready and extreme contrast is the more "organized" system in socialist states in which graduates are assigned to jobs.

548 ARNOW, PHILIP. Bridging the gap from school to work. *Occupational Outlook Quarterly,* 1968, vol. 12, no. 4, pp. 28-31.

This article deals with the relationship between the high unemployment rate among youth and the present system of school-work transition. The author identifies and explores questions bearing on this relationship, including the inability of the economy to absorb graduating students because of a lack of low-skilled jobs, employers' attitudes toward hiring inexperienced youth, and the relation between educational preparation and later work experience. He suggests that schools may aid in increasing the rate of absorption through improvements in vocational education and counseling beginning at the junior high school level, cooperative work-study programs, increased involvement of business and professional groups, staggered graduations, and special attention to poverty youth.

549 BROWN, NEWELL. *After college . . . what? A career exploration handbook*. New York: M. W. Lads, 1968, 246 pp. $2.95.

This career guidebook for college students combines lively and practical discussion with a do-it-yourself appraisal. It describes 11 fallacies about career decisions and discusses emotional and value attitudes concerning careers. A special section provides useful career classifications and information on opportunities, qualifications, and potential salaries.

550 COLLEGE PLACEMENT COUNCIL. Series of Research Monographs. Bethlehem, Pa.: College Placement Council, 1968-1970.

This series of monographs centers on the early postcollege job attitudes, satisfactions, and turnovers. They are based on data supplied mainly by the National Opinion Research Center (NORC). In general, the reports dispel as a "somewhat universal myth" the notion that college graduates are increasingly disenchanted with private business and industry. Another general interpretation is that business might well consider recruitment a long-term procedure, rather than an annual one-shot visit to college campuses. This recommendation is made partly because of career uncertainties and delays involved in students' draft situations. Individual reports in the series are: No. 1, *Attitudes of College Students Toward Business Careers*, $2.50. No. 2, *The College Graduate: His Early Employment and Job Satisfaction*, $3. No. 3, *The College Graduate: Turnover and Mobility,* $3.

551 COOPER, ALVA C. Administration of placement, in Asa S. Knowles (Ed.), *Handbook of college and university administration*. Vol. 1. *General*. New York: McGraw-Hill, 1970, sec. 5, pp. 227-249.

This chapter provides a concise overview of principles and practices of placement administration. Individual sections describe the various types of placement services; the organization of facilities; personnel qualifications; organization of student, alumni, employer, and information files; automation of operations; and legal implications of corporation and government recruitment. The author also provides a useful outline of desirable placement office files concerning students, references, alumni, employers, information, office procedures, etc.

552 KAUFFMAN, WARREN E. (ED.) *College placement annual, 1971*. Bethlehem, Pa.: College Placement Council, 1970, 640 pp. Free.

This guide is sponsored by the eight regional placement associations of the United States and Canada for the benefit of graduating seniors seeking employment. It includes a series of articles describing the current employment situation for college graduates and provides suggestions concerning employment interviews, preparing resumes, etc. The bulk of the publication consists of brief statements from 2,000 corporate and government employers describing the nature of each organization and the types of positions open. (Also annotated in section 1.7.)

553 PRINCETON MANPOWER SYMPOSIUM. *The transition from school to work*. Princeton, N. J.: Industrial Relations Section, Princeton University, 1968, 282 pp.

The major thread of the discussion at this symposium was the recognition of the changes that must be made in the American system of education to cope with the problems that one-third of today's youth are encountering in the job market. Some of the obstacles identified were the shrinking proportion of low-skill entry jobs, the increasing reluctance of young people to take such jobs, residence and transportation barriers, and a nationwide failure to place high priority on efforts to cope with the problem. One difficulty cited was the inadequacy of job-counseling programs in the schools in the light of evidence that 8 out of 10 high school dropouts have never received counseling on job training or opportunities. Participants expressed support for the potential of cooperative education. They also advocated try-out periods of employment during the school year, so that work experience could become an integral part of school preparation for career development. The conference also explored what industry and government can do to train disadvantaged youth to be adequately qualified employees.

554 ROSENTHAL, NEAL H., AND HEDGES, JANICE N. Matching sheepskins with jobs. *Monthly Labor Review,* 1968, vol. 91, no. 11, pp. 9-15.

This article projects that by 1975 the overall demand for college-trained workers will come out even with supply but warns of sharp imbalances in some important fields. Projections for 1966-75 based on research conducted by the United States Bureau of Labor Statistics indicate that there will be too few doctors, dentists, engineers, and physical scientists, and too many teachers, mathematicians, and life scientists. Oversupply can be headed off in some fields such as science, where students can switch majors with little difficulty. The authors warn that oversupply of teachers should alert women to the need for broadening their occupational horizons; informed occupational counseling can encourage students to prepare for uncrowded fields, but only increasing enrollments and educational facilities will insure adequate supplies in specialized occupations.

555 SHARP, LAURE M. *Education and employment: The early careers of college graduates.* Baltimore, Md.: Johns Hopkins Press, 1970, 162 pp. $9.

This book summarizes findings and interpretations derived from studies of recent college graduates. The author concludes that colleges and universities have succeeded in their "work preparatory" role, leading undergraduates toward early specialization. The undergraduate major was found to have the greatest impact on career selection and success, while the quality or prestige of the undergraduate institution had little effect on career development, except in the field of business. Students seemed to view education as a life-long process and were willing to combine study with work and family life. Further findings identified low undergraduate grades and the career and role choices unique to women as obstacles to graduate study. The study includes a useful section on the effect of military service on the transition from education to work.

556 SUPER, DONALD E., AND CRITES, JOHN O. *Appraising vocational fitness by means of psychological tests.* New York: Harper & Row, 1962, 688 pp. $12.

This volume is a revision of the classic work which first appeared in 1949. It is not a drastic revision, for most of the instruments dealt with in the first edition are still the most widely used. Some tests and inventories discussed in the first edition have been replaced by more refined instruments, and a few others have been published since the first edition. This volume is designed for the test user—the counselor in school, college, or community agency and the personnel worker in business, industry, or government who uses standard tests for educational and vocational appraisal. The aim is to give him an adequate knowledge and understanding of the available tests and instruments, and some skill in using them.

557 U.S. BUREAU OF LABOR STATISTICS. *Education and jobs: A series of pamphlets to guide young people to jobs that match different levels of education and training.* Wash., D. C.: Government Printing Office, 1968.

This is a series of brief pamphlets that list a number of jobs that match various levels of education and training. The packet includes five pamphlets listing jobs for which: (1) apprenticeship training is available; (2) a high school education is preferred but not essential; (3) a high school education is generally required; (4) junior college, technical institute, or other specialized training is usually required; and (5) a college education is usually required. The pamphlets give a brief summary of the qualifications and training needed, and also the employment opportunity trends for each of the occupations listed. This material gives an especially graphic view of the relation of education to work as it is expressed in the job market. (Also annotated in section 1.7.)

558 U.S. DEPARTMENT OF LABOR. *Report of the Secretary of Labor on manpower research and training under the Manpower Development and Training Act of 1962.* Wash., D. C.: Government Printing Office, 1966, 216 pp. $1.25.

This report is divided into sections covering description and evaluation of manpower research and training programs, program support and community involvement, reports of manpower advisory committees, and future developments. The appendix includes the text of the Manpower Development and Training Act of 1962, guidelines for research grants and contracts, and availability and location of research reports.

559 WOLFBEIN, SEYMOUR L. *Occupational information: A career guidance view.* New York: Random House, 1968, 142 pp. $3.95; paperback $1.95.

Wolfbein addresses himself to three major developments that he contends should be a part of the basic knowledge of teaching and counseling personnel: (1) the increase in school enrollments and its effects on the guidance process, (2) the resultant importance of making specific occupational information available to counseling personnel, and (3) the wealth of material relevant to the work environment now available. He concludes by stressing the need for flexibility and adaptability in each person's education and in the educational process itself. The author also urges recognition of the shortage of skilled craftsmen and the use of fiscal and monetary policy to maintain high employment.

II. *The System*

SECTION 7: ORGANIZATION AND ADMINISTRATION

Organization and administration involve implementation of policies that determine the access characteristics of an educational system. These processes include consideration of the role of higher education in American society, of national priorities that affect education, of how those priorities are expressed in the organization of the system, and of the administration of individual institutions and programs. In short, access is very much dependent upon how the educational system is organized and administered. Considerable power is vested in institutions, in departments within those institutions, and in the traditional independence of individual teachers and professionals. But there is also great pressure to tighten governance and control and to insist that education be held accountable and serve the public interest.

It therefore seems likely that planning, administration, and coordination of postsecondary educational programs will be continuously fraught with incompatible tensions. Efforts to coordinate and manage access to higher education are as dangerous as they are necessary. But it also seems highly likely that the power politics in the educational enterprise will support the inertia of the present system so that fundamental changes in administrative control will not occur quickly.

Of the associations concerned with the organization and administration of higher education, the American Council on Education (1102) is on most counts the most prominent. Its journal, *Educational Record* (1320), and its newsletter, *Higher Education and National Affairs* (1373), are influential and widely read. Equally prominent among two-year institutions is the American Association of Junior Colleges (1097). Its journal (1332) and numerous publications have contributed to the unusual leadership of the association. There are a number of organizations that provide similar leadership. The larger associations that are actively involved in access problems are annotated in section 12.1.

Two other types of organizations that play an important role are special commissions and coordinating boards. The former (see section 12.6) exert momentary influence and provide national guidelines and goals. The latter (see section 12.5) are critically important administrative agencies that are too new to have yet settled into a clear pattern. Three "super" coordinating agencies deserve special mention.

The Education Commission of the States (1178) is a relatively new association that promises to develop a new seat of power built on the relationship between higher education and state government. Its journal, *Compact* (1316), and its newsletter, *Higher Education in the States* (1374), are the best sources of current information on statewide coordination. The Southern Regional Education Board (1180) and the Western Interstate Commission for Higher Education (1181) are two regional associations that play an increasingly important role in coordination and planning. Both have active publication programs.

Among the publications especially related to this area, the *Harvard Educational Review* (1321), *Change Magazine* (1312), and *Daedalus* (1317) should be mentioned as outstanding and influential journals that give consistently intelligent treatment to important philosophical issues in education. Finally, *The Chronicle of Higher Education* (1355) stands in a class by itself. It does an outstanding job of detailed coverage of current developments in higher education.

7.1—*HISTORY AND PHILOSOPHY.* The literature of this area consists of books on the history of higher education and significant essays related to the underlying philosophy of access to higher education. The authors are typically well-known professors and educational leaders. There is no comprehensive history of college admissions, but several overlapping works at least cover a considerable time span (see 560, 561, and 564). An especially important historical and current analysis of access to higher education is Jencks and Riesman's *Academic Revolution* (568).

560 BOWLES, FRANK. *The refounding of the College Board, 1948-1963: An informal commentary and selected papers.* New York: College Entrance Examination Board, 1967, 336 pp. $4.50.

This anthology of Bowles's papers and speeches covers his 15-year tenure as chief executive of the College Board. They are arranged chronologically beginning with 1948, when the Board had just transferred the administration of its testing program to Educational Testing Service, through the period of rapid growth and development of important new areas of service in the 1950s and early 1960s. They provide illuminating insight into the thinking that went into Bowles's concern for broadening the concept of admissions to a concept of access to higher education that includes social forces, barriers to opportunity, and all of the educational and administrative procedures involved in the transition from school to college.

561 BROOME, EDWIN CORNELIUS. *A historical and critical discussion of college admission requirements.* New York: Columbia University, 1903. New York: College Entrance Examination Board, 1963, 157 pp. (Reprint). $2.

This 1903 critique of admissions requirements has been reprinted by the College Board not as a period piece of historical perspective but for the intrinsic value of its perception of the tie between college admissions and the public interest. When Broome speaks of the "increased popular demand for advanced studies in what is sometimes called the 'people's college'—the public high school—for that institution is at home, easily accessible, and free," he describes today's "people's college"—the community college. He reports the trend to make entrance examinations "tests of power rather than acquisition of facts that shift from stultifying memoriter work to that more quickening sort which calls for independent thought." His final plea that colleges "offer no obstruction to those young men who though penniless have the stuff in them to profit by a college education" expresses today's goals in yesterday's words.

562 BRUBACHER, JOHN S., AND RUDY, WILLIS. *Higher education in transition: A history of American colleges and universities, 1636-1968.* (Rev. ed.) New York: Harper & Row, 1968, 529 pp. $12.

Brubacher and Rudy present here a revision of their 1958 history of American higher education, expanded to include developments from 1958 to 1968. The book is basically chronological in arrangement; however, the focus throughout is on certain major areas of concern, such as curriculum, administration, academic freedom, and student life, showing how the conduct of higher education has been affected by changing social attitudes on these matters. The authors trace the developments brought about by "three hundred thirty years of ferment," beginning with the early influences that shaped the colonial colleges, and conclude that American higher education "remains in a state of dynamic evolution."

563 CLARK, BURTON R. The "cooling-out" function in higher education. *American Journal of Sociology,* 1960, vol. 65, pp. 569-576.

The term "cooling-out function," borrowed from psychiatric descriptions of adaptation to failure, describes the way junior colleges provide gentle letdowns from the unattainable ambitions of low-performing students. The ideology of equal opportunity is popularly assumed to mean unlimited access to a college education regardless of past record, and college aspiration is widely encouraged as a means of moving upward in job status. However, once admitted, large numbers of students are doomed to failure when they cannot meet required standards of performance. The "hard" answer is the unequivocal dismissal meted out at universities after the first year. The "soft" answer is the junior college technique for disengaging a failing student from his goal of transfer to a four-year college. Preentrance testing, interviews, special "Orientation to College" courses all are used by counselors—"agents of consolation"—to provide advice, self-assessment, and alternative goals. Clark points out that one dilemma of the cooling-out role is that it must be kept away from public scrutiny and camouflaged so that the student does not perceive his rejection. However, cooling-out may also be interpreted as an opportunity to provide career exploration appropriate to the student's ability. Thus the junior college becomes a place where everyone is admitted and everyone succeeds. See also Clark's *Cpen Door College* (747), which considers the operation of this social policy in a landmark study of one community college.

564 FUESS, CLAUDE M. *The College Board: Its first fifty years (1900-1950).* New York: College Entrance Examination Board, 1950, 222 pp. $4.

The work of the College Entrance Examination Board has been a significant factor in the development of admissions processes in American higher education. Fuess traces the history of the Board from its inception in 1899 to the reorganization that took place in 1947. In particular, the book clarifies the role played by the Board early in the century in creating some bases for order in the prevailing chaos of admissions requirements. Fuess began a personal association with the Board in the 1920s; this volume is an informal and readable account of the personalities and problems he encountered as the Board's chief custodian for financial affairs.

565 GARDNER, JOHN W. *Excellence: Can we be equal and excellent too?* New York: Harper & Row, 1961, 171 pp. $4.95.

In this volume, the author analyzes the problem of achieving excellence in our kind of society—i.e., a society which cherishes the ideal of equality. Gardner discusses the decline of hereditary privilege, the search for talent, the sorting-out function of education, alternatives to college, and many other aspects of the problem of the simultaneous achievement of both equality and excellence. He suggests that there are many kinds of excellence and that "every institution in our society should contribute to the fulfillment of the individual." The pursuit of excellence "implies a striving for the highest standards in every phase of life." This famous essay is perhaps more successful in describing the problem than suggesting practical solutions; nonetheless, it represents an unusually thoughtful and important book.

566 HANDLIN, OSCAR, AND HANDLIN, MARY F. *The American college and American culture: Socialization as a function of higher education.* New York: McGraw-Hill, 1970, 104 pp. $4.95.

This historical essay deals with the development of the American college as a force for the socialization of youth. The authors trace parallel shifts in the social order and in expectations from higher education. Thus, during the colonial period, colleges were expected to emphasize Christian values, but after the revolution the more secular attributes of an informed citizenry were stressed. The industrial age brought with it the additional demand for vocational preparation. In all three of these periods there was a consensus concerning the model toward which the young should be socialized. The authors contend that the proliferation of the pressures placed on higher education after 1930—e.g., the training of technologists and "organization men," the rise of the disciplines, the growing commitment to universal higher education, and the development of higher education as a "growth" industry—prevented a similar consensus from developing, and are the basis for the present crises in today's colleges.

567 HUTCHINS, ROBERT M. *The learning society.* New York: Praeger, 1968, 142 pp. $4.50.

Hutchins considers the question of educational goals and suggests that the aim of education should be manhood not manpower. All men and women should be afforded the opportunity to continue their education and achieve their full potential as human beings. Since a human being acts in a human way when he thinks, Hutchins argues that the most effective means to this goal is through a liberal, theoretical education. He questions in some detail the value of vocational education from the standpoints of both theory and of practice. Much of this volume is an expansion of basic themes first laid down 35 years ago in his book *The Higher Learning in America.* However, Hutchins now discusses how in a world entering the 21st century machines might do for modern man what slavery did for the privileged few in ancient Athens. With the increase of leisure, the vision of the learning society may yet come into its own, and if so "a world community learning to be civilized, learning to be human, is at least a possibility."

568 JENCKS, CHRISTOPHER, AND RIESMAN, DAVID. *The academic revolution.* Garden City, N. Y.: Doubleday, 1968, 580 pp. $10; paperback $4.95.

This volume describes the recent ascendance of higher education within American society (the "academic revolution"), and discusses the amazing success and unprecedented academic competence of many institutions. It contains penetrating analyses of some broad topics, including social stratification and mass higher education (see 933 for a separate annotation of this important chapter), the conflict between the generations, and the "public–private" controversy. It also describes the characteristics of some types of undergraduate institutions —church-related, Negro, and community colleges—as well as graduate and professional schools. Lewis B. Mayhew calls this a "cold bleak book which attempts to show not how higher education is ideally visualized, but how it actually is." The authors conclude that American higher education has not had much effect on the rate of social mobility or the degree of equality in American society, and that a meritocracy runs the risk of overvaluing technical competence. The book is a landmark in the literature of higher education—perhaps not always right, but usually impressive, and always thought provoking.

569 REICH, CHARLES A. *The greening of America.* New York: Random House, 1970, 399 pp. $6.95.

In this widely read and influential book, Reich presents a quasi-historical analysis of the youth culture that evolved in the 1960s. He describes the major changes in American society as changes in "consciousness," or "reactions to a way of life that existed before and an adaptation to new realities." According to Reich, the era of Consciousness I began with the individualism and enterprise of the early pioneers and ended with industrialism and widespread corruption. Consciousness II developed during the rise of the corporate state and was a reaction to the failure of the individual to deal with the industrial era successfully. As a result, the corporate organization expanded and began to take on a life of its own, estranged from human values, causing widespread alienation and "impoverishment of life." Consciousness III emerged among the young in response to the domination of man by economic and technological interests. This new mentality stresses the capability of each individual to construct his own life, develop his own moral and aesthetic values, and use technology as a tool in this development. Reich argues that changes in education are central to a new way of life. Education must "enable man to make use of technology, control it and give it direction, cause it to serve values we have chosen." Education should stress humanistic values, prepare the individual for change, but primarily lead him to develop his own potential and uniqueness.

570 RIESMAN, DAVID. *Constraint and variety in American education.* Lincoln, Neb.: University of Nebraska Press, 1958, 137 pp. $1.50.

In this book, Riesman applies a sociological analysis of intellectual life to current developments in American education and culture. The first chapter, dealing with the "homogenization" of academic institutions, discusses the emergence of national institutional models and the effects of their standards on colleges of all levels. Riesman further relates the preeminence of the American university to a decline in experimentation and innovation. The second chapter examines the emerging strength of the disciplines, with special reference to the social sciences, tracing their development as "veto groups" that control inquiry but simultaneously protect the scholar. In addition, problems in the establishment of interdisciplinary study programs are elaborated in light of increasing specialization. In the final chapter, Riesman suggests a "counter-cyclical" policy for secondary education, stressing that schools should provide contrast to, rather than imitation of, the prevailing culture.

571 RUDOLPH, FREDERICK. *The American college and university: A history.* New York: Knopf, 1962, 516 pp. $6.95; paperback Vintage, $2.95.

In this well-written and highly regarded history, Rudolph concentrates on the question: "How and why and with what consequences have the American colleges and universities developed as they have?" He traces this development from the founding of Harvard to the present time. Rudolph succeeds in creating a sense of historical understanding through a combination of well-chosen scholarly and anecdotal material. In addition to treating the major turning points in higher education, specific chapters deal with the extracurriculum, the education of women, the rise of football, and the effects of progressivism on the universities.

572 WHITEHEAD, A. N. *The aims of education and other essays.* New York: Free Press, 1967, 247 pp. $1.95.

In this classic collection of addresses delivered in the early 1900s, Whitehead elaborates an educational philosophy which has remained relevant to the educational problems of succeeding decades. The central theme of the collection— education as a stimulant and guide for the self-development of students—is developed in the first three papers. Whitehead maintains that the aim of education is "acquisition of the art of the utilization of knowledge." This acquisition is related to the growth of the student and is governed by the complementary essentials of freedom and discipline. Whitehead relates this theme to specific areas of the preuniversity curriculum, including technical and liberal education, the place of the classics, and the mathematics curriculum. He further discusses the "imaginative acquisition of knowledge" as the role of the modern university. Though much of the material is outdated, the continuing impact and value of the book lie in Whitehead's generalist approach and in the strong practical and theoretical foundation of his ideas.

7.2—NATIONAL GOALS. Various groups periodically prepare statements concerning national objectives that bear upon access to higher education. In some cases these are essentially pronouncements, in others, detailed analyses of future problems and needs. Some of the more prominent reports are included in this section. They include statements concerning the de-

sirability of universal higher education. The first was that given in 1947 by
the Truman Commission (583) which stated that the time had come for education through the fourteenth grade to be available in the same way that
secondary education is available. The Carnegie Commission on Higher
Education has undertaken various analyses of the extent of educational
opportunity (e.g., 574). Several groups have cited the need for a continuing
national body to monitor educational opportunity and the utilization of
human resources.

573 AMERICAN ACADEMY OF ARTS AND SCIENCES. *A first report: The Assembly on
University Goals and Governance.* Cambridge, Mass.: AAAS, 1971, 51 pp.

A call to action that would reform and revitalize every facet of higher education is the theme of this initial report of the Assembly, established in 1969 by the
American Academy of Arts and Sciences. The report was written by Martin
Meyerson, president of the University of Pennsylvania, and Stephen R. Graubard of Brown University. It lists 85 "theses" for change which should prove
valuable reading for everyone concerned with higher education. A few examples
of the suggested changes are: (1) opportunities for the disadvantaged should be
vastly increased; (2) the "involuntariness" of attendance should be ended, and
opportunities should be broadened for older adults; (3) an "educaid" program
should provide deferred payment covering most college expenses; (4) universities should open up opportunities for graduate and professional training to
women, and be willing to hire them at all levels; (5) admission to graduate and
professional schools by national examination should be offered as an alternative
to the bachelor's degree requirement.

574 CARNEGIE COMMISSION ON HIGHER EDUCATION. *The open-door colleges:
Policies for community colleges.* New York: McGraw-Hill, 1970, 74 pp. $1.95.

This monograph recommends goals for the development and support of community colleges. These recommendations pertain to a variety of objectives and
operating characteristics of community colleges, but the main thrust of the report stems from the Commission's position that there should be a community
college within commuting distance of every potential student, except for those
in sparsely populated areas. The Commission here recommends the need for
from 230 to 280 new colleges by 1980 (a substantial reduction from earlier
recommendations). The Commission suggests the number of colleges it feels
are needed in each state, and estimates that the addition of these new colleges
would put some 95 percent of the population within commuting distance of a
community college. These estimates stand in contrast to Willingham's independent study (688) which indicates that 375 additional colleges in optimal locations would put two-thirds of the population in most states near an accessible
institution.

575 CARNEGIE COMMISSION ON HIGHER EDUCATION. *Less time, more options:
Education beyond the high school.* New York: McGraw-Hill, 1971, 45 pp.
$1.95.

This report offers recommendations for breaking the traditional lockstep pattern of high school and college attendance. Suggested modifications include:
(1) increasing the options for "stopping-out" of college through creation of
service and employment opportunities with the help of national, state, and
municipal programs, as well as private employers; (2) shortening the length of
undergraduate education; and (3) giving credit for education outside the formal
college. The Commission also urges establishment of a four-level degree structure, composed of an A.A., B.A., M.PHIL., and D.A. (Doctor of Arts) or PH.D., to
reduce the number of dropouts and provide more points for career reassessment.

Other recommendations include a decrease in emphasis on certification through formal higher education; the creation of more educational opportunities for older segments of the population; and the universal availability of two years of post-secondary education.

576 COLUMBIA UNIVERSITY, AMERICAN ASSEMBLY. *Goals for Americans: The report of the President's Commission on National Goals.* Englewood Cliffs, N. J.: Prentice-Hall, 1960, 372 pp. $1.95.

This book combines the report of the Eisenhower Commission on National Goals with a series of invitational "summit" essays submitted for consideration in the drawing up of the goals. These papers were contributed by leading authorities in areas of public concern; they discuss science, technological change, urban society, education, the role of the U.S. in world affairs, etc. The essay on education was written by John Gardner. The Commission's goals for education are: (1) The consolidation of small and inefficient school districts to reduce the total number from 40,000 to 10,000. (2) The establishment of a high-level board of education in every state. (3) The improvement of teachers' salaries at all levels. (4) The development of two-year colleges within commuting distance of most high school graduates. (5) A doubling of graduate school capacity. (6) A new emphasis on education throughout life, with a stress on adult education.

577 EDUCATIONAL POLICIES COMMISSION. *Universal opportunity for education beyond the high school.* Wash., D. C.: National Education Association, 1964, 36 pp. $1.25; paper self-cover 35 cents.

This statement discusses ways and means of accomplishing a national goal set by the Educational Policies Commission—i.e., to provide in every population center at least two years of education beyond high school. It is argued that since this additional education benefits society in general, the opportunity should be available free of all cost (including cost of transportation to the nearest public college). Those who wish to resume their education after years spent in military service, child rearing, or limited-education jobs should be included. The general education faculty should look for teachers who are competent in their field, but are not aspiring to narrow specialization. Because of the enormous costs, the Commission, sponsored by NEA and AASA (American Association of School Administrators) expects the burdens to be shared by all levels of government, but rejects tuition charges and selectivity in admission as contravening the goal.

578 EDUCATIONAL POLICIES COMMISSION. *American education and the search for equal opportunity.* Wash., D. C.: National Education Association, 1965, 37 pp. $1.25; paper self-cover 35 cents.

This pamphlet spells out a bill of particulars for bringing equal opportunity into the nation's classrooms. The Commission lists principles that strike both at the prejudices that thwart efforts at equalization, and at the conditions of the disadvantaged themselves. The recommendations start with the concept of the elementary schools as a congenial place where true individualization of program replaces grade-level lockstep. Disadvantaged children need constant reassurance as to their personal worth, and reading and verbal skills should have top priority. The education of teachers for the disadvantaged should be predicated on the need to empathize with the circumstances of life of the disadvantaged. Teachers should have administrative support, freedom to experiment in the classroom, and a role in planning the educational program. Opportunities should be made available for the continuing education of adults, and parents should be drawn into the school world. While these goals are well stated and unquestionably worthy, they stand somewhat in contrast to many of the realities of the school situation. (See for example 599.)

579 GORDON, KERMIT (ED.) *Agenda for the nation.* Wash., D. C.: Brookings Institution, 1968, 620 pp. $8.95.

These penetrating and authoritative essays on major domestic and foreign policy issues were designed as briefings for the incoming leadership of the Republican administration. Written by top-level experts in their fields, they take stock of the situation as of 1968 and weigh alternative courses of action. In the field of education, Ralph Tyler outlines a program for improving elementary and secondary schools, and Clark Kerr reviews the state of higher education. Other chapters dealing with domestic issues consider budget alternatives after Vietnam, housing, antipoverty policies, and the Negro and the urban crisis.

580 KIMBALL, SOLON, AND McCLELLAND, JAMES E. JR. *Education and the new America.* New York: Random House, 1962, 402 pp. $6.75; paperback $1.95.

In this book the authors attempt to answer questions concerning the changing role of education in modern society. They present their views in an anthropological–philosophical framework, observing the role of education as the transmission of culture and its goal as individual commitment. The first section deals with education in agrarian America and the emergence of the progressive philosophy as agrarianism gave way to industrialism. The authors then describe the evolving "culture of the metropolis," with emphasis on contemporary values and the relation of the individual to the organization, and finally review the present role of the educational system in support of corporate society. In the second section the authors define the failure of the educational system as the inability to create an "integrated commitment," or a dedication to society which also "sustains and enhances individuality." By describing commitment in earlier societies, the authors show that modern society demands a different type of commitment and thus a different type of education. They believe education must create commitment by institutionalizing mental and emotional habits necessary for the individual to relate to the complex world; they outline theoretical proposals for this kind of education from the preschool through high school years.

581 McGRATH, EARL J. (ED.) *Universal higher education.* New York: McGraw-Hill, 1966, 258 pp. $5.95.

In this volume, a pathfinding conference sponsored by the Intitute of Higher Education of Teachers College, Columbia University, is described by McGrath as an "exercise in prediction" on "how to translate the politically accepted goal of universal higher education into reality." This book contains texts of the 12 papers read at the conference. The ramifications of universal higher education for a broad spectrum of educational concerns are treated. For example: the social, political, and economic consequences; the impact on admissions, curriculum, and governance; the implications for manpower planning. Some of the material has been superseded by later literature on the topic, but the volume remains valuable as an overview of universal higher education. (For individual chapter annotations, see 220, 662, and 706.)

582 NATIONAL ASSOCIATION OF STATE UNIVERSITIES AND LAND-GRANT COLLEGES, AND AMERICAN ASSOCIATION OF STATE COLLEGES AND UNIVERSITIES. *Recommendations for national action affecting higher education.* Wash., D. C.: NASULGC and AASCU, 1969.

In November 1968 this policy statement was jointly adopted by the National Association of State Universities and Land-Grant Colleges and the American Association of State Colleges and Universities. The statement contains a number of recommendations concerning national priorities. Highlights include: (1) Expansion of postsecondary educational opportunity for all who may benefit from it, with special emphasis on programs for disadvantaged students. (2) A national institutional grants program and expansion of student aid programs. (3) Increased funding for academic facilities and housing. (4) Widespread support of education and research to include fellowship programs; increased support for basic research; institutional development programs; and increased support for programs in the health fields. (5) Adequate support for research programs aimed at urban problems. (6) Substantially increased funding for the Community Services and Continuing Education Act. (7) Federal support for programs designed to improve the quality of the natural environment. (8) Prompt administrative or legislative action to minimize the disruptive effect of selective service calls on graduate and professional education. (9) Support for programs of international and cultural exchange which will assure a truly international dimension in American higher education.

583 PRESIDENT'S COMMISSION ON HIGHER EDUCATION. *Higher education for American democracy.* Wash., D. C.: Office of Education, U.S. Department of Health, Education and Welfare, 1947.

This report of the Truman Commission has probably been cited in reference to universal higher education more than any other document. It was the first prominent national group to declare that "the time has come to make education through the fourteenth grade available in the same way that high school education is now available."

584 PRESIDENT'S TASK FORCE ON HIGHER EDUCATION. *Priorities in higher education: Report.* Wash., D. C.: Government Printing Office, 1970, 31 pp. 30 cents.

This Presidential Task Force was commissioned to determine major federal and institutional priorities for higher education in the 1970s. Resulting recommendations include continuing federal support of the expansion of postsecondary educational opportunity and continued aid to high-quality graduate and professional programs. The Task Force recommended immediate federal assistance to disadvantaged students, health education programs, and tax incentives for private support of higher education. The group also defined the major institutional priorities as clarification of institutional purposes, improvement of curriculum and instructional method, and efficient use of resources. The group suggested the establishment of a national academy of higher education, chartered by but independent of the federal government, to serve as a center for the analysis of higher education as a national resource.

585 SCHULTZE, CHARLES L., HAMILTON, EDWARD K., AND SCHICK, ALLEN. *Setting national priorities: The 1971 budget.* Wash., D. C.: Brookings Institution, 1970, 192 pp. $6.50; paperback $2.95.

This book explains the 1971 federal budget as a set of decisions made about national priorities "in the crucible of limited resources." It discusses some alternatives available, and explains the reasoning behind the difficult choices actually made by President Nixon. Of the $200.8 billion total budget, the President recommended an expenditure of $71.8 billion for defense. The budget of the Department of Health, Education, and Welfare is one of the few to show an increase, but this is largely a result of the $5.9 billion built-in increases in Social Security, Medicare, etc. In education the Administration is confronted with two basic problems: (1) fiscal mismatch—resources to support education are not located where needs are greatest; (2) quality—schools are not as effective as they could be. The administration faces stronger Congressional and public pressure with respect to elementary and secondary education than with respect to higher education. The budgetary strategy is to redirect existing programs. The authors warn: "This approach is certain to provoke political and bureaucratic struggles. In the 1970 budget this approach led to the creation of a powerful education lobby and the near stalemate on education appropriations." The decision against major support for education programs (principally assistance to elementary and secondary education) reflects the view that too little is yet known about their effectiveness to justify large budgetary increases.

586 TASK FORCE ON HIGHER EDUCATION. *Report on higher education.* Wash., D. C.: Government Printing Office, 1971, 130 pp. 75 cents.

This report of an independent task force, funded by the Ford Foundation and chaired by Frank Newman, has received major attention in both governmental and educational circles. The group was asked to examine the major problems facing the nation's colleges and universities in the 1970s and to determine how the functioning of the system meshes with the public interest. The group stressed the need for development of new educational enterprises and the establishment of funding programs to encourage innovation. These enterprises would provide educational "entrepreneurs" with creative opportunities for breaking the lock-step pattern of college attendance. Additional recommendations include changing the structure of accrediting agencies to mirror the public interest; increasing resources for off-campus education; establishing regional examining universities to grant equivalent credit and degrees; and regional television colleges to develop means of providing education through the new media. It also recommended increased autonomy for individual campuses, state use of project grants, and expansion of noncollege programs. An extensive bibliography is listed for each section of the report.

587 U.S. OFFICE OF EDUCATION. *Background readings in American education.* Wash., D. C.: Government Printing Office, 1965, 80 pp. 35 cents.

This booklet contains a variety of historical comments on the nature of American education which were selected and edited for use at the 1965 White House Conference on Education. It begins with a promotional tract about Harvard College published in 1643, includes the Truman Commission enunciation of the need for equality of opportunity, and ends with discussions of current issues. It provides a broad range of background readings on all these topics. It includes selections by statesmen, philosophers, and educators, including Thomas Jefferson, Ralph Waldo Emerson, Horace Mann, John Dewey, Alfred North Whitehead, Robert Hutchins, and Lyndon B. Johnson.

588 U.S. OFFICE OF EDUCATION. *Progress of public education in the United States of America 1967-68: Report for the Thirty-First International Conference on Public Education.* Wash., D. C.: Government Printing Office, 1968, 50 pp. 50 cents.

This report provides a synopsis of the status of U.S. public education in 1966–67. It gives statistics covering enrollment, teacher supply, retention and achievement of pupils, financial support, and vocational education. It was prepared for the Thirty-First International Conference on Public Education, sponsored by UNESCO and the International Bureau of Education. Some of the highlights reported are as follows: 3 out of every 10 persons were directly involved in the educational process—57 million young students and 3 million adults. The number of high school graduates in 1967 equaled more than 75 percent of the nation's 17-year-olds. Average expenditures per pupil (elementary and secondary) rose to an estimated $750, compared with $449 a decade ago. In relation to the gross national product, expenditures are more than three times as great as they were during the middle 1940s. Total expenditures for vocational education have more than quadrupled in the past decade. The proportion of college graduates among young adults almost doubled between 1950 (7.7 percent) and 1966 (14 percent).

589 U.S. OFFICE OF EDUCATION. *Trends in postsecondary education.* Wash., D. C.: Government Printing Office, 1970, 261 pp. $2.50.

This volume contains a number of papers commissioned by the U.S. Office of Education in connection with the preparation of proposals regarding universal education through the thirteenth and fourteenth grades. The papers are concerned with the feasibility and practical consequences of moving toward this national goal. They include such topics as financial requirements, the problem of relevance for new types of students, the role of junior colleges, and the necessary faculty resources. Together the papers provide a useful status and reference document with respect to universal opportunity for higher education.

7.3 — CURRENT ISSUES. This section contains two related types of material—literature of contemporary issues and futurist literature that attempts to anticipate the course of events and conditions that will subsequently characterize higher education and society. These range from professional prognostication (591) to popular works such as the very readable *Future Shock* (601).

590 CAFFREY, JOHN (ED.) *The future academic community — continuity and change.* Wash., D. C.: American Council on Education, 1969, 327 pp. $7.

To say that this book comprises the proceedings of the ACE annual meeting of 1968 on the future of American education does not begin to convey the sense of urgency brought to scholarly discussions of the future. It starts with editor Caffrey's charge that common future-making, "hanging together," is the only way for all segments of the academic community—faculty, students, specialists, administrators, and governing boards—to accomplish change without sacrificing continuity. The format includes invitational papers presenting views from within the educational community, on-the-spot reactions and commentary, and important keynote speeches by national leaders with outside horizons. Of unusual interest is the chapter by Constantinos Doxiadis, internationally known city planner, who connects trends in urbanization with planning for universities.

591 ELAM, STANLEY, AND MCLURE, WILLIAM P. (EDS.) *Educational requirements for the 1970's: An interdisciplinary approach.* New York: Praeger, 1967, 266 pp. $6.50.

An interdisciplinary conference held at the University of Illinois and sponsored by Phi Delta Kappa explored the impact of forces for change on requirements of the educational system in the decade of the seventies. This volume contains presentations by experts in economics, political science, sociology, science, education, and government planning, as well as the ensuing discussions. Problems discussed included interactions between race relations and economic planning; school curriculums and social welfare; goal priorities and costs; government subsidies and government interference. The authors seem to concur that "Today, more than ever before, the educational system and the requirements of that system cannot be isolated from the needs, goals, and expectations of the nation as a whole."

592 EURICH, ALVIN C. (ED.) *Campus 1980: The shape of the future in higher education.* New York: Delacorte, 1968, 326 pp. $6.95; paperback $2.45.

The shape higher education will take by 1980 is the substance of these 17 essays by well-known educators. Some of the challenges that editor Eurich outlines as high-priority issues are: (1) how best to involve the universities as "brain-power centers" in solving social problems; (2) how to allocate financial and educational resources most effectively to serve student population explosions; (3) how to provide meaning and focus for individual students; and (4) how to develop curriculum and instruction to serve a new breed of students. The contributors discuss these broad-spectrum problems from the perspectives of their own fields of interest in higher education.

593 HARCLEROAD, FRED F. (ED.) *Issues of the seventies: The future of higher education.* San Francisco: Jossey-Bass, 1970, 192 pp. $7.75.

This volume contains papers presented at a 1969 conference of the American College Testing Program. Conference participants address themselves to three critical areas of decision in higher education. In Part One, *Society's Concerns,* O. Meredith Wilson urges that education "make credible the ethic expressed in the Declaration of Independence"; Max Lerner discusses the potential of universities to provide minorities with access to jobs, power, and a sense of identity. In Part Two, *Student Needs,* Robert S. Powell Jr., and Harold Taylor both recommend that students be given some of the decision-making power, especially regarding curriculum and faculty appointments. Part Three, *Institutional Response,* contains papers by Daniel Robinson and Robert Heinich suggesting uses of technology and communication media for improving the quality of college management and undergraduate teaching. Ralph Tyler sums up with a discussion of conditions required for effective learning, and concludes that academic excellence and equality of opportunity can be compatible.

594 MAYHEW, LEWIS B. (ED.) *Higher education in the revolutionary decades.* Berkeley, Calif.: McCutchan, 1967, 466 pp. $12.50.

This collection of articles centers on the impact on higher education of the post-World War II revolutions—the population explosion, the growth of cybernetics, the revolt of colonial peoples, the development of modern weapons systems, the growth of technology and automation, and the exponential increases in knowledge. Mayhew points out that some of the problems brought to light in the wake of pressure for rapid change in the higher education system were dysfunctions of long standing; others "derive directly from the revolutionary decade." The readings are well selected and well annotated to provide the basic backdrop for many of the problems besetting higher education in the 1970s.

595 MAYHEW, LEWIS B. *Colleges today and tomorrow.* San Francisco: Jossey-Bass, 1969, 255 pp. $7.75.

In this volume, new directions for future policies in American higher education are proposed to change the pattern of failure in coping with student unrest and urban and minority problems. Mayhew warns that colleges and universities are on "the verge of imminent impotence" because of their lack of response to undergraduate needs and demands. He blames student revolt and radicalism for cuts in educational appropriations and for the intrusion of political officials into academic decisions. He recommends procedural frameworks for dealing with student protest. He finds these were lacking in every major campus upset since 1964. The frameworks should include delegation of authority to a campus judicial system, with procedures for indictments, hearings, and appeals made explicit. He indicts higher education for its lack of response to the problems of urbanization as shown by (1) teaching about urban problems that has not gone deeper than the "descriptive level"; and (2) the failure to locate new institutions in the inner city, which has limited opportunities for minority students.

Other chapters discuss the relevance of the present curriculum and the place of general education in the future. He predicts that the liberal arts undergraduate college can prevail in years to come if it: (1) seeks its own objectives; (2) recognizes reality in staffing, even to the extent of rejecting the PH.D. as a prerequisite; (3) operates as economically as possible; and (4) produces human beings demonstrably better equipped for the complex world of the future. The author's prodigious knowledge of higher education is well applied in this comprehensive overview of current issues and possible solutions.

596 MAYHEW, LEWIS B. *Arrogance on campus.* San Francisco: Jossey-Bass, 1970, 155 pp. $6.50.

In this book Mayhew argues that arrogance among students, faculty, and administrators was the major cause of the crises in colleges and universities in the 1960s. He cogently describes the historical evolution of this widespread arrogance, and traces the erosion of administration from the development of faculty syndicalism and self-interest and student irrationality and romanticism. Mayhew believes that the key to peace in the universities is the restoration of legitimate power to the administration and trustees, and the development of a system of legislative checks and balances. Within this framework, faculty and students would have a voice in specific areas of concern and would accept limitation of power in others. Mayhew further argues that the appropriate area of institutional response to student revolt is curricular reform, and recommends a four-dimensional curricular model that serves developmental and intellectual needs of students. Further recommendations include legislative guidelines for dealing with dissident faculty, and a revised theory of academic freedom that would protect faculty members but not relieve them of individual responsibility for their actions. Finally, Mayhew argues for an increased responsiveness from the university to the larger society through reassessment of the research role, random admissions procedures, concentration on teaching, institutional candor, and establishment of a new academic morality. The book is characterized by the author's usual engaging and forthright style.

597 McCONNELL, T. R. *The redistribution of power in higher education.* Berkeley, Calif.: Center for Research and Development in Higher Education, University of California, 1971, 67 pp. $2.

In this monograph McConnell discusses the changing structure of power and influence in the university. He describes the new personal and social values that affect educational priorities, which in turn affect relationships among the major constituents of the university. McConnell concludes that external forces will become more important in shaping institutions of higher learning, and that most institutions will become campuses of systems, with danger to academic freedom resulting. He predicts a long period of turbulence and conflict.

598 SANFORD, NEVITT (ED.) *The American college.* New York: John Wiley, 1962, 1,084 pp. $12.95; paperback $8.50.

The American College has become a classic in the literature of higher education. The volume runs over a thousand pages and a shorter version entitled *College and Character* was released by the same publisher in 1964. The abbreviated version presents the essential arguments but eliminates much of the discussion of research methodology. In general, the book argues that higher education should be more responsive to the facts and principles of the behavioral sciences. The authors have undertaken to map out the field of higher education as an area of intellectual inquiry, and to construct a basis in theory for the interpretation of existing research.

The authors begin first with the student, summarizing what is known and what might be known about the characteristics, susceptibilities, and potentialities of those who enter college. Next they turn to the college environment and consider the influences which arise within the college. Then follow chapters on the behavior of students in college, on patterns of interaction between students and particular processes of the college, and, finally, on effects upon students of the college experience. Many of these chapters are still basic references; others may be dated but contain valuable ideas, references, and status reports. It is a good place to start reading on any general problem in higher education, particularly if it deals with students.

599 SILBERMAN, CHARLES E. *Crisis in the classroom: The remaking of American education.* New York: Random House, 1970, 553 pp. $10.

In this thought-provoking review of contemporary education, Silberman combines theoretical discussion with dramatic vignettes ("ITEMS") to alert both layman and professional to "what is wrong and what needs to be done." He sees the crisis in education as the lack of attention to moral purposes, to the ends as well as the means of the educational process. He discusses the specific failure of the urban schools in educating minority groups, the general failure of all public schools to produce students able to take responsibility for their own education, and reviews reasons for the failure of recent reforms. Succeeding chapters detail possible reforms in elementary and high schools. Silberman describes successful innovative primary and secondary schools in the United States and England, to illustrate how the educational system could be changed. The final section deals with restructuring American education through reforms of teacher education. Silberman states that "the education of educators should be the central purpose of the college," and stresses that teaching in some form should be an integral part of the undergraduate training program.

600 TAYLOR, HAROLD. *Students without teachers: The crisis in the university.* New York: McGraw-Hill, 1969, 333 pp. $7.95.

Taylor indicts American universities for the "crisis of neglect," which forced students to turn to other students for intellectual and moral leadership. His exposition of the student radical movement places the blame on the bureaucracy of the university hierarchy, which he feels has brought about "educational bankruptcy." The answer he sees is to revitalize education in the spirit of the landgrant concept of "service to all citizens." This would "reestablish the student at the center of the university community." His experiences as president of Sarah Lawrence College support his argument that the small experimental college can reconstitute education by bringing students into the mainstream of educational decisions. He presents many concrete suggestions for reforming teaching and learning along these lines.

601 TOFFLER, ALVIN. *Future shock.* New York: Random House, 1970, 505 pp. $8.95.

This fascinating book documents in mind-boggling detail the seemingly simple and obvious fact that things are changing, and change is often unsettling. Not content to leave the message in those simple terms, the author cites innumerable examples of the increasing impermanence and transience of life. For the average person bombarded with change, novelty, and increasing diversity, the urgent problem is to develop strategies for survival. One such strategy suggested by the author is a new form of education designed to teach us how to maintain mental balance and cope with life in an ad-hoc world. What the book may lack in reliable profundity, it makes up in perceptive and relentless documentation of the accelerating pace of life. At the least it is fascinating reading, with entertaining writing by a writer with a keen ear for alliteration (e.g., "Catholics, cliques, and coffee breaks," or "the psychic cake-mix").

602 TROW, MARTIN. Reflections on the transition from mass to universal higher education. *Daedalus,* 1970, vol. 99, pp. 1-43.

Trow describes the dilemma of American higher education as a serious loss in equilibrium between scholarly autonomy and public service, resulting from massive enrollment jumps and involvement in controversial social issues. He explains how this crisis in confidence has affected his own university, the Berkeley campus of the University of California. The trustees, reacting to public resentment of radicals, intervene in the academic domain—a serious threat to the university's capacity to sustain a climate of excellence. In Berkeley's eagerness to help solve urban problems, militant black students, whom Trow considers not typical of the black community as a whole, have been recruited. As a result, he claims, the thrust of black campus leadership is to operate as a base for revolutionary political action. Another factor in the politicalization of the campus is the "involuntary student" syndrome. This results from the transformation to universal higher education and the locking-in to college of young men who want to avoid the draft. Even within the academic community, Trow sees evidence of breakdown in governance, and predicts that the situation may worsen to the point where "governance will be carried on by political students, the minority of academic men who enjoy polemical politics, and hapless administrators." He fears progressively more repressive sanctions, more confrontation, and further losses in autonomy and academic freedom.

603 U.S. OFFICE OF EDUCATION. *Contemporary issues in American education.* Wash., D. C.: Government Printing Office, 1965, 158 pp. 60 cents.

This volume contains valuable background papers prepared by 18 prominent educators who served as consultants to the 1965 White House Conference on Education. The papers were designed to stimulate discussion by the panelists and participants. They cover a wide range of topics: jobs and dropouts; automation and job obsolescence; teacher education and evaluation; the role of the states; overseas programs and foreign students; talented and handicapped students; graduate and undergraduate education; desegregation; innovation; and urban schools. However, two noticeable omissions—student activism and women's rights—indicate the swift changes in focus occurring in a few years' time.

604 WOODRING, PAUL. *The higher learning in America: A reassessment.* New York: McGraw-Hill, 1968, 236 pp. $6.95; paperback $2.95.

In this book, Woodring draws upon his wide-ranging knowledge gained as education editor of the *Saturday Review* (1960-66). He describes the present state of higher education and offers recommendations for solutions to some of the more urgent problems. The first part details characteristics of institutions and offers definitions of prestige, selectivity, and quality. The second part treats the student population, with special attention to student unrest, characteristics of student activists, and changes in sexual mores. The third part examines the conflicting loyalties of the professor, and investigates the administrative and governing structures. In the final section, Woodring identifies and offers solutions for major problems facing higher education, including selection for admission, funding, degree structure, specialization, undergraduate teaching, and the future of liberal education. He concludes with a plan for the restructuring of the present system involving three levels: The first level would comprise three years of liberal education leading to a bachelor's degree. The student would then choose a major specialized field and continue one or two years of professional study, which would qualify him for a master's degree. He could then choose to continue for a doctorate degree if he wished. This program would solve a major problem by "shifting the responsibility for planning and teaching the program of liberal education to those who believe in it." See 218 and 575 for similar proposals.

605 YAMAMOTO, KAORU (ED.) *The college student and his culture: An analysis.* Boston: Houghton Mifflin, 1968, 493 pp. $7.75.

This book is an anthology of outstanding research contributions to the understanding of a college student from many dimensions: the characteristics he brings to college; the subcultures that are important in his college adjustments, transitions, and changes; and the impact of college on the student. The first and last sections deal with the broad spectrum of the university today and tomorrow. Among the many well-known contributors are Clark Kerr, Kenneth Keniston, Alexander Astin, C. Robert Pace, Burton Clark, David Riesman, and Ralph Tyler. The book follows in the tradition of Nevitt Sanford's *The American College* (598), and while there is slight overlap, it is a useful complement to Sanford's book.

7.4 – *GOVERNANCE AND PLANNING*. The process of governance and planning is central and has a controlling effect on many aspects of access to higher education. It is, of course, a large field, and the references presented here are highly selected. Some of this literature is based upon research or theoretical analysis; most is descriptive and concerned with process.

There are three principal areas covered. One is long-range planning, particularly with respect to social objectives. Another is administration, and in this case the definitive reference is the *Handbook of College and University Administration* edited by Knowles (615). Third, the broad area of governance includes such questions as the roles of trustees, administrators, faculty, and students; the dynamics of governance and control; and relationships with legislative bodies. Corson's book (608) remains a standard reference even though it is more than a decade old. *Campus and Capitol* (620) is an especially useful reference on the respective roles of higher education and state government. It also has a very good bibliography.

606 AMERICAN ASSOCIATION FOR HIGHER EDUCATION AND NATIONAL EDUCATION ASSOCIATION TASK FORCE. *Faculty participation in academic governance.* Wash., D. C.: AAHE, 1967, 67 pp. $1.25.

This investigation found that a main source of faculty unrest was dissatisfaction with their role in academic decision-making. The greatest discontent and support of unionization showed up at public junior colleges and "emerging" four-year colleges. A concept of "shared authority" is the central recommendation to alleviate the situation. It should be implemented partly by an academic senate with authority to settle "aggregate" issues that affect the faculty as a whole. A formal appeals procedure is also recommended to resolve disputes involving individual faculty members and the administration. Although hesitant to endorse strikes, the Task Force concludes, "There are no decisive reasons why the faculty should be denied the opportunity to strike, in terms of either society's essential needs or the long-run interests of the institution."

607 CARTTER, ALLAN M., CONANT, JAMES B., LONGENECKER, HERBERT E., AND ALLEN, JAMES E. JR. The Compact for Education: Views from higher education. *Educational Record,* 1966, vol. 47, pp. 79-115.

These four articles deal with the background and rationale for the Compact for Education, and provide a forum for leaders in higher education to air supportive and opposing viewpoints of implementing the Compact by means of an educational commission of the states. The concept derived from Conant's 1964 book *Shaping Educational Policy,* which recommended the creation of a new body to provide more coordinated planning at all levels of education in the U.S. Some of the voluntary higher education associations expressed misgivings that "it was a bad idea . . . to involve educational and political leaders in a policy-oriented organization," and objected that it threatened institutional autonomy. Conant defends the commission as "not a mechanism for action, but rather a mechanism for stimulating wise action by the states." He sees a vital need for cooperative approaches to the many problems of state planning, policy decisions, and financial support for higher education. Longenecker, president of Tulane University, speaking for the opposition, argues that the Compact would establish a new system for the governance of higher educational institutions that "would be a major step toward the degradation of our colleges and universities to the status of state agencies." Allen writes in support of the Compact, pointing out the need for "a vigorous renaissance in state educational leadership – a commitment to the reforms necessary to make the states strong and fully effective in the governance of education."

608 CORSON, JOHN J. *Governance of colleges and universities.* New York: McGraw-Hill, 1960, 209 pp. $5.95.

In this highly regarded study, Corson examines the status of institutional governance (as of 1960) from the vantage point of his long experience as a management consultant in public administration. The study focuses on the decision-making process in the context of educational goals, student and faculty affairs, alumni relations, finance, relations with private and public agencies and the general public. In view of the "unprecedented demands for adaptability, expansibility, and creativity" facing higher education in the decades ahead, he feels that the academic community must unite in "dynamically improving collaboration" to eliminate inflexibility and tradition-bound practices. He also outlines the roles of major administrative officers in higher education, and compares their functions with those of leaders in other organizations. This remains a valuable book even though radical changes during the 1960s date much of the material.

609 DODDS, HAROLD W. *The academic president—educator or caretaker?* New York: McGraw-Hill, 1962, 294 pp. (Out of print)

This informal book could almost be termed a "job description" of the academic presidency. Based partly on distilled wisdom from Dodds's tenure as President of Princeton, and partly on interviews with other academic presidents, it concentrates on how to keep the essence of the job—educational leadership—from being diluted by daily pressures from the many constituencies of a university. Dodds's prescient description of the strains that "behemoth" size place on this role keeps the book from being a view from an ivory tower. He warns that if enormous growth makes a university a "coldly impersonal melange of unrelated parts, . . . radical surgery or imaginative reorganization" would be called for. He proposes an apprenticeship approach that would equip more young faculty men for later leadership. The book contains much practical advice, both for search committees looking for new presidents, and administrators in need of perspective.

610 ELAM, STANLEY, AND SWANSON, GORDON I. (EDS.) *Educational planning in the United States.* Itasca, Ill.: Peacock, 1969, 216 pp. $6.50.

This volume includes papers delivered at the Symposium on Educational Planning sponsored by the Phi Delta Kappa Commission on Education, Manpower, and Economics. Conference participants focused on the present status of educational planning; planning as a separate profession with distinctive training and standards; the planning of adjustments in the educational system; and a theoretical outline of the science of planning.

611 ERIC CLEARINGHOUSE ON HIGHER EDUCATION. *Governance.* Compendium Series of Current Research, Programs and Proposals, No. 1. Wash., D. C.: ERIC Clearinghouse on Higher Education, 1970, 23 pp.

This booklet contains a listing of recently completed and ongoing research dealing with governance. Following a brief introductory comment on the scope of the research, each project is listed with a brief description including the major goals and methodology, the beginning and expected completion dates, the principal investigator, and the source of funding. Finally, the items listed are indexed by author and sponsoring agency.

612 HARTNETT, RODNEY T. *College and university trustees: Their backgrounds, roles, and educational attitudes.* Princeton, N. J.: Educational Testing Service, 1969, 79 pp. $2.

Student unrest has catapulted the trustee from corporate anonymity into the public spotlight as a policy maker responsible for many significant and controversial decisions. This report brings the academic trustee into focus as an individual. More than 5,000 trustees, representing 536 colleges and universities, responded to a questionnaire on their backgrounds, attributes, and attitudes.

Despite wide diversity, the typical trustee was found to fit the stereotype of the white, well-educated, middle-aged, successful business or professional man. At private universities, nearly 50 percent were business executives. On matters of academic freedom, trustees of institutions in New England and the middle Atlantic states were found to be the most liberal; trustees of public junior colleges appeared to be the most conservative. On questions of academic governance, the trustees feel a responsibility for presidential appointments and decisions on "external" affairs such as finances and the physical plant, but in other areas prefer to delegate authority to the administration. They are wary of faculty and student participation in governance. Trustees typically do not follow up their attendance at board meetings by reading the literature of higher education; for the most part, they were unfamiliar with books and journals on the subject. This study supplies useful comparisons for institutions engaged in self-studies of their systems of governance.

613 HENDERSON, ALGO D. Control in higher education: Trends and issues. *Journal of Higher Education,* 1969, vol. 40, pp. 1-11.

Henderson discusses two types of group-participative frameworks—corporate and collective bargaining. He concludes that the corporate model has the best potential for attaining the "only real security for the academic program—the acceptance of goals and roles by both the academic and the public interest." The corporate setup functions successfully in the complex administration of a large university, but it is increasingly the focus of radical hostility. He conjectures that opening board membership to students and faculty would broaden the educational perspectives of the business members, who in turn are charged with interpreting the university to the public. The other kind of participative model—the collective bargaining approach—he sees as unsuited for a university. Emphasizing the need to keep political decisions distinct from educational ones, he recommends state constitutional provisions as the best protection for the university against political interference. Although comprehensive planning for the location, size, and financial needs of higher education are properly political in nature, he stresses that decisions on program, environment, and research should be the clear domain of the individual institution.

614 KNORR, OWEN A. (ED.) *Long-range planning in higher education.* Boulder, Colo.: Western Interstate Commission for Higher Education, 1965, 128 pp. $3.

This publication includes the papers presented at the Sixth Annual Institute on College Self Study for College and University Administrators. The topics include design and change in American higher education; planning in the college or university; study in institutional planning; autonomy and coordination between the institution and the system; housing the educational program; long-range financial planning; system analysis in planning; and resources for planning.

615 KNOWLES, ASA S. (ED.) *Handbook of college and university administration.* Vol. 1 *General.* Vol. 2 *Academic.* New York: McGraw-Hill, 1970. Vol. 1, 1,100 pp., $35. Vol. 2, 1,300 pp., $35. Boxed set $60.

This encyclopedic handbook is designed to provide the administrator in higher education with an overall view of general operating procedures and with models of administrative practice. The chapters are written in a concise and practical how-to style by 160 practitioners in the major areas of college administration. Volume 1 covers general administration: legal aspects; governing boards; planning, space requirements, and institutional research; public relations, development, and alumni relations; nonacademic personnel administration; physical plant administration; and business and financial administration. Volume 2 covers academic administration: legal aspects; academic affairs; admissions; learning resources; adult education; academic personnel administration; student personnel administration; athletics; health programs; religion; and campus–community facilities and enterprises. Selected sections and chapters are annotated separately throughout this volume. Individual contributions vary in quality, but, as a whole, the handbook is a very valuable reference.

616 KROEPSCH, ROBERT H. Regional cooperation in higher education. *Compact,* 1970, vol. 4, no. 2, pp. 35-38.

This brief article traces the development of the three major regional coordination boards of higher education: the Southern Regional Education Board (1180), the Western Interstate Commission for Higher Education (1181), and the New England Board of Higher Education (1179). The author identifies similarities and differences in the official processes of organization, charters, cooperative programs, financing, and the role of the coordinating agency.

617 MCCONNELL, T. R., AND MORTIMER, KENNETH P. *The faculty in university governance.* Berkeley, Calif.: Center for Research and Development in Higher Education, University of California, 1971, 201 pp. $3.50.

This work is based on studies of Fresno State College, the Twin Cities campus of the University of Minnesota, and the University of California at Berkeley. The authors explore organizational roles of the faculty in internal government, in relationships with administration and governing boards, and in response to external constraints. They also document the degree of decentralization in each system, and weigh the possible effects of further autonomy against the need for central administrative control. From these studies the authors conclude that a faculty senate must be limited in size to be effective. They found that such bodies tend to be oligarchical in nature, and that committees were unaccountable to the senate. They further recommend joint faculty–administrative participation in decision making, and stress the need for strong administrative leadership. Finally, the authors conclude that conflict is a normal state of affairs and should be institutionalized through open debate and democratic processes.

618 MCGRATH, EARL J. (ED.) *Cooperative long-range planning in liberal arts colleges.* New York: Teachers College, Columbia University, 1964, 108 pp. $3.

This small volume contains eight useful papers prepared for a working conference of college presidents. It includes practical discussions and exemplary data on various aspects of long-range planning in the liberal arts college. Topics include: quality and cost of liberal arts programs; a continuing program of institutional research; the relation of admissions policies to institutional purpose; and the involvement of faculty members in institutional policy formulation.

619 MILLETT, JOHN D. *Decision making and administration in higher education.* Kent, Ohio: Kent State University Press, 1968, 161 pp. $5; paperback, $1.95.

This well-known volume of essays presents a clear and cogent analysis of major problems and recent developments in educational administration. The author draws on his wide experience, including 11 years as a state university president. The first paper discusses new patterns of decision-making emerging not only within the institutional structure but also in the authority of external agencies of government. Millett examines the relative power of the president, the faculty, and the governing board, and reviews the development of collective bargaining and the effects of student demands for power. He also analyzes the increasing control by federal and state governments and its effect on administrative policies and practices.

The second paper discusses the planning process. It traces the historical background and defines four substantive issues involved in planning: objectives of the institution; enrollment; programs; and resources. The third paper investigates systems analysis as a method of studying organizations in combination with cost-effectiveness studies and planning–programming–budget sequences. The final papers discuss methods of financing higher education and the structure of communications in the university.

620 MINTER, W. JOHN (ED.) *Campus and capitol: Higher education and the state.* Boulder, Colo.: Western Interstate Commission for Higher Education, 1966, 192 pp. $3.50.

This publication includes the papers presented at the Eighth Annual College Self Study Institute sponsored by WICHE and the Center for Research and Development in Higher Education at Berkeley. Seven leading educators discuss the most important dimensions of the growing interdependence between government and higher education. The book also contains a very useful annotated bibliography.

In his paper, Samuel Gould underlines the increasing interest in higher education among politicians, and warns that the erosion of the independence of a university may be very subtle. Universities, he contends, should have their basic freedom of action guaranteed by constitutional authority. Daniel Aldrich suggests that the identity of an institution is the image established by the idiosyncrasies and dynamics of internal constituents, and the freedom that they may exercise in establishing this identity determines institutional autonomy. Lyman Glenny provides a useful discussion of current patterns of coordination (see 657). The role of the federal government in higher education is considered by John F. Morse. He refers to a conviction in Congress and the White House that the federal government must play a major role in financing higher education, and suggests that it is up to higher education to articulate the priorities. Charles Benson continues this theme and points out the gross inequities in federal disbursements. He suggests that "one solution might be to provide the states with block grants to use in strengthening all higher education within their boundaries." Fred Harrington tells the story of the Compact for Education. Finally, T. R. McConnell examines the university and the state and contends that "state governments should determine only the resources available to the university and leave the effective expenditure of those funds to the institution." It seems safe to say that this suggestion falls on less sympathetic ears in the 1970s than when it was first made.

621 ORGANIZATION FOR ECONOMIC CO-OPERATION AND DEVELOPMENT. *Social objectives in educational planning.* Wash., D. C.: OECD, 1967, 309 pp. $6.50.

This volume includes papers presented at the 1967 Paris conference of the OECD Study Group in the Economics of Education. The theoretical basis for the conference was the belief that the educational process *creates* ability, and the resulting theme was the implementation of equal educational opportunity in OECD countries. The major concern of the Study Group was an investigation of the social and economic elements involved in the "democratization of educational participation." The papers examine elements related to democratization, including performance of the schools, effectiveness of specific educational policies and measures, research needed to increase this effectiveness, and development and planning requirements.

622 PALOLA, ERNEST G., AND PADGETT, WILLIAM. *Planning for self-renewal: A new approach to planned organizational change.* Berkeley, Calif.: Center for Research and Development in Higher Education, University of California, 1971, 118 pp. $2.

One of the major crises facing higher education in recent years is the questioning of basic aims and purposes. In this volume the authors examine institutional planning in four states in an effort to determine planning methods that may be helpful in meeting this qualitative crisis. Three major types of planning were identified: *expedient* planning dealing primarily with logistical problems; *substantive* planning involving examination and determination of major long-range policies; and *mixed* planning combining features of both. The authors investigate institutional characteristics fostering each type of planning, and present case studies of colleges where substantive planning has been successful.

From this analysis, the authors define five key conditions of institutional self-renewal, suggest a model for long-range planning, and outline organizational and structural requirements for planning offices. The authors conclude that self-renewal is primarily facilitated by emphasis on qualitative development, strong educational leadership, wide participation in the planning process, and use of outside experts.

623 PETERSON, RICHARD E. *The crisis of purpose: Definition and uses of institutional goals.* Report 5. Wash., D. C.: ERIC Clearinghouse on Higher Education, 1970, 13 pp.

The author discusses the critical role of institutional goals and how they fit into the process of long-range planning and systems of management accountability. He briefly summarizes research on institutional goals and describes useful strategies for defining goals and coming to agreement on their priority. An extensive bibliography is included.

624 RAUH, MORTON A. *The trusteeship of colleges and universities.* New York: McGraw-Hill, 1969, 206 pp. $7.95.

This book is a practical examination of the role of the trustee and the key issues of concern to trustees. Individual chapters treat the characteristics and responsibilities of trustees; the selection of a president; the relationships between the president, the faculty, the students, and the board; finance and management; development; and public relations. Further chapters discuss the mechanics of board organization, the initiation of new trustees, and composition of the board. Special attention is devoted to the problems and issues of the trusteeship in the public university, the junior college, and the Catholic college.

625 ROURKE, FRANCIS E., AND BROOKS, GLENN E. *The managerial revolution in higher education.* Baltimore, Md.: Johns Hopkins Press, 1966, 182 pp. $8.

This book analyzes the impact of new managerial techniques on administrative systems of higher education. Data are based on questionnaires and interviews at over 300 colleges and agencies. The authors define the adoption of these new techniques as an attempt to "rationalize" the universities' administrative and decision-making structures. Chapters are devoted specifically to use of computers and automation, institutional research, and allocative decisions based on quantitative data gathering. Final sections investigate the effects of these techniques in educational policy making with regard to shifts in group control over policy and changes in actual decisions.

626 UNITED NATIONS EDUCATIONAL, SCIENTIFIC AND CULTURAL ORGANIZATION, INTERNATIONAL INSTITUTE FOR EDUCATIONAL PLANNING. *Educational planning: A directory of training and research institutions.* (2nd ed.) Paris: Unesco, 1968, 235 pp. $3.

This international directory lists the activities, staff, and publications of 130 institutions in 36 countries. It represents a world-wide community of scholars and practitioners devoted to educational planning, and is a valuable source of information on the international scope of education research related to planning.

627 WILSON, LOGAN. Changing university governance. *Educational Record,* 1969, vol. 50, pp. 388-404.

This article is noteworthy for its forthright indictment of faculty who have condoned or vacillated over "criminal trespass, property destruction, and interference with majority rights to teach and learn." Wilson, president of the American Council on Education, charges that "not only does such behavior weaken the internal structure of the university, it also invites outside interference." To forestall this retrograde "devolution" in governance, he warns that clear bases of authority must be established. He defends the university administrator as being far removed from the "authoritarian devil" of the revolutionary student litany; in fact, he points out that administrative independence of action is limited on one side by state planning and coordinating boards, and on the other, by faculty authority over appointments and educational decisions. He criticizes the "ambivalent feelings" of faculty, who want a strong role in policy making, but are often reluctant to give necessary time. He concludes that it is crucial for professors to broaden their participation in university affairs; "the implication that if universities will not govern themselves, they will be governed by others" is more ominous for faculty than for any other group in the academic community.

628 WILSON, LOGAN (ED.) *Emerging patterns in American higher education.* Wash., D. C.: American Council on Education, 1965, 292 pp. $4.

This book provides a forum for leaders of higher education to air their opinions on recent developments and innovations in American colleges. Many of the articles discuss the conflict between the concepts of institutional autonomy and institutional cooperation. Three factual sections deal with changes within institutions; the emergence of state systems; and cooperative arrangements among institutions on the local, interstate, and regional levels. National organizations in higher education and the role of professional associations are also assessed. The effect of national policy on higher education is considered in the closing essays. Although the authors assert that colleges and universities must make responsible plans for the future, they also argue that a certain measure of institutional autonomy is necessary for the maintenance of academic freedom.

629 ZWINGLE, J. L. Governing boards, in Asa S. Knowles (Ed.), *Handbook of college and university administration.* Vol. I. *General.* New York: McGraw-Hill, 1970, sec. 2, 80 pp.

This section reviews theoretical considerations and the practical operation of governing boards. Individual sections discuss the concept of the board, its current role in higher education, and the types and titles of representative boards. Further sections examine the composition of boards and their legal authority. The author also provides a comprehensive review of bylaws, including such topics as: methods of election or appointment, alumni representation, student representatives, and committees of the board. The chapter also includes sample charters and bylaws and a checklist for rating governing board policy manuals.

7.5—MANAGEMENT INFORMATION. Demands of educational accountability have exacerbated an already existing problem of retrieving and interpreting information necessary for sound administrative practice. Consequently, since the late 1960s there has been a surge of activity and interest in the development of modern business methods in higher education.

References in this section include material on management information systems, programming–planning–budgeting methods, and educational accountability. While this movement is commonly regarded as inevitable and necessary, there is in many quarters well-reasoned reservation concerning the dangers of introducing control mechanisms that may in some instances add arbitrariness at the expense of wisdom, procedure instead of action, and short-sighted economy in the place of long-range social good. Some such dangers will have to be risked in order to accomplish social objectives and protect public interests.

630 BANGHART, FRANK W. *Educational systems analysis.* New York: Macmillan, 1969, 315 pp. $8.95.

This volume provides a useful introduction to the application of systems analysis to educational administration. It covers the following major topics: a general background to systems analysis, information systems, applications of systems, and system technology. The book is self-contained and well illustrated, but it moves fast and does not dilute the topic.

631 CAFFREY, JOHN, AND MOSMANN, CHARLES J. *Computers on campus.* Wash., D. C.: American Council on Education, 1967, 207 pp. $3.

Many problems associated with processing larger and larger numbers of applications, aid awards, student needs, etc., sooner or later become problems of electronic data processing—whether to install a computer or how to use the one already on hand. This book is based on visits to over 50 colleges. It describes the variety of ways colleges use computers to support daily operations and administrative services as well as research. Administrators will likely find this a useful nontechnical introduction to a complex but increasingly necessary tool.

632 CASASCO, JUAN A. *Planning techniques for university management.* Wash., D. C.: American Council on Education, 1970, 77 pp. $2.50.

This report provides a brief description of the progress that has been made in using computers in systems analysis in academic administration on individual campuses. It includes brief and relatively nontechnical annotations of selected programs and projects concerned with computer applications to university planning.

633 DONOHUE, JAMES P., AND McKINNEY, JOHN R. Information systems for administrative control, in Asa S. Knowles (Ed.), *Handbook of college and university administration.* Vol. I. *General.* New York: McGraw-Hill, 1970, sec. 3, pp. 94-123.

This chapter provides a concise summary of information dealing with the goals and practical operation of information systems used in institutional management. Individual sections discuss planning for an information system; the costs of computing and the role of the computer; methods of reporting; structure of the system; necessary personnel; and physical site considerations.

634 EDUCATION COMMISSION OF THE STATES. Accountability '70. *Compact,* 1970, vol. 4, no. 5, pp. 1-27.

Early in 1970 the concept of accountability became both fashionable and threatening in education. At its simplest the term has come to mean that administrators will be held responsible for managing the educational enterprise so that concrete outcomes can be evaluated in relation to specific budgeted objectives. This issue of *Compact* contains a number of articles on various aspects of accountability in elementary, secondary, and higher education. It also includes a series of brief articles on "national assessment," a major project designed to facilitate evaluation of educational outcomes.

635 EDUCATIONAL TESTING SERVICE. *Proceedings of the Conferences on Educational Accountability.* Princeton, N. J.: ETS, 1971. (Multilithed)

The concept of educational accountability has many applications and ramifications. This conference was especially valuable in representing the views of individuals highly respected in educational administration at the secondary and higher levels, in educational evaluation, and in instruction, as well as representatives from teachers' unions and private business.

636 FARMER, JAMES. *Why planning, programming, budgeting systems for higher education?* Boulder, Colo.: Western Interstate Commission for Higher Education, 1970, 24 pp.

This brief monograph is designed for senior administrators in higher education. It is intended to provide an understanding of the nature of programming-planning-budget techniques, their advantage for decision-making, their approximate cost, the effects of their use, and how they are implemented. It is a very limited introduction but should be useful in providing a basic overview.

637 HARTLEY, HARRY J. *Educational planning-programming-budgeting: Systems approach.* Englewood Cliffs, N. J.: Prentice-Hall, 1969, 290 pp. $8.95.

Systematic program-planning-budgeting methods (PPBS) were developed in the armed forces and introduced successively in private industry and the federal government. In the late 1960s PPBS became a natural complement to the concept of accountability. PPBS is variously viewed as a salvation or as a menace. This book describes the methods in theory and in practice with numerous examples and illustrations.

638 HARTNETT, RODNEY T. *Accountability in higher education: A consideration of some of the problems of assessing college impacts.* New York: College Entrance Examination Board, 1971, 21 pp. $1.

This excellent paper discusses the importance of measuring outcomes of higher education and the many pitfalls in doing so. The author clarifies the distinction between such terms as accountability, evaluation, institutional research, and cost-benefit analysis. In particular, he contrasts evaluation as being primarily concerned with effectiveness while accountability is concerned with effectiveness and also efficiency. He goes on to explain that management information systems can only succeed in supporting the accountability function if institutional objectives are clearly stated. A constant dilemma is the fact that those objectives defined carefully enough to permit reliable measurement tend to be trivial, while "important" objectives tend to be ambiguous. It is a paper that ought to be read by those held accountable and also by those doing the accounting.

639 HEFFERLIN, JB LON, AND PHILLIPS, ELLIS L. JR. *Information services for academic administration.* San Francisco: Jossey-Bass, 1971, 160 pp. $6.50.

This practical and useful book was prompted by the urgent needs of college administrators to obtain reliable information. Its numerous annotations of information sources are designed to aid college presidents and senior administrators in coping with the proliferation of specialized educational organizations. The book also includes sections on communication within and between campuses, workshops, consulting services, and information centers. There is also a very good chapter on publications. The annotations are well chosen and well written. The authors conclude with a realistic discussion of ways to expedite information gathering. A principal recommendation is for more metainformation systems — centers, mechanisms, and publications which specialize in selecting critical information and telling people where it can be found.

640 HUFF, ROBERT A. *Focus on MIS: A report on the WICHE-ACE higher education management information systems seminar.* Boulder, Colo.: Western Interstate Commission for Higher Education, 1970, 22 pp.

This report provides a useful brief overview of management information systems. It includes impressions from various observers at a national seminar on information systems. This report is a companion for the much more detailed papers presented at the meeting (see 644).

641 JOHNSON, CHARLES B., AND KATZENMEYER, WILLIAM G. (EDS.) *Management information systems in higher education: The state of the art.* Durham, N. C.: Duke University Press, 1969, 191 pp. $6.

The papers included in this volume resulted from a seminar on management information systems held at Duke University. The basic thesis of the book is that "the existence of the computer and the competence to utilize it in the development of management information are making the creation of management information systems imperative to ethical administrative practice in complex institutions." The book includes a discussion of basic principles and procedures involved in the development of management information systems, the development of large-scale multiinstitutional systems, and the potential of modeling or simulation techniques as a tool in problem solving. The volume is intended as a source book for those considering the development of a management information system, and it includes illustrations of the application of various modeling techniques to specific problems.

642 LAWRENCE, BEN, WEATHERSBY, GEORGE, AND PATTERSON, VIRGINIA W. (EDS.) *Outputs of higher education: Their identification, measurement, and evaluation.* Boulder, Colo.: Western Interstate Commission for Higher Education, 1970, 130 pp. $3.50.

This volume is concerned with one of the most difficult problems in planning and managing higher institutions—the identification and measurement of outputs. Ten well-informed writers contributed these papers to a symposium held in May 1970. While all the papers are directed to the general problem of determining outputs of higher education, they range from conceptual analysis to specific approaches to measurement, and from research-based systems approaches to narrative discussions of the general problem. Though somewhat uneven and certainly not definitive, the volume does provide valuable progress toward the problem of specifying educational objectives and knowing whether they have been achieved.

643 MILLER, JAMES L. JR. *State budgeting for higher education: The use of formulas and cost analysis.* Ann Arbor, Mich.: Institute of Public Administration, University of Michigan, 1965, 228 pp. $3.50.

This study describes formulas for budget requests and cost analysis used to work out appropriations for public higher education in California, Kentucky, Florida, Indiana, and Texas. The author discusses the need for further investigation of such matters as the significance of measurement units, the effects on innovation and creativity, and the long-term accuracy of a formula as institutions grow and change. It is useful background reading for educators and officials concerned with planning and financing of public higher education.

644 MINTER, W. JOHN, AND LAWRENCE, BEN (EDS.) *Management information systems: Their development and use in the administration of higher education.* Boulder, Colo.: Western Interstate Commission for Higher Education, 1969, 114 pp. $3.50.

This volume contains a series of papers presented at a national symposium on management information systems. It includes discussion of various types of systems and such special problems as measures of performance and effectiveness. The papers vary from fairly technical presentations to practical case histories describing applications on individual campuses. For a brief overview of the topic see 640.

645 ORGANIZATION FOR ECONOMIC CO-OPERATION AND DEVELOPMENT. *Methods and statistical needs for educational planning.* Wash., D. C.: OECD, 1967, 363 pp. $8.50.

This volume provides a detailed but generally nontechnical handbook of methods for educational planning in large systems. It includes topics such as elements of an educational flow model; sociological aspects of educational planning; methods of cost analysis; and international comparisons. The emphasis is on broad, long-range policy considerations rather than short-term administrative decisions.

646 ORGANIZATION FOR ECONOMIC CO-OPERATION AND DEVELOPMENT. *Budgeting, programme analysis and cost-effectiveness in educational planning.* Wash., D. C.: OECD, 1968, 304 pp. $4.20.

This volume contains papers from a conference of the same name held in 1968. It focuses primarily on the integration of short-run and long-run aspects of educational planning, and the relationship between objectives and implementation. Papers by well-known authors are concerned with such problems as the budget as an instrument of planning; cost effectiveness in local schools; allocation of resources to education; and the role of cost models in educational planning.

647 ROUECHE, JOHN E., BAKER, GEORGE A. III, AND BROWNELL, RICHARD L. *Accountability and the community college: Directions for the 70's.* Wash., D. C.: American Association of Junior Colleges, 1971, 46 pp. $3.

This monograph suggests what junior colleges should do in response to the challenge of accountability—the responsibility for student success or failure. The authors assert that the traditional assumption that the student is exclusively responsible for his educational achievement is no longer valid for the open-door community college philosophy. They see the first step as the responsibility of the junior college president and staff to identify goals, and submit a model framework for translating these goals into action. They emphasize the importance of changing instructors' orientation from imitation of four-year college status ambition to acceptance of the student as he is.

648 THOMAS, J. ALAN. Cost-benefit analysis and the evaluation of educational systems, in Educational Testing Service, *Proceedings of the 1968 Invitational Conference on Testing Problems.* Princeton, N. J.: ETS, 1969, pp. 89-100.

This article provides a brief introduction to the economic model of cost–benefit analysis as applied to education. The author describes the basic rationale for evaluating the budget and performance of an educational system through systematic comparison of relevant input and output measures.

7.6—SYSTEM COORDINATION. The rationale of the modern planning and management system applies equally well to mechanisms for statewide coordination. Most states now have some means for central coordination; ten years ago very few did. The literature is consequently all fairly recent. Glenny wrote perhaps the best known early treatment in 1959 (655).

There are several types of literature involved. There is literature concerned with the theory and form of state coordination. McConnell's book (660) is an outstanding example. There are many additional publications on the process of coordination, including the political relationships, major issues, and the question of how such coordination should and does actually work. The best recent work of this type is a book by Berdahl (650).

There are also periodic reports on the status of statewide coordination and state-by-state descriptions of current master plans and coordinating agencies. The best recent reference of this type is a report prepared by Abrahams (649). In addition to the highly visible coordination of public systems, there are a surprising number of consortia among small groups of public and private institutions. Moore's description is a standard reference (663).

649 ABRAHAMS, LOUISE. *State planning for higher education.* Wash., D. C.: Academy for Educational Development, 1969, 194 pp.

This especially useful document summarizes certain critical information concerning the planning and coordination of higher education in each of the 50 states. The state profiles identify the major planning agencies in each state and include responsible officers and addresses as of December 1969. In addition to a brief description of overall planning and coordination in each state, the profiles include statements concerning the coordination and governance of the following six types of institutions and programs: public institutions, private institutions, medical institutions, facilities, student financial aid, and postsecondary vocational technical education. Such information does become dated rapidly, but at this writing the Abrahams' compendium provides the most comprehensive factual summary of planning and coordination on a state-by-state basis.

650 BERDAHL, ROBERT O. *Statewide coordination of higher education.* Wash., D. C.: American Council on Education, 1971, 285 pp. $7.

This comprehensive study focuses on the potential effectiveness of state coordinating agencies as mediators between the state and institutions of higher education. The author begins by distinguishing academic freedom from university autonomy, and examines both procedural and substantive aspects of autonomy. He then traces the evaluation of various types of state agencies. The second part analyzes the structure, functions, and relationships of agencies, with special attention to membership, staff, planning, and evaluation. The third part explores problems in the relationships between the state and private higher education, the federal government, and the public school system. Finally Berdahl offers conclusions and recommendations concerning requirements for agency structure and functions.

651 CARNEGIE COMMISSION ON HIGHER EDUCATION. *The capitol and the campus: State responsibility for postsecondary education.* New York: McGraw-Hill, 1971, 153 pp. $2.95.

The major theme of this report is that state governments must take the initiative to continue and expand quantitative and qualitative accomplishments in public higher education. The report cautions against a single national system of higher education, and identifies the federal role as one of providing specialized and supplemental funds. Despite the Commission's position that the state should broaden its scope of responsibility to provide universal access to higher education, they warn that the growing dominance of state governors should be held in check. Concern is expressed over the "development of heavy-handed regulatory councils" but the Commission does single out two functions—long-range planning and consultation on current issues—that need to be the domain of a state coordinating agency. Guidelines are suggested for state planning and for the functions of coordinating agencies. The report also sets criteria for the amount of state financial support that should be forthcoming, and singles out states that need to take emergency action. Additional recommendations refer to the support of educational attainment, college access rates, and provision of free-access colleges in individual states.

652 CHAMBERS, M. M. *Voluntary statewide coordination in public higher education.* Ann Arbor, Mich.: University of Michigan Press, 1961, 68 pp. (Out of print)

The importance of preserving voluntary state-level planning for higher education against the threat of compulsory "strait-jacketing" of state control is the theme of this book. The author reports the workings of voluntary coordination systems in nine states where (as of 1960) they play a primary role in developing state institutions of higher education. He argues that no evidence is available to demonstrate that central governing boards produce better efficiency, better service to the people of the state, or superior universities. In refuting views expressed by Glenny (see 655), Chambers argues that Glenny "tends to underestimate the ill effects of extending the tentacles of noneducational state fiscal offices into the management of colleges and universities." In 1971 the author's own state of Indiana was one of the few remaining that still relied upon voluntary coordination.

653 COX, LANIER, AND HARRELL, LESTER E. *The impact of federal programs on state planning and coordination of higher education.* Atlanta, Ga.: Southern Regional Education Board, 1969, 235 pp. $2.50.

This study was occasioned by the change in policy of administering federal aid to higher education from direct grants to institutions to that of funding state agencies. This change dates from the Higher Education Facilities Act of 1963, which involved state agencies in administering programs, and also designated the private sector of higher education as eligible for aid. The study examines the impact of both types of funding on state planning and coordination, and the reactions of educational and governmental leadership. Interviews with governors, college presidents, and state agency representatives were conducted in six southern states and five others that represent both the governing and coordinating mode of state organization. The direct-aid system was usually endorsed by governors and state agencies, although a majority of coordinating boards raised objections to this system based on the discontinuity of purpose occurring when the state is not involved. A preponderant majority of institutional presidents expressed approval of the state-coordinated programs, although there was majority opposition to extending it to cover graduate education programs.

654 FIVE COLLEGE LONG RANGE PLANNING COMMITTEE. *Five college cooperation: Directions for the future.* Amherst, Mass.: University of Massachusetts Press, 1969, 228 pp. $5.

This report weighs the arguments for planned cooperation, the specific areas where cooperation would be most advantageous, and ways and means of implementing a consortium for five closely aligned New England colleges — Amherst, Smith, Mount Holyoke, Hampshire, and the University of Massachusetts. The conclusion is that "The five institutions should move deliberately and thoughtfully toward academic complementarity," keeping in mind that institutional autonomy and individual diversity should not be sacrificed. The report discusses the financial advantages of allocating financial resources on a cooperative basis for expensive new programs and technology, such as computers and video tapes, and the educational advantages of faculty exchange, increased variety of courses, and broader opportunities for graduate study. The insistence of student demands for coeducation is cited as another reason for joint decision-making. The report urges that no decision on coeducation should be undertaken unilaterally without prior consultation with the other colleges. It also points out advantages of cooperation in many specific areas, including programs for disadvantaged students, a field office for urban and regional studies, summer programs, overseas study, a common calendar, and continuing education. The report sets up a detailed framework for governance and makes suggestions for joint fund raising.

655 GLENNY, LYMAN A. *Autonomy of public colleges.* New York: McGraw-Hill, 1959, 325 pp. (Out of print)

Glenny defines the "challenge of coordination" as the problem of achieving goals of economy, efficiency, and reduction of competition for funds without destroying the initiative, flexibility, and diversity of public colleges and universities. The breadth of view of this 1959 report on how individual states approach this challenge makes this book important background reading for administrators. Glenny describes and assesses three types of state-level coordinating frameworks: (1) "governing agency" — a single board which coordinates and governs all public institutions of higher learning; (2) "coordinating agency" — a board with limited powers; and (3) voluntary systems — in which the individual institutions meet and coordinate on matters of common concern, usually appropriations. He concludes that the greatest deficiencies are in overall failure of agencies and staffs to understand the concept and importance of imaginative planning. Not only do they fall down in long-range planning for capital improvement and program development, but they also "are seriously inadequate in their collection and analysis of data." Suspicions that state coordination would bring homogenization of institutions have not been borne out, he says, though he does caution that states which stress extension centers of existing institutions may be stifling diversity in types of institutions. He also warns prophetically that colleges and universities must modernize their business administrative practices if they wish to stave off greater intrusion of state economy-minded agencies.

656 GLENNY, LYMAN A. State systems and plans for higher education, in Logan Wilson (Ed.), *Emerging patterns in American higher education.* Wash., D. C.: American Council on Education, 1965, pp. 86-103.

This article provides a useful brief overview of the development of state coordination in the early 1960s. The author describes the primary models and the major trends in coordination during this formative period.

657 GLENNY, LYMAN A. Politics and current patterns in coordinating higher education, in W. John Minter (Ed.), *Campus and capitol.* Boulder, Colo.: Western Interstate Commission for Higher Education, 1966, pp. 27-46.

In this paper a noted director of a state board explores recent trends in state coordination of higher education. He suggests that states have experimented with three different types of coordinating systems. The first of these is the voluntary council made up of public college and university board members. The second type is the single governing–coordinating board responsible for all state supported institutions of higher education. Finally, an increasing number of states are turning to a "Higher Board" which is superimposed over the governing boards of individual institutions or systems.

A general trend toward the creation of citizen boards has been accelerated by three factors: (1) Coordinating agencies are exercising increasing leadership in formulating and advocating policies, and the policy-making branches of government show reluctance to extend significant power to boards composed primarily of institution presidents and governing-board members. (2) Increasing numbers of federal grant programs are being state oriented rather than institution oriented. (3) Private institutions are becoming more involved in statewide policy making and coordination. Glenny places particular emphasis on the political leadership role of coordinating agencies and on the influence of federal grant programs in strengthening that role.

658 HURLBURT, ALLAN S. *State master plans for community colleges.* Wash., D. C.: American Association of Junior Colleges, 1969, 46 pp. $2.

This useful monograph reviews briefly many aspects of state planning for community college systems. The author uses master plans in 19 states to establish general principles and basic procedures for statewide planning. He further reviews relevant literature dealing with the planning process and analyzes such major areas as curriculum, occupational education, transfer programs, special facilities, enrollment and admissions, faculty qualifications, finance and administration, and the role of the state. The final sections deal with the presentation and establishment of plans and suggest areas for future research.

659 MAYHEW, LEWIS B. *Long range planning for higher education.* Studies in the Future of Higher Education Report No. 3. Wash., D. C.: Academy for Educational Development, 1969, 221 pp. (Multilithed)

This comprehensive report examines current trends in long-range planning for colleges and universities and projects the broad outlines of American higher education to 1980. Mayhew describes three different master plans (California,

Florida, and Michigan), and then discusses the general structure of statewide planning and coordination. He presents an overview of master plans, discusses voluntary coordination and institutional long-range planning, and concludes with an assessment of planning and coordination. Information in this rapidly developing area becomes dated quickly, but Mayhew provides generalizations and an analytic framework which go considerably beyond a status report. For example, the report includes a wide variety of tabular data on such topics as: (1) states having master plans; (2) agencies preparing plans or their equivalent and the date of preparation; (3) assumptions on which plans are based; (4) scope and specificity of plans; (5) states with central planning agencies; (6) interrelationships between the central agency and other planning groups; and (7) the degree of planning by state. The final table lists all 50 states and notes the current state of development on a continuum from completed master plan to no plan or study. It also includes a helpful summary of the common denominators of features and provisions in master plans, and gives a general evaluation of the plans.

660 McConnell, Thomas R. *A general pattern for American public higher education.* New York: McGraw-Hill, 1962, 198 pp. $5.50.

This book argues the case for diversity and flexibility in planning the expansion of public higher education. McConnell points out ways in which education can "challenge the brilliant while serving the ordinary" as it fills the educational needs of a democratic industrialized society. He argues that universities should be free to concentrate on advanced undergraduate and graduate education. This is accomplished by channeling the open-door function to the junior colleges, and by encouraging a system of public four-year colleges with sound offerings in liberal studies. This kind of system should, he cautions, provide "a succession of choice-points" so that students can change direction within an institution, or transfer to another type of system. It is basically the hierarchical model followed by California (see 689) and many other states in the 1960s.

661 McConnell, T. R. The coordination of state systems of higher education, in Logan Wilson (Ed.), *Emerging patterns in American higher education.* Wash., D. C.: American Council on Education, 1965, pp. 129-140.

In this paper McConnell analyzes the extent and effectiveness of coordination in higher education both in Great Britain and the United States. His appraisal of the Robbins Report (816), which urged a broad expansion in opportunities for higher education in Britain, is that "it expanded the citadel, but did not breach it." The "almost tragic expenditure" of scarce British resources to start seven new universities argues for more effective coordination; this cannot wait, McConnell asserts, "for the measured and somewhat voluntary body of busy vice-chancellors." He predicts that universities in both Britain and the U.S. will need to become deeply involved in efforts to accomplish large-scale expansion of opportunities for higher education. In evaluating statewide coordination of higher education in this country, McConnell expresses a reversal of his previous views and criticizes the inadequacy of voluntary systems. He sees coordination as inevitable, and argues that it should be the responsibility of educational bodies, rather than external agencies, such as legislatures or state departments of finance. He also deprecates the effectiveness of voluntary cooperation in accomplishing differentiation of functions and programs within the institutional system, and argues that "unnecessary duplication of programs can only lead to educational enfeeblement."

662 McConnell, Thomas R. State systems of higher education, in Earl J. McGrath (Ed.), *Universal higher education.* New York: McGraw-Hill, 1966, pp. 19-39.

This paper presents a rationale for the coordination of state systems under conditions of universal higher education. McConnell discusses the role of state systems in differentiating the education functions among various types of institutions to provide for wide variation in clientele; the changing concept of the two-year college; and the possibility that new types of institutions will be established to provide two-year terminal education. He further examines the processes of student choice and distribution in a state system.

663 MOORE, RAYMOND S. *A guide to higher education consortiums: 1965-66.* Wash., D.C.: Government Printing Office, 1967, 175 pp. $1.25. *Consortiums in American higher education: 1965-66: Report of an exploratory study.* Wash., D. C.: Government Printing Office, 1968, 47 pp. (Out of print)

These two reports provide factual data and interpretive analysis of an Office of Education study of consortiums set up to provide interinstitutional cooperation in solving problems of higher education. The comprehensive guide consists of two detailed tables listing pertinent facts about nearly 1,300 consortiums. The *Report* gives a brief overview of the history and rationale of the consortium movement, and presents some conclusions based on this study. Among the findings are: (1) A decisive factor in the success of such a cooperative arrangement is narrowness of purpose; large consortiums whose activities are directed to a single goal, such as data processing, computer networks, etc., are more effective than small bilateral arrangements involving broad-scope decisions. (2) A successful consortium must maintain a flexible approach to cooperation—participating institutions must be willing to share decision-making, even to the extent of modifying traditionally guarded prerogatives.

Institutions of diverse size and type of control can maintain successful consortiums; many colleges and universities have entered into cooperative affiliation with non-degree-granting institutions such as the National Laboratories or the Smithsonian Institution. Most consortiums retain administrative control within the institutions rather than assigning control to an independent board of trustees.

664 PALOLA, ERNEST G., LEHMANN, TIMOTHY, AND BLISCHKE, WILLIAM R. *Higher education by design: The sociology of planning.* Berkeley, Calif.: Center for Research and Development in Higher Education, University of California, 1970, 580 pp. (Out of print)

This is the final report of a three-year study of statewide planning for higher education and its impact on institutions of higher learning in California, Florida, Illinois, and New York. These sociological studies of planning were the first to make use of a theoretical framework. Four dimensions are developed as yardsticks for comparing higher education systems: (1) the degree of differentiation; (2) the distribution of authority; (3) the type of planning—comprehensive versus fragmented; and (4) the level of educational autonomy. The study makes some general assessments of successes and failures in planning efforts. The record indicates success in keeping up with demands for expansion of enrollment, in selling budgetary needs to legislatures, and in achieving a realistic degree of individual differences among campuses. The authors maintain, however, that preoccupation with financial and enrollment strains has prevented planning leadership from coming to grips with the "qualitative crisis." They feel that higher education has lost its "can do no wrong" status, and see the mood of the future as one of more restrictive policies and tighter control by government agencies.

665 PALTRIDGE, JAMES G. *California's Coordinating Council for Higher Education.* Berkeley, Calif.: Center for Research and Development in Higher Education, University of California, 1966, 193 pp. $2.

This case study analyzes major changes and developments in organization and operation during the California Council's first five years of existence, and relates the causes of these changes to principles of organization theory. Paltridge identifies and traces three major areas of change: internal organization, membership, and organizational change resulting from the Council's involvement in federal programs. The author attempts to explain the effect of these changes on basic coordinating structure. He further develops specific hypotheses concerning organizational change in coordinating bodies with relation to growth and conflict, goal definition, and decision-making.

666 PALTRIDGE, JAMES G. Toward a systems model for state coordination. *Educational Record*, 1969, vol. 50, pp. 71-77.

Paltridge suggests an organizational "systems model" for a state agency responsible for coordinating educational planning. He suggests that the "unavoidable" conflicts between educators and legislators can best be ironed out in an organizational framework that assigns explicit areas of decision-making, with public policy the domain of legislators, and educational policy that of educators. Other suggested guidelines for increasing the effectiveness of coordinating agencies are: (1) Representatives of the general public should have a voting majority on the board. (2) Professional staff of the coordinating agency should be independent of the staffs of both educational institutions and state agencies. (3) The authority structure inherent in statutory coordination can protect the autonomy of all institutions. (4) Clearly defined roles and functions of existing institutions, with provisions for innovative change and modification, would reduce institutional competition.

667 SOUTHERN REGIONAL EDUCATION BOARD. *Expanding opportunities: Case studies of interinstitutional cooperation.* Atlanta, Ga.: SREB, 1969, 44 pp. $1.

This report analyzes five cases of interinstitutional cooperation among liberal arts colleges in the South serving either predominantly black or predominantly white students. Included are examples of cosponsorship of a joint seminar and a shared department established through merging of faculty and resources; a tricollege consortium established to eliminate unnecessary duplication in a particular geographic area; a five-college consortium of black church-related schools; and the merger of two colleges related to two different churches. Each section reviews the historical development, including sources of difficulty; describes present administrative structures; and assesses potential for future success.

668 SOUTHERN REGIONAL EDUCATION BOARD. *New directions in statewide higher education: Planning and coordination.* Proceedings of the 19th SREB Legislative Work Conference. Atlanta, Ga.: SREB, 1970, 56 pp.

This booklet records papers and discussions from the 19th annual Legislative Work Conference sponsored by the SREB to discuss the role of the state in higher education. The participants, including educators and legislators, dealt with issues such as coordinating powers of state planning agencies in graduate education; the relationships between the state planning board and the legislature; interinstitutional and interstate cooperation; and the impact of federal and state funding for private schools.

669 SOUTHERN REGIONAL EDUCATION BOARD. *Summary of state legislation affecting higher education in the South, 1971.* Atlanta, Ga.: SREB, 1971, 43 pp. (Mimeographed)

This convenient annual document summarizes the major state legislation affecting higher education in the South. The succinct state reports are written by professional journalists, and a brief regional summary is included. See 670 for an almost identical report covering the western states.

670 WESTERN INTERSTATE COMMISSION FOR HIGHER EDUCATION. *Summary of state legislation affecting higher education in the West: 1970.* Boulder, Colo.: WICHE, 1970, 58 pp.

This convenient annual document summarizes the major state legislation affecting higher education in the West. Succinct state reports are written by professional journalists, and a brief regional summary is included. See 669 for an almost identical report covering the southern states.

671 YARRINGTON, ROGER (ED.) *Junior colleges: 50 states/50 years.* Wash., D. C.: American Association of Junior Colleges, 1969, 297 pp. $2.50.

The phenomenal growth of junior colleges—mushrooming from 780 in 1965 to 1,000 in 1970—is documented in this collection of case histories of junior college systems developed in individual states. This expanded version of an earlier report describes the junior college systems in 28 states; a brief summary of the status of junior colleges in the other 22 states is also provided. It is a valuable handbook on how to plan, legislate, and pay for statewide junior college systems. Although a wide range of jurisdictional and budgetary systems are tailored to the situation in individual states, some useful general guidelines are suggested. Critical steps in developing a successful system include "persistent leadership, cooperation among educators, citizen awareness, careful studies, and legislative planning."

7.7—SYSTEM PLANNING STUDIES. Because of the money involved, the magnitude of the decisions, and the potential for social good or harm, one might naively imagine that there is a large body of careful studies that explain and justify the actions of governing boards, coordinating commissions, and state planners. In actual fact there is extremely little work of this sort published, and practically all of what is available has been published somewhat informally by agencies, boards, commissions, etc., rather than in professional journals or by established publishers. One can say, however, that some of the reports available are very useful.

Most studies fall into one of three categories. There are background reports for the development of a master plan or coordinating agency. A good example is Pliner's report (685) on higher education in Louisiana. There are also studies or surveys of students that provide information useful for coordination or the development of system-wide programs. An unusually good example is Knoell's (682) report on educational opportunity in New York state. Finally, there are a limited number of studies that provide information useful for the evaluation and improvement of existing master plans, programs, or coordinating mechanisms. These studies may be local (675), state (672), or national (688) in their application. It seems unlikely that state agencies will be able to discharge their responsibilities to their own satisfaction until such comprehensive background studies become commonplace.

672 CALIFORNIA COORDINATING COUNCIL FOR HIGHER EDUCATION. *The undergraduate student and his higher education: Policies of California colleges and universities in the next decade.* Sacramento, Calif.: CCHE, 1969, 114 pp. (Multilithed)

This report reviews the impact of the state master plan and related educational policies on the undergraduate student. The report was intended as a first step in the application of recent research on students to the development of new state policies. Specific chapters discuss the selection process, factors affecting persistence and attrition, institutional policies including probation and advanced standing, and the diversion of students to junior colleges.

This excellent report is unusually comprehensive and useful as a model study of the operation of a state system. It vividly illustrates how much one can learn about the operation of a master plan by collecting appropriate data on student experiences and attainment. It also represents a perceptive but regrettably rare wedding of research and educational policy.

673 CALIFORNIA LEGISLATURE, JOINT COMMITTEE ON HIGHER EDUCATION. *The challenge of achievement*. Sacramento, Calif.: Joint Committee on Higher Education, 1969, 158 pp.

This report to the California Legislature summarizes a comprehensive and elaborate study of higher education in the state. The report considers present operation of the system, equality of opportunity, attrition, financing, and governance. A sweeping reorganization of public higher education in California is the keynote recommendation of this report. Changes suggested by the Committee included the following proposals: (1) The University of California and State College systems should be consolidated into a one-board system, with statewide responsibility for governance, planning, and financing. Junior colleges would also come under the jurisdiction of this board. (2) Major commitments should be undertaken to realize equality of opportunity in higher education. This would call for adequate funding to provide guidance and academic and financial aid along the lines recommended in the Martyn report (989). (3) Tuition and other student charges should not be increased. One of the most significant alternatives proposed is a system of withholding income tax. (4) Campuses in metropolitan areas should mount a joint effort to solve urban problems by working with University Extension, public schools, and black and Mexican American leadership.

674 CASASCO, JUAN A. *Corporate planning models for university management*. Report 4. Wash., D. C.: ERIC Clearinghouse on Higher Education, 1970, 16 pp.

This useful report outlines corporate planning techniques and applies those methods to the problems of university management. Aimed at top-level administrators, this article stresses the need for organized planning based on predetermined goals and systematic methods. It also details the basic features of three corporate models, and incorporates features of each into a proposed university planning model. Each section is well illustrated.

675 CHICAGO PUBLIC SCHOOLS, STUDY COMMITTEE ON HIGHER EDUCATION. *Higher education in the Chicago public schools*. Part I: *The Chicago teachers colleges*. Part II: *The Chicago City Junior College*. Study Report No. 10. Chicago: Board of Education of Chicago, 1964. (Mimeographed)

These comprehensive reports on the status of higher education in Chicago teachers colleges and the Chicago City Junior College contain discussions of the administrative policies, student body characteristics, enrollment, curriculum, building facilities, and plans for the future. An exemplary aspect of the study is its detailed analysis of student residential patterns and their effect upon the accessibility of nine units of Chicago City Junior College. Over the years the Chicago school system has done very careful research and planning on this particular aspect of educational opportunity.

676 COMMISSION TO STUDY NON-PUBLIC HIGHER EDUCATION IN ILLINOIS. *Strengthening private higher education in Illinois*. Springfield, Ill.: Illinois Board of Higher Education, 1969, 142 pp. Free.

Illinois was among the first states to give special attention to the relation of private institutions to the state's public colleges and universities. This report transmits the recommendations of a prominent commission appointed by the state. In the judgment of the commission, the evidence "clearly and persuasively supports the conclusion that financial assistance to the private institutions from public funds is imperative." It recommended that such funding be provided and suggested means for doing so.

677 DARLEY, JOHN G. *Promise and performance; A study of ability and achievement in higher education.* Berkeley, Calif.: Center for the Study of Higher Education, University of California, 1962, 191 pp.

This study investigates the rationale that the diversity attributed to American higher education consciously reflects and serves the enormous range of diversity in student ability, characteristics, and goals. In order to assess how selection processes affect institutional diversity, Darley compared 1952 and 1959 data, using both a national sample of types of colleges and a longitudinal study of student educational patterns in four states—Minnesota, Wisconsin, Ohio, and Texas. He finds that diversity is not a product of rational organization, but rather of "unrelated historical trends, empire building, and competition, leading frequently to duplication rather than differentiation." He criticizes the system for "loss of human capacity" that occurs at several points: (1) Loss from high school to college. Fifty percent of students in the top half of their high school graduating class do not go on to college. (2) Loss from college entry to graduation. Here he points to the high withdrawal rates of superior students. Forty percent of able men students and forty-five percent of able women do not complete four years of college. There were sharp variations among types of colleges in their holding ability; at private coeducational colleges in Minnesota, 73 percent of able students finished. This valuable study may have been ahead of its time. The finding which especially surprised many readers was the very wide variation in student aptitudes from college to college.

678 FERRIN, RICHARD I. *A decade of change in free-access higher education.* New York: College Entrance Examination Board, 1971, 75 pp. $1.50.

This study of the change in accessibility within U.S. higher education is in many ways a follow-up to 688. In that study Willingham identified those colleges that were free-access (low-cost and nonselective) in 1968 and then undertook a state-by-state analysis of the proximity of such institutions to various populations. Ferrin did a similar analysis for 1958, and described the nature of accessibility changes between 1958 and 1968. Several components of change included: (1) new colleges; (2) increased selectivity in existing colleges; (3) increased costs of existing colleges; (4) college closings; (5) college relocations; and (6) increased urbanization. Although new colleges brought free-access higher education within commuting distance of nearly 50 million additional people over the decade, approximately half that gain was erased by a combination of the other components. The final chapter summarizes regional developments and indicates the major problems that continue to limit accessibility across the country.

679 FLORIDA SELECT COUNCIL ON POST-HIGH-SCHOOL EDUCATION. *Florida post-high-school education: A comprehensive plan for the 70's. A report to the Florida legislature.* Tallahassee: SCPHSE, 1970, 72 pp.

The Council was established in 1969 to assess the current status of public and independent postsecondary education in Florida. Their report presents a comprehensive state plan for education beyond the secondary level. Major recommendations include the establishment of a State Planning Council for higher education, local coordinating agencies in each community college district, and a Florida Independent Higher Education Commission. Further recommendations deal with the organizational structure of these boards, articulation between community colleges and state universities, institutional capacities and area needs, and educational programs at various levels. The Council also emphasized the need for review of vocational–technical programs, and recommended that career guidance and industrial orientation be an integral part of secondary education. Of particular interest is Florida's pioneer role in establishing new state upper-division universities, Florida International and Florida Atlantic. These institutions, like community junior colleges, are projected to draw a large proportion of students from lower socioeconomic backgrounds, as well as job-holding students who need part-time educational opportunities.

680 HOOD, ALBERT B. *What type of college for what type of student?* Minneapolis, Minn.: University of Minnesota Press, 1968, 84 pp. $2.75.

This monograph provides an excellent example of a statewide study of transition from secondary school to college. The questionnaire and test data were obtained for virtually all Minnesota high school graduates, and follow-up information was obtained from those who went to college in Minnesota. The report focuses upon such problems as evaluating college choice; academic achievement levels in different colleges; and the academic achievement of rebels and introverts in different types of colleges. The authors cite various implications for high school counselors, college student personnel workers, and educational planners. However, the primary value of the report probably lies in the normative data it provides and in its systematic approach to the problem of understanding access to higher education in the state.

681 INDIANA STATE POLICY COMMISSION ON POST HIGH SCHOOL EDUCATION. *An Indiana pattern for higher education.* Indianapolis, Ind.: Indiana State Policy Commission on Post High School Education, 1968, 148 pp. (Multilithed)

This report is a good example of a study undertaken to provide background and recommendations concerning the development of statewide planning. The Indiana State Policy Commission was established in 1967 to examine the existing state educational institutions, the needs for different kinds of post-high school education, the establishment of new institutions, and statewide coordination. Major recommendations included establishment of a statewide planning and coordinating Board of Regents; the development of a system of comprehensive community colleges; the appointment of an advisory council on education for the health professions; and the conversion of regional campuses of the state university into autonomous institutions.

682 KNOELL, DOROTHY M. *Toward educational opportunity for all.* Albany, N. Y.: State University of New York, 1966, 220 pp.

The general goal of this excellent model study was to provide a fairly comprehensive assessment of the postsecondary education needs which the State University of New York might meet through some type of two-year college. Of particular concern were persons living in urban centers of population who had not been reached by the traditional institutions in the state's system of higher education.

The original research included interviews with urban high school seniors not planning on college; with trustees, administrators, and faculty members in the two-year colleges; and with students who had withdrawn from the two-year colleges in order to seek employment. In addition, the report includes six background papers on various aspects of extending opportunity, particularly with respect to urban disadvantaged youth. The book is well written and contains many useful insights on a variety of problems concerning educational opportunity. The following are among the conclusions suggested in the report: (1) While not all young people need further formal education, many of high ability are not motivated to attend college. (2) Higher education must be made as attractive as possible to these people, and efforts must be made to overcome the social and economic barriers to higher education which many still face. (3) Better counseling in the community colleges must be accompanied by better articulation with public school guidance programs. (4) There is need for expansion in the university system in order to provide a full spectrum of occupational and liberal education programs, including remedial and developmental work. (5) Programs which combine study and supervised work experience are recommended for many young people. (6) Before considering the creation of a new type of institution, the state university should look to its present two-year colleges to expand opportunity,

683 LINS, L. JOSEPH. *Post-secondary educational preferences of high school seniors: A survey of Spring 1968 Wisconsin high school seniors.* Madison, Wis.: Coordinating Council for Higher Education, 1969, 97 pp.

This report presents data from a 1968 survey of graduating high school seniors in Wisconsin. It is one of the best examples of a study undertaken to aid statewide planning of new facilities by determining the proportion of students planning to attend some form of post-high school education or training. In addition, the survey examines factors affecting choice of college; characteristics of able students not planning postsecondary education; and the effects of the secondary school, financial aid opportunity, housing, college location, and characteristics of parents on the decisions of high school graduates. A follow-up study of these students was conducted in 1970. (See 485.)

684 NEW YORK STATE DEPARTMENT OF EDUCATION, SELECT COMMITTEE ON THE FUTURE OF PRIVATE AND INDEPENDENT HIGHER EDUCATION IN NEW YORK STATE. *New York State and private higher education.* Albany, N. Y.: New York State Education Department, 1968, 155 pp.

The Select Committee, chaired by McGeorge Bundy, was appointed in 1967 to examine the current status of private higher education in New York State. The purpose was to determine "how the state can help preserve the strength and vitality of private and independent institutions, yet at the same time keep them free." Major recommendations include direct financial assistance from the state to private institutions; amendment of the state constitution to allow aid to schools with religious affiliations; strengthening the Board of Regents to meet fiscal and educational responsibilities to private as well as state schools; and development of a strong informational network, including a Commission on Independent Colleges, on which to base statewide educational decisions.

685 PLINER, EMOGENE. *Louisiana higher education: Coordination and planning.* Report No. 3. Baton Rouge, La.: Public Affairs Research Council of Louisiana, 1966, 149 pp. $2.

This volume reports an unusually comprehensive study of the needs of higher education in the state of Louisiana. It starts with a detailed summary of coordination of higher education in other states, continues with a description of higher education in Louisiana as it existed at the time the report was written, and ends with a series of observations and recommendations. Principal among these are detailed suggestions regarding the need for a statewide coordinating agency. The report provides a useful model of a thorough background study for the development of statewide coordination.

686 SOUTH DAKOTA MASTER PLAN ADVISORY COMMITTEE. *A master plan for public higher education in South Dakota.* Pierre, S. D.: South Dakota Regents of Education, 1970, 31 pp. (Mimeographed)

This provisional report presents a summary of recommendations resulting from a background study conducted by the South Dakota Master Plan Committee. The report received outside attention for its recommendation to decrease from seven to four the number of state colleges and universities, and to remodel course structure at the various schools so that each of the campuses is "unique and exceptionally strong in certain areas."

687 VIRGINIA STATE DEPARTMENT OF EDUCATION. *A study of educational and occupational aspirations of Virginia's 1966-67 high school seniors.* Richmond, Va.: Division of Educational Research and Statistics, Virginia State Department of Education, 1969, 79 pp.

This study reports data gathered from 95 percent of Virginia's high school seniors. The study was undertaken to provide information for the planning of more effective educational programs as well as general data relating to development of the state's human resources. The report focuses on three major areas: the differences in background and aspirations of public versus private, male versus female, and college preparatory versus vocational high school seniors; major factors influencing educational aspirations; and a comparison of background and school achievement between those students considering and those definitely planning a college career. The study represents an important prototype of a first step state agencies need to take in providing information necessary for educational planning and coordination.

688 WILLINGHAM, WARREN W. *Free-access higher education.* New York: College Entrance Examination Board, 1970, 240 pp. $6.50.

An important barometer of equal opportunity for higher education is its accessibility to potential students. This book is concerned with the extent and nature of this accessibility. Of all colleges in the country, the author has identified those which are free-access on the basis of the following definition: the college should charge no more than $400 in annual tuition; it should be de facto nonselective in the sense that at least one-third of its freshmen were below-average students in high school; it should be within 45 minutes commuting time from a student's home. The author has estimated what proportion of various populations of people—blacks, whites, urban and rural dwellers, residents of different states—live within commuting distance of a free-access college. These data describing the educational demography of higher education are presented on a state-by-state basis with a variety of other information related to the resources and organization of higher education in each state. The data revealed dramatic differences in the accessibility of higher education from state to state. The author identifies various factors which limit accessibility in different areas, and cites statewide planning and coordination as a primary means for organizing and monitoring educational opportunity in the public interest.

7.8—MASTER PLANS. It is not easy to tell what is and what is not a state master plan for higher education. Neither title nor intent seems sufficient as a basis for discrimination, but most writers 'agree that roughly half of the states have by now prepared a comprehensive document that states the rationale, policy guidelines, and governing authority for a substantial portion of postsecondary institutions in the state. As Mayhew (659) has noted, there is a predictable sameness about most master plans, and they exhibit relatively little imagination in developing diverse forms of institutions and organizational arrangements.

The California master plan (689) has been quite influential across the country. California's reputation for being a step ahead of most states in most matters has paid off in revealing after a decade that its master plan has great strengths but also some troublesome weaknesses. The access characteristics of that model are well illustrated in several prototype master plans included in this section. These plans also illustrate deviant characteristics of other models that may have significant effects upon the access process in those states.

689 CALIFORNIA MASTER PLAN, Coordinating Council for Higher Education, 1020 Twelfth Street, Sacramento, California 95814. (916) 455-7933.

One of the earliest and most comprehensive of all state master plans, the California model has received considerable national attention. Partially enacted into law under the Donahoe Act of 1960, the plan affects all public higher education in the state. In addition, representatives of private institutions are included in the Coordinating Council (1182) also created by the Donahoe Act. The Master Plan reaffirmed California's intention to provide tuition-free public higher education, and its desire to place a junior college within commuting distance of virtually every state resident. In 1970 the state university and state colleges adopted a policy of charging tuition, even though both systems had been charging instructionally related "fees" for several years. But California remains the only state where community colleges continue to be tuition free. The plan specifies that the state colleges are to select their freshmen from the top one-third and the university from the top one-eighth of California public high school graduates; the junior colleges are to admit all high school graduates. It also recommends that private institutions adopt rigorous admissions standards. In 1971 various revisions of the plan were deliberated by both the state legislature and the Coordinating Council for Higher Education. The California hierarchical model of three layers of higher education has been widely accepted throughout the country, and has been successful on many counts in its home state. In many respects California is a showcase state for higher education. But there have been serious problems in funding, providing space for transfer students, and serving the special educational needs of urban minorities.

690 FLORIDA PLAN FOR HIGHER EDUCATION, State Board of Education, The Capitol, Tallahassee, Florida 32304. (904) 599-5732.

Florida has been the site of significant innovation and improvement in the accessibility of higher education during the 1960s. Although only modest attention has been given to the role of private institutions, the developing plan for public higher education includes: (1) the establishment of two-year colleges within commuting distance of most residents, and (2) the creation of senior institutions offering upper division courses only within or near major urban areas. Largely upon the recommendations of a comprehensive 1956 study, the number of two-year colleges increased from 5 in 1957 to 27 in 1970. The advent of upper-division institutions has been more recent; two have been in operation for some time, and two others were scheduled to open in the fall of 1972 in Miami and Jacksonville. The state department of education, through the commissioner and his staff, coordinates all public education in the state, including higher education's two components—the Division of Universities and the Division of Community Colleges. Numerous planning documents have been created to guide educational planning within the state, but no formal master plan has been developed. The recent study *Florida Post-High-School Education: A Comprehensive Plan for the 70's* (679) comes the closest to being a master plan.

691 ILLINOIS MASTER PLAN, Board of Higher Education, 119 South Fifth Street, Room 500, Springfield, Illinois 62706. (217) 525-2551.

The Illinois Master Plan was developed by the Board of Higher Education in three phases. In its first phase, published in 1964, the plan proposed: development of two- and four-year commuter institutions; promotion of technical and semitechnical programs, primarily in junior colleges; and organization of a state junior college coordinating board. It also proposed creation of a state guaranteed loan program and a much more substantial state scholarship program, both of which would be available to students attending public or private institutions within the state. The second phase, published in 1966, focused attention on urban and disadvantaged youth. It called for a new grant program based on student need rather than on scholarship. It also recommended the creation of upper-division commuter institutions, and the stabilization of lower-division enrollments at residential senior institutions, thereby concentrating future enrollments in commuter colleges and universities. This phase also created five systems of public higher education, each with unique functions and governed by a separate board that is responsible to the Board of Higher Education. The recently completed third phase involves professional and graduate programs. With respect to access, the Illinois plan is basically a hierarchical model similar to that of California. A significant variation is the provision of space for junior college transfers in upper-division colleges.

692 CITY UNIVERSITY OF NEW YORK MASTER PLAN, 535 East 80 Street, New York, New York 10021. (212) 879-3600.

The tuition-free City University of New York consists of all public higher educational institutions in New York City, although CUNY shares with SUNY administrative responsibility for the several community colleges. For many years New York City has provided high quality, low-cost higher education for its residents. Recently that principle has been extended to a much broader segment of the city's population than ever before. In 1966 the City Board of Higher Education committed itself to providing postsecondary educational opportunities for all high school graduates within the near future. The unusually comprehensive 1968 Master Plan set the date for such provisions at 1975. It also recommended that CUNY assess and attempt to meet the changing manpower needs of the city, and that in doing so it create new colleges with specific orientations. Events helped to revise the timetable of "open admissions" (see 216) so that in the fall of 1970 the University began accepting all New York City high school graduates as of June 1970 and thereafter. As a result of this decision, first-time enrollments in CUNY's two- and four-year colleges rose from 19,000 in 1969 to 35,000 in 1970. While the University found it necessary to expand its tutorial and counseling services as a result of "open admissions," it abided by a Master Plan suggestion and continued to operate three programs specially designed for underprepared students—SEEK, College Discovery, and Educational Skills Centers (see 1252 for descriptions of these programs).

693 STATE UNIVERSITY OF NEW YORK MASTER PLAN, Office of the Chancellor, 8 Thurlow Terrace, Albany, New York 12201. (518) 474-4060.

The State University of New York has primary administrative responsibility for all public higher education outside New York City, and shared responsibility for community colleges within New York City. SUNY developed its first system-wide plan in 1960. The plan specifically called for the development of accessible community colleges throughout the state, and between 1960 and 1970 the number of such institutions increased from 18 to 37. The 1964 Master Plan for all higher education in the state urged the development of new community colleges, establishment of several urban centers, improvement of transfer opportunities for two-year college graduates, and expansion of programs in continuing education. SUNY's revised plan, published in 1968, again called for improved transfer opportunities, more emphasis on the needs of continuing-education students, and state legislation to enhance the participation of private institutions in future planning. The plan also recommended that financial aid be available to part-time as well as to full-time students. Community colleges were urged to seek out disadvantaged students and create special programs for them. A 1969 Master Plan recommendation stated: "As a present and realistic goal for calculated-risk admissions, each campus of the university will reserve a significant and appropriate proportion of new admissions annually for disadvantaged applicants who may lack preparation, but who show potential for making good use of the opportunity for higher education." In 1970 SUNY created a 50-man citizens' commission to examine several urgent problems including "open admissions."

694 OHIO MASTER PLAN, Ohio Board of Regents, 88 East Broad Street, Columbus, Ohio 43215. (614) 469-2575.

In 1971 the Ohio Board of Regents published a new Master Plan. The most significant recommendation affecting access was a request that state law be changed to allow public four-year colleges to set their own admissions policies while maintaining open admissions among the limited number of public two-year institutions. They also recommended that the 19 two-year branch campuses be called General Colleges and become as comprehensive and autonomous as feasible, and that new two-year campuses be created in areas of sufficient population density not currently served by such campuses. The Plan further called for the development of Job Education Centers at two-year colleges for both high school graduates and dropouts. In line with this interest in manpower planning, the Board suggested that the number of students entering the state's postsecondary institutions be regulated by the demands of the economy.

The contribution and financial plight of private institutions were recognized as the Board recommended assistance through student aid, direct aid, capital assistance, and partial reimbursement for educating public two-year college graduates. Ohio ranks 46th among states in per capita support for higher education, and the plan called for major increases in state support rather than in student charges. One of the most innovative recommendations was that Ohio University's Independent Study Through Correspondence program be expanded to provide opportunities to obtain an associate degree and a baccalaureate in appropriate subject matter areas. As of this writing none of these recommendations has been enacted into law.

SECTION 8: STRUCTURE OF THE SYSTEM

The structure of education is quite diverse, and many sections throughout this volume contain references relevant to the special characteristics of different types of institutions. In this section the emphasis is on educational forms, institutional types, and learning environments. In particular, we are concerned with the character and role of different segments of the educational structure, and how such differentiation affects access to higher education.

There are many ways to describe the structure of education. The intent here is merely to provide categories for the literature concerning those major forms that are relevant to the access process. We are mainly concerned with higher education, but secondary education is included because of its very important relationship to access to higher education.

There are several reasons why the structure of higher education has a critical bearing upon the access process. Mass higher education necessarily means a diverse group of students with a variety of special interests and problems which in turn imply the need for institutional and programmatic specialization. Master plans for public higher education typically specify structural specialization for political, economic, and manpower reasons in addition to educational considerations. Furthermore, there is an existing institutional diversity that serves special roles and special constituencies.

One of the principal problems in guiding college-bound students is to help them understand and evaluate differences among colleges in relation to their own interests and aspirations. Conversely, admissions policies of an institution must begin with the consideration of the institution's form and role, and both have a heavy bearing on whether the outcome (section 5.2) will be beneficial from the standpoint of student or institution.

8.1 – *SECONDARY EDUCATION.* The high school and the student's experiences in it have a critical bearing upon access to higher education. There is, however, surprisingly little good research specifically on this point. There is some material of interest in section 1 on student guidance and section 9.3 on motives to attend college. The major study of the high school's effect on students' educational attainment is the Coleman Report (948), and there are several articles related to it in section 10.1.

The literature on secondary education is extensive, and this section makes no effort to cover it all. There are included, however, several basic references on the American high school (see 710 in particular) and some research of special significance such as the Project TALENT *Studies of the American High School* (702) and Venn's study of occupational education at the secondary level (713).

There are various associations concerned with secondary education such as the National Catholic Education Association (1124) and the National Association of Independent Schools (1120). Of course, the National Education Association (1128) is the umbrella organization for public education throughout the country. Its many affiliates at the state and national level are primary sources of information through countless journals, meetings, and newsletters. The American Association of Secondary School Administrators, an affiliate of NEA, is particularly prominent in secondary education.

695 BARCLAY, JAMES R. Approach to the measurement of "teacher press" in the secondary curriculum. *Journal of Counseling Psychology,* 1967, vol. 14, pp. 552-567.
   This study is concerned with the identification of variables associated with teacher judgments of student performance. Students in Oakland, California high schools who had been nominated as closest to and farthest from their teachers' concepts of the ideal student were compared on 80 intellective, personality, motivational, and vocational variables. The results indicated that students had "personality-motivational-vocational" profiles that seemed to reflect influence of teachers' judgment in various curriculum areas. Thus teacher attitudes about students are confirmed as an important element in environmental press.

696 BOYLE, RICHARD P. The effect of the high school on students' aspirations. *American Journal of Sociology,* 1966, vol. 71, pp. 628-639.

This is a sociological study of variations in college aspirations of Canadian high school girls relative to the socioeconomic composition of their school. It is synthesized with findings of four similar studies. The results of the five pieces of research indicate that working-class students at predominantly middle-class high schools plan to attend college much more frequently than those at predominantly working-class high schools.

697 COLEMAN, JAMES S. Style and substance in American high schools, in College Entrance Examination Board, *College admissions.* No. 6: *The American high school.* New York: College Entrance Examination Board, 1959, pp. 9-21.

Coleman discusses the differences in the substance or quality of the education offered in high schools and differences in style—i.e., attitudes toward intellectual activity. The "plush" suburban school, he feels, is often faced with the problem of counterbalancing the overemphasis on social activities which fosters a nonchalant attitude toward the intellectual opportunities. He concludes that the standards and values current among students are primarily the responsibility of the school. These descriptions of prevailing attitudes of students in 1959 are particularly interesting in comparison to sharply different attitudes of today's secondary students, but Coleman's discussion of differences among high schools is still quite relevant.

698 CONANT, JAMES B. *The comprehensive high school.* New York: McGraw-Hill, 1967, 95 pp. $1.95.

In 1959 Conant published *The American High School Today: A First Report to Interested Citizens.* This second report is based on written replies to a questionnaire sent to 2,000 comprehensive high schools of medium size. It is primarily concerned with opportunities for studying a variety of subjects in American high schools.

Several recommendations were made by Conant in *The American High School Today.* The present study surveyed the situation regarding many of these recommendations, and tables are presented which show the relative performance of 33 selected states. The following were among the criteria of interest to Conant: (1) the ratio of students to guidance counselors; (2) the student load of English teachers; (3) the opportunities for advanced academic work; (4) the opportunities for four years of study in a single foreign language; (5) offerings in advanced mathematics and in "new" science curriculums; (6) offerings in vocational education; (7) opportunities for a student to take five academic subjects plus art or music and physical education.

The data show a wide variation among the states on these criteria. The report contains very few interpretations of questionnaire returns but Conant does conclude that in the 10 years since the first report, "considerable progress has been made in the teaching of mathematics, science, and foreign languages." These findings provide a valuable reference to limited but critical characteristics of the comprehensive high school.

699 EBEL, ROBERT L. Educational programs—secondary schools, in Robert L. Ebel (Ed.), *Encyclopedia of educational research.* (4th ed.) New York: Macmillan, 1969, pp. 410-413.

This brief article reviews the literature dealing with important innovations in secondary school programs during the 60s. These include new kinds of schools, new educational opportunities outside the conventional establishment, independent study, flexible scheduling, work-study programs, and the Advanced Placement Program.

700 EURICH, ALVIN C. (ED.) *High school 1980: The shape of the future in American secondary education.* New York: Pitman, 1970, 304 pp. $8.50.

Eurich diagnoses the American high school as being "in trouble," as evidenced by the spread of student unrest to the high school level, its failures with ghetto youth, and widespread charges that its programs are not relevant. He feels the solution lies in speeding up the process of educational reform. These essays, contributed by prominent educators, relate this premise to the topics of urban education, the changing student, curricular reform, professional staff, and management of educational resources. The concluding essay by Oettinger is pessimistic about the prospects for change; he asserts "The American school system seems almost ideally designed to resist change. It combines the rigidity of a military organization with the fragmentation of small business."

701 FENTON, EDWIN. Working with high schools: A professor's testimony. *School Review,* 1961, vol. 69, no. 2, pp. 157-168.

The author, a professor at Carnegie Institute of Technology, left his post for a year to teach Advanced Placement courses in a Pittsburgh high school. This highly personal article describes his experience. He concludes that there are untapped resources in both the student body and the faculty which can be mined by better cooperation between high schools and colleges — a development he sees as highly desirable.

702 FLANAGAN, JOHN C., DAILEY, JOHN T., SHAYCOFT, MARION F., ORR, DAVID B., AND GOLDBERG, ISADORE. *Studies of the American high school.* Palo Alto, Calif.: Project TALENT Office, American Institutes for Research, 1962. $8.50. (Mimeographed)

This monograph contains a comprehensive report of the first results of the Project TALENT findings concerning the characteristics of American high schools. The sample of 1,353 American secondary schools was classified into 17 categories in order to relate specific school characteristics to measured outcomes. Some tentative conclusions are drawn. Levels of achievement vary markedly. The average achievement for students in specific schools ranges from the 5th to the 95th percentile for individuals. The upper three-fourths of the graduates in some schools are better prepared than the upper tenth in some other schools. Thus class rank is of limited value as a screen for college entrance unless the college draws from a very homogeneous group of high schools. The authors conclude that "There is no single factor accounting for excellence of results in schools, and the credit for effective learning has to be distributed among a very large number of different types of effective practices and treatments." The four factors which seem to be most important are teacher salaries, teacher experience, number of books in the school library, and expenditure per pupil. The data also indicate some factors which seem unlikely to be *prime* causes of school excellence. Among these are school size, average class size, age of building, and suburban location. The authors also regard the 17-group taxonomy taken in conjunction with non-curriculum-linked tests, such as the Abstract Reasoning Test, as a useful "yardstick" for comparing selected school outcomes on both an absolute and a relative basis.

703 FRIEDENBERG, EDGAR Z. *Coming of age in America.* New York: Random House, 1963, 300 pp. $7.95; paperback $1.95.

In this widely read book, Friedenberg examines the American adolescent in the typical secondary school. Starting with the thesis that "the most important effect of life in a mass society is on the values of the people who share it," he conducted interviews and psychological tests with students in nine high schools to determine student values and decision-making processes. Results demonstrate the influence of the student's institution and peer group on value formation. The author asserts in unequivocal terms that students were subtly required to subordinate personal independence and goals to institutional norms, and those who resisted were rejected by the institution as well as by their fellow students.

Friedenberg's conclusions rest on the belief that education for conformity is destructive both to the individual and to his society.

704 HAVIGHURST, ROBERT J., AND NEUGARTEN, BERNICE L. *Society and education.* (3rd ed.) Boston: Allyn and Bacon, 1967, 538 pp. $9.50.

This comprehensive textbook in the sociology of education has been updated for the second time in less than 10 years to keep pace with fast-moving social changes affecting educational problems and opportunities. This revised edition is built around the view of the school as "an agent of social urban renewal, now the major domestic problem." The opening chapters discuss the role of the school in the social class structure; social mobility and the school as a "sorting and selecting agency" are important subtopics. Other sections view the school in relationship to the family and peer groups, and in the context of the local community — particularly the metropolitan complex of inner city and suburbs. The book also deals with interrelationships between the school and the problems of the wider society, including population growth, race relations, changing industrial patterns, juvenile delinquency, etc. The final chapter focuses on the various roles of the teacher in the classroom and community.

705 HEMPHILL, JOHN K., RICHARDS, JAMES M., AND PETERSON, RICHARD E. *Report of the senior high-school principalship.* Vol. I. *The study of the secondary-school principalship.* Wash., D. C.: National Association of Secondary-School Principals, 1965, 104 pp.

This comprehensive study surveyed almost 70 percent of the nation's secondary school principals in the early 1960s to provide basic information on the overall characteristics of the job. The questionnaires covered such factors as background and formal preparation, on-the-job activities, problems, rewards, opinions, and school characteristics. In general, the principal was found to be a well-educated individual who has come up through the ranks of secondary school teaching. His financial compensation was found to be comparable to that of an associate professor at an average college or university. He reports much satisfaction in his work, though he feels it does not carry as much prestige as it should. Events of the late 1960s that put the high school principal on the front line in confrontations and issues of social change in the schools were not yet a factor; in this survey the principals report the most frequent source of pressure was "athletic-minded" groups.

706 HOWE, HAROLD II. How will more schooling affect the high schools? in Earl J. McGrath (Ed.), *Universal higher education.* New York: McGraw-Hill, 1966, pp. 122-139.

In this paper Howe briefly discusses some of the changes in high school organization, curriculum, and staffing which may result from universal higher education. In addition he traces the slow pace of previous change in secondary schools and urges educators to develop a rationale for change and to construct appropriate models.

707 KAPEL, DAVID E. *Effects of Negro density on student variables and the post-high-school adjustment of male Negroes.* Palo Alto, Calif.: Project TALENT Office, American Institutes for Research, 1968, 80 pp. $3.

With data from Project TALENT, the author undertook to determine how racial composition and other environmental factors of the high school affect post high school adjustment of male Negroes. The scarcity of subjects limited the scope of the research, but the author suggests that the percentage of Negroes attending a school may not be as important as regional and community differences among schools.

708 MCDILL, EDWARD L., MEYERS, EDMUND D. JR., AND RIGSBY, LEO C. Institutional effects on the behavior of high school students. *Sociology of Education*, 1967, vol. 40, pp. 181-199.

This sociological study examined the extent to which variations in the educational and social environments or "climates" of 20 comprehensive public high schools in seven geographical regions affected the academic behavior of individual students. The tentative conclusion is that schools with a strong commitment to academic competence turn out students who tend to conform to these standards. The findings are also termed a "direct assessment of the effects of high school climates on academic performance."

709 MEYER, JOHN W. High school effects on college intentions. *American Journal of Sociology*, 1970, vol. 76, pp. 59-70.

This paper finds that there is both a positive and negative aspect in the small observed effect of the secondary school on the individual student's aspirations. While high-status schools tended to encourage students in moving upward, they also increased competitive pressure. Thus a student's self-appraisal is influenced inversely by the ability of his peers in his own school—a finding similar to that of James A. Davis in "The Campus as Frog Pond" (see 26).

710 PEARSON, JIM B., AND FULLER, EDGAR (EDS.) *Education in the states. Vol. I. Historical development and outlook.* Wash., D. C.: National Education Association, 1969, 1,475 pp. $50. FULLER, EDGAR, AND PEARSON, JIM B. (EDS.) *Education in the states. Vol. II. Nationwide development since 1900.* Wash., D. C.: National Education Association, 1969, 763 pp. $12.50.

The first of these two volumes that resulted from an intensive study of state departments of education conducted by the Council of Chief State School Officers undertakes to trace the historical development of state departments of education and the central school agencies of Puerto Rico, American Samoa, Guam, the Panama Canal Zone, and the Virgin Islands. Each chapter includes a wealth of data on early beginnings of the state department on size, internal function and organization, policy directions, and rate of development. In addition the chapters include organizational charts and a selected bibliography for each state.

Volume II of this massive study deals with areas of nationwide concern to all state departments of education. These include: the impact of federal programs, constitutional and legal bases for state action, relationships with state governments, state financing of elementary and secondary education, the curriculum, occupational education, and adult education. Additional chapters examine student personnel services, teaching professions, and relationships with higher education. Each chapter is well documented and includes a selected bibliography.

711 RAMSØY, NATALIE ROGOFF. College recruitment and high school curriculum. *Sociology of Education*, 1965, vol. 38, pp. 297-309.

The author examines the adequacy of American high school curriculums for preparing students for college entrance by using data from three national surveys (1955, 1958, and 1960). She concludes that college preparatory instruction is scarce relative to pupil demand for it, particularly in smaller high schools. In all three studies a larger percentage planned to attend college than had taken the college preparatory program. Data from the 1955 survey showed that in high schools with minimal college preparatory programs, 10 times as many seniors were planning to enter college as had taken a college preparatory program. The author suggests that these "late college deciders" are handicapped when they enter college by the relatively meager curricular offerings of their high schools. There are no comparable data for a recent period but the Coleman report (948) does provide similar information with heavy emphasis on disadvantaged schools.

712 TROW, MARTIN. The second transformation of American secondary education, in Reinhard Bendix and Seymour Martin Lipset (Eds.), *Class, status, and power.* (2nd ed.) New York: Free Press, 1966, pp. 437-449.

The transformation of the American educational system is traced first from an elitist preparatory to a universal high school system, and now to a universal college preparatory system. Trow contends that the difficulties in accomplishing the second transformation stem from the need to redo the programs of existing institutions rather than a simple task of building new ones. Several problems that may arise are analyzed: (1) The "comprehensive" nature of a high school may have to be altered to place greater emphasis on differences in academic ability among both students and teachers. The shortage of qualified and motivated teachers may limit their use to classes for the most talented students. (2) Low-achieving terminal students may be classified as "second-class" as the expectation of universal college attendance increases, with resulting sociological and psychological damages. (3) As the parent groups become better educated, they are less willing to accept the statements of professional educators, and educators must expect to turn controversy and challenge into fruitful dialogue.

One suggested experiment would be the establishment of one or two academically selective high schools in each major city, where some of the gains and losses of institutional differentiation can be observed and experimental programs developed for later application to comprehensive schools. Trow's observations are generally very helpful in clarifying the effect of universal higher education on the secondary school.

713 VENN, GRANT. *Man, education, and manpower.* Wash., D. C.: American Association of School Administrators, 1970, 281 pp. $6.

This book is primarily concerned with career education in the secondary schools. It suggests many innovative local and state-level manpower policies designed to implement a goal of career orientation, rather than "second-class" vocational education. Venn scores the federal manpower programs of the sixties for bypassing educational institutions—"those best able to develop new skilled and technical manpower," and concentrating on remedial programs. The end result, he feels, is that the decade ended with almost as large a pool of disadvantaged and unskilled workers as when it began. He contends that the prevailing concept of vocational education—one "designed for somebody else's children" —fails either to provide an education or to train skilled workers. He suggests new roles for schools, year-round operation, and grass-roots approaches to manpower planning.

8.2—*VOCATIONAL EDUCATION.*

Vocational education is a large, loosely organized field that grew rapidly during the 1960s. Much of the pertinent literature is published under the auspices of the federal government or special research groups. The references cited here include descriptions of vocational education, statistics of enrollment and programs, and studies of vocational education's functions, organization, and relation to industry.

Important problems include the role of vocational education in society (see 714), the organization and planning of vocational education (722), and the relation of educational programs to actual job requirements. The literature on the latter problem is found in section 6.3. Other pertinent sections are Career Information Sources (1.7), Occupational Structure (6.4), and Transition to Work (6.5).

In addition to the U.S. Office of Education (1143) two important organizations concerned with vocational education are the American Association of Junior Colleges (1097) and the American Vocational Association (1108). The principal periodicals of those two associations are good sources of information (*American Vocational Journal,* 1311, and *Junior College Journal,* 1332). There are also important research centers concerned with vocational education at Ohio State University (1162) and the University of Wisconsin (1163).

714 ADVISORY COUNCIL ON VOCATIONAL EDUCATION. *Vocational education: The bridge between man and his work.* Report of the Advisory Council on Vocational Education. Wash., D. C.: Government Printing Office, 1968, 220 pp. $2.25.

The Advisory Council on Vocational Education was established by Congress in 1966 to evaluate the nation's program of vocational education and appraise the results of the Vocational Education Act of 1963. Advisory Councils are to convene every two years, and the first Council published this report based on an appraisal of two-years' experience under the Act. The report begins with a review of vocational education since 1964, discussing in some detail such topics as growth and development, finance, administration, research, teacher education, and vocational guidance. Part II gives an evaluation and assessment of the existing situation in vocational education, listing both the achievements and the limitations of the programs. Part III presents the 26 specific recommendations of the Council.

715 BARLOW, MELVIN L. (Ed.) *Vocational education: Sixty-fourth yearbook of the National Society for the Study of Education.* Vol. 64, Part I. Chicago, NSSE, 1965, 301 pp. $5.

This compendium of papers by specialists in vocational education provides a comprehensive treatment of the field. Chapters cover a wide variety of topics, including recent social and economic trends, the technological context, vocational education in the secondary school and beyond, impact of federal and state legislation, and the vocational curriculum. Further papers discuss organization, administration and finance, responsibilities of nonpublic agencies, and research in the field.

716 BELITSKY, A. HARVEY. *Private vocational schools and their students: Limited objectives, unlimited opportunities.* Cambridge, Mass.: Schenkman, 1969, 186 pp. $7.95.

Belitsky presents an overview of that frequently ignored segment of education—the proprietary vocational school. He discusses the social role of the institution, its operation and personnel, and characteristics of its students. Data were based upon a 40 percent return to a questionnaire sent to some 2,400 institutions. The author recommends that public schools undertake joint ventures with private vocational schools, and that proprietary institutions upgrade their programs and initiate voluntary accreditation.

717 BRANDON, GEORGE L. Vocational and technical education, in Robert L. Ebel (Ed.), *Encyclopedia of educational research.* (4th ed.) New York: Macmillan, 1969, pp. 1506-1522.

This article provides a concise summary of research dealing with vocational education, and an outline of major trends and influences in the field. Specific sections discuss the changing nature of vocational education, with special emphasis on technicians and their changing roles and competition in the vocational market. Further sections describe the current status of work in vocational research centers supported by private and federal sources. The article includes a fairly extensive bibliography.

718 BURT, SAMUEL M. *Industry and vocational-technical education.* New York: McGraw-Hill, 1967, 520 pp. $12.95.

This book is described as the first comprehensive study examining industry-education cooperation and its effect on occupational training. Part I presents an overview of the field and illuminates the need for cooperation. Part II describes present cooperation in conducting manpower and skill needs surveys; developing curriculums; counseling and recruiting students; and evaluating school programs. Legislation and organization are reviewed in Part III. Specific sections deal with federal and state regulations, the structure of advisory committees, joint apprenticeship training bodies, and the functions of the industry program coordinator and regional associations.

719 EDUCATION COMMISSION OF THE STATES. State action—vocational education and community colleges. *Compact,* 1970, vol. 4, no. 4, pp. 18-27.

Most of this issue is concerned with vocational education. The article cited here is a valuable state-by-state summary of actions concerning vocational education and the community college. Content of individual sketches varies but includes such information as enrollment, expenditures, establishment of new institutions and programs, current studies, and future needs in the state.

720 HARRIS, NORMAN C. *Developments in technical and vocational education.* New Dimensions in Higher Education No. 23. Wash., D. C.: U. S. Office of Education, 1967, 115 pp. (Multilithed)

This "status report" on the role of higher education in middle manpower development deals with jobs requiring a combination of cognitive and manual skills. The report begins with an analysis of the dichotomy between the liberal arts and practical training. The author comments on middle manpower occupations in industry, science, business, health, agriculture, and service, and notes available educational programs in these areas. He concludes that the community college will assume the major responsibility for middle manpower development. He also discusses the major problems facing these schools, including status; weaknesses in counseling programs; the ideological split between academic and vocational programs; faculty shortage; and reluctance to attempt innovative teaching techniques. The annotated bibliography provides excellent source material.

721 KAUFMAN, JACOB J., HU, TEH-WEI, LEE, MAW LIN, AND STROMSDORFER, ERNST W. *A cost-effectiveness study of vocational education: A comparison of vocational and nonvocational education in secondary schools.* University Park, Pa.: Institute for Research on Human Resources, Pennsylvania State University, 1969, 301 pp. $5.

The authors of this study were the first to attempt to develop a theoretical framework for obtaining cost-benefit data needed to answer the question: "Should the U.S. invest more money in vocational education, given investment opportunities in other educational curricula?" Two related issues, the effect of vocational-technical education on the dropout rate and on short-run shortages in needed skills, were also examined. The findings indicated that vocational-technical education is a worthwhile investment. An equally important result was the indication that further generalization was hampered by the inadequate development of cost-benefit theory as it applies to education. The authors suggest that additional cost-benefit studies will require that individual institutions maintain adequate data to determine the efficiency of specific programs and allow analysis of alternate program possibilities.

722 KOTZ, ARNOLD (ED.) *Occupational education: Planning and programming.* Vols. I and II. Menlo Park, Calif.: Stanford Research Institute, 1967. Vol. I, 207 pp. $5. Vol. II, 477 pp. $5.50. Both $9.50.

This report summarizes a major study of occupational education. A survey in 6 states and 11 communities provided background information for a conference at which many noted writers contributed papers. This two-volume report includes a full account plus selected discussions among participants. The study was designed to identify significant issues in planning and programming and to investigate the decision-making processes involved. Volume I includes a section on objectives and goals, including discussion of the role of vocational education in the reduction of unemployment and social tensions. The second section reviews alternative programs, including the deferment of occupational choices, cooperative training programs, the "organic" curriculum, and cooperation between manpower development and training programs.

Volume II includes sections examining program structure and budgeting with recommendations for multiyear programs. Budgets display total costs and focus on planning final outputs. Further sections deal with the conduct of analytical studies and problems of evaluation. In addition, the study suggested that careful establishment of priorities and allocations would minimize the conflict between economic efficiency and social objectives. New analytical approaches to the decision-making process are discussed and applied to more general educational areas. The appendix includes a useful checklist for school and program evaluation.

723 MERCER, CHARLES V. Public postsecondary occupational education in the United States, in U. S. Office of Education, *Trends in postsecondary education,* Wash., D. C.: Government Printing Office, 1970, pp. 239-249.

This chapter provides a convenient and useful overview of vocational education in the four major types of public institutions providing such programs: community colleges, postsecondary schools, four-year colleges, and combination secondary/postsecondary schools. The author comments on the inadequate data available but does provide valuable summary statistics on institutions, types of programs, and enrollment in different sections of the country. He concludes that most students take jobs that are relevant to training they have received in vocational programs, though completion rates are "alarmingly low" in some instances.

724 Moss, JEROME (CHAIRMAN) Vocational, technical, and practical arts education. *Review of Educational Research,* 1968, vol. 38, no. 4.

This issue reviews and evaluates selected major research efforts in the fields of vocational, technical, and practical arts education since 1962. The report is divided into problem areas including manpower supply and demand; career development; curriculum and instruction; and organization staffing and evaluation of programs. Each area is followed by a bibliography of research reports.

725 STOCK, WILLIAM E., AND PRATZNER, FRANK C. *Review of research on student selection and the prediction of success in occupational education.* Minneapolis, Minn.: Minnesota Research Coordination Unit in Occupational Education, University of Minnesota, 1969, 48 pp. (Mimeographed)

This synthesis of research on selection and prediction of success in vocational programs reviews the current status of the field and indicates problems for future investigation. The authors suggest that research, prediction, and selection in occupational education are generally inadequate. They propose more full-time certified counselors, utilization of paraprofessional assistants, planning and follow-up studies, and improved in-service programs in counseling. They also describe a proposed selection, guidance, and placement center for a state or region that would serve as a clearinghouse for present programs and research efforts.

726 SWANSON, J. CHESTER (DIRECTOR) *Leadership role, functions, procedures and administration of vocational-technical education agencies at the state level.*

Vol. I. *A nationwide survey of status and organization, 1966-67.* Berkeley, Calif.: School of Education, University of California, 1968, 70 pp. (Multilithed)

This project undertook to assess the leadership role of state agencies in implementing goals of vocational–technical education. The report contains valuable factual information about the organization, enrollment, staff, and expenditures in vocational education in each state. The author concludes that: (1) Individual differences of state directors' personality, experience, and leadership qualities are probably more significant determinants of the quality of a state vocational–technical program than is the position of the state director in the educational hierarchy. (2) Problems resulting from the current trend toward separation of state-level administration of secondary and postsecondary vocational–technical education may be expected to increase in complexity. (3) Existing vocational–technical education programs "are not yet fully geared toward meeting the needs of urban youth or of adults residing in industrial centers."

727 U.S. OFFICE OF EDUCATION. *State reports of vocational-technical program development.* Wash., D. C.: Government Printing Office, 1967, 48 pp.

This publication presents a concise state-by-state review of developments in vocational–technical education. Topics include construction of facilities, changes in program content, enrollment trends, and expansion of existing programs due to the opening of new occupational fields.

728 U.S. OFFICE OF EDUCATION. *Vocational education and occupations.* Wash., D. C.: Government Printing Office, 1969, 292 pp. $2.25.

This report links vocational–technical education programs and occupations, and provides a means for evaluation and improvement of results of occupational education. It outlines a system which defines and classifies vocational programs offered by state and local school systems, and links these programs to occupations in all areas of the economy. Part I contains a list summarizing and coding the substantive content of vocational programs. Part II lists dictionary codes, titles, and worker-trait groups related to the various programs.

729 U.S. OFFICE OF EDUCATION. *Vocational and technical education: Annual report, fiscal year 1968.* Wash., D. C.: Government Printing Office, 1970, 175 pp. $2.

Increasing national interest in vocational education was reflected in the passage of the Vocational Education Act of 1963. This volume discusses the effects through 1968 of the increased funding and program flexibility provided by the Act. It examines enrollments and trends, ancillary services, administration of vocational education, and needs and projections for the future. A major aim of vocational education is to fill gaps in manpower supply caused by technological and social changes. Another major aim is to create educational/vocational opportunity for minority and poor students. The report notes that "Vocational education programs of the future will need to be characterized by accessibility, flexible scheduling, orientation to adult needs, and more extensive guidance and counseling services." The appendix includes extensive statistical information on enrollments, expenditures, etc.

8.3 – COLLEGE ENVIRONMENTS. The literature on college environments is mostly attributable to researchers in psychology and sociology. It is a new field that has seen intensive work since the late 1950s. This work started at Syracuse University with the work of Robert Pace and George Stern and also at National Merit Scholarship Corporation where much of the early work on the effect of different types of colleges on student aspirations first flourished (see section 5.2).

There have been several interrelated problems in this research. One is how to characterize educational institutions for different programmatic or research purposes. Astin (732) has done a great deal of work on this question. Another problem of great interest has been the relationship between the college environment and the student's interests and needs (744). Both of these problems are central to the most immediate and practical question concerning college environments—the need for an improved means of describing colleges in the guidance and admission process (see Pace, 740, and Clark, 737).

730 ASTIN, ALEXANDER W. Classroom environment in different fields of study. *Journal of Educational Psychology,* 1965, vol. 58, pp. 275-282.

This study examines differences in classroom environment in various fields of study. Data on instructor and student behavior (e.g., instructor was enthusiastic, seats were assigned, students argued in class), were gathered from 4,109 students majoring in 19 fields at 246 colleges. Significant and interesting differences in classroom environment were found among the 19 fields. Astin interprets the findings in support of his hypothesis that college environment is affected by the relative proportions of students and faculty in the various fields.

731 ASTIN, ALEXANDER W. *Who goes where to college?* Chicago: Science Research Associates, 1965, 125 pp. $5.50; paperback $3.25.

The purpose of this study was to learn more about the characteristics of students at different institutions, and to get some indication of how successful institutions are in attracting the kinds of students who can benefit most from their particular programs. Data for the study were collected by means of a questionnaire administered to 127,212 students who composed the entering freshman classes at 248 colleges and universities throughout the country. Information was collected about the student's socioeconomic background, academic and extracurricular achievement in high school, and future educational and vocational plans. From the questionnaire data and other known information, 52 measures were obtained which were reduced to a set of six "freshman input factors": intellectualism, aestheticism, status, leadership, pragmatism, and masculinity.

In addition the environmental assessment technique (733) was used to describe 1,015 colleges on selectivity, size, and six orientations: realistic, scientific, social, conventional, enterprising, and artistic. This book reports the first effort to describe a large population of colleges on the basis of research-based information. (Also annotated in section 1.6.)

732 ASTIN, ALEXANDER W. *The college environment.* Wash., D. C.: American Council on Education, 1968, 187 pp. $3.

In this well-known study, Astin attempted to identify and measure important differences in college environments, to systematically document their diversity, and to examine the relationship of environment to the college's impact upon its students. He defined environment as a composite of 275 stimuli from the peer, classroom, administrative, and physical environments. A questionnaire concerning these stimuli was administered to 30,500 students in 246 colleges. Findings indicated extensive qualitative and quantitative differences in institutional environments. Results suggested that certain aspects of college environment were determined by student input while others were not. Astin points out implications of the findings for administration, faculty, guidance and counseling departments, and future research. The study is probably the most comprehensive examination of "real life" aspects of college environments ever undertaken.

733 ASTIN, ALEXANDER W., AND HOLLAND, JOHN L. The environmental assessment technique: A way to measure college environments. *Journal of Educational Psychology*, 1961, vol. 52, pp. 308-316.

This pioneering article describes a simple method for measuring college environment that has been used in many studies. It involves counting the number of students in different major fields in the institution. The method yields six measures to be used along with size and average intelligence of the student body. These are: realistic, intellectual, social, conventional, enterprising, and artistic. See 731 for an extensive application of the method.

734 BARTON, ALLEN H. *Organizational measurement and its bearing on the study of college environments*. Research Monograph No. 2. New York: College Entrance Examination Board, 1961, 82 pp. $2.50.

In this book, the author surveyed literature on social organizations to develop categories of variables and organizational measurements applicable to a wide spectrum of environments. The chapters are organized around major classifications of variables: input, output, environmental social structure, attitudes, and activities. Each section includes a description of appropriate organizational measures. The appendix and bibliography detail references specifically dealing with college variables.

735 BERDIE, RALPH F. A university is a many-faceted thing. *Personnel and Guidance Journal*, 1968, vol. 45, pp. 768-775.

The College and University Environment Scales (CUES) were administered to various groups at a large university. Results indicated consistent differences among colleges and some sex differences. The authors concluded that CUES can be used to generalize about parts of a university but not the entire institution.

736 CENTRA, JOHN A., AND LINN, ROBERT L. On interpreting students' perceptions of their college environments. *Measurement and Evaluation in Guidance*, 1970, vol. 3, no. 2, pp. 102-109.

This study explores the relation between objective characteristics of colleges and student perceptions of college environment measured by the College and University Environment Scales (CUES). Results indicated that CUES scores can be predicted to a substantial degree ($r = .60-.80$) from characteristics such as college size and average SAT score, but student perceptions of environment still vary considerably when such characteristics are held constant.

737 CLARK, BURTON R. College image and student selection, in Kaoru Yamamota (Ed.), *The college student and his culture: An analysis*. Boston: Houghton Mifflin, 1968, pp. 178-192.

In this widely read paper, Clark discusses the influence of a college's public image on student self-selection. He defines content and power as two components of college public image and describes the historical development of the strong public image of Reed College and its influence on applicants. In addition, Clark describes content and salience of public image through student perceptions at Reed, Antioch, Swarthmore, and San Francisco State College, and suggests that highly powerful images are characteristic of small private and highly selective colleges. Public schools are less rigid and permit flexible adjustment to outside pressures. Clark concludes that the function of images is to attract a pool of students with specific values and expectations for recruitment and selection.

738 CLARK, BURTON R., AND TROW, MARTIN. The organizational context, in Theodore M. Newcomb and Everett K. Wilson (Eds.), *College peer groups*. Chicago: Aldine, 1966, pp. 17-70.

This chapter deals with social forces and organizational conditions as determinants of student subculture. The authors discuss four major types of sub-cultures—collegiate, vocational, academic, and nonconformist. They then examine broad movements in American life, such as change in vocational structure, and institutional variables including authority structure, size, complexity, and autonomy, which shape the strength and distribution of the four subcultures on a variety of campuses. The chapter concludes with a discussion of social conditions resulting in an increasing vocational orientation among students and the resulting tension between the academic and vocational subcultures. The authors suggest that structural innovation such as creation of small communities within the larger organization may produce a more favorable environment for the development of values and interests of each student group.

739 NEWCOMB, THEODORE M. Campus environment as a factor in admissions, in College Entrance Examination Board, *College admissions policies for the 1970s*. New York: College Entrance Examination Board, 1968, pp. 126-136.

In this paper, Newcomb discusses the interdependence of environment, program, and admissions, and their relation to the innovation necessary for the solution of problems facing universities in the next decade. He reports results of two studies at Bennington College, demonstrating that development of a concrete college image led to a static campus environment and limited the student selection process. Newcomb believes this process occurs in many schools and results in neglected populations of potential applicants. He suggests the establishment of small units within complex institutions with interdependent policies of admissions and program especially designed to serve these neglected student groups and other potential candidates for admission.

740 PACE, C. ROBERT. Five college environments. *College Board Review,* Spring 1960, no. 41, pp. 24-28.

In this study the College Characteristics Index (CCI) was administered to a sample of 32 institutions to determine the factors which differentiate basic types of colleges. Factorial analysis identified five types of college environments: (1) humanist and reflective; (2) scientific and competitive; (3) practical and status-oriented; (4) group welfare and organization-oriented, and (5) aggressive and impulsive. These correspond generally to the five scales later incorporated in the College and University Environment Scales (CUES) developed by the author.

741 PACE, C. ROBERT. College environments, in Robert L. Ebel (Ed.), *Encyclopedia of educational research.* (4th ed.) New York: Macmillan, 1969, pp. 169-173.

In the past decade there has been a broadening of social science research in exploring new ways of describing and measuring the characteristics of college environments. The author, well-known for his work in developing the early systematic means of characterizing college environments, reports on the latest research extending these methods. This article provides a useful brief review of the major types of research on college environments.

742 PERVIN, LAWRENCE A. Performance and satisfaction as a function of individual-environment fit. *Psychological Bulletin,* 1968, vol. 69, pp. 56-68.

This review examines performance and satisfaction as a function of the interaction between the characteristics of the individual and those of the interpersonal and noninterpersonal environments. The author reviews relevant theoretical positions and discusses alternative models for the analysis of interactions or transactions between individuals and environments. He discusses three questions: (1) Should one study the perceived or "actual" environment? (2) What units should be employed, and should they be the same for individuals and environments? (3) What is the nature of the process involved in individual–environment relationships?

743 RAND, LEONARD P. Effect on college choice satisfaction of matching students and colleges. *Personnel and Guidance Journal,* 1968, vol. 47, pp. 34-49.

Students and counselors often approach the college decision process with the intention of "fitting" the student to the college. This study examined satisfaction with college choice for over 7,000 students in 28 colleges. Degree of match between student and college was based upon measures of scholastic potential, personality, interest, and cultural orientation. The relationship between satisfaction and matching was reported to be minimal and complex.

744 STERN, GEORGE G. *People in context: Measuring person-environment congruence in education and industry.* New York: John Wiley, 1970, 402 pp. $13.95.

This book pulls together the work of one of the most highly regarded researchers on the problem of measuring college environments. The Activities Index catalogued personality measures of 10,000 students, and the College Characteristics Index (CCI) was used to analyze 100 institutions; the goal was to identify characteristics of student personalities and college environments in comparable psychological dimensions. Although the work was expected to supply a new basis for classifying colleges, the resulting subgroups provided empirical corroboration of the familiar labels. The detailed statistical analyses of these subgroups—independent liberal arts, denominational, university-affiliated liberal arts, business administration, engineering, and teacher training—show that the characteristics of students are generally appropriate to the college they choose.

Stern makes projections for the future as to how universal access to higher education may revise the characteristics he has identified in today's colleges. Although increasing vocational orientation has already made substantial inroads on the liberal arts curriculum, he feels "quality in education is still most closely associated with breadth, not specialization, and the orientation toward ideas rather than technology that characterizes the small liberal arts college cannot yet be dismissed as an irrelevant anachronism." However, much of the basic organizational structure he considers to be obsolete, and he looks towards "elimination of grades as a coercive device, joint participation in curriculum change, and the withdrawal of custodial supervision, as structural changes pointing to the future of the college community."

745 TROW, MARTIN. The campus viewed as a culture, in Hall T. Sprague (Ed.), *Research on college students.* Boulder, Colo.: Western Interstate Commission for Higher Education, 1960, pp. 105-123.

Aside from its substantive value, this article has special historical interest because Trow describes here four student cultures that have subsequently been very frequently used, particularly in sociological literature. The four cultures—collegiate, vocational, academic, and nonconformist—were devised on an a priori basis. The cultures differ with respect to the extent to which students are (1) involved with ideas and (2) identified with the college. For example, the nonconformist deals with ideas but does not identify with the college. These categories, though undoubtedly oversimplified, do conveniently distinguish some of the broad differences which characterize college students.

8.4—*COMMUNITY COLLEGES*. The community college movement has generated a substantial new literature since the mid-1960s. Much of that literature is concerned with the organization and development of new community colleges. The American Association of Junior Colleges (1097) has exerted active leadership in sponsoring and developing these publications. Some of the issues related more specifically to the access process include the problem of developing adequate student personnel services (753) for diverse groups of "new" students (748) and the role conflicts typified by Roueche's monograph, *Salvage, Redirection or Custody?* (757). In addition to the *Junior College Journal* (1332), which is the most important source of current information concerning community colleges, AAJC publishes a number of newsletters including *Junior College Research Review* (1376) prepared in conjunction with the ERIC Clearinghouse for Junior Colleges (1450).

746 BLOCKER, CLYDE E., PLUMMER, ROBERT H., AND RICHARDSON, RICHARD C. JR. *The two-year college: A social synthesis.* Englewood Cliffs, N. J.: Prentice-Hall, 1965, 298 pp. $9.95.

This book combines a theoretical approach with critical analysis of the junior college and its relationships to the sociopolitical and educational structures of society. It also includes broad coverage of financial, administrative, student-personnel, and faculty aspects of the junior college. The authors conclude that the junior college should reverse its allocation of resources on transfer versus technical programs. At the moment it devotes 75 percent of its efforts to liberal arts transfer programs, but, they say, "a proper redefinition of its role would channel more than half its resources into training technicians." They view remedial roles as having dubious effectiveness, asserting that such programs "make extravagant claims, which, in effect, cannot be supported." In planning, they recommend that federal funds be channeled into state master plans which locate new two-year colleges by population need rather than by political opportunism. They see as a myth the idea that the two-year college is low-cost education, and feel that if anything, more funds are needed.

747 CLARK, BURTON R. *The open door college: A case study.* New York: McGraw-Hill, 1960, 207 pp. $6.95.

This is a classic study of the role of the junior college in higher education. Clark's analysis derives from his intensive case study of one junior college – San Jose Junior College – during the years 1953–57. He concludes that the multiplicity of roles of the junior college blurs the sharpness of its educational focus. Its open-door admission policies serve a mass clientele, drawing heavily from lower socioeconomic groups, yet its educational status depends on how well its transfer students achieve in four-year colleges, not on job performance of vocationally trained two-year students. His clear evaluation of the problems and potential of junior colleges make this a landmark study.

748 CROSS, K. PATRICIA. The role of the junior college in providing postsecondary education for all, in U. S. Office of Education, *Trends in postsecondary education.* Wash., D. C.: Government Printing Office, 1970, pp. 181-195.

This article is a "state of the junior college" appraisal of its accomplishments toward the goal of universal postsecondary education. It defines criteria for judging these accomplishments; describes how state master plans, educational leaders, and faculty view the junior college mission; and concludes with statistics on how well it has performed so far in meeting these criteria. The conclusion is one of optimism regarding the "capacity and spirit" of the two-year colleges in providing universal postsecondary education, tempered with concern that they must do more than erase financial, geographic, and other barriers; they must provide a "productive" education, particularly for those in the lower half of ability and socioeconomic levels.

749 GLEAZER, EDMUND J. JR. An introduction to junior colleges, in Edmund J. Gleazer Jr. (Ed.), *American junior colleges.* (7th ed.) Wash., D. C.: American Council on Education, 1967, pp. 3-60.

The introduction to this standard reference volume on the junior college presents a brief but comprehensive review of the junior college movement. Gleazer analyzes the historical background, the development of state and national master plans, organization and administration, and funding of two-year colleges. He also reviews trends in programs, services, and changing clientele. The second part of the chapter is devoted to occupational education and deals with types and problems of occupational programs in relation to manpower needs.

750 MARTORANA, S. V., AND HUNTER, PAULINE F. (EDS.) *Administering the community college in a changing world.* Buffalo Studies, II, No. 1. Buffalo, N. Y.: University Council for Educational Administration and the School of Education, State University of New York at Buffalo, 1966, 209 pp.

This report contains the proceedings of a seminar on community college administration attended by 40 professors of educational administration. It was planned to promote discussion of external and internal factors affecting the directions junior colleges may take in the decade ahead. The external factors included social and cultural change, new economic approaches to school finance, and the effects of occupational change and urbanization. The internal factors were those influencing the leadership of the institution, such as the changing nature of the students and faculty–administrative relationships. A number of leaders in the community college movement are represented among the authors.

751 MEDSKER, LELAND L. Community college education, in Robert L. Ebel (Ed.), *Encyclopedia of educational research.* (4th ed.) New York: Macmillan, 1969, pp. 173-184.

This article covers recent studies on the community college, ranging from history to legislation, finance, students, programs, and governance. It concludes with a discussion of how the dichotomy of roles of the community college hampers the development of a distinct identity. This conflict develops from a duality of purpose—on the one hand to provide academic preparation for four-year college programs, and on the other to provide nontraditional terminal education for new kinds of students.

752 MEDSKER, LELAND, AND TILLERY, DALE. *Breaking the access barriers: A profile of two-year colleges.* New York: McGraw-Hill, 1971, 183 pp. $6.95.

This useful volume presents a statistical profile of junior colleges and provides information on clientele, functions, programs, administrative control, staffing, financing, and planning. A separate chapter is devoted to private junior colleges. University extension centers, technical institutes, and other two-year institutions are treated briefly. The authors trace the evolution of the junior college and describe characteristics of junior college students, curricular programs, and the junior college in the urban setting. Their recommendations include the following: review of master plans for community colleges in the context of all post-secondary education; increase of financial support from state and federal government; increase of financial aid to community college students; development of policies governing sharing of funds between independent and state colleges; and a nationwide program to develop faculty and administrators for junior colleges.

753 RAINES, MAX R. The student personnel situation. *Junior College Journal,* 1966, vol. 36, no. 5, pp. 6-8.

A national committee for appraisal and development of junior college student personnel programs was appointed by the American Association of Junior Colleges to examine and make recommendations concerning student personnel functions in two-year institutions. The committee judged that three-fourths of the junior colleges in the country have not developed adequate student personnel programs, and only 1 institution in 10 has adequate leadership to upgrade those programs. The committee defined basic functions in five areas: admissions, registration, and records; placement and financial aids; student activities; guidance and counseling; and the central administrative unit. Ten critical needs and recommendations were also listed. This is an important report for all those interested in the community colleges because it dramatizes the gap which exists between personnel resources and the professional assistance community college students especially need.

754 RARIG, EMORY W. JR. (ED.) *The community junior college: An annotated bibliography.* New York: Teachers College Press, Columbia University, 1966, 113 pp. $4.

This annotated bibliography provides brief discussions of the literature dealing with eight aspects of the community junior college: history, functions and purposes, organization and administration, students, programs, personnel, facilities, and research.

755 RIESMAN, DAVID, GUSFIELD, JOSEPH, AND GAMSON, ZELDA. *Academic values and mass education: The early years of Oakland and Monteith.* Garden City, N. Y.: Doubleday, 1970, 332 pp. $7.95.

This book examines the first 10 years in the history of Oakland College, a two-year commuter branch of Michigan State University, and of Monteith College, a four-year commuter college within Wayne State University. Both institutions were designed to bring rigorous academic standards to nonselected commuter students. The authors were primarily interested in investigating how academic and intellectual values can come alive for these students who are often the first college generation in their families and have come to college because college-going has become "the thing to do."

In addition, the study demonstrates how the two institutions developed in response to the ideals of founders, faculty, and administration, and to the needs of students and community. The authors outline implications for general educational reform. They stress the crucial role of administration, especially in the recruitment and training of faculty, and point out that financial security within a parent institution has a beneficial effect on innovation. The development of educational programs at these colleges underlines the importance of faculty as student advisors and the pooling of faculty experience in evaluative sessions.

756 ROBERTS, DAYTON Y. (ED.) *Junior college local and state relations.* Gainesville, Fla.: Florida Institute of Higher Education, University of Florida, 1968, 66 pp. Free.

This pamphlet includes papers delivered at the Southeastern Regional Junior College Conference in 1968. The theme of the conference was the relationship between junior colleges and their outer environment. Topics included principles of state and local relations, educational reporting, financial management, and also state and local relationships with regard to curriculum, occupational programs, and public relations functions.

757 ROUECHE, JOHN E. *Salvage, redirection, or custody? Remedial education in the community junior college.* Monograph Series, ERIC Clearinghouse for Junior College Information, American Association of Junior Colleges. Wash., D. C.: AAJC, 1968, 67 pp. $2.

This report offers some blunt criticisms of remedial programs in community junior colleges; not only are they failing to make headway in overcoming students' deficiencies, but the colleges are sidestepping evaluative research on such programs. Roueche sees in the research scarcity a fear on the part of the colleges that their institution will be in jeopardy if the public thinks that millions of dollars have been wasted on the remedial programs. He reports in detail on the remedial approaches of five California community colleges that have defined their goals and attempted to evaluate the results. In one case fewer than five in a hundred remedial students ever qualified for transfer or technical programs. He has some positive suggestions for rethinking goals and implementing "imaginative" approaches that could help give real substance to the open-door admissions policy.

758 SOUTHERN REGIONAL EDUCATION BOARD. *New challenges to the junior colleges: Their role in expanding opportunity for Negroes: A progress report.* Atlanta, Ga.: SREB, 1970, 23 pp.

This pamphlet reports findings and implications of the first phase of a three-part study designed to improve the contribution of the junior college to black students in the South. Four hundred high school and junior college students along with faculty, parents, and community leaders were interviewed to determine attitudes toward and assessments of the junior college. Findings indicated that: (1) black students attend junior colleges because of low costs, proximity, and special programs; (2) they feel two-year institutions are inferior to senior colleges; and (3) they have similar attitudes regarding terminal as opposed to continuing programs. Students were satisfied with the quality of teaching but found discrimination in attitudes of some teachers as well as white students. The students maintained that more attention should be given to special needs of black students including courses in black studies and improvement of remedial and compensatory programs and standardized tests.

8.5 – *SENIOR INSTITUTIONS*. This heading includes state colleges, private liberal arts colleges, institutions with a religious orientation, and universities. These form the backbone of American higher education, and there is naturally a very large body of literature pertinent to their role and operation. Most of this literature is cited in appropriate sections and the selected references included here deal with the purpose, the past, and the future of the senior institution. Section 12.1 lists a number of important associations with which different types of senior institutions are affiliated.

759 BROWN, J. DOUGLAS. *The liberal university.* New York: McGraw-Hill, 1969, 263 pp. $7.95.

This is a pragmatic analysis of the organization and operation of a liberal university by the provost and dean emeritus of Princeton University. His background as an expert in industrial organization and relations makes this a useful source book for university administrators. The book is concerned with only one institution, but what it loses in generality it gains in depth.

760 CAMERON, BEN F. JR. Survival of the fittest. *College Board Review,* Spring 1963, no. 50, pp. 7-11.

Just before the college admissions bulge of 1964-65, most educators in private institutions looked optimistically to the influx of students as new life blood. This article correctly predicted the serious financial straits and survival problems of small private colleges. In concise and very readable language the author outlines the historical role of these colleges and current forces undermining that role. The author also anticipates another conclusion now commonly accepted: the small private college serves an increasingly important social function in offering diversity in higher education.

761 COMMAGER, HENRY STEELE. Has the small college a future? *Saturday Review of Literature,* Feb. 21, 1970, vol. 53, pp. 62-64, 88-90.

Noted historian Commager appraises the small liberal arts college as caught in an educational squeeze—what can it do better than a good secondary school in the first two years, and better than a university or professional school in the last two? He gives five answers: (1) Stay simple, small, and relatively unorganized—as an alternative to the computerized, dehumanized multiversity. The impersonality of the giant educational machine aggravates discontent in students and demoralization in faculty. (2) Speed up the process of formal education. Cutting the college span to three years would increase by one-fourth the number of students who could be educated for the same expenditure of resources. (3) Dispense with parietal rules, but at the same time involve students in the governance of the college. (4) Resist the demand for "relevance" when the term is interpreted to mean that nothing is relevant that happened before yesterday. (5) Involve students in the creative arts.

762 DUNHAM, E. ALDEN. *Colleges of the forgotten Americans: A profile of state colleges and regional universities.* New York: McGraw-Hill, 1969, 206 pp. $5.95.

This highly praised book gives a good feel for the tensions and forces prevalent at state colleges and regional universities. One major issue is the drive on many of these campuses for equal status with major state universities. This includes equal opportunity for PH.D. programs and research grants. The author contends that these institutions cannot possibly compete with the prestige universities in the production of research scholars and are doomed to failure if they try. He further contends that the time has come to create a new doctoral degree, the doctor of arts, which will cut across all departments and will emphasize teaching rather than research preparation. In a "radical recommendation," Dunham suggests that this degree might well be offered by state colleges to meet the expanding need for trained teachers in their own institutions as well as in the junior colleges. The crucial factor is that the institutions must be committed to the new degree to the extent that they are willing not only to hire graduates of the program but also to promote them and give them tenure as well.

763 GRAUBARD, STEPHEN R., AND BALLOTTI, GENO A. (EDS.) *The embattled university.* New York: George Braziller, 1970, 451 pp. $3.95.

The major portion of this book originally appeared in the Fall 1969 and Winter 1970 issues of *Daedalus* and grew out of intellectual concern with the ferment in colleges and universities. The first part deals with the major issues which surfaced during the last decade. It includes essays by Stanley Hoffmann on university dissent from a historical perspective; Erik Erikson on a psychoanalytic interpretation of dissidence in youth; Clark Kerr, Morris Abram, and Daniel Bell on university governance; and Martin Trow and Edgar Friedenberg on the purposes of the university in modern society. The second part reproduces a dialogue on university governance and on higher education in industrial societies sponsored by the American Academy of Arts and Sciences.

764 GREELEY, ANDREW M. *From backwater to mainstream: A profile of Catholic higher education.* New York: McGraw-Hill, 1969, 184 pp. $6.95.

The development of Catholic higher education is traced from "slum to suburb" in this book, the first of a Carnegie Commission series analyzing major types of U.S. colleges and universities. Profiles of individual Catholic colleges were drawn from data obtained on National Opinion Research Center team visits. The diversity found in the 350 U.S. Catholic colleges dispels the myth that the church dominates the system in a "monolithic hierarchy."

In describing the history of Catholic colleges the author notes that they were founded to protect the religious faith of immigrants from the secularizing influence of American public education, as well as to train clergy. In their early years, the colleges were for the most part "static in educational philosophy, rigid in discipline and traditional in curriculum." As Catholics became prosperous suburban Americans in increasing numbers, their children rejected the authoritarianism and compulsory religious tradition. Consequently Catholic colleges are now entering the mainstream of American higher education by adopting the same professional standards, but they face an identity crisis of deciding what is uniquely Catholic about their educational contributions.

Financial crises plague Catholic institutions, since most of them live off tuition and contributions; endowments are practically nonexistent. The author believes that Catholic higher education could make a major educational contribution by assuming leadership with programs emphasizing the development of cognitive elements of the personality in a context of concern for total personality development.

765 KERR, CLARK. *The uses of the university.* Cambridge, Mass.: Harvard University Press, 1963, 140 pp. $2.95. New York: Harper & Row, 1963 (paperback). $1.60.

These highly regarded and seminal essays were delivered at Harvard in 1963 as the Godkin Lectures. Kerr describes the characteristics unique to the American university in its transformation from landgrant beginnings, to the federal grant multiversity of the 60s, to the "city of intellect" of the future. The multiversity grew in response to the massive impact of federal programs begun in World War II. Although the project method of making grants directly to individual researchers was highly productive of scientific progress, some of its side effects have stirred criticism. It was charged with creating pockets of scientific affluence, headed by a scientist–professor oriented more to Washington than to his own institution, and more to research than to teaching.

Kerr believes the policy of massive federal aid should be applied to current problems facing higher education. The best techniques of the government–scientist partnership could well be borrowed in other disciplines and broadened to provide a federal orientation to the total functions of a university. Kerr recommends the establishment of a National Foundation for Higher Education, modeled along the lines of the National Science Foundation. He forecasts that the future of the American university will hinge on how well it adjusts to three important challenges: the great increases in enrollment, the knowledge explosions that create new fields of study, and the involvement of the university in society's problems.

766 MORISON, ROBERT S. (ED.) *The contemporary university: U.S.A.* Boston: Houghton Mifflin, and American Academy of Arts and Sciences, 1966, 364 pp. $6.50.

These penetrating essays on the contemporary university are in large part a collection of articles from *Daedalus.* Many of the articles, though representing the distillation of several years of scholarly work by eminent educators and administrators, are timely enough to be corroborated by today's headlines. They discuss the role conflicts of the university as it struggles to maintain educational integrity while it accepts obligations as a "knowledge industry"; as it attempts to solve the problems of the affluent society as well as those of the disadvantaged society.

767 NEVINS, ALLAN. *The state universities and democracy.* Urbana, Ill.: University of Illinois Press, 1962, 171 pp. $2.95.

This illuminating and lively history of the land-grant colleges traces the stops and starts of democracy in bringing to reality the vision of free college education. It derives from a series of lectures Nevins delivered at the University of Illinois to celebrate the centennial of the signing of the Morrill Land Grant Act of 1862. Nevins describes the early struggles of the land-grant colleges—financial mismanagement of land grants, popular opposition, and censure by religious denominations—and terms the 100-year-outcome as "the most impressive set of agencies for higher education in the world."

768 TRENT, JAMES W., WITH GOLDS, JENETTE. *Catholics in college: Religious commitments and the intellectual life.* Chicago: University of Chicago Press, 1967, 366 pp. $9.

In the light of past history and contemporary research, Catholic education is characterized here as "anti-intellectual." Primary data were secured from the Omnibus Personality Index (OPI), administered in 1959 and 1963 to Catholic students, with supporting data from studies of selected colleges, National Merit Scholars, and national samplings of the College and University Environment Scales (CUES). The dominance of the Irish clergy and the immigrant background of the Catholic school population are cited as historical factors in the charge that Catholic institutions value unquestioning acceptance and character building above intellectual freedom of inquiry. The authors maintain that the church has ignored earlier indictments for meager contributions of the church educational system to intellectual life. As specific shortcomings they cite: (1) failure to do a good job in areas where Catholic education should be strong—in liberal arts, particularly theology and philosophy; (2) proliferation of small and weak colleges; and (3) failure to upgrade seminary education of future teachers.

8.6—NEGRO COLLEGES. For many years the predominantly Negro college was synonymous with educational opportunity for many blacks. The effort to expand educational opportunity by integrating white institutions was a mixed blessing to these black institutions. Several serious efforts to assay the status and future of the black college have been met with all degrees of reception—agreement, alarm, and indignation. The predominantly Negro colleges are largely in the South. They suffer several increasingly serious problems. Their financial condition is frequently precarious. On many campuses there is a serious problem of maintaining quality programs that are relevant to the individual needs of blacks. As a final irony, these problems are made all the more severe by new competition with white institutions for black students and faculty.

The United Negro College Fund (1133) and the Office for Advancement of Public Negro Colleges (1131) represent two efforts to improve support for Negro institutions. An important periodical is the *Journal of Negro Education* (1329).

769 BOWLES, FRANK. What's ahead for our Negro colleges? *College Board Review,* Fall 1965, no. 57, pp. 16-19.

This article deals with the present and future status of the predominantly Negro college. Bowles concentrates on two problems: the financial situation in the colleges, and the need to attract a larger group of more able students. Possible solutions are offered, including a redefinition of educational goals; a plan to determine need for financial support; cooperative arrangements; and improvements in graduate counseling and educational research.

770 BOWLES, FRANK, AND DECOSTA, FRANK A. *Between two worlds: A profile of Negro higher education.* New York: McGraw-Hill, 1971, 326 pp. $7.95.

This volume describes and analyzes the "between two worlds" status of traditionally Negro colleges as "following the formal models of white education but adapted to the tolerances and expedients of an isolated culture." Part I traces the development of these institutions from pre-Civil War days to the present, and includes thumbnail descriptions of the major groups of schools now enrolling large numbers of Negro students. Part II examines the problems confronting these institutions through detailed portraits of five Negro colleges and Merritt College, a community college in California with an enrollment 35 percent Negro. The authors also examine the resources and aspirations of Negro students and investigate the rate of entry of graduates of Negro colleges into the professions. They conclude that the future of Negro colleges is a question of "the political and financial readiness of the nation to provide full equality of opportunity for Negroes, even at the cost of establishing large-scale student and institutional support programs." The authors' specific recommendations include immediate establishment of research and development centers attached to one or more colleges; the stimulation of community college development to speed enrollments; and foundation support for projects to aid Negro students interested in entering professional schools after graduation. They also recommend federal support for professional programs at Negro colleges; for training of personnel and guidance counselors; and for the formation of a planning and consultant body for Negro education.

771 CARNEGIE COMMISSION ON HIGHER EDUCATION. *From isolation to mainstream: Problems of the colleges founded for Negroes.* New York: McGraw-Hill, 1971, 83 pp. $1.95.

This report of the Carnegie Commission on Higher Education spells out guidelines for the massive infusion of money necessary to bring Negro colleges to their rightful place as centers of intellectual leadership for the black community. This document draws heavily on the Carnegie report, *Between Two Worlds* (770), and discusses the financial outlay necessary to accommodate expanding enrollments, provide student financial aid, upgrade faculties, and fund new programs. The report concludes with recommendations for dividing up these tasks among the federal government, state governments, foundations, the business community, the colleges themselves, and other cooperating institutions.

772 JAFFE, A. J., ADAMS, WALTER, AND MEYERS, SANDRA G. *Negro higher education in the 1960's.* New York: Praeger, 1968, 290 pp. $12.50.

This book questions the value of a college education obtained in Negro colleges of the South. A "panel of experts" rated the colleges as good, fair, or poor, where poor was defined as colleges "offering inferior schooling and unlikely candidates for improvement." Three interrelated surveys conducted in 1965–66 provided data on the colleges, students, and projections for enrollments up to 1975. While all enrollments in Negro colleges have risen from 1962 to 1965, the largest increase (43 percent) occurred at the colleges rated poor.

The authors hold that a significant factor in this trend is the increase in federal student loans and work-study funds, and therefore the implications of perpetuating mediocrity should be faced in setting educational policies and allocating funds for the future. In support of the educational goal of providing the Negro student with a college education of sufficient caliber to enable him to leave the ghetto and hold his own against white competition, they oppose escalating support for the poor or even those fair colleges that show little potential for improvement. Instead they urge the "broad and swift expansion" of integrated public two-year colleges, modeled after those of California and Florida. The book is termed a "classic exposition of institutional racism" by reviewer Elias Blake Jr. in the August 1970 issue of *Harvard Educational Review*. See 774 for a very different evaluation of the predominantly Negro college.

773 JENCKS, CHRISTOPHER, AND RIESMAN, DAVID. The American Negro college. *Harvard Educational Review*, 1967, vol. 37, pp. 3-60.

The dilemmas facing American Negro colleges are here described as similar to those confronted earlier by colleges founded to serve ethnic and religious minorities. As the clientele becomes assimilated into American life, the students seek mainstream colleges, leaving a dwindling rationale for existence of the narrowly focused college. This problem is acerbated by the educational deficiencies of most Negro colleges, which Riesman and Jencks rate as "near the tail end of the academic procession in terms of student aptitudes, faculty creativity and intellectual ferment." Even the best colleges—the Negro "Ivy League"—are appraised as "comparable to fairly typical state colleges, near the middle of the academic procession." The authors contend that the future of these schools hinges on what kind of students they can attract now that white colleges have opened broad opportunities for Negro admissions. If Negroes educated in white colleges fare better in graduate schools and careers than graduates of Negro colleges, the authors suggest that more and more Negroes will choose white colleges—much as Catholic and Jewish students prefer prestige to parochial colleges.

Riesman and Jencks do not foresee any significant group of Negroes "for whom an all-Negro college will represent the best choice." They expect that the wealthy elite private Negro colleges will continue as before in catering to the social aspirations of the Negro middle class. They suggest several directions for struggling nonelite colleges: (1) Become a community college with service programs for all ages; e.g., Upward Bound, adult job training, prenatal health care, and legal assistance. (2) Develop a "black" curriculum. Although "most Negro colleges want no part of black nationalism," the authors feel that out of 70 private colleges, one or two might go this route. (3) Become a residential secondary school. Instead of competing with better colleges, they are urged to "compensate for the mediocrity of inadequate secondary schools." See the Summer 1967 issue of *Harvard Educational Review* for "Four Responses and a Reply" (779).

774 LeMelle, Tilden J., and LeMelle, Wilbert J. *The black college: A strategy for relevancy.* New York: Praeger, 1969, 144 pp. $10.

This book supplies blueprints for using the potential of the black colleges to achieve the goal of black self-determination based on the "power of competitive attitudes and marketable abilities." Written by two black educators, the focus is upon "pragmatic realism"—an approach that goes beyond the diagnosis of Negro college problems and suggests programs for action. The LeMelles defend the traditional Negro colleges against the charge of being "educational disaster areas," and argue that they have made unique contributions despite being relegated to a "statusless" position in education.

Nevertheless they do fault the traditional college for failing to fulfill its goal of social development of black Americans. Some of their suggestions are: (1) consortiums of black colleges that would coordinate planning, cooperative research, and faculty exchange programs; (2) mergers of some small private colleges into educationally effective and financially sound institutions; (3) a National Manpower Development and Utilization Center that would provide "practical incentive" for curriculum revision; and (4) a new alignment of decision-making power that would replace the tendency to centralize authority in the office of the president.

775 McGrath, Earl J. *The predominantly Negro colleges and universities in transition.* New York: Teachers College Press, Columbia University, 1965, 204 pp. $4.75; paperback $2.75.

Massive federal funding for less-than-prestigious Negro colleges and universities is recommended by McGrath in this 1965 report on the characteristics, needs, and prospects of Negro institutions. He feels that widespread consolidation of overlapping and educationally debilitated institutions is not the answer in view of the tremendous unserved needs of Negro students. The federal policy of making grants to institutions of proven excellence militates against Negro colleges who need across-the-board support in huge doses to reach the threshold of quality. In comparing Negro and white institutional characteristics, McGrath notes important differences: (1) Negro colleges enroll a preponderance of women. (2) Nearly half these schools are sponsored and partially supported by religious denominations.

He proposes establishing a planning center at one of the great universities which could provide experienced counsel and field service in coordinating efforts on a state, regional, and interinstitutional level. His recommendations for improving educational quality are: (1) Graduate work at a number of Negro state colleges should be phased out and opportunities broadened at predominantly white graduate schools. (2) Terminal technical programs should be removed from four-year colleges since junior colleges can and should fulfill this obligation. (3) New programs preparing for careers in business, computer fields, and government service should be provided. (4) Liberal arts should be strengthened; e.g., science programs are woefully weak and inadequate in preparation for graduate work. (5) Remedial programs found to be most effective should be expanded.

776 MORRIS, EDDIE W. Admissions in predominantly Negro colleges; A view from the inside. *College and University,* 1969, vol. 44, pp. 130-145.

The author contends that the survival of Negro colleges depends upon their ability to compete successfully with white colleges for above-average black students. He warns that they face "impending doom" unless they can change the image of most Negro colleges. White colleges are seeking Negro students in such wholesale numbers they are skimming the cream of the crop the Negro colleges depend on for their student strength. He feels that the Negro admissions officer must not only struggle to upgrade quality; he must also guard against the admission of students who will use the college as a school for black nationalism.

Another reported difficulty is that middle-class Negroes want their children to attend prestigious white colleges. It is essential, Morris points out, that the Negro colleges have additional financial support to improve their facilities and faculties and broaden their curricular opportunities if they are to be successful in recruiting a wider spectrum of students. Otherwise, he warns, Negro colleges will be left to fulfill only the compensatory educational function.

777 OFFICE FOR ADVANCEMENT OF PUBLIC NEGRO COLLEGES. *Public Negro colleges: A fact book.* Atlanta, Ga.: OAPNC, 1969, 21 pp.

This reference guide to public predominantly Negro colleges and universities contains listings of 34 colleges and information on programs, resources, and enrollments.

778 SOUTHERN REGIONAL EDUCATION BOARD. *New careers and curriculum change.* Atlanta, Ga.: SREB, 1968, 61 pp.

In June 1968 a writing conference was convened at Warren Wilson College to consider curriculum change in the traditionally Negro college for new career opportunities. This publication resulted from that conference. The first section of the book examines some current social, cultural, and economic changes that demand prompt accommodation in the college curriculum. A second section deals with specific subject matter areas and suggests a wide range of curriculum innovations designed to complement existing programs. A brief third section considers various procedures for change, and a final section advances recommendations for action based on the major conclusions of the conference participants. The guidelines seem useful and sound and are certainly applicable beyond the realm of the traditionally Negro college. This booklet should be of value to any higher education institution seeking to implement program change.

"The American
Negro college." Four responses and a reply. *Harvard Educational Review,*
1967, vol. 37, pp. 451-459.

Four Negro leaders in education vehemently refute the Riesman–Jencks
charges of low educational quality of Negro colleges as "unsubstantiated
generalizations" based on grossly unfair comparisons with elite white colleges.
They deplore the "shattering effect" on the morale of Negro education to have
such "unscholarly" efforts published by authors with scholarly reputations.
They defend Negro colleges as striving to serve the most deprived youth in the
most underfinanced institutions.

Riesman and Jencks reply that this vignette is only part of a comprehensive
study of American colleges and universities as products of history and current
social forces. They explain that their perspective was not one of invidious comparison, but rather of suggestions for better educational alternatives. Their
appraisals of Negro colleges as third-rate imitators of white prestige colleges
should not be construed as arguments for closing them, but rather as suggestions
for ways to strengthen their educational programs in nonimitative ways.

8.7–*CONTINUING EDUCATION.* There are many forms of continuing education that have thrived without a great deal of attention. Until recently there has been relatively little research, evaluation, or formal organization of what is now sometimes called nontraditional learning. The categories of continuing education overlap a good deal. A somewhat arbitrary
grouping would include the following: adult education (793), correspondence study (797), extension and evening college (802), education in business and industry (794), college-level education in the military (806), and
educational television (783). See section 13.6 for annotated illustrations of
these various forms of continuing education; see entry 805 for a comprehensive guide to programs.

A comprehensive survey of adult education was published in 1965 (790).
The new interest in continuing education is due partly to the recognition of
a heightened need for retraining; the increased educational opportunity that
nontraditional forms can offer; and the mounting cost of developing formal
institutions. One response has been keen interest in the development of
external degree programs (800).

780 Alford, Harold J. *Continuing education in action.* New York: John Wiley,
1968, 153 pp. $6.95.

This book reports the experiences of 10 residential continuing educational
facilities located in universities and sponsored by the W. K. Kellogg Foundation. The author traces the evolution of the centers outlining educational philosophy, facility design and construction, course planning, in-service training and
research programs, and administration and finance. A list of 79 continuing education centers is also provided. This book is especially designed for universities
contemplating establishment of continuing education centers.

781 Arbolino, Jack N., and Valley, John R. Education: The institution or the
individual. *Continuing Education,* 1970, vol. 3, no. 4, p. 6, 55.

This brief statement proposes the establishment of a National University
which would award degrees based upon examination without residency re-

quirements. As arguments in favor of their proposal the authors emphasize the cost of the present structural models of higher education and their inflexibility in meeting the needs of nontraditional students.

782 BURKETT, J. E., AND RUGGIERS, PAUL G. (EDS.) *Bachelor of Liberal Studies: Development of a curriculum at the University of Oklahoma.* Brookline, Mass.: Center for the Study of Liberal Education for Adults at Boston University, 1965, 107 pp.

There are several major barriers to the adult's attainment of a degree in liberal studies: ordinary class schedules, rigid course requirements, and residence requirements. This book tells the story of a successful attempt to break through those barriers. The report encompasses the philosophical concepts of continuing liberal education for adults and how-to-do-it descriptions of the Bachelor of Liberal Studies degree developed at the University of Oklahoma. Three years of deliberations by a faculty committee went into framing the curriculum on a "central learning–central problems" approach. The pathfinding program combines independent study with three-weeks residence study in area seminars; the curriculum is individually adjusted to the level of each student's prior attainment.

783 CARNEGIE CORPORATION OF NEW YORK, COMMISSION ON EDUCATIONAL TELEVISION. *Public television: A program for action.* New York: Bantam Books, 1967, 284 pp. $1.

This study of noncommercial television focused on the potential of community-owned stations for service to the general public. The Commission conducted surveys, interviews, and studies of public television systems in this country and abroad. They concluded that an expanded system of educational television was necessary and outlined proposals for this expansion. Major recommendations included increased federal, state, and local support for existing stations, and the establishment of a national "Corporation for Public Television." In addition, the Commission recommended enlarged federal support for public television and continued study and research for the improvement of instructional television.

784 CLARK, HAROLD F., AND SLOAN, HAROLD S. *Classrooms in the stores: An account of education and research in American retailing.* Sweet Springs, Mo.: Roxbury Press, 1962, 123 pp. (Out of print)

This book summarizes a study of the educational and research activities of 36 large retail corporations. The authors conclude that the total amount of formal education conducted by retail establishments is extremely limited. Despite the title, much of this brief report is concerned with research on retailing and formal retail programs in higher education.

785 CLARK, HAROLD F., AND SLOAN, HAROLD S. *Classrooms in the military: An account of education in the Armed Forces of the United States.* New York: Teachers College Press, Columbia University, 1964, 154 pp. $3.95.

This book presents an overview of educational programs in the armed services. Brief chapters outline programs in on-duty education for enlisted personnel and officers, off-duty programs, correspondence courses and residence study at civilian colleges, and evaluations of military education by former service personnel. For a much more extensive and recent guide to education in the military, see 806.

786 CLARK, HAROLD F., AND SLOAN, HAROLD S. *Classrooms on Main Street: An account of specialty schools in the United States that train for work and leisure.* New York: Teachers College Press, Columbia University, 1966, 162 pp. $3.95.

This volume is the fourth in a series of studies (see 784 and 785 for annotations of two others in the series) on nontraditional education. It gives a brief account of the 35,000 specialty schools scattered throughout the country which offer training in a wide range of subjects. The authors begin with a brief history of the origin and development of these schools, and then describe their regulation and control, the nature and scope of their curriculums, and their administrative procedures.

787 FLAUGHER, RONALD L., MAHONEY, MARGARET H., AND MESSING, RITA B. *Credit by examination for college-level studies: An annotated bibliography.* New York: College Entrance Examination Board, 1967, 233 pp. $3.

This bibliography covers the transfer student, credit by examination, and the unaffiliated student and sources of instruction open to him. Included are 308 nonevaluative annotations of books, articles, and periodicals available in 1966.

788 HECHINGER, FRED M. What tearing down the "walls" can do. *The New York Times,* Sunday, December 27, 1970, Section E, p. 7.

The "University Without Walls" experiment funded by the U.S. Office of Education is described in this article. Seventeen colleges and universities will waive fixed requirements to allow 75 to 100 students per institution to "learn by doing," with the only stipulation that they must complete an identifiable contribution in their field of interest to be eligible for a degree. The rationale is to provide older, action-minded students with opportunities for independent study.

789 HOPPE, WILLIAM A. (ED.) *Policies and practices in evening colleges 1969.* Metuchen, N.J.: Scarecrow Press, 1969, 253 pp. $7.50.

This volume reports on a survey of policies and practices in evening colleges carried out by the Research Committee of the Association of University Evening Colleges. Usable returns were received from a total of 107 institutions. In addition to a general summary, policies and practices for individual institutions are described in the following areas: admissions policies, terminology, fees, faculty and faculty recruitment, scheduling and research, general policies, and student recruitment.

790 JOHNSTONE, JOHN W. C., AND RIVERA, RAMON J. *Volunteers for learning.* Chicago: Aldine, 1965, 624 pp. $15.

Volunteers for Learning is the detailed report of a massive National Opinion Research Center study on adult education in America. The study, begun in 1962 and sponsored by the Carnegie Corporation, reviews the extent and nature of adult participation in continuing education.

The research consisted of four basic phases: Phase I, a national survey of the educational activities of the adult population; Phase II, an intensive study of the reactions of adults to continuing education; Phase III, case studies of adult education facilities in four middle size American cities; and Phase IV, an inquiry into the postschool educational experiences of youth.

The principal findings of the study are summarized in the form of answers to 20 key questions. About 25 million American adults were found to have been active in some form of continued education during the twelve-month period covered by the survey, but those from the lower class who would benefit the most were the least likely to avail themselves of the opportunity.

791 KNOWLES, ASA S. (ED.) Adult education, in Asa S. Knowles (Ed.), *Handbook of college and university administration.* Vol. II, *Academic.* New York: McGraw-Hill, 1970, sec. 5, 115 pp.

This section includes eight chapters reviewing the administration of the major components of adult education in institutions of higher learning. These include adult education degree programs, higher continuing education, cooperative and general extension programs, correspondence study, service programs in community colleges, and educational assistance programs. In addition, one chapter is devoted to the admission and counseling of adult students. Each chapter concludes with a brief selected bibliography.

792 KNOWLES, MALCOLM S. *The adult education movement in the United States.* New York: Holt, Rinehart and Winston, 1962, 335 pp. $7.95.

This comprehensive history examines the development and structure of the adult education movement. Part I traces the emergence of adult education institutions from the colonial period to the present, stressing the influence of social change on institutional growth, and the corresponding effect of adult education on the development of national culture. Part II examines the nature of coordinating organizations within the field. In Part III Knowles concludes with a theoretical discussion of the developmental and coordinating processes in adult education and comments on possible future trends.

793 KNOWLES, MALCOLM S. *Higher adult education in the United States.* Wash., D. C.: American Council on Education, 1969, 105 pp. $3.

This overview of higher adult education provides a comprehensive, succinct assessment of the present state of the field. Introductory chapters present a historical synopsis and discuss internal and external forces influencing change. Other chapters summarize these changes in curriculum and teaching, organization and administration, personnel, and financial policies. The author also identifies societal trends and contemporary issues affecting adult higher education. The appendixes include a suggested system for classification of policy issues and practices, suggested operational objectives and evaluative questions, and guidelines for the structure of the university extension. The annotated bibliography provides extensive material for further reading.

794 LAUWERYS, JOSEPH A., AND SCANLON, DAVID G. (EDS.) *Education within industry: World year book of education 1968.* New York: Harcourt, Brace & World, 1968, 382 pp. $12.95.

This extensive volume of brief papers by international experts provides a comprehensive review of the state of education and training conducted by industrial enterprises in developing and advanced nations. Section I discusses theoretical and philosophical questions concerning education within industry. Section II reviews the historical development of national policies regarding technical education. The final section is devoted to case studies of educational and training programs arranged by companies in many countries. They focus on the demands of the employer and the requirements for trained staff.

795 LEVIN, MELVIN R., AND SLAVET, JOSEPH S. *Continuing education: State programs for the 1970's.* Lexington, Mass.: D. C. Heath, 1970, 139 pp. $10.

This study sponsored by the Massachusetts Advisory Council on Education examines problem areas and presents a comprehensive program model for state commitment to continuing education. The authors adopt a broad definition of continuing education. It encompasses traditional programs such as adult basic education and occupational training, staff training, career development programs for government personnel, and "citizen-client" programs concerned with consumer, driver safety, and environmental education. The first chapter details a cost–benefit analysis of continuing education, indicating that state funds invested in such programs yield significant benefits. The second chapter examines the disparity between current demand and existing programs. The final section details a model plan for establishment of strong state-supported continuing education including program recommendations as well as guidelines for strengthening state administrative leadership.

796 MACKENZIE, OSSIAN, AND CHRISTENSEN, EDWARD L. (EDS.) *The changing world of correspondence study: International readings.* University Park, Pa.: Pennsylvania State University Press, 1971, 376 pp. $12.50.

This volume is the first international compilation of important papers dealing with correspondence study. Specific sections treat classic studies and pioneer experiments, early institutions, academic acceptance, problems in instruction and curriculum, and use of media technology. Further sections review theoretical aspects of correspondence work and report current policy and practice in selected areas of the world. Each section is followed by a selected bibliography.

797 MacKenzie, Ossian, Christensen, Edward L., and Rigby, Paul H. *Correspondence instruction in the United States.* New York: McGraw-Hill, 1968, 261 pp. $6.95.

This study of correspondence instruction presents a comprehensive evaluation of the potential of this mode of education. The book traces the origin and development of private and university sponsors of correspondence programs, and discusses present problems in finance, staffing, public relations, credit, and accreditation. The authors also analyze the instructional technique and offer a model for course evaluation. The final chapter is devoted to an examination of future problems facing correspondence programs, including the competition of new media.

798 Monroe, Margaret E. *Library adult education: The biography of an idea.* New York: Scarecrow Press, 1963, 550 pp. (Out of print)

This book traces the history of library adult education as a major factor in shaping the program of public library service. Monroe describes events of the years 1920–1955 and continues with an examination of exemplary adult education library programs.

799 National Home Study Council. *Directory of accredited private home study schools 1970.* Wash., D. C.: NHSC, 1970.

This pamphlet from the Accrediting Commission of the National Home Study Council lists 133 schools and a wide variety of subjects offered.

800 Pifer, Alan. Is it time for an external degree? *College Board Review*, Winter 1970-71, no. 78, pp. 5-10.

In this article, Pifer discusses the need and rationale for the external degree; describes programs in Australia, South Africa, and Great Britain; and surveys current American attitudes and experiments. He outlines a proposal for an instructional program involving the establishment of a new private college operating with contract support from the state. This college would have a nucleus of full-time faculty responsible for curriculum and would conduct instruction through programmed correspondence graded by computers.

801 Rogin, Lawrence, and Rachlin, Marjorie. *Labor education in the U.S.* Wash., D. C.: National Institute of Labor Education, American University, 1968, 275 pp. $3.50.

This report is a survey of educational programs designed to meet the needs and interests of labor union members. Data obtained from questionnaire responses in 1965–66 provided information on the educational activities of specific unions, as well as on union–university joint educational courses, conferences, and special projects.

802 Sanders, H. C., et al. (Eds.) *The Cooperative Extension Service.* Englewood Cliffs, N. J.: Prentice-Hall, 1966, 436 pp. $11.50.

This valuable reference, authored by 41 specialists, presents a thorough examination of the cooperative extension service. Part I covers historical development, functions and objectives, and organizational arrangements. Part II discusses the contributions of the behavioral sciences to extension work. Further sections deal with program development, planning and effecting change, reporting and public relations, personnel training, and future trends. Each section is supplemented with extensive bibliographies, and the appendixes include texts of the Morrill Act and other relevant legislative measures. The broad scope of well-balanced theoretical and practical material makes this a unique reference in the field.

803 SHARON, AMIEL T. *College credit for off-campus study.* Report 8. Wash., D. C.: ERIC Clearinghouse on Higher Education, George Washington University, 1971, 15 pp.

This report summarizes ways in which individuals learn outside the traditional classroom. The author describes the major methods of off-campus learning, including correspondence study, service-related courses, educational television, and independent study. He discusses the awarding of college credit, and concludes with a recommendation for the establishment of external degree programs.

804 SMITH, ROBERT M., AKER, GEORGE F., AND KIDD, J. R. (EDS.) *Handbook of adult education.* New York: Macmillan, 1970, 594 pp. $15.

This book of selected articles by 39 specialists was issued by the Adult Education Association. It provides a comprehensive assessment of the current status of the field. The readings are divided into three sections. The first describes the general status of adult education, including papers on social setting, information resources and services, teacher training, and present research and theory. The second section examines programs in colleges and universities as well as in outside agencies such as the armed forces, labor unions, business and industry, health and welfare agencies, and religious institutions. The final section is devoted to program areas, including curriculum, sensitivity training, vocational programs, continuing education for professional workers and women, and education for civic responsibility. The appendixes identify participating organizations as well as general information sources.

The volume is an unusually comprehensive reference to the whole field of continuing education. The editors point out, however, that the field is changing rapidly and there is relatively little good information concerning program evaluation, statistics, or systematic research in the field. Consequently these articles are informative though frequently exhortative and may become dated quickly in some areas.

805 THOMSON, FRANCES C. (ED.) *The New York Times guide to continuing education in America.* New York: Quadrangle Books. (In press)

This encyclopedic source book is an educational "first," aimed at a growing constituency—adults who seek opportunities in education as a lifetime process. Recognizing the growing acceptance of this concept of education, the College Board undertook this project to collect comprehensive information on courses and programs available. The resulting handbook lists offerings in 2,281 accredited institutions. It also contains information on how to get a high school equivalency certificate, how to secure college credit through the College-Level Examination Program, a section on accreditation, and a section on how to make use of the book. [*Editor's note:* Published in March 1972. $12.50.]

806 TURNER, CORNELIUS P. (ED.) *A guide to the evaluation of educational experiences in the armed services.* Wash., D. C.: American Council on Education, 1968, 527 pp. $10.

In 1945 the American Council on Education established the Commission on Accreditation of Service Experiences to assist institutions in evaluating military educational programs. This guide is a primary service of the Commission. In this 1968 edition some 8,814 formal service school programs are included. These programs have been evaluated by civilian educators expert in the academic areas concerned, and recommendations are provided to assist college officials in assigning credit.

The *Guide* includes three basic divisions: Part I lists the formal service school courses offered by the various branches of the armed services. Part II describes two national testing programs (General Educational Development and College-Level Examination Program) through which military personnel may receive appraisal of their educational achievements. The index gives all of the courses included in the *Guide* listed by service offering the program. The 1968 *Guide* does not include any credit recommendations at the secondary school level. However, the Commission will provide credit recommendations at the high school level to appropriate officials upon request. The *Guide* is the recognized authority on creditibility of work undertaken in the armed services. (Also annotated in section 1.6.)

807 VALENTINE, JOHN A. The external degree. Speech presented to the American Association of Colleges, Washington, D. C., January 10, 1972. New York: College Entrance Examination Board, 14 pp. (Multilithed)

This speech is an important progress report on the concept of the external degree. Valentine, executive secretary of the Commission on Non-Traditional Study, describes three important British moves in this direction: (1) "External" students at the University of London can earn a degree by passing the same or similar examinations as those taken by resident students. (2) The Council for National Academic Awards, a unique degree-granting agency, is empowered to set up and accredit course programs in non-credit-awarding institutions. (3) The Open University was launched in January 1971, to improve access to quality higher education for the British working class. It plans to provide television and correspondence courses and innovative programs for its 25,000 students. It cost about one-third as much per student to develop and about one-fourth as much to operate as a traditional college.

The U.S., by contrast, has no counterpart to the Council for National Academic Awards, nor has it initiated as widespread changes as the British. Nonetheless, Valentine describes some important developments such as the Regents External Degree Program of the New York State Education Department and the "catered" instruction approach of Empire State College. He sees as the common denominator of nontraditional programs three characteristics: (1) people of all ages who want to learn and are capable of learning; (2) learning centered in many different kinds of places and circumstances; and (3) learning freed from constraints of academic schedules.

8.8 — *INTERNATIONAL EDUCATION.* International education is a very broad field, and the literature relevant to access to higher education is limited here to certain types of problems. One topic of general interest is comparative access models in different countries. The Organization of Economic Cooperation and Development (1138) and UNESCO (1139) are two organizations that have been very active in sponsoring work in this area.

A second topic of broad interest is the international movement of students. This includes the procedures for admitting students as well as guides designed for students and practitioners. Organizations that have been especially active in sponsoring conferences and publishing materials related to this movement of students are those represented on the National Liaison Committee. These include the American Association of Collegiate Registrars and Admissions Officers (1096), the Council of Graduate Schools, the Institute of International Education (1135), the National Association of Foreign Student Affairs (1118), and the College Board (1112).

808 AACRAO-AID PARTICIPANT SELECTION AND PLACEMENT STUDY COMMITTEE. *AACRAO-AID Participant Selection and Placement Study: Report to the Office of International Training*. Wash., D. C.: American Association of Collegiate Registrars and Admissions Officers, 1971. (Multilithed)

This is a report on an AACRAO study of 1,100 participants in the AID academic training program which educates foreign nationals who then return to their home country. The purpose was to evaluate general procedures and formulate guidelines for selection and placement of foreign students. The report presents data on the demographic characteristics of the students, their educational qualifications, academic performance in the U.S., the role of English language proficiency, the predictive accuracy of test scores, and the general efficacy of the selection and placement process. Findings indicated that the AID selection and placement program was unusually successful in choosing students who fulfilled their training objectives. The authors suggest success resulted from a selection process which emphasized maturity and demonstrated ability in the specific field rather than overall academic record.

809 ARNOLD, RUTH. *World education series: Do-it-yourself evaluation of foreign student credentials*. Wash., D. C.: American Association of Collegiate Registrars and Admissions Officers, 1966, 42 pp. $1.

This publication is a valuable aid in interpreting the credentials of foreign students applying for admission to American colleges. It contains general information on foreign secondary education; it also has helpful information for evaluating foreign degrees of students seeking admission to American graduate and professional schools. AACRAO also issues companion reports on individual countries in this World Education Series, with special emphasis on the academic placement of students from that country in U.S. educational institutions.

810 BEREDAY, GEORGE Z. F., AND LAUWERYS, JOSEPH A. *Church and state in education: World year book of education 1966*. New York: Harcourt, Brace & World, 1966, 386 pp. $12.95.

Each *Year Book* treats educational problems of international concern from many important angles. The 1966 *Year Book* gives an overview of how individual nations are coping with the two recurrent problems in church–state relations in education: the attitude of the state toward the teaching of religion in public schools, and the question of state financial support for church-controlled schools. Various articles cover the historical, national, theoretical, and practical aspects of the problem. The introduction compares the adjustments made in countries with varying socioreligious makeups: Communist countries; Western Christianity countries, subdivided into ones with a dominant religion, those with a dominant religion but with strong opposition, and multi-denominational countries; and Asian and African countries. See 1440 for an annotation and complete listing of the *World Year Book of Education*.

811 BOWLES, FRANK H. Contrasts in education: Europe and the U.S. *College Board Review*, Winter 1962, no. 46, pp. 13-18.

Bowles identifies the divergent development of the common school in the United States and Europe as the primary reason for contrasting attitudes toward higher education. In Europe the common school developed laterally, selecting students off into other forms of secondary education not preparatory for the university. In America the common school eventually developed into the comprehensive high school which qualifies all students for some form of college, and selection takes place at the transition between secondary and higher education.

Within this historical context, Bowles reviews differences in university standards, alternative opportunities, requirements, institutional control, sources of financial support, and attitudes toward student employment. He stresses that the differences are consequences of contrasting environments which lead to contrasting views of the purposes and functions of higher education. The article is an especially good introduction to comparative aspects of access to higher education.

812 BOWLES, FRANK. *Access to higher education.* Vol. I. *The international study of university admissions.* Paris: United Nations Educational, Scientific and Cultural Organization, and International Association of Universities, 1965, 212 pp. $3.

The landmark international study of university admissions was the first major project carried out under a joint UNESCO-IAU Research Programme in Higher Education. The first problem chosen for study was the broad question of university admissions—who does or does not have access, how and why? A joint steering committee, composed of a full-time director and an international commission of nine experts examined admissions operations in 12 countries.

This volume, the director's report, is based on data from national and international sources, from personal observation, and from the 12 admissions studies. In summarizing conclusions drawn from the studies, Bowles notes that expansion of preuniversity education unaccompanied by expansion in higher education has resulted in inadequate satisfaction of enrollment demands. Various mechanisms have been used to limit admissions; nevertheless, the number of students entering higher education in 1960 was almost double the number in 1950.

Bowles suggests that the basic problem of regulating admissions is the development of appropriate methods for selection which reflect the structure and aims of the educational system. He presents questions bearing on the choice of operating procedures and follows each with an outline of possible solutions based on experiences encountered in actual practice. Bowles concludes that the imbalance between demand and capacity for higher education has forced the creation of a set of barriers to entrance. He suggests that control by examination be replaced by control through orientation or guidance and through advice based on student performance. See 823 for the reports on individual countries.

813 BURN, BARBARA B. *Higher education in nine countries: A comparative study of colleges and universities abroad.* New York: McGraw-Hill, 1971, 387 pp. $7.95.

This book is a recent and important contribution to the literature of international education. It provides a detailed comparison of current trends and developments in higher education in different countries. In the introduction, Clark Kerr discusses methods of evaluation and comparison of national systems. Individual chapters examine higher education in eight industrialized countries: France, Great Britain, Canada, Australia, West Germany, Sweden, Japan, and the Soviet Union. Topics covered include structural and functional components of the systems, enrollment trends, government relations, internal governance, finance, student characteristics and student aid, changes, and reform. Each section concludes with a list of institutions and references. Also included is a chapter dealing with higher education in India, an economically less-developed nation. The study concludes with a commentary by James Perkins discussing the significance of developments in higher education abroad for colleges and universities in the United States. The appendix lists annotated references by country.

814 CHORAFAS, DIMITRIUS N. *The knowledge revolution: An analysis of the international brain market.* New York: McGraw-Hill, 1968, 142 pp. $2.45.

The basic tenet of this volume is that the brain drain from Europe to the United States is "merely a symptom of a basic disease in the European economic system." The first section examines the reasons for the migration of highly trained scientists and technologists. Primary considerations are the availability of greater professional opportunity and greater financial rewards provided through skillful management and planning techniques. The author also discusses the "hidden" brain drain, the employment of foreign nationals by American overseas corporations. The second section deals with the knowledge revolution, and analyzes the American success in the development of human resources. In the final section the author outlines a program to aid Europe in keeping its university graduates at home. He stresses the immediate need for large investment in research and development, long-range planning for curricular relevance, close university–industry cooperation, and opportunity for continuing education.

815 COLLEGE ENTRANCE EXAMINATION BOARD. *Financial planning for study in the United States: A guide for students from other countries*. New York: College Entrance Examination Board, 1970, 42 pp. Single copies free.

This small but useful booklet is designed to provide foreign students with information on financial aspects of study in the United States. Specific sections deal with estimated costs, including travel, tuition, books, living expenses for married and single students, and additional costs for orientation, entertainment, and vacations. Further sections detail financial aid opportunities from government, foundation, university, and other private sources; describe application procedures; and discuss currency restrictions and bank policies. A sample budget form is included. (Also annotated in section 2.5.)

816 COMMITTEE ON HIGHER EDUCATION. *Higher education*. Report of the Committee appointed by the Prime Minister under the Chairmanship of Lord Robbins. London: Her Majesty's Stationery Office, 1963, 335 pp. $1.80. With Appendices $18.18.

The Robbins Committee Report is generally considered one of the most comprehensive and sophisticated national investigations of access to higher education. The report includes an historical survey, international comparisons, data relating to British student populations, the structure of finance, and administration of British institutions. The major recommendation of the Committee was an 80 percent increase in full-time students over a 10-year period in order to meet expanding demands for higher education. An appendix in several volumes provides a great deal of valuable information on such topics as the demand for higher education, characteristics and performance of students, and problems of student finance.

817 COUNCIL OF GRADUATE SCHOOLS. *University, government, and the foreign graduate student*. New York: College Entrance Examination Board, 1969, 57 pp. $1.25.

This book is the result of the 1967 Wingspread Colloquium on university and national policy relating to the foreign graduate student. The major theme of the Colloquium was mechanisms for sharing the responsibility for foreign graduate student exchange among the graduate school, the university, the government, or other sponsoring agencies. Albert G. Sims summarizes the colloquium observations and recommendations including guidelines for policies dealing with international research, institution-to-institution arrangements for selection, and financial support of graduate students.

818 FORTIER-ORTIZ, ADOLFO. *Problems of university admissions in Latin America: A Report to the Trustees of the College Entrance Examination Board*. New York: College Entrance Examination Board, 1963, 36 pp. $.25.

This report summarizes a study of university admissions problems in Latin America. It describes the general structure and opportunity in secondary and higher education, with emphasis on recent developments that have promoted expansion. The author also examines the current system of university admissions and outlines the problems universities face when growth of secondary schools exceeds that of colleges and universities.

819 FOSTER, J. F., AND CRAIG, T. (EDS.) *Commonwealth universities yearbook.* (47th ed.) London: Association of Commonwealth Universities, 1970, 1,874 pp. Wash., D. C.: American Council on Education. $24.

This volume is the standard reference on universities in Great Britain and other countries of the Commonwealth. It is designed to facilitate contact and cooperation among institutions. Each institution is treated in a separate chapter containing lists of faculty by subject headings, administrative staff, recent statistics, and general information in a wide variety of areas. Introductions discuss the general background to university education in each country. The appendixes include an outline of admissions requirements, a description of the Commonwealth Fellowship plan, data on foreign students, and a short bibliography. The *Yearbook* is also annotated in section 1.6 (88).

820 HAWES, GENE R. *Entering higher education in the United States: A guide for students from other countries.* New York: College Entrance Examination Board, 1969, 42 pp. Single copies free; $10 per 100 copies.

This pamphlet provides concise information for foreign students entering higher education in the United States. Individual sections discuss opportunities for study in the U.S., basic qualifications for entrance, admissions preparations, offices providing information and services, selection of program and institution, and application procedures. A glossary provides definitions of American academic terms, and a bibliography of basic references and directories is also included.

821 INSTITUTE OF INTERNATIONAL EDUCATION. *Handbook on international study for U.S. nationals.* (5th ed.) New York: Institute of International Education, 1970, 293 pp. $7.

This fifth edition of the *Handbook* includes complete information on study abroad for U.S. nationals. Listings include major universities, programs offered, fees, regulations, and requirements in Africa, North and South America, Eastern Europe and the USSR, the Far East and South-Central Asia, the Near and Middle East, Oceania, and Western Europe. Additional listings include awards for study and research abroad, U.S. college-sponsored academic year programs abroad, summer study abroad, special programs, organizations and agencies providing services to students going abroad, and government regulations affecting study abroad.

822 INSTITUTE OF INTERNATIONAL EDUCATION. *Open doors 1970.* New York: IIE, 1970, 81 pp. $3.

This report is the primary source of statistical information concerning the flow of international students to and from the United States. Charts and tables give data on field of study, academic level, length of stay, institutions attended, and sources of support to exchange students. Information is also provided on foreign scholars in the United States and American faculty abroad.

823 INTERNATIONAL STUDY OF UNIVERSITY ADMISSIONS. *Access to higher education.* Vol. II. *National Studies.* Paris: United Nations Educational, Scientific and Cultural Organization, and International Association of Universities, 1965, 648 pp. $9.50.

This volume includes the complete data on university admissions resulting from the joint UNESCO-IAU study of 12 countries. This project was the first attempt to examine admissions problems according to a standard outline applied to widely varying structures and practices. Each section includes a general introduction to the national system of higher education, a description of the admissions process, current problems, general evaluation, and a selected bibliography. Countries studied include Brazil, Chile, France, India, Japan, the Soviet Union, the United Arab Republic, Great Britain, the United States, New Zealand,

Senegal, and South Africa. A separate report dealing with direct financial aid to students in Great Britain is also included. See 812 for the director's overview of the project.

824 JAMESON, SANFORD (ED.) *The admission and placement of students from the Pacific–Asia area: A workshop report.* Wash., D. C.: National Association for Foreign Student Affairs, 1969, 93 pp. $1.50.

This workshop report reviews educational systems of 10 Pacific–Asian countries. Individual sections review each country's educational background, present structure, grading system, quality factors, and special characteristics. The sections conclude with a selected bibliography and recommendations on the admission and placement of applicants in United States institutions. Sample credentials from each country are reproduced in the appendix.

825 MICHIE, ALLAN A. *Higher education and world affairs.* New York: Education and World Affairs, 1968, 96 pp.

This overview of international education is especially directed to institutions establishing or assessing international programs. The author reviews the various activities which comprise international education and discusses institutional conditions necessary for effective cooperation and organization. The book includes an extensive bibliography and suggestions regarding available governmental and private financial resources.

826 NATIONAL ASSOCIATION FOR FOREIGN STUDENT AFFAIRS, AND AMERICAN ASSOCIATION OF COLLEGIATE REGISTRARS AND ADMISSIONS OFFICERS. *A guide to the admission of foreign students.* Wash., D. C.: NAFSA, 1971, 20 pp.

This pamphlet is a compact guide to the process of admitting foreign students. It includes information on responses to initial letters of inquiry, necessary information for admissions decisions, making and communicating the admissions decision, a list of services offered by agencies in the international field, and a basic bibliography. The pamphlet is typical of the useful guides published by NAFSA (1118). Other publications include: *The Foreign Student Advisor and His Institution in Educational Exchange, Our Emergency Situation Involving Foreign Students,* and *Advisor's Manual of Federal Laws and Federal Agencies' Regulations Affecting Foreign Students.*

827 NATIONAL LIAISON COMMITTEE ON FOREIGN STUDENT ADMISSIONS. *The foreign graduate student: Priorities for research and action.* New York: College Entrance Examination Board, 1971, 98 pp. $1.25.

This book reports highlights of a 1970 Wingspread Colloquium that was concerned with the need for a new frame of reference for policies on the admission of foreign graduate students to U.S. institutions. The increasing demands on American higher education to fulfill social goals of open access, coupled with gloomy financial outlooks, are cited as factors that call for realistic justifications of support for foreign students: universities must establish that "foreign students are vital contributors, both here and at home." In addition, participants stressed the need for more systematic research, especially in the area of financial aid and the utility of master's degree programs. They also urged continued support of government fellowship programs. The appendix includes a review of relevant research and a bibliography.

828 ORGANIZATION FOR ECONOMIC CO-OPERATION AND DEVELOPMENT. Guidelines for educational policy in the seventies. *OECD Observer,* 1970, vol. 47, pp. 37-43.

This brief informative report summarizes recommendations from the OECD Conference on Policies for Educational Growth. Papers presented at the conference indicated that increased expenditures for education had not improved equality of educational opportunity. Proposals for future policy dealt with integration of educational and societal goals, effective allocation of resources, and organization of planning and innovation. The article presents useful comparative data on educational resources, enrollment, and distribution of students in higher education by socioeconomic level in various countries.

829 PIKE, ROBERT M. *Who doesn't get to university . . . and why: A study on accessibility to higher education in Canada.* Ottawa: Association of Universities and Colleges of Canada, 1970, 210 pp. $7.50.

In 1965 the Association of Universities and Colleges of Canada resolved to set up a special committee to study all aspects of accessibility to postsecondary education including financial assistance to students. The resulting study provides an unusually comprehensive view of access to higher education in Canada. The report is divided into two approximately equal parts—one devoted to a demographic analysis of educational attainment and the causes of social differentials in university participation; a second part gives a history of student financial aid in Canada, the characteristics of present programs, and the extent to which they cover present needs.

830 SANDERS, IRWIN T., AND WARD, JENNIFER C. *Bridges to understanding: International programs of American colleges and universities.* New York: McGraw-Hill, 1970, 285 pp. $7.95.

This report examines international studies programs in the context of recent financial and organizational crises. The authors trace the rise of area studies, student exchange, overseas research programs, and study centers, and describe the effects of foundation and government cutbacks during the last decade. In addition, they identify internal program weaknesses including lack of feedback, inadequate preparation of staff and students, as well as insufficient orientation programs for visiting foreign students. The authors conclude that due to the current financial squeeze it will be necessary for universities to agree to a division of responsibility for area programs. Implications for the undergraduate curriculum suggest modification of existing courses, rather than expansion. The authors point out possibly desirable changes in financing, personnel policies, physical facilities, and other administrative policies. It is one of a series of profiles of American colleges and universities sponsored by the Carnegie Commission on Higher Education.

831 STUDY OF EDUCATION AT STANFORD. *Report to the university.* Vol. IX. *Study abroad.* Stanford, Calif.: Stanford University, 1968, 79 pp.

This ninth report in the Stanford Study of Education series describes and evaluates the university's Overseas Campus Program established in 1958. It provides a useful description of a well-known program at one institution, and summarizes recommendations with regard to policy direction, faculty and student selection, curriculum, and campus location.

832 UNITED NATIONS EDUCATIONAL, SCIENTIFIC AND CULTURAL ORGANIZATION. *World surveys of education.* Vol. IV. *Higher education.* Paris: Unesco, 1966, 1,433 pp. $38.

This very large volume is the fourth in a series of *World Surveys of Education* sponsored by Unesco. It is designed to offer a global view of higher education by giving comprehensive information on provisions for higher education in virtually every country and territory of the world. Introductory chapters are devoted to a world survey of education, 1957-1961; analysis of school-age and school-going populations; and the progress of higher education since 1930. Another section is concerned with the changing patterns, the intellectual and human aspects of higher education, and future perspectives. The major portion of the book offers a verbal and tabular description of systems of higher education in each country and territory with regard to development, institutions, administration and organization, finance, students, graduate training, and special problems.

833 UNITED NATIONS EDUCATIONAL, SCIENTIFIC AND CULTURAL ORGANIZATION. *Access to higher education in Europe: Comparative background documents and report of the conference.* Vienna: Unesco, 1967, 139 pp. $4.

This booklet is an outgrowth of a Conference of Ministers of Education of European members of Unesco on access to higher education. In addition to a summary of conference proceedings and recommendations, the three comparative background studies presented to the session are reproduced. These studies include comparative statistical data on access in member countries; access investigated from the social, economic, and cultural origins of students; and access in relation to present and future needs of the development of the community.

834 UNITED NATIONS EDUCATIONAL, SCIENTIFIC AND CULTURAL ORGANIZATION. *Study abroad, including vacation study.* (17th ed.) Paris: Unesco, 1968, 683 pp. $5.

This encyclopedic reference work provides information on more than 200,000 scholarships, fellowships, and other grants for foreign study or educational travel to virtually every country of the world. Opportunities sponsored by international organizations – including members of the U.N. system, intergovernmental and nongovernmental programs – are grouped in one section, with information printed in English, French, and Spanish. Another section details opportunities offered by individual countries, with information printed in the national language of the country concerned, or that normally used for official international communications. The offerings are listed according to fields of study, and information for making application is included. A separate section lists information on vacation study abroad.

835 U.S. BUREAU OF LABOR STATISTICS. *Transition from school to work in selected countries.* Wash., D. C.: U.S. Department of Labor, 1970, 57 pp.

This paper summarizes research on the transition from school to work in 14 countries comparable to the United States in political and economic development. The study investigated the role of general education, vocational guidance, vocational training, and initial experiences of the young worker on the job.

836 WARREN, HUGH. *Vocational and technical education: A comparative study of present practice and future trends in ten countries.* Monographs on Education, VI. New York: United Nations Educational, Scientific and Cultural Organization, 1967, 22 pp. $4.

This valuable comparative study describes vocational and technical education in 10 European countries. The first three chapters consider the individual nations with respect to systems of general education; vocational education and the training of the skilled worker; and technical education and training. Following chapters compare the various systems concerning objectives and methods in specific occupational areas, routes provided for access to higher technological education, and future trends. The appendixes reproduce specimen programs of study in each country. (For additional information on vocational and technical education, see section 8.2.)

8.9 – *URBAN EDUCATION.* It is commonly agreed that urban education is one of the more critical problems of contemporary American culture. It coexists with the familiar problems of drugs, poverty, bureaucratization, a crumbling environment, crime, and the lack of a stable community. In only limited respects, however, have writers succeeded in dealing with problems of urban education in a manner that seems convincingly urban rather than simply one aspect of a problem in secondary education, compensatory education, financing education, etc.

Despite this lack of disciplinary coherence, some highly useful reports have been published in recent years on important aspects of access to higher education in the great cities. Two influential books concerned with the urban schools are Conant's *Slums and Suburbs* (844) and Toffler's *School House in the City* (856). Knoell (850) has recently provided an especially useful description of the problems of the urban student in gaining access to higher education.

Organizations of special interest with respect to urban education include the Committee on Economic Development (1166), the Urban Coalition (1134), and the Center for Urban Education (1111). Two useful periodicals are the *Center Forum* and the *Urban Affairs Newsletter* (1394).

837 BEBOUT, JOHN E. Urban extension. *American Behavioral Scientist,* 1963, vol. 6, no. 6, pp. 24-45.

This paper examines the idea of urban extension—the use of university resources, knowledge, and personnel to effect urban change. Part I traces the development of this idea and reviews basic principles of extension service management. Part II deals with the principal functions of the university extension: as a clearinghouse, counselor, and consultant; and as a sponsor of policy seminars and conferences, special education courses, and demonstration projects. Part III evaluates the role of the urban agent, who is responsible for communicating knowledge of the urban environment to the community. In the final section the author discusses the role of the extension in supplying a "noncoercive integrative influence" to shape a consensus on basic metropolitan goals.

838 BERNSTEIN, ABRAHAM. *The education of urban populations.* New York: Random House, 1967, 398 pp. $4.50.

This book presents a wide-ranging assessment of urban education. Bernstein examines the characteristics of the urban problems including family structure, the sociology of ignorance, and the connection between militancy and intelligence. He recommends in-school programs as well as improvements in recruitment and training of teachers, administrative procedures, and curricular psychology. Bernstein believes the central philosophy directing these changes must involve a commitment to enhancement of the cultural background of urban students, rather than an imposition of white middle-class values.

839 COMMITTEE FOR ECONOMIC DEVELOPMENT. *Innovation in education: New directions for the American school.* New York: CED, 1968, 75 pp. $1.

This study is concerned with innovation in elementary and secondary education. It urges the use of new technological resources and proposes methods of analyzing the cost–benefit ratios for new programs. Finally the report calls for improved organization for change, emphasis on both basic and applied educational research, continuous cost–benefit analysis, and the establishment of a national Commission on Research, Innovation, and Evaluation in Education.

840 COMMITTEE FOR ECONOMIC DEVELOPMENT. *The schools and the challenge of innovation.* New York: CED, 1969, 358 pp. $7.95; paperback $4.

This collection of papers commissioned by the CED Subcommittee on Efficiency and Innovation focuses on four major issues affecting innovation in instruction at the secondary level. Part I examines the improved use of human and economic resources and includes papers on finance, effective allocation, and government cooperation. Part II deals with improvements in educational evaluation and research. The challenge to teachers of innovation in curricular context and technology is discussed in Part III. The final section reviews design and costs of various instructional systems including audiovisual programs, instructional television, and computer-assisted instruction.

841 COMMITTEE FOR ECONOMIC DEVELOPMENT. *Training and jobs for the urban poor.* New York: CED, 1970, 78 pp. $1.25.

This policy statement by the Committee for Economic Development Research and Policy Committee makes recommendations concerning improvements in manpower training and employment programs necessary to relieve poverty conditions in urban areas. These recommendations deal with improvements in remedial and job training programs, incentives for business participation, and federal funding for manpower development programs with state and local planning and administrative agencies. Further recommendations include the establishment of a public Jobs Corporation which would provide jobs for marginal and hard-core workers.

842 COMMITTEE FOR ECONOMIC DEVELOPMENT. *Education for the urban disadvantaged from preschool to employment.* New York: CED, 1971, 86 pp. $1.50.

This policy statement by the Committee for Economic Development suggests that improved education for the disadvantaged is the best hope for breaking the poverty cycle. The report lists seven imperatives through which schools might bring pupils up to a minimum standard of achievement; each is supported by a chapter of the text. The recommendations include preschooling for all children, providing a sense of community through the school, developing total instructional systems, accountability of the schools for their products, and equalization in distribution of school resources.

843 COMMUNITY COLLEGE PLANNING CENTER. *Community colleges in urban settings.* Stanford, Calif.: CCPC, Stanford University School of Education, 1964, 20 pp.

This booklet provides valuable information and support for locating new community colleges in inner-city depressed areas. It reflects many viewpoints—architectural, economic, educational, and sociological. The report is based on a two-day work conference convened by the Community College Planning Center at Stanford; it provides both rationale and knowhow. Planners who feel that the high cost of downtown land puts it out of reach as a site choice will find here suggestions for obtaining federal help in land acquisition and explanations of how vertical planning can offset initial land costs. The concluding arguments cite benefits in both human and urban renewal and urge that "variety and diversity are as necessary for the ecology of society as they are for natural ecology."

844 CONANT, JAMES B. *Slums and suburbs.* New York: McGraw-Hill, 1961, 147 pp. $3.95.

The bitter contrasts between slum and suburban high schools described by Conant in 1961 make this a prophetic book. He warns of the "social dynamite" building up in unemployed out-of-school youth in big city slums. Far from being dated, however, his 1961 proposals are still relevant and controversial a decade later. He argues for decentralized administration and parental involvement to bring the schools closer to the needs of the people in each neighborhood. He urges that the schools take on the responsibility for the vocational–educational outcomes of youth up to age 21. Conant perceives some shortcomings in well-financed suburban schools—mainly the unrealistic pressure of parents to get their children into highly selective colleges. This creates a devastating competitiveness and a downgrading of vocational, noncollege preparatory programs that is frustrating to less able students.

845 DENTLER, ROBERT A., AND WARSHAUER, MARY ELLEN, *Big city dropouts and illiterates.* New York: Praeger, 1968, 140 pp. $10.

The major conclusion of this study is that urban educational and welfare programs that deal directly with the problem of school dropouts and adult illiteracy are "irrelevant if not futile." The authors used various statistical analyses to compare the dropout and illiteracy rates for 131 U.S. cities in terms of economic, social, and demographic differences. They argue that "high school withdrawal should be viewed ecologically," as a function of poverty levels, occupational mix, economic opportunity, and social mobility. The findings indicate that cities with higher proportions of dropouts tend to have higher than average expenditures on education and welfare. They conclude that the real answer lies in eliminating economic insecurity, which can only be accomplished by a combination of economic growth in urban areas and more diversified social insurance that protects against unemployment and disability.

846 FANTINI, MARIO D. Alternatives for urban school reform. *Harvard Educational Review,* 1968, vol. 38, no. 1, pp. 160-175.

Fantini describes the crisis in urban education as its failure to educate low-income minority children. He outlines the basic patterns of urban school improvement, and the assumptions, practice, and promise of each. Fantini defines the basic alternatives as compensatory education, desegregation, model subsystems, parallel systems, and total system reform. He believes the most promising alternative to be total reform, either by providing new leadership and leaving the structure unchanged, by reorganization of the system into autonomous districts, or by the merger of school systems in two political jurisdictions. Fantini advocates a form of decentralization which includes parental and community involvement in the school system. He believes effective community participation would lead to increased community responsibility for the education of its children, increased respect for the complicated task of school administration, and increased political strength for financial support.

847 HERRIOTT, ROBERT E., AND ST. JOHN, NANCY H. *Social class and the urban school: The impact of pupil background on teachers and principals.* New York: John Wiley, 1966, 289 pp. $8.95.

In contrast to the many studies of social class and educational status of individual students, the research reported here is concerned with the impact of social class on the total educational environment. This large-scale study classified schools in 41 cities into four different socioeconomic status (SES) levels; comparative analyses were made of the attitudes, behavior, ambitions, and job satisfactions of the teachers and principals. The authors conclude that teachers do serve quite different roles in high and low SES schools, but their data did not support the common assumption of a greater class gap between pupil and teacher in the low as compared with the high SES school. They note the need for additional research to investigate how increased expenditures on low SES schools might affect behavior and attitudes of teachers and principals.

848 KERR, CLARK. *The urban-grant university: A model for the future.* New York: City University of New York, 1968, 15 pp. (Available from ERIC, No. ED-025198)

In this paper Kerr discusses the structure, responsibilities, and controversy relating to the establishment of urban-grant universities whose main focus would be the solution of urban problems. Kerr suggests that an urban-grant institution should be established in each city over 250,000. According to the proposal, each institution would make direct application to the federal government for grants to be awarded on the basis of merit of program presented. The federal government would then make land available as part of urban renewal programs, locating new institutions in educational parks or as central stations in urban transportation systems. Money from the federal government would assist institutions in the development of a city-oriented curriculum, experiment stations, and intensified urban extension.

The urban-grant institution would take major responsibility for: (1) assuring access to minority groups by moving directly into the ghetto; (2) providing a framework for interaction with city public schools; and (3) improving the urban environment, health services, and cultural activities. Kerr outlines the internal and external political problems the new institution would face and stresses the role of the trustees as buffers between the university and the surrounding community.

849 KLOTSCHE, J. MARTIN. *The urban university: And the future of our cities.* New York: Harper & Row, 1966, 149 pp. $4.50.

This volume traces the growth and development of the urban university as a major segment of American higher education. The author discusses the unique characteristics of the urban university and its potential for solving urban problems. He examines the structure of the urban campus, the characteristics of the urban student, and the university's role as a cultural center. Klotsche believes that the urban university can play a dynamic role in improving urban environments by contributing to urban theory and policy, by providing trained manpower, by sending the scholar into the community, by offering places for interaction for urban residents, and by becoming actively involved in redevelopment. He also recommends that the university provide opportunity for continuing education, cooperative and compensatory programs for poverty groups, and for training in the creative arts.

850 KNOELL, DOROTHY M. *People who need college: A report on students we have yet to serve.* Wash., D. C.: American Association of Junior Colleges, 1970, 182 pp. $2.50.

This highly regarded study of attitudes, characteristics, and potential of 1,000 black students was undertaken in 1968 by the AAJC in cooperation with community colleges in five major cities: St. Louis, San Francisco, Fort Worth, Dallas, and Philadelphia. The major objectives of the study were: to construct matrices of college attendance data for samples of both black and white high school graduates to facilitate recruitment; to examine the extent to which black high school graduates are attending local community colleges; to assess aspirations of black youth not attending college; and to explore the usefulness of new testing programs such as the Comparative Guidance and Placement Program (CGP) in assessing special abilities of disadvantaged youth. The findings demonstrated the importance of the community college in the education of urban populations. Community colleges were successful in recruiting disadvantaged youth of academic ability; the author concludes that the community colleges could do more to develop the full potential of less able students while they are still in high school and to insure their successful performance after admission. Parts of this study are also summarized in *Black Student Potential* (1073).

851 LAUWERYS, JOSEPH A., AND SCANLON, DAVID G. (EDS.) *Education in cities: World year book of education 1970.* New York: Harcourt, Brace & World, 1970, 420 pp. $12.95.

This volume of papers presents a comparative analysis of the effect of urbanization on educational systems at all levels. The introductory section discusses foundations of urban education, guidelines for study of the topic, and urban functions of educational institutions. Following sections detail case studies in selected cities throughout the world. These studies review urban growth in each area and examine the methods that have been attempted to educate mushrooming urban populations. The studies further point out particular problems arising from different kinds of urban development such as the rise of shanty towns, the decay of city centers, and the establishment of new towns. They also underscore the importance of the school and university in transmission of attitudes and skills necessary for urban life.

852 McMurrin, Sterling M. (Ed.) *Functional education for disadvantaged youth.* New York: Committee for Economic Development, 1971, 120 pp. $3.

This volume contains four papers focusing on the participation of education, business, and industry in providing the disadvantaged student with an education relevant to his life. The first paper defines the concept of functional education and suggests curricular change necessary for its implementation. The second discusses the role of the public school in preparing youth for employment. The author suggests operational principles for vocational education programs and elaborates a system of employment education in the ghetto from elementary school through the post-secondary level. The third paper suggests seven strategies for success in vocational programs and presents two exemplary case studies. The final paper deals with education and urban youth from the perspective of manpower development.

853 National Commission on Urban Problems. *Building the American city: Report to the Congress and to the President of the United States.* Wash., D. C.: Government Printing Office, 1968, 504 pp. $4.50.

It is commonly assumed that the quality of the immediate environment is a major urban problem that affects education, opportunity, and all aspects of life. This comprehensive report on the cities deals with urban government and finance, building and housing codes, zoning laws, and environmental improvement. Recommendations of the Commission include methods for increasing subsidized housing and lowering construction costs with improvements in codes and regulations, tax revision, state responsiveness, and planned urban growth.

854 Randolph, H. Helen. *Urban education bibliography: An annotated listing.* New York: Center for Urban Education, 1968, 98 pp. $1.

This annotated review of literature brings together research reports, articles, books, and other more fugitive publications concerned with the many aspects of urban education. The bibliography is designed to serve a wide audience: researchers, teachers, students, administrators, and policymakers. The references are primarily from material produced from September 1964 through December 1965.

The bulk of the material included here focuses on minority group integration into the educational, social, and economic institutions of the country; the inner-city schools; their curriculums and teaching techniques; the involvement of community and parents; and, finally, the role of school boards, politics, and bureaucratization as they affect these schools. In addition, the review notes research areas where data are lacking, and lists other bibliographies.

855 Southern Regional Education Board. *The emerging city and higher education.* Atlanta, Ga.: SREB, 1963, 46 pp.

This report includes papers presented at the Tulane University Institute for Deans and Directors of Adult Education. The theme of the conference was the development of higher adult education in an urban setting. The papers deal with a variety of related topics such as the impact of the emerging city on adult education, education for civic policy, the role of the university extension administrator, and specific curriculums for adult education including urban studies programs.

856 Toffler, Alvin (Ed.) *Schoolhouse in the city.* New York: Praeger, 1968, 255 pp. $5.95; paperback $2.50.

This volume includes selected papers delivered at a 1967 conference sponsored by the School Planning and Educational Facilities Laboratories at Stanford University. The papers reflect an assumption of the interdependence of the school and city, the need for administrative reorganization, and the importance of the physical plant and its effect on educational programs. The contributors come from government, sociology, psychology, civil rights groups, urban planning, and architecture. They analyze and suggest solutions to major urban problems and present case studies of school systems in Pittsburgh, Baltimore, and Brooklyn.

857 URBAN AMERICA, INC., AND URBAN COALITION. *One year later.* New York: Praeger, 1969, 122 pp. $1.25.

This report evaluates the national response to the Kerner Commission recommendations regarding correction of slum conditions and social division. The first section describes poverty, education, and environment in the ghettos. The second deals with (1) the scope of violence and response; (2) crime and the community; (3) city government and the ghetto; (4) rising black militancy, and white reaction. The report concludes that the intervening year saw "not even a serious start" toward necessary changes in national priorities, programs, and institutions.

III. *The Students*

SECTION 9: DISTRIBUTION OF TALENT

How students are distributed within higher education is partly a question of how one describes students. Two important ways of describing students are according to (1) their abilities and personal qualities and (2) the characteristics that define their social identification and status. The sorts of students who do and do not attend different forms of postsecondary education define the distributional aspects of access to higher education.

Distribution is a key aspect of access to higher education because it is one of the primary criteria of how the access process works. Evidence of an effective match between educational programs and student talents and interests portends a favorable educational outcome. In this sense the distribution is economically efficient and promises to enhance the general welfare.

The distributional character of access to higher education also gives important evidence of the social outcome of the process. Who goes to college from what social group is the primary indication of the extent to which the access process is egalitarian, meritocratic, or hereditary in its distribution of privilege. Of the following five areas of interest, the first two include primarily work of psychologists. The last three areas include work of both psychologists and sociologists, but especially the latter. This literature appears largely as articles in a variety of professional journals.

=======

9.1—*THE NATURE OF ABILITY.* An understanding of distribution of talent naturally requires an appreciation of what talent is. The literature of this area describes human abilities and how they are organized (for example, see 867). The role of heredity and environment in the formation of intellectual ability is a very old topic of psychological study. For several decades, individual researchers have tended to lean toward either hereditary factors (860) or environmental influences (869). A closely related issue is whether there are racial differences in hereditary influences and whether racial differences in the observed pattern of abilities are a proper basis for favoring different pedagogical methods (871).

These various issues have become socially explosive. The workings of the culture place a premium on certain abilities which have demonstrated relationship to outstanding performance in socially valued activities. In turn these abilities influence access and educational opportunity. Of course, the problem arises due to unequal distribution of valued abilities and heavy emphasis on certain abilities in the educational process. Consequently, the measurement and understanding of socially valued traits is especially important.

858 ANASTASI, ANNE. The formation of psychological traits. *American Psychologist,* 1970, vol. 25, pp. 899-910.

For many years psychologists have examined the components of intellect and behavior through factorial analysis. This statistical technique describes the interrelationships of traits, but as the author explains, it reveals very little concerning their etiology. With intense recent interest in social differences and compensatory education, the question of how traits develop has become especially important. In this article Anastasi provides a very useful summary of the literature on the topic. She gives special consideration to developmental studies, comparative studies of group differences, and experimental investigations.

859 BLOOM, BENJAMIN S. *Stability and change in human characteristics.* New York: John Wiley, 1964, 283 pp. $9.95.

Longitudinal studies in which the same individuals have been repeatedly measured at different points in their lives are analyzed to show the possibilities of quantitative measurement of the development and growth of selected human characteristics. "Stable characteristic" is used to describe attributes which (1) have an underlying structure, such as height, general intelligence, reading comprehension; (2) can be measured quantitatively; and (3) are cumulative in nature, i.e., "nonreversible." Since these characteristics are strongly affected by environmental influence during the rapid growth period of early childhood, Bloom emphasizes the need for much more longitudinal study in order to improve quantitative measurement of environmental factors.

He points out that more precise knowledge of the influence of such factors will place new responsibility on the home, school, and society to consider the social consequences of deprivation. Among the most important questions are: (1) How much can early deprivation be compensated for in later years? (2) To what extent and at what age levels can environmental improvement accomplish change in intelligence and school achievement? He concludes "A society which places great emphasis on verbal learning and rational problem solving and which needs highly skilled and well-trained individuals cannot ignore the enormous consequences of deprivation as it affects the development of general intelligence." The book has been quite influential in establishing national programs and policies in education because it dramatizes the tremendous importance of the first few years of life.

860 BURT, CYRIL. The inheritance of mental ability. *American Psychologist,* 1958, vol. 13, pp. 1-15.

This classic article provides a detailed analysis of the statistical evidence concerning the genetic component in mental ability. The author concluded that intelligence is largely inherited, and his analysis has formed the basis for much subsequent writing on the topic from a hereditary standpoint.

861 COOLEY, WILLIAM W., AND LOHNES, PAUL R. *Predicting development of young adults.* Palo Alto, Calif.: Project TALENT Office, American Institutes for Research, 1968, 233 pp. $5.

Project TALENT pioneered a new style of large-scale, programmatic research into the long-range implications of personality development of youth. In 1960 Project TALENT tested and inventoried almost half a million American secondary students, grades 9 through 12. In the first stages of the follow-up program the subjects were contacted by questionnaire during their first year out of high school, and again after five years.

In this research the authors: (1) reduce approximately 100 test scores in the high school measurement battery to 22 basic personality factors, which are employed as predictors; (2) reduce the many-categoried educational and occupational follow-up items to a rather simple set of categories which are employed as nominal criterion variables; (3) use multiple-group discriminant analysis as the primary analytic method for relating personality profiles to career adjustment variables; and (4) identify trends and generalizations concerning career development of youth. The report is lengthy and technical but contains much valuable and basic data not available elsewhere.

862 DEUTSCH, MARTIN, AND BROWN, BERT. Social influences in Negro-white intelligence differences. *Journal of Social Issues,* 1964, vol. 20, no. 2, pp. 24-35.

This study is based upon Negro and white children but deals largely with social deprivation. The authors were concerned with the effect of social status on intellectual functioning. From a variety of data they cite the "striking fact" that the Negro ranks lower on most social variables. They conclude that "the Negro group is a socially deprived one and that whatever other measures and functions are sensitive to social effects will also reflect this deprivation." They suggest that when it is possible to classify and measure the elements and variables in social deprivation it will be possible to account for differences in intelligence test scores that are attributable to environmental influences.

863 DEUTSCH, MARTIN, KATZ, IRWIN, AND JENSEN, ARTHUR R. (EDS.) *Social class, race, and psychological development.* New York: Holt, Rinehart and Winston, 1968, 423 pp. $8.50.

This comprehensive collection of 11 papers by well-known educational experts attempts to examine and clarify the present state of knowledge concerning social and biological influences on intellectual development. Part I deals with biogenetic perspectives and discusses research on the traditional nature–nurture problem and its relation to racial and social class intelligence differences. Part II includes three papers reviewing basic processes in intellectual development and the influence of the home environment. Social and psychological factors influencing the disadvantaged child's will to learn are discussed in Part III. These papers examine Negro self-identity, the influence of teacher expectations on performance, and Negro performance in desegregated schools. Part IV includes four papers on compensatory education and environmental intervention.

864 DREGER, RALPH M., AND MILLER, KENT S. Comparative psychological studies of Negroes and whites in the United States: 1959-1965. *Psychological Bulletin Monograph Supplement,* 1968, vol. 70, no. 3, part 2, 58 pp.

Dreger and Miller reviewed comparative psychological studies of Negroes and whites in 1960; this paper covers the period 1959–1965. The report lists research on physical influences on psychological and psychosocial functions, physical and motor development, psychophysical functions, intellectual functions, the level of educational and occupational aspiration, temperament, social perceptions and attitudes, mental illness, crime, and family organization. The authors identify significant books of the period and discuss trends in the research literature. They note the fact that while there is no way to make generalizations as to intellectual ability, some specific abilities appear to have differential racial patterns. They conclude that researchers are beginning to understand that reactions are not the simple product of heredity or environment, but of complex combinations of many variables, such as cultural goals, geographic locale, language development, peer relations, role expectancies, gene patterns, neurological status, and sex.

865 ECKLAND, BRUCE K. Genetics and sociology: A reconsideration. *American Sociological Review,* 1967, vol. 32, pp. 173-194.

Eckland explains why sociologists originally erected a barrier between themselves and the hard sciences, and why they should now change this posture. He describes four sociological problems in which the integration of genetic and social processes is especially significant: (1) the possibility of man's genetic character being altered by a combination of differential fertility rates (favoring the lower classes) and assortative mating; (2) how regression toward the mean (exhibited when bright parents produce a dull child or vice versa) causes the contradiction between our institution of the nuclear family and its control over the individual, and our goal of most efficiently educating and employing human resources; (3) the problem of whether or not standardized tests can measure genetically endowed intelligence; and (4) the problem of designing a "vertical mobility" system that puts the most intellectually capable persons on top. The author concludes that our survival will soon demand that we face issues involving a confrontation between the principles of social heredity and those of the meritocracy. In his view, the second, while not more equitable, is more rational.

866 ERLENMEYER-KIMLING, L., AND JARVIK, LISSY F. Genetics and intelligence: A review. *Science,* 1963, vol. 142, pp. 1477-1479.

In a survey of 52 studies from eight countries over the past 50 years, the authors assembled correlation coefficients bearing upon the relationship between heredity and intelligence. The survey revealed a consistency in the accumulated data relating mental functioning to genetic potentials and showed that intragroup resemblance in intellectual abilities increases in proportion to the degree of genetic relationships, regardless of environmental communality. The authors acknowledge that environment is not without effect upon intellectual functioning, but emphasize that intellectual expression "results from the patterns laid down by the genotype under given environmental conditions."

867 GUILFORD, JOY P. *The nature of human intelligence.* New York: McGraw-Hill, 1967, 538 pp. $14.75.

There have been several schools of thought on the nature of intelligence. These range from the idea that intelligence is one general trait manifested in somewhat different ways by different individuals to the notion that intelligence is composed of a number of only partially related abilities. The most recent and the most elaborate theory concerning the "structure of intellect" is due largely to Guilford's research and theoretical development. This book gives a somewhat technical but comprehensive description of the author's theory of intellect. It hypothesizes many types of abilities which vary according to the content, the mode of operation, and the product of the intellectual process. This theory has attracted special attention because of its implications for utilizing a wide variety of potentially useful traits which might characterize various socially deprived groups to a greater extent than is true of traditional measures of scholastic aptitude.

868 HOLLAND, JOHN L., AND RICHARDS, JAMES M. JR. Academic and nonacademic accomplishment in a representative sample of students taking the American College Tests. *College and University,* 1967, vol. 43, pp. 60-71.

The authors begin with the premise that a better record of a student's non-academic competencies is needed if we are to find students who will be out-standing outside the classroom and in later life. For their study they took a three percent representative sample of the group of approximately 612,000 students tested by ACT between November 1964 and 1965. A checklist of extracurricular accomplishment was developed to obtain scores in six nonacademic areas of accomplishment. The correlations between the nonacademic achievement scales, ACT tests, and high school grades supported earlier findings that academic and nonacademic achievements are essentially independent of one another. The present study used the largest and most diverse student sample ever obtained to examine the relationships in question. The authors conclude that the present emphasis in colleges and universities on academic potential has led to neglect of other equally important talents.

869 HUNT, J. McVICKER. *Intelligence and experience.* New York: Ronald Press, 1961, 416 pp. $8.

Jensen (see 870) assembled considerable evidence favoring the proposition that intellectual abilities are largely inherited. This book by Hunt is probably the most extensive, well-developed, and prominent opposing view. The author uses Piaget's work and hundreds of experimental studies of learning and cognition to argue that intellectual performance is largely determined by environment and early development.

870 JENSEN, ARTHUR R. Social class, race, and genetics: Implications for education. *American Educational Research Journal,* 1968, vol. 5, pp. 1-42.

One conviction underlies Jensen's analysis: refusal to recognize a biological as well as an environmental basis to differences in educability will only harm efforts to understand the diversity of human capacities and to facilitate the humanitarian goals of a free society. He reviews the current status of knowledge about hereditary sources of variance in intelligence and educability. Also, past efforts to develop tests for pinpointing genetic or environmental influences as sources of intellectual differences between races and social classes are critically analyzed.

Jensen cites evidence of characteristic patterns of different types of abilities which are consistent at different socioeconomic levels within the same racial group. Such patterns which seem independent of social class but common to racial groups are taken as a basis for treating different groups differently in educational situations. He argues that an optimal individual Instruction × Pupil interaction would help to prevent us from running all children through a standard schooling format, thereby alienating those incapable of a certain kind of learning to the point of eliminating the chances they might have of entering upon any path of educational fulfillment.

871 JENSEN, ARTHUR R. How much can we boost IQ and scholastic achievement? *Harvard Educational Review*, 1969, vol. 39, pp. 1-123.

Jensen argues that compensatory education programs have failed to produce lasting changes in the IQ and achievement of disadvantaged children and the basic premises of these programs should be reexamined. He contends that tests and the history of test development indicate that the concept of intelligence correlates closely with the probability of acceptable performance in occupational endeavor. If we were a hunting culture, "general intelligence" would probably involve visual acuity and running speed. The tests that measure general intelligence in our society define it primarily as the ability to abstract and conceptualize for problem solving. The author argues that several lines of evidence indicate that genetic inheritance is of equal or greater importance than environmental influences in determining this ability for abstraction and conceptualization. The environment operates as a threshold variable—deprivation can inhibit reaching full potential, but intensive, enriched educational experiences cannot push a child above his potential.

Obviously, Jensen notes, there are kinds of mental abilities other than those stressing abstract reasoning. Associative learning ability rather than cognitive skill, for example, is demonstrated by the child of low IQ who nevertheless can quickly learn the names of all the children in the playground and the rules to all the games in two or three days. Different ethnic groups definitely have different patterns of mental abilities because of their peculiar genetic inheritances (see 870). He reasons that schools presently stress a type of education that emphasizes IQ and requires certain prerequisites—an attention span sufficiently long to listen to the teacher's instruction, the ability to comprehend verbal utterances, to inhibit large-muscle activity, to voluntarily rehearse newly-learned behavior, etc.—to operate in the active–passive, teacher–student relationship. Children who consistently meet with failure in this traditional method of teaching have succeeded when other modes of learning were utilized. If the goal is helping each person to reach his full potential, the educational system should recognize the diversity of mental abilities and provide flexibility in instructional techniques and occupational objectives. See the next issue of this same journal for reactions to this controversial article (vol. 39, no. 2).

872 MCNEMAR, QUINN. Lost: Our intelligence? Why? *American Psychologist*, 1964, vol. 19, pp. 871-882.

In this presidential address before the Seventy-Second Annual Convention of the American Psychological Association, McNemar reviewed the various attacks on the concept of general intelligence from Thurstone's factor analysis approach to the more recent stress on creativity as a "better" measure of productivity. He discusses several of the multitest batteries, and concludes that their ability to provide better predictors of achievement in school has not been demonstrated. After pointing out the methodological shortcomings of several of the recent studies of creativity, the author concludes that the concept of general intelligence, although maligned by some and discarded by others, still has a "rightful place in the science of psychology and in the practical affairs of man."

873 NICHOLS, ROBERT C. The resemblance of twins in personality and interests. NMSC Research Reports, vol. 2, no. 8. Evanston, Ill.: National Merit Scholarship Corporation, 1966, 23 pp.

The California Psychological Inventory (CPI), the Vocational Preference Inventory (VPI), and the Objective Behavior Inventory (OBI), were administered to 319 pairs of fraternal twins of the same sex, and to 498 pairs of identical twins. The correlations for both male and female sets showed significantly greater similarity between identical than fraternal twins. The author could not make definite conclusions on the cause of various personality traits, though, because of three factors: (1) There was not agreement between the results for boys and those for girls so that "whatever was making identical twins more alike than fraternal ones was not the same or was not operating the same way in both sexes." (2) Many of the differences in similarity between the two kinds of twins were too large to be accounted for by genetics. (3) The findings were inconsistent with those of an earlier twin study also based upon the CPI. Nichols concludes that perhaps the twin method is inapplicable to personality inventories based on self-reports because identical twins are more likely to have the same "random" experiences than fraternal twins. He cites the need for continued diligence in seeking some way of obtaining reproducible results with the twin method.

874 NICHOLS, ROBERT C. Heredity, environment, and school achievement. *Measurement and Evaluation in Guidance,* 1968, vol. 1, pp. 122-129.

The author provides a brief but informative summary of recent research on the genetic and environmental factors involved in school achievement. He contends that there is substantial evidence of the importance of the genetic factor and suggests that a rough ordering from least to greatest of the main determinants of individual differences in ability might be as follows: the school factor, the family factor, and the genetic factor. At the same time he does not see this as cause for undue pessimism since there is evidence of strong interaction between heredity and environment. He concludes with a suggestion that "educational effects may be considerably enhanced once we know enough to administer the right educational experience at the right time to the right genotype."

875 NICHOLS, ROBERT C. Nature and nurture in adolescence, in J. S. Adams (Ed.), *Understanding adolescence.* Boston: Allyn and Bacon, 1968, pp. 101-127.

In this chapter Nichols provides a very useful summary of evidence concerning the effects of hereditary and environmental factors in various aspects of adolescent behavior. The author considers first the relationship between intelligence and academic achievement, particularly as this relationship is affected by the school, the family, and genetic factors. Other brief sections summarize information concerning hereditary and environmental components in different mental abilities, personality and interest, and mental disorder.

876 SCHOENFELDT, LYLE F. The hereditary components of the Project TALENT two-day test battery. *Measurement and Evaluation in Guidance,* 1968, vol. 1, pp. 130-140.

The purpose of this study was to determine the extent to which individual differences in the Project TALENT test battery could be attributed to genetic factors. Results were based upon statistical analysis of the performance of fraternal and identical twins on: a general intellectual factor, three different aptitudes, two types of educational achievement, and five areas of special knowledge. Each type of ability and achievement contained significant components of genetically related variability. None of the five types of special knowledge had a significant heredity component.

877 WERTS, CHARLES E. The many faces of intelligence. *Journal of Educational Psychology,* 1967, vol. 58, pp. 198-204.

To further illuminate the controversy about academically adept students being accepted into college over those capable of creativity in "real life," the author examined the relationship between the high school grades and extracurricular achievements of over 127,000 college freshmen in fall 1961. Students with high grades formed a greater percentage of the achievers in scientific, literary, leadership, speech, drama, music, and art areas than did students with low grades. They also tended to win recognition in several of these areas while the "majority of students with low grades did not show any extracurricular achievement." These results contradict the work of Holland and others (868). See the same journal for a rebuttal by Holland and Richards (same issue, pp. 205-209).

9.2 — STUDENT CHARACTERISTICS. This section is mostly concerned with personal, biographical, and intellectual characteristics of students in general and of students at different types of colleges. The data are quite diverse and detailed. Most of this sort of normative information necessarily comes from large surveys and national testing programs. A particularly valuable source of information about student characteristics has been Project TALENT (885). The best source of current information about the characteristics of students entering different types of colleges each year is the annual survey undertaken by the American Council on Education (881).

878 ABE, CLIFFORD, AND HOLLAND, JOHN L. *A description of college freshmen. I. Students with different choices of major field.* ACT Research Report No. 3. Iowa City, Iowa: American College Testing Program, 1965, 53 pp.

This report provides interesting information on characteristics, achievements, and attitudes of some 12,000 college freshmen in 31 institutions of higher education. Values and attitudes expressed by the students were summarized into several broad areas and used to describe differences among students choosing different major fields.

879 ADAMS, JAMES F. (ED.) *Understanding adolescence: Current developments in adolescent psychology.* Boston: Allyn and Bacon, 1968, 386 pp. $8.95.

This book is intended as a text in adolescent psychology. Written by a variety of contributors, the chapters cover a wide spectrum of topics and deal with theories of development, physiological changes, problems of transition from childhood, hereditary versus environmental character determinants, cognitive development, values, and attitudes. Further chapters treat contemporary topics including activism and apathy, sex education, sociological views on the disadvantaged, the privileged adolescent, vocational training and counseling, and the role of educational institutions in development. See 875 for Nichols' chapter on heredity and environment.

880 AMERICAN COLLEGE TESTING PROGRAM. *College student profiles: Norms for the ACT assessment.* Iowa City, Iowa: ACT, 1966, 292 pp. $3.50.

The American College Testing Program has summarized in this volume the results of the ACT assessment for some 400 higher institutions. Profile information is provided for various groups of students and types of institutions in different regions of the country. While the report is a useful reference to the ACT program, a shortcoming is its provision of normative information which is seriously nonrepresentative for some types of institutions and regions.

881 AMERICAN COUNCIL ON EDUCATION, OFFICE OF RESEARCH. *National norms for entering college freshmen — Fall 1970.* ACE Research Reports, vol. 5, no. 6. Wash., D. C.: ACE, 1970, 100 pp.

Each year since 1965 the Office of Research of the American Council on Education has carried out a survey of entering freshmen in a representative group of colleges and universities across the nation. The normative data in this particular report are based upon some 180,000 students entering 275 institutions. The questionnaire, a copy of which is included in the volume, was designed to elicit a wide range of biographical and demographic data and expressions of career plans, student behaviors, and attitudes. The data are weighted in order to be representative of the nation's freshman population, and summary statistics are presented for men and women at various types of colleges. These normative reports provide valuable annual indications of changes in the character of entering freshmen; the data thus filed form the basis for follow-up studies and a continuing program of research (see 1156).

882 COLEMAN, JAMES S. *The adolescent society.* New York: Free Press, 1961, 368 pp. $8.50.

This sociological study of high school students documents the character of adolescent society in the late 1950s. Extensive research was conducted in 10 northern Illinois high schools, each one chosen to represent a different sociological situation, and with clear differences in their status systems. The book takes as a starting point the development of an adolescent subculture as a concomitant of an industrialized society; Coleman points out that the "natural processes" of education within the family have been supplanted by educational institutions that segregate adolescents for longer and longer training periods. As a result, he finds that adolescent subcultures operate quite apart from adult society, and dispense rewards in the form of distribution of status. Rewarded activities were found to vary from school to school, but in all cases athletics was extremely important for boys, and social success with boys was extremely important for girls. The status value of academic success was found to vary from school to school. The book concludes with a discussion of how educational attainment could be integrated into the status systems. In general it is particularly noteworthy for its interesting descriptions of the variations in types of adolescent status systems.

883 CROSS, K. PATRICIA. *The junior college student: A research description.* Princeton, N. J.: Educational Testing Service, 1968, 56 pp. $1.

This study provides a valuable synthesis of findings of recent research and presents a description of the characteristics of junior college students. The author discusses academic characteristics, socioeconomic background, finances, self-concepts, interests and personality characteristics, reasons for attending college, reactions to college, choice of vocation and major field of study, and educational and occupational aspirations. An especially useful concluding chapter identifies some "knowns" and "unknowns" regarding the characteristics of junior college students as suggested by the available research.

884 DREW, DAVID E. *A profile of the Jewish freshman.* ACE Research Reports, vol. 5, no. 4. Wash., D. C.: American Council on Education, 1970, 53 pp.

This special report was commissioned by the American Jewish Committee and takes advantage of the fact that the Cooperative Institutional Research Program of the American Council on Education maintains a current data bank on a representative sample of American college freshmen. The report includes relatively little narrative but a great deal of statistical information on Jewish men and women students at different types of higher institutions. Comparative data on students expressing a preference for other religions is also included. The report is based upon the same type of student characteristics, plans, and attitudes contained in ACE's annual *National Norms for Entering College Freshmen* (881). It presents a picture reasonably close to the familiar stereotype of the Jewish student—upper middle class, liberal, verbally oriented, and a high academic achiever.

885 FLANAGAN, JOHN C., ET AL. *The American high school student.* Palo Alto, Calif.: Project TALENT Office, American Institutes for Research, 1964, 738 pp. $10.

Project TALENT is an extensive study of American youth including follow-up into adult life. A comprehensive battery of tests and instruments was developed to measure aptitudes, abilities, knowledge, interests, activities, and backgrounds of high school students. In 1960 this two-day battery was administered to a stratified random sample of about 440,000 students constituting about five percent of the American high school population. This publication provides the first detailed information from the study; more than 2,000 items of information were collected about each student. The project represents the first comprehensive survey of its kind. Follow-up studies have provided particularly valuable data. See 1405 for a list of Project TALENT reports.

886 HEIST, PAUL. Student characteristics: College and university, in Robert L. Ebel (Ed.), *Encyclopedia of educational research.* (4th ed.) New York: Macmillan, 1969, pp. 1318-1329.

This article provides a concise and useful overview of research concerned with the characteristics of college students. It includes a 100-item bibliography emphasizing work published in the 1960s. One section is devoted to students in other countries.

887 KOOS, LEONARD V. *The community college student.* Gainesville, Fla.: University of Florida Press, 1970, 580 pp. $17.50.

This book provides a synthesis of research and descriptive literature dealing with late adolescence. It gives a comprehensive profile of a major portion of students enrolled in community colleges. Part I summarizes studies of physical, mental, and social development; sexual and dating behavior; and vocational and recreational interests. Part II focuses on student aptitude; socioeconomic status; academic competence; personal characteristics, attitudes, and interests; and personal problems. Part III points out the implications of the research for curriculum development and student personnel program structure. Koos also includes a chapter on adult education and the adult student. Each section is followed by a selected bibliography.

888 RICHARDS, JAMES M. JR., AND BRASKAMP, LARRY A. *Who goes where to junior college?* ACT Research Report No. 20. Iowa City, Iowa: American College Testing Program, 1967, 19 pp.

This study investigated differences in student characteristics between: (1) two- and four-year college students and (2) students at various types of two-year colleges. Compared with his counterpart at a four-year college, the junior college student was found to be less talented, and vocationally rather than intellectually motivated. The authors extrapolate that a two-year student is likely to be the first in his family to attend college, and that "for him college primarily is an instrument of social mobility." Correlations were computed between student body characteristics and a factorially derived description of institutional environments. Students at colleges rated high on conventionalism, high cost, or private control, were found to have many similarities with students at four-year colleges.

889 SCHOENFELDT, LYLE F. Post-high-school education, in John C. Flanagan et al., *Project TALENT one-year follow-up studies.* Palo Alto, Calif.: Project TALENT Office, American Institutes for Research, 1966, pp. 91-129.

In this chapter Schoenfeldt elaborates on previous studies which compared Project TALENT students who entered a junior college with those who entered a four-year college, and those who either enrolled in some kind of technical school or did not attend any post-high school institution. The findings showed that junior college students were more similar to non-college students in terms of ability, and to four-year college students in socioeconomic background. Another conclusion was that ability facilitated college entrance to a much greater degree than socioeconomic level. Males entering four-year colleges were considerably higher on all measures of ability, information, and socioeconomic environment than those in the other groups. Interest, ability, and information variables were found to differentiate females entering a four-year college or nursing school from the remaining groups. The chapter is especially valuable in reporting a variety of normative information about students in these various groups.

890 SCHOENFELDT, LYLE F., BAYER, ALAN E., AND BROWN, MARSHA D. Delayed and normal progress college students: A comparison of psycho-social characteristics and career plans. *American Educational Research Journal,* 1970, vol. 7, pp. 235-250.

This article provides the most comprehensive information available concerning the characteristics of students who delayed their entrance into college following high school. Other sources of data indicate that roughly one college freshman out of eight is a delayed entrant. In this study those students who delayed college entrance for a year were generally of lower ability and lower socio-economic status. They were more likely black, relied on savings or bank loans to go to college, had friends who did not attend college, and had changed career goals.

891 SEIBEL, DEAN W. *A study of the academic ability and performance of junior college students.* Princeton, N. J.: Educational Testing Service, 1965, 44 pp.

This study is one of four which provides follow-up information on the college performance of a representative national sample of high school seniors. Data on ability characteristics and college grades and academic status are provided for students at two- and four-year colleges. Students who attended four-year colleges were of higher average ability than those who attended two-year institutions, however there was considerable overlap. The proportion of junior college students completing the first year in good standing was somewhat smaller than that of four-year college students (61 percent compared to 78 percent), and the proportion on probation was nearly twice as great among junior college students (21 percent compared to 11 percent). However, the proportion of junior college students dismissed for academic reasons was only slightly higher than those dismissed from four-year institutions. In general, boys seemed to fare much worse than girls during the first year regardless of what type of college attended.

892 SHAYCOFT, MARION F. *The high school years: Growth in cognitive skills.* Palo Alto, Calif.: Project TALENT Office, American Institutes for Research, 1967, 376 pp. $5.

This report analyzes the growth in cognitive skills of 7,500 twelfth graders who had been part of the original ninth-grade Project TALENT sample in 1960. The findings showed a substantial amount of growth in the three-year period; the larger gains tended to be associated with school-taught subjects. In general, the amount of course work taken in subject areas had a direct effect on test performance in those areas. Reading comprehension seemed to improve somewhat more for students taking many academic courses than for those taking lighter academic loads. Significant differences in score changes were found among schools; the author recommends further research to determine the critical ways in which the more effective schools differ from the less effective ones. Some suggested implications are that remedial efforts should not be postponed until high school, and that research is needed to determine the relationship between vocational programs and reading competence. This work underscores the critical nature of verbal aptitude and the fact that disadvantaged youth show limited improvement in this skill during the high school years.

893 SHAYCOFT, MARION F., DAILEY, JOHN T., ORR, DAVID B., NEYMAN, CLINTON A. JR., AND SHERMAN, STUART E. *Studies of a complete age group—age 15.* Palo Alto, Calif.: Project TALENT Office, American Institutes for Research, 1963, 288 pp. $8.50.

In order to develop national norms on a representative sample of an age group,

Student Characteristics

rather than just on those members of the age group who are in high school, an attempt was made to locate and test a sample of all 15-year-olds. The sample consisted of roughly four and one-half percent of 15-year-olds in school taken from the regular Project TALENT sample, and slightly less than one-half of one percent of all other 15-year-olds. An effort was made to locate and test all members of this sample, and if they were not in school, to find out when and why they had dropped out. A special questionnaire was developed to elicit this and other significant information about the dropouts. Except for a very few localities with large concentrations of disadvantaged groups, there were hardly any 15-year-olds not attending school. Most of those not in school who were located could not be tested, either because of inadequate reading and writing skills, or unwillingness to participate. The data from those who did participate showed that almost all the dropouts were very poor readers; this factor is cited as evidence of the need to intensify efforts in the early grades to improve reading and other basic skills of weaker students.

894 TILLERY, DALE. *SCOPE state profile grade nine 1966. SCOPE state profile grade twelve 1966. SCOPE grade ten profile 1967. SCOPE grade eleven profile 1968.* New York: College Entrance Examination Board.

SCOPE (School to College: Opportunities for Postsecondary Education) is a four-state study of student decision-making which seeks to determine how, when, and why students make decisions about post-high school education and careers, and the relative influence that parents, schools, and peers have on the nature of those decisions. The six-year project, sponsored by the Center for Research and Development in Higher Education at Berkeley and the College Entrance Examination Board, involved nearly 90,000 students in California, Illinois, Massachusetts, and North Carolina.

Information about 9th- and 12th-grade students as a basis for longitudinal studies was collected during the spring of 1966. Several groups of variables were examined, among them: academic ability test scores; family and home milieu; parental expectations; self-evaluation; values; perceptions of school; information-seeking activities; occupational preferences; and intellectual predisposition. The follow-up phases of the project are designed to find out how well students do after high school graduation and how they view their decisions in retrospect. This series of 14 reports provides useful summary statistics on the responses of students to the SCOPE surveys in the first two years of the project.

895 UNIVERSITY SYSTEM OF GEORGIA, REGENTS. *Normative data for the 1969-70 freshman class — University System of Georgia.* Atlanta: RUSG, 1970, 94 pp.

Since the fall of 1957 the Board of Regents of the University System of Georgia has published an annual monograph containing descriptive statistics about the fall-quarter entering freshmen in University System institutions. In these monographs the freshman class is described in terms of total score on the Scholastic Aptitude Test, academic record achieved in high school, and average freshman grades. Equations for predicting freshman grades are reported. The primary purpose of this publication is to provide University System institutions with summary statistics about their entering freshman class and with data useful in advising prospective students concerning their probable success in college. It represents one of the earliest statewide efforts to coordinate information concerning college admissions.

9.3—MOTIVES TO ATTEND COLLEGE. One of the more interesting areas of research literature is that concerned with what motivates students to go to college. Most has been written by psychologists and sociologists and is concerned with the influence of peers, parents, and the contextual effects of community and school. Unfortunately, much of this work suffers from inadequate statistical or experimental control so the results are often contradictory and difficult to interpret. A highly selected group of references is included in this section.

896 BEEZER, ROBERT H., AND HJELM, HOWARD F. *Factors related to college attendance.* Cooperative Research Monograph No. 8, Wash., D. C.: Government Printing Office, 1963, 42 pp.

This report is based on the findings of three statewide surveys conducted in Arkansas, Indiana, and Wisconsin under the sponsorship of the U.S. Office of Education. These three surveys were integrated with other recent studies of factors influencing college attendance. The authors suggest several conclusions from an analysis of the combined findings of the studies cited: (1) Lack of motivation is probably the greatest deterrent to college attendance for capable youth. (2) Insufficient funds constitute a serious barrier for some. (3) Parental attitudes toward higher education are an important influence, and special attention should be given to improving parental attitudes toward college training for girls. (4) Large numbers of minority students do not pursue their education beyond high school, and this represents one of the greatest wastes of potential talent in the country. (5) College attendance varies from state to state, and attention must be given to equalizing the opportunities for college training among different regions of the country. (6) The effect of peer pressure might be utilized to increase college attendance if leaders among the better students were encouraged to continue their education at the college level. Some of the information of this report is spotty but it is one of the more comprehensive early reports on the topic.

897 COHEN, ARLENE G., AND GUTHRIE, GEORGE M. Patterns of motivation for college attendance. *Educational and Psychological Measurement,* 1966, vol. 26, pp. 89-98.

The authors undertook a factor analysis of a number of statements concerning motives for attending college. The primary motives identified in an initial analysis and a replication were: intellectual development; vocational preparation; to satisfy parental and social demands; economic gains; leadership; and to serve society.

898 COLE, CHARLES C. JR. *Encouraging scientific talent.* New York: College Entrance Examination Board, 1957, 259 pp.

How many talented young people, particularly capable science students, do not go on to college, and what inducements might attract more of them to do so? These are the primary questions to which this classic study was addressed. The study included a questionnaire survey on college plans, science interest, and financial needs of a five percent sample of public high school seniors in 1955. This was the first national study of access to higher education. The author concluded that the intellectual wastage was approximately 200,000 18-year-olds a year. Cole felt that 100,000 new scholarships would salvage the students who are held back by financial reasons. Another 100,000 who are not motivated to continue need to have their interest aroused, beginning in the early grades. He proposed many specific remedies, including improvement of teaching; federal, state, and local aid to schools; and an increase in efforts to attract women into science.

899 COWHIG, JAMES D., AND NAM, CHARLES B. *Farm population: Educational status, college plans, and occupational status of farm and nonfarm youths, October 1959.* Series Census-ERS, No. 30. Wash., D. C.: U.S. Bureau of the Census, 1961, 33 pp. 50 cents.

The October 1959 *Current Population Survey* provided information concerning the educational plans of high school seniors, college students, and persons 16 to 24 years old not enrolled in school. Much of the information is dated but does provide, for this period, valuable bench-mark data concerning students' perceptions of their reasons for their continuing or not continuing their education.

900 HALLER, ARCHIBALD O., AND BUTTERWORTH, C. E. Peer influences on levels of occupational and educational aspirations. *Social Forces,* 1960, vol. 38, pp. 289-295.

This article provides contradictory evidence to the common assumption that peers influence educational aspiration. The study was undertaken in 1957 of all 17-year-old boys in Lenawee County, Michigan, a site study that presented a full range of American class levels and a high degree of exposure to knowledge about advanced education. The peer-pair was selected as the unit of analysis. The control variables included social class status; measured general intelligence of the subjects; and the degree to which parents desired high social achievement for the subject. The evidence provided little or no support of the assumption of peer influence.

901 HERRIOTT, ROBERT E. Some social determinants of educational aspiration, in Kaoru Yamamota (Ed.), *The college student and his culture: An analysis.* Boston: Houghton Mifflin, 1968, pp. 104-122.

This detailed examination of educational aspiration presents a variety of multiple and partial regression analyses which are quite useful in identifying the interrelationships among self-assessment, expectations perceived from others, and educational aspiration. As would be expected, aspiration was found to be substantially related to self-assessment and expectations of others. Additional analysis indicated that the most important self-assessment is intellectual performance, and the most influential expectation from others is that of friends of the same age.

902 HOLLINSHEAD, BYRON S. *Who should go to college.* New York: Columbia University Press, 1952, 190 pp. (Out of print)

This famous book was sponsored by the College Board on behalf of the Commission on Financing Higher Education. It was perhaps the first comprehensive examination of the question of who should go to college and what steps might be taken to finance and motivate those students who should be encouraged to continue their education. The proposed answers reflect a marked change in social attitudes toward higher education over the past two decades. Heavy emphasis is placed upon private funding to assist the top quarter of the age group in attending college.

903 JAFFE, A. J., AND ADAMS, WALTER. *American higher education in transition.* New York: Bureau of Applied Social Research, Columbia University, 1969, 239 pp.

This report presents an overview of various short- and long-term trends with special emphasis on access to college. Recent reports and articles from specific projects are summarized, but the authors rely heavily upon special follow-up data from a Census Bureau survey.

Specific topics include the following: (1) the high school dropout and college entrance; (2) the over-age student; (3) changes in the educational establishment; (4) recent trends in college attendance; (5) financial characteristics of college planners and entrants; (6) nonfinancial characteristics of college planners; (7) entrants to two- and four-year colleges; (8) nonentrants to college; (9) family structure, socioeconomic class, and college attendance; and (10) occupational expectations and reality.

In a summary of findings the authors make several observations. They see a significant lessening of financial barriers to college attendance, chiefly due to the rise of the public two-year college. Failure to enter the college preparatory curriculum, unfavorable self-image, and counseling against college attendance are cited as deterrents that require further study. The authors also report that many students are unrealistic about the relationship between educational attainment and future employment.

904 KANDEL, DENISE B., AND LESSER, GERALD S. Parental and peer influences on educational plans of adolescents. *American Sociological Review,* 1969, vol. 34, pp. 213-223.

In this study the authors report that agreement on educational goals is higher with the mother than with the best friend at school. While agreement with the friend increases with greater intimacy, agreement with the mother remains at the same level irrespective of the adolescent's closeness to his parents. These findings are interpreted as a contradiction to the notion of a separate adolescent subculture isolated from parental influence. See 901 for variant results.

905 MEDSKER, LELAND L., AND TRENT, JAMES W. *The influence of different types of public higher institutions on college attendance from varying socioeconomic and ability levels.* Berkeley, Calif.: Center for Research and Development in Higher Education, University of California, 1965, 110 pp. (Out of print)

This study investigated socioeconomic and ease-of-access factors affecting college attendance. The sample constituted 10,000 high school graduates of 1959 representing 16 communities with various access situations—no public college, public junior college, freshman–sophomore university extension center, nonselective state college, and one metropolitan center. Total enrollment figures for September 1959 showed half the men and 37 percent of the women continuing their education. The extent of waste of talent may be seen in 25 percent of the men and 33 percent of the women in the top ability quintile who did not go on to college. Socioeconomic status was found to be more important than ability in determining college plans, and the report finds "The value placed upon education by the family unit becomes the mainspring of the motivational factor which affects college attendance." Where parents strongly encouraged college plans, 75 percent enrolled in college. The highest entrance rates were found in communities with public junior colleges. At-hand facilities were a strong inducement for high-ability students from low socioeconomic backgrounds to continue; 53 percent of such students were enrolled where their home community offered a public junior college, in contrast to 22 percent entering college from communities with no public facility. The complexity of the many factors underlying college decisions and their implications for future planning are discussed in the concluding chapter.

906 MEYER, JOHN W. High school effects on college intentions. *American Journal of Sociology,* 1970, vol. 76, pp. 59-70.

This paper finds that there is both a positive and a negative aspect in the small observed effect of the secondary school on the individual student's aspirations. High social status of a school tends to encourage college attendance, while the contextual effect of high aptitude among peers discourages college attendance. This finding is similar to that reported by Davis (see 26).

907 SEWELL, WILLIAM H. Community of residence and college plans. *American Sociological Review,* 1964, vol. 29, pp. 24-38.

The authors analyze here the well-known fact that probability of attending college varies systematically with community size. These data indicate that the percentage of students with college plans increases from 21 percent for those living on farms to 42 percent for those from large cities. Whereas intelligence and socioeconomic status explain most of the differences associated with community size, there does remain a residual tendency for able rural boys not to attend college.

908 SEWELL, WILLIAM H., AND ARMER, J. MICHAEL. Neighborhood context and college plans. *American Sociological Review*, 1966, vol. 31, pp. 159-168.

This study of educational aspiration among students in the Milwaukee metropolitan area indicates large differences among neighborhoods with different occupational composition. These differences were greatly diminished or wiped out completely when effects due to sex, socioeconomic status, and intelligence were controlled. The author concludes that neighborhood context itself probably accounts for relatively little of the variance in college plans. See 934 for evidence of a positive relationship between educational aspiration and status in the immediate peer group.

909 SEWELL, WILLIAM H., AND ORENSTEIN, ALAN M. Community of residence and occupational choice. *American Journal of Sociology*, 1965, vol. 70, pp. 551-563.

The proportion of students choosing high-status occupations typically increases with the size of the community. Results of this study indicate that controlling effects due to sex, intelligence, and socioeconomic status eliminates such community differences in occupational choice for girls but not completely for boys. This study is a companion to 907 which examines community of residence and college plans.

910 SPADY, WILLIAM G. Lament for the letterman: Effects of peer status and extracurricular activities on goals and achievement. *American Journal of Sociology*, 1970, vol. 75, pp. 680-702.

The author's analysis points to the student's role in the peer group as an important source of student aspiration. Participation in extracurricular activities (especially athletics) is strongly associated with high status perceptions and stimulates a desire for further status after high school. The resultant aspiration for college "backfires" when activities such as athletics stimulate future goals without providing the skills required for their fulfillment. The author concludes "The survival beyond high school for such students is considerably less likely than for their peers with sounder resources."

911 WILSON, ALAN B. Residential segregation of social classes and aspirations of high school boys. *American Sociological Review*, 1959, vol. 24, pp. 836-845.

This was one of the early and influential studies which documented wide differences in educational aspiration among boys who attended schools characterized by different social climates. These differences in aspiration persisted even after introduction of various control variables such as intelligence, mother's education, father's occupation, etc. While the author is undoubtedly correct that the ethos of the school does affect aspiration, an important methodological weakness of the article lies in the fact that critical variables were controlled individually and not simultaneously.

9.4–WHO GOES TO COLLEGE? This section includes the primary data on how many and what students are going to college. Information is typically based upon longitudinal surveys, and the sources of data are actually quite limited. Only a few states have made systematic efforts to examine the conditions of educational opportunity, and national studies are infrequent. Much of the available information comes from the Census Bureau (919, for example) or Project TALENT (see 917).

Three types of information are of special interest: the access rate or the proportion of high school graduates attending college; normative data on characteristics of young people who do and do not continue education immediately after high school; and analyses of the variables associated with attendance and nonattendance. By far the best source of information on the latter point is Chapter 5 of the final report of the Commission on Human Resources and Advanced Training (918).

For reasons that are hard to understand there is no routine and reliable source of information on the annual rate of access to college. A report from the Bureau of Labor Statistics (920) does give an estimate of the proportion of high school graduates attending college each fall, but this simple and useful statistic does not begin to give an adequate picture of the access process with respect to different types of students and conditions. The last comprehensive data were provided by Project TALENT in the early 1960s.

912 BAIRD, LEONARD L., AND HOLLAND, JOHN L. *The flow of high school students to schools, colleges, and jobs*. ACT Research Report No. 26. Iowa City, Iowa: American College Testing Program, 1968, 19 pp.

This follow-up survey of 1966 high school seniors one year after graduation examined academic and nonacademic ability in relation to college and vocational choices. The sorting process between high school and college largely reflected variations in academic aptitudes, with students enrolled at four-year institutions having the highest ability. However, nonacademic talents were found to be much in evidence among the groups who were working, married, or attending other types of institutions. The authors conclude that it is misleading to label those who do not go on to four-year colleges as "less talented"; their choices represent a different use of talent—not "talent loss."

913 BERDIE, RALPH F. *After high school—what?* Minneapolis, Minn.: University of Minnesota Press, 1954, 240 pp. $4.25.

This is one of the classic early statewide studies of who goes to college. All Minnesota high school seniors of 1950 were given questionnaires concerning their plans for education after high school. A follow-up study a year later found a reasonably close relationship between plans expressed and actual placement. The study documents one of the major concerns of the early 1950s—the talent waste of the many superior students who did not go on to college. It analyzes how various psychological, geographic, cultural, and economic factors relate to this waste, and makes recommendations for salvaging some of the talent lost. The suggestions emphasize: (1) broadening testing to identify talented students; (2) increasing the supply of well-trained counselors to help motivate superior students; and (3) involving parents in the counseling and college planning programs. The findings of this report were quite influential in the development of counseling and testing over the following decade.

914 BERDIE, RALPH F., AND HOOD, ALBERT B. *Decisions for tomorrow: Plans of high school seniors after graduation*. Minneapolis, Minn.: University of Minnesota Press, 1965, 195 pp. $4.75.

This volume was based upon a survey of 46,000 Minnesota high school seniors in 1961. It is a replication of a similar study made a decade earlier (913) in which students were asked for information concerning their post-high school plans, and then followed up to determine actual outcomes. This report contains a detailed comparison of the studies, plus several chapters on the relation of school, personal values and attitudes, and socioeconomic variables to college attendance. Other chapters are devoted to students planning to enter military service, trade school, nursing, and business school. Coming as it did soon after Sputnik, the study reflects special interest in high-ability students.

915 BERDIE, RALPH F., AND HOOD, ALBERT B. How effectively do we predict plans for college attendance? *Personnel and Guidance Journal,* 1966, vol. 45, pp. 487-493.

This study examines the extent to which college attendance can be predicted from a variety of ability, achievement, socioeconomic, and personality variables. With a statewide population, multiple correlation coefficients of about 0.6 were obtained. See 509 for a much more detailed national analysis.

916 BERDIE, RALPH F., LAYTON, WILBUR L., HAGENAH, THEDA, AND SWANSON, EDWARD O. *Who goes to college?* Minneapolis, Minn.: University of Minnesota Press, 1962, 56 pp. $1.50.

This study is valuable as a longitudinal study of college ability using data collected over a 21-year period. Minnesota started a statewide testing program in 1928, and gradually broadened the collection of information to include all high school juniors, junior college, and liberal arts college freshmen. This report, comparing freshman aptitudes of 1938 and 1959, finds that the average ability has remained constant. The data do indicate more differentiation in the average student aptitude among colleges in 1959 than in 1938.

917 FLANAGAN, JOHN C., ET AL. *Project TALENT one-year follow-up studies.* Palo Alto, Calif.: Project TALENT Office, American Institutes for Research, 1966, 365 pp. $5.

This report deals with follow-up studies of the 1960 Project TALENT sample of 400,000 high school students undertaken one year after high school completion. These follow-up studies are primarily concerned with career development: the nature of employment and job satisfaction; the type and extent of post-high school education; and long-range career plans. The report contains data on the following: (1) the characteristics of students who selected different types of post-high school education (see 889); (2) the attributes of students attending different colleges and selecting various college majors; (3) the extent to which young people change career plans between high school and one year after high school; and (4) the implications of these results for educational guidance. A computer measurement system for guidance programs in American schools is advocated which could handle: (1) the student cumulative record; (2) the student progress report; (3) the appraisal of curriculum and staff; (4) the projection of vocational potentials for students; (5) the periodic monitoring of individual learning prescriptions; and (6) the management of various alumni services. (See 1243 for a description of such a program subsequently in operation.)

918 FOLGER, JOHN K., ASTIN, HELEN S., AND BAYER, ALAN E. The flow of students through the educational system, in John K. Folger, Helen S. Astin, and Alan E. Bayer, *Human resources and higher education.* New York: Russell Sage Foundation, 1970, pp. 147-196.

This chapter from a book reviewed elsewhere (509) presents the most detailed analysis available of the distribution of students through the educational system from high school graduation to admission to graduate school. Multiple and partial regression analyses are presented for each of six critical distribution points: college attendance or nonattendance; junior college or senior college attendance; completion of nonselective or selective senior college; dropping out or completing senior college; delayed completion of senior college or completion in five years; and termination of college with baccalaureate or continuation with graduate school.

Each analysis simultaneously considers 38 variables grouped into the following categories: ability, interests, temperament, socioeconomic, ethnic–religious, residence, family, high school, college commitment, and marital status. Each of the six major analyses are carried out in various ways so as to clarify the relationship of each variable to the choice situation. These relationships are shown in their simple form and also when all other variables are held constant. Altogether the analyses are unusually comprehensive, sophisticated, and useful. They supply the basic data for many questions concerning the movement of students through higher education.

919 FOLGER, JOHN K., AND NAM, CHARLES B. *Education of the American population.* Census Monographs, 1960. Wash., D. C.: Government Printing Office, 1967, 290 pp. $2.25.

This study extracts from the vast backlog of 1960 census statistics valuable data on three educational topics: enrollment of students, characteristics of teachers, and educational attainments of the adult population. In response to requests for interpretations of census and statistical data that "would illuminate major current problem areas," the authors have included analyses and well-chosen tables of educational differences among important groups of the population. They also provide a reference to historical sources of statistical information going back to the census of 1840.

920 HAYGHE, HOWARD. Employment of high school graduates and dropouts. *Monthly Labor Review,* 1970, vol. 93, no. 8, pp. 35–42.

Each year the Bureau of Labor Statistics prepares a Special Labor Force report based upon the Current Population Survey carried out by the Bureau of the Census the previous October. This report contains current national data on the employment and educational status of 16- to 21-year-olds, and special analyses of recent high school graduates. Data obtained from this October 1969 survey showed that 60 percent of the male high school graduates of June 1969 and 47 percent of the female had continued on to college. Other significant findings on youths 16 to 21 years old are: (1) Seventy-five percent of the whites and 57 percent of the Negroes were high school graduates. (2) The unemployment rate for dropouts was nearly twice that of graduates. (3) Unemployment was much higher among Negro youths than among whites, and educational achievement did not seem to be a determining factor. Job discrimination, quality of schooling, and geographic location seemed to have more bearing. (4) Family income has a strong relationship to the likelihood of a young person's finishing high school. Eighty-four percent of the youths whose family income was $7,500 or more finished high school, compared to only 40 percent of those whose families had incomes of $3,000 or less. Comparable annual reports may be found in the same journal as follows: June 1969, pp. 36–43; December 1968, pp. 6–12; July 1967, pp. 15–21; June 1966, pp. 643–649; June 1965, pp. 637–643; May 1964, pp. 522–529; July 1963, pp. 772–779; May 1962, pp. 502–509; May 1961, pp. 463–470; and May 1960, pp. 500–506. Special Labor Force Reports containing the same information are 5, 15, 21, 32, 41, 54, 66, 85, 100, and 108. They provide the only annual direct indicator of the proportion of high school graduates going on to college the next fall, and are a primary reference on the transition from school to work.

921 NAM, CHARLES B., AND COWHIG, JAMES D. *Farm population: Factors related to college attendance of farm and nonfarm high school graduates, 1960.* Series Census-ERS, No. 32. Wash., D. C.: U.S. Bureau of the Census, 1962, 18 pp.

This follow-up study was an outgrowth of a cooperative study conducted by the Census Bureau and the Department of Agriculture in conjunction with the 1959 population survey. Data from that survey on college plans of high school seniors and their personal and family characteristics were combined with data collected in a follow-up questionnaire on college attendance and school records.

The report deals with high school dropouts, the relation of stated college plans to actual attendance. Analysis of college attendance and demographic, socioeconomic, and ability measures is supplemented by a multiple regression analysis in which the relative importance of the several variables is assessed.

Several findings are of special interest. Fifty-three percent of the 1960 high school graduates indicated plans to attend college, but only 42 percent did so in 1960, and those who did were from families of higher socioeconomic status and ranked higher on measures of ability. A lower proportion of rural graduates attended college, but they were more "realistic" in their stated college plans than were nonfarm students. Roughly twice as many graduates from white collar families attended college as from families headed by farmers or manual or service workers. Occupational differences occurred even when family income and student ability levels were similar. Finally, about 70 percent of graduates enrolled in a college preparatory curriculum attended college, but only 20 percent of those enrolled in other curriculums did so. See 925 for similar data almost a decade later.

922 PREDIGER, DALE. Biographical data differentiating college attenders from non-attenders at various ability levels. *Measurement and Evaluation in Guidance,* 1970, vol. 2, pp. 217-224.

This analysis was based upon 20,000 high school senior males who participated in the 1960–61 data collection of Project TALENT. The purpose of this study was to analyze the relationship of biographical information to college attendance within six different levels of scholastic ability. The proportion of students attending college ranged from 16 percent in the lowest ability group to 86 percent in the highest. Within each ability group it was possible to substantially improve the prediction of college attendance on the basis of biographical information. The types of items which were useful for such prediction did not seem to vary systematically from one ability level to another. This latter point is perhaps the most significant finding of the study, but the author did not present any systematic content analysis (other than categorization) of the significant items at different ability levels.

923 SCHOENFELDT, LYLE F. Education after high school. *Sociology of Education,* 1968, vol. 41, pp. 350-369.

In this study of the post-high school educational–occupational choices of a sample of American high school students, the usual division of two groups (college versus noncollege) was expanded as follows: four-year colleges, junior colleges, armed forces schools (males), nursing schools (females), technical institutes (males), business schools (females), trade schools, and no post-high school education. The study presents the proportions of persons selecting various alternatives after graduation and assesses differences among students along the four basic variables of ability, interest, temperament, and family background.

The findings confirm that both ability and socioeconomic level directly affect educational decisions; however, ability facilitates college entrance to a significantly greater degree than does socioeconomic level. During the four-year period of the follow-up surveys, the percentage of students reporting some further education beyond high school increased 11 percent. The article is based upon analysis of Project TALENT data and includes much valuable bench-mark information concerning access to college at the national level.

924 SEIBEL, DEAN W. Prediction of college attendance. *Vocational Guidance Quarterly,* 1963, vol. 11, pp. 265-272.

This study provides national normative information concerning the probability of college attendance for students at different score levels of the Preliminary Scholastic Aptitude Test, which is the most widely used eleventh-grade test for guidance and scholarship purposes. The multiple prediction of college attendance on the basis of PSAT and high school grades was 0.57.

925 U.S. BUREAU OF THE CENSUS. *Population characteristics. Factors related to high school graduation and college attendance: 1967. Current Population Reports,* Series P-20, no. 185. Wash., D. C.: Government Printing Office, 1970, 10 pp. 15 cents.

A Bureau of the Census survey collected data from a nationwide sample of high school seniors in October 1965 to provide information on factors affecting future educational status. A follow-up questionnaire was administered in February 1967. Student characteristics were tallied and related to high school record, graduation or nongraduation, and college attendance. Specific factors investigated were the student's place of residence (metropolitan–nonmetropolitan), age, race, sex, parents' education, occupation, and income. The report thus provides valuable normative data on the relationship between these various characteristics and educational attainment. In general the results are consistent with common assumptions. For example: (1) High family income was closely associated with both high school graduation and propensity to attend college. (2) The likelihood that a student would graduate from high school and attend college increased with the level of his parents' education. (3) While senior girls were more likely to graduate than were senior boys, male graduates were more likely to attend college than were female graduates. (4) Forty-seven percent of the graduates had gone on to college by February 1967; about one-half of those who planned to attend a junior college had not done so by the following year. (The entire series of *Current Population Reports* is annotated in 1418.)

926 WERTS, CHARLES E. A comparison of male vs. female college attendance probabilities. *Sociology of Education,* 1968, vol. 41, pp. 103-110.

The ratio of males to females in a large sample of college freshmen was computed for numerous groups of students: various fathers' occupations; different levels of fathers' education; and students' levels of academic achievement in high school. The ratio of males to females was almost 1 to 1 among those students whose fathers were in the "intellectual" category, including such occupations as psychologist, physicist, and college professor; the ratio of males to females was almost 2 to 1 when the fathers were unskilled. Similarly, the ratio of male to female college students was much higher among offspring of fathers with a grammar school education than with graduate degrees. Males and females appear equally likely to attend college when their grades are B+ or better (despite the fact that more girls make high grades), but males with grades of C or D were three times as likely to attend college as were females with such grades.

9.5 – *SOCIAL MOBILITY.* Several types of important distributional problems can be listed under the general heading of social mobility. There is special interest in the relation of parental educational status to that of offspring. When compared across age levels, this analysis gives evidence of the extent and trend in intergenerational mobility. An important aspect of this interest is the relationship of higher education to social stratification; namely, does higher education tend to equalize social privilege or reinforce existing class lines? There is no simple answer to this question. A very useful and interesting series of studies by Sewell concerning social status and educational aspiration illustrates the complexities of the problem. The most careful analysis of education and social stratification is that of Jencks (933).

927 ANDERSON, C. ARNOLD. A skeptical note on the relation of vertical mobility to education. *American Journal of Sociology,* 1961, vol. 66, pp. 560-570.

The results of this study using data from England, Sweden, and the United States lead the author to question the assumption that social mobility is heavily dependent upon formal education. The data did indicate a great deal of upward and downward social mobility, though most of the upwardly mobile were persons of typical rather than superior education. Since many better educated sons of upper class fathers descended the occupational status scale, the author concludes that factors other than schooling play a major part in mobility.

928 BAYER, ALAN E. Birth order and college attendance. *Journal of Marriage and the Family,* 1966, vol. 28, pp. 480-484.

Data from a follow-up study of 50,000 high school seniors in 1960 are used here to analyze the influence of birth order on college attendance. Only children were found to be the most likely to attend college, but within families there was no difference between first and last born in likelihood of college attendance. The child in the intermediate ordinal position is consistently least likely to attend college. Hypotheses from earlier studies that younger siblings have lower capacity for academic attainment is contradicted by these findings, as is the theory that financial resources are less available to younger siblings.

929 COHEN, ELIZABETH G. Parental factors in educational mobility. *Sociology of Education,* 1965, vol. 38, pp. 404-425.

The author reports here an intensive study of two groups of 50 high school boys of working class background matched on intelligence. One group was planning to attend college; the other was not. Interviews with parents indicated significantly different attitudes between the two groups. Parents of upwardly mobile students tended to have a favorable attitude toward college and encouraged upward mobility for either vocational reasons (the father) or social reasons (the mother). Parental encouragement to get good grades in secondary school did not predict mobility.

930 DUNCAN, OTIS DUDLEY, AND HODGE, ROBERT W. Education and occupational mobility: A regression analysis. *American Journal of Sociology,* 1963, vol. 68, pp. 629-644.

The authors present a detailed analysis of the relationship between occupational level and educational attainment. Data based upon more than 1,000 males indicated a correlation of about 0.3 between respondents' occupational scores and those of their fathers. The respondents' educational attainment was correlated about 0.4 or 0.5 with occupational status. This latter relationship held approximately constant from 1940 to 1950 despite the fact that educational attainment increased, and there was decreasing dispersion in number of school years completed. This fact would suggest increasing importance of education for social mobility though that conclusion has been questioned (see 933).

931 ECKLAND, BRUCE K. Academic ability, higher education, and occupational mobility. *American Sociological Review,* 1965, vol. 30, pp. 735-746.

Using follow-up data on some 1,300 men who enrolled at the University of Illinois, the author analyzes the interrelated effects of class origin, academic ability, and college graduation on occupational achievement. All three variables were associated with occupational achievement, but graduation from college was by far the dominant factor. The occupational achievement of dropouts tended to be affected by class status but not by ability. Occupational achievement of college graduates was not greatly affected by either ability or class status. Arguing that employers evidently assume that colleges do a good job of sorting out less able students as they compete for degrees, the author concludes "A college degree is evidently so crucial that jobs are allocated with little regard for the likelihood that colleges perform only moderately well as sorters of talent."

932 HALSEY, A. H., FLOUD, JEAN, AND ANDERSON, C. ARNOLD (EDS.) *Education, economy and society: A reader in the sociology of education.* New York: Free Press, 1961, 625 pp. $8.50; paperback $4.95.

This volume reprints a number of classics in the sociology of education. Especially useful sections are concerned with (1) education, social mobility, and the labor market; (2) the selection process in education; (3) social factors in educational achievement; and (4) the changing social functions of schools and universities. A number of the reprinted articles are concerned with British education.

933 JENCKS, CHRISTOPHER. Social stratification and higher education. *Harvard Educational Review,* 1968, vol. 38, pp. 277-316.

In this important and unusually perceptive essay, Jencks analyzes a variety of evidence on the relationship between class status and access to higher education. The author recognizes that higher education is an important route to a good job, but judges that "the middle class have always made disproportionate use of this tool for self-advancement, and the gap is not narrowing." He feels that class differences in motivation probably play the decisive role in maintaining the middle class advantage. Even if access to higher education became more equal, Jencks cautions that this would not necessarily make American life more satisfactory. He identifies the central problem as inequality, not the need for more social mobility. The article offers a comprehensive and provocative view of many subtle aspects of the social role of higher education. It is a later and shorter version of Chapter 5 of *The Academic Revolution* (568). This revision is tighter and more cogent. It is a classic which should be read carefully by anyone seriously interested in the nature and effect of educational opportunity.

934 McDILL, EDWARD L., AND COLEMAN, JAMES. Family and peer influences in college plans of high school students. *Sociology of Education,* 1965, vol. 38, pp. 112-126.

While some research has indicated that the contextual effects of the high school are not an important determinant of college attendance (see 509), this study focused upon the possible effect of social status within the school upon educational aspiration. The data did indicate that individuals with low status were less likely to attend college than those with high status. Furthermore, the effect was greater in the senior year than in the freshman year in high school. In these data, educational aspiration seemed more closely related to status in the school than to parents' education.

935 SEWELL, WILLIAM H., HALLER, ARCHIBALD O., AND PORTES, ALEJANDRO. The educational and early occupational attainment process. *American Sociological Review,* 1969, vol. 34, pp. 82-92.

The authors present a "path model" designed to clarify the social and psychological antecedents of educational and occupational attainment. They propose a causal sequence which starts with the parents' social position and the individual's mental ability. Further links in the causal chain include school performance followed by outside influence, then by educational and occupational aspiration, and finally by actual attainment. The model proved useful when tested with a sample of Wisconsin youth. The paper is also useful because it brings together several lines of sociological research on social mobility.

936 SEWELL, WILLIAM H., HALLER, ARCHIBALD O., AND STRAUS, MURRAY A. Social status and educational and occupational aspiration. *American Sociological Review,* 1957, vol. 22, pp. 67-73.

This article was one of the first to present convincing data indicating that educational aspiration is related to social status even after the effect of intelligence is controlled. Data based upon virtually all high school seniors in the state of Wisconsin showed that educational and occupational aspiration varied directly with family status for both boys and girls within the same intelligence stratum. It was left to later research to separate the effects of family cultural status and family income.

937 SEWELL, WILLIAM H., AND SHAH, VIMAL P. Socioeconomic status, intelligence, and the attainment of higher education. *Sociology of Education,* 1967, vol. 40, pp. 1-23.

Using various methods such as cross-tabulations and path analysis, the authors examine here the relative influence of socioeconomic status and measured intelligence on college planning, college attendance, and college graduation. While both factors had considerable effect, socioeconomic status seemed more important for females while intelligence level seemed more important in the case of males. The article contains numerous useful footnotes on previous research in this area.

938 SEWELL, WILLIAM H., AND SHAH, VIMAL P. Parents' education and children's educational aspiration and achievements. *American Sociological Review,* 1968, vol. 33, pp. 191-209.

The authors followed a representative group of Wisconsin high school seniors for a seven-year period and examined the relationship between education of the parents and several other variables such as college attendance and college graduation. The results indicated that father's education had a slightly stronger effect than mother's education on educational attainment for males, while both father's and mother's education have almost equal effect for females. The authors conclude that consistently high educational achievement of the parents inspires educational achievement in the offspring, and that discrepancy in the parents' education is of negligible value in explaining variation in educational outcomes.

939 SEWELL, WILLIAM H., AND SHAH, VIMAL P. Social class, parental encouragement, and educational aspirations. *American Journal of Sociology,* 1968, vol. 73, pp. 559-572.

In their continuing analysis of the educational aspiration and achievement of Wisconsin's youth, the authors used in this study a variety of multivariate methods of analysis to examine the relationships of several variables to college plans. The findings indicated that socioeconomic status, intelligence, and parental encouragement all had substantial independent relationships to college plans, and that all taken together could not completely account for social class differences in educational aspiration. The authors also conclude, however, that parental encouragement plays a powerful role, particularly with respect to the more able students from relatively high socioeconomic levels.

940 SPADY, WILLIAM G. Educational mobility and access: Growth and paradoxes. *American Journal of Sociology,* 1967, vol. 73, pp. 273-286.

This paper presents evidence of an educational paradox—that democratization of educational opportunity has not facilitated educational and social mobility for the lowest socioeconomic groups; in fact the probability that youths with poorly educated fathers will complete college has decreased. Moreover, if the father's education is held constant, the educational outcomes for Negroes are consistently lower than those for whites. An illustration of racial and status difference is that in the youngest age cohort, 63 percent of the sons of white college graduates completed college, in contrast to the one percent of the nonwhites with grade school–educated fathers. A possible explanation lies in the fact that a specific low level of parental education now signifies lower relative status than was previously true.

SECTION 10: EDUCATIONAL OPPORTUNITY

The literature concerning educational opportunity is limited and quite new, but very important. More than any other topic it reflects the new attitude about college admissions and makes access to higher education a societal rather than primarily an institutional issue.

What educational opportunity should mean is a key philosophical question because access to higher education is a principal means whereby an increasing proportion of the population expresses its aspiration and defines its social roles. Consequently, the whole matter of who is granted what form of educational opportunity is now recognized as a pivotal issue.

Educational opportunity used to mean that bright but poor young people should have a chance to go to college. There is now great pressure that colleges create opportunities that are adaptable to students with widely divergent interests and abilities. Opportunity for higher education has certainly lost whatever passive and paternalistic qualities it may have had. It now represents one of the key intersections of social, political, and economic forces. Consequently, it bears an important relationship to material in Section 7 concerned with the philosophy and national goals of higher education and that in subsection 3.1 on national admissions policy.

10.1 — *DISCRIMINATION AND EQUALITY*. There is a large literature on social discrimination, and in the past decade a considerable technical and popular literature has been developed on the more specific issue of educational equality. Most of the publications in this area are essays or reports based upon surveys. There are three general types of problems.

First, there is the difficult philosophical problem of defining educational opportunity in terms that have clear educational and operational implications. A set of very useful articles concerned with this section is found in 953. A second type of literature covers the broad issue of prejudice, racism, and other forms of social and educational inequality. Glock and Siegleman (952) have prepared a brief but useful book of readings related to this issue. Finally, there is the problem of defining the conditions of inequality and describing the effects of discrimination. There is a great deal of excellent anecdotal literature in this area and several important surveys and reports. The Coleman Report (948) is especially notable; it has been called the most important piece of educational research in our time. There are also a number of articles concerned with reanalyses and reinterpretations of the original data.

941 BOWLES, SAMUEL S. Towards equality of educational opportunity?, in Editorial Board, *Harvard Educational Review, Equal educational opportunity.* Cambridge, Mass.: Harvard University Press, 1969, pp. 115-125.

The author contends that very substantial changes are necessary if equality of educational opportunity is to be achieved. He feels that equality will require allocation of unequal amounts of resources for educating Negro as compared to white children and poor as compared to rich children. He rejects the notion that the educational system alone bears the responsibility for achieving equal opportunity, and doubts that real change will come about without a major and improbable redistribution of political power within society.

942 BOWLES, SAMUEL, AND LEVIN, HENRY M. The determinants of scholastic achievement—an appraisal of some recent evidence. *Journal of Human Resources,* 1968, vol. 3, pp. 3-24.

This study challenges the findings of the Coleman Report, *Equality of Educational Opportunity* (948). The Coleman Report, a massive survey done for the U.S. Office of Education, has generated widespread public and legislative concern about the great disparities in educational opportunity. Bowles and Levin take issue, however, with the statement that school resources and per-pupil expenditures have little bearing on academic achievement, and that the only important factor is the effect of a student's peers. They charge that shortcomings in both data and analysis make these findings "particularly inappropriate for policy-makers attempting to assess the likely effects of radical changes in resources devoted to schoolings." In evaluating research flaws, they point out that: (1) refusals of large numbers of inner-city districts to participate led to a high nonreturn ratio (41 percent), and overloaded the sample with suburban schools; and (2) assigning the arithmetic mean of the responses to the "no responses" on a particular question is "an ingenuous treatment which has probably created severe measurement error." They also charge inadequate methods of determining social background and of measuring school resources and teacher–pupil ratios.

Although the Report cautiously qualified its finding that Negro pupils performed better in integrated schools, many commentaries have quoted this finding as conclusive. Bowles and Levin appraise the evidence here as showing a "minuscule" improvement, and conclude "The report simply does not provide conclusive evidence one way or the other." Although they concede that the survey was hampered by time constraints as well as the more serious difficulty of measuring the impact of different influences on achievement, their position remains "agnostic." See 946 for a reply.

943 CARNEGIE COMMISSION ON HIGHER EDUCATION. *A chance to learn.* New York: McGraw-Hill, 1970, 31 pp. $1.

This special report on equal opportunity in higher education is the second in a series submitted by the Carnegie Commission. The first report, *Quality and Equality: New Levels of Federal Responsibility for Higher Education* (150), appeared in December of 1968 and focused upon the essential role of the federal government in preserving margins of academic excellence and expanding educational opportunity.

The present report concentrates upon the goals, agenda, and policies for achieving equality of opportunity for higher education for an increasingly diverse student population. Both short- and long-range goals are suggested. By 1976 the report recommends that all economic barriers and inequities in curriculums, policies, and facilities be removed, and that the quality of lower levels of education be improved substantially. By the year 2000, the Commission believes that all remaining barriers to equality of educational opportunity must be removed so that ethnic origin, geographic location, age, and quality of prior schooling no longer circumvent access to higher education or success within it. The report includes a checklist to facilitate appraisal of equality of educational opportunity by individual institutions.

944 CLARK, KENNETH B. (ED.) *Racism and American education: A dialogue and agenda for action.* New York: Harper & Row, 1970, 164 pp. $1.95.

This volume presents an edited record of dialogues from a conference on racism sponsored by the President's Commission for the Observance of Human Rights Year. The participants, all representing expertise in a wide variety of fields, discussed themes relating to racism and school structure, competition, educational systems, separatism versus integration, black studies, all-black institutions and black self-image, teacher training, and the role of unions. The final section presents 20 recommendations for effecting attitudinal, structural, and educational change. Among these is a call for colleges to orient their programs and activities more toward contemporary social issues and give students credit for curriculum-related work in communities.

945 COLEMAN, JAMES S. Equal schools or equal students? *Public Interest,* 1966, vol. 4, pp. 70-75.

The primary virtue of this article is the fact that it provides a six-page digest of the Coleman Report (948). Like any useful summary, it hits the highlights, but the reader should be aware that some of those highlights have been the subject of considerable controversy and criticism.

946 COLEMAN, JAMES S. Equality of educational opportunity: Reply to Bowles and Levin. *Journal of Human Resources,* 1968, vol. 3, pp. 237-246.

This reply to criticism of the Coleman Report (see 942) is perhaps less interesting for its substantive rebuttal than for its comment on the natural history and sociology of massive social research. Coleman's response makes clear the extreme difficulty of undertaking such work in a way that is satisfactory from a research standpoint. As a result the social resistance to this type of result hamper its effectiveness and undermine sincere efforts to bring modern methods of inquiry to bear upon serious social problems. Coleman's comments further illustrate that the matter is often exacerbated by the fact that highly qualified experts easily disagree on what constitutes appropriate methodology and defensible interpretation.

947 COLEMAN, JAMES S. The concept of equality of educational opportunity, in Editorial Board, *Harvard Educational Review, Equal educational opportunity.* Cambridge, Mass.: Harvard University Press, 1969, pp. 9-24.

In this chapter Coleman traces the shifts that have occurred in the interpretation of the "equality" concept. The first stage in the evaluation of the concept was the belief that all children must be exposed to the same curriculum in the same school. The second stage assumed that equality of opportunity meant providing different curriculums for different occupational futures. The third stage was seen in the southern states' doctrine of "separate but equal" facilities. The Supreme Court ruling that separation by race was inherently unequal led to a new assumption—that "equality of opportunity depends in some fashion upon effects of schooling." Thus the definition of equal opportunity shifted from emphasis on an equal distribution of educational resources to an emphasis on equality of student achievement. This emphasis on output as the measure of equality of opportunity represents "a notable shift, and one which should have strong consequences for the practice of education in future years." This article is especially valuable in clarifying the fundamental philosophies that have guided educational practice and political attitudes. It illustrates, for example, that the heredity–environment controversy is to some extent a false issue because current social philosophy demands that education produce more equal status regardless of how present unequal status may have come about.

948 COLEMAN, JAMES S., CAMPBELL, ERNEST Q., HOBSON, CAROL J., MCPARTLAND, JAMES, MOOD, ALEXANDER M., WEINFELD, FREDERIC D., AND YORK, ROBERT L. *Equality of educational opportunity.* Wash., D. C.: Government Printing Office, 1966, 737 pp. $4.25.

This massive survey was an all-out effort to document the extent and effects of racial segregation in U.S. public schools. With approximately 900,000 students as a sample, the study was carried out at the request of Congress by the National Center for Educational Statistics, under the direction of sociologist James Coleman. The study also focused on the degree of equality of educational opportunity, student achievement on standardized tests, and the possible interrelationships between student achievement and school characteristics. The results spell out the degree of segregation: the majority of American children attend schools that are largely segregated. Among minority groups, Negroes are by far the most segregated. The findings also document the extent of inferior educational opportunity for Negroes: nationally, their school resources are not commensurate with those of white students—in textbooks, libraries, science and language laboratories, as well as in curriculum offerings, competence of teachers, etc. The average minority student scores below the average white student on standardized achievement tests; in the South differences are greater than in other regions of the country.

The authors suggest that when socioeconomic factors are controlled "It appears that differences between schools account for only a small fraction of differences in pupil achievement." However, they conclude that differences in school quality have a greater impact on achievement of minority students than on that of white students. The complicated and highly controversial study has generated a number of reanalyses and reinterpretations. See 942, 946, 953, 959.

949 COLLEGE ENTRANCE EXAMINATION BOARD. *Barriers to higher education.* New York: College Entrance Examination Board, 1971, 151 pp. $3.50.

These papers were presented at the 1970 Wingspread Conference on Barriers to Higher Education. Topics include the uses and abuses of standardized tests, the question of test validity for disadvantaged students, and proposals for new models of evaluation of the admissions process. Other topics especially relevant to the access problems of minority/poverty students were the organization of higher education, open admissions policies, creation of more effective programs for disadvantaged students, and the financial barrier. The general theme of the colloquium was the need for change in both institutions and programs.

950 DYER, HENRY S. School factors and equal educational opportunity, in Editorial Board, *Harvard Educational Review, Equal educational opportunity.* Cambridge, Mass.: Harvard University Press, 1969, pp. 41-59.

Dyer surveys three earlier studies of the effects of schooling on achievement and cognitive development in which the conclusions apparently differ from those of the Coleman Report. He is one of the few writers to suggest (probably correctly) that Coleman's nearly exclusive use of verbal ability as a measure of achievement caused an underestimate of school effects. "This underestimate is further exacerbated by the confining of the analysis to ethnic subsamples in which the schools, pupils, and pupil achievement are likely to be so homogeneous as to prevent important relationships from appearing."

Dyer asserts that on both of these counts "The Coleman results have the unfortunate, though perhaps inadvertent, effect of giving school systems the false impression that there is not much they can do to improve the achievement of their pupils." He suggests several school characteristics which do seem to affect achievement, and notes that these are, for the most part, hard-to-change characteristics. Thus, educators will have to fight off pressures to attempt instant improvement by concentrating on the easy-to-change characteristics rather than on slow changes which are more likely to make a real difference.

951 FERRIN, RICHARD I. *Barriers to universal higher education.* New York: College Entrance Examination Board, 1970, 54 pp. $3.40. (Available through ERIC, No. ED 038 924)

This paper provides one means of analyzing the accessibility of higher education. It outlines four barriers that discourage many young people, particularly minority low-income youth, from attending college: the financial, the academic, the motivational, and the geographic. It discusses these barriers in the perspective of recent social history and documents efforts throughout the country that have been designed to reduce them. These efforts can be grouped into five categories: (1) new two-year colleges; (2) federal, state, and private scholarship and loan programs; (3) special college preparatory programs; (4) comprehensive talent-search programs; and (5) modification of admissions requirements. The author concludes that these measures have been only partially successful toward attaining a goal of universal higher education because of the magnitude and complexity of the problem.

952 GLOCK, CHARLES Y., AND SIEGELMAN, ELLEN (EDS.) *Prejudice USA.* New York: Praeger, 1969, 194 pp. $2.25.

The premise that America's major social institutions offer the greatest hope for reducing prejudice and discrimination is the underlying tenet in these studies. They stem from a "Five Year Study of Anti-Semitism in America," and a March 1968 symposium, "Patterns of Prejudice," both sponsored by the University of California. Chapters describe the status quo in education, the church, politics, mass media, and industry as compared with the institutional ideal. The barrier of "self-delusion" is cited as a major factor in all areas of society, on the grounds that those who could be most instrumental in leading change often deny the existence of their own prejudice.

A final chapter contains several general conclusions and recommendations. School efforts to reduce segregation and discrimination are termed only half-solutions unless they can dissolve the prejudice that causes the discrimination. The basic requirements for all social institutions are to undertake a commitment to the goal of tolerance, to blueprint specific plans toward that end, and to bring adequate resources to the effort. The program should be a coordinated attack, not a piecemeal effort by each school, church, or newspaper. The authors also offer some concrete suggestions for industry: to develop a commitment to the goal from top-level executives down through middle management and foremen, to examine hiring procedures to avoid a "credentials gap," and to go out into the community for recruitment of workers.

953 HARVARD EDUCATIONAL REVIEW, EDITORIAL BOARD. *Equal educational opportunity.* Cambridge, Mass.: Harvard University Press, 1969, 274 pp. $6.50.

This especially valuable book is an expanded issue of the *Harvard Educational Review,* devoted entirely to various aspects of the question of equality of educational opportunity. Highly qualified writers speak on such issues as the concept of equal opportunity; the role of motivation, social class, and the school; and policy issues such as alternative public school systems, compensatory education, and problems in implementing programs. For annotations of individual articles see 941, 947, 950, 955, and 958.

954 KATZ, IRWIN. Review of evidence relating to effects of desegregation on the performance of Negroes. *American Psychologist,* 1964, vol. 19, pp. 381-399.

On the basis of this review, the author suggests that school desegregation has a variety of favorable and detrimental influences on Negro performance. He suggests that minority group newcomers in integrated classrooms are likely to have a low expectancy of academic success partly due to the intimidating perception of prestige and power in the white majority group; a consequent fear of failure is detrimental to performance. On the other hand he cites the facilitating incentive effect of white standards of academic performance. Reports on the academic progress of Negro children in the segregated schools indicate that any or all of the situational factors may be operative in specific instances. He cites the need for research on cognitive functioning of Negroes in biracial situations, and lists several implications for educational practice. These include raising the educational standards of Negro schools so that minority children will not face a transfer shock; working with parents to help them prepare children for schooling; training teachers to develop awareness of the emotional needs of children in biracial situations; and abandoning homogeneous ability grouping which tends to "freeze teachers expectations, as well as children's own self-images."

955 KATZ, IRWIN. Academic motivation, in Editorial Board, *Harvard Educational Review, Equal educational opportunity.* Cambridge, Mass.: Harvard University Press, 1969, pp. 60-69.

Katz examined the hypothesis that Negro children benefit in predominantly white classrooms from social exposure to the academic motivation already developed by white children. Low-achieving Negro children in segregated schools were found to have "such stringent and rigid standards as to be utterly dysfunctional." Katz asserts that these children have "been socialized to self-imposed failure," and he reports further evidence that this problem relates to lack of prior rewards at home and parental demands for school achievement. He sees similar implications in the Coleman Report that Negro achievement increased with the proportion of white students at a school, and concludes "a modest self-concept is not detrimental to Negro academic performance, provided children can depend upon the environment to dispense rewards in a fair and equitable way."

956 KENDRICK, S. A., AND THOMAS, CHARLES L. Transition from school to college. *Review of Educational Research,* 1970, vol. 40, pp. 151-179.

Research on the problems of disadvantaged youth is reviewed in the perspective of the past few decades, current crises of confidence in research, and future goals that need clarification. The authors note that the extent of racial segregation in higher education was only brought into public scrutiny as recently as 1966. The assassination of Martin Luther King precipitated demands for dynamic and immediate social change; educational research is under fire as being antithetical to this change, and unable to provide "now" answers.

Educational research of the 1950s was oriented to a "manpower" viewpoint. By the end of that decade scholars were questioning the definition of talent as formal academic ability to the exclusion of social, entrepreneurial, and creative abilities. The 1960s brought change from the goal of providing financial aid to a few able students to that of opening college doors to most, if not all, students. The idea of "talent search," the authors assert, is no longer acceptable to the black community. Caution is voiced that open access cannot mean much gain if it is implemented by assigning minority students to general curriculums, a common but unsatisfactory method of providing universal secondary education.

Guidance and compensatory programs are both found wanting in what they have accomplished for the disadvantaged. Research on the success of compensatory programs is limited, but the evidence points to the conclusion that "existing compensatory programs have made little impact in eradicating the problems of disadvantaged college students, nor have the majority of colleges accepted this area as their responsibility." The authors conclude that the emerging dominance of public higher education and the appearance of state master plans will have more effect on disadvantaged students than any present or likely future idea for compensatory programs.

957 MACK, RAYMOND W. (ED.) *Prejudice and race relations.* Chicago: Quadrangle Books, 1970, 271 pp. $6.95; paperback $2.45.

This is a collection of informative and highly readable articles from the Sunday *New York Times Magazine* dealing with many aspects of racial discrimination. The book begins with some essays on the genetic arguments concerning intelligence, and ends with discussions of future options for Americans — "Paths to Separatism or Integration." It also includes profiles of black leaders, and three essays on race relations in other countries.

958 MOYNIHAN, DANIEL P. Sources of resistance to the Coleman Report, in Editorial Board, *Harvard Educational Review, Equal educational opportunity.* Cambridge, Mass.: Harvard University Press, 1969, pp. 25-38.

In this article, Moynihan interprets the reasons for the quick pigeon-hole treatment accorded to the Coleman Report by the education, reform, and research establishments. He feels that the study did not receive proper attention despite its being one of the largest research projects in the history of social science prepared by a staff of leading social scientists. He suggests that it failed to come out with the answer that these groups expected to hear — that inequalities in school facilities are largely responsible for inequalities in achievement. The educational establishment's silence is understandable, Moynihan asserts, since it showed the ineffectiveness of the massive federal funds being pumped into school facilities for minority groups. He postulates that the educational establishment resists research on institutional grounds, and that reform groups resist it on ideological grounds. Thus reformers rejected the Coleman Report when it did not support their assumptions, even though it is "the most powerful social science case for school integration that has ever been made." Moynihan discusses what he interprets as the research establishment's predisposition to direct their studies toward the "neutral" area of institutional change, and a corresponding reluctance to pay heed to problems of personal and individual development.

959 NICHOLS, ROBERT C. Schools and the disadvantaged. *Science,* 1966, vol. 154, pp. 1312-1314.

Nichols reviews the major findings of the Coleman Report and points out several problems in the study. He criticizes the interpretation of some correlations as indicating causation, and suggests several areas where the study lacked adequate control of variables. He concludes that the survey "suffers from problems common to all nonexperimental studies in attempting to assess the effects of natural experiments, which are so messy that one can never be certain that all the relevant variables have been taken into account or that the correlations observed in the natural setting would continue to hold if the variables were artificially manipulated."

The revolutionary finding that "schools with widely varying characteristics differ very little in their effects" is too astonishing to be accepted on the basis of one imperfect study. What seems to be needed is "additional study of differential school effects with better controls for input."

960 U.S. COMMISSION ON CIVIL RIGHTS. *Racial isolation in the public schools.* Wash., D. C.: Government Printing Office, 1967. 2 vols. Vol. 1, 276 pp., $1. Vol. 2, *Appendices,* 293 pp., $1.

This report addresses the problem of de facto school segregation resulting from housing patterns, school districting and finance, economic stratification, and urban–suburban population shifts. In 1965 the Civil Rights Commission was asked by President Johnson to undertake a fact-finding investigation to determine the extent of racial isolation in the public schools, the factors that contribute to it, and the relationships between school segregation and educational outcomes. The study finds that the key factors are "rigidly discriminatory" housing practices of private enterprise, coupled with federal housing programs which have intensified concentrations of the poor and nonwhite within central cities. The report documents that housing policies, with attendant declines in property tax resources for education, and geographical pupil-assignment policies, result in racial segregation and inequalities of school facilities. Compensatory programs are considered in detail, but they are found to be of "limited effectiveness," because "the problems stem, in large part, from racial and social class isolation in schools which are themselves isolated by race and social class." Instead they recommend legislative action to bring federal aid to school construction and to low- and moderate-income housing, and to prohibit discrimination in the sale or rental of housing. They also urge that Congress adopt a standard of integration, copied after the criterion used by Massachusetts and New York, that defines racial imbalance as a school with more than 50 percent Negro enrollment. This report is a carefully documented basic reference that provided part of the groundwork for subsequent desegregation policy and action.

961 U.S. Office of Education, Educational Research Information Center. *Catalog of selected documents on the disadvantaged.* Wash., D. C.: Government Printing Office, 1966, *Number and author index,* 130 pp. 65 cents. *Subject index,* $3.

This bibliography lists 1,740 reports covering many aspects of education for the disadvantaged. Topics include curriculum, teaching guides, tests and measurements, public relations materials, implementation, and evaluation. Most of the reports were obtained from 23 exemplary programs which are listed in the report. All of the reference material is available through the ERIC system. The report comes in two volumes. One contains a sequential listing of each of the 1,740 documents; the other contains a word list index compiled from these studies.

10.2–*EQUITY IN SELECTION.* As long as educational opportunity is a social issue and as long as there is differential access to various institutions and programs, the equity of the selection process will be a matter of much concern. It is difficult to deal with some of the problems involved. Not only do they become politicized and emotionally charged, they also include technical problems that are difficult to solve and equally difficult to describe.

The literature of this area comes under three quite different headings. First, there is the matter of social bias in selection. This involves simply the description of de facto conditions of unequal representation of minority groups in higher education. Egerton's report on state universities and black Americans (969) is a good example. Second, there are various complicated questions concerning test bias. Stanley and Porter have provided a useful review of important aspects of this literature (974). Third, there are those questions of policy that relate directly to the recruitment and selection of minority/poverty students or any other group of special interest. An already classic article is Kendrick's essay (971) "The Coming Segregation of Our Selective Colleges."

These topics are closely related to subsections 9.1 and 9.4 which provide more material on the de facto conditions of measured ability and educational attainment. Other related sections of literature include institutional admissions policy (subsection 3.2) and recruitment and selection (subsection 3.3).

962 BLUMENFELD, WARREN S. *Selecting talented Negro students: Nominations vs. test performance.* NMSC Research Reports, Vol. 5, No. 6. Evanston, Ill.: National Merit Scholarship Corporation, 1969, 8 pp.

This report provides information concerning the characteristics of students who participate in a scholarship program when different methods of student identification are used. The third National Achievement Scholarship Program identified students by two methods: (1) all U.S. high schools were asked to nominate talented Negro students; and (2) high-scoring Negro students were identified on the National Merit Scholarship Qualifying Test. For each five students who entered the competition, one was identified by nomination only, one by test only, and the remainder were both nominated and identified by the test. Information about these students indicated that those identified by the test tended to have higher test scores, lower high school grades, higher socioeconomic status, and they attended larger and better-equipped high schools than those identified by nominations.

963 BRAZZIEL, WILLIAM F. Black-white comparability in college enrollment. *Journal of Human Resources,* 1970, vol. 5, no. 1, pp. 106-116.

The author starts with the premise that black–white comparability in jobs and housing will never be realized until comparability in college enrollment and graduation for Negroes is achieved. One can argue that the opposite is more likely true. Nevertheless, he provides interesting comparative statistics which indicate for example that the gap between the percentage of Negro and white college graduates has widened in the last 30 years (two percent versus six percent in 1940, and eight percent versus fifteen percent in 1967). The author also discusses the need for more scholarship and grant money for Negro students, expansion of Negro colleges, more new colleges in Negro communities, and greater effort to enroll black students in predominantly white institutions.

964 CALIFORNIA COUNCIL FOR EDUCATIONAL OPPORTUNITY, AND COLLEGE ENTRANCE EXAMINATION BOARD (SPONSORS). *Statewide seminar on race and poverty in higher education.* San Mateo, Calif.: College of San Mateo, 1968, 28 pp.

This booklet reports the proceedings of a statewide seminar held in San Mateo, California. It summarizes both the formal presentations and action resolutions submitted by an ad hoc minority caucus. Following the opening sessions, minority representatives insisted on redefining the workshop discussion agenda. Resolutions were posed on the following items: (1) Institutions should have to appoint members of minority groups on all levels of administration in order to qualify for federal funds. (2) The basis for financial aid should be need, not grades. (3) Minority student organizations or interest groups should determine admission and retention of marginal minority students; admissions tests should not be required. (4) Counseling programs should be revamped at the eighth- and ninth-grade levels to motivate minority students to college aspirations. Counselor selection should be based "on the degree of commitment toward the students."

965 CARVER, RONALD P. Designing an aural aptitude test for Negroes: An experiment that failed. *College Board Review,* Winter 1968-69, no. 70, pp. 10-14.

Traditional scholastic aptitude tests have frequently been criticized on the grounds that they represent the middle-class culture in ways which are unfair to minority youth. Furthermore, such tests require reading skill that does not take advantage of a possibly superior aural facility of urban black youth. Consequently, the College Board commissioned the development of an aural test specifically for low-income Negro boys. The test contained items of interest to this particular group of students, and the difficulty of the items was appropriate for their level of achievement. It was hypothesized that such a specially designed test would narrow the gap normally shown between aptitude scores of low-income Negroes and middle-income whites. The test was unsuccessful, however, because the average score difference between the two groups of students was essentially the same on the experimental test as on a traditional aptitude test. The experiment certainly does not prove that such a test is not feasible, but it does document an interesting and unusual approach to the problem of black–white score differences on traditional scholastic tests.

966 CLEARY, T. ANNE. Test bias: Prediction of grades of Negro and white students in integrated colleges. *Journal of Educational Measurement*, 1968, vol. 5, pp. 115-124.

The purpose of this study was to examine the relationship of college grades to Scholastic Aptitude Test scores for Negro and white students in integrated colleges in order to determine the existence of test bias in the SAT. By the definition used in this study "a test is biased if the criterion score predicted from the common regression line is consistently too high or too low for members of the subgroup." Matched samples of Negro and white students and a random sample of white students were studied at each of three state-supported institutions. Correlations were computed between the pairs of variables available for each group within each school, and analysis of covariance was used to determine whether the relationship of grades to SAT scores was different for the different groups of students. The author concludes that there is little evidence that the Scholastic Aptitude Test is biased as a predictor of college grades.

967 CLEARY, T. ANNE, AND HILTON, THOMAS L. An investigation of item bias. *Educational and Psychological Measurement*, 1968, vol. 28, pp. 61-75.

The problem of test bias has been a matter of increasing concern among educators, particularly as it relates to minority subgroups. In this research, test bias is explored in terms of individual test items. An item of a test is said to be biased for members of a particular group if, on that item, the members of the group obtain an average score which differs from the average score of other groups by more or less than expected from performance on other items of the same test.

This study examined the variation of Preliminary Scholastic Aptitude Test (PSAT) item scores in different racial and socioeconomic (SES) groups. SES was defined from items concerned with father's occupation, father's and mother's education, and a home index. In four separate analyses there was no significant relationship between item scores and race. The authors conclude that, "given the stated definition of bias, the PSAT for practical purposes is not biased for the groups studied."

968 DYER, HENRY S. Toward more effective recruitment and selection of Negroes for college. *Journal of Negro Education*, 1967, vol. 36, pp. 216-229.

The author starts by assuming that the recruitment and selection of Negroes for college is an indispensable process by which society attempts to make the most of its people by helping them make the most of themselves. He contends that the effectiveness of this recruitment process is hindered by intercollegiate competition for candidates, and suggests that in order to close the educational gap between Negroes and whites we must shift our focus from the most talented to the most disadvantaged. He urges a coordinated mobilization of resources and well-organized recruiting programs such as Upward Bound, but suggests that the coordinated program must be enormously increased if it is to be adequate to the need.

969 EGERTON, JOHN. *State universities and black Americans: An inquiry into deseg-regation and equity for Negroes in 100 public universities.* Atlanta, Ga.: Southern Education Foundation, 1969, 96 pp. $1.

This is a 1968 report on the extent of racial desegregation in 100 universities belonging to the National Association of State Universities and Land-Grant Colleges. Data from eight predominantly white institutions showed that: (1) Under two percent of all full-time undergraduates were black. The same percentage held for graduate and professional school enrollments in those institutions. (2) Of these, nearly half were freshmen. (3) Less than one percent of all full-time faculty positions were held by black Americans. Thirty-nine institutions providing figures on degree award ratios said that less than one percent of all degrees went to blacks in 1967–68. The 18 predominantly Negro institutions included in the survey enrolled almost twice as many blacks as the 80 predominantly white institutions. Feeling that there is little reason to suppose that the ratio of black Americans is much higher in the public and private institutions not included in the survey, the author concludes that desegregation in American higher education has largely been token. His data and conclusion were widely quoted.

970 FISHMAN, JOSHUA A., DEUTSCH, MARTIN, KOGAN, LEONARD, NORTH, ROBERT, AND WHITEMAN, MARTIN. Guidelines for testing minority group children. *Journal of Social Issues,* 1964, vol. 20, no. 2, pp. 129-145.

This set of useful and thoughtful guidelines cites three major difficulties in the use of standardized tests with minority group children: (1) They may not provide reliable differentiation in the range of the minority group's scores. (2) Their predictive validity for minority groups may be quite different from that normally found in other groups. (3) The validity of their interpretation is very much dependent upon an understanding of the social and cultural background of the child. A number of cautions and suggestions are offered with respect to each of these problems. The report concludes with the thought that tests are among the most important evaluative and prognostic tools that educators have at their disposal. Consequently, it is extremely important that they not be used routinely, but in a conscientious effort to discover what lies behind the test scores. Frequently, a test is useful for determining the magnitude of the deprivation to be overcome or to evaluate a child's current performance with his previous performance. Finally, the report suggests that proper use of tests depends upon intelligence, good will, and a sense of responsibility to make the proper interpretation and undertake the proper compensatory action.

971 KENDRICK, S. A. The coming segregation of our selective colleges. *College Board Review,* Winter 1967-68, no. 66, pp. 6-13.

In this speech given at the College Board annual meeting in 1967, Kendrick warns of the possibility that a stratified system of American higher education may emerge—in which selective colleges will enroll white students almost exclusively, while increasing numbers of Negro and other disadvantaged youth will attend open-door or nonselective colleges. The chief reason given for this de facto segregation is that the distribution of verbal ability in the existing population of Negro twelfth graders is far lower than that in the white population. He estimates that only 10 to 15 percent of all Negro high school seniors would score 400 or above on the verbal SAT, while only one or two percent would score 500 or above. Since the evidence shows that these scores fairly predict Negro performance in college course work, he points out that "this very real difference . . . cannot be wished away by saying that the tests are biased." The importance of verbal ability as a predictor of college-level work, and the futility of expecting to improve verbal ability at the twelfth-grade level are cited as the critical factors in this dilemma. Moreover, he predicts that the selective colleges will also be in competition with the less selective colleges for the small number of highly verbal Negro seniors. To avert this progressive segregation he offers several suggestions: (1) selective colleges might design instruction to suit the needs, ability, and background of students with low verbal ability; (2) colleges should make a concerted effort to help improve the early education of these students. He calls for extensive and candid discussion of what is being done now for Negroes at selective colleges. Kendrick's analysis and his recommendations had considerable impact on the selective colleges in the period following Martin Luther King's death.

972 MANNING, WINTON H. The measurement of intellectual capacity and performance. *Journal of Negro Education*, 1968, vol. 37, pp. 258-267.

This paper discusses the dichotomy between the role that intelligence testing has played in opening up educational opportunity and the criticisms that test bias locks the verbally disadvantaged black student into inferior opportunity. Tests are useful forecasts of future performance for black as well as white students in guidance, selection, and evaluation. However, the saturation of tests with verbal aptitude is a handicap for the ghetto child whose cultural poverty is reflected in his distinctly different form of language—termed "public" as compared with the "formal" language he encounters in school and tests. The author feels that the seriousness of this linguistic barrier calls for major improvements in measurement theory based on further study of psycholinguistics and cognitive development.

973 SHUEY, AUDREY M. *The testing of Negro intelligence.* (2nd ed.) New York: Social Science Press, 1966, 578 pp. $6.50.

This large volume summarizes studies of Negro–white differences in mental test performance in America over the past 50 years. Approximately 380 original investigations were included which employed some 80 psychometric tests designed to measure intelligence or some aspect of behavior related to it. There are studies examining young children and school children, high school and college students, armed forces personnel and veterans, deviates—both gifted and retarded, delinquents and criminals, migrants, and racial hybrids. At every age level and under a variety of conditions, it was found that Negroes regularly score below whites, and the persistent mean differences are significant both from a statistical and practical standpoint. The "regularity and consistency" in test results lead the author to suggest that there is a genetic basis for the differences. The report documents a large amount of data, but it comes close to belaboring repetitive findings within a limited reference, and contains relatively little information concerning the social and developmental conditions associated with the topic.

974 STANLEY, JULIAN C., AND PORTER, ANDREW C. Correlation of Scholastic Aptitude Test scores with college grades for Negroes versus whites. *Journal of Educational Measurement*, 1967, vol. 4, pp. 199-218.

College Board Scholastic Aptitude Test verbal and mathematical test scores correlated rather well with freshman grades in three essentially all-Negro coeducational four-year state colleges in Georgia over the six academic years 1959–60 through 1964–65. The mean coefficients of correlation were not significantly lower for the men in these colleges than for the predominantly white men in 15 other Georgia state colleges. Mean coefficients were somewhat lower for the Negro women than for the predominantly white women. The median multiple correlation for predicting freshman-year grade point averages within the predominantly Negro colleges (composite of SAT-V and SAT-M scores and average high school grades) was 0.595 for men and 0.645 for women.

In view of the detailed analysis of the Georgia data and several related studies, the authors conclude that SAT-type test scores are about as correlationally valid for Negroes competing with Negroes and taught chiefly by Negroes as they are for whites competing chiefly with whites and taught chiefly by whites.

They further suggest that in predicting college grades with an "academic aptitude" test, the paramount consideration is to choose a well-prepared test of appropriate difficulty for the persons tested. Because the criterion (usually freshman grade-point average) will probably be influenced by cultural factors in some of the same ways as the test score, correlation of test scores with typical grades is likely to be substantial even for culturally disadvantaged college freshmen. Usually, including high school average or rank along with test scores in the predictor composite improves prediction of college grades.

975 TEMP, GEORGE. *Validity of the SAT for blacks and whites in thirteen integrated institutions. Journal of Educational Measurement,* 1971, vol. 8, pp. 245-251.

Objections to the use of admissions tests for minority students are based partially upon the assumption that such tests underpredict the college grades of such students. This study of the validity of the SAT at 13 institutions provides the most comprehensive data on the question. The results tend to support the following generalizations: (1) A single equation cannot be used to predict grade-point averages for both blacks and whites in many of the institutions studied. (2) If grade predictions from SAT scores are based upon suitable separate equations, then the black students as a group are predicted to do about as well (or better than) they actually do. Since the data demonstrated that a general conclusion could not be drawn for all institutions, the author recommends that admissions officers do continuing institutional self-studies on differential predictive validity for whites and blacks.

10.3 — OPPORTUNITY PROGRAMS. There are hundreds if not thousands of programs of one sort or another that are designed to create access situations beneficial to individuals with inadequate opportunity. These programs are largely quite new and naturally more emphasis has been placed upon program development than on developing literature. There is, however, a substantial informal literature and a limited number of important books and articles.

Major topics include the theory and practice of compensatory education (986); analysis of programmatic needs (989); and descriptions of special guidance, admissions, and educational programs. The College Board has recently published a directory (979) of 800 such programs. Examples of individual programs are described in subsections 13.4 and 13.5.

976 ALTMAN, ROBERT A., AND SNYDER, PATRICIA O. (EDS.) *Minority students on the campus: Expectations and possibilities.* Boulder, Colo.: Western Interstate Commission for Higher Education, 1971, 219 pp. $3.50.

This book combines the raw stuff of minority students' thinking about their role in higher education with the dispassionate objectivity of educational research reporting. The papers were presented at the 1970 College and University Self-Study Institute sponsored jointly by WICHE and the Berkeley Center for Research and Development in Higher Education at the University of California. The urgency of the situation is expressed in the summing-up by keynote speaker William Birenbaum — "It will do no good to talk about innovation, experimentation, or accommodating new students . . . until we confront and change the reality of the power dynamics which currently govern American institutions of higher education." The volume serves a useful purpose in describing the life of the minority student on campus, the personnel programs that attempt to serve him, and a brief view of minority culture curriculums.

977 BLOOM, BENJAMIN S., DAVIS, ALLISON, AND HESS, ROBERT. *Compensatory education for cultural deprivation*. New York: Holt, Rinehart and Winston, 1965, 179 pp. $3.50.

This report is based on papers generated at the Research Conference on Education and Cultural Deprivation held at the University of Chicago in 1964. Thirty-one scholars and educators formulated a series of generalizations about education and cultural deprivation and their implications for schools. Recommendations to implement these generalizations covered areas of national, school–community, and school responsibilities. Citing the importance of undoing the damage of deprivation in early childhood, the report recommends that a national commission of teachers and other specialists should be created to develop programs for special nursery schools and the first three years of elementary school. Schools and communities are urged to shoulder responsibility for nutrition programs, work–study programs, and development of peer societies to help adolescents acquire meaningful value patterns. Recommendations for the school are outlined as part of the "all-out effort to halt the cumulative deficits in learning achievement at the later grades."

978 CLARK, KENNETH B. Alternative public school systems. *Harvard Educational Review*, 1968, vol. 38, pp. 100-113.

Clark contends that American public education suffers from "pervasive and persistent" inefficiency, particularly in the schools provided for Negro and other underprivileged children. He proposes a strategy for improving education in ghetto schools by providing some competition. The paper includes a discussion of alternatives such as industrial demonstration schools and schools operated by the Department of Defense.

979 COLLEGE ENTRANCE EXAMINATION BOARD. *A chance to go to college: A directory of 800 colleges that have special help for students from minorities and low-income families*. New York: College Entrance Examination Board, 1971, 294 pp. $3. (Out of print)

This book was based upon a nationwide survey of higher institutions. It includes annotations of a wide variety of programs designed for minority/poverty students. They vary from fairly common open-door programs with no special characteristics to unusual programs containing a number of well-organized components and directed specifically to the needs and interest of a particular group of students. Each program was briefly annotated so that the student can see what special activities, assistance, and facilities may be available at each college. There is also an introductory section that offers advice to the student about how he might find a college program that suits his needs. The book was distributed free early in 1971 to a large mailing including all secondary schools in the country.

980 EGERTON, JOHN. *Higher education for "high risk" students*. Atlanta: Southern Education Foundation, 1968, 59 pp. Single copy free.

This 1968 survey found that programs for admitting "high risk" students had made little headway at predominantly white colleges and universities. Of 210 institutions considered likely to have inaugurated such programs, only 20 to 25 reported substantial involvement; almost half of those responding (76) had no programs for these students. Private universities were in the forefront; two-thirds reported some involvement, in contrast to the 60 percent of the public institutions who said they had no "high risk" programs. The programs that were in existence were found to be largely inspired by a single individual, with leadership coming more often from administrators — admissions officers, social workers, and counselors—than from faculty. The advocates of high-risk admissions expressed a commitment to public service, a sense of social responsibility, and a desire to have racial and socioeconomic diversity in their student body. The uninvolved institutions said they were hampered by lack of funds, political worries, lack of faculty support, institutional inflexibility, and prior commitment to regular students. The report concludes with descriptions of some of the programs, singling out Antioch and Wesleyan as outstanding in this area.

981 ERIC CLEARINGHOUSE ON HIGHER EDUCATION. *Recruiting disadvantaged students.* Compendium Series of Current Research, Programs and Proposals, No. 3. Wash., D. C.: ERIC Clearinghouse on Higher Education, George Washington University, 1970, 28 pp.

This pamphlet is a compilation of a few published studies and selected opportunity programs for disadvantaged students. It contains a summary review of admissions criteria and procedures, and then lists the details and scope of programs of some 50 individual institutions.

982 FERRIN, RICHARD I. *Developmental programs in Midwestern community colleges.* Higher Education Surveys, Report No. 4. New York: College Entrance Examination Board, 1971, 50 pp. Free.

About three-fourths of all students in formal developmental programs either continue in college or leave with a definite job opportunity, according to developmental program directors of community colleges in the Midwest. This study, conducted in early 1971, examined the extent and nature of special educational and support services for educationally disadvantaged students in midwestern community colleges. Results indicated that one student in nine was involved in remedial courses, special academic skill services, and/or formal developmental programs. Remedial courses continue to be offered by most colleges, but institutions are turning increasingly to one or both of the other two approaches. Brief descriptions of 16 programs are included.

983 GOODRICH, ANDREW L. *Community services for the "new student" at inner city community colleges.* East Lansing, Mich.: Kellogg Community Services Leadership Program, Michigan State University, 1970, 32 pp.

This report discusses the general role of the community college in serving minority/poverty students in the inner city, and describes prototype programs in six community colleges.

984 GORDON, EDMUND (ISSUE ED.) Education for socially disadvantaged children. *Review of Educational Research,* 1970, vol. 40, no. 1, 179 pp.

This issue reviews research related to the educational development of disadvantaged children from four perspectives: socialization, ethnic desegregation, decentralized participation, and transition to postsecondary education. Curriculum modification was purposely not included since no substantial curriculum progress had been reported since it was covered in the 1965 review.

In his introduction, editor Gordon gives critical appraisal to the research on the disadvantaged. Several factors impeding research are: (1) tendency of researchers to look for generic treatments or one solution for the disadvantaged; (2) excessive studies depending on quantitative measures and static variables to the neglect of qualitative analysis; and (3) the tendency to look at relationships between single variables, instead of the examination of multiple interaction in the generation of behavior change. He concludes "The quality of many large scale programs is indeed questionable."

985 GORDON, EDMUND W. Programs and practices for minority group youth in higher education, in College Entrance Examination Board, *Barriers to higher education.* New York: College Entrance Examination Board, 1971, pp. 109-126.

In this paper one of the foremost authorities on compensatory education discusses the recent history of special programs for minority/poverty students in higher education. One of his themes is the general conclusion that the administrative processes of open admissions are still more influenced by considerations of meritocracy than those of democracy. He regards developments in this area as anemic in relation to the magnitude of the problem. Furthermore, Gordon feels that the history of higher education will reveal to all but the most biased that ways have been found in the past to admit and provide the collegiate credential to selected members of the population whose qualifications have been money, political contacts, or athletic ability rather than traditional academic criteria. Gordon makes the interesting proposal that colleges might assume a compromise posture by admitting half of their students on traditional meritocratic grounds and half on social grounds, and then educate and credential both by the most appropriate means.

986 GORDON, EDMUND W., ET AL. Collegiate compensatory programs for disadvantaged youth. (Tentative title) New York: College Entrance Examination Board (in preparation).

This well-written and wide-ranging study represents perhaps the best attempt to date to describe current developments in collegiate compensatory education. Material in this book ranges from a comprehensive review of the literature to concrete suggestions that readers are encouraged to try in their local situations. Specifically, the book provides examples of operational programs and describes not only activities and ideas that seem to be working well, but also some which have not worked well. In a chapter devoted to the presentation of a rationale and strategy for ethnic studies programs, the authors state conclusively that "ultimately ethnic studies is not just a label to be hung on another separate, lonely, little department of the university; it is a means and an inspiration to rethink and reorganize those significant fields of thought." Other sections of this volume present case studies and selected student reactions. An entire chapter is devoted to the College Readiness Program (CRP) of the College of San Mateo (California). CRP was generally regarded as being one of the most effective compensatory programs operating during the late 1960s, and readers interested in a detailed account of how this program came into being, the dynamics that made it effective, and a description of the events that led to its demise will find considerable information here. In summary, this book is a practical handbook that should be of significant value both to those interested in an overview of the compensatory education movement and to those looking for concrete, "how to" suggestions.

987 GORDON, EDMUND W., AND WILKERSON, DOXEY A. *Compensatory education for the disadvantaged. Programs and practices: Preschool through college.* New York: College Entrance Examination Board, 1966, 299 pp. $4.50.

This well-known comprehensive guide to compensatory education programs for the disadvantaged combines descriptive information with critical evaluation. An outgrowth of a research project sponsored by the College Board and the National Scholarship Service and Fund for Negro Students, it gives a nationwide overview of programs, from preschool through college, discusses the inadequacies of existing approaches, and suggests some possibilities for the future. It provides useful information on teacher recruitment, preparation and in-service training, curriculum innovation, and the role of the parents and the community. Also included is a detailed "Directory of Compensatory Practices," containing city-by-city outlines of past and present programs. See 986 for a more recent treatment by the same author.

988 HILLSON, HENRY T., AND MYERS, FLORENCE C. *The Demonstration Guidance Project 1957-1962.* New York: George Washington High School, Board of Education, 1963, 31 pp.

The Demonstration Guidance Project, one of the first major compensatory programs, received a great deal of attention. This program demonstrated fairly conclusively that it is possible to raise the sights and achievement of minority/poverty students in the urban ghetto if sufficient resources are made available. Other activities modeled after this project have tended to cut back on those resources and fail to yield the results obtained in this landmark project.

989 MARTYN, KENNETH A. *Increasing opportunities for disadvantaged students: Final report.* Los Angeles: California State College at Los Angeles, 1969, 225 pp.

Recommendations in this report to the Joint Committee on Higher Education of the California Legislature urge the enactment of a $25 million program to overcome the barriers to higher education for substantial numbers of disadvantaged youth. The major components of the program are: (1) $16 million to support 8,000 students directly, at an annual cost of $2,000 per student; (2) $7.5 million to establish community tutorial centers and summer institutes that would help to surmount the academic barriers for disadvantaged students. Recommendations concerning the geographic hurdle call for subsidizing the construction of housing near appropriate campuses. Mexican American and black students at California State College at Los Angeles testified at hearings of the legislative committee held on the campus in May 1968. Their views and recommendations, combined with evaluations of existing programs, form the basis for this report. It provides a comprehensive model study of statewide problems of educational opportunity of minority students.

990 MCDILL, EDWARD L., MCDILL, MARY S., AND SPREHE, J. TIMOTHY. *Strategies for success in compensatory education: An appraisal of evaluation research.* Baltimore, Md.: Johns Hopkins Press, 1969, 83 pp. $5; paperback $1.95.

This brief book describes some of the problems involved in evaluating the success of compensatory education programs. It summarizes evaluative research on Head Start, Title I, and Upward Bound programs, and also includes a brief description and analysis of several selected local programs. The authors' general theme is that the outcomes of these evaluations are complex, ambiguous, and often subject to conflicting interpretations.

991 MOORE, WILLIAM, JR. *Against the odds: The high-risk student in the community college.* San Francisco: Jossey-Bass, 1970, 244 pp. $8.50.

This is a book about high-risk students written by a black who grew up in the ghetto and calls himself a high-risk student. The author is president of Seattle Central Community College, and he contends that, for the most part, the open-door community college has failed to meet the needs of those students labeled "high-risk." "Entrance examinations and other selection techniques are screening out more—not fewer—students from the community college. The dropout rate of low achievers in the open-door college continues to increase, while the number of these students who get into the regular college (as opposed to the remedial program) continues to decrease."

The author provides a great many practical suggestions in his consideration of the problem as it relates to the student, the teacher, the counselor, the administrator, and the curriculum. He notes that "a whole new professional attitude and a genuine commitment from faculties and administrators will have to emerge" if the high-risk student is to receive the assistance he needs. But he is convinced that the high-risk student can be educated, and his personal experience adds vitality and force to his argument.

992 NICHOLS, DAVID C., AND MILLS, OLIVE (EDS.) *The campus and the racial crisis.* Wash., D. C.: American Council on Education, 1970, 309 pp. $7.

The 44 papers presented in this book discuss the campus as "cauldron" in the racial crisis involving society as a whole. As the theme of the 1969 Annual Meeting of the American Council on Education, it provided a forum for the expression of opinion of representatives of the education community, the black community, the federal government, and other concerned sectors of society. Discussions centered around the pressures for racial equality and institutional policies in the areas of admissions, curriculum, financial aid, and the overall responsibilities of higher education in the face of revolutionary social pressures. "Potential for change" is suggested as an admissions policy that would help achieve equality of opportunity, and "bridging education" is recommended to help compensate for inadequate preparation.

993 PASSOW, A. HARRY, GOLDBERG, MIRIAM, AND TANNENBAUM, ABRAHAM J. (EDS.) *Education of the disadvantaged: A book of readings.* New York: Holt, Rinehart and Winston, 1967, 503 pp. $8.95.

In this excellent collection of readings, the nature of the disadvantaged student and the causes of his difficulties are explored by leading sociologists, educators, and psychologists. The articles are largely research based and deal with both theoretical issues and practical problems. Wherever available, reports of promising school provisions for the disadvantaged and special instructional adaptations are included even though no evaluation of the consequences of such programs is available. The book covers five basic areas: the nature and setting of the educational problem; disadvantaged minority groups; socio-psychological factors affecting school achievement; education for the disadvantaged; and teachers for the disadvantaged. Throughout the volume, theory and research are clearly related to educational programs and practices.

994 RIESSMAN, FRANK. *Strategies against poverty.* New York: Random House, 1969, 114 pp. $6.95.

This book contrasts three general antipoverty approaches and discusses more specific strategies in some of the human service fields. The three major strategies considered are: (1) the Alinsky conflict model that is directed toward increasing the power of the poor through creating conflict; (2) the welfare crisis strategy designed to produce a "run" on the welfare system that would pressure the government to grant a guaranteed annual income; and (3) the New Careers model, developed by the author and Arthur Pearl. The latter is aimed at providing employment opportunities for poor people. The author stipulates that the ultimate test of a strategy is whether it affects related variables beyond its immediate impact—"the multiplier effect." He develops the thesis that the New Careers strategy has an important multiplier effect on the various dimensions of poverty in that it provides significant potential for positive reorganization of the education, health, and welfare service systems. (See 531 for more on the New Careers movement.)

995 SOMERVILLE, BILL. Can selective colleges accommodate the disadvantaged? Berkeley says "yes." *College Board Review,* Fall 1967, no. 65, pp. 5-10.

This article describes one of the earliest successful programs of recruiting minority students in a large, very selective institution. The program became prominent partly because of its success and partly because of unusual attention accorded Berkeley for other reasons. The author describes here the problems of making a program work and cites the need for massive aid to give these students help in getting admitted, all the necessary financial support, and all of the academic help needed to stay in college.

996 SOUTHERN REGIONAL EDUCATION BOARD, INSTITUTE FOR HIGHER EDUCATIONAL OPPORTUNITY. *The black community and the community college. Ac-*

tion programs for expanding opportunity: A project record. Atlanta, Ga.: SREB, 1970, 61 pp. (Multilithed)

Earlier research by the Institute for Higher Educational Opportunity had indicated that there were a variety of personal and administrative factors which tended to inhibit the enrollment of black students at the public community colleges in the South. This study summarizes the experience of a number of programs and activities in community colleges which seem effective in recruiting, enrolling, and meeting the special needs of black students. The report also includes a section that describes the implications of this study for statewide planning and coordination.

997 TRENT, WILLIAM T. *College compensatory programs for disadvantaged students.* Report 3. Wash., D. C.: ERIC Clearinghouse on Higher Education, George Washington University, 1970, 15 pp. Free.

This report reviews the general features, problems, and implications of special programs for disadvantaged students at colleges and universities. It also includes an annotation of programs at 18 institutions. The annotation includes a description of the goal and operation of the program, a profile of the target student, the institution's own evaluation of the program, and some indication of cost and source of funds.

998 U.S. OFFICE OF EDUCATION. *National Conference on Education of the Disadvantaged.* Wash., D. C.: Government Printing Office, 1966, 86 pp. 55 cents.

This report summarizes the discussions of the National Planning Conference on Education for Disadvantaged Children, held in 1965. It was called by U.S. Commissioner of Education Harold Howe to explore ways of using funds available under the new Title I legislation to wipe out inequality of educational opportunity. Each state sent a delegation representing the educational leaders who would be implementing the Title I Act, and they were joined by government officials, community action specialists, and civil rights leaders. The report synthesizes the views exchanged by the participants on approaches and programs that hold the most potential for improving the quality of education for the disadvantaged. It concludes with the major addresses given by leaders of the Johnson Administration.

999 U.S. OFFICE OF EDUCATION. *Office of Education programs for the disadvantaged.* Wash., D. C.: Government Printing Office, 1966. 20 cents.

The Office of Education supports a wide variety of programs intended partially or primarily for disadvantaged students. This brief report summarizes the programs under the following headings: research, training, school instruction, vocational education, adult education, student financial aid, supplementary activities and services, and construction and equipment. Reference to each program includes specifications of the enacting law, a description of the program, who is eligible, and the administrative unit within the Office of Education.

1000 U.S. OFFICE OF EDUCATION. *It works series: Summaries of selected compensatory education projects.* Wash., D. C.: Government Printing Office, 1970, 33 pp. 20 cents per pamphlet.

This series of pamphlets summarizes the 31 most successful compensatory education programs selected in a nationwide evaluation of projects by the American Institutes for Research. There is also available a separate booklet describing each project—its specific program activities, staffing, and budget. The five secondary programs are: Junior High Summer Institutes, New York, N.Y. (OE-37026); Project R-3, San Jose, Cal. (OE-37040); College Bound Program, New York, N.Y. (OE-37032); Expanded Language Arts, Buffalo, N.Y. (OE-37050); and Summer Upward Bound, Terre Haute, Ind. (OE-37049).

SECTION 11: SELECTED STUDENT GROUPS

In any large social process such as access to higher education, there are always individuals who get short-changed, excluded, or dealt with in a manner that doesn't facilitate individual growth or insure a fair and economically efficient society. Various preceding sections elaborate the fact that the access process needs to operate in a fashion that minimizes such ineffectiveness. The problem takes on a new dimension, however, when identifiable social groups are systematically treated ineffectively or unfairly. Such a condition suggests more than mere inefficiency. It might suggest a breakdown in the system, formal or *de jure* inequities, or the necessity to rethink the principles upon which the whole access process is based.

For these considerations the access process must include special interest in problems of important groups of students. This is partly for the simple reason of fair representation. Special groups have special guidance problems, peculiar problems of equity in financial aid and admissions, personal and educational problems that reflect their group character, and always the threat of open prejudice or unconscious bias. But in the end those groups that have legitimate interests that are not being well served do get attention; the groups represented here are the most visible examples.

11.1—*STUDENT ACTIVISTS*. The literature on student activism is heavy on description, surveys, and analysis of what is going on. Higher education has never experienced such convulsions as those of the late 1960s and early 1970s. There is understandably great emphasis on describing the nature of student protest, how to cope with confrontation and crises, and how to reform those aspects of education that do need change.

The problems and the literature tend to fall into three broad categories. There is the continuing social criticism by young people that has centered primarily on war, racism, and hypocrisy. There is the radicalism of the New Left that seemingly attacks the university because it is vulnerable rather than from a desire to reform it as an institution. And finally there is a complex set of issues concerned with educational reform. These include matters of curriculum, governance, grading, treatment of students, etc.

All of these issues bear an important relation to access to higher education because they threaten to change the role of higher education and how students relate to institutions. There are a number of important references included in section 11.1. Of special interest are the report of the Commission on Student Unrest (1018), Keniston's book on *The Uncommitted* (1009), and an extensive set of readings edited by Foster and Long (1005).

1001 ALTBACH, PHILIP G. *A select bibliography on students, politics, and higher education.* Cambridge, Mass.: Center for International Affairs, Harvard University and United Ministries in Higher Education. 1970, 65 pp. $2.50.

This bibliography presents selected comparative and cross-cultural research on the causes and impact of student activism. The sections deal with theoretical and general material relating to the student and society, international student politics, foreign students, and publications. The major portion is devoted to publications from the major regions of the world, with 81 countries represented.

1002 ASTIN, ALEXANDER W. Personal and environmental determinants of student activism. *Measurement and Evaluation in Guidance,* 1968, vol. 1, pp. 149-162.

This longitudinal study of student activism involved data collected from entering freshman classes at 246 institutions in fall 1966, and follow-up data collected one year later. The predictive value of various student input measures was explored by means of multiple regression analysis. In addition, the relative contribution of environmental variables was examined using the institution as the unit of analysis.

The findings indicated that activists differ from nonactivists in several respects. They are more likely to be politically liberal, have relatively well-educated and affluent parents, have no particular religious preference, and have an interest in artistic expression. The bulk of colleges and universities in the United States experienced little or no protest activity during 1966-67 over the issues of the Vietnam War or racial discrimination; however, protests against administrative policies were frequent. Some institutions experienced protests of this type that involved a majority of their students. A principal conclusion of the author was that environmental factors play almost no part in the emergence of social protest, whereas student input characteristics proved to be fairly accurate predictors of this type of protest (e.g., Vietnam, discrimination).

1003 CALDWELL, WALLACE F. The changing legal relationships between students and universities. *College and University,* 1970, vol. 45, pp. 245-265.

This article is a reference source on the development of legal protection of student rights under the First Amendment. The author provides a detailed and technical summary of the major court cases since 1960 that deal with student rights. He points out key issues and concludes with a brief discussion of the effects of judicial involvement on administrative authority.

1004 ERIKSON, ERIK H. (ED.) *Youth: Change and challenge.* New York: Basic Books, 1963, 284 pp. $7.50.

This volume contains a series of essays on youth, most of which were first published in *Daedalus* during the winter of 1961-62. The main focus was the key psychological and sociological aspects of modern youth and their environment. Contributors include such notables as Erik Erikson, Bruno Bettelheim, Talcott Parsons, Arthur Goldberg, and Kenneth Keniston. An international perspective is provided by papers on the youth of Japan, France, and Russia. Finally, Joseph Kauffman and Robert Coles record their impressions of American youth in the Peace Corps and in the civil rights movement. The book provides a perceptive view of the problems and social commitments of modern youth prior to the convulsive reactions during and after the mid-1960s.

1005 FOSTER, JULIAN, AND LONG, DURWARD (EDS.) *Protest! Student activism in America.* New York: William Morrow, 1970, 596 pp. $10.

This large book attempts a scholarly, comprehensive, and factual examination of student protest. Thirty-one mostly original chapters were contributed by activists as well as educators. The results of three inclusive surveys of the incidence of protest and an extensive bibliography are included.

Part I is an introductory discussion of the conflict and Part II is an in-depth analysis of the protesters. Part III includes case studies of protests at seven institutions—Indiana, Wisconsin, San Francisco State, Colorado, Princeton, Howard, and Ohio State. Part IV deals with changing patterns of power in educational institutions. Part V presents perspectives on black protest, activism in Catholic colleges, student government, *in loco parentis,* and the influence of the courts.

The final chapter predicts that student activism will remain a long-term influence on higher education, and that the kinds of social control previously used in our colleges have lost validity. The conclusion is that adequate and constructive response to protest, perhaps even a comprehensive restructuring of higher education, is now necessary.

1006 GADDY, DALE. *The scope of organized student protest in junior colleges.* Washington, D. C.: American Association of Junior Colleges, 1970, 26 pp. $2.

This report describes the results of a survey of 600 junior colleges concerning the characteristics of student protest. Findings indicated that two-fifths of the respondents had experienced protest incidents. The majority of these colleges were large public, open-door institutions, with a small number of minority and radical students. The report further details the protests with regard to geographic location, existing administrative procedures for protest control, the issues involved, and faculty participation. On the basis of these data, Gaddy offers recommendations for reforms including increased accessibility of administrators, participation of students and faculty in governance, attention to off-campus issues such as the draft, and responsiveness to curricular and financial needs of minority groups.

1007 HODGKINSON, HAROLD. Student protest—an institutional and national profile. *The Record,* 1970, vol. 71, pp. 537-555.

This article reports results of a survey of presidents of 1,230 institutions that was undertaken to identify characteristics of institutions that did and did not experience protest activity. Institutions are analyzed with regard to location, size, type of control, age, degrees awarded, and student and faculty characteristics. The article concludes with a recommendation for "selective decentralization" in decision-making, letting individuals participate in decisions directly affecting them.

1008 JACOBS, PAUL, AND LANDAU, SAUL (EDS.) *The new radicals: A report with documents.* New York: Random House, 1966, 333 pp. $8.95; paperback $1.95.

This is a basic reference in the literature concerning the New Left. The beginning chapters consider the movement's basic themes and the historical forces that gave rise to the movement. Next, attention is given to the roles played by such factions as the Student Non-Violent Coordinating Committee, the Students for a Democratic Society, the Free Speech Movement, and the Vietnam Anti-war Campaign. Finally, the book includes an impressive collection of documents including such classics as "The Port Huron Statement" and "On the New Left" by C. Wright Mills.

1009 KENISTON, KENNETH. *The uncommitted: Alienated youth in American society.* New York: Harcourt, Brace & World, 1965, 500 pp. $8.50; paperback (Dell) $2.45.

In this classic and highly praised study, Keniston explores the characteristics of alienated intellectuals and the psychological and societal origins of their alienation. The first section reports results of intensive clinical studies of students focusing on psychological factors such as ideology, behavior, family context, and fantasy life. In the second section Keniston examines alienation as a response to the stresses and demands of modern technological society and isolates several factors that predispose certain individuals to reject societal values. Keniston concludes that alienation is a response to early development and social stress. He cites the tensions created by chronic social change, the shattering of traditional community, the separation of work and family, the constant emphasis on high performance, and the declining belief that everything is attainable. He feels that the alienated individual can only become integrated through societal changes leading to an increased capacity for "commitment, dedication, passionate concern and care."

1010 KENISTON, KENNETH. *Young radicals: Notes on committed youth.* New York: Harcourt, Brace & World, 1968, 368 pp. $6.95; paperback $2.45.

This is one of the better known books on student activism. It is based on in-depth interviews with 14 young radicals who worked in the national office of Vietnam Summer, a 1967 antiwar program. Of primary interest were the psychological, social, and historical forces that led to the political commitment of these young people.

The author begins with a summary of the nature of the radical commitment he found in this group of movement leaders. Next, he discusses the personal roots of radicalism and the steps by which these particular young men and women came to think of themselves as radicals. He then turns to the tensions and frustrations, the rewards and satisfactions of movement work as reported by his subjects. Finally, he examines "the broader historical context within which they work and on which they seek to have an effect."

1011 KENISTON, KENNETH. What's bugging the students? *Educational Record,* 1970, vol. 51, pp. 116-129.

In this article Keniston analyzes the causes of campus unrest. He bases his discussion on a psychohistorical theory of conflict among three student groups: those "solidly in" the existing society, those "tenuously in," and those "effectively excluded." He reviews the characteristics and issues of discontent that have led to the polarization of these groups. Finally, Keniston offers recommendations for administrative response to conflict including equitable responses to legitimate grievances of each student group, development of institutional mechanisms for expression of conflict, redefinition of educational goals and resources, increase in institutional autonomy, maximal involvement of students in governance, and support of student political involvements. In the fall 1970 issue of the same journal Andrew M. Greeley takes sharp issue with Keniston's analysis and recommendations.

1012 KNORR, OWEN A., AND MINTER, W. JOHN (EDS.) *Order and freedom on the campus.* Boulder, Colo.: Western Interstate Commission on Higher Education, 1965, 100 pp. $3.50.

This book reports edited papers and discussions of the Seventh Annual Institute on College Self-Study for College and University Administrators. The participants, including well-known educators as well as activist students, dealt with topics such as changing patterns of authority, rights and responsibilities of faculty and students, academic freedom, institutional accountability, student unrest and reform, and the Berkeley revolt of 1964.

1013 KUNEN, JAMES S. *The strawberry statement.* New York: Random House, 1969, 176 pp. $4.95; paperback $1.25.

This well-written personal account of the Columbia riots of 1968 stands out from similar literature for its honest portrayal of the combined confusion and dedication of a "college revolutionary." In addition to personal reflection, Kunen chronicles the major events at Columbia with insight as well as wit.

1014 LIPSET, SEYMOUR MARTIN (ED.) *Student politics*. New York: Basic Books, 1967, 403 pp. $10.

In this volume internationally prominent educators focus on the almost universal phenomenon of student unrest and the factors that encourage or inhibit it. These essays are divided into sections covering these topics: approaches to the study of student political behavior, comparative perspectives, student politics in Western countries, student politics in Latin America, and student politics in India. The general tone of the papers is that the importance of student roles has lately become overwhelming; student agitation has had a great influence in shaking and overthrowing some governments and the effects of student action on the educational process has been at times negative, and at times positive.

1015 NEWFIELD, JACK. *A prophetic minority*. New York: Signet Books (New American Library), 1966, 158 pp. 95 cents.

This volume is a study of the origins and present status of the New Left. The author, a member of Students for a Democratic Society and editor of the *Village Voice,* regards the movement not as an isolated phenomenon, but as part of a larger development in society. He describes the growing split between the New Left and the old Leftist-Socialist and Communist groups in the 1940s and 1950s that culminated in the emergence of a group of concerned activist students during the early days of the civil rights movement. He reviews the foundations of the Student Non-Violent Coordinating Committee and SDS and describes the organizations and personalities of the present radical left. For Newfield, the new radicals possess a prophetic insight into the problems of American society. He describes the New Left movement as an ethical revolt against poverty, war, racism, and the dehumanization of the modern corporate state. Though the author underlines the validity of the New Left philosophy, he criticizes the radicals for failing to provide creative alternatives and for their "nihilism, romanticism, irrationalism, and anti-intellectualism."

1016 PETERSON, RICHARD E. *The scope of organized student protest in 1967-68*. Princeton, N. J.: Educational Testing Service, 1968, 60 pp. $1.50.

Using a questionnaire addressed to the dean of students, the author surveyed all the regionally accredited, four-year, degree-granting institutions in the United States regarding the dimensions of organized student protest during the year 1967-68. The study was nearly identical to one he conducted in 1964-65, and thus enabled tentative statements regarding trends in organized protest during the three-year period.

The following are among the conclusions offered: (1) Issues pertaining to instruction, faculty, or freedom of expression rarely caused protest; issues bearing on personal freedoms or student participation in college governance generated protest somewhat more often. (2) The Vietnam War was the issue that most frequently triggered student activism. (3) Institutional quality, defined as the proportion of faculty doctorates, was significantly correlated only with protests over the war. (4) The extent to which a college is residential or commuter generally had little or no relationship to the incidence of protest. (5) Generally speaking, activists constitute a small minority on campus, ranging from about four to nine percent depending on the type of issue. (6) The number of campuses experiencing protest over the war almost doubled in the interval between 1965 and 1968 as did the number of colleges reporting student left groups.

1017 PETERSON, RICHARD E. Reform in higher education—demands of the left and right. *Liberal Education,* 1969, vol. 55, pp. 60-78.

In this engagingly written overview of the current political scene in American colleges and universities the author suggests that authority in higher education has been seriously eroded. Governance often occurs through a trade-off of demands among a host of competing power blocs. The author sorts these competing parties into four categories which he labels the Anarchist Left, the Reformist Left, the Nostalgic Right, and the Upright Right. The main purpose of this paper is to outline some of the demands that are being pressed by these various groups.

The Anarchist Left "seek a revamped university in which the students, acting communally, can determine the nature of their educational and personal experiences." The Reformist Left is made up of a number of rather disparate power blocs such as black student groups, local teachers' unions, and great foundations. The Nostalgic Right is composed principally of older faculty members who yearn for the ivory tower of bygone days and can be counted on to voice their outrage whenever the college is planning an innovation. Finally the Upright Right are depicted as spirited citizens and groups from off campus who are "strong in moral certitude yet frightened that their values are being threatened." Peterson concludes with the observation that college administrators should accept the fact of conflict and become experts in conflict resolution.

1018 PRESIDENT'S COMMISSION ON CAMPUS UNREST. *The report of the President's Commission on Campus Unrest.* Washington, D. C.: Government Printing Office, 1970, 537 pp. $2.50.

The Scranton Commission was established after the Kent and Jackson State tragedies to investigate causes and impact of campus unrest across the nation. Sections of the report deal with the roots of student protest, the evolution of the black student movement, the treatment of disorder by university law enforcement agencies and the government, along with special reports on Jackson and Kent State. The commission's recommendations to the President, government, law enforcement, the university, and the students are based on themes of understanding, reconciliation, and shared national commitment. An annotated bibliography containing material used in the report is reproduced in the appendix.

1019 SMITH, ROBERT, AXEN, RICHARD, AND PENTONY, DEVERE. *By any means necessary: The revolutionary struggle at San Francisco State.* San Francisco: Jossey-Bass, 1970, 370 pp. $9.75.

This is a firing-line narrative of the background and events of the strike at San Francisco State College in early 1969, as seen by former president Robert Smith and two of his top colleagues over a two-year period. The major lesson they draw is the fragility of the higher education institution when it becomes the battleground of alienated white students, militant ethnic minorities, and the New Left against the conservative right. They see the State conflict as prophetic of the widespread campus violence in 1970. All factions used the argument that high moral commitment justified the "by any means" tactics. This is termed a "powerful threat that negates the essence of higher education." The final chapter paints Hayakawa as the "authoritarian, managerial" president and describes the situation as a power struggle that "decimated classes, and embittered and polarized the faculty."

11.2—TALENTED STUDENTS. Since the shock of Sputnik there has been special interest in the education of talented students. This interest seemed especially associated with national pride, but it did develop a useful realization of the importance of the most talented segment of society, and the special access problems of maintaining curriculum continuity as these students are moved from secondary schools to appropriately challenging college course work. There are three areas of special interest that are only partly related.

The overriding issue is effective identification and utilization of talent on a national basis. Wolfle (1039) has provided representative readings. Section 6.2 also contains relevant references on human resources. Another problem is the appropriate educational treatment of talented students. A book by Cohen (1022) contains useful readings and section 4.2 includes references on Advanced Placement (1220), the only national program specifically designed to aid in the articulation of educational programs for talented students between secondary and higher education. A third very different interest is the psychological and psychometric study of creativity. This was an especially active field in the early 1960s (see edited works by Taylor).

1020 ASTIN, ALEXANDER W. Personal and environmental factors associated with college dropouts among high aptitude students. *Journal of Educational Psychology*, 1964, vol. 55, pp. 219-227.

The picture of high aptitude dropouts presented by the results of this study seems to reflect the period in which it was undertaken—the early 1960s. These talented dropouts came from lower socioeconomic backgrounds and tended to have lower educational aspirations. Only a few years later the problem of the talented dropout was usually seen to be a much more complicated educational and social problem (see 1026).

1021 BRIDGMAN, DONALD S. Where the loss of talent occurs and why, in College Entrance Examination Board, *The search for talent*. New York: College Entrance Examination Board, 1960, pp. 30-45.

The purpose of the study was to determine from available information the extent to which the country's talented youth carry through their formal education to the point of college graduation.

The findings indicated that of those in the top 30 percent ability level, from 75 to 80 percent of the boys and about 55 percent of the girls who graduate from high school enter college. This gives a combined sex figure of about 66 percent which may be compared with that of 48 percent secured by Dael Wolfle in 1954. Thus this study was one of several that documented the improvement in attracting talented youth to college but also laid the groundwork for expanded student aid programs by identifying financial restraint as a major cause of limited educational attainment.

1022 COHEN, JOSEPH W. (ED.) *The superior student in American higher education*. New York: McGraw-Hill, 1966, 299 pp. $7.95.

Honors programs in American higher institutions have a long history, beginning with the private eastern colleges that took the initiative in providing special programs for talented students in the early decades of the century. With the founding of the Inter-University Committee on the Superior Student (ICSS), a coordinated effort was initiated to extend the concept of honors programs throughout higher education. This volume summarizes the eight-year work of the ICSS, and explores the major problems and possible means of attacking them.

The volume begins with a history of the honors movement including the founding and work of the ICSS. Next the needs and desires of the superior student are discussed; this is followed by several chapters on honors programs and what they can mean to various types of higher institutions. Special attention is given to the question of how the honors curriculum might differ from the ordinary curriculum. The honors approach discussed in this book also seeks to counter the current overwhelming trend toward specialization.

1023 COLLEGE ENTRANCE EXAMINATION BOARD. *The search for talent*. New York: College Entrance Examination Board, 1960, 131 pp. $3.

This volume includes papers presented at the Seventh Annual Admissions

Colloquium of the College Board. The papers provide excellent background on such topics as the identification of talented students, the development of talent, and barriers to such development. (See 1021 and 1028 for annotations of individual papers.)

1024 COPLEY, FRANK O. *The American high school and the talented student.* Ann Arbor, Mich.: University of Michigan Press, 1961, 92 pp. (Out of print)

This 1961 study provides a broad look at how high schools can prevent talent waste by providing college-level work for gifted students. Writing from the educational perspectives of a classics professor, Copley concludes that enrichment in high school courses is a better answer than early college admission, which may penalize emotional immaturity in high-ability students. His observations of schools already using Advanced Placement, independent study, and other types of enrichment programs resulted from his work as liaison consultant to high schools for the University of Michigan Honors Program. The author provides valuable suggestions to schools and teachers wishing to broaden and deepen high school experiences for their top students.

1025 DURR, WILLIAM K. *The gifted student.* New York: Oxford University Press, 1964, 296 pp. $5.95.

This is a source book on the course content and teaching strategies for gifted student programs at the elementary and secondary levels. It includes chapters on identification, grouping, acceleration, motivation, and guidance. Other chapters describe a variety of enrichment activities and materials.

1026 HEIST, PAUL (ED.) *The creative college student: An unmet challenge.* San Francisco: Jossey-Bass, 1968, 253 pp. $7.75.

Are colleges and universities failing in their responsibility to educate the highly creative student? In spring 1966 a conference sponsored by the Center for Research and Development in Higher Education at the University of California at Berkeley addressed this question. A number of the chapters in this provocative volume were originally presented at that conference. A general theme of the papers is that colleges "fail as often as they succeed" in educating those students recognized as highly creative. A surprising number of highly creative young people are dissatisfied with their college experiences, and the result is a disturbingly high attrition rate (50 to 80 percent in one study).

Chief among the problems identified by the creative was the rigidity of curriculum and academic experiences. The consistent use of a single set of unimaginative classroom procedures, the lack of quality and stimulation in teaching, the "pressure-cooker" learning climate, and the traditional grading methods are cited as testimony to a pervading insensitivity to individual needs and interests. The authors assert that genuine improvement will require some rather basic changes. College faculty must be trained as teachers and learn to respond to the interests and aspirations of individuals. Colleges must broaden the definition of their goals, allow for more flexible programs, and enrich their curricular offerings.

1027 HOLLAND, JOHN L. Creative and academic performance among talented adolescents. *Journal of Educational Psychology,* 1961, vol. 52, pp. 136-147.

This study was based on 75 types of information from approximately 1,000 National Merit finalists. The purpose was to examine the differences that may exist between students who are especially creative and students who are especially high academic achievers. The findings indicated that creative students are more often independent, intellectual, expressive, asocial, consciously original, and have high aspirations for achievement. The high academic achievers were more persevering, sociable, and responsible, and were more likely to have parents with authoritarian attitudes.

1028 MacKinnon, Donald W. What do we mean by talent and how do we test for it?, in College Entrance Examination Board, *The search for talent*. New York: College Entrance Examination Board, 1960, pp. 20-29.

In this article MacKinnon discusses some characteristics of the creatively talented individual and gives some suggestions regarding the identification of such talent. Creative individuals are characterized by originality, independence, cognitive flexibility, complexity of personality, lack of defensiveness, commitment to sustained endeavor, sense of personal identity, breadth of interests, and a preference for intuition. They score high on theoretical and aesthetic values and are somewhat inclined toward introversion. They are, of course, fairly intelligent, but "above a certain minimum level of intelligence there is no one-to-one relationship between intelligence and creativity." The author concludes that the effective identification of talent requires more than aptitude, intelligence, and achievement scores. In addition to these the task requires the employment of measures of interests and values and "such aspects of total personality functioning" as are described in this article.

1029 Mayhew, Lewis B. The superior student, in Asa S. Knowles (Ed.), *Handbook of college and university administration*. Vol. II. *Academic*. New York: McGraw-Hill, 1970, sec. 2, pp. 96-101.

This chapter briefly reviews major theoretical studies and pioneer programs for gifted students. The author also discusses administrative guidelines for developing programs for superior students, for program evaluation, student selection, program structure, and administrative responsibility.

1030 National Education Association. *Administration procedures and school practices for the academically talented student*. Washington, D. C.: NEA, 1960, 223 pp. $1.25.

This book outlines administrative procedures for the development of accelerated programs for academically talented high school students. Specific chapters deal with administrative coordination, identification, enrichment, and grouping of students as well as appropriate curricular and guidance programs. Some of this material can apply equally well to higher education. The volume includes an extensive bibliography.

1031 National Merit Scholarship Corporation. *Review of research*. NMSC Research Reports, vol. 6, no. 1. Evanston, Ill.: National Merit Scholarship Corporation, 1970, 20 pp.

The National Merit Scholarship Corporation has conducted research on its talented participants since the inception of the program. This productive and influential research program currently emphasizes longitudinal studies of Merit Scholars, studies of talented Negro students, and studies of participants in the national talent search. This report summarizes work in progress and includes annotations of previously completed studies.

1032 Nichols, Robert C. *The origin and development of talent*. NMSC Research Reports, vol. 2, no. 10. Evanston, Ill.: National Merit Scholarship Corporation, 1966, 20 pp.

This review of research on talent considers the characteristics of talented students and the origin and development of talent. Comparisons of National Merit Scholarship finalists with college students in general showed a disproportionately large percentage of boys and Jews, a predominance of firstborn children among Merit finalists, and a tendency for them to come from families of higher socioeconomic status. In assessing personality traits, the author finds that the evidence suggests that "able students tend to be intellectually autonomous, audacious, and aggressive." He evaluates college environments as having little effect on career plans, intellectual achievement, or personality; his interpretation is that able students are like "cannon balls"—with so much momentum they will achieve at whatever college they attend. He feels that plausible explanations for high incidence of firstborn children among the Merit finalist group are more likely to be found in psychological factors which tend to put younger siblings at a developmental disadvantage. His evaluation of heredity and environment as factors in the origin of talent distinguishes between two categories of environment—developmental and educational influences; he sums up by saying, "At present differences in quality of schools and colleges are not a major source of differences in ability." He concedes, however, that the effects of differential access to college have not been adequately investigated.

1033 NICHOLS, ROBERT C. *Where the brains are.* NMSC Research Reports, vol. 5, no. 5. Evanston, Ill.: National Merit Scholarship Corporation, 1969, 17 pp.

It is probably safe to assume that a large majority of the more academically talented eleventh graders in the country are tested in the National Merit Scholarship competition. Nichols capitalizes on this circumstance in producing estimates of the intellectual level of the population in each of the 50 states and more than 200 metropolitan areas. His findings indicate that talented students tend to be concentrated in areas with large populations that are economically well off and have a high educational level, a high proportion of foreign born, a low proportion of nonwhites, and low fertility. Of course, the data provide interesting comparisons among cities and states, but they also provide very useful demographic information for research purposes.

1034 TAYLOR, CALVIN W. (ED.) *Creativity: Progress and potential.* New York: McGraw-Hill, 1964, 241 pp. $8.95.

The first three of the University of Utah's series of national research conferences on creativity were concerned with reports of individual research projects (see 1036). This fourth in the series was a small work conference intended to summarize research findings to date and to discuss promising new directions for research on creativity.

1035 TAYLOR, CALVIN W. (ED.) *Widening horizons in creativity.* New York: John Wiley, 1964, 466 pp. $11.50.

This volume reports the proceedings of the fifth University of Utah Conference on Creativity. It is unusual in two respects. The participants were selected after an extensive nationwide nomination process, and the volume reports the papers and the discussion essentially verbatim. Topics include historical reports, creative process studies, education and development of creativity, criterion and prediction studies, and creativity in special fields and settings.

1036 TAYLOR, CALVIN W., AND BARRON, FRANK (EDS.) *Scientific creativity: Its recognition and development.* New York: John Wiley, 1963, 419 pp. $10.95.

This useful volume contains selected material from the first three University of Utah national conferences on creativity. It includes a number of landmark papers by 29 leaders in the field.

1037 TERMAN, LEWIS M., AND ODEN, MELITA H. *Genetic studies of genius.* Vol. 5, *The gifted group at mid-life: Thirty-five years' follow-up of the superior child.* Stanford, Calif.: Stanford University Press, 1959, 187 pp. $5.50.

In 1921 Lewis Terman began his famous genetic studies of genius that were to become the most comprehensive longitudinal analyses of human talent. He screened thousands of third- through eighth-grade pupils throughout California on the basis of teacher rankings, a group intelligence test, and finally the Stanford-Binet individually administered test. More than 1,500 children were selected, practically all of whom had IQs of 140 or above. Terman maintained contact with 95 percent of this sample by means of questionnaires and personal letters over a period of 35 years. The trailblazing study is unique in a number of ways: its duration, the value of the data collected, the confidentiality of the information, and the personal relationship between the investigator and his subjects.

The five volumes and the many articles based on this massive study provide an unmatched wealth of information about the development of talented individuals. Prior to this study the common folklore held that especially talented children generally developed into maladjusted, ineffective adults. Perhaps the major conclusion of this study was the undeniable correction of that misconception. All of Terman's evidence indicated that the gifted child is far more apt to become an intellectually superior, vocationally successful, well-adjusted adult than is the average child.

1038 U.S. OFFICE OF EDUCATION, BUREAU OF RESEARCH. *Provisions for talented students: An annotated bibliography.* Washington, D. C.: Government Printing Office, 1966, 61 pp. 25 cents.

This annotated bibliography describes a variety of reports and materials concerning programs and practices for the education of academically, creatively, and artistically talented children. Most of these materials were prepared for limited audiences and have never been listed in the education indexes or bibliographies. It is a useful source of information on differentiated education for talented elementary and secondary school students.

1039 WOLFLE, DAEL (ED.) *The discovery of talent.* Cambridge, Mass.: Harvard University Press, 1969, 316 pp. $9.50.

This collection of lectures by 11 distinguished psychologists records the Bingham lecture series from 1956 to 1965. They deal with the process of "finding the talented, encouraging their advancement and making known their potentialities." Specific chapters deal with such topics as diversity of talent, nurturing talent, identification and conservation of talent, and hereditary and environmental influences. As a group these lectures constitute an unusually rich source of current thought concerning the value of talent.

11.3 — *WOMEN STUDENTS*. The largest minority and the one with potentially the most socially revolutionary grievances is by all odds women. The women's liberation movement has generated prolific literature describing the nature of the problem, but there is relatively little research and scholarly writing on the broad problem of women's rights in society and the role of higher education. Anticipating the educational implications of this movement is all the more difficult because the movement is not highly focused and a substantial number of women have yet to decide which aspects of liberation they favor.

There are various problems. Perhaps the most flagrant is the occupational bias that seems to be very slowly reaching the public consciousness. The most subtle problem is perhaps that of the female role. Even when male chauvinism runs rampant, it is not always recognized, even by women, to say nothing of men. Popular references on these problems are *The Feminine Mystique* (1043) and *Sexual Politics* (1048). Traditionally prominent educational organizations concerned with women's rights are the American Association of University Women (1100) and the National Association of Women Deans and Counselors (1123).

There are limited references to the educational problems of women (see 1040 and 1060), but this seems due for the most part to the fact that the matter has not been studied carefully and described well. A comprehensive documentation of the occupational experiences of women immediately out of college would likely describe a national scandal. The more difficult problem is that of providing real educational opportunity in a social structure that is not at all well designed to provide it. As many writers have commented, the biological revolution will likely raise entirely new possibilities and social decisions regarding sex relationships, family structure, and other attributes of society that have defined woman's role.

1040 BERNARD, JESSIE. *Academic women.* University Park, Pa.: Pennsylvania State University Press, 1964, 331 pp. $8.95.

This pioneering study of academic women examines the effect of sex differences on the learning process and career patterns, investigates the combination of career and family life, and explores the problem of supply and demand for highly trained women. The author uses systematic sociological data and personal biographical material to analyze the motivations and backgrounds of academic women and evaluate their contribution to the total academic enterprise. Bernard found that women receiving the doctorate were superior in test intelligence to men of the same group, yet significantly lower in publication productivity. Further investigation revealed academic position a better predictor of productivity than sex.

1041 CROSS, K. PATRICIA. College women: A research description. *Journal of the National Association of Women Deans and Counselors,* 1968, vol. 32, pp. 12-21.

This useful article is a synthesis of findings from four major student surveys dealing with self-perception, interests, attitudes, and goals. Responses underscored differences between college men and women with regard to socioeconomic level, parental encouragement, socialization, reasons for college attendance, grade achievement, and satisfaction with the college experience. Most women students planned at least part-time careers but considered marriage and family life their primary fulfillment. The author urges flexibility in undergraduate curriculum and specifically suggests independent study programs as basic preparation for both the career and housewife roles.

1042 CROSS, K. PATRICIA. *The undergraduate woman.* AAHE Research Report No. 5. Washington, D. C.: American Association for Higher Education, 1971, 6 pp.

This report summarizes current research on undergraduate women and indicates implications for future practice. The report reviews measures of academic ability including test scores, grades, and academic motivation—all of which indicate little difference between men and women in academic potential. Further research indicates women's career aspirations are hampered by lack of parental support and the general counsel to choose a "realistic" career goal. Studies of the equality of educational opportunity indicate that women from the lower socioeconomic levels are the major group of well-qualified students not attending college. The author suggests state colleges may improve the educational opportunity for women by diverting women in elementary education to college-level teaching and offering counseling and broader informational programs stressing the wide range of career opportunities. She also suggests that universities should examine practices that discriminate against women including limitation of dormitory space, insufficient counseling programs, and bias against women faculty members.

1043 FRIEDAN, BETTY. *The feminine mystique.* New York: Norton, 1963, 384 pp. $6.95; paperback (Dell) 1970, $1.25.

This book, first published in 1963, was one of the earliest to popularize the role conflicts of the college-educated suburban housewife. Friedan defines the "mystique" as the image of total feminine fulfillment through home and family. She traces the historical development of the mystique, discussing the influence of Freud and the social sciences, and examines the perpetuation of the image by the educational system and advertising. Friedan's theory derives support from scholarly analysis, interviews with housewives, and her own personal experience as wife, mother, and career woman. She concludes that women, as well as men, need to establish identity through creative work outside the home and that higher education is the key to discovery of the appropriate vocation.

1044 GINZBERG, ELI, BERG, IVAR E., BROWN, CAROL A., HERMA, JOHN L., YOHALEM, ALICE M., AND GORELICK, SHERRY. *Life styles of educated women.* New York: Columbia University Press, 1966, 224 pp. $7.

The women's liberation movement gained momentum soon after this study of 300 women was published. It is consequently interesting to speculate how the results might have differed if these highly trained women had been queried regarding their career/family roles some five years later. In 1965 the authors concluded that their respondents do not lead constricted and discontented lives but have the freedom of action to allow them to realize most of their goals even though there is some discrimination and prejudice. Despite these now questionable generalizations the book does contain a useful final chapter that identifies many problems women face in education and employment. Suggested solutions emphasize action on fairly visible restraints rather than the more subtle social inequities dramatized by the liberation movement.

1045 KATZ, JOSEPH, COMSTOCK, PEGGY, AND LOZOFF, MARJORIE M. *Educational and occupational aspirations of adult women.* Report to the College Entrance Examination Board. Stanford, Calif.: Institute for the Study of Human Problems, Stanford University, 1970, 261 pp. (Mimeographed)

This study analyzes the role conflicts of college educated women. Chapter I examines career choice and autonomy among students at two quite different institutions—Stanford University and San Jose City College. Chapters II and III investigate the attitudes of alumnae of Stanford and Santa Rosa Junior College toward career and family life. The findings indicate that traditional social attitudes often inhibit occupational development of women students. In addition, alumnae respondents, while relatively content with their roles as wives and mothers, often expressed dissatisfaction with educational and occupational development, leading the authors to recommend a variety of programs to assist women in utilization of time and skills. The final chapters examine the image of women in popular women's magazines and present an extensive annotated bibliography.

1046 LEWIS, EDWIN C. *Developing woman's potential.* Ames, Iowa: Iowa State University Press, 1968, 389 pp. $7.50; paperback $3.50.

Starting from the premise that "women represent the largest area of waste in human resources," counseling psychologist Lewis argues that this talent loss can be averted by changes in society's attitudes, not by political or legal action. Such changes require that women learn to view themselves as individuals and make career plans commensurate with their special qualifications. His objective discussion of current research on attitudes concerning the roles of women in education, homemaking, and career provide clues for developing this kind of self-concept. The author defines one hurdle to consistency of career planning for women as the "discontinuity" of the different phases of a woman's life, with sudden and unrelated change in role from student, to wife, to mother. Since the supporting research data for each chapter are grouped in separate appendixes, the book serves both a professional and popular readership.

1047 McGuigan, Dorothy Gies. *A dangerous experiment: 100 years of women at the University of Michigan.* Ann Arbor, Mich.: Center for the Continuing Education of Women, University of Michigan, 1970, 136 pp. $2.50.

This lively book traces the history of coeducation at the University of Michigan from 1870 to the present day. The author describes the background of the first women to enter the university, their motivations, and the hostility and anger they encountered. She further discusses the first women medical students, the developments leading to the establishment of the position of dean of women, and the later careers of the first women graduates. The final chapter is devoted to a review of the current status of women at the university. The author observes that though progress has been made, discrimination still exists both in opportunities open to women at the university and in later employment patterns.

1048 Millett, Kate. *Sexual politics.* Garden City, N. Y.: Doubleday, 1970, 393 pp. $7.95.

In this pioneering work, Millett attempts to formulate the ideas and principles underlying the women's liberation movement into a theoretical framework. The first section discusses the patriarchal bias in society and examines male domination as a political force. In further chapters Millett traces historically the social relationship between the sexes, outlining the advances of the early feminists and their frustration by political and ideological reaction after World War II. The final chapters are devoted to an analysis of sexual oppression in the works of D. H. Lawrence, Henry Miller, Norman Mailer, and Jean Genet.

1049 Neuman, Rebecca R. The educational needs of women, in Kaoru Yamamoto (Ed.), *The college student and his culture: An analysis.* Boston: Houghton Mifflin, 1968, pp. 470-476.

This brief article examines the needs, attitudes, capacities, and expectations of women and the most appropriate educational framework for a dual role in the family and the larger society. The author directs her discussion especially to the counselor who must understand the reality of sex differences and must recognize and face difficult value questions in dealing with women students.

1050 Oltman, Ruth M. *Campus 1970: Where do women stand?* Research Report of a Survey on Women in Academe. Washington, D. C.: American Association of University Women, 1970, 25 pp. (Mimeographed)

This report finds that American colleges and universities pay only lip service to equality of opportunity for women. Data were obtained from a questionnaire sent to 750 institutions holding corporate membership in the American Association of University Women. Ninety percent of the schools reported that their promotion policies were the same for both men and women faculty, yet in reality women were rarely found in upper-echelon tenured positions and department chairmanships. Oltman concludes that at every level—"student body, administration, faculty, and trustees—women are under-represented or placed in positions with little power in decision-making." The author calls for new opportunities at the policy-making level in both teaching and administration, the elimination of nepotism, and the examination of institutional policies that may contribute to "covert or overt" discrimination. The appendix contains the official resolution of the Board of Directors of AAUW, passed in November 1969, urging "new efforts to achieve equal status and a complete range of alternatives for women."

1051 Patterson, Gardner. The education of women at Princeton: A special report. *Princeton Alumni Weekly,* 1968, vol. 69, no. 1, 74 pp.

Coeducation at traditionally all-male and all-female colleges has long been a hotly debated topic. In the late 1960s several of these institutions, including Princeton, made headlines by opening their doors to members of the opposite sex. This issue of the Princeton alumni magazine contains the complete committee report of the desirability and feasibility of admitting women to the under-graduate college. The committee examined the effects the admission of women might have on various facets of the university, including number and quality of male applicants, structure of the curriculum, and social and intellectual life. In addition they thoroughly examined financial aspects including the effect on the operating budget and additional capital expenditures required. The report concluded with a recommendation for the admission of 1,000 women on a coeducational rather than a coordinate basis.

1052 PRESIDENT'S COMMISSION ON THE STATUS OF WOMEN. *American women.* Washington, D. C.: Government Printing Office, 1963, 86 pp. $1.25.

This commission's report provides a comprehensive but concise description of the status of women with respect to education and training, home and community services, private employment, labor standards, basic income security, and legal treatment. Further sections summarize advances in the position of American women during the twentieth century. A number of simple basic charts are included.

1053 SOLDWELL, BETTE J. (ED.) Problems and opportunities challenging women today. *Journal of the National Association of Women Deans and Counselors,* 1970, vol. 34, no. 1, 48 pp.

This issue of the *Journal of the National Association of Women Deans and Counselors* is devoted to an examination of the problems facing the professional woman and the role of the counselor in aiding women students to reach their full potential. Eight articles are included, dealing with topics such as the historical role of women, counseling women for responsibilities, the role of value formulation in helping women to make their own decisions, female role perception as a factor in counseling, and attitudes of high school age students concerning marriage.

1054 UNITED NATIONS EDUCATIONAL, SCIENTIFIC AND CULTURAL ORGANIZATION. *Comparative study on access of girls and women to higher education.* Paris: Unesco, 1967. (Multilithed)

Even though this Unesco study reports spectacular gains from 1958 to 1963 in the number of women enrolled in higher education in its member countries, opportunities for women are still found to be circumscribed in fields of study and career possibilities. Even the proportion of women students to the total enrollment is a modest one—less than 30 percent in 62 percent of the countries. Career and marriage are considered an either/or decision in most countries. By and large, the study showed that women pursue traditionally feminine courses of study and are denied access to scientific disciplines in almost every country. Women in the USSR and socialist countries of eastern Europe are found to have broader educational and job opportunities, particularly in science. The report gives the text of a resolution adopted by the Economic and Social Council in 1967 urging that the member states promote access of women to higher education on conditions of equality with men and to all jobs and professions for which they are qualified.

1055 U.S. BUREAU OF LABOR STATISTICS. Women at work: A special section. *Monthly Labor Review,* 1970, vol. 93, no. 6, pp. 3-44.

A major section of this issue was devoted to a series of articles concerning the status of women in the labor market. Most of the literature concerning the woman's cause deals with social or educational matters; this reference is complementary and particularly useful because it contains a great deal of information about vital but somewhat obscure government labor statistics and programs. The topics include discrimination against women in the labor market, manpower demand for women in the 1970s, and trends in women's employment patterns.

1056 U.S. Department of Labor. *College women seven years after graduation: Resurvey of women graduates – class of 1957.* Washington, D. C.: Government Printing Office, 1966. 40 cents.

This longitudinal survey is a follow-up study of a selected sample of 6,000 college graduates investigated originally in 1957. The study focuses on the interrelated influences of undergraduate education, postgraduate specialization, family and community activities, and work careers. It attempts to answer questions concerning reasons for increased demand for paid employment, obstacles in availability and attainment of jobs, quality of attachment of women to the labor force, interest in continuing education, and the importance of volunteer activities. The findings indicated a rising interest of college women in paid employment and continuing education, and widespread desire for participation in economic or community activities. Though a significant number had jobs commensurate with ability and education, the career aspirations of many women appeared restricted by social attitudes and economic forces. The primary influence affecting the economic status of women was asserted to be the generally high national level of economic activity. The rising demand for trained workers created a favorable attitude toward women among employers and created a favorable climate for legislation improving work opportunities.

1057 U.S. Department of Labor, Wage and Labor Standards Administration. *Trends in educational attainment of women.* Washington, D. C.: Government Printing Office, 1969, 19 pp. (Mimeographed)

This report presents data on educational attainment of women during the period 1900-1968. The charts and tables cover such statistics as high school graduates, degree recipients, and labor force participation rates of women of different educational levels.

1058 University of Michigan, Center for Continuing Education of Women. *Careers for college women: A bibliography of vocational materials.* Ann Arbor, Mich.: CCE, University of Michigan, 1968, 61 pp. $1.

This bibliography lists a large number of pamphlets and brochures providing information on occupations for college-educated women. The occupations listed cover a wide variety of academic fields in business, humanities, the sciences, and social service. Some are specifically directed to women; others simply describe the career opportunity.

1059 Watley, Donivan J., and Kaplan, Rosalyn. Career or marriage? Aspirations and achievements of able young women. *Journal of Vocational Behavior,* 1971, vol. 1, pp. 29-43.

A 1965 follow-up study of career and/or marriage plans of 833 women National Merit Scholars during the years 1956-1960 found that 85 percent planned to pursue a career. This finding is cited as a sharp contrast to earlier studies indicating that most gifted women do not undertake careers. Fifty-two percent of these women Scholars reported that they were already involved in a career. However, the authors also characterize these able young women as "very marriage oriented," with "multiple expectations and plans for themselves as wife-mother and as active contributors in their career fields." This study is a particularly valuable source of data because it focuses on a group of very talented women who are naturally at the center of many concerns of the women's liberation movement.

1060 Westervelt, Esther M., and Fixter, Deborah A. *Women's higher and continuing education: An annotated bibliography with selected references on related aspects of women's lives.* New York: College Entrance Examination Board, 1971, 67 pp. $1.50.

This annotated bibliography provides valuable short cuts through the rapidly mounting literature on the roles and rights of women. It gives extensive and up-to-date coverage of the main topic of education, pays secondary attention to the employment of women, and includes representative samples of the literature on other social and cultural aspects. The impetus for change in the status of women has so rapidly outdated works once considered basic references that the authors characterize research done in the 1950s as of "questionable relevance" for the 1970s.

11.4—BLACK STUDENTS. The civil rights movement has been a significant force in American society since the mid-1950s and it has generated a very large literature, much of which is relevant to access to higher education. The items included here are especially selected as prototypes or because of particular relevance to the access process.

There are many books and studies concerned with the documentation of conditions of Negro life, social status, and problems of inequality. Parsons' and Clark's *The Negro American* (1077) provides representative readings. A second burgeoning literature is concerned with cultural identity, black pride, and black studies in higher education (see 1078). There is also a much smaller body of work concerned with educational aspiration of black students and the conditions of access and achievement in higher education. In addition to references in this particular section, there are a number of other relevant citations in section 8.6 on the Negro college; section 9.1 on the nature of ability; and all of section 10 on educational opportunity.

There are many organizations concerned with educational opportunity and social rights of blacks. Two that are especially relevant to access to higher education are the U.S. Commission on Civil Rights (1141) and the National Association for Afro-American Education (1117). Important periodicals include the *Journal of Negro Education* (1329), the *Civil Rights Digest* (1313), and the *Race Relations Reporter* (1388).

1061 BAYER, ALAN E., AND BORUCH, ROBERT F. Black and white freshmen entering four-year colleges. *Educational Record,* 1969, vol. 50, no. 4, pp. 371-386.
National normative data compiled for 300,000 college freshmen in 1968 provide this profile of black students—their numbers, backgrounds, and aspirations. The authors conclude that stepped-up minority recruiting had made little impact on the numbers of black students enrolling. Although 12 percent of the college age population were black, only 5-6 percent of college students were black, and of those, 40-50 percent were enrolled in predominantly black institutions. Black students were found more likely to be women, to be older students from low-income urban families, and to have below average aptitude scores. Their educational aspirations are high, with future goals of entering business, teaching, social sciences, or health-related fields. A follow-up study of 1,966 entering students indicated that black students have a relatively high "survival rate."

1062 BORGEN, FRED H. *Able black Americans in college: Entry and freshman experiences.* NMSC Research Reports, Vol. 6, No. 2. Evanston, Ill.: National Merit Scholarship Corporation, 1970, 21 pp.
This study summarizes college choices and freshman performances of 1,744 able black students who had done well in the National Achievement Scholarship Program. Highly selective white colleges drew the students from the highest

socioeconomic and educational backgrounds. Private Negro colleges and less selective white colleges both attracted similar middle-class students. Students from the South and from the least advantaged educational and economic backgrounds tended to enroll in public Negro colleges. The author concludes that it is probable that the low and high selectivity white colleges are enrolling black students with important attitudinal differences.

1063 BURGDORF, KENNETH. *Outstanding Negro high school students: A one-year followup.* NMSC Research Reports, Vol. 5, No. 4. Evanston, Ill.: National Merit Scholarship Corporation, 1969, 12 pp.

This report analyzes the results of a one-year follow-up questionnaire submitted to outstanding Negro students who had participated in the first National Achievement Scholarship Program in 1965. Their names and addresses and competition status had been sent to almost 1,500 colleges as a means of encouraging colleges to seek talented Negro students. All of the top ranking scholars enrolled in four-year colleges, and 97 percent planned to return to college. Even in the lowest group, only an estimated eight percent were not accepted by any college, and 87 percent expected to return for their second year. Burgdorf points out that these figures are well above the national average for both white and nonwhite students.

1064 CENTRA, JOHN A. Black students at predominantly white colleges: A research description. *Sociology of Education,* 1970, vol. 43, no. 3, pp. 325-339.

This study provides a useful picture of the characteristics, activities, goals, and perceptions of 249 black students at predominantly white colleges. It also includes a comparison with a matched group of white students at the same institutions. In many respects, the two groups of students were quite similar, but there were "impressive" differences in a number of important aspects of student life and extracurricular activity. The results gave evidence of alienation and social isolation of black students, but this seemed to vary a great deal from campus to campus. While black and white students may be reasonably well integrated on some campuses, the author suggests that some student bodies exist almost as "two nations."

1065 CENTRA, JOHN A., LINN, ROBERT L., AND PARRY, MARY ELLEN. Academic growth in predominantly Negro and predominantly white colleges. *American Educational Research Journal,* 1970, vol. 7, no. 1, pp. 83-98.

The authors examine the relationship between the academic achievement of seniors on the Graduate Record Examination (GRE) and the scholastic aptitude of entering freshmen for students at predominantly black and predominantly white colleges. Seven colleges of each type were matched according to purpose, type of control, and ability level of students. The results were interpreted to indicate that neither group of colleges was any more or less effective in student academic growth as measured by the GRE test. That is, at the same aptitude level there was no indication that students are likely to learn more at either type of institution. The authors note that this particular group of colleges is not representative of predominantly white or predominantly black colleges.

1066 CLARK, KENNETH B. *Dark ghetto: Dilemmas of social power.* New York: Harper & Row, 1965, 253 pp. $5.95.

In this highly regarded examination of the black ghetto, Clark analyzes the psychological fate of men confined to depressed areas with no access to economic and social mobility. The book grew out of Clark's own experiences during a 40-year residency in Harlem and his tenure as director of Harlem Youth Opportunities Unlimited (HARYOU). Specific chapters deal with the social dynamics, psychology, and pathology of the ghetto. Further chapters treat ghetto schools, the black power structure, and possible strategies for transformation of ghetto conditions. Clark's relatively moderate stance is apparent in his conclusion that "white and Negro must fight together for the rights of human beings — to make mistakes and aspire to human goals."

1067 CLARK, KENNETH B., AND PLOTKIN, LAWRENCE. *The Negro student at integrated colleges.* New York: National Scholarship Service Fund for Negro Students, 1963, 59 pp.

This well-known report gained a great deal of attention because it was one of the first reports to provide documentary evidence of success of black students at predominantly white colleges. A follow-up study of 1,278 students aided by the National Scholarship Service and Fund for Negro Students indicated that the gross dropout rate was about 33 percent. Various other types of information attested to the success of those students who did remain in college, and at that time the report provided particularly valuable information concerning the life of the black student on the white campus.

The report includes a variety of evaluations and implicit recommendations. Many were undoubtedly valuable in furthering the access and adjustment to higher education of subsequent groups of black students. Some interpretations, such as the conclusion that, "Scholastic Aptitude Test scores are not clearly associated with college grades," were not well founded and were contradicted by subsequent research (see 974).

1068 CLEAVER, ELDRIDGE. *Soul on ice.* New York: McGraw-Hill, 1968, 210 pp. $5.95; paperback (Dell) 95 cents.

This collection of essays and letters was written while Cleaver was an inmate of Folsom State Prison. It presents a dramatic personal portrait of black identification and struggle. The book is similar to the *Autobiography of Malcolm X* in its description of forces that shaped the author's life and attitudes, but different in its brilliant literary style and wealth of scathing cultural critique.

1069 COUNSELING PSYCHOLOGIST EDITORIAL BOARD. Black students in higher education. *Counseling Psychologist,* 1970, vol. 2, no. 1, 43 pp.

This issue of the *Counseling Psychologist* was sponsored by the American College Personnel Association and the Division of Counseling Psychology of the American Psychological Association. It contains essays by seven black Americans on significant aspects of black culture that relate to education. These include black pride, black life in a white university, white miseducation of blacks, and a black view of standardized tests. The collection should be very useful in improving awareness of black attitudes and culture.

1070 CRAMER, M. RICHARD, BOWERMAN, CHARLES E., AND CAMPBELL, ERNEST Q. *Social factors in educational achievement and aspirations among Negro adolescents.* Vol. I. *Demographic study.* Vol. II. *Survey study.* Chapel Hill, N. C.: Institute for Research in Social Science, University of North Carolina, 1966, Vol. I, 266 pp.; Vol. II, 384 pp. (Mimeographed)

This two-volume work analyzes social factors relating to educational achievement and goals of Negro adolescents. Volume I reports on a demographic study of certain correlates of educational performance in 11 southern states, with primary focus on whether the same variables predict performance for both Negroes and whites in the same way. The survey compared rates of school attendance, age-grade retardation, dropouts, and college entrance. Community characteristics found to be the best general predictors of the level of absolute Negro and white performance were median adult education, per-pupil expenditure, and population per household. The first two variables were found to have positive correlation with performance; household size was a negative correlate. The authors conclude that assumption of causality predicates the following recommendations: (1) raising the level of education among adults, (2) raising the level of school expenditures, and (3) encouraging programs for limiting family size.

Volume II reports on a questionnaire survey of 16,000 boys and girls in Alabama, Mississippi, North Carolina, and Virginia. The survey investigated relationships between several variables and educational plans. In general, the same factors were found to be related to educational planning for both races. Scholastic ability, academic commitment, and grades were strongly associated with aspiration. The strongest single variable in accounting for racial difference in aspiration derived from indexes of socioeconomic status.

1071 HARTNETT, RODNEY T. Differences in selected attitudes and college orientations between black students attending traditionally Negro and traditionally white institutions. *Sociology of Education,* 1970, vol. 43, pp. 419-436.

This study examined the characteristics of black students attending either integrated institutions or traditionally Negro colleges. The results indicated that black students entering integrated institutions have higher aptitude, are more independent, more likely to be liberal, and have higher educational aspirations than those entering predominantly Negro colleges. The author points out, however, that these differences are highly related to scholastic aptitude, and he suggests that the presence of activist black students on selective college campuses bears more than a coincidental relationship to admissions policy.

1072 JABLONSKY, ADELAIDE. Media for teaching Afro-American studies. *IRCD Bulletin,* 1970, vol. 6, nos. 1 & 2, 23 pp.

This report annotates a number of filmstrips and records designed for use in black studies programs. Each is described and reviewed briefly. Information is provided on how to order these and related materials from the ERIC Information Retrieval Center on the Disadvantaged (see 1456).

1073 KNOELL, DOROTHY M. *Black student potential. A summary of the study: People who need college.* Washington, D. C.: American Association of Junior Colleges, 1970, 78 pp. $2.

This excellent study is concerned with the educational aspirations of black youth in five major cities. The author prepared this condensed, nontechnical summary for general audiences. (See 850 for a more detailed annotation of the original technical report.)

1074 LANE, HUGH W. (MODERATOR) The black agenda for higher education. *College Board Review,* Spring 1969, no. 71, pp. 5-27.

This article records trenchant views of black education expressed by four black activist educators at a program session of the 1968 annual meeting of the College Board. Hugh Lane, president of the National Scholarship Service and Fund for Negro Students, served as moderator. Preston Wilcox, chairman of the National Association of Afro-American Education, stressed that the black agenda for higher education must not be a replica of the white agenda. Blacks do not want to be "wasps" and their education must promulgate a pride of identity, which can only be achieved if black people are in control of black education. Edgar Beckman, assistant professor of German at Wesleyan University, called for a black university whose "most comprehensive function will be generating the intellectual apparatus, the new values, concepts, and criteria, the models, the policies, and the procedural guidelines which must inform and support the black man's new perception of himself." Jeff Donaldson, a graduate art student at Northwestern University, notes the "almost total exclusion of African and Afro-American artistic materials from school and college curriculums," and stresses the need for art and knowledge that will serve the cause of the black struggle.

1075 MARSH, GEORGIA. Junior colleges and Negroes. *Southern Education Report,* 1968, vol. 4, no. 2, pp. 10-17.

This article describes the effect on Negro enrollments when Florida phased out its 10 remaining Negro junior colleges in 1964-65, in compliance with the

Civil Rights Act. The expected spurt in Negro enrollments did not materialize in the 26 predominantly white junior colleges; only 8 reported any increase, while 15 reported a drop in Negro enrollment. Lack of aggressive recruitment, the Negro student's fear of failure, and failures of colleges to supply relevant programs or to advertise the existence of such programs were suggested as deterrent factors. Miami-Dade Junior College is cited as one institution that did make significant and successful efforts to overcome these problems. Negro enrollment figures at this college showed a steady increase from 1965 to 1967, when the student body included 1,284 Negroes. Miami-Dade's recruitment program brought high school and junior high students and guidance counselors to their campus for orientation, and also sent out teams of student and college staff members to visit high schools.

1076 MORGAN, GORDON D. *The ghetto college student: A descriptive essay on college youth from the inner city.* ACT Monograph Three. Iowa City, Iowa: American College Testing Program, 1970, 64 pp. $3.

Using interviews with inner-city students as his prime data source, Morgan builds an essay describing some of the problems and conditions that influence the education of the ghetto student. The picture emerging from the interviews indicates that black students demand equal treatment from teachers and administrators and also demand a relevant education. The students voiced doubt and suspicion of the university's ability to meet the needs of black people. Morgan stresses the need for a philosophy of ghetto education and "toleration for departures from middle class values" in order to give the inner-city students a chance to succeed.

1077 PARSONS, TALCOTT, AND CLARK, KENNETH B. (EDS.) *The Negro American.* Boston: Houghton Mifflin, 1965, 1966, 781 pp. $10; paperback (Beacon) $3.95.

This collection of papers by 30 well-known civil rights leaders and scholars addresses itself to the black struggle for full equality with special attention to the contradictory realities of social need and political power. Individual chapters deal with historical factors as well as the social, economic, and personal consequences of American racial patterns. Further chapters discuss various sectors of society that are in the process of change and proposals for national policies on education and housing. The authors conclude by examining the status of the civil rights movement and the black man's identification with Africa, and present perspectives on integration and revolution.

1078 ROBINSON, ARMSTEAD L., FOSTER, CRAIG C., AND OGILVIE, DONALD H. *Black studies in the university: A symposium.* New Haven, Conn.: Yale University Press, 1969, 231 pp. $1.95.

This volume records the Symposium on the Afro-American Experience sponsored by the Black Student Alliance at Yale University in May 1968. It is addressed to the intellectual, political, and social issues involved in the establishment of an Afro-American program. Included are papers on the intellectual validity of the Afro-American experience, black philosophy as an organizing principle for an Afro-American studies curriculum, a black perspective for a social science curriculum, the establishment of a funded Center for the Study of the Black Experience, and relations between the university and the surrounding community. The final draft of the program adopted by Yale in December 1968 is reproduced in the appendix.

1079 U.S. BUREAU OF LABOR STATISTICS, AND U.S. BUREAU OF THE CENSUS. *The social and economic status of Negroes in the United States 1969.* Current Population Reports, Series P-23, No. 29. Washington, D. C.: Government Printing Office, 1970, 96 pp. $1.

This report, prepared jointly by the Bureau of the Census and the Bureau of

Labor Statistics, is the third in a series of statistical reports about the social and economic condition of the Negro population of the United States. Current data are presented in tables showing the changes that have taken place in income, employment, education, housing, health, and other major aspects of life.

Negroes have continued to make gains in their level of living; however, they are still quite disadvantaged compared with white Americans in terms of educational and occupational attainment. Negro family income reached an average (median) of $5,400 in 1968, about double the median at the end of World War II. However, this was only 60 percent of the white family median of $8,900, and despite the gains of the past few years, the movement toward income equality is still very slow.

There has been a marked increase in school enrollment among Negroes, particularly the very young (ages three to four) and those at the college level. The percent of Negro men 25 to 34 years old completing four or more years of college has increased from 3.9 percent to 7.6 percent between 1960 and 1969. High school completion for Negro men in the 25- to 29-year bracket rose from 36 percent in 1960 to 60 percent in 1969.

About three-fourths of the total growth in the Negro population since 1960 has occurred in the central cities of the metropolitan areas. As a result, 55 percent of the total Negro population now resides in central cities compared with 26 percent of the white population.

1080 WILLINGHAM, WARREN W. *Admission of minority students in Midwestern colleges.* Higher Education Surveys, Report No. 1. New York: College Entrance Examination Board, 1970, 27 pp.

This is the first of a series of regional surveys on current problems of higher education designed by the College Board to close the customary time lag between collection of data and publication of results. This study deals with the extent of involvement of 129 midwestern four-year institutions in recruiting and enrolling minority freshmen. The findings indicated that three out of five institutions were working actively to enroll minority students, using special recruitment methods involving minority staff and students, special programs, and direct contact with schools. Financial support was found to be an overriding concern, since 41 percent of minority students required full financial aid, as contrasted with 13 percent of the total incoming freshmen. The respondents reported that seven out of ten minority freshmen returned the following year.

11.5—OTHER MINORITY / POVERTY STUDENTS. There are, of course, an almost indefinite number of minority/poverty groups that could be studied from the standpoint of access to higher education, but groups other than blacks and urban students have received relatively little attention. This is partly because some minority groups do not have serious access problems, but also because some groups seem to blend into the background and lack social cohesion and identification. For example, there is very little literature on access problems of poor whites as a group.

There is one group of whites, however—those living in rural areas—that are frequently poor and have received close attention for quite some time (see 1093). Another much smaller but important minority that frequently lives in rural areas is the American Indian. An extensive study of the education of Indian youth has recently been completed (1092).

Americans of Spanish heritage constitute a large and diverse minority group with special problems. These include large numbers of Mexican Americans in the West and the Southwest, a substantial population of Puerto Ricans in a few major cities, and a significant Cuban population in the greater Miami area. These Spanish-language groups share the access problems of any poor minority (see 1085 and 1090); there is also the additional complication of bilingualism.

1081 ANDERSON, JAMES G., AND JOHNSON, WILLIAM H. Stability and change among three generations of Mexican-Americans: Factors affecting achievement. *American Educational Research Journal*, 1971, vol. 8, pp. 285-309.

This survey explored characteristics of Mexican American families that have differential effect on school achievement. A stratified sample included Mexican Americans from several generations. The persistence of Spanish as the major language spoken in the home, and the lack of improvement in socioeconomic and educational level of parents all act to maintain a substantial gap between Mexican American families and other families even after three generations. Mexican American families seemed to value formal education just as much as did other families in the sample. In comparison with other students, Mexican Americans were found to do equally well in mathematics, but not as well in English—an understandable outcome of bilingualism in the home. The authors stress their finding that a favorable self-image is especially important to the student's success in both English and mathematics.

1082 BARRIOS, ERNIE (ED.) *Bibliografía de Aztlán (An annotated chicano bibliography)*. San Diego, Calif.: Centro de Estudios Chicanos Publications, San Diego State College, 1971, 147 pp. $3.95. (Mimeographed)

This excellent and extensive annotated bibliography of literature dealing with Chicanos is intended to help the Chicano develop a positive self-identity. The well-written annotations include recommendations on how the materials can be most effectively utilized. However, the user may be hampered by the lack of introductions to the individual chapters, which list 12 areas including contemporary Chicano history, educational materials, history of Mexico, political science, and sociology. There is a short overall introduction presented in both Spanish and English tracing the historically negative approach of Anglo-American writers in presenting the Chicano story.

1083 BERRY, BREWTON. *The education of the American Indians; a survey of the literature*. 1968 (Available from ERIC, No. ED 026 545)

This survey of the literature of the American Indian covers a number of topics: (1) the measurement of intelligence, (2) the effects of cultural deprivation, (3) language barriers, (4) the school environment, and (5) the Indian college student. An extensive bibliography is included.

1084 BURCHINAL, LEE G. (ED.) *Rural youth in crisis: Facts, myths, and social change*. Washington, D. C.: Government Printing Office, 1965, 401 pp. $1.25.

This extensive collection of papers was prepared by a number of scholars for the National Committee for Children and Youth. It includes sections on the nature of the rural community, the physical and mental health of rural youth, and juvenile delinquency in rural areas. A section on rural education documents the educational status of youth in rural areas, describes the educational and occupational aspirations of these youths, and describes the special character of educational problems in rural areas. The report is primarily narrative; it contains a number of references, but relatively little quantitative information.

1085 CARTER, THOMAS P. *Mexican Americans in school: A history of educational neglect*. New York: College Entrance Examination Board, 1970, 235 pp. $4.

This study examines educational problems of Mexican Americans in the southwestern states. The author visited over 250 schools, educators, and special projects. Although he stresses the need for more data before anything but tentative conclusions can be drawn, Carter does discuss three interrelated factors that influence the Mexican American child during his school years. These are: (1) the nature of the complex system of subcultures in which he grows up, (2) the quality of the education that is available to him, and (3) the nature of the local society and the opportunity that it affords the minority group. He calls for innovations that will make school a relevant, exciting, and significant experience for these children, starting with the elimination of rote teaching, rigid curriculums, biased teachers, and an overstressing of middle-class norms.

1086 EAST SIDE UNION HIGH SCHOOL DISTRICT. *1969 follow-up study of dropouts and graduates of 1962-63 and 1964-65 with special reference to problems encountered by Mexican-American leavers.* San Jose, Calif.: East Side Union High School District, 1969, 46 pp. Free.

This study is of special interest for its information on the educational patterns and attitudes of Mexican American dropouts. The percentage of Mexican Americans enrolled in this school district remained stable—around 30 percent—over the 10-year period 1956-1966. Although progress has been made in the number who stay and graduate, the dropout rate is still a major problem for these students. The recommendations for helping the Mexican American youth seem valuable, down-to-earth, and applicable to other minority groups.

1087 EGERTON, JOHN. *Cubans in Miami: A third dimension in racial and cultural relations.* Nashville, Tenn.: Race Relations Information Center, 1969, 26 pp.

This brief report gives a compelling and personal account of the 400,000 Cuban citizens who have taken refuge in the United States during the 1960s. A quarter of a million now live in the greater Miami area and make up 20 percent of that county's population. With case histories and depth reporting the author captures the personal drama and social impact of this substantial new minority and its special problems.

1088 FISHMAN, JOSHUA A., COOPER, ROBERT L., MA, ROXANA, ET AL. *Bilingualism in the barrio: The measurement and description of language dominance in bilinguals.* Washington, D. C.: Bureau of Research, U.S. Office of Education, 1968, 2 vols. (Mimeographed)

This pathbreaking study deals with the measurement and description of bilingual populations. The goal of the researchers was to study a small network of bilinguals and then to develop methods for studying widespread and stable bilingualism in large and complex social environments. The authors derived a variety of instruments and methods for measurement of bilingualism from the disciplines of psychology, sociology, and linguistics.

These techniques were administered in 28 studies of Spanish-English bilinguals living in a Puerto Rican neighborhood in New Jersey in order to assess the relationship between these measures and their relative utility as predictors of four proficiency variables.

Results of the study stressed the need for an interdisciplinary approach to the study on bilingualism. The study dramatizes the controlling effects of bilingualism on social behavior, educational aspiration, and personal identification.

1089 GLAZER, NATHAN, AND MOYNIHAN, DANIEL PATRICK. *Beyond the melting pot: The Negroes, Puerto Ricans, Jews, Italians, and the Irish of New York City.* (2nd ed.) Cambridge: Massachusetts Institute of Technology Press, 1970, 363 pp. $10; paperback $1.95.

Written in 1963, this book is a perceptive inquiry into the dynamics of life in New York City and the centrality of ethnic heritage. The volume concentrates on the role of the "old stock" and the Negroes, Puerto Ricans, Jews, Italians, and Irish. Many other ethnic minorities, such as Greeks, Chinese, and Latin

Americans are also treated briefly. The authors engagingly discuss each group's history, struggles, religion, politics, interaction with other groups, and current status. This edition contains an added 90-page "view from 1970."

Contrary to some expectations, the authors point out that total assimilation, i.e., "the melting pot" has not yet been realized. Immigrant groups do not maintain old-country characteristics, but replace them with common experiences as "Italian-Americans" or "Irish-Americans," and thus ethnicity has remained important. Even though the national aspect of ethnicity has rarely survived significantly beyond the third generation, religious and racial aspects have become increasingly important. This volume has been highly praised as one of the most insightful inquiries into American minorities. Its candor is refreshing.

1090 GREBLER, LEO, MOORE, JOAN W., AND GUZMAN, RALPH C. *The Mexican-American people: The nation's second largest minority.* New York: Macmillan, 1970, 777 pp. $14.95.

This comprehensive volume is the result of a four-year interdisciplinary study of the socioeconomic position of the nation's second largest minority. A wealth of original research material gathered from numerous field tours, interviews, and special reports is analyzed in comparison with the experience of other minority groups. Each section of the book is the result of a group of studies with a specific focus: Parts I and II describe the setting and historical background, the environment of the Southwest, and the patterns of immigration, work, and settlement. Part III details socioeconomic conditions and includes data on population patterns, education and income, job opportunity, and housing segregation. Part IV examines the relationship between the individual and the social system, social structure, and the tenacity of ethnic culture. Part V is especially interesting as it investigates the role of the church as an agency of socialization and interethnic contact. Part VI concentrates on the effort of Mexican Americans to influence their environment through the political process.

The authors conclude that Mexican Americans are demonstrating a growing potential for greater participation in the larger society. Findings indicated increasing internal diversity, and documented strong generational, cultural, and political differentiation. The authors suggest that this diversity as well as the previously underrated assimilative potential and the rapid urbanization of the group have altered the minority's relationship to society. This process has become clear through changing attitudes and more dramatically through increasing militancy among the youth. The volume concludes with recommendations for assistance necessary to aid the Mexican American community in meeting the challenge of full participation in the American system.

1091 HALLER, ARCHIBALD, O. Education and the occupational achievement process, in President's National Advisory Commission on Rural Poverty, *Rural poverty in the United States.* Washington, D. C.: Government Printing Office, 1968, pp. 149-169.

The gap in educational achievement between the population as a whole and the rural South and Southwest is postulated as the main mechanism limiting occupational achievement. In analyzing the social psychological factors affecting low achievement in rural groups, the author designates ability, socioeconomic status, and the influence of "significant others" as key variables. More research is needed in learning how to identify who the "significant others" are and how they influence individual and occupational decision-making. In the middle of his study the author "discovered" the importance of the self-concept as it relates to educational aspiration. Consequently he puts special stress on identifying what educators call underachievers and recommends that at least three educational achievement variables should be measured at all age levels — grades, standardized achievement test scores, and school continuation.

1092 HAVIGHURST, ROBERT J. *The education of Indian children and youth: Summary report and recommendations.* Series IV, No. 6. Minneapolis, Minn.: Center for Urban and Regional Affairs, University of Minnesota, 1970, 65 pp. $1.

This summary report is part of a massive National Study of American Indian Education undertaken during 1967-70 to provide government agencies and Indian leadership with baseline information for fund allocation and educational planning. Geographical isolation, extreme poverty, the Indian tribal culture, the public versus federal Indian boarding schools, and the growth of urban Indian population are discussed in this report. The report recommends greater involvement of Indian leadership in responsibility for education of Indian children, a privately financed Commission on Indian Education, and substantial revision of curriculum to include Indian language and culture. It also suggests that boarding schools for elementary school age children be replaced as far as possible by day schools serving nutritious meals. The final reports of research conducted in Indian communities will be available from the ERIC Clearinghouse at New Mexico State University, Las Cruces. This report includes basic information about the national study, and gives a description of the research papers.

1093 PRESIDENT'S NATIONAL ADVISORY COMMISSION ON RURAL POVERTY. *Rural poverty in the United States.* Washington, D. C.: Government Printing Office, 1968, 601 pp. $5.75.

This comprehensive collection of research reports provided background information for *The People Left Behind*—recommendations submitted to the President by the National Advisory Commission on Rural Poverty. They represent an important contribution to understanding the problems of rural poverty and provide insights toward possible solutions. Topics include the interrelationships between rural and urban America, the problems of migration and assimilation in urban centers, health care, family planning, and the economics of poverty. The chapter on education is reviewed separately (see 1091).

IV. *Access Agents*

SECTION 12: ORGANIZATIONS

There are many types of organizations that serve an important role in mediating the access process. They may serve this function either through the activities and programs of the organization or through the work of individual professionals who identify with the organization. The actual functions organizations serve vary widely but they tend to fall into the general categories of research, program administration, or forum activities such as professional meetings and other forms of communication.

Many of these formal organizations have considerable influence that is in some sense apart from that of the teaching institutions. One should not mistakenly assume, however, that there are no other seats of power in determining national policy. Some of the most important are not represented here because their life is too temporary or not readily open to public scrutiny in the same way that one can describe a professional association, research center, etc. These include legislative committees, pressure groups in Washington, public media, inner circles in the executive branch, informal establishment groups, and transitory manifestations of "people power."

These quasi groups are extremely important in determining the major thrust of legislation, appropriations, and programs that affect millions of people. At the same time, the influence of these informal groups operates within the bounds of existing organizations, programs, professional affairs, and political realities of the time. These influential organizations are annotated in the following sections.

12.1 – *ASSOCIATIONS*. These are mostly professional associations and associations of institutions. Several are not actually membership-based but fit better in this category than elsewhere. The associations are important because they are frequently near the cutting edge of ideas and new developments. Several of these organizations sponsor programs that play a major role in access to higher education. They are an important source of publications and information concerning programs, recent research, and the status of current problems.

There are innumerable associations that have some relationship to the access process. The ones included here either play a major role or they represent the interest of special groups of students or institutions. *The Encyclopedia of Associations* gives information on more than 13,000 associations in the United States.

1094 AMERICAN ACADEMY OF ARTS AND SCIENCES, 280 Newton Street, Boston, Massachusetts 02146. (617) 522-2400.

The American Academy of Arts and Sciences is a prestigious society of scholars founded in 1780. The scope of its interests is very broad – promoting knowledge and research in "every art and science which may tend to advance the interest, honor, dignity, and happiness of a free, independent, and virtuous people." The academy awards highly respected honors, sponsors a variety of educational activities, provides funds for research projects, holds an annual meeting, and produces several publications. Its journal *Daedalus* frequently publishes excellent issues on various topics broadly related to access to higher education.
Annual meeting: Second week in May
Newsletter: *AAAS Bulletin* (8 per year)
Journal: *Daedalus* (1317)
Informational document: *Records of the Academy* (annual)

1095 AMERICAN ASSOCIATION FOR HIGHER EDUCATION, One Dupont Circle, N. W., Washington, D. C. 20036. (202) 293-6440.

The American Association for Higher Education is more than 100 years old. It was formerly part of the National Education Association (1128) but is now an independent group of faculty members, administrators, trustees, and graduate students from all types of institutions. Believing that matters such as the teaching-learning process, decision-making, academic freedom, economic representation, and institutional goals are not separate interests but common interests that can best be served by a coming together of all who share them, AAHE seeks to provide this opportunity. The organization represents its members' interests through publications, conferences, projects dealing with current issues, and liaison with other national organizations and policy groups.
Annual meeting: March

Newsletter: *College and University Bulletin* (1357)
Journal: *Journal of Higher Education* (1327)
Informational document: *Invitation to Membership in the American Association for Higher Education*
Special annual reports:
  Current Issues in Higher Education (1431)
  A.A.H.E. Bibliography on Higher Education (1477)

1096 AMERICAN ASSOCIATION OF COLLEGIATE REGISTRARS AND ADMISSIONS OFFICERS, One Dupont Circle, N. W., Washington, D. C. 20036. (202) 293-6230.

The American Association of Collegiate Registrars and Admissions Officers was established in 1910. It is composed of over 1,700 institutions with some 5,000 member representatives. AACRAO emphasizes the advancement of higher education and the enhancement of professional growth in offices of admissions, records and registration, and related functions. To accomplish its purposes the association holds an annual meeting, maintains a national office to provide continuing service, publishes a professional journal, conducts research projects, and establishes committees to study current problems in education.
Annual meeting: April
Newsletter: *Newsletter* (1383) (for members only)
Journal: *College and University* (1314)
Informational document: *AACRAO*

1097 AMERICAN ASSOCIATION OF JUNIOR COLLEGES, One Dupont Circle, N. W., Washington, D. C. 20036. (202) 293-7050.

The American Association of Junior Colleges, established in 1920, is a nonprofit organization composed of over 825 member institutions plus a number of independent individuals and associations. Its purpose is to represent the interests and stimulate professional development of American two-year institutions. Frequent workshops, conferences, and seminars, as well as consultant and information services, are implemented by various commissions coordinated by the Council on Research and Service. These are directed especially toward improvement of teaching, curriculum, administration, student guidance services, and communication with local, state, and national communities. AAJC has a very active publications program (1485) directed particularly to problems of planning and organizing new colleges.
Annual meeting: February
Newsletters:
  Occupational Education Bulletin (1387)
  Junior College Research Review (ERIC) (1376)
  PR Exchange
  Awareness (6 per year)
  Community Service
  National Council of Independent Junior Colleges
Journal: *Junior College Journal* (1332)
Informational document: Annual report
Other: Numerous special reports covering a wide range of topics from planning to administration to curriculum

1098 AMERICAN ASSOCIATION OF STATE COLLEGES AND UNIVERSITIES, One Dupont Circle, N. W., Washington, D. C. 20036. (202) 293-7070.

The American Association of State Colleges and Universities was established in 1961, having grown out of organizations dating back to 1915. It acts as a vehicle for coordinated action and research programs, a clearinghouse for information, a liaison with federal departments and programs, and a cooperative mechanism through which its 265 member institutions work on problems of common interest. AASCU's Committee on Urban Affairs carries on projects whereby urban institutions can help to meet the needs of disadvantaged youth,

AASCU has a close working relationship with the National Association of State Universities and Land-Grant Colleges (1121).
Annual meeting: November
Newsletters:
  MEMO (1379)
  Urban Affairs Newsletter (1394)
Informational document: *AASCU*

1099 AMERICAN ASSOCIATION OF UNIVERSITY PROFESSORS, One Dupont Circle, Suite 500, Washington, D. C. 20036. (202) 466-8050.

The American Association of University Professors was founded in 1915 to serve the interests of teachers and research scholars. AAUP is now the largest organization in higher education. It has more than 90,000 members, 1,250 chapters, 45 state and regional conferences, and a national staff of 60. Major concerns of the AAUP include: defending academic freedom and tenure, developing the faculty role in academic government, representing economic and other professional interests, shaping federal and state relations to higher education, upholding professional responsibilities, and aiding junior colleges and developing institutions.
Annual meeting: Spring
Newsletter: *Academe* (1346)
Journal: *AAUP Bulletin* (1303)
Informational document: *A Special Invitation to Prospective Members*

1100 AMERICAN ASSOCIATION OF UNIVERSITY WOMEN, 2401 Virginia Avenue, N. W., Washington, D. C. 20037. (202) 338-4300.

The American Association of University Women, founded in 1882, is a large and politically influential organization composed of women graduates of AAUW-qualified colleges. It conducts a study-action program in four topics selected in alternate academic years and organizes implementation committees for each topic. AAUW annually awards graduate fellowships to nearly 100 women scholars. About half the fellowships are awarded to women from other countries for study in the United States. In 1958 the AAUW Educational Foundation was established to conduct research and educational projects, and provide occasional reports and monographs.
Biennial meeting: June
Journal: *AAUW Journal* (1304)
Informational document: *AAUW: What It Is*

1101 AMERICAN COLLEGE TESTING PROGRAM, P. O. Box 168, Iowa City, Iowa 52240. (319) 351-4470.

The American College Testing Program was established in 1959. ACT collects, analyzes, and reports information for use in educational planning by college-bound students, their high schools, and colleges. The program has emphasized measuring a student's academic and nonacademic potential (1218) and has maintained an active research program (1155). ACT also operates research and special reporting services for colleges (1217), financial aid services (1215), a career-planning profile system (1234), and maintains field offices to assist schools and colleges in using ACT data and services.
Meetings: Various workshops and seminars
Newsletter: *ACTivity* (1347)
Informational documents:
  The American College Testing Program
  ACT and the Two-year College
  Using ACT on the Campus
  Annual report

1102 AMERICAN COUNCIL ON EDUCATION, One Dupont Circle, N. W., Washington, D. C. 20036. (202) 833-4700.

The American Council on Education, established in 1918, is a council of 215 national and regional education associations, 1,363 higher education institutions, and 83 affiliated institutions and organizations. It works for the establishment and improvement of educational standards, policies, and procedures. The council investigates educational problems of general interest and enlists appropriate agencies to solve such problems; stimulates experimental activities by institutions and groups of institutions; keeps in touch with pending legislation affecting educational matters; acts in a liaison capacity between educational institutions and agencies of the federal government; and through its publications, makes available to educators and the general public widely used handbooks, informational reports, and volumes of critical analyses of social and educational problems. For many years ACE has been a very influential organization in higher education. It has an unusually strong publications program and has recently developed a dynamic research program (1156) on student development.

Annual meeting: October
Newsletters:
   Higher Education and National Affairs (1373)
   Report on Questionnaires (12 per year)
Journal: *Educational Record* (1320)
Informational document: *A Brief Statement of Programs and Activities*

1103 AMERICAN ECONOMIC ASSOCIATION, 1313 21st Avenue South, Nashville, Tennessee 37212.

The American Economic Association promotes economic research, publishes economic monographs, and encourages "perfect freedom in all economic discussion." Its membership of 18,000 comprises about 45 percent from higher education, 35 percent from private business and industry, and 14 percent from federal, state, and local governments. The remainder are from nonprofit organizations or are self-employed. AEA has published several series of monographs on special economic topics.

Annual meeting: December
Journals:
   The American Economic Review (1507)
   Journal of Economic Literature (4 per year)

1104 AMERICAN EDUCATIONAL RESEARCH ASSOCIATION, 1126 Sixteenth Street, N. W., Washington, D. C. 20036. (202) 223-9485.

The American Educational Research Association has a membership of more than 10,000 researchers and administrators. In order to encourage and improve educational research and its application, AERA conducts research training sessions and annual conferences and also deploys task forces and special interest groups to work on current educational problems. Its eight divisions include administration, curriculum and objectives, instruction and learning, measurement and research methodology, counseling and human development, history and historiography, the social context of education, and school evaluation and program development. AERA became independent of the National Education Association (1128) in 1968. It has grown rapidly and has become the primary professional organization for educational researchers.

Annual meeting: Spring. Also, research training sessions
Newsletter: *Educational Researcher* (1364)
Journals:
   American Educational Research Journal (1306)
   Review of Educational Research (1343)
Informational document: *An Introduction to the Association*
Other:
   Encyclopedia of Educational Research (1466)
   Handbook of Research on Teaching (436)
   AERA Monograph Series on Curriculum Evaluation (six volumes now available)

Readings in Educational Research
Research in Teacher Education: A Symposium
Review of Research in Education (1973)

1105 AMERICAN PERSONNEL AND GUIDANCE ASSOCIATION, 1607 New Hampshire Avenue, N. W., Washington, D. C. 20009. (202) 483-4633.

The American Personnel and Guidance Association has a membership of 29,000 individuals. It was established in 1952 to serve its members and the public through programs designed to advance the broad educational aspects of guidance, counseling, and student personnel work. APGA is composed of eight divisions: American College Personnel Association, National Vocational Guidance Association, American School Counselor Association, Association for Measurement and Evaluation in Guidance, Association for Counselor Education and Supervision, Student Personnel Association for Teacher Education, National Employment Counselors Association, and American Rehabilitation Counseling Association. These divisions are individually quite active in sponsoring meetings, publications, and other activities relevant to their special interests. The Association also works through the Commission on Human Rights and the National Office on Non-White Concerns to increase opportunity for all individuals.

Meetings:
    National convention – spring
    Regional, state, and local meetings
Newsletter: *The Guidepost* (1372)
Journals:
    Personnel and Guidance Journal (1341)
    Other journals published by each division
Informational documents: Available on all eight divisions

1106 AMERICAN PSYCHOLOGICAL ASSOCIATION, 1200 Seventeenth Street, N. W., Washington, D. C. 20036. (202) 833-7600.

The American Psychological Association was founded in 1892 and has over 31,000 members. Its membership includes most of the qualified psychologists in the country. It is an important association not because it is especially involved with access to higher education as an organization, but because psychologists constitute by far the largest group of researchers working in the access area. APA comprises 31 divisions; those most closely related to access to higher education are: divisions 5 (evaluation and measurement), 15 (educational psychology), and 17 (counseling psychology).

Annual meeting: September
Newsletter: *APA Monitor* (monthly)
Journals: 14, including
    American Psychologist (1308)
    Journal of Counseling Psychology (1324)
    Journal of Educational Psychology (1326)

1107 AMERICAN SOCIOLOGICAL ASSOCIATION, 1722 N Street, N. W., Washington, D. C. 20036. (202) 833-3410.

The American Sociological Association was founded in 1905. It is the principal nationwide organization of sociologists with a membership of some 15,000. Its members are active researchers in several fields connected with access to higher education – particularly manpower utilization, the distribution of talent, and the special interests of various groups of students.

Annual meeting: August
Journals:
    American Sociological Review (1310)
    Sociology of Education (1344)
    Other journals are also published but do not directly relate to education
Informational document: *The American Sociological Association*

1108 AMERICAN VOCATIONAL ASSOCIATION, 1510 H Street, N. W., Washington, D. C. 20005. (202) 737-3722.

The American Vocational Association, founded in 1906, is a federation of state-affiliated associations with a membership of nearly 50,000 teachers, supervisors, administrators, and others interested in the development and improvement of vocational and practical arts education. AVA's divisions cover agriculture, business and office education, distributive education, home economics, industrial arts, trade and industrial education, technical education, guidance, health occupations, manpower development training, and research. Its areas of interest include industrial cooperative training programs, part-time classes for adults, supervisory and foreman training, technical training at subcollege levels, and occupational preparation at the secondary level. AVA members also work in career development and guidance programs. The association also works with major government agencies in the interest of vocational education.
Annual meeting: December
Newsletters:
  AVA Member-gram (1349)
  AVA Washington Letter (issued when needed)
  AVA Washington Desk (monthly)
Journal: *American Vocational Journal* (1311)
Informational document: Annual report

1109 ASSOCIATION FOR INSTITUTIONAL RESEARCH, James K. Morishima, Secretary, Director of Institutional Educational Research, University of Washington, Seattle, Washington 98195. (206) 543-2385.

The Association for Institutional Research is a professional association of over 900 institutional researchers and others interested in the field. It seeks to improve the operation of higher educational institutions by advancing institutional research. AIR provides the opportunity for the exchange of ideas and keeps members informed of new developments and techniques through its collections of papers, annotated bibliographies, and conventions. Management, planning, evaluation, and student development are areas of special continuing interest. The association grew out of the National Institutional Research Forum, established in 1960, and assumed its present character in 1965.
Annual meeting: May
Newsletter: *AIR Newsletter* (1348)
Informational document: *The Association for Institutional Research*
Other:
  Proceedings of annual meeting – various topics
  An Annotated Bibliography of Institutional Research (441)

1110 ASSOCIATION OF AMERICAN COLLEGES, 1818 R Street, N. W., Washington, D. C. 20009. (202) 265-3137.

The Association of American Colleges is a national organization of undergraduate colleges of liberal arts and sciences. It seeks to promote improvement in the quality of undergraduate education. Founded in 1915, its membership now comprises more than 850 public and private institutions. AAC has three standing commissions focused on major areas of concern to the undergraduate college: liberal learning, religion in higher education, and institutional affairs. The association's services include publications, annual meetings, research projects, and legislative and public information on issues relating to the areas of its concern.
Annual meeting: January
Journal: *Liberal Education* (1333)
Informational document: *Background on the Association of American Colleges*

1111 CENTER FOR URBAN EDUCATION, 105 Madison Avenue, New York, New York 10016. (212) 889-7277.

The Center for Urban Education is a nonprofit organization supported by the United States Office of Education and other funding agencies. Its main goal is to improve education for city children by promoting effective community involvement and improving the quality of teaching in urban school systems. CUE provides programs for both the urban school and the urban community. School programs include new instructional materials for early childhood education and elementary grades. Community programs offer training for those adults who are interested in assuming leadership in matters that concern both school and community.

Other CUE services include evaluation of urban programs, basic research and policy studies, and planning for school desegregation. The center maintains an extensive library on urban education that is open to the public. It organizes conferences and seminars and produces a variety of publications and films related to urban education.

Informational document: *Your CUE To Action*

1112 COLLEGE ENTRANCE EXAMINATION BOARD, 888 Seventh Avenue, New York, New York 10019. (212) 582-6210.

The College Entrance Examination Board, founded in 1900, is a nonprofit membership organization of more than 1,500 colleges and universities, secondary schools, urban school systems, and education associations. Representatives of the members serve on committees that consider the Board's programs and participate in the determination of its policies and activities. Many aspects of high school to college transition are included among its present programs: Admissions Testing Program (1219), Advanced Placement Program (1220), College Scholarship Service (1211), College-Level Examination Program (1222), Comparative Guidance and Placement Program (1225), Test of English as a Foreign Language (1232), Decision-Making Program (1238), and PSAT/NMSQT (1230). Through its various offices and with the affiliation of the Educational Testing Service (11·15), the Board carries on a wide variety of student and institutional services, research and development activities (1165), conferences and workshops, and an extensive publications program highly focused on problems of access to higher education.

Annual meeting: Fall
Also, colloquiums, regional conferences, seminars, training institutes, workshops
Newsletters:
College Board News
Financial Aid News (1368)
Journal: *College Board Review* (1315)
Informational documents:
Fact sheets on various programs
Numerous publications listed in catalog (1488)

1113 COLLEGE PLACEMENT COUNCIL, P. O. Box 2263, 65 East Elizabeth Avenue, Bethlehem, Pennsylvania 18001. (215) 868-1421.

The College Placement Council is the principal organization of college placement and recruitment personnel. It was created in 1956 by the eight regional College Placement Associations in the United States and Canada. CPC provides an informational link between 1,300 accredited four-year colleges and universities and 2,100 employers in business, government, and industry. Services include research, computerized placement, meetings and workshops, and publications. College Placement Services, Inc., an independent affiliated organization, provides placement assistance for predominantly Negro colleges.

Annual meeting: June
Newsletter: *Placement Perspective*
Journal: *Journal of College Placement* (1322)
Research reports: *Salary Survey,* provides beginning salary rates offered by employers to candidates in selected key curriculums at all degree levels

Special publications:
A Bibliography of Selected Research and Statistical Studies Pertaining to College Trained Manpower 1960-66
Supplement to the above bibliography
College Placement Annual (110 and 552)
Series of research monographs on post-college job attitudes, satisfactions, and turn-over (550)
Career Counseling and Placement in Higher Education
Manpower Resources of the Traditionally Black Colleges

1114 COUNCIL FOR THE ADVANCEMENT OF SMALL COLLEGES, One Dupont Circle, N. W., Suite 750, Washington, D. C. 20036. (202) 659-3795.

The Council for the Advancement of Small Colleges is the only national education association that serves solely the small, private, independent four-year colleges of liberal arts and sciences. It is a service organization that seeks to help its 100 member colleges (half are accredited) improve their educational and administrative processes. CASC implements its program through regional and national workshops, consultant services, research, publications, and federal representation. Current special projects include a series of seminars and institutes for the training of administrators and trustees, workshops on academic innovation, and proposal-writing seminars.
Annual meeting: March
Newsletters:
CASC Newsletter (1353)
Memos to the Membership (irregular)
Informational document: *The Council for the Advancement of Small Colleges*

1115 EDUCATIONAL TESTING SERVICE, Princeton, New Jersey 08540. (609) 921-9000.

Educational Testing Service was formed in 1947 when the Carnegie Foundation for the Advancement of Teaching, the American Council on Education (1102), and the College Entrance Examination Board (1112) decided to create a new agency to operate their existing testing programs and to serve as a national center for psychometric research and service. ETS develops and administers many testing programs including those of the College Board, the Graduate Record Examination Board, various professional schools, etc. ETS is especially well-known for its large and diverse research program (1167). It also publishes its own tests and carries on a number of programs designed to serve educational institutions at all levels. In 1970 ETS established the ERIC Clearinghouse on Tests, Measurement, and Evaluation (1454).
Meeting: Invitational Conference on Testing Problems—fall
Newsletters:
ETS Developments (1366)
Education Recaps (1363)
Research reports: ETS Research Bulletin (1401)
Informational document: Annual report
Other:
Numerous research reports
ETS Tests and Measurement Kit (414) describes all programs and services and includes information on topics in measurement

1116 NATIONAL ACADEMY OF EDUCATION, 723 University Avenue, Syracuse, New York 13210. (315) 477-8677.

The National Academy of Education was founded in 1965 by distinguished scholars "to create a forum which will set the highest standards for educational inquiry and discussion." A main function is to stimulate fruitful lines of research. The academy operates without governmental status or support. The current membership is comprised of outstanding university scholars who have made notable contributions to research on education. Activities of the academy include semiannual meetings for discussion of research and policy questions, task force studies leading to advisory reports and publications, programs of support to identify and encourage promising scholars of education at the early postdoctoral stage, and cooperation with the National Academy of Sciences in the joint NAS/NAE Committee on Basic Research in Education.

1117 NATIONAL ASSOCIATION FOR AFRO-AMERICAN EDUCATION, 68-72 East 131st Street, Harlem, New York 10037. (212) 690-7010.

The National Association for Afro-American Education is a clearinghouse for several national and local organizations concerned with the education of black students and their access to higher education. NAAAE maintains information about most black educational organizations in addition to other types of information. Some of the affiliated and related organizations include local AAAE organizations, Afram Associates (a private, nonprofit consultation firm), Students Organization for Black Unity (SOBU), United Negro College Fund (1133), National Scholarship Service and Fund for Negro Students (1130), and the Council on Education of the Congress of African People. NAAAE is currently working on a comprehensive directory of black educator organizations.

1118 NATIONAL ASSOCIATION FOR FOREIGN STUDENT AFFAIRS, 1860 Nineteenth Street, N. W., Washington, D. C. 20009. (202) 462-4811.

NAFSA is the major professional association for those engaged in the international educational exchange of students and scholars. Membership includes academic institutions and individual members located in colleges, universities, private organizations, business organizations, and community and governmental agencies.

NAFSA serves as a source of professional training, as a guide to standards of performance and programs, and as a spokesman for educational exchange programs. The association has several professional sections and commissions that represent special professional responsibilities and conduct conferences and workshops (e.g., foreign student advisers, teachers of English as a second language).

Annual meeting: April
Newsletter: *NAFSA Newsletter* (1380)
Informational document: *National Association for Foreign Student Affairs*

1119 NATIONAL ASSOCIATION OF COLLEGE ADMISSIONS COUNSELORS, 9933 Lawler Avenue, Skokie, Illinois 60076. (312) 676-0500.

The National Association of College Admissions Counselors, established in 1937, is composed of over 2,200 public and private secondary schools, higher education institutions, and educational organizations concerned with admissions and financial aid. The organization seeks to establish and maintain high professional standards in college admissions guidance and to develop and expand relationships among secondary schools and higher education institutions. NACAC has recently become active in attempting to increase minority opportunity through its member institutions. It also operates a nonprofit clearinghouse for college admissions named ASK US available to member colleges and to students seeking undergraduate college admission.

Annual meeting: Fall
   Also state, regional, and national workshops, seminars, and conferences
Newsletter: *National ACAC Newsletter* (1381)
Journal: *National ACAC Journal* (1337)
Informational document: *What Is National ACAC?*

1120 NATIONAL ASSOCIATION OF INDEPENDENT SCHOOLS, Four Liberty Square, Boston, Massachusetts 02109. (617) 542-1988.

Founded in 1962, the National Association of Independent Schools is the major service organization for independent elementary and secondary schools and associations. It sponsors research, some educational tests, a publications program, educational conferences and workshops, and a quarterly journal.

Annual meeting: March
Newsletter: *NAIS Report* (4 per year)
Journal: *The Independent School Bulletin* (4 per year)

1121 NATIONAL ASSOCIATION OF STATE UNIVERSITIES AND LAND-GRANT COLLEGES, One Dupont Circle, N. W., Washington, D. C. 20036. (202) 293-7120.

The National Association of State Universities and Land-Grant Colleges is composed of 118 major state universities and land-grant institutions. It provides consultation, cooperation, stimulation, and acts as a vehicle for united effort for member institutions. Its major activities include research, information distribution, soliciting support for public higher education and public Negro institutions, and conducting activities related to international programs of member institutions. The association endeavors to increase minority opportunity through its Office for Advancement of Public Negro Colleges (1131), and by its efforts to keep tuition at public institutions low. NASULGC, which works closely with the American Association of State Colleges and Universities (1098), evolved from several forerunner organizations dating back to the 1880s. It assumed its present character in 1963. The association prepares numerous reports on federal action and student finance, annual and periodic surveys, guidance materials, voluntary support, and information on public Negro colleges.

Annual meeting: November
Newsletters:
   The Circular Letter (1356)
   For Your Information (approximately 20 per year)
   International Letter (members only)
Informational document: *1971 Fact Book*

1122 NATIONAL ASSOCIATION OF STUDENT FINANCIAL AID ADMINISTRATORS, Richard Tombaugh, Director of Central Office, Purdue University, Lafayette, Indiana 47907. (317) 749-3676.

The National Association of Student Financial Aid Administrators was founded in 1969. It is made up of administrators and counselors of student financial aid and others concerned with aid support and administration. NASFAA attempts to promote and coordinate plans and programs for more effective student financial aid, to facilitate communication, and to serve as a national forum on financial aid matters. It recently established a national placement service.

Newsletter: *NASFAA Newsletter*
Journal: *Journal of Student Financial Aid* (1330)

1123 NATIONAL ASSOCIATION OF WOMEN DEANS AND COUNSELORS, 1201 Sixteenth Street, N. W., Washington, D. C. 20036. (202) 833-4256.

The National Association of Women Deans and Counselors, established in 1916, is a major professional organization for women holding positions in student personnel, guidance, and administration in colleges and secondary schools. Associated with the National Education Association (1128), NAWDC strives to improve personnel and guidance services with particular emphasis on the special needs of women. The 2,500 members are served through an annual meeting, summer workshops, a placement bureau, and publications.

Annual meeting: Spring
Newsletter: *NAWDC Newsletter* (irregular)
Journal: *Journal of the National Association of Women Deans and Counselors* (1331)

1124 NATIONAL CATHOLIC EDUCATIONAL ASSOCIATION, One Dupont Circle, Suite 350, Washington, D. C. 20036. (202) 293-5954.

The National Catholic Educational Association, founded in 1904, is the oldest and largest professional organization of Catholic educators in the United States. Its membership includes nearly 6,000 individuals and about 11,000 Catholic

schools. NCEA is concerned with the betterment of Catholic education from pre-school through graduate and continuing education. It conducts research, sponsors lecture series, participates in litigation affecting Catholic education, conducts regional conferences and workshops, and sponsors a publications program.
Annual meeting: Easter week
Journal: *Momentum* (5 per year)
Informational document: *The NCEA Platform*

1125 NATIONAL COALITION FOR RESEARCH ON WOMEN'S EDUCATION AND DEVELOPMENT, State University of New York at Stony Brook, Stony Brook, New York 11790.

The National Coalition for Research on Women's Education and Development is a membership corporation organized in 1971. Members are colleges, universities, and education agencies active in innovations in women's education and/or research pertinent to it. Its purpose is to stimulate, conduct, coordinate, and disseminate research on women's education and development. The Coalition's National Center is located at the State University of New York at Stony Brook.
Informational document: *Description of the National Coalition for Research on Women's Education and Development*

1126 NATIONAL COMMISSION ON ACCREDITING, One Dupont Circle, N. W., Washington, D. C. 20036. (202) 296-4196.

The National Commission on Accrediting is an independent educational agency supported by colleges and universities to improve the operation and effectiveness of accreditation in higher education. The commission grants recognition to qualified accrediting agencies, helps to improve accrediting standards and practices, fosters increased cooperation among accrediting agencies, recommends action concerning accreditation to its 1,400 member institutions, and carries on other activities related to accreditation. NCA is concerned with accreditation of colleges and universities, professional schools, junior colleges, and technical institutes. It recognizes nearly 40 accrediting agencies of professional schools and the following regional associations which grant general accreditation and carry on their own programs and activities.

Middle States Association of Colleges and Secondary Schools, 225 Broadway, New York, New York 10007.

North Central Association of Colleges and Secondary Schools, 5454 Lake Shore Drive, Chicago, Illinois 60615.

Southern Association of Colleges and Secondary Schools, 795 Peachtree Street, N. E., Atlanta, Georgia 30308.

New England Association of Colleges and Secondary Schools, 50 Beacon Street, Boston, Massachusetts 02108.

Northwest Association of Secondary and Higher Schools, 3731 University Way, N. E., 104, Seattle, Washington 98105.

Western Association of Schools and Colleges, Accrediting Commission for Senior Colleges, c/o Mills College, Oakland, California 94613.

Western Association of Schools and Colleges, Accrediting Commission for Junior Colleges, c/o Modesto Junior College, Modesto, California 95350.

Report series: *Procedures of Accrediting Education in the Professions: A Series of Reports* (529)
Informational documents:
Facts about the Commission
List of Recognized Accrediting Agencies
Annual report (522)

1127 NATIONAL COUNCIL ON MEASUREMENT IN EDUCATION, Irvin J. Lehmann, Secretary-Treasurer, Office of Evaluation Services, Michigan State University, East Lansing, Michigan 48823. (517) 355-1912.

The National Council on Measurement in Education seeks to improve measurement practices and techniques in the instructional setting. The membership consists of more than 2,000 individuals — mostly college instructors in measurement and other personnel in schools and research agencies who are concerned with measurement practice. It is the principal association primarily interested in applied educational measurement.

Annual meeting: Spring (held with American Educational Research Association, 1104)
Newsletters:
> *Measurement News* (1378)
> *NCME Newsletter*
> *Measurement in Education* (1377)

Journal: *Journal of Educational Measurement* (1325)

1128 NATIONAL EDUCATION ASSOCIATION, 1201 Sixteenth Street, N. W., Washington, D. C. 20036. (202) 223-9400.

The National Education Association, composed of over one million teachers, administrators, and specialists, works for better schools and for the improvement of the professional status of teachers. It is a large and complex parent organization consisting of 35 departments, national affiliates, and associated organizations including the American Association for Higher Education (1095) and the National Association of Women Deans and Counselors (1123). NEA produces numerous and varied educational materials, serves as a clearinghouse for ideas, provides a consultative service, and meets various needs of education through its departments, affiliates, associated organizations, and committees. While its activities have been traditionally focused on elementary and secondary education, in 1969 NEA created the National Higher Education Association to provide members at that level with personal and professional services. NHEA is comprised of the National Faculty Association of Community and Junior Colleges, the National Society of Professors, and the National Association of College and University Administrators.

Annual meeting: July
Newsletters:
> *NEA Reporter* (8 per year)
> *Higher Education Forum* (NHEA) (6 per year)

Journal: *Today's Education* (1345)
Informational document: *NEA Handbook*
Other: Produces over 500 new books, booklets, leaflets, filmstrips, slides, and other graphic communications media annually. See catalog (1492)

1129 NATIONAL HOME STUDY COUNCIL, 1601 Eighteenth Street, N. W., Washington, D. C. 20009. (202) 234-5100.

The National Home Study Council, established in 1926, is the standard-setting agency for private home study schools. Its independent accrediting commission was set up in 1955 and approved by the United States Office of Education in 1959 as a nationally recognized accrediting agency. It establishes educational, ethical, and business standards; examines and evaluates private home study schools in terms of these standards; accredits those that qualify; and supplies lists of accredited schools. NHSC attempts to progressively raise its standards, employing procedures similar to those of other educational accrediting agencies. At present over 150 schools and school divisions are accredited by NHSC.

Newsletter: *NHSC News* (1385)
Informational documents:
> *Directory of Accredited Private Home Study Schools*
> *Accredited Home Study Courses for Industry Training* (for companies interested in setting up a tuition refund program)
> *A Counselor's Guide to Home Study Training*

1130 NATIONAL SCHOLARSHIP SERVICE AND FUND FOR NEGRO STUDENTS, 1776 Broadway, New York, New York 10019. (212) 757-8100.

The National Scholarship Service Fund for Negro Students is the only national organization offering a free college advisory and referral service designed specifically for black high school juniors and seniors. No minimum test scores or grade averages are required of applicants. NSSFNS uses a computerized system to advise students (more than 16,000 in the class of 1970) of colleges most likely to grant them admission and financial aid. It sends information about the students to college admissions officers and carries on related activities facilitating the movement of black students from high school to college. NSSFNS also maintains a limited Supplementary Scholarship Fund for counselees (1214). More than 3,000 post-secondary institutions participate in the referral program.

Newsletter: *NSSFNS News*
Informational documents:
   What is NSSFNS?
   Right On With Education for Black Students!

1131 OFFICE FOR ADVANCEMENT OF PUBLIC NEGRO COLLEGES, National Association of State Universities and Land-Grant Colleges, 805 Peachtree Street, N. E., Suite 577, Atlanta, Georgia 30308. (404) 874-8073.

The National Association of State Universities and Land-Grant Colleges established the Office for Advancement of Public Negro Colleges in 1968. OAPNC gathers information about the nation's public Negro colleges, presents their case for general support to potential donors, and helps build development staffs at the institutions. Its services are available to all degree-granting public predominantly Negro institutions.

Newsletter: *Advancement Newsletter* (published periodically)
Informational document: *Public Negro Colleges: A Fact Book* (777)

1132 UNION FOR EXPERIMENTING COLLEGES AND UNIVERSITIES, Antioch College, Yellow Springs, Ohio 45387. (513) 767-7331.

The Union for Experimenting Colleges and Universities seeks to foster and encourage research and experimentation in higher education. Its members currently include about 20 innovative colleges and universities of diverse sizes and academic purposes. The central staff of UECU is housed at Antioch College, but the Union has future plans to develop three or four area centers for research and experimentation at member institutions. Programs of the union include: (1) Project Changeover, a series of summer workshops for college professors to develop innovative teaching; (2) Field Study Centers where students and faculty work together in off-campus settings on various problems of human and social needs; (3) University Without Walls, an undergraduate degree program providing highly individualized and flexible programs of learning for students of all ages (19 colleges and universities are participating in this program); (4) a graduate school of the union especially designed for those whose educational goals are not met by the usual PH.D. programs. UECU also was the main force behind the development of *Change Magazine* (1312).

Newsletter: *UECU Notes* (5-6 per year)

1133 UNITED NEGRO COLLEGE FUND, 55 East 52nd Street, New York, New York 10022. (212) 751-0700.

The United Negro College Fund represents a group of 36 predominantly Negro four-year colleges and universities that are private and accredited. UNCF solicits contributions and bequests, develops and administers educational programs of benefit to member institutions, and serves as a center for information concerning the higher education of Negroes. Since its establishment in 1944, it has contributed over $110 million to assist member colleges, providing funds for student aid, faculty salaries, teaching equipment and libraries, and continued development of educational programs.

Informational document: Packet of information concerning the purposes and activities of UNCF and information for applicants to member colleges

1134 URBAN COALITION, 1819 H Street, N. W., Washington, D. C. 20005. (202) 223-9500.

The Urban Coalition was formed in 1968 to enable social, political, and religious leaders to combine resources and efforts in combatting urban problems. Rather than operate its own programs, the national office helps communities to organize local coalitions and to strengthen and form programs especially suited to the needs of the particular area. Special concerns include employment, education, housing, economic development, youth, the aging, and communications; educationally related activities include provisions for basic education, job training, work-study and compensatory programs, anti-illiteracy programs, elimination of financial barriers to higher education, and student motivation. The Urban Coalition Action Council (a separate organization) handles all legislative activities.

Informational document: *An Urban Coalition in Your Community*

12.2—*AGENCIES*. There are a limited number of major federal (and quasi-public) agencies that play a very important role in access to higher education. Their functions include the administration of major programs, data collection and reporting, and funding federally supported activities. They have an important impact on the access process because they reflect major activities and also influence the development of such activities.

There are countless such agencies from the local to the federal level. The few included here for the most part are very large and have many subdivisions. They provide most of the routinely collected facts and statistics reported in section 14.4. The *Directory of Information Resources in the United States: Federal Government* describes a large number of federal agencies.

1135 INSTITUTE OF INTERNATIONAL EDUCATION, 809 United Nations Plaza, New York, New York 10017. (212) 867-0400.

The Institute of International Education is a private nonprofit agency that has worked for the dissemination of ideas, knowledge, and skills among nations through the exchange of students, scholars, artists, and leaders, and has assisted in developing educational programs to serve the economic, political, and social needs of new and emerging nations. Its academic exchange programs include more than 110 countries and involve about 1,300 American students and 6,000 foreign students annually. The IIE also serves as an information clearinghouse and provides consulting services on all phases of educational and cultural exchange. It publishes numerous studies, directories, handbooks, guides, surveys, and informational brochures and is an especially good source for material dealing with the movement of students to and from the United States. It also conducts research, workshops, and conferences and maintains a reference library on United States and foreign educational systems and institutions.

Informational document: *This Is IIE*

1136 NATIONAL SCIENCE FOUNDATION, 1800 G Street, N. W., Washington, D. C. 20550. (202) 655-4000.

The National Science Foundation is a federal agency for advancing all fields of science in the United States. It does this primarily through supporting research, encouraging improvements in science education, and fostering scientific information exchange. NSF itself does not conduct research or carry out educational projects, but supports research primarily through providing colleges with funds for upgrading research and science education activities and for equipment and specialized facilities. NSF also encourages curriculum modernization and helps scholars, science teachers, and students to obtain advanced or supplementary training.

Informational document: *Guide to Programs*
Also, various leaflets describing individual NSF programs in detail

1137 OFFICE OF ECONOMIC OPPORTUNITY, 1200 Nineteenth Street, N. W., Washington, D. C. 20506. (202) 254-5840.

The Office of Economic Opportunity was created in 1964 under the Economic Opportunity Act (1290) to bring together all levels of government in a unified, intensified approach "to eliminate the paradox of poverty in the midst of plenty in this Nation." OEO has attempted to establish educational and training programs to help those in poverty gain access to more productive living through the offices of legal services, VISTA, health affairs, operations, and program development; through the community action agencies; and through various special emphasis programs. OEO has initiated numerous innovative programs including Upward Bound (1272), Head Start, Neighborhood Youth Corps, Job Corps (1287), Follow Through, and Mainstream. As these programs have moved from the experimental to a more permanent stage, other agencies have taken up their administration.

1138 ORGANIZATION FOR ECONOMIC COOPERATION AND DEVELOPMENT, OECD Publications Center, Suite 1207, 1750 Pennsylvania Avenue, N. W., Washington, D. C. 20006. (202) 298-8755. Main Headquarters, 2 rue André-Pascal, 75 Paris 16, France.

The Organization for Economic Cooperation and Development includes 21 European and North American countries plus Japan. It strives to promote economic growth, employment, higher living standards, and financial stability in member countries; to contribute to economic expansion of developing nations; and to further multilateral, nondiscriminatory expansion of world trade. Member countries work together in committees covering various aspects of economic activity, including such fields as education, manpower, and social affairs. OECD provides a forum for working out policies through shared ideas and makes economic knowledge available through its publication of factual findings and policy recommendations (1493). The OECD Information Service at headquarters provides further answers to general or specific inquiries from public media and private individuals. This agency has sponsored and published some of the most advanced work on educational innovation and planning in relation to manpower resources and needs. A publications catalog is free on request (1493).

Informational document: OECD: History, Aims and Structure

1139 UNITED NATIONS EDUCATIONAL, SCIENTIFIC AND CULTURAL ORGANIZATION, The U.S. National Commission for Unesco, U.S. Department of State, Washington, D. C. 20520. (202) 655-4000. Main Headquarters, Place de Fontenoy, Paris 7, France.

Unesco is an agency of the United Nations and includes 125 member countries. Its purpose is to contribute to peace and security by promoting collaboration among the nations through education, science, and culture. Its three main functions include international intellectual cooperation, assistance to member countries, and promotion of peace and human rights and mutual understanding among peoples. These functions are carried out through conferences, clearinghouse services, research on racial problems, and publications. One of its primary concerns in recent years has been the extension of higher educational opportunity throughout the world. See 812, 833, and 1054 for annotations of its access studies, and 1496 for information on the catalog of Unesco educational publications.

Informational document: *Unesco: What It Is, What It Does, How It Works*

1140 U.S. BUREAU OF THE CENSUS, U.S. Department of Commerce, Washington, D. C. 20233. (202) 735-2000.

The Census Bureau collects a variety of demographic and economic data in areas such as agriculture, business, foreign trade, industry, population, housing, governments, and transportation. The bureau carries out quinquennial and decennial censuses, monthly and annual surveys, and other periodic inquiries. Educational information is gathered primarily through the decennial censuses and monthly population surveys. The types of educational information collected include data on school enrollment, educational attainment, characteristics of male college graduates, and annual proportion of high school graduates matriculating at college. Series of the *Current Population Reports* (1418) of particular interest to educational researchers and practitioners are P-20 (Population Characteristics), P-23 (Special Studies), P-25 (Population Estimates and Projections), and P-60 (Consumer Income). See 1448 for an annotation of the bureau as a data source.
Informational documents:
  Bureau of the Census *Catalog* (1497)
  1970 Census Users' Guide (1482)

1141 U.S. COMMISSION ON CIVIL RIGHTS, 801 Nineteenth Street, N. W., Washington, D. C. 20425. (202) 382-1228.

The commission is an independent, bipartisan fact-finding agency established by Congress in 1957 as part of the executive branch. It investigates violations of civil rights; serves as a clearinghouse for civil rights information; analyzes federal laws and policies with respect to denials of equal protection; and submits reports of its activities, findings, and recommendations to the President and Congress. Its activities cut across several fields, including education and matters of equal access. Its primary purpose is to make the public and policy-makers aware of what is actually occurring throughout the country; it achieves this purpose partly by means of its journal, *Civil Rights Digest* (1313), its various monographs, such as *Racism in America,* and its reference collection available for on-site use or interlibrary loan. The commission is not adequately staffed to answer specific questions, but it does respond to requests for materials on general civil rights topics.
Journal: *Civil Rights Digest* (1313)

1142 U.S. DEPARTMENT OF LABOR, Washington, D. C. 20210. (202) 393-2420.

The Department of Labor carries out activities in five major areas: employment and unemployment, labor-management relations, wage and labor standards, international labor, and labor statistics. Employment and unemployment under the Manpower Administration and labor statistics under the Bureau of Labor Statistics are directly related to access to higher education. The former investigates the needs of the unemployed and underemployed and administers all public employment, work-experience, and training programs of the department. Program examples include the Job Corps (1287), Public Service Careers (1288), JOBS (Job Opportunities in the Business Sector), and apprenticeship information centers. The Bureau of Labor Statistics collects, analyzes, and distributes data on employment, unemployment, wages, prices, jobs, productivity, and working conditions. It is consequently a vital resource for researchers. Refer to 1447 for a more detailed description of the Bureau of Labor Statistics, and see the *1970 Manpower Report of the President* (503) for an extensive treatment of the functions and activities of the Manpower Administration.
Informational document: Annual report

1143 UNITED STATES OFFICE OF EDUCATION, 400 Maryland Avenue, S. W., Washington, D. C. 20202. (202) 963-1110.

The United States Office of Education (USOE) is a unit within the Department of Health, Education, and Welfare. It collects and disseminates all types of information on education at all levels, administers federal financial aid programs for students and institutions, supports educational research, and cooperates with other federal agencies on the educational aspects of their programs. USOE is a very important agency; it is also large, complex, and frequently reorganized. There are several bureaus, centers, and institutes that may be grouped for analytic purposes into five substantive categories: elementary and secondary education; postsecondary education; instructional resources; planning, research, and evaluation; and organizational and administrative services. Following are brief descriptions of the two categories that deal most directly with questions of access to higher education. Several useful documents providing other information about USOE are listed at the end of this annotation.

Postsecondary Education. The Bureau of Higher Education administers the four federal student financial aid programs, special programs designed to increase the access and retention in higher education of disadvantaged students and ex-military personnel, the graduate fellowship program, and the financial institutional support programs. It also provides assistance to institutions for overall improvement, facilities planning, and upgraded community service programs. The bureau also determines the eligibility of institutions to receive federal aid. In addition the bureau has inaugurated through contractual arrangements a series of evaluations of the impacts of the federal programs within their jurisdiction.

The Institute of International Studies, created in 1968, is involved primarily with programs for graduate students, faculty members, and other international educational and governmental personnel, but it also jointly administers a program with AID (Agency for International Development) that brings several hundred foreign students from developing countries to the United States annually for training in whatever field they choose at whatever level they qualify. The institute also provides advisory determination of the academic credentials of foreign students coming into this country, a service available to any institution that desires to use it.

The Bureau of Adult, Vocational, and Technical Education deals primarily with activities at the secondary level or below, but it also administers some funds utilized at the postsecondary level. For example, at least 15 percent of the basic state vocational-education grants must be used for postsecondary education. Exemplary vocational, cooperative education, and work-study programs may also secure support. In addition, the bureau is responsible for programs of manpower institutional training whereby unemployed or underemployed people are either made ready for the job market or are helped to upgrade their abilities. This program is particularly designed for unemployed heads of families rather than teenage high school dropouts, although a number of the latter do participate. Other programs developed primarily for the 15- to 21-year-old group include work-study and cooperative vocational education, two efforts which seek to combine learning with earning.

Planning, Research, and Evaluation. The units within this area conduct surveys, administer research programs, disseminate research results and other educational information, and engage in program planning and evaluation for all levels of education. The National Center for Educational Statistics (1443) gathers, stores, analyzes, and disseminates statistical data to show the condition and progress of American education. It relates educational statistics to critical public issues and provides quantitative information for decision and policymakers at all levels. Its main source of higher educational data comes through the annual Higher Education General Information Survey (HEGIS), discussed in more detail in 1443.

The Office of Program Planning and Evaluation undertakes analytical studies on various topics and suggests appropriate federal courses of action. Two recent investigations include a comprehensive study of community colleges and an analysis of the status and impact of vocational-education programs in selected major cities. The office also provides technical assistance to the various bureaus within USOE that might be engaged in planning and evaluation of their individual program responsibilities.

The National Center for Educational Research and Development processes research proposals and monitors contracts and grants in support of research or related activities within all levels of education. In addition to allocating grants to organizations and institutions for work on specific projects, it administers funds to agencies initiated by USOE. These include:

- ten university-based research and development centers that bring together resources and talents from many disciplines to seek basic knowledge for educational improvement,
- eleven regional educational laboratories that have as their mission the systematic conversion of research knowledge into improved educational practice,
- two university-based policy research centers whose goal is to anticipate and plan for educational needs through the end of this century.

NCERD also conducts a regional research program through USOE's nine regional offices. This program allocates funds to college and university personnel engaged in short-term projects requiring no more than $10,000. One purpose of this program is to encourage faculty members of small institutions to participate in educational research, although personnel of large schools are also eligible.

A new office, the National Center for Educational Communications, was established in early 1970 to improve and enlarge the program of educational research and materials dissemination. Among its activities are the administration of the ERIC system (1449) and a program of evaluation, interpretation, and distribution of research findings in succinct, nontechnical language to nonresearch audiences responsible for educational decisions and change.

Although many bureaus and centers of USOE do have their separate publication catalogs, the reader interested in a wide range of topics is advised to utilize the annual USOE publications catalog (1499) which may be secured through the Government Printing Office.

Documents of general interest include:

Where the Money Is – American Education *Guide to OE Programs*
How the OE Assists College Students and Colleges
American Education (1305)
Office of Education Programs for the Disadvantaged (999)
Office of Education Support for Research and Related Activities
Annual report of the Department of Health, Education, and Welfare

1144 U.S. TRAINING AND EMPLOYMENT SERVICE, Manpower Administration, U.S. Department of Labor, Washington, D. C. 20210. (202) 961-3641.

Operating within the Department of Labor, the U.S. Training and Employment Service maintains 2,400 public employment offices with job-market information in all 50 states, the District of Columbia, and United States territories. The offices are prepared to offer occupational counseling and testing and to assist in job recruitment and placement. Special services are provided for persons with employment problems – veterans, older workers, the young and inexperienced, members of minorities, migrant workers, the handicapped, and the disadvantaged. USTES conducts various types of research, including development of procedures, standards, and evaluation of training programs. It also carries out surveys and analyses of the nation's occupational structure.

Journals:

Area Trends in Employment and Unemployment
Employment Service Statistics
Rural Manpower Developments

12.3 – *FOUNDATIONS*. The large foundations are among the more influential organizations in the country. This section includes the major ones that are especially concerned with some aspect of access to higher education. A very large number are listed in the *Foundation Directory*.

The foundations are of special interest for several reasons. Several of the major ones tend to be interested in such social issues as educational opportunity. The staffs of the more prominent foundations tend to be influential and innovative and can draw upon flexible financial resources as seed money for social change. Consequently, the activities of the foundations are frequently indicative of new developments even though they are often criticized for being too conservative.

1145 Carnegie Corporation of New York, 437 Madison Avenue, New York, New York 10022. (212) 753-3100.

The Carnegie Corporation of New York, established in 1911, provides financial assistance to institutions and organizations actively engaged in the advancement and diffusion of knowledge. The corporation's present emphasis is on education (including education of the disadvantaged, higher and professional education, early childhood education, and educational research) and certain aspects of governmental affairs. Of its $12-13 million in annual grant appropriations, about 40 percent aids United States higher education, including organizations emphasizing access. The *Carnegie Quarterly* (1352) describes current projects in detail; the annual report provides a financial report and a review of various projects.

1146 Danforth Foundation, 222 South Central Avenue, St. Louis, Missouri 63105. (314) 862-6200.

The Danforth Foundation was established in 1927. Of its $6 to $8 million annual grant expenditure, about 65 percent goes toward higher education, with emphasis on the strengthening of teaching and curriculum, institutional development and management, education for the disadvantaged, and student growth including religious and social concerns. The foundation also spends another $4 million in administering several programs of its own, including graduate fellowships, faculty workshops, and other assistance to college personnel. The annual report briefly describes the various programs and lists foundation grants and awards.

1147 Esso Education Foundation, 49 West 49th Street, New York, New York 10020. (212) 974-2273.

The Esso Education Foundation was established in 1955 to aid public and private higher education in the United States. It seeks particularly to encourage creative and innovative solutions to institutional problems. Experimental and research projects receive nearly half of Esso's $3.1 million annual grant expenditure. The Foundation also sponsors *Change* (1312), a bimonthly journal of academic criticism and commentary designed to stimulate reform and innovation on the nation's campuses. The annual report lists all grants and defines areas of interest.

1148 The Ford Foundation, 320 East 43rd Street, New York, New York 10017. (212) 573-5000.

The Ford Foundation, established in 1936, seeks to contribute to the solution of national problems, mainly by granting funds to institutions. It focuses on experimental, demonstration, and developmental efforts that are likely to produce significant advances in the public interest. The foundation grants over $225 million annually for projects concerned with education, international understanding and assistance, national affairs, educational television, humanities and the arts, population studies, and other research activities. In education it attempts to advance quality at all levels; to equalize opportunities; and to improve management, teaching, and curriculum. About a third of its annual funds go toward higher education in the United States.

About the Ford Foundation, a list of publications, and the annual report are available from the Office of Reports.

1149 EDWARD W. HAZEN FOUNDATION, 400 Prospect Street, New Haven, Connecticut 06511. (203) 865-8824.

The Hazen Foundation, established in 1925, is particularly interested in projects of a pioneering nature. It has engaged in the improvement of liberal higher education, student personnel work, the place and effects of religion in higher education, higher education and world affairs, and international cultural exchanges. A major portion of its funds (some one-third million annually) assists international higher education and education in developing societies. The brief biennial report comments on reports, awards, and studies carried on under the auspices of the Foundation.

1150 W. K. KELLOGG FOUNDATION, 400 North Avenue, Battle Creek, Michigan 49016. (616) 965-1221.

The W. K. Kellogg Foundation, established in 1930, emphasizes practicality and the application of knowledge to "help people help themselves." Operating in North and South America, Europe, and Australia, the foundation concentrates its efforts on health, agriculture, education, health professions education, and expanded programs and opportunities in higher education. Of its more than $16 million for program payments in 1970, over one-third assisted United States higher and continuing education. The annual report, available on request, describes grants and programs.

1151 CHARLES F. KETTERING FOUNDATION, 5335 Far Hills Avenue, Dayton, Ohio 45429. (513) 434-7300.

The Charles F. Kettering Foundation, established in 1927, conducts and sponsors programs in four major areas: elementary and secondary education, biological science, world order and peace, and citizen involvement in public affairs. The Kettering Foundation uses its funds to sponsor its own affiliated projects in education and science, as well as in making grants-in-aid. The Institute for Development of Educational Activities, Inc. (/I/D/E/A), which is the foundation's educational affiliate, develops systems and materials to speed constructive change in elementary and secondary schools. The foundation's Charles F. Kettering Research Laboratory and its offshoot, Kettering Scientific Research, Inc., perform basic biological research. In addition to these projects, the Charles F. Kettering Foundation supports the creative efforts of others to solve some of society's major problems. The Kettering Foundation's annual report gives an overall view of the types of research supported. The annual reports of the Charles F. Kettering Research Laboratory and /I/D/E/A deal exclusively with developments in biological science and education.

1152 RUSSELL SAGE FOUNDATION, 230 Park Avenue, New York, New York 10017. (212) 689-6622.

The Russell Sage Foundation was established in 1907 for the improvement of social and living conditions in the United States. In carrying out its purpose, the foundation conducts research under staff direction or in close collaboration with other institutions and supports programs designed to improve the utilization of social science knowledge. Major areas of interest include the social sciences and human biology, social control, education and human resources, a visiting scholar program, law and the social sciences, and mass media and the social sciences. The foundation publishes numerous books, including a number on various topics pertinent to higher education. The annual report presents a description of its activities, toward which it disburses nearly $2 million annually.

1153 ALFRED P. SLOAN FOUNDATION, 630 Fifth Avenue, New York, New York 10020. (212) 582-0450.

The primary areas of interest of the Alfred P. Sloan Foundation, established in 1934, are education, science and technology, economics and management, related social problems, and cancer research. Of its $16 million paid out in grants annually, about three-fourths has assisted higher education, including major grants to colleges and universities, a college science program and science research fellowships, student scholarships, and Negro college development. The foundation is phasing out its scholarship program and emphasizing a changing set of particular programs, the first of which seeks to expand minority opportunity in medicine and management, and to advance neuroscience research. The annual report provides a thorough descriptive and evaluative overview of existing or projected grants and programs for scientific research, related social problems, and aid to education.

12.4 – RESEARCH CENTERS. There are an indefinite number of research centers in the country, but only about a score that have substantial technical resources and make frequent important contributions to problems of access to higher education. These research centers form the major programmatic research effort and supply most of the basic access data not routinely collected by federal agencies.

These research centers produce many influential publications and several basic types of information. These include normative data from such agencies as Educational Testing Service (1167) and American Council on Education (1156), survey data from such centers as the National Opinion Research Center (1174), planning information from coordinating agencies like Western Interstate Commission for Higher Education (1177) and Southern Regional Education Board (1176), and information concerning educational developments from such laboratories as the Center for Research and Development in Higher Education (1161) and the National Laboratory for Higher Education (1172).

1154 ACADEMY FOR EDUCATIONAL DEVELOPMENT, 437 Madison Avenue, New York, New York 10022. (212) 758-5454.

The Academy for Educational Development, a nonprofit planning organization, has been carrying on research projects for educational institutions, government agencies, and other organizations since 1962. The academy's projects range from master plans for states to national planning for the United States Office of Education to specialized studies for individual institutions. These projects have included planning for higher education, development of improved educational practices, studies related to communications, and editorial projects. In addition to its own research staff, AED also utilizes the services of other educators and specialists on a consultant basis.

Research reports: Reports on research published intermittently
Informational document: *Academy for Educational Development*

1155 AMERICAN COLLEGE TESTING PROGRAM, Research and Development Division, P. O. Box 168, Iowa City, Iowa 52240. (319) 351-4470.

The American College Testing Program's (1101) Research and Development

Division was established in 1959 when the ACT Program was initiated. The Division conducts basic and applied research focusing on students in transition from high school to college. Topics include college student development, vocational psychology, psychometrics, and the financing of higher education. ACT Postdoctoral Summer Research Fellowships are offered annually to encourage research in higher education. The Research and Development Division also operates a Research Service (1217) offering free prediction, description, and financial aid planning services to colleges participating in the ACT program, in addition to other at-cost services to any educational institution. A new Research Institute was begun in 1969, in which basic research in the social sciences is conducted in collaboration with researchers on college and university campuses.
Newsletter: *ACTivity* (1347)
Research reports:
  ACT Research Reports (1397)
  ACT Monographs
Informational document: *ACT Research Services for Colleges and Universities*

1156 AMERICAN COUNCIL ON EDUCATION, One Dupont Circle, N. W., Washington, D. C. 20036. (202) 833-4700.

In 1965 the American Council on Education (1102) established an Office of Research to conduct a broad program of studies on substantive problems in higher education. Its major ongoing project is the Cooperative Institutional Research Program, a long-range longitudinal study on student development. These data have been developed into a computerized system enabling outside researchers to carry out their own analyses. (See 1441.) The office has used the available data to study such topics as attrition, black students, and junior college students. Information has also been gathered for analyses pertinent to such issues as campus unrest, open admissions policies, and compensatory higher education. ACE's Research Office is also well known for its annual survey of the characteristics of entering college freshmen.
Research reports: ACE Research Report Series (1396)
Informational document: *Implications of a Program of Research on Student Development in Higher Education* (ACE Research Report Series, vol. 2, no. 6, 1967)

1157 AMERICAN INSTITUTES FOR RESEARCH, 135 North Bellefield Avenue, Pittsburgh, Pennsylvania 15213. (412) 683-7600.

American Institutes for Research is a nonprofit organization established in 1947. It is engaged in a broad spectrum of research and development activities for governmental agencies, industrial organizations, and foundations. AIR research projects tend to focus on individual development, social improvement and adaptation, and national and international change. For more than 10 years AIR has conducted Project TALENT (1445), a research activity of major importance in understanding access to higher education. Other projects are concerned with innovative curriculums, career development, and instruction. AIR presently operates in five locations (Pittsburgh; Palo Alto; Washington; Kensington, Maryland; and Bangkok), with research activities in each.
Newsletter: *Behavioral Sciences Newsletter for Research Planning* (1350)
Research reports: Reports on projects published intermittently
Informational documents:
  American Institutes for Research
  Annual report

1158 THE BROOKINGS INSTITUTION, 1775 Massachusetts Avenue, N. W., Washington, D. C. 20036. (202) 483-8919.

The Brookings Institution was established in 1927 as an independent organization devoted to research and publication in the fields of economics, government, and foreign policy. It also conducts seminars on public issues, provides research opportunities for scholars, and maintains conference facilities. In addition to its three research areas with some 125 studies typically in progress,

Brookings operates a computer center and an advanced study program. Research is carried on by Brookings staff and by scholars in residence from other institutions.

Newsletter: *Brookings Bulletin*
Research reports:
    Research Report Series (approximately 20 per year, $5)
    Reprint Series (numerous copies annually, $5)
Informational documents:
    Brookings Program
    The Brookings Institution Annual Report

1159 BUREAU OF APPLIED SOCIAL RESEARCH, Columbia University, 605 West 115th Street, New York, New York 10025. (212) 280-4024.

The Bureau of Applied Social Research is the Columbia University Graduate Faculties research laboratory for training and research in the social sciences. Research is carried on by a core staff of professional researchers and by faculty and students, primarily in the fields of communication and public opinion; education; international and comparative research; manpower and population; the professions; and urban, community, and poverty problems. BASR has studied student financial aid, admissions, higher education opportunities of the disadvantaged, student activism, career planning, the relationship of student attitudes to college entrance, and university involvement in the urban crisis. The bureau had its beginnings in 1937 and assumed its present name and orientation in 1944. It is often regarded as the first research center of its kind.

Newsletter: *The Bureau Reporter* (4-5 per year)
Research reports: Numerous reports and articles
Informational document: *Bureau of Applied Social Research: A Report of the Years 1968 and 1969*

1160 CARNEGIE COMMISSION ON HIGHER EDUCATION, 1947 Center Street, Berkeley, California 94704. (415) 849-4474.

The Carnegie Commission on Higher Education was established in 1967 to help provide guidance for the development of American colleges and universities. To carry out this mandate, the commission has held seminars and conferences around the country, has asked experienced investigators in the fields of higher education and social and behavioral sciences to conduct research and write monographs on important topics, and has put forth its own recommendations in monograph form. Before the commission completes its work with a final report in 1972, it intends to have investigated the functions, structure, and governance of higher education; innovation and change; demand for higher education; and expenditures, available resources, and their effective use.

Research reports: Numerous special reports on subjects of public interest (see 1398 for a listing)
Informational document: *Carnegie Commission on Higher Education: General Information, November, 1970*

1161 CENTER FOR RESEARCH AND DEVELOPMENT IN HIGHER EDUCATION, 1947 Center Street, Berkeley, California 94720. (415) 642-5040.

The Center for Research and Development in Higher Education was established in 1956 at the University of California at Berkeley. In 1965 it became one of the nine research and development centers sponsored by the United States Office of Education. The center has undertaken research on a variety of subjects: school to college student flow, undergraduate psychological growth and personality development, faculty impact on students, governance patterns, regional and national educational planning systems, graduate and professional programs, educational philosophies, institutional objectives, and academic innovation. The center is now concentrating on educational programs for the "new" students—those who are educationally disadvantaged and/or unconventional.

In addition to publishing its research results, the center also conducts conferences, seminars, and workshops.

Newsletter: *The Research Reporter* (1393)
Research reports: Reports frequently cited in newsletter
Informational document: *The Center for Research and Development in Higher Education*

1162 CENTER FOR RESEARCH AND LEADERSHIP DEVELOPMENT IN VOCATIONAL AND TECHNICAL EDUCATION, The Ohio State University, 1900 Kenny Road, Columbus, Ohio 43210. (614) 486-3655.

The Center for Research and Leadership Development in Vocational and Technical Education, established in 1965, is an interdisciplinary unit on the Ohio State campus. The major program areas for its research, development, training, and dissemination are as follows: state leadership, teacher education, curriculum development, vocational-technical education for the occupationally disadvantaged, vocational development and adjustment, and the change process in vocational-technical education. The ERIC Clearinghouse on Vocational and Technical Education (1455) is part of the Center.

Newsletter: *Centergram* (1354)
Other publications:
> *Abstracts of Instructional Material in Vocational and Technical Education* (AIM) (quarterly)
> *Abstracts of Research and Related Materials in Vocational and Technical Education* (ARM) (quarterly)

Informational documents:
> "Information on The Center for Research and Leadership Development in Vocational and Technical Education"
> *Centergram* (January issue)
> "Publications of the Center for Vocational and Technical Education" (November 1970)

1163 CENTER FOR STUDIES IN VOCATIONAL AND TECHNICAL EDUCATION, University of Wisconsin, Social Science Building, 1180 Observatory Drive, Madison, Wisconsin 53706. (608) 262-5393.

The Center for Studies in Vocational and Technical Education was established in 1964 under a grant from the Ford Foundation. The functions of the center are: research and study in vocational and technical education; the maintenance of a national depository and clearinghouse for publications in the field; publication of research findings; sponsorship of conferences, workshops, and seminars; and the promotion and support of graduate study in the field. Although sources of funds have been reduced and the center is functioning on a reduced scale, it continues to be a major research center for the field of vocational and technical education. A list of its reports and other publications is available from the center.

Journal: *Journal of Human Resources* (1328)
Informational document: Center news is reported in the annual report of the Industrial Relations Research Institute, same address

1164 CENTER FOR THE STUDY OF EVALUATION, UCLA Graduate School of Education, Los Angeles, California 90024. (213) 825-4711.

The Center for the Study of Evaluation is devoted exclusively to the development of new theories and methods of analyzing and evaluating educational programs and systems. One of eight educational research and development centers sponsored by the United States Office of Education, CSE was established in 1966 at UCLA to aid educators in determining accurately the impact of their programs. Study projects dealing with evaluation at all levels are conducted on instructional programs, educational systems, and methodology and services. CSE's products, procedures, and methodology are intended for evaluation specialists, teachers, administrators, and others concerned with the improvement of educational practices.

Newsletter: *Evaluation Comment* (1367)
Research reports: *CSE Reports* (variable, 15-30 per year)

Informational documents:
Evaluation in Education
Products for Improving Educational Evaluation (1970 annual report to the U.S. Office of Education)

1165 COLLEGE ENTRANCE EXAMINATION BOARD, 888 Seventh Avenue, New York, New York 10019. (212) 582-6210.

The College Entrance Examination Board (1112) sponsors or carries out research on a variety of problems concerning transition from secondary school to college. Its research focuses on such issues as financing higher education, student guidance, educational opportunity, identification of talent, educational planning and coordination, and administration of admissions programs and financial aid. Much of the research is conducted in cooperation with university and college personnel or Educational Testing Service (1167). In addition, the Board established an Access Research Office in 1968, which undertakes research and prepares reports directly pertinent to access to higher education; e.g., status of free-access higher education, a series of Higher Education Surveys on current issues, and this volume. The Board also provides a free Validity Study Service for colleges and universities.

Newsletters:
College Board News
Financial Aid News (1368)
Research reports:
College Entrance Examination Board Research and Development Reports (1399)
Higher Education Surveys (1402)
Other special publications (see catalog 1488)
Informational documents:
Fact sheets on various programs
Numerous publications listed in catalog (1488)

1166 COMMITTEE FOR ECONOMIC DEVELOPMENT, 477 Madison Avenue, New York, New York 10022. (212) 688-2063.

The Committee for Economic Development (CED) is an independent, non-profit, research and educational organization of 200 leading businessmen and educators. Supported largely by contributions from business, foundations, and individuals, CED's objective is to promote economic growth by raising living standards and broadening opportunities for individuals. With the help of advisory boards of distinguished economists and social scientists, CED trustees sponsor research and formulate policy recommendations in four major areas of public policy: (1) the national economy; (2) the international economy; (3) education and urban development; and (4) the mangement of federal, state, and local government. These recommendations are published as Statements on National Policy. In addition, background papers of particular merit are frequently published.

1167 EDUCATIONAL TESTING SERVICE, Princeton, New Jersey 08540. (609) 921-9000.

Educational Testing Service (1115), founded in 1947, is a national nonprofit organization connected with measurement, research, and other services to education, government, and professions. ETS publishes tests and administers testing and service programs for sponsors such as the College Board, the Law School Admissions Council, the Graduate Business Admissions Council, and the Graduate Record Examinations Board. ETS assists test users in applying measurement techniques, and conducts a large program of educational and measurement research in many fields. Research topics include test theory, personality measurement, cultural diversity and the disadvantaged, career and vocational development, and evaluation of educational programs and systems. ETS has a close working relationship with the College Board (1165) and conducts many studies for the Board.

Newsletters:
ETS Developments (1366)
Education Recaps (1363)
Research reports: ETS Research Bulletins (1401)
Informational document: Annual report

1168 INSTITUTE FOR SOCIAL RESEARCH, University of Michigan, P. O. Box 1248, 426 Thompson Street, Ann Arbor, Michigan 48106. (313) 764-8354.

The Institute for Social Research was established at the University of Michigan in 1946 to advance understanding of society and behavior. It is composed of four basic research groups: Survey Research Center, Research Center for Group Dynamics, Center for Research on Utilization of Scientific Knowledge, and Center for Political Studies. With a large staff of interviewers and researchers, the institute carries on individual studies and continuing programs in consumer economics, behavior of groups and organizations, youth and family life, public health, political behavior, and education. ISR currently publishes about 300 books, monographs, reports, articles, and special documents annually.
Newsletter: *ISR Newsletter* (quarterly)
Research reports:
Twenty-Five Years of Social Research: A Report
Varied reports on research published frequently
Informational document: *The University of Michigan/Institute for Social Research: A Report on Recent Activities*

1169 INSTITUTE FOR THE QUANTITATIVE ANALYSIS OF SOCIAL AND ECONOMIC POLICY, University of Toronto, 150 St. George Street, Toronto 5, Canada. (416) 928-4854.

The Institute for the Quantitative Analysis of Social and Economic Policy was established by the University of Toronto in 1967 to encourage quantitative social science research and to develop useful information through the establishment of close relationships with government and business. While most research presently deals with various aspects of economics, the institute has gained recognition for its work on systems analysis for efficient resource allocation in higher education. This institute project on program planning and budgeting is known as CAMPUS.
Research reports: Numerous reports, technical papers, reprints, policy papers, working papers, monographs published intermittently
Informational document: *A Research Progress Report on Systems Analysis for Allocation in Higher Education*

1170 INSTITUTE OF HIGHER EDUCATION, Teachers College, Columbia University, 525 West 120th Street, New York, New York 10027. (212) 870-4891.

The Institute of Higher Education conducts research related to organization, administration, and financing of the educational programs of institutions and state systems of higher education. In addition, it provides consultative services to institutions. The institute includes two centers: one focuses on adult learning and development; the other focuses on community colleges. The institute has published various research reports. At this writing it is undergoing reorganization and plans to publish a regular report series on its work.

1171 LEAGUE FOR INNOVATION IN THE COMMUNITY COLLEGE, Suite 925, 1100 Glendon Avenue, Los Angeles, California 90024. (213) 477-7255.

Organized in 1968, the league consists of 14 leading community college districts, representing 39 colleges that are especially interested in innovation. Major activities include workshops, conferences, and exchange programs for faculty in addition to securing funds to support league projects. These include

planning a systems approach for general education of career students; initiating an experimental vocational college; conducting an institute on new developments in teaching physics; and holding a variety of conferences on student personnel work, computer-assisted instruction, and educational development.
Newsletter: *Jottings* (irregular, about twice a year)

1172 NATIONAL LABORATORY FOR HIGHER EDUCATION, Mutual Plaza, Durham, North Carolina 27701. (919) 688-8057.

Formerly called the Regional Education Laboratory for the Carolinas and Virginia, NLHE is one of 11 regional laboratories established under the Elementary and Secondary Education Act of 1965 (1292). The only laboratory in the network whose major responsibility is in higher education, NLHE works toward the improvement of educational practice through conducting research, preparing materials and products for field testing, disseminating prototype systems, and publishing reports of its activities. Its two major programs are concerned with administrative services in four-year institutions and instruction in the junior college.
Newsletter: *Educational Development* (bimonthly)
Research reports: Books, papers, and articles published intermittently

1173 NATIONAL MERIT SCHOLARSHIP CORPORATION, 990 Grove Street, Evanston, Illinois 60201. (312) 869-5100.

The National Merit Scholarship Corporation has carried on a testing and scholarship program (1213) since 1955 to identify and encourage talented students. Taking advantage of data available through the Merit and Achievement Programs, NMSC has completed studies on a variety of topics, including the effects of financial assistance on college-going decisions, college selection, career choice, talented Negro youth, and output differences among colleges.
Research reports: NMSC Research Reports (1404)
Informational document: Annual report

1174 NATIONAL OPINION RESEARCH CENTER, University of Chicago, 6030 South Ellis Avenue, Chicago, Illinois 60637. (312) 684-5600.

The National Opinion Research Center is a nonprofit social research institute established in 1941 and affiliated with the University of Chicago. With its research staff and national corps of interviewers, NORC has conducted over 1,000 surveys in health and welfare, occupations and professional training, mass communications, economics and business, national and international political affairs, education, community affairs and intergroup relations, and methodology and theory. To make its resources available to independent researchers, NORC established the Survey Research Service (see 1444) in 1963, which provides data collection, data processing, and consultation on a contractual basis for organizations and individuals with varied research needs. In the 1960s NORC produced several important monographs related to access to higher education.
Research reports:
  NORC Monographs in Social Research
  NORC Reports (numbered series produced by multilith)
Newsletter: *NORC Newsletter* (irregular)
Informational documents:
  NORC Social Research, 1941-1964: An Inventory of Studies and Publications in Social Research
  Bibliography of Publications, 1941-1960
  Supplement to the above (December, annually)
  Survey Research Service (descriptive brochure)

1175 NATIONAL PLANNING ASSOCIATION, 1606 New Hampshire Avenue, N. W., Washington, D. C. 20009. (202) 265-7685.

The National Planning Association is an independent, nonpartisan, nonprofit organization established in 1934 to bring together leaders from business, labor, agriculture, and the professions to develop plans for more effective use of the nation's resources by all sectors of the economy. It carries on research through its centers for economic projections, priority analysis, and economic programming, and through an international division. Of special value in higher educational planning are the association's detailed 5- and 10-year economic and demographic projections for the nation, regions, states, and 224 metropolitan areas. NPA also conducts manpower studies, including the effects of differing national priorities on manpower requirements. NPA's membership consists of more than 3,000 individuals, corporations, and organizations that support its activities and make use of its data and numerous publications.

Periodicals:
  Projection Highlights ($30 per year)
  Looking Ahead ($15 per year)
  Both publications $40 per year
Research reports:
  National Economic Projections Series
  Regional Economic Projections Series
  ($500 per year for both, $300 per year for one for nonprofit organizations, educational institutions, and government agencies; others, $600 and $350)
Informational documents:
  For Better Decisions Today . . . (a brief description of the Economic Projections Series)
  Biennial report

1176 SOUTHERN REGIONAL EDUCATION BOARD, 130 Sixth Street, N. W., Atlanta, Georgia 30313. (404) 875-9211.

The Southern Regional Education Board is a highly regarded compact of 14 states working toward regional cooperation in planning and effective multistate use of higher educational resources. Among its varied activities the Board conducts and promotes research in higher education through its research staff and through individuals at various universities. SREB conducts regional workshops in institutional research and higher educational issues. It examines such topics as higher educational financing, educational opportunity, planning and coordination, curriculum change, operation of community college systems, problems of Negro colleges, and computer use. See 1180 for a further description of SREB's coordinating activities.

Newsletters:
  Regional Action (1389)
  Regional Spotlight (1390)
Research reports: Research Monograph Series (1408)
Informational document: Annual report

1177 WESTERN INTERSTATE COMMISSION FOR HIGHER EDUCATION, P. O. Drawer P, Boulder, Colorado 80302. (303) 449-3333.

The Western Interstate Commission for Higher Education, an effective compact of 13 states, works to improve education through interstate and institutional cooperation. Among its many activities, the commission identifies problems; develops and implements programs; collects, analyzes, and disseminates information; and conducts a large management information systems project intended to provide for systematic collection and use of data in institutional and state higher education management. WICHE has recently conducted surveys on urban and minority programs and has also encouraged community college programs that focus upon recruiting minorities and developing courses for potential mental health workers. See 1181 for further information on WICHE's activities as a coordinating commission.

Newsletter: *WICHE Reports on Higher Education* (1392)
Informational documents:
  This is WICHE
  Annual report

12.5—*COORDINATING BOARDS.* Practically every state has one or more central agency for the purpose of coordinating postsecondary education. These agencies play an increasingly important role in monitoring and facilitating access to higher education. This section includes only a few illustrations of state boards and regional coordinating agencies. A very useful book by Abrahams (649) describes statewide coordination in individual state profiles (see also sections 7.6, 7.7, and 7.8).

Regional Commissions

1178 EDUCATION COMMISSION OF THE STATES, 300 Lincoln Tower, 1860 Lincoln Street, Denver, Colorado 80203. (303) 255-3631.

The primary goal of the Education Commission of the States is to encourage a working relationship among state governors, legislators, and educators for the improvement of education. Representatives of the 43 member states and territories periodically come together to identify and discuss common problems and authorize research on those that seem most critical. Established in 1966, ECS gives attention to educational issues related to elementary, secondary, and higher education. In postsecondary education a number of activities have been initiated, including the development of four national task forces concerned with student assistance, community and junior colleges, statewide planning, and vocational education in higher education. New projects are planned in the area of graduate education and the structure and governance of higher education. Other activities include the writing of a number of papers concerning federal legislation for higher education, and the publication of a monthly bulletin entitled *Higher Education in the States* (1374). The commission also maintains a library of published and unpublished reports and studies on key educational issues across the country. Its journal, *Compact* (1316), is a good source of information concerning current educational issues of special public and political interest. *Legislative Review* (1361) supplies information on pending legislation.

1179 NEW ENGLAND BOARD OF HIGHER EDUCATION, 20 Walnut Street, Wellesley, Massachusetts 02181. (617) 235-8071.

The New England Board of Higher Education was formed in 1955 to help coordinate all higher education, both public and private, in the six New England states. It assists the states and their institutions in expanding educational opportunities, while improving institutional and program quality. The board conducts research; assists in initiating and developing plans and programs to meet regional and institutional needs; serves as an information center; administers higher educational contracts between institutions and/or governments; provides consulting services to institutions, agencies, and governments; and administers federally and privately financed education programs.

1180 SOUTHERN REGIONAL EDUCATION BOARD, 130 Sixth Street, N. W., Atlanta, Georgia 30313. (404) 875-9211.

The Southern Regional Education Board has played an important and influential role since it was established in 1948. SREB is a compact of 14 states that works directly with state governments, academic institutions, and other agencies to foster regional cooperation in planning, action, and effective multistate use of higher educational resources. SREB membership consists of the governor of each compact state and four others appointed by him. The board examines the role of higher education, promotes innovative solutions to educational problems of the South, conducts and sponsors research (see 1176), and offers consultation services to states and institutions. SREB has a very active publications program. It publishes several newsletters (e.g., 1369, 1389, and 1390), and frequent reports and monographs (see 1408) bearing upon various aspects of access to higher education.

1181 WESTERN INTERSTATE COMMISSION FOR HIGHER EDUCATION, P. O. Drawer P, Boulder, Colorado 80302. (303) 449-3333.

The Western Interstate Commission for Higher Education was formed in 1951 by the 13 western states. Each state is represented by three commissioners. WICHE seeks to improve educational programs, opportunities, and facilities through interstate and interinstitutional cooperation. The commission helps institutions to improve their programs, administration, and management; works to increase the supply of specialized manpower; carries on studies and disseminates information for states, institutions, and the public; and acts as administrative agent for interstate educational projects. See 1177 for a description of WICHE's research activities. WICHE has no authority over states or institutions, but builds consensus based on joint deliberation. It has exercised leadership in many areas, particularly the development of management information systems (e.g., see 644). WICHE publishes a variety of reports and a newsletter (1392).

State Commissions

1182 COORDINATING COUNCIL FOR HIGHER EDUCATION, 1020 Twelfth Street, Sacramento, California 95814. (916) 445-7933.

The Coordinating Council for Higher Education was established in 1960 to advise the California governor, legislature, and the governing boards of the three segments of public higher education (the university, state colleges, and community colleges) concerning finance, program development, new facilities, and statewide higher education planning in general. The council is made up of members representing both public and private education and the state at large. It reviews and makes recommendations on annual budget and capital outlay requests, interprets the functional differentiation among the three segments, develops plans for the orderly growth of higher education (689), administers California's participation in federal programs, and conducts applied research on topics related to institutional planning and operation, educational programs, and student needs. The council has no governing authority but has exercised substantial influence in the state. Part of this influence has been due to the extensive published research of an unusually active staff.

1183 COLORADO COMMISSION ON HIGHER EDUCATION, 719 State Services Building, Denver, Colorado 80203. (303) 892-2115.

The Colorado Commission on Higher Education, established in 1965, is a coordinating board working in cooperation with the various governing boards of public higher educational institutions within the state. The commission maintains a comprehensive plan for public higher education in Colorado; reviews and makes recommendations to state administrative agencies on appropriation requests, capital construction, long-range planning, new degree and nondegree programs, and new state-supported higher educational institutions; conducts studies to further state planning and to help institutions efficiently use staff and facilities; and administers federal higher education legislation. The commission has broad responsibilities but limited policy-making authority.

1184 ILLINOIS BOARD OF HIGHER EDUCATION, Room 500, 119 South Fifth Street, Springfield, Illinois 62706. (217) 525-2551.

The Illinois Board of Higher Education was created in 1961 to expand educational opportunities through planning and coordination of public higher education in the state. It is empowered to conduct studies and continuously formulate a state master plan for public higher education. The first phase of the master plan (691) was developed in 1964 and quickly gained acceptance within the state and recognition nationally. The board also has responsibility for analyzing and making recommendations on budget requests; approving all new programs of instruction, research, or service, including new branches or campuses; establishing a comprehensive information system for all state universities and colleges; recommending legislation and advising the governor on higher education; and administering certain federal education programs. Through the 1960s the Illinois Board established a model of effective central coordination without actual governing authority.

1185 BOARD OF REGENTS, University of the State of New York, Education Bldg., Room 102, Albany, New York 12224. (518) 474-5880.

The Regents of the University of the State of New York, established in 1784, is the oldest continuous state board of education in America. The Regents coordinate planning and development for all levels of New York education, elementary through graduate and professional schools, both public and private. The Board of Regents is concerned with overall planning, policy formulation, and supervision of New York's education system. It administers the Regents Examinations (1231) and an extensive financial assistance program for college students (1209). It investigates pertinent problems and conducts studies with the assistance of various advisory committees, and it makes recommendations for legislative action. In addition the Regents' responsibilities include the establishment of admissions standards to all professions except law and licensing of qualified practitioners as well as development and supervision of libraries, museums, and historic sites. In sum, the Regents have more comprehensive responsibilities and a broader base of authority than any other state higher education coordinating body in the nation.

1186 OHIO BOARD OF REGENTS, 88 East Broad Street, Room 770, Columbus, Ohio 43215. (614) 469-2575.

The Ohio Board of Regents was created in 1963 as the administrative agency for planning and coordinating public higher education. One of its first activities was to develop and implement a state master plan. Other major responsibilities of the board include: (1) reviewing and making recommendations on appropriations for current operations and capital improvements; (2) advising the governor and General Assembly on higher educational matters and recommending legislation; (3) approving the establishment of new degree programs and new two-year colleges, technical institutes, branches, and academic centers; (4) working toward common action among colleges and universities; and (5) administering various federally funded programs involving both public and private institutions. As with most boards of this type, it does not have governing authority over individual boards of trustees and must make its impact largely on the strength of its planning and advisory activities. See 694 for an annotation of the Ohio Master Plan.

12.6—*SPECIAL COMMISSIONS*. A number of public and semipublic commissions have been convened to study special problems that have an important bearing on the access process. The work of these commissions is important because it tends to be competent, visible, and influential. Of the commissions listed here some have been nationally prominent; others are less so but highly focused on specific access problems.

1187 CARNEGIE COMMISSION ON HIGHER EDUCATION, 1947 Center Street, Berkeley, California 94704.

The Carnegie Commission on Higher Education was established by the Carnegie Foundation for the Advancement of Teaching to provide guidance for the future development of colleges and universities. The commission is concerned with these major areas of inquiry: the functions, structure, and governance of higher education; innovation and change; the demand for higher education; expenditures; and availability and effective use of resources. The commission has published numerous special statements and reports of investigations. (See 1398 for a list.) A final report will be published at the completion of the commission's work. See 1160 for a more extensive exploration of its research functions.

1188 COMMISSION ON ENGLISH.

The Commission on English was established by the College Entrance Examination Board in 1959 to propose recommendations for the improvement of the teaching of English in high schools and colleges. The final report of the commission, *Freedom and Discipline in English* (285), was published in 1965.

1189 COMMISSION ON HUMAN RESOURCES AND ADVANCED EDUCATION.

The Commission on Human Resources was established in the mid-1960s by the American Council of Learned Societies, the American Council on Education, the National Research Council, and the Social Science Research Council. Its purpose was to study the development and utilization of human resources with special emphasis on the development of high-level talent and professions associated with graduate degrees. The final report *Human Resources and Higher Education* (509) was published in 1970.

1190 COMMISSION ON NONTRADITIONAL STUDY, 888 Seventh Avenue, New York, New York 10019.

The Commission on Nontraditional Study was established under joint sponsorship of the College Entrance Examination Board and the Educational Testing Service in March 1971. Its purpose is to study and recommend ways to expand opportunities for postsecondary learning. One interim report is scheduled to appear before the commission submits its final report in 1973.

1191 COMMISSION ON TESTS.

The Commission on Tests was established in 1967 by the College Entrance Examination Board to undertake a critical review of the Board's testing function in American education. The final *Report of the Commission on Tests* (1354), Volume I — *Righting the Balance* and Volume II — *Briefs,* was published in 1970.

1192 COMMITTEE ON STUDENT ECONOMICS.

The Committee on Student Economics was established by the College Entrance Examination Board in late 1970 to examine the role of parents and students in meeting costs of higher education. The committee plans to sponsor studies and make policy recommendations concerning financing practices.

1193 NATIONAL COMMISSION ON URBAN PROBLEMS.

The National Commission on Urban Problems was established by President Johnson in 1967 to study the problems of urban environment; to review zoning, housing and building codes, and taxation and development standards; and to recommend ways in which the federal government, private industry, and local communities can increase the supply of low-cost housing. The major report of the commission, *Building the American City* (853), was published in 1968.

1194 PRESIDENT'S COMMISSION ON CAMPUS UNREST.

The Commission on Campus Unrest was established by President Nixon after the tragedies at Kent and Jackson State. The commission conducted several months of public hearings and intensive investigations. The major report, *The Report of the President's Commission on Campus Unrest* (1018), was published in September 1970.

1195 PRESIDENT'S COMMISSION ON HIGHER EDUCATION.

The Truman Commission was established in 1946 to examine national priorities in higher education. Its major report *Higher Education for American Democracy* (583) was published in 1947. A key recommendation was for universal availability of education through the fourteenth grade.

1196 PRESIDENT'S COMMISSION ON NATIONAL GOALS.

The President's Commission on National Goals was established by President Eisenhower in 1959 to "develop a broad outline of coordinated national policies and programs and to set up a series of goals in various areas of national activity." The major report of the commission, *Goals for Americans: The Report of the President's Commission on National Goals* (576), was published in 1960.

1197 PRESIDENT'S COMMISSION ON THE STATUS OF WOMEN.

The Commission on the Status of Women was established by President Kennedy in 1960 to assess the position of women and the roles they play in the home, in the economy, and in society. The final report of the commission, *American Women* (1052), was published in 1963.

1198 PRESIDENT'S TASK FORCE ON HIGHER EDUCATION.

The President's Task Force on Higher Education, chaired by James S. Hester, was established by President Nixon in October 1969 to determine federal and institutional priorities for higher education in the 1970s. The major report of the commission, *Priorities in Higher Education* (584), was published in August 1970.

1199 TASK FORCE ON HIGHER EDUCATION.

This Task Force was an independent group initiated by the Department of Health, Education, and Welfare in 1969 and funded by the Ford Foundation. With Frank Newman as chairman, its charge was to examine the major problems facing the nation's system of higher education in the 1970s and to determine how the functioning of the system matches the public interest in education. The final report of the Task Force, *Report on Higher Education* (586), was submitted in March 1971.

SECTION 13: PROGRAMS

For the purposes of the guide, the term "programs" has been used to designate activities that serve an important function in carrying out various procedural aspects of access to higher education. The choice of what general classes of programs to represent is somewhat arbitrary. The categories included here are either especially important or relatively new types of activities not always well described in formal literature.

13.1—*FINANCIAL AID***.** It seems generally agreed that the greatest single barrier to higher education is financial need. Consequently, over the past

decade substantial state and federal programs have supplemented institutional and private sources of student aid. The annotations in this section include all of the major federal programs, four of the largest state programs,
and several prototype private programs selected from a very large number;
they do not include institutional programs. These annotations simply give a
brief indication of the history of each program, its mode of operation, level
of funding, and number of students involved.

Federal

1200 College Work-Study Program, Division of Student Financial Aid, Bureau
of Higher Education, U.S. Office of Education, Washington, D. C. 20202.
(202) 962-3871.

The College Work-Study Program was established in 1964 as one of the major
federal student aid programs. It provides grants to eligible higher education institutions to assist in the operation of educationally related work-study programs
for full-time students needing part-time employment. A student may work an
average of 15 hours a week during regular academic periods and up to 40 hours
during vacations. Jobs are located on campus or at an approved nonprofit
agency. Preference is given to students from low-income families although other
needy students may receive aid when funds and jobs are available. In 1970-71
the federal government contributed about $199 million (80 percent of the stu-
dents' wages) for 375,000 students. See 1290 for an annotation of the legislation
authorizing the Work-Study Program.

1201 Educational Assistance for Veterans Program, Veterans Administration Benefits Office, 2033 M Street, N. W., Washington, D. C. 20036. (202) 347-
1121.

The Educational Assistance for Veterans Program, popularly known as the
GI Bill, was created to restore lost educational opportunities, facilitate vocational readjustment, and provide higher education to veterans. Veterans on
active duty for over six months or discharged for a service-connected disability
are eligible for financial assistance (up to $175 per month with no dependents for
a maximum of 36 months, based on service time). Servicemen currently on
active duty who have served more than 180 days may also receive up to $175
per month toward educational expenses. In the fiscal year 1970 approximately
1.2 million veterans received educational or training benefits totaling over
$938.8 million in support of work in high school, vocational school, higher edu-
cation, or on-the-job-training. See 1301 for an annotation of authorizing legislation.

1202 Educational Opportunity Grants Program, Division of Student Financial Aid, Bureau of Higher Education, U.S. Office of Education, Washington,
D. C. 20202. (202) 962-4110.

The Educational Opportunity Grants Program, established in 1965, is the
major federal student aid program specifically intended to make higher education possible for undergraduate students of exceptional financial need who, without an EOG, could not attend college. Full-time undergraduates progressing normally toward a degree are eligible for renewable grants of $200 to $1,000
awarded directly by the participating college or university, with the agreement
that the institution will provide an equal amount of financial assistance from
other sources. In 1970-71, 290,500 students were assisted through grants totaling over $164 million. Item 1295 describes the authorizing legislation.

1203 Guaranteed Loan Program, Division of Student Financial Aid, Bureau of
Higher Education, U.S. Office of Education, Washington, D. C. 20202. (202)
962-2677.

The Guaranteed Loan Program for college and vocational students enables undergraduate and graduate students to borrow directly from private lenders to help pay for postsecondary education. Loans of up to $1,500 per academic year are guaranteed by a state or nonprofit agency or insured by the federal government. For a student whose adjusted family income is less than $15,000 a year, the federal government will pay the interest up to seven percent while the student is in school. In 1970-71 over one million loans were granted from a fund of $1 billion contributed by many sources. A comprehensive study of this program may be found in *A Study of Federal Student Loan Programs* (160). See 1295 for an annotation on the program's authorizing legislation.

1204 NATIONAL DEFENSE STUDENT LOAN PROGRAM, Division of Student Financial Aid, Bureau of Higher Education, U.S. Office of Education, Washington, D. C. 20202. (202) 962-0183.

The National Defense Student Loan Program was established in 1958. It provides institutionally administered loans of up to $1,000 annually with a maximum of $5,000 ($2,500 for graduate and professional students, maximum for both graduate and undergraduate study $10,000). Loans are available to financially needy students taking at least half the normal academic workload and maintaining good academic standing in an accredited public or nonprofit postsecondary education institution. In 1970-71 the federal government contributed $236.5 million toward loans to over 560,000 students. A comprehensive study of this and other federal loan programs may be found in *A Study of Federal Student Loan Programs* (160). See 1299 for an annotation of the National Defense Education Act.

1205 SOCIAL SECURITY PROGRAM, Social Security Administration. Local offices throughout the United States.

The Social Security Program, although seldom recognized as such, is one of the major sources of student aid. The Program provides monthly benefits for children of deceased, disabled, or retired workers who worked long enough in employment or self-employment covered by social security to qualify for benefits. Unmarried children under 18, or between 18 and 22 if they are full-time students, may receive whatever monthly benefits they are entitled to under their parents' Social Security account. At the end of 1970, approximately 540,000 students between 18 and 22 were receiving benefits at a rate of about $45 million per month. The benefit payments are administered through the Social Security Administration. Further information is available from local Social Security offices. Their addresses are in local telephone directories.

1206 WAR ORPHANS' AND WIDOWS' EDUCATIONAL ASSISTANCE PROGRAM, Veterans Administration Benefits Office, 2033 M Street, N. W., Washington, D. C. 20420. (202) 347-1121.

Through the War Orphans' and Widows' Educational Assistance Program the Veterans Administration provides opportunities to students whose education would otherwise be impeded by the death or total disability of a parent as a result of military service. Financial assistance for higher education is available for students between 18 and 26 at the rate of $175 per month for full-time study, for up to 36 months. Although approximately 190,000 children of veterans are eligible, fewer than half have applied for the available benefits. Wives of disabled veterans or widows are eligible for similar educational benefits. In fiscal year 1970 over 45,000 students received War Orphan benefits totaling over $41.6 million; over 7,000 widows received educational benefits of approximately $6.6 million. A fact sheet entitled *Federal Benefits for Veterans' Dependents* is available from the Government Printing Office; any Veterans Administration office will supply complete information.

1207 CALIFORNIA STATE SCHOLARSHIP PROGRAM, COLLEGE OPPORTUNITY GRANT PROGRAM, STATE GRADUATE FELLOWSHIP PROGRAM, California State Scholarship and Loan Commission, 714 P Street, Sacramento, California 95814. (916) 445-0880.

The California State Scholarship and Loan Commission administers three programs of student financial aid for residents attending a higher education institution in California. State Scholarships of $150 to $2,000 for tuition and fees at an accredited college in California are based on academic achievement and promise (as evidenced by high school grades and College Board Scholastic Aptitude Test scores) and on financial need. Some 16,000 students received a total of $13.8 million in 1970-71. The average state scholarship award in California is the highest among all major state aid programs. College Opportunity Grants of tuition plus subsistence are available to minority/poverty students. Opportunity Grants are initiated primarily at public community colleges and may be transferred to four-year colleges. In 1970-71, $1,772,000 was awarded to 1,720 students under this program. State Graduate Fellowships for tuition and fees are available for students contemplating a college teaching career in California. In 1970-71, 938 fellowships totaling $950,000 were awarded.

1208 ILLINOIS STATE SCHOLARSHIP PROGRAM, Box 607, 730 Waukegan Road, Deerfield, Illinois 60015. (312) 945-1500.

The Illinois State Scholarship Commission offers three comprehensive programs for Illinois residents seeking higher education within the state: (1) State Scholarships are renewable competitive awards of up to $1,200 annually for tuition and fees at an approved Illinois college or university. They are based on American College Testing Program scores, high school rank, and financial need. (2) The Commission also administers a renewable noncompetitive Monetary Awards Program. The maximum award for 1971-72 is $1,200, not to exceed tuition and fees at an approved Illinois college (public or private). Monetary Awards are available for undergraduate work only, and the student must be a resident of the state of Illinois and a citizen of the United States. (3) The Illinois Guaranteed Loan Program offers low-cost loans for collegiate and vocational students who are residents of Illinois and United States citizens. They must be enrolled in full-time courses of study at approved schools in the United States (and some foreign countries). In 1970-71 Illinois awarded a total of over $33 million to 48,000 students who demonstrated financial need.

1209 NEW YORK STATE SCHOLARSHIP PROGRAM, Regents Examination and Scholarship Center, 99 Washington Avenue, Albany, New York 12210. (518) 474-5907.

The comprehensive New York State Scholarship Program, begun in 1913, was for many years far larger than any other state aid program. Still ranking first or second by most criteria, it presently provides varied types of financial assistance for higher education in New York for state residents. The average award in New York is relatively low, but a distinctive aspect of the aid program is the fact that the vast majority of high school graduates are eligible, and far more students receive such state aid in New York than in any other state. There are two major programs: (1) Competitive Regents Scholarships of $250 to $1,000 (renewable) are given each year to 19,500 first-time freshmen, including 600 nursing students. These awards are based on Regents Scholarship and College Qualification Tests (1231) and on financial need. (2) Noncompetitive Scholar Incentive Awards of $100 to $600 depending upon family income are given students who demonstrate ability to complete an approved postsecondary course and whose net taxable family income is not over $20,000.

Other aid programs include the State University Scholarship Fund, the War Service Scholarships for Veterans, scholarships to children of deceased or disabled veterans, and a guaranteed loan program for full- or part-time students studying within or out of the state. Each year over $70 million is distributed to more than 220,000 college students. The booklet entitled *Handbook on Scholarships and Grants* provides a detailed description of New York's programs; a variety of pamphlets intended for students is also available. See also 165 for a comprehensive study of New York aid programs.

1210 PENNSYLVANIA STATE SCHOLARSHIP PROGRAM, Pennsylvania Higher Education Assistance Agency, Towne House, Harrisburg, Pennsylvania 17102. (717) 787-1490.

The Pennsylvania State Scholarship Program, established in 1966, provides scholarships based on financial need. For tnose demonstrating financial need, awards range from $100 to 80 percent of tuition and fees (limited to $800). They cover tuition and fees for Pennsylvania residents at approved private and public degree-credit institutions both within and outside the state, and at nondegree-credit institutions and community colleges in Pennsylvania. Current-year high school graduates planning to attend a degree-credit institution must receive a qualifying score on the College Board Scholastic Aptitude Test; no test is required of students in nondegree-credit programs. In 1969-70 about 88,000 students received a total of $51.4 million in scholarships. In dollar volume Pennsylvania's program is twice as large as that of any other state. It has a small Education Incentive Program.

Private

1211 COLLEGE SCHOLARSHIP SERVICE, College Entrance Examination Board (1112), 888 Seventh Avenue, New York, New York 10019. (212) 582-6210.

The College Scholarship Service was established in 1954 by the College Entrance Examination Board to facilitate a more equitable system of financial aid distribution and administration. CSS operates a need analysis service and acts as a clearinghouse for family financial information required by colleges. On the basis of the Parents' Confidential Statement, CSS prepares estimates of a student's resources and financial need and forwards copies of these estimates to colleges designated by the student. As a membership organization within the College Board, CSS also sponsors national and regional conferences for member organizations, sponsors research on student financial aid, and puts out a variety of publications of special interest to aid officers. The *Manual for Financial Aid Officers* (176) provides a detailed description of aid administration and need analysis and the *College Scholarship Service Fact Sheet* presents a concise description of CSS activities. For other publications see 184, 195, 196, 201, and 1368.

1212 UPPER DIVISION SCHOLARSHIP PROGRAM, College Entrance Examination Board (1112), 888 Seventh Avenue, New York, New York 10019. (212) 582-6210.

The Upper Division Scholarship Program awards scholarships to selected minority graduates of community colleges to continue their education in senior institutions. The program was established in 1970 and is funded by the Ford Foundation (1148) at about $2 million a year. Since June 1971, UDSP has been directed and administered by the College Board. Eligible students include blacks, Mexican Americans, Puerto Ricans, and American Indians who are nominated by their own two-year colleges. The Program is expected to assist approximately 1,000 students annually, with awards ranging from 20 to 80 percent of total educational expenses. UDSP is a major step toward combating the general lack of financial aid for students planning to transfer from two- to four-year institutions.

1213 National Merit Scholarship Corporation, 990 Grove Street, Evanston, Illinois 60201. (312) 869-5100.

The National Merit Scholarship Corporation is the major private scholarship program in the country. It seeks out the most academically and intellectually gifted high school students in the nation and provides many of them with scholarships for higher education. In a highly competitive program, winners are selected on the basis of scores on the Preliminary Scholastic Aptitude Test/National Merit Scholarship Qualifying Test (1230) and the Scholastic Aptitude Test, school record and recommendations, and biographical information. In 1970-71 more than 1,000 students received the unrestricted one-time $1,000 scholarships based on merit alone, and more than 2,000 received four-year sponsored scholarships of $100 to $1,500 annually. The stipend accompanying the four-year awards is based on the winner's financial need. NMSC has sponsored an important and influential research program (1173) since 1955. In 1964 NMSC established a National Achievement Scholarship Program that aids more than 300 outstanding Negro students each year. NMSC publishes a *Guide* that describes the structure and administration of the scholarship program and includes a listing of other publications related to the Merit Program.

1214 National Scholarship Service and Fund for Negro Students, 1776 Broadway, New York, New York 10019. (212) 757-8100.

The National Scholarship Service and Fund for Negro Students (1130) assists black high school juniors and seniors in obtaining admission and financial aid at postsecondary institutions. A source of special guidance rather than a primary source of funds, NSSFNS uses a computerized system to match students with appropriate colleges and provides a variety of programs to assist students and to improve guidance services. It does, however, maintain a Supplementary Scholarship Fund to help fill the gap between students' total resources and college costs. Scholarships range from $200 to $600 and are renewable for two years. Renewal is not dependent upon a specific grade-point average. *What is NSSFNS?* and *Right On With Education For Black Students* contain general information about the organization and its programs; *NSSFNS Reference Materials* is a guide to sources of funds; and *NSSFNS Student Information Booklet* gives advice and information for students on how to apply to college and obtain financial aid.

1215 Student Need Analysis Service, American College Testing Program (1101), P. O. Box 168, Iowa City, Iowa 52240. (319) 351-4470.

ACT's Student Need Analysis Service (SNAS) assists financial aid officers in the equitable allocation of resources by providing a consistent estimate of the student's ability to pay for his education. A Comprehensive Financial Aid Report (CFAR) is prepared on the basis of information received from the student and his parents and is sent to institutions selected by the student. The CFAR includes general, financial, and academic information as well as an analysis of need. The student fee is the only charge for the service. *ACT Financial Aid Services* provides general information about the program; *Handbook for Financial Aid Officers* (173) is the technical manual for institutions using the service; *Financial Aid for College: A Guide for Students and Parents* is a brief information brochure for participants.

1216 Youth Opportunities Foundation, P. O. Box 45762, Los Angeles, California 90045. (213) 670-7664.

The Youth Opportunities Foundation was organized in 1964 by a group of successful Mexican Americans. Its purpose is to help combat the inability of many talented Spanish-speaking young people to secure a higher education because of economic handicaps. With support from industry, community contributors, and other foundations, in 1970-71 YOF gave nearly $100,000 in grants and work-study to about 300 California students selected on the basis of ability and need. The Foundation also develops and carries out other educational and vocational programs such as seminars in bilingual education, cultural activities for children, and the publication of bilingual books for children. From 1965 to 1970 the Foundation participated in the development and execution of the Malabar Reading Project, which succeeded in raising the academic achievement of 1,400 Mexican American elementary school children in reading and other subjects by as much as 650 percent. The annual status report describes the Foundation, its scholarship program, other educational projects, and programs planned for the future.

13.2 — *TESTING.* Colleges vary greatly in selectivity, character, and programs; students vary greatly in background, interest, and capabilities. Consequently, the access process creates problems of admission, guidance, placement, credit practices, scholarship selection, and other specialized problems such as the foreign student's competence in the English language. These problems create the need for a variety of programs to evaluate student achievement and other characteristics as well as research programs to judge the operation and outcome of the admissions process.

The items in this section include all of the major national testing programs related to college admissions, several prominent statewide testing programs, and several research services that serve in part to assist in the evaluation of the access process. The annotations describe the nature of the program and its operation and identify sources of additional information.

1217 ACT RESEARCH SERVICES, American College Testing Program (1101), P. O. Box 168, Iowa City, Iowa 52240. (319) 351-4470.

The American College Testing Program (1101) offers a variety of research services; some are free, and others are provided at cost. There are four types of services for colleges and universities: (1) descriptive services including the Class Profile and the Institutional Self-Study Service; (2) predictive services including a basic analysis of academic potential and a more detailed study of predicted grades in college courses; (3) financial aid planning services including a profile of aid applicants or a management aid service; and (4) several special types of analysis for subgroups or systems. An additional service provides secondary schools with a profile of college-bound students. For information consult *ACT Research Services for Colleges and Universities.* Two other publications, *Your College Freshmen* (437) and *Your College-Bound Students* are designed for interpretation and use of the research services on college and high school campuses respectively.

1218 ACT STUDENT ASSESSMENT PROGRAM, American College Testing Program (1101), P. O. Box 168, Iowa City, Iowa 52240. (319) 351-4470.

The ACT Student Assessment Program is designed to measure a prospective college student's academic and nonacademic potential as well as to obtain a profile of his activities and interests by means of four objective tests (English, mathematics, social studies, and natural sciences) and a student profile section. The Program is intended to assist in the admissions process and also in guidance and course placement. The three-hour test is administered five times a year to approximately one million students at test centers throughout the United States and overseas. For further details, *Quiz for College Presidents* serves as a general information brochure; *Using ACT on the Campus* provides a guide for the use of ACT services at institutions of higher education; the *Student's Booklet* gives the student both an evaluative description of his ACT scores and general information concerning planning for college, the admissions process, and financial aid; and the *Counselor's Handbook* offers information on the use of ACT services in precollege guidance.

1219 ADMISSIONS TESTING PROGRAM, College Entrance Examination Board (1112), Box 592, Princeton, New Jersey 08540. (609) 921-9000.

The College Board Admissions Testing Program consists mainly of two components: the Scholastic Aptitude Test (SAT) and the Achievement Tests. The SAT, given to over 1.6 million students annually, is a three-hour objective test designed to measure basic verbal and mathematical abilities. The Achievement Tests are one-hour objective tests that measure level of accomplishment in any one of 15 subject fields. Both test batteries are administered several times a year throughout the world at designated test centers. Achievement Tests are also administered on some college campuses by special arrangement for placement purposes. For the first time in May 1971, composite reading-listening tests were administered in five modern foreign languages at U.S. testing centers.

For information on test centers, dates, fees, etc., consult the *Bulletin of Information: College Board Admissions Tests*. For details on test content and format, obtain brochures on each program: *A Description of the College Board Achievement Tests* and *A Description of the College Board Scholastic Aptitude Test*. For information on the fee-waiver program for needy students, contact a Regional Office of the College Board. For interpretive information, see *College Board Score Reports: A Guide for Counselors and Admissions Officers* (406). Technical information about the psychometric characteristics of the tests is available in *The College Board Admissions Testing Program*.

1220 ADVANCED PLACEMENT PROGRAM, College Entrance Examination Board (1112), 888 Seventh Avenue, New York, New York 10019. (212) 582-6210.

The Advanced Placement Program provides course descriptions and the assistance of professional consultants to help secondary schools establish college-level courses for their stronger students. It sets, administers, and grades examinations based on these courses. It sends the examination grades, together with supporting materials, to the students' colleges, thus enabling the college to grant appropriate placement and credit. In 1969-70 Advanced Placement Examinations consisting of essay and objective questions were given to 55,442 students in 11 subject-matter areas: American history, biology, chemistry, English, European history, French, German, Latin, mathematics, physics, and Spanish. The examinations are administered in the third week of May, and most students take them at their own high schools. For the 1971 examinations there was a new offering in French language. In May 1972 the Program also included examinations (or evaluations) in studio art, art history, and music. Students participating in this Program generally take college-level courses and examinations in only one or two subjects. The Program, therefore, has tended to enrich the educational programs of such students rather than to reduce the number of years of their schooling. Further information is available in the free publication *A Guide to the Advanced Placement Program*.

1221 COLLEGE BOARD VALIDITY STUDY SERVICE, College Entrance Examination Board (1112), Princeton, New Jersey 08540. (609) 921-9000.

This service offers colleges an opportunity to study the effectiveness of secondary school records, College Board test scores, and other measures in predicting both overall college success and success in selected areas of the college curriculum. The program is free of charge and provides information that may be helpful in student selection, course placement, and guidance and counseling. *A Staff Aid for the Interpretation and Implementation of Validity Studies* (453) explains the technical aspects of a validity study. For information concerning participation in the program see *Designing Validity Studies and Collecting Data.*

1222 COLLEGE-LEVEL EXAMINATION PROGRAM, College Entrance Examination Board (1112), Box 1821, Princeton, New Jersey 08540. (609) 921-9000.

The College-Level Examination Program was established to provide a national program of examinations to evaluate the academic achievement of those who have reached the college level of education either in or outside the college classroom. It serves colleges and universities by enabling them to develop procedures for placement, accreditation, and admission of transfer or unaffiliated students; it serves individuals by providing a systematic way of validating the learning they have acquired; it serves business, industry, government, licensing agencies, and other organizations by making available a reliable method of assessing a person's educational level.

The Program includes two kinds of examinations: the General Examinations, which measure achievement in five basic liberal arts areas (English composition, humanities, mathematics, natural sciences, and social sciences-history), and the Subject Examinations, which measure achievement in 28 widely taught undergraduate courses. New Subject Examinations continue to be developed. In 1970-71 approximately 650 colleges and universities indicated they would award credit based upon scores from these tests. For further information on the test dates, test centers, and fees, write for the *Bulletin of Information for Candidates.* For specific details about the nature of the tests themselves, write for *A Description of the General Examinations, A Description of the Subject Examinations,* and *College Credit by Examination through the College-Level Examination Program.*

1223 COLLEGE PROFICIENCY EXAMINATION PROGRAM, New York State Education Department, 99 Washington Avenue, Albany, New York 12210. (518) 474-3703.

The College Proficiency Examination Program was established in 1963 by the Regents of the State of New York to enable individuals to obtain college credit by means of examination without formal classroom preparation. The tests cover material included in regular college courses and measure the knowledge expected of a student who completes the course in college. Most New York higher institutions, as well as many from other parts of the country, grant credit or advanced standing for acceptable CPE performance. CPEs are currently offered in arts and sciences, professional education, health education, nursing sciences, and modern foreign languages; new examinations are developed periodically. By 1970 nearly 10,000 examinations had been taken, well over 7,000 college credits have been granted on the basis of College Proficiency Examinations, and several hundred additional CPEs have been accepted as meeting New York State and New York City teacher certification requirements. *The New York College Proficiency Examination Program* presents the background of the program, suggested study aids, special adult degree programs, examination descriptions, and policy statements of participating institutions.

1224 COLLEGE QUALIFICATION TESTS, The Psychological Corporation, 304 East 45th Street, New York, New York 10017. (212) 679-7070.

The College Qualification Tests are a series of three ability tests (verbal, numerical, and information) developed primarily for use by colleges in admission, placement, and guidance procedures. The tests, which are designed to measure knowledge of vocabulary, mathematics, science, and social studies, require a total time of approximately one and one-half hours. They are admin-istered by individual institutions at their convenience. The *College Qualifica-tion Tests Manual* provides technical and administrative information.

1225 COMPARATIVE GUIDANCE AND PLACEMENT PROGRAM, College Entrance Ex-amination Board (1112), Box 592, Princeton, New Jersey 08540. (609) 921-9000.

The Comparative Guidance and Placement Program includes tests, question-naires, and related services. It is designed to: (1) aid two-year colleges in cur-ricular guidance and course placement of their entering students; (2) help stu-dents learn about themselves and aid them in making educational decisions and career choices; and (3) assist colleges in identifying students who need remedial courses, help in basic study skills, financial aid, employment, housing, and voca-tional or personal counseling. It is expressly not concerned with the selection and admission of students.

The test battery is administered by the individual institution and requires approximately three and one-half hours of testing time. It includes a biograph-ical inventory, a comparative interest index, and test sections on vocabulary, reading, sentence construction, mathematics, inductive reasoning, and integra-tive reasoning. After three years of experimentation, the program became fully operational for use with 1969-70 freshmen. As of June 1971 there were approxi-mately 195 participating institutions distributed throughout the United States. Four publications useful for an understanding of CGP are *Announcement, Using Your CGP Report, CGP: What It's Like,* and *CGP In Action* (five parts). All are available without charge. A more technical aid is the *Interpretive Manual for Counselors, Administrators, and Faculty* (306).

1226 FLORIDA STATEWIDE TWELFTH GRADE TESTING PROGRAM, University of Florida, Board of University Examiners, 408 Seagle Building, Gainesville, Florida 32601. (904) 392-1715.

This program is conducted in all Florida high schools each fall to provide com-parable ability and achievement data on all seniors. The results of these five 40-minute objective tests of academic ability in English, social studies, natural science, and mathematics are used for both guidance and admission purposes. Florida's state universities generally require a specified composite score for admission, whereas community colleges tend to accept students with a broad range of scores. For further information see the pamphlet *Florida Statewide Twelfth Grade Testing Program.*

1227 GENERAL EDUCATIONAL DEVELOPMENT TESTING SERVICE, American Coun-cil on Education (1102), One Dupont Circle, Washington, D. C. 20036. (202) 833-4700.

General Educational Development tests are principally used to appraise the educational development of adults who have not completed their formal high school education. The test battery consists of comprehensive examinations in English composition, social studies, natural sciences, literature, and mathe-matics; each takes about two hours to complete, although no time limits are set. Annually about 350,000 civilians and 100,000 military personnel take the tests at 1,750 centers throughout the United States and overseas, primarily in order to earn a high school equivalency certificate or qualify for admission to post-secondary education. Traditionally all tests have been presented in English, but a Spanish language version has recently become available. For more informa-tion on the GED see *Opportunities for Educational and Vocational Advance-ment.*

1228 INSTITUTIONAL RESEARCH PROGRAM FOR HIGHER EDUCATION, Educational Testing Service (1115), Princeton, New Jersey 08540. (609) 921-9000.

The Institutional Research Program for Higher Education was established by Educational Testing Service in 1965 in response to the growing interest of many colleges and universities in undertaking institutional evaluation and self-study. The instruments offered through IRPHE are the College Student Questionnaires for the study of student activities and background characteristics; the College and University Environment Scales, Second Edition, for the study of the college atmosphere or "climate"; the Survey of College Achievement to measure academic achievement; the Institutional Functioning Inventory which asks faculty members, administrators, and students for their perceptions and opinions of their college or university; and the Student Instructional Report which gives faculty members an opportunity to have their students respond in a systematic way to courses and instruction. All are used to describe groups, not to assess individuals. IRPHE also offers extensive data-processing options and professional assistance in research design and data interpretation. Other instruments in preparation are also designed to assist colleges in effecting educational change in a variety of areas. For example, currently under development are the Institutional Goals Inventory, an instrument to aid institutions in defining their goals; and a self-study instrument, Student Reactions to College, which is designed specifically for use in two-year colleges. The pamphlet *Institutional Research Program for Higher Education* provides a general description of the program.

1229 NATIONAL ASSESSMENT OF EDUCATIONAL PROGRESS, Office of the Staff Director, 300 Lincoln Tower, 1860 Lincoln Street, Denver, Colorado 80203. (303) 255-3631.

National Assessment of Educational Progress is a very large data-gathering project designed to provide systematic information about knowledge, skills, understanding, and attitudes of young people in this country. The idea for this project developed in the U.S. Office of Education in 1963. Through funding from the Carnegie Corporation and the Ford Foundation, the Committee on Assessing the Progress of Education was established in 1964. The Committee planned and developed the project and in 1969-70 conducted the first stages of the study.

Data in three subject fields (science, writing, and citizenship) were collected from four age groups—9-, 13-, and 17-year olds, in addition to young adults between 26 and 35. The first reports of the project were released in June 1970 by the Education Commission of the States (1178), the sponsoring agency. These reports carry no scores or norms—just individual exercises (questions, items) along with the percent choosing or producing each response for each exercise. Thus the reader makes his own evaluation of the exercise and the results.

Many additional reports in these three subject areas as well as in seven others are scheduled. Inquiries regarding National Assessment reports should be addressed to the Superintendent of Documents, Government Printing Office, Washington, D. C. Additional information about the National Assessment project can be secured from the Staff Director in Denver, Colorado.

1230 PRELIMINARY SCHOLASTIC APTITUDE TEST/NATIONAL MERIT SCHOLARSHIP QUALIFICATION TEST, College Entrance Examination Board (1112), Box 589, Princeton, New Jersey 08540. (609) 921-9000.

The Preliminary Scholastic Aptitude Test, a two-hour version of the Scholastic Aptitude Test, has been used since 1959 in secondary school guidance programs. Like its longer and more widely used counterpart, it measures verbal and mathematical abilities by means of multiple-choice questions. In 1971 the College Board and the National Merit Scholarship Corporation (1173) entered into an agreement which substantially reduced duplicate testing. The PSAT became known as the PSAT/NMSQT and, in addition to its use by schools for guidance, is now also used by the NMSC in the selection of scholarship recipients.

The test is administered by individual schools on a specific date each fall. The majority of students who take the PSAT/NMSQT are high school juniors, but a school may administer it to any student who wants a general estimate of his ability to do work at various colleges. Well over one million students took the PSAT/NMSQT in the fall of 1971. For further information see the annual *Announcement;* more technical information can be found in *The PSAT/NMSQT Interpretive Manual for Counselors and Administrators.*

1231 REGENTS SCHOLARSHIP AND COLLEGE QUALIFICATION TEST, Regents Examination and Scholarship Center, 99 Washington Avenue, Albany, New York 12210. (518) 474-5907.

The Regents Scholarship and College Qualification Test serves both as the primary basis for awarding 19,500 New York Regents scholarships (1209), and as the State University admissions test. The six-hour test of general scholastic aptitude and subject matter achievement examines the ability to think clearly and critically and to apply knowledge. It is composed entirely of multiple-choice questions. The test is described in *The Opening Door* (165), which includes a review of the psychometric aspects of the program.

1232 TEST OF ENGLISH AS A FOREIGN LANGUAGE, College Entrance Examination Board (1112) – Educational Testing Service (1115), Box 899, Princeton, New Jersey 08540. (609) 921-9000.

Test of English as a Foreign Language (TOEFL) is a test of English proficiency for foreign applicants to colleges and universities in the United States. It is cosponsored by the College Entrance Examination Board and Educational Testing Service. Annually more than 45,000 students take the test during one of the four administrations at the 340 test centers throughout the world. Specific information about the program is available in *Test of English as a Foreign Language: Bulletin of Information for Candidates.*

1233 WASHINGTON PRE-COLLEGE TESTING PROGRAM, 1400 N. E. Campus Parkway, Room 460, University of Washington, Seattle, Washington 98105. (206) 543-1792.

This five-hour test, taken primarily by high school juniors throughout the state of Washington, measures achievement in verbal skills, mathematics, mechanical reasoning, and spatial ability. It is a cooperative enterprise of the high schools and colleges in Washington and is designed as a guidance and planning tool. It serves as the basis for one of the most comprehensive statewide college guidance programs in the nation. Scores are used to predict success in up to 43 college subject areas as well as several vocational fields. For further information see the *Counselor's Manual* or the *Student Instruction Booklet.*

13.3 – *GUIDANCE AND ADMISSIONS SYSTEMS.* The access process involves massive numbers of students and increasingly complex education/career alternatives. Add to these quantitative problems the insistence that counselors give attention to the problems of individual students and consider every possibility for individual opportunity and expression. It quickly becomes obvious that one-to-one relationships in guidance and admissions are neither feasible nor effective. These pressures have stimulated the development of complex new systems to retrieve and display information, to keep students as well as professionals informed of facts and alter-

1234–1236

―――――――――

13.3
Guidance and
Admissions
Systems

natives, and also to simplify the massive operations involved in guidance and admissions.

This section includes examples of the following types of guidance and admissions systems: Computer-assisted guidance (1244), computer-assisted admissions and related administrative operations (1246), programs of common admissions within an educational system (1248), and special secondary guidance programs (1242).

There are many local and generally more limited applications similar to those described. These items are highly selected because they represent either institutional prototypes, national programs, or activities that have received a good deal of attention.

Guidance

1234 CAREER PLANNING PROFILE, American College Testing Program (1101), P. O. Box 168, Iowa City, Iowa 52240. (319) 351-4470.

The Career Planning Profile was developed by the American College Testing Program to help those students considering vocational-technical curriculums beyond high school. The service provides a guidance-oriented system of continuing collection and reporting of information to the student and the institution. The first stage of CPP is the collection of information about the student through a student information survey, a vocational interest inventory, and a battery of academic and special ability measures. The second stage is a follow-up of the student after he has partially completed his program. The third stage is designed to assist the institution in following up its students in their jobs in order to evaluate job satisfaction and success. Career Planning Profile was field tested in 1969-70 and made operational the following year. Information concerning the operation and technical aspects of the program is available in *Handbook for the ACT Career Planning Profile*.

1235 COLLEGE LOCATER SERVICE, College Entrance Examination Board (1112), Box 2602, Princeton, New Jersey 08540. (609) 921-9000.

The College Locater Service provides high school students with an initial screening of colleges and acquaints the student with institutions that meet his stated specifications. With the help of an introductory guide, the student completes a checklist designed to determine institutional characteristics that are related to his educational preferences and requirements. The checklist also allows the various characteristics to be ranked in order of importance to the student. In response to the checklist, the student receives a report with capsule information on as many as 40 colleges that best meet his specifications.

1236 COMPUTERIZED VOCATIONAL INFORMATION SYSTEM, Willowbrook High School, Villa Park, Illinois 60181. (312) 834-9400; also 833-8075.

The Computerized Vocational Information System has been described as "one of the most impressive systems" operating in 1970. It gives students in grades 7 through 14 access to a large mass of information about occupations, apprenticeships, local job opportunities, technical and specialized schools, four-year and community colleges, and military opportunities. Students relate ability, interest, and school achievement to occupational and educational choice by prepared scripts that allow for trying alternative paths. Students "converse" with the computer via TV-like terminals, multichoice response on a keyboard, and printed copies of desired information. CVIS now operates at Willowbrook High School, College of DuPage, Naperville Community High School, York High School, and Glen Crest Junior High School.

1237 COUNSELING INFORMATION SYSTEM 9/10, Follett Educational Corporation, 1010 West Washington Boulevard, Chicago, Illinois 60607. (312) 666-5858.

Counseling Information System 9/10 is a computer-based group guidance service designed to help students develop decision-making skills and make specific educational-vocational plans. It also involves parents in the counseling process. CIS 9/10 provides ninth- and tenth-grade students with guidance materials and information in the form of experience tables built on a school's own graduates. It also provides a system of classroom group guidance wherewith counselors help students relate their levels of success in high school to future course selections and levels of post-high school aspiration.

1238 DECIDING: A DECISION-MAKING PROGRAM FOR STUDENTS, College Entrance Examination Board (1112), 888 Seventh Avenue, New York, New York 10019. (212) 582-6210.

The Decision-Making Program is a new and important contribution of the College Board to the guidance field. It is a course of study in the development of decision-making skills, designed for students in junior and senior high schools. The Decision-Making Program consists of student and leader materials that may serve as a basis for a school guidance program, as a major component for a school-wide decision-making curriculum, or as a part of the teaching of such subjects as English, social studies, science, or health education. The program stresses recognition and evaluation of personal values, acquisition and application of pertinent information, and development of effective strategies. In order to teach decision-making skills, the program uses exercises, discussions, outside activities, role-play, and simulations. A desirable feature of the Decision-Making Program is its flexibility; it can take from 15 to 45 class periods, depending upon the depth and nature of the activities included.

1239 EDUCATIONAL AND CAREER EXPLORATION SYSTEM, ASDD Mohansic Laboratory, IBM Corporation, 2651 Strang Boulevard, Yorktown Heights, New York 10598. (914) 245-6000.

The experimental Educational and Career Exploration System was developed by IBM in consultation with Donald Super and others. It is designed to supplement high school guidance services through computer-based learning. The student first converses with the computer via a projector which displays information and questions. He responds to the questions on a keyboard, and a typewriter prints messages for him. Three information banks for exploring occupations, major areas of post-high school study, and post-high school educational institutions are available. The computer stores a school data profile and a self-description profile that each student may relate to the educational and occupational information.

1240 EDUCATIONAL GUIDANCE INFORMATION SYSTEM, College Entrance Examination Board (1112), 888 Seventh Avenue, New York, New York 10019. (212) 582-6210.

Educational Guidance Information System is an experimental guidance program for high school students. Through special questionnaires and cognitive tests, EGIS collects information from students about their abilities and aspirations, interprets this information, and returns it to students in the form of personalized planning guides. The student booklet *Looking Ahead*, which accompanies the planning guides, helps each student interpret his own guide and introduces him to the importance of planning for his future through a decision-making framework. Schools are provided materials to guide counselors in the use of reported data and in leading group discussions of the decision-making process.

[*Editor's note:* This experiment was completed in late 1971]

1241 GUIDANCE INFORMATION SYSTEM, 1616 Soldiers Field Road, Boston, Massachusetts 02135. (617) 254-5613.

Guidance Information System was developed by Interactive Learning Systems, a private firm in Boston. It is a computerized data retrieval program for junior and senior high school students. The system provides extensive information in four areas: occupations, vocational and technical schools, colleges and universities, and scholarships and financial aids. Guided by prepared materials, students communicate with the ILS computer in Boston via a teletypewriter terminal located at their school. The computer prints immediate responses on the teletypewriter. GIS was successfully field tested in over 60 high schools across the country and became operational in 1969.

1242 INFORMATION SYSTEM FOR VOCATIONAL DECISIONS, Graduate School of Education, Harvard University, Cambridge, Massachusetts 02138. (617) 495-3425.

Information System for Vocational Decisions was an early and unusually comprehensive program for computer-based guidance. The system was developed jointly by Harvard University Graduate School of Education, New England Educational Data Systems, and the Newton (Massachusetts) Public Schools. A general cutback in federal funding halted further development of the system as of July 1969, but it had considerable influence on work in this field. The program was designed to facilitate responsible decision making by individuals at levels from elementary school through retirement in four areas of living: education, occupation, military service, and family. Interacting directly with the computer, the student had access to a data bank of information about career options and student characteristics, instruction units in decision-making, and supervised practice in decision-making through simulated decision problems. See 75 for further information about the system.

1243 PROJECT PLAN, American Institutes for Research (1157), 1791 Arastradero Road, Palo Alto, California 94306. (415) 328-3550.

Project PLAN (Program for Learning in Accordance with Needs) was initiated in 1966 as a cooperative project of American Institutes for Research, Westinghouse Learning Corporation, and 12 school districts. PLAN is computer-assisted for planning and monitoring the educational development of students in grades Kindergarten through 12. Computer terminals at individual schools help teachers plan individual students' lesson sequences, monitor and evaluate their progress, and provide continuous information that is valuable for the students' career development. Effective educational planning through and beyond secondary school is a central function of the program. PLAN represents an unusually comprehensive longitudinal approach to individualized instruction and guidance. (See also 64.)

1244 SYSTEM OF INTERACTIVE GUIDANCE AND INFORMATION, Educational Testing Service (1115), Princeton, New Jersey 08540. (609) 921-9000.

The System of Interactive Guidance and Information is a developmental project of the Educational Testing Service. It is a computer-assisted system designed to improve career decision-making, particularly among junior college students. After an introductory overview of the entire system, the student is free to proceed at will in four subsystems: values, information, prediction, and planning. He will be able periodically to combine elements from the four subsystems to rank options in a way that "combines subjective utility and objective probability." The intent is not merely to provide information, but to help the student learn to understand and make his own decisions. The project director describes the program in 68. An illustrated description of the program entitled *SIGI: A Computer-based System of Interactive Guidance and Information* is available from ETS.

Admissions

1245–1247

*13.3
Guidance and
Admissions
Systems*

1245 COMMON ADMISSIONS PROGRAM, California State Colleges, 5670 Wilshire Boulevard, Los Angeles, California 90036. (213) 938-2981.

The Common Admissions Program is a new admission application procedure instituted for the 1971-72 academic year among the 19 California State Colleges. Using a single application form and paying a single $20 fee, applicants indicate a college of first choice and as many as three alternate choices, filing their application with the first-choice college. Before the uniform system-wide filing period of one month begins, categories and quotas of applicants for each college are established. All applications submitted during the filing period are given consideration regardless of the date received. When all applications have been reviewed and selections made, applicants are notified of their status. Space reservations and requests for transcripts and test scores are then sent to those who can be accommodated at a college of their choice. Late applications are processed on a first come-first served basis only after all unaccommodated on-time applicants have opportunity to select an open state college. Beginning in 1972-73 financial aid applications will be included in the Common Application Form. Financial aid commitments will be granted only after the student obtains a space reservation at a particular college.

1246 COMPUTERIZED STUDENT RECORD SYSTEMS

A number of institutions have developed computerized record systems to facilitate decision-making concerning students. Bucknell University, for example, has been operating a computerized admissions system for about five years, using a second generation computer to complete data on 5,000 applicants. With the development of total systems concepts and a more sophisticated third generation computer, several colleges and universities now have student record systems comprising a master data bank with the capacity to add, correct, or report data at any time. Each office (admissions, guidance, registrar, alumni) has independent access to the data bank and develops its own program for maximum usage. Among the institutions already utilizing such systems are New Mexico State University, Regis College, University of Cincinnati, Brigham Young University, University of California at Santa Barbara, William Rainey Harper College, Oklahoma State University, the U.S. Air Force Academy, and Tarant County Junior College.

1247 COOPERATIVE ADMISSIONS INFORMATION SYSTEM, College Entrance Examination Board (1112), 888 Seventh Avenue, New York, New York 10019. (212) 582-6210.

The Cooperative Admissions Information System was developed by IBM and the College Entrance Examination Board. It is a computer-based, model system designed to assist colleges in preparing admissions and financial aid information for use in selection, counseling, and research. CAIS assembles student credentials (application, test scores, high school transcript) as well as college evaluations and decisions. This creates a comprehensive admissions data bank from which the institution can request standardized reports with comprehensive student profiles and a full range of data for planning, evaluation, and decision-making. The system also monitors admissions/financial aid decisions and checks for missing information. Several colleges may cooperatively use CAIS while maintaining individual control and access to the system. An early version of CAIS was used for several years by 12 private women's colleges in the East. A later version, designed for a third generation computer, is currently operative in the 10 state colleges of Massachusetts and a new version should be available as of fall 1971. The IBM 1401 University Admissions Information System, a similar system designed specifically for large, multicollege universities, is currently operative at Catholic University in Washington, D. C., Lynchburg College in Lynchburg, Virginia, and North Carolina Central University in Durham. Systems similar to UAIS exist at the University of Massachusetts and New York University.

1248 SINGLE APPLICATION METHOD, Associated Colleges of the Midwest, 60 West Walton, Chicago, Illinois 60610. (312) 664-9580.

The Single Application Method represents a significant and successful effort on the part of a private consortium of 12 colleges to reduce the cost and wasted effort generated by multiple applications. SAM is a program whereby a student can apply to several ACM colleges with one application, one fee, and one set of credentials, which are sent to his first-choice college. If the student is not admitted to the first-choice institution, the application is forwarded in order of preference to others listed by the applicant. Information is available from cooperating colleges that are identified in current college directories (see 1.6 for a listing).

13.4—SPECIAL ADMISSIONS. A very large number of institutions have established various types of special admissions programs for minority/poverty students. *A Chance to Go to College* (979) briefly describes some 800 such programs. The few examples included here are either prominent programs or unusual in their structure and application. They range from statewide operations to activities of single colleges; most have been in operation for several years. The annotations provide a very brief description and place emphasis on those functions that seem unique or instrumental in the success of the program.

1249 ANTIOCH COLLEGE, Antioch New Directions Program, Office of Admissions, Yellow Springs, Ohio 45387. (513) 767-7331.

The Antioch New Directions Program was established in 1970 for the primary purpose of increasing social and cultural diversity within the Antioch community. As a way of implementing the college's long-standing principle of student diversity, the Program involves a concerted effort to recruit, select, and enroll students from low-income and working-class backgrounds, those from various ethnic groups, and those who are not necessarily in the traditional college age group. Students who have been working or serving in the armed services will also be recruited. In the entering class of 1970, about 140 students (approximately 20 percent of the class) were identified as New Directions students. This Program replaces the Antioch Program for Interracial Education that was established in 1965 with major funding from the Rockefeller Foundation. There are no special application procedures or requirements for prospective students interested in the Antioch New Directions Program. The February 1 deadline is observed for both admission and financial aid applications. Accepted students with substantial financial need will usually receive a "package" award consisting of some combination of Antioch College grant, Educational Opportunity Grant, long-term loan, and part-time campus job.

1250 CALIFORNIA STATE COLLEGE AT FULLERTON, New Educational Horizons, 800 North State College, Fullerton, California 92634. (714) 870-2484.

Established in 1968 as one of California's Educational Opportunity Programs (1251), the New Educational Horizons program provides "comprehensive educational services for culturally different students." It includes recruitment, financial aid, tutorial help, professional counseling and academic advice, and extracurricular involvement. The heart of the program is the tutorial group, usually consisting of an upper-division white tutor and an entering black or brown student who interact on both social and academic levels. A "faculty friends group" has also been developed in which interested faculty members meet informally with those in the NEH program. The staff reports that this has been highly successful not only for the students but also for the faculty members. Another useful adjunct to the main program is the "general assistance corporation, which involves a group of interested people throughout Orange County who are willing to provide professional services, such as reduced fees for eyeglasses and dental care, and assistance in job placement." In 1969-70 approximately 250 students were involved in NEH.

1251 CALIFORNIA STATE COLLEGES, California Educational Opportunities Programs, Division of Student Affairs, 5760 Wilshire Boulevard, Los Angeles, California 90036. (213) 938-2981.

In 1966 the California legislature provided for the establishment of Educational Opportunities Programs at the state college and university level, and by 1970 programs enrolling nearly 10,000 minority/poverty students were in operation on each of the nine university campuses and at the 19 state colleges. A complete EOP "package" generally includes recruitment, admission, tutoring, financial counseling and aid, and housing. Since individual campuses develop their own programs, there are great differences in approach, numbers involved, and services provided. Acceptance into an EOP program is based not only on the usual (high school record and references) but also on the unusual (cultural and economic background and statement of commitment or motivation). Two successful programs are described in 1250 and 1260.

1252 CITY UNIVERSITY OF NEW YORK, CUNY Educational Opportunity Programs, 535 East 80th Street, New York, New York 10021. (212) 360-2154.

CUNY operates three special programs for disadvantaged youth: SEEK, College Discovery, and Educational Skills Centers.

SEEK (Search for Education, Elevation, and Knowledge) was established in 1966 and operates on seven CUNY four-year campuses. In an effort to encourage poverty youth to enter and stay in college, SEEK offers tuition waivers, payment of books and fees, weekly stipends (that may be as high as $50), counseling, tutoring, and remedial services throughout the undergraduate years. In some cases housing is provided. About 6,000 students were enrolled in 1970-71, and if past trends continue, approximately one-half will graduate within five years. SEEK also operates an Employment Development Program that arranges summer and part-time jobs for SEEK students and also provides counseling to both the student and the employer.

A similar and equally effective program that operates on CUNY's 6 two-year college campuses is the College Discovery Program. CDP students may enroll in either a transfer or career program. Nearly 3,000 were enrolled in 1970-71.

The Educational Skills Centers provide both vocational training and remedial work for students who wish to continue their studies. These centers operate under various names on all two- and four-year campuses. They have markedly increased the number of students served since the inception of "open admissions." Two other centers, called Urban Centers, perform similar functions in off-campus settings. They are located in Brooklyn and Manhattan and together serve 400-500 students. (See 1277 for further discussion of Urban Centers.)

1253 COLLEGE OF SAN MATEO, College Readiness Program, 1700 West Hillsdale Boulevard, San Mateo, California 94402. (415) 341-6161.

The College Readiness Program officially began in 1966 at the College of San Mateo and quickly gained national prominence as a dynamic program for minority students. Through active recruitment efforts, enrollment in CRP increased from 39 to nearly 400 by fall 1968, while the dropout rate over the same period decreased from 90 percent to 15 percent. The key ingredients in the program were tutoring, counseling, participation in regular college courses, development of a sense of achievement and unity among those involved, staff concern with nonacademic as well as academic matters, and the provision of necessary financial aid. In large part the program operated outside the general college framework, with attendant advantages and disadvantages. This factor, among others, was instrumental in bringing about a dramatic upheaval and reorganization of CRP in 1969. The Program continues to provide tutoring, counseling, and financial aid, but it is now open to all disadvantaged students and has been expanded to the two new San Mateo District Colleges, Cañada and Skyline.

1254 NAIROBI COLLEGE, 1627 Bay Road, East Palo Alto, California 94303. (415) 323-3169.

Nairobi College is a two-year, private, open-door college without walls. If an applicant accepts the philosophy of the college and is willing to assume the responsibility of community work and self-development, he is admitted without consideration of previous academic experience. In fall 1969, Nairobi opened as a tuition-free college committed to serving racial-ethnic communities and to educating people of color for community leadership. The educational program includes a staff-student team system of 7 to 15 students, a core curriculum, extensive student involvement in college governance, and required community service. Courses are conducted in faculty homes and in a variety of social service agencies in East Palo Alto. In 1970-71 Nairobi enrolled 250 students, 190 full time.

1255 NAVAJO COMMUNITY COLLEGE, Many Farms Rural Post Office, Chinle, Arizona 86503. (602) 781-6302.

Established in 1969, Navajo Community College is the first college on an Indian reservation and the first to be governed by an Indian board of regents. The college primarily serves Navajos, although admission is open to all students; a small number of the 311 enrolled in 1970-71 were non-Indians. Neither high school graduation nor the ability to speak English is required for admission. The college is dedicated to helping students acquire a positive self-image and a clear sense of identify by fully developing their capacities. Navajo Community College operates a curriculum that includes an A.A. degree program, vocational-technical training, a GED program (1227), an off-campus program of English instruction for non-English-speaking Navajos, and Navajo cultural studies.

1256 NEW YORK STATE DEPARTMENT OF EDUCATION, Higher Education Opportunity Program, Albany, New York 12210. (518) 474-5313.

In 1969 New York established the Higher Education Opportunity Program to provide support services, such as tutoring, counseling, and financial aid assistance, to disadvantaged students already enrolled at public and private colleges throughout the state. Beginning in 1970, however, the program focused exclusively on private institutions. During 1970-71 HEOP used its $4 million to fund programs involving 53 private colleges and over 3,500 students. In a few cases two or more institutions pooled resources to offer more comprehensive and effective programs.

1257 NEW YORK STATE DEPARTMENT OF EDUCATION, New York Higher Education Opportunities Programs, Albany, New York 12210. (518) 474-5313.

With the coming of "open admissions" to its City University, the State of New York has been thrust into the vanguard of those states seeking to expand educational opportunity for disadvantaged students. In addition to its financial outlay for open admissions in 1970-71, the state also allocated $17 million for collegiate special opportunity programs. This level of funding is a reflection of the high retention rates of students involved in past programs. For example, 82 percent of all 1969-70 "opportunity students" returned to college in fall 1970.

See 1252 and 1256 for annotations of specific programs. The CUNY programs are particularly large, comprehensive, and well known. The program among private colleges illustrates an unusual relationship between the state government and private institutions.

1258 SOUTHERN ILLINOIS UNIVERSITY AT EDWARDSVILLE, Experiment in Higher Education, Edwardsville, Illinois 62025. (618) 692-2000.

Southern Illinois University established the Experiment in Higher Education in fall 1966. This well-known program seeks to develop in low-income, underachieving young people from East St. Louis the academic skills necessary for successful completion of four years of college. The program is designed for two calendar years (four quarters each year). Students are prepared to compete at the junior level on the main campuses of Southern Illinois University or elsewhere. The program includes a completely redesigned curriculum, a work-study program, a staff of paraprofessionals called teacher-counselors, and learning-teaching techniques such as programmed instruction, mimeographed textbooks, and videotape.

1259 U.S. OFFICE OF EDUCATION, Special Services for Disadvantaged Students, Division of Student Special Services, 400 Maryland Avenue, N. W., Washington, D. C. 20202. (202) 962-7150.

Special Services for Disadvantaged Students is the third in a series of federal programs designed to bring disadvantaged students into the educational mainstream. The other two, Upward Bound (1272) and Talent Search (1268), provide funds to projects that seek to identify students not yet in college; Special Services supports projects designed to help disadvantaged students stay in college once admitted. In its first year of operation (1970), the program awarded funds to 146 colleges and universities to provide counseling, tutoring, career guidance, and other educational services.

1260 UNIVERSITY OF CALIFORNIA AT LOS ANGELES, Educational Opportunities Program, Los Angeles, California 90024. (213) 825-2127.

Under the aegis of California Educational Opportunities Programs (1251), UCLA operates two programs. The larger one enrolls primarily minority students who do not quite meet the university entrance requirements but who show particular promise of academic success. These students receive tutoring, on-campus housing, and financial aid according to need, but are enrolled in a normal undergraduate curriculum. The second program, called the High Potential Program, is for minority students who have not completed high school or who have not functioned well in high school but appear able to perform successfully in college if given the chance. In addition to receiving the same services as regular EOP students, those in "Hi Pot" are provided three quarters of academic skill courses, after which they are admitted to regular undergraduate status. The program enrolled about 300 students in 1970-71.

1261 URBAN EDUCATIONAL CENTER, 105 Dodge Street, Providence, Rhode Island 02907. (401) 521-7823.

The Urban Educational Center of Rhode Island was established in June 1968 as an inner-city arm of the Rhode Island system of higher education. Its specific purpose is to provide a center where people can come to learn what they want to know. Modeled on the "free university" notion, the postsecondary community is highly flexible and is developed in response to community needs and demands. Students may pursue individual courses or become enrolled in certificate or diploma courses that may be taken for institutional credit. In addition, students may take up to 27 college credits (authorized through the University of Rhode Island) at the Center. Admission is open to any Rhode Island resident seeking to further his education. There are no fees of any kind; required books are provided. On-the-spot counseling is available to students at all times. Courses are offered both at the Center and in satellite classrooms throughout Providence and the state of Rhode Island.

1262 WESLEYAN UNIVERSITY, Educational Opportunity Program, Middletown, Connecticut 06457. (203) 847-9411.

Wesleyan's Educational Opportunity Program is most notable for successful admission and retention of minority students by intensive and effective use of conventional methods. Wesleyan was one of the first highly selective institutions that chose to incorporate racial and economic diversity into its student body. In 1964 only 2 of the 350 enrolled freshmen were minority students, but by 1969 over 20 percent were. In selection, careful attention has been given to previous academic performance and "overall personal strength." Thus, most minority students are not high risk; for example, in 1969, only 5 of the 68 minority freshmen ranked in the bottom half of their high school class, and the average Scholastic Aptitude Test scores were verbal 545 and mathematical 571. Support programs for these students include frequent and intensive faculty counseling, tutoring by other students, reduction of course loads, extensive financial aid (96 percent received aid in 1969), a prefreshman summer term, and a science support program. Attrition of minority students from 1964 to 1969 was approximately 16 percent.

13.5 – TALENT SEARCH. A decade ago talent search meant locating very bright young people who had performed well in high school but did not plan to attend college. The emphasis has since shifted somewhat from academic performance to the less definite but equally significant qualities of motivation and potential. Talent search operations typically help minority/poverty youth define realistic educational and vocational aspirations and gain access to appropriate postsecondary programs.

There are a great many talent search programs. The few representative examples included here focus on different types of students in different situations. In particular these selected programs reflect the different approaches that are being used to locate and assist talented but disadvantaged youth.

1263 ASPIRA, INC., 296 Fifth Avenue, New York, New York 10001. (212) 244-1110.

The goal of Aspira, Inc. is to accelerate the development of Puerto Rican leadership from within Puerto Rican communities. Founded in 1961 in New York City, it is funded by both governmental and private agencies and has now established affiliate agencies in Newark, Philadelphia, Chicago, and San Juan. Aspira operates on the assumption that a committed and effective leadership is not possible without education and thus seeks to keep Puerto Rican young people in high school and to motivate them to attend college. It has established Aspira Clubs in about two-thirds of the New York City high schools where students participate in workshops and engage in activities designed to foster leadership development and cultural identity. They also receive tutoring, educational counseling, and career guidance. Aspira attempts to facilitate placement and the financial aid necessary for every student desiring postsecondary education. During the academic year 1968-69, 5,000 students received counseling, and more than 900 were placed in some postsecondary institution.

1264 COLLEGE BOUND, New York City Board of Education, 141 Livingston Street, Brooklyn, New York 11201. (212) 624-2725.

College Bound is a consortium of over 100 colleges and universities, including virtually all those in the Greater New York area, as well as the New York City Public School System, the New York and Brooklyn Diocesan School Systems, and Aspira, Inc. Established in 1967 with both foundational and New York City Board of Education support, College Bound works with high school students likely to drop out of high school or to graduate with only a general diploma. High schools select approximately 3,000 of these ninth- and tenth-grade students each year to receive an intensive educational program in preparation for admission to college. In addition to an initial seven-week summer session, the program includes small classes, double sessions of English, group and individual counseling, and cultural enrichment that continue until graduation. Family aides work with the students' parents to keep them informed, stimulate their interest, and help in any way possible. Cooperating colleges provide preadmission counseling, tutorial help, and general supplemental assistance to geographically proximate College Bound high schools. They also guarantee to accept and provide financial aid to needy students who complete the program with an academic diploma and a minimum grade average of 70. Approximately one-third of the students who began the program in 1967 enrolled in college in fall 1970.

1265 COLLEGE DISCOVERY AND DEVELOPMENT PROGRAM, City University of New York, New York, New York 10023. (212) 262-5460.

The College Discovery and Development Program, inaugurated in 1965, seeks to discover and develop the college potential of disadvantaged youth who would be unlikely to enter college without the benefit of intensive and long-range educational support. The university works with the Board of Education to identify several hundred such youth at the end of the ninth grade. These students are enrolled in one of five Development Centers located in high schools in each borough. Four-fifths of the first CDDP group were sufficiently motivated through the range of services and activities provided through these centers that they graduated from high school and gained admission automatically to a unit of the university.

1266 EDUCATION WAREHOUSE, 700 Massachusetts Avenue, Cambridge, Massachusetts 02139. (617) 868-3560.

The Education Warehouse, funded largely by Talent Search (1268), operates in a city where two-thirds of the population are foreign born, children of foreign born, black, or poor. Established in 1969, the Warehouse offers a wide range of support and outreach services. These include tutoring, both inside the two public high schools and in neighborhood drop-in study centers; English instruction for Spanish- and Portuguese-speaking people, Spanish instruction to police and medical personnel who have considerable contact with non-English-speaking people; and technical expertise for community action groups. The Warehouse also gathers data and maintains files on the nature of various postsecondary opportunities. The staff counsels approximately 200 people weekly, about 60 percent of whom are of high school age. During the academic year 1970-71 about 300 people were placed in colleges, technical institutes, or job training programs.

1267 EDUCATIONAL CLEARINGHOUSE OF CENTRAL LOS ANGELES, 3945 South Western Avenue, Los Angeles, California 90062. (213) 296-6123.

The Educational Clearinghouse of Central Los Angeles is sponsored by the California Council for Educational Opportunity, but is funded largely through Talent Search (1268). ECCLA works primarily with black high school students. Its three general objectives include the immediate placement of these students in institutions of higher learning, the infusion of the idea that "college is possible" into the surrounding black communities, and the training of both professional and nonprofessional individuals in the techniques of talent identification and development. ECCLA becomes aware of potential college students through cooperation with the public school system, government agencies, and local community organizations. The ECCLA staff annually counsels and advises several thousand students, both in individual and group sessions. They help students with admissions and financial aid applications, admissions test preparations, fee waivers, and trips to various campuses for interviews. ECCLA also works directly with institutions in an effort to obtain specific commitments for admission and aid. Approximately 2,000 ECCLA students applied to college for fall 1970, and nearly half were accepted.

1268 EDUCATIONAL TALENT SEARCH PROGRAM, Division of Student Special Services, U.S. Office of Education, 400 Maryland Avenue, N. W., Washington, D. C. 20202. (202) 962-7150.

The purpose of the Educational Talent Search Program is to identify poor, unmotivated young people with exceptional potential and encourage them to complete high school and undertake postsecondary education. Established in 1966, the program annually provides funds to more than 80 diverse projects throughout the country. While the majority of projects provide information on financial aid, career guidance, and college admissions to low-income urban students, a few reach into rural areas and attempt to overcome the apathy toward education that often exists. For examples of projects at least partially supported by Talent Search funds, see 1263, 1266, 1267, 1270, and 1271. The pamphlet *Search '68,* published by the U.S. Office of Education, describes all projects funded by Talent Search in 1968-69.

1269 PROJECT OPPORTUNITY, Southern Association of Colleges and Schools, 795 Peachtree Street, Suite 592, Atlanta, Georgia 30308. (404) 875-8011.

Project Opportunity is a demonstration talent search and encouragement program funded primarily by the Ford Foundation, administered by the Southern Association of Colleges and Schools, and operating in cooperation with the College Board. The project helps minority/poverty students develop their full potential by providing a highly personal guidance program over a long-term period. Begun in 1964, Project Opportunity operates at 11 centers in 8 southern states. Each center is staffed by a school counselor who is assisted by volunteers from the local school system and one or more of the 16 sponsoring colleges. Students participating in the project are identified at the seventh or eighth grade and continue their association with the project throughout high school. Of the first group of 417 Project Opportunity students who graduated from high school in 1970, 85 percent continued with some form of postsecondary education.

1270 PROJECT STAY, 1302 Guadalupe Street, San Antonio, Texas 78207. (512) 226-5387.

Project STAY (Scholarships to Able Youth) is sponsored by the Federation of Settlement Houses and Neighborhood Centers, but supported largely by Talent Search (1268). It works almost exclusively with Mexican American young people who have the ability to continue secondary education and beyond, but who are likely to discontinue their schooling because of personal circumstances. Operating in the barrios, the Project staff contacts those students identified through high school counselors, teachers, social workers, family, and other individuals. They counsel both these students and their parents to stimulate interest in further education, to give information about available financial aid, and to assist in filling out required forms. The staff attempts to discover additional sources of financial aid so that finances will not be a barrier to college attendance for any able youth. Project STAY also provides occupational interest testing and sponsors lectures and seminars by local Mexican American adults who are well acquainted with the problems students face. Since economic factors constitute a critical barrier to education for these students, part-time job development is an important feature of the program.

1271 SET-GO, Central YMCA Community College, 211 West Wacker Drive, Chicago, Illinois 60606. (312) 222-8205.

SET-GO (Support and Encouragement for Talent—Gateway to Opportunity) is a federally sponsored Talent Search Project (1268) established in 1968. It attempts to identify and counsel inner-city Chicago youths and reenroll them in formal education at the high school or college level or in other suitable training programs. Although it is a program sponsored by the Central YMCA Community College, its staff of six "street and outreach workers" has placed students in various colleges across the nation, including Harvard and several state colleges. SET-GO serves a diversity of ethnic groups living primarily in Chicago's West Side and South Side districts, although the program has taken its workers throughout the city and surrounding suburbs. Members of the staff do whatever they can to motivate and help finance young people who they judge have the potential to continue their education. SET-GO's workers walk the streets where the dropouts are, speak their language, and remain in constant contact with interested individuals. It placed nearly 1,000 young people in college in fall 1970.

1272 UPWARD BOUND, Division of Student Special Services, U.S. Office of Education, 400 Maryland Avenue, N. W., Washington, D. C. 20202. (202) 962-3710.

Upward Bound is a precollege program designed to help high school students from low-income families develop the skills and motivation necessary for success in college. Begun on a national basis in 1966, Upward Bound programs annually serve approximately 25,000 students through about 300 colleges and universities across the nation. Students admitted to the program generally have completed the tenth or eleventh grade, but typically have not had the preparation, motivation, or opportunity to realize or demonstrate their talents. They are brought to a college campus for six to eight weeks during the summer where they participate in a variety of academic, social, and cultural activities. During the academic year the Upward Bound staff continues to meet the students through classes on Saturdays, tutorial or counseling sessions during the week, and periodic cultural enrichment programs. The success of the program can be measured by lower high school dropout rates and higher college admission and retention rates than is true for similar students not in Upward Bound. Of those Upward Bound students graduating from high school, over 75 percent plan to go to postsecondary schools. According to program evaluations, however, Upward Bound has had limited impact upon the educational processes of the schools from which students have come.

13.6—*NONTRADITIONAL LEARNING*. There is a vast amount of postsecondary educational activity. These programs range from highly specific job training to liberal adult education, from federally sponsored and operated programs to private enterprise, from the level of the welfare recipient and social dropout to that of the advanced graduate student.

There are innumerable individual programs in many different settings. The selected examples included here fall into several categories: college and university nonresident programs, education in business and industry, education in the military, independent study, and various career-oriented programs. There are an even larger number of unaffiliated programs that are not represented here; e.g., community education in the secondary schools, library and museum programs, informal individual study.

1273 ADULT DAY PROGRAMS, Northeastern University, 360 Huntington Avenue, CH 102, Boston, Massachusetts 02115. (617) 437-2400.

Northeastern University's Adult Day Programs are specifically designed to satisfy the need of many adults, both men and women, for college courses offered on a part-time basis during the day that carry credit toward a college degree. Courses may be taken during the day on the Boston and/or Burlington campus leading to degrees in over 30 different fields within the general areas of liberal arts, business administration, law enforcement, education, and health science. The "open admissions policy" of University College, of which Adult Day Programs is a part, allows a student to freely register for up to 40 quarter hours of credit (approximately 20 courses or workshops), with matriculation into a formal degree program at the 40 quarter-hour checkpoint if the student has maintained a C average or better. Free program advisement is also available at both campuses during daytime hours. There are approximately 2,000 adults presently taking courses in Adult Day Programs of University College. A good descriptive catalog is available.

1274 BACHELOR OF LIBERAL STUDIES PROGRAM, University of Oklahoma, 1700 Asp Avenue, Norman, Oklahoma 73069. (405) 325-1061.

The Bachelor of Liberal Studies degree, one of several baccalaureate degrees offered by the University of Oklahoma, was launched in 1961 as "A New Frontier in Adult Education." The program consists of faculty-guided independent study in humanities, natural sciences, social sciences, and interarea studies; residential seminars; and comprehensive examinations. The student's level of prior learning, measured by placement tests, determines the amount of work necessary in each area. Students proceed at their own pace, generally completing the degree in about four years. In its first 10 years of operation, 2,650 students from all 50 states and several foreign countries enrolled in the B.L.S. program. A Master of Liberal Studies degree is also offered. Brochures (*BLS* and *MLS*) and information are available from the College of Liberal Studies office. See 782 for a detailed description of the program's background, development, and implementation.

1275 CENTERS FOR CONTINUING EDUCATION, W. K. Kellogg Foundation, 400 North Avenue, Battle Creek, Michigan 49018. (616) 965-1221.

The W. K. Kellogg Foundation (1150) has provided financial assistance for 10 prototype centers for continuing education. Each center is virtually a self-contained residential college designed for adult university-oriented education. The first was established in 1951 at Michigan State University, and subsequent centers have been established at the universities of Georgia, Nebraska, Oklahoma, Chicago, Notre Dame, and New Hampshire, at California State Polytechnic College, Columbia University, and Oxford University in England. The centers provide conferences and institute programs, credit and noncredit classes, correspondence and independent study, radio and television facilities, audiovisual libraries and studios, and a wide variety of special programs. See *Continuing Education in Action* (780) for a complete report.

1276 LA SALLE EXTENSION UNIVERSITY, 417 South Dearborn Street, Chicago, Illinois 60605. (312) 427-4181.

La Salle Extension University is one of the largest private correspondence institutions in the country. It offers a variety of courses, for which no previous training is required. These include many high school courses, business-related subjects, and such electives as foreign language and art. Since its establishment in 1908, La Salle has served over 2,000,000 students. Brochures on individual programs are available on request.

1277 SUNY URBAN CENTERS, State University of New York, Central Administration, Thurlow Terrace, Albany, New York 12202. (518) 457-4149.

SUNY Urban Centers, the first of which were established in 1966, are non-degree-granting institutions with a major focus on technical and vocational training, remedial education, and college preparatory courses for disadvantaged urban young adults. Counseling and vocational guidance are available to supplement the programs. Many students are subsequently placed in jobs in the community or they enter community colleges and other private or public college programs. The Urban Centers, operated by community colleges under contracts with the State University of New York, enrolled approximately 10,594 students in 1970-71.

The six centers are located in Brooklyn, Buffalo, the Capital District (Albany, Troy, and Schenectady), Farmingdale, Manhattan, and Rochester. The budget allocation for 1970-71 was $6.4 million. *Urban Centers Progress Report* offers a detailed, interesting account of the purposes and functions of the programs at the various centers.

1278 TV COLLEGE OF THE CITY COLLEGES OF CHICAGO, 5400 North St. Louis Avenue, Chicago, Illinois 60625. (312) 588-2000.

Since 1956 the TV College of the City Colleges of Chicago has provided opportunities for adults and college-age students to take a wide variety of subjects (at present about 75 different courses) through open-circuit television. Students watch TV lectures, send in written assignments, and take examinations at one of the college campuses. By 1970 more than 130,000 individuals had taken courses; more than half were for credit. Since 1956 more than 300 students have received the Associate of Arts degree entirely by television courses, for which only a minimal fee is charged. All college services, including counseling and library, are available to TV students. Periodic informative reports that describe the scope and the progress of TV College are published by the City Colleges of Chicago. TV College has also produced special noncredit series with federal and private funding, including the recent color series *Man and His Art,* filmed in the Art Institute of Chicago.

1279 UNIVERSITY OF CALIFORNIA EXTENSION, Office of the President, 2200 University Avenue, Berkeley, California 94720. (415) 642-7571.

Many universities have extension divisions. The university extension of the University of California is unusual in its size and scope. It provides continuing education through credit and noncredit programs on all nine university campuses, in communities throughout the state, and in worldwide correspondence instruction. Programs are open to those who have attended college and to any other adult who can benefit from university-level study. They range from one-day conferences and short lecture series to courses of two or more quarters and certificate programs requiring up to several years. Over 9,000 programs are available with nearly 300,000 registrations or more than 19,000 full-time equivalent students. Emphasis is placed on professional advancement, enhancement of cultural and intellectual vitality, improved capability to deal with political and social issues, and utilization of university resources in the solution of urban problems. The annual report of University of California Extension briefly describes extension programs at the various university campuses. Extension catalogs are available from the university extension office on the individual campuses.

Military

1280 U.S. ARMED FORCES INSTITUTE, Department of Defense, Madison, Wisconsin 53713. (608) 256-2651.

The U.S. Armed Forces Institute, established in 1942, enables military personnel in all branches of the service to further their educational development while on active duty. USAFI's mission is to provide educational services and materials on subjects normally taught in civilian academic institutions up to and including graduate study. The institute provides over 200 correspondence and group study courses in pre-high school, high school, college, and technical subjects that may be taken directly through USAFI. In addition, more than 6,000 correspondence courses are offered through extension divisions of 44 colleges and universities. About half of the 305,000 participating personnel are taking college-level work. USAFI also offers an integrated program for the general educational development of military personnel, from basic literacy through high school equivalency. Some 100,000 servicemen successfully complete the high school General Educational Development tests (1227) annually, and a large number of others participate in the College-Level Examination Program (1222). The USAFI program is actually administered by education officers at the various military installations throughout the world. The *USAFI Catalog* is the primary source of information for the entire program.

Business and Industry

1281 AMERICAN INSTITUTE OF BANKING, American Bankers Association, 1120 Connecticut Avenue N. W., Washington, D. C. 20036. (202) 467-4000.

The American Institute of Banking is the educational and training arm of the American Bankers Association. It is a good example of an industry-wide education, training, and certification program. AIB strives to meet some of the educational needs of local banks at a lower cost than that required when each bank handles its needs alone. The institute provides training in banking skills, formal and informal education for general banking knowledge, and development of management skills. The educational programs are conducted through chapters (about 20 large ones) and study groups offering classroom instruction, correspondence study, study teams for group correspondence work, accelerated in-bank study for college graduates and experienced employees, and skills training. The *AIB Catalog* offers detailed information on programs offered, admissions requirements, etc.

1282 GENERAL ELECTRIC COMPANY, Educational Relations, 570 Lexington Avenue, New York, New York 10022. (212) 750-2000.

General Electric supports the educational interests of its employees through five programs: (1) tuition refunds, (2) educational loans for employees and their families undertaking full-time college study, (3) company courses covering a wide range of specific business and technical areas, (4) cooperative advanced course and degree arrangements with several universities, and (5) manpower development programs that supplement on-the-job experience. At least 50 percent of the employees from all levels of the organization participate in one or more programs in any given year. *General Electric Careers,* an informational booklet directed to recent college graduates considering employment at GE, provides additional information on these programs.

1283 GENERAL MOTORS CORPORATION, Placement and College Relations, 3044 West Grand Boulevard, Detroit, Michigan 48202. (313) 556-2312.

General Motors Corporation provides educational assistance through the following programs: (1) the General Motors Institute, which grants baccalaureate degrees in engineering and industrial administration in a five-year work-study program; (2) the GM Tuition Refund Plan, under which GM employees receive a refund of full tuition costs and compulsory fees up to $500 per year; (3) the GM Graduate Fellowship Plan, under which selected employees may obtain a leave of absence and receive a grant to cover stipend plus costs of tuition and fees for advanced study in engineering, science, or business administration;

and (4) scholarships to college students and grants to educational associations. Three booklets, *GM Educational Opportunities, Educational Assistance for GM Salaried Employees,* and *Your Pathway to Progress* offer information on specific programs.

1284 INTERNATIONAL BUSINESS MACHINES CORPORATION, Armonk, New York 10504. (914) 765-1900.

IBM provides educational training for both employees and customers. Employee training includes job training for those who must learn new knowledge or skills to perform their jobs effectively, various management-level training programs, and voluntary programs of career development, including company-conducted courses and tuition-refund support for outside study. Professional courses, offered to customers for a fee, are intended primarily for users of IBM equipment. In addition, IBM offers tuition programs for experienced data-processing professionals at its Systems Science Institutes.

1285 WESTERN ELECTRIC COMPANY, Corporate Education Center, P. O. Box 900, Princeton, New Jersey 08540. (609) 639-0123.

Western Electric conducts a range of educational programs that include (1) job training for hourly employees at each step up the job ladder; (2) live-in programs in engineering, computer science, business management, and executive training ranging from one week to six months at its Corporate Education Center; (3) up to $350 a year in tuition refunds for anyone taking job-related courses; and (4) support of a small number of middle-management personnel in various university executive training programs including the Sloan Fellowship Program (1153).

Unions

1286 INTERNATIONAL UNION, UNITED AUTOMOBILE, AEROSPACE AND AGRICULTURAL IMPLEMENT WORKERS OF AMERICA, 8000 East Jefferson Avenue, Detroit, Michigan 48214. (313) 926-5474.

The United Auto Workers Union is the nation's second largest union with about 1,500,000 members and more than 1,650 locals. It conducts one of the most comprehensive educational programs of any organization of its type. The UAW maintains a $20 million education center near Onaway, Michigan that offers a wide variety of combined family education/recreation and leisure time activities. In addition to a liberal tuition refund program, UAW provides literature, summer institutes, films, and discussion groups on topics ranging from leadership training, to the nature and effects of automation and technology, to an understanding of national social issues and federal legislation. The union maintains what is described as the largest labor film library in the western world. It offers a wide variety of paperback books on social, economic, historical, and labor-oriented issues for sale to its members at a 20 percent discount. It also initiated an Associate Degree in Labor Studies program in 1966 that is now offered at four Michigan community colleges and includes large numbers of UAW workers among its participants.

Federal Job Training

1287 JOB CORPS, Manpower Administration, Department of Labor, 1111 Eighteenth Street N. W., Washington, D. C. 20210. (202) 382-6134.

The Job Corps was established in 1964. It strives to serve those disadvantaged young men and women aged 16 to 21 most in need of a residential training program. Public school dropouts, the individually poor, and those living in a family with an annual income of under $3,000 are eligible. The Job Corps trains enrollees to become productive citizens and places them in jobs, other training programs, secondary schools or colleges, or the armed forces. The program also tests, develops, and disseminates new techniques for working with disadvantaged youth. Enrollees receive room and board, financial assistance, and other benefits.

1288 PUBLIC SERVICE CAREERS PROGRAM, Manpower Administration, 1741 Rhode Island Avenue, N. W., Washington, D. C. 20021. (202) 961-4323.

The Public Service Careers Program is a Labor Department activity that grew out of the New Careers movement (531). It was established to meet manpower needs of state, local, and federal agencies while establishing career opportunities for disadvantaged workers. To help remove barriers to employment and advancement, the program offers remedial or advanced education, skill training, vocational and personal counseling, and transportation and child care services. Public Service Careers also helps agencies update their recruiting and selection methods and restructure jobs so that unskilled workers can be hired and trained to fill them. Most present New Careers projects in human service agencies will also be part of the new program. The program operates on the principle of "hire now, train later, and educate for higher positions." The pamphlet *Public Service Careers: Jobs of Advancement in Public Agencies* provides a description of the program and lists regional Manpower Administration offices where further information may be obtained. Information is also available from the National Civil Service League Clearinghouse for Public Manpower Information, 1028 Connecticut Avenue, N. W., Washington, D. C. 20036.

1289 WORK INCENTIVE PROGRAM, Administration Building, 2815 Bladensburg Road, N. E., Washington, D. C. 20018. (202) 832-5210.

Work Incentive Program (WIN) provides education, services, and opportunities to AFDC (Aid to Families with Dependent Children) recipients 16 years of age and over to enable them to become economically independent. In addition to job placement, work experience, and counseling, WIN provides the training necessary to obtain jobs, such as basic and remedial education, vocational training, etc. The program uses the resources of local public and private colleges, high schools, and vocational schools. This nationwide activity was authorized by a 1967 Amendment to the Social Security Act (1300). It has placed more than 50,000 welfare recipients in jobs or skill-training programs. The pamphlet *Work Incentive Program: From Welfare to Wages* gives a brief description of the program.

13.7—FEDERAL LEGISLATION. Practitioners and researchers in education sometimes fail to appreciate the importance of federal legislation. There are innumerable Congressional bills that have some bearing on access to higher education, but a limited number have had a truly dramatic effect over the past decade. Items in this section include the large packages of educational legislation and a few important prototypes of more specialized acts. Taken as a whole this legislation has had a decisive impact on student financial aid, professional development, institutional facility construction, compensatory education, and vocational education.

1290 ECONOMIC OPPORTUNITY ACT OF 1964, PL 88-452. Administered by: Office of Economic Opportunity, 1200 Nineteenth Street, N. W., Washington, D. C. 20506. (202) 655-4000.

The Economic Opportunity Act of 1964 was enacted to strengthen and coordinate efforts to combat poverty by opening opportunities for education, training, and work. It provided funds and organization for youth programs (Job

Corps, 1287, work-training and work-study programs, 1200); urban and rural community action, health affairs, and other special programs including adult basic education; and grants to higher education institutions and other organizations for research and development in these areas.

1291 EDUCATION PROFESSIONS DEVELOPMENT ACT OF 1967, PL 90-35. Administered by: U.S. Office of Education, Washington, D. C. 20202. (202) 963-1110.

The Education Professions Development Act of 1967, an amendment of the Higher Education Act (1295), was enacted to improve the quality of teaching and to help meet personnel shortages. It provided (1) opportunities for educational agencies and institutions to develop training programs for teachers in elementary, secondary, vocational, and higher education; (2) fellowships for teachers, administrators, and educational specialists; (3) a Teacher Corps to attract and train teachers for poverty area schools; (4) a Career Opportunities Program to attract and train veterans and low-income persons for careers in education.

1292 ELEMENTARY AND SECONDARY EDUCATION ACT OF 1965, PL 89-10. Administered by: U.S. Office of Education, Washington, D. C. 20202. (202) 963-1110.

The Elementary and Secondary Education Act of 1965 was a major bill designed to strengthen and improve educational quality and opportunities in elementary and secondary schools. It provided very substantial financial assistance for the education of children of low-income families, for library and instructional materials, for the establishment of supplementary education services, for furtherance of educational research and training, and for strengthening state departments of education. Major research activities funded through this act include regional educational laboratories (1172), ERIC centers (1449), and research and development centers (1161 and 1162).

1293 HEALTH MANPOWER ACT OF 1968, TITLE II, NURSE TRAINING, PL 70-490. Administered by: Division of Nursing, Bureau of Health Manpower Education, National Institutes of Health, Bethesda, Maryland 20014. (301) 496-6985.

Title II, Nurse Training, of the Health Manpower Act of 1968 is a good example of "categorical" federal support for critical professional training. It provides grants to assist in the construction, extension, and rehabilitation of facilities for public and nonprofit private schools of nursing; grants for special projects to improve the quality of nursing education; traineeships to prepare nurses as teachers, supervisors, administrators, and clinical specialists; loans with up to 100 percent cancellation for student borrowers who subsequently work full time as nurses in certain hospitals; scholarships; and contracts to recruit disadvantaged students into nursing. Approximately 60 percent of Title II funds is designated for student assistance.

1294 HEALTH PROFESSIONS EDUCATION ASSISTANCE ACT OF 1963 AND 1965 AMENDMENTS, PL 88-129, PL 89-290, PL 89-709, PL 89-751, and PL 90-490. Administered by: Division of Physician and Health Profession Education, National Institutes of Health, Bethesda, Maryland 20014. (301) 496-6907.

The Health Professions Education Assistance Act of 1963 and its 1965 Amendments were designed to (1) increase the supply of physicians, dentists, and other professional health personnel; (2) improve the educational quality of schools; (3) assist schools in serious financial straits; and (4) provide financial assistance for students. Among other provisions, these acts authorized grants for construction and rehabilitation of teaching and health research facilities, long-term loans to full-time students, and scholarship grants to health professions schools for needy students.

1295 HIGHER EDUCATION ACT OF 1965, PL 89-329. Administered by: U.S. Office of Education, Washington, D. C. 20202. (202) 963-1110.

The Higher Education Act of 1965 was one of the major legislative accomplishments in education during the Johnson administration. It was designed to strengthen the educational resources of colleges and universities and to provide financial assistance for students in postsecondary education. The act provided funds to improve undergraduate instruction, support developing institutions, improve the quality and quantity of teachers, increase library and educational media resources, set up community service and continuing education programs, develop a Talent Search Program (1268), and provide financial aid for students through the Educational Opportunity Grants Program (1208), the Guaranteed Student Loan Program (1203), and the revised College Work-Study Program (1200).

1296 HIGHER EDUCATION AMENDMENTS OF 1968, PL 90-575. Administered by: U.S. Office of Education, Washington, D. C. 20202. (202) 963-1110.

The Higher Education Amendments of 1968 continued the legislative program of the 1960s by amending the Higher Education Act (1295), National Defense Education Act (1299), National Vocational Student Loan Insurance Act, and Higher Education Facilities Act (1297). It provided substantial federal funds for programs designed to increase educational opportunity. The act extended and expanded the Educational Opportunity Grants Program (1202), Guaranteed Student Loan Program (1203), College Work-Study Program (1200), and National Defense Student Loan Program (1204). It also authorized six new higher education programs assisting both students and institutions: the Cooperative Education Program, Special Services for Disadvantaged Students (1259), Education for the Public Service, Networks for Knowledge, Improved Graduate Programs, and Law School Clinical Experience Program. *The Higher Education Amendments of 1968* (Government Printing Office, 1969) provides a good summary and analysis.

1297 HIGHER EDUCATION FACILITIES ACT OF 1963, PL 88-204. Administered by: U.S. Office of Education, Washington, D. C. 20202. (202) 963-1110.

The Higher Education Facilities Act of 1963 was enacted to assist colleges and universities to accommodate rapidly growing numbers of youth aspiring to higher education. It provided grants and loans (up to 50 and 75 percent of project cost, respectively) to assist public and nonprofit undergraduate and graduate institutions, junior and community colleges, and technical institutes to build or improve academic facilities, to expand on-campus extension and continuing-education programs, and to improve health care for students and employees. The act was instrumental in making possible the vast expansion of higher education in the mid to late 1960s.

1298 MANPOWER DEVELOPMENT AND TRAINING ACT (Title II-B, PL 87-415, as amended, 76 Stat. 23, USC 571-2628). Administered by: U.S. Office of Education, Department of Health, Education, and Welfare, Washington, D. C. 20202. (202) 963-7132.

This act is designed to provide funds to train unemployed and underemployed people and thereby help them obtain a job or upgrade their skills. Individuals are referred by state employment service offices to training programs conducted by the state vocational education agency or by a private training organization operating under contract, or they may receive on-the-job training from an employer after being hired. Although much of the education and training is for entry-level employment, some corresponds to postsecondary career training, and brief refresher training for professionals is permitted to enable them to find other employment in their professions.

1299 NATIONAL DEFENSE EDUCATION ACT, PL 85-864. Administered by: U.S. Office of Education, Washington, D. C. 20202. (202) 963-1110.

Coming in the wake of Sputnik, the National Defense Education Act was passed in 1958 to improve the education of the nation's talented youth and to insure well-trained manpower for national defense needs. Two major impacts on access to higher education have been the student loan programs (1204) and provisions for the establishment and maintenance of guidance, counseling, and testing programs. Other provisions authorized National Defense Fellowships for graduate students; strengthened science, mathematics, and modern foreign language programs and instruction; supported media research and experimentation; established area vocational-education programs; and improved state statistical services and education agencies.

1300 SOCIAL SECURITY ACT, PL 74-271. Administered by: Social Security Administration, Department of Health, Education, and Welfare, Washington, D. C. 20201. (202) 783-5666.

Social Security offers retirement, hospital, and medical insurance to the aged, but its provisions for disability and survivors' insurance have particular significance with respect to financial aid for higher education. Disability insurance provides monthly cash benefits to a disabled worker and his dependents, and survivors' insurance provides both a lump sum death payment and monthly cash payments to dependents of deceased workers. A child of a retired, disabled, or deceased worker receives benefits until age 22 if a full-time student, but only until age 18 if not a full-time student. A disabled child, however, can receive benefits for as long as he remains disabled, if his disability began before age 18. Thus, on a national level, social security is a substantial source of financial aid.

1301 VETERANS' READJUSTMENT BENEFITS ACT OF 1966, PL 89-358. VETERANS' PENSION AND READJUSTMENT ASSISTANCE ACT OF 1967, PL 90-77. Administered by: Veterans Administration, Washington, D. C. 20420. (202) 347-1121.

The educational provisions of the Veterans' Readjustment Benefits Acts of 1966, 1967, and 1970 are intended to provide vocational readjustment and restore lost educational opportunities. These acts extend the benefits of previous GI Bills to veterans and certain dependents of veterans of the "Vietnam era." Benefits include educational assistance allowance for secondary and higher education, special training for the educationally disadvantaged, educational and vocational counseling, employment placement service, and various training programs (flight, farm cooperative, apprenticeship, etc.). See 1201 for a description of the Educational Assistance for Veterans Program.

1302 VOCATIONAL EDUCATION ACT OF 1963, PL 88-210. Administered by: U.S. Office of Education, Washington, D. C. 20202. (202) 963-1110.

The Vocational Education Act of 1963 was enacted to improve the availability of quality vocational education to high school students, graduates, and dropouts; to working persons who need additional training; and to the educationally handicapped. This act provided grants to states for developing and expanding programs, building new vocational schools, and aiding needy vocational students through part-time employment. Related activities supported under this act include teacher training, program evaluation, experimental projects, development of instructional materials, and state administrative improvement.

v. *Sources of Information*

SECTION 14: PERIODICALS

This section includes five types of periodical publications that are especially important sources of information pertaining to access to higher education. Many individual reports and articles in these periodicals have been annotated at appropriate places in preceding sections. The purpose of these annotations is to describe the nature of the periodicals as information sources.

Periodical literature has shortcomings as a form of communication, but it serves vital functions. Specialized regularly appearing publications focus attention on individual disciplines, problem areas, and professional affairs. They are the prime source of most types of current information including program developments, original research reports, statistical data, and contemporary ideas. Periodicals are the initial source of a great deal of the information that is later published in book form. Also, periodicals serve a unique archival function by maintaining in one source a chronicle of research findings, interpretations, and values in specialized fields of professional endeavor and intellectual inquiry.

Because of this specialized archival function, periodicals are especially useful in understanding the various parts of a complex multi-discipline like access to higher education. Familiarity with these sources greatly facilitates locating material in unfamiliar fields. Furthermore, books and secondary references become dated, but knowing the right newsletter or journal can very quickly bring the reader up to date on an otherwise obscure topic. Consequently, this section includes a fairly large number of periodicals. Some of them are very general and quite valuable; others are perhaps not quite so consistently striking in quality but provide valuable information in specialized areas.

14.1–*JOURNALS*. There are hundreds of journals in education. The 40 or so in this section include many of the most prominent, particularly those that include material of special relevance to the access process. The annotation attempts to give the reader some indication of what he can expect to find in the journal—what sort of content, what sort of language and style, who reads the journal, and routine information concerning subscription. Also, the annotations include information on circulation and readership of each journal and newsletter as reported by the publication.

1303 *AAUP Bulletin,* American Association of University Professors (1099), One Dupont Circle, N. W., Washington, D. C. 20036. (202) 466-8050. Frequency: quarterly. Price: $4.50 per year. Usual length: about 100 pp.

As the official journal of AAUP, the *Bulletin* presents Association news, reports of its various committees, and articles written primarily by its members. Committee reports include AAUP position statements, discussions of committee activities, and explanations of cases investigated by the Association. Articles tend to focus on governance, academic reform, and job concerns rather than on issues arising within any particular academic discipline. Both articles and reports are fairly concise, so that the reader receives information on a number of topics within a single issue. Circulation exceeds 90,000.

1304 *AAUW Journal,* American Association of University Women (1100), 2401 Virginia Avenue, N. W., Washington, D. C. 20037. (202) 338-4300. Frequency: 7 per year. Price: $3 per year. Usual length: about 50 pp.

This attractive, well-organized journal includes numerous articles on women's roles but also presents discussions on issues such as ecology, foreign policy, and education at all levels. Material on higher and continuing education is presented in most issues and is generally oriented toward opportunities and programs for women. The circulation of 175,000 includes, for the most part, women college graduates, but the timeliness and quality of the articles deserve a wide readership of both sexes.

1305 *American Education,* Superintendent of Documents, U.S. Government Printing Office, Washington, D. C. 20402. Frequency: 10 per year. Price: $4.50 per year. Usual length: 30-40 pp.

With articles written for the most part by professional journalists interested in education, *American Education* primarily provides interesting success stories of projects funded by the U.S. Office of Education. Projects cut across all age levels from preschoolers to senior citizens, and the articles offer readers a wealth of new ideas. Once a year, usually in November, the periodical lists critical information on all types of programs funded by the Office of Education, including the amount of each appropriation and who may apply. *American Education* is distributed to about 35,000 educators.

1306 *American Educational Research Journal,* American Educational Research Association (1104), 1126 Sixteenth Street, Washington, D. C. 20036. (202) 223-9485. Frequency: quarterly. Price: $8 per year. Usual length: about 200 pp.

This journal is a principal publication of the 10,000-member American Educational Research Association. It publishes original reports of experimental and theoretical studies in education at all levels. The reports are often pertinent to current educational issues, but the content and style are that of a research journal. Although the studies vary widely from governance to student self-concepts, a large proportion deal with some facet of the classroom learning process.

1307 *American Journal of Sociology,* University of Chicago Press, 5801 Ellis Avenue, Chicago, Illinois 60637. (312) 753-3301. Frequency: bimonthly. Price: institutions $15 per year; individuals $10 per year. Usual length: 175-225 pp.

This university-based journal publishes technical sociological research reports. Although most of the reported studies have not been conducted in educational settings, the few that have been comprise some of the most significant literature on educational and social mobility. In addition, each issue contains 15-20 book reviews. The *Journal* has a circulation of 9,400, largely to members of the American Sociological Association.

1308 *American Psychologist,* American Psychological Association (1106), 1200 Seventeenth Street, N. W., Washington, D. C. 20036. (202) 833-7600. Frequency: monthly. Price: $10 per year. Usual length: 100-120 pp.

This is the primary professional journal of APA, and much of the content is concerned with associational affairs or matters of general professional interest to psychologists in many different fields. Consequently, most of the material is not directly related to access to higher education, but periodically there are especially important articles concerned with the nature of ability, the social context of testing and behavioral research, and similar general topics. Most of the 33,000 circulation goes to APA members.

1309 *American Scholar,* Phi Beta Kappa, 1811 Q Street, N. W., Washington, D. C. 20009. (202) 265-3808. Frequency: quarterly. Price: $5 per year. Usual length: 175-200 pp.

Labeled "a quarterly for the Independent Thinker," this influential and intellectual journal presents articles and lengthy book reviews that cover a range of socially important topics. Although quite scholarly, the material is generally both readable and stimulating. The few articles that focus on higher education typically discuss broad issues of interest to both the professional educator and the thoughtful noneducator. The circulation of 40,000 includes an unusually diverse audience of professionals, executives, housewives, scientists, educators, and students.

1310 *American Sociological Review,* American Sociological Association (1107), 1001 Connecticut Avenue, N. W., Washington, D. C. 20036. (202) 347-7140. Frequency: bimonthly. Price: organizations $20 per year; individuals $15 per year. Usual length: about 200 pp.

This official journal of the American Sociological Association presents technical reports of research undertaken by sociologists on a wide variety of problems. Each issue also contains reviews of 50 to 75 recent books. The journal is a standard sociological periodical of primary interest to those within the discipline though it frequently includes articles that bear upon access to higher education. There are 19,000 subscribers, most of whom are ASA members or libraries.

1311 *American Vocational Journal,* American Vocational Association (1108), 1510 H Street, N. W., Washington, D. C. 20005. (202) 737-3722. Frequency: monthly, except June, July, August. Price: $6 per year. Usual length: 75-100 pp.

This readable, popularly styled journal features articles of interest both to classroom teachers and to those involved in planning and evaluation of vocational education. The *Journal* describes federal developments concerning vocational education in a regular "Washington" column and also enlists federal labor and education leaders to write articles. As the foremost journal in its field, the *American Vocational Journal* is received by over 52,000 readers, including the teachers, educational administrators, counselors, and job supervisors who constitute the majority of the American Vocational Association.

1312 *Change Magazine,* NBW Tower, New Rochelle, New York 10801. (914) 235-8700. Frequency: 10 per year. Price: $10 per year. Usual length: 60-80 pp.

Change, a new and experimental magazine, takes broadside approaches to the most controversial issues in higher education. Its stimulating and provocative articles, written by well-known educators and journalists, address not only professional educators, but a popular audience as well. Its articles generate a lively letters-to-the-editor section; other regular features include reports on the Washington scene, book reviews, reports from the campuses, etc. Circulation is about 16,000.

1313 *Civil Rights Digest,* U.S. Commission on Civil Rights (1141), Superintendent of Documents, U.S. Government Printing Office, Washington, D. C. 20402. (202) 655-4000. Frequency: quarterly. Price: 35 cents per copy. Usual length: about 50 pp.

With this journal the Commission on Civil Rights seeks to stimulate interest in current civil rights issues. Many articles focus on some aspect of minority education. Writers come from diverse occupations and present material that is both interesting and to the point. The *Digest* is circulated to over 20,000 readers, a large portion of whom are in governmental or private organizations and schools.

1314 *College and University,* American Association of Collegiate Registrars and Admissions Officers (1096), One Dupont Circle, Suite 330, Washington, D. C. 20036. (202) 293-6230. Frequency: quarterly. Price: $8 per year. Usual length: 80-100 pp.

This journal presents research reports and fairly brief articles on professional affairs and topics of particular interest to registrars and admissions officers. The research reports are written in nontechnical language. Each summer edition consists of the proceedings of the most recent annual meeting and a subject and author index to articles published in the journal during the preceding academic year. Circulation is approximately 6,000.

1315 *College Board Review,* College Entrance Examination Board (1112), Box 592, Princeton, New Jersey 08540. (609) 921-9000. Frequency: quarterly. Price: $2 per year. Usual length: 25-30 pp.

The *College Board Review* is an attractively designed quarterly that provides a forum for the exchange of information and opinion on all matters related to the school-to-college transition. It probably contains articles on more of the issues included in the taxonomy of this guide than any other single journal. Articles range from a discussion of current national issues to practical admissions and financial aid problems. In addition, each issue contains information on College Board programs, activities, and publications. The circulation of 20,000 goes primarily to admissions officers, financial aid officers, guidance counselors, and administrators.

1316 *Compact,* Education Commission of the States (1178), 300 Lincoln Tower, 1860 Lincoln Street, Denver, Colorado 80203. (303) 255-3631. Frequency: bimonthly. Price: $6 per year. Usual length: 40-50 pp.

Compact is an important source of information concerning statewide coordination, planning, and governance of education at all levels. It typically focuses on a single topic in each issue. Examples of recent topics are: performance contracting, occupational education, drug abuse, interstate cooperation, and state aid to private education. October issues present annual meeting proceedings of the Education Commission of the States. A main strength of *Compact* derives from its broad spectrum coverage of viewpoints of the political, business, and education communities concerning important educational issues. It reaches 13,000 readers, including researchers, administrators, and professors. It is sent free to many legislators and government officials.

1317 *Daedalus,* American Academy of Arts and Sciences (1094), 280 Newton Street, Brookline, Massachusetts 02146. (617) 522-2400. Frequency: quarterly. Price: $8 per year. Usual length: 200-400 pp.

As the journal for the American Academy of Arts and Sciences, whose members are elected for outstanding scholarly achievements, *Daedalus* maintains a high level of scholarship in its articles. Issues are often devoted to the proceedings of conferences on topics of major concern to the leadership in higher education; virtually all issues appear in expanded form as hardcover or paperback books. *Daedalus* has a circulation of about 50,000.

1318 *Demography,* Population Association of America, P. O. Box 14182, Benjamin Franklin Station, Washington, D. C. 20044. (202) 393-3253. Frequency: quarterly. Price: $15 per year. Usual length: about 150 pp.

Although *Demography* only occasionally includes a paper with an educational focus, its numerous discussions of population growth and residential distribution should be of interest to researchers on access to higher education. Authors are primarily sociologists, demographers, and economists. Their articles tend to be technical and international in scope. Its circulation of over 2,000 goes primarily to members of the Population Association.

1319 Education Supplement: "Education in America," *Saturday Review,* 380 Madison Avenue, New York, New York 10017. (212) 983-5555. Frequency: monthly. Price: $10 per year for entire magazine. Usual length: 15-20 pp.

"Education in America" is a monthly supplement included in the weekly *Saturday Review.* Sponsored by the Kettering Foundation (1151), it provides perceptive and well-written articles on a wide variety of educational topics. Normally, each issue focuses on a topic of major public interest such as campus disruptions, education of the disadvantaged, and open admissions, and includes at least one article describing innovative programs. Additional regular features include editorials, letters to the editor, and book reviews. As a forum for the discussion of major educational issues of national interest, it is one of the most informative series available. Circulation of the *Saturday Review* is 630,000.

1320 *Educational Record,* American Council on Education (1102), One Dupont Circle, Washington, D. C. 20036. (202) 833-4758. Frequency: quarterly. Price: $10 per year. Usual length: about 100 pp.

Educational Record, the journal of the influential American Council on Education, serves as a forum for discussion of current issues. Its articles present a wide range of viewpoints of particular value to higher education administrators involved in decision-making. Book reviews and commentary are also regular features, and on occasion policy statements of ACE are made public through the *Record*. It is distributed to 10,000 readers, primarily college administrators.

1321 *Harvard Educational Review,* Longfellow Hall, 13 Appian Way, Cambridge, Massachusetts 02138. (617) 495-3432. Frequency: quarterly. Price: $10 per year. Usual length: 150-175 pp.

Harvard Educational Review presents articles of opinion and research on education at all levels. It ranks with the most respected journals, and is published by Harvard graduate students in education. Its primary focus is on elementary and secondary education, but occasionally it includes articles on higher education. From time to time, the *Review* devotes an entire issue to one subject. For example, the winter 1968 issue focused on "Equal Education il Opportunity," and 15 leading educators spoke to the research and policy issues involved. The *Review* has a circulation of 13,500 and is read primarily by administrators, researchers, and professors.

1322 *Journal of College Placement,* College Placement Council, Inc. (1113), P. O. Box 2263, Bethlehem, Pennsylvania 18001. (215) 868-1421. Frequency: quarterly. Price: $18 per year (includes five other publications). Usual length: 100-125 pp.

This journal is devoted to the interests of college placement and industrial recruitment officers. Articles include essays on relevant social issues, surveys of college graduates, aspects of career counseling, and placement and recruitment functions. Most authors are directly involved in either college placement or corporate recruitment. As the standard college placement journal in the country, each issue presents a calendar of upcoming regional association meetings, news of College Placement Council projects and activities, reviews of career-information literature, and a host of corporate recruitment advertisements. There are about 5,000 subscribers.

1323 *Journal of College Student Personnel,* American College Personnel Association, Division of American Personnel and Guidance Association (1105), 1607 New Hampshire Avenue, N. W., Washington, D. C. 20009. (202) 483-4633. Frequency: bimonthly. Price: $12 per year. Usual length: about 80 pp.

As the official journal of the American College Personnel Association, this publication reports on the problems and issues confronting student personnel workers. Most articles are research reports; some focus on the student and the complexities of college life, others investigate the functions and operations of the counseling center and its staff. The research itself is usually highly practical, not especially technical, and uneven in quality. Circulation is about 8,000.

1324 *Journal of Counseling Psychology,* American Psychological Association (1106), 1200 Seventeenth Street, N. W., Washington, D. C. 20036. (202) 833-7600. Frequency: bimonthly. Price: $10 per year. Usual length: about 100 pp.

This is the standard technical journal for theory and research in counseling and related activities. Particular attention is given to articles dealing with the developmental aspects of counseling as well as with diagnostic, remedial, and therapeutic approaches. Articles are not restricted to studies within educational settings, but include business, religious, and military institutions as well. The *Journal* has a circulation of 9,000, composed for the most part of counseling psychologists and researchers.

1325 *Journal of Educational Measurement,* National Council on Measurement in Education (1127), Irvin J. Lehman, Secretary-Treasurer, Office of Evaluation Service, Michigan State University, East Lansing, Michigan 48823. (517) 355-1912. Frequency: quarterly. Price: $10 per year. Usual length: 60-80 pp.

Most journals concerned with educational measurement are both technical and abstruse. This journal makes an effort to focus on practical problems, but much of the material is specialized. Articles are more likely to be concerned with methodology than with the substantive outcome of measurement. The authors are typically psychologists who specialize in measurement. The *Journal*'s circulation is 2,700, distributed primarily to members of NCME.

1326 *Journal of Educational Psychology,* American Psychological Association (1106), 1200 Seventeenth Street, Washington, D. C. 20036. (202) 833-7600. Frequency: bimonthly. Price: $10 per year. Usual length: 80-100 pp.

This is a technical journal; it publishes original investigations and theoretical papers dealing with problems of learning, teaching, and the psychological development of the individual. Most studies deal with complex types of behavior, especially in educational settings. Papers concern all levels of education. Issues are circulated to 9,000 readers and are of primary interest to educational psychologists and research specialists.

1327 *Journal of Higher Education,* Ohio State University Press, 2070 Neil Avenue, Columbus, Ohio 43210. (614) 422-6930. Frequency: monthly, except July, August, September. Price: organizations $10 per year; individuals $8 per year. Usual length: 80-90 pp.

This well-established though not especially colorful journal consists primarily of essays on general education and academic reform. The majority are written by college and university faculty. Informative and useful sections of the *Journal* include two regular features: "Trends and Tangents" and "Book Reviews." The *Journal*'s stature and financial base have been strengthened by its recent affiliation with the American Association for Higher Education (1095), and its new editor seeks to include more research-based articles. The 5,500 subscribers include educators and students in the higher education community.

1328 *Journal of Human Resources,* University of Wisconsin Press, P. O. Box 1379, Madison, Wisconsin 53701. (608) 262-1116. Frequency: quarterly. Price: organizations $16 per year; individuals $8 per year. Usual length: 125-130 pp.

Since its inception in 1966, this successful journal has emerged as the foremost periodical of its type. Its primary emphasis is on the role of education and training in enhancing productive skills, employment opportunities, and income. It also includes articles on general manpower, health, and welfare policies as they relate to the labor market and to economic and social development. The articles report studies of critical, timely issues that, despite their technical format, are generally readable and should be of interest to those concerned with educational outcomes. There are currently about 2,000 subscribers. The majority are institutions and organizations, probably because the *Journal* is not sponsored by an association and relatively few individuals think of human resources as a primary professional interest. The authors are primarily economists and sociologists.

1329 *Journal of Negro Education,* Bureau of Educational Research, Howard University, Washington, D. C. 20001. (202) 387-6100. Frequency: quarterly. Price: $5 per year. Usual length: 80-100 pp.

Each issue of the *Journal of Negro Education* features short reports on research relating to Negro education. Authors represent a variety of disciplines; articles generally focus on elementary and secondary students, often comparing black and white students and the learning environment. Each summer issue is devoted to essays and research on a single theme. In 1970 the theme was "Black Studies in American Education," and in 1971 it was "Strategies for Educational Change." The *Journal* has a circulation of 3,300 and goes primarily to high school and college libraries, counselors, and other concerned individuals.

1330 *Journal of Student Financial Aid,* National Association of Student Financial Aid Administrators (1122), Richard Tombaugh, Director of Central Office,

Purdue University, Lafayette, Indiana 47907. (317) 749-3676. Frequency: 2 per year. Price: $4 per year. Usual length: about 50 pp.

This new journal attractively presents articles dealing with matters relating to financial support for college students. In particular, articles focus on significant issues in financial aid administration, descriptions of innovative programs, and reports of research projects. Articles are typically well written and timely. This journal is of primary interest to those concerned with student aid. Copies are sent to about 3,000 individuals, including all members of the National Association of Student Financial Aid Administrators.

1331 *Journal of the National Association of Women Deans and Counselors,* National Association of Women Deans and Counselors (1123), 1201 Sixteenth Street, N. W., Washington, D. C. 20036. (202) 833-4256. Frequency: quarterly. Price: $7.50 per year. Usual length: 40-50 pp.

Essays and research reports in this journal focus primarily on college student personnel work and postsecondary education of women. Articles tend to be readable, practical, and of general value to student personnel workers of both sexes. Typically very little space is given over to Association news and affairs, but most of the 3,000 journal recipients are members of the Association.

1332 *Junior College Journal,* American Association of Junior Colleges (1097), Publisher Services, Inc., 705 Prince Street, Alexandria, Virginia 22314. (703) 836-3231. Frequency: monthly, except combined for June-July, August-September, December-January. Price: $4.50 per year. Usual length: 60-80 pp.

This popular, well-designed journal is both highly informative and enjoyable to read. Its brief articles cover virtually every facet of junior college education, from curriculum design to professional affairs and educational accountability. Each issue typically has two or three articles on interesting programs under way at particular colleges. The *Journal* also includes campus news items, a calendar of events, job openings, recent publications, and extensive advertisements. It is the standard periodical of the junior college community; each issue goes to over 45,000 subscribers.

1333 *Liberal Education,* Association of American Colleges (1110), 1818 R Street, N. W., Washington, D. C. 20009. (202) 265-3137. Frequency: 4 per year. Price: $5 per year. Usual length: about 125 pp.

This journal is not as esoteric as its title and design might suggest. It consists primarily of essays that deal with a variety of important educational issues. Each March issue carries the proceedings of the Association of American Colleges' annual meeting. Other issues include as a regular feature a section describing recent interesting developments on member college campuses. *Liberal Education* has a circulation of about 5,000 and is read primarily by academic administrators.

1334 *Manpower,* Manpower Administration, U.S. Department of Labor, Superintendent of Documents, U.S. Government Printing Office, Washington, D. C. 20402. (202) 393-2420. Frequency: monthly. Price: $7 per year. Usual length: 32 pp.

This attractive monthly journal of the Manpower Administration presents articles that illustrate progress in job opportunities. Contributions are written by journalists or personnel involved with manpower programs and usually focus on successful job training programs across the country or on problems that still need solutions. Occasionally, an entire issue will be devoted to a single topic, such as "Making Prison Training Work" (January 1971). *Manpower* has over 20,000 subscribers and is of primary interest to state employment services, regional manpower offices, and a variety of educational groups.

1335 *Measurement and Evaluation in Guidance,* Association for Measurement and Evaluation in Guidance, American Personnel and Guidance Association (1105), 1607 New Hampshire Avenue, N. W., Washington, D. C. 20009. (202) 483-4633. Frequency: quarterly. Price: $6 per year. Usual length: about 60 pp.

This journal publishes research on various measurement and evaluation instruments and their usefulness and relation to guidance and counseling at all levels. Some articles are theoretical and oriented toward the measurement specialist; others are more practical and intended for administrators, counselors, or personnel workers. In the fall 1970 issue, *Measurement and Evaluation in Guidance* began a test review section that should prove helpful. It has a circulation of about 3,000 and is of primary value to professionals involved with secondary and collegiate counseling and testing centers.

1336 *Monthly Labor Review,* Bureau of Labor Statistics (1447), Superintendent of Documents, U.S. Government Printing Office, Washington, D. C. 20402. (202) 961-2327. Frequency: monthly. Price: $9 per year. Usual length: 100-125 pp.

Whereas *Manpower* (1334) and *Occupational Outlook Quarterly* (1339) are oriented toward the individual worker, *Monthly Labor Review* depicts the overall national labor picture. Articles written primarily by Department of Labor staff members factually describe labor conditions and trends. The *Review* regularly reports major labor agreements and developments in industrial relations, and reviews the relevant literature. A large portion of each issue is devoted to current labor statistics. The *Review* is of primary interest to manpower specialists, economists, labor managers, lawyers, and professors. Even though somewhat dry and technical, it is a primary source of important information concerning employment. The circulation exceeds 16,000.

1337 *National ACAC Journal,* National Association of College Admissions Counselors (1119), 9933 Lawler Avenue, Suite 500, Skokie, Illinois 60076. (312) 676-0500. Frequency: quarterly. Price: $6 per year. Usual length: 20-30 pp.

This journal concentrates on counseling, admissions, and financial aid. Articles written primarily by practitioners in these areas deal largely with college admissions policies, practices, and office procedures. There are also occasional short essays on general educational problems. This is a primary journal for anyone interested in school-to-college transition. Circulation is about 5,000.

1338 *NEA Research Bulletin,* National Education Association (1128), 1201 Sixteenth Street, N. W., Washington, D. C. 20036. (202) 833-5469. Frequency: quarterly. Price: $2 per year. Usual length: 25-30 pp.

This very informative series contains summaries of research and experimentation presented in a concise readable format. All articles are written by NEA staff members and include material particularly helpful to elementary and secondary school teachers and administrators. Articles present information related both to the educational process (e.g., computer-assisted instruction) and to job-related concerns (e.g., rights of nontenured teachers). Most issues have numerous figures and tables that are also likely to be of value to researchers. Circulation is over 110,000.

1339 *Occupational Outlook Quarterly,* Bureau of Labor Statistics (1447), Superintendent of Documents, U.S. Government Printing Office, Washington, D. C. 20402. (202) 393-2420. Frequency: quarterly. Price: $1.50 per year. Usual length: 30-40 pp.

Whereas *Manpower* (1334) focuses on job training, *Occupational Outlook Quarterly* typically describes and discusses particular job categories ranging from cowpunchers to sewage plant operators. Written primarily by Department of Labor staff members, articles contain information on the nature of the job, its requirements, and future demands for such positions. The journal is attractive and simply written and serves as a valuable, practical resource for those who counsel youth about career opportunities as well as for young people themselves. Descriptions of recent Special Labor Force Reports (1412) are presented regularly. *Occupational Outlook Quarterly* has a circulation of 30,000 and is sent primarily to guidance personnel at secondary and higher education levels.

1340 *OECD Observer,* Organization for Economic Cooperation and Development (1138), OECD Publications Center, Suite 1207, 1750 Pennsylvania Avenue, N. W., Washington, D. C. 20006. (202) 298-8755. Frequency: bimonthly. Price: $3.50 per year. Usual length: 42 pp.

Printed in English and French, the *OECD Observer* is an attractive news magazine that chronicles the economic development of the 22 OECD countries. Articles sometimes focus on a particular economic issue in a single country, others discuss and display comparative data for one or more subjects throughout all member countries. Occasionally, the journal publishes important articles on comparative information concerning access to higher education in different countries. But, in general, it is a prime source of information about the relationship of educational planning to manpower resources and economic development. There are 1,200 subscribers in the United States, but this is only a small percentage of the world circulation. The journal appeals primarily to top-level planners and international specialists.

1341 *Personnel and Guidance Journal,* American Personnel and Guidance Association (1105), 1607 New Hampshire Avenue, N. W., Washington, D. C. 20009. (202) 483-4633. Frequency: monthly, except July and August. Price: $15 per year. Usual length: 75-90 pp.

As the official journal of the American Personnel and Guidance Association, this publication provides professional information to its diverse membership. Virtually all issues are addressed to counseling and guidance problems or modes of operation. The *Journal* is a practical resource. It carries many book reviews and a regular feature, "In the Field," which includes reports of programs, practices, and techniques. From time to time, entire issues are devoted to discussions related to a theme of critical current importance. Directed to the common interest of counselors and personnel workers at all educational levels, the *Journal* has a circulation of 35,000 — mostly APGA members.

1342 *Phi Delta Kappan,* Phi Delta Kappa, Eighth Street and Union Avenue, Box 789, Bloomington, Indiana 47401. (812) 339-1156. Frequency: monthly, except July and August. Price: $6.50 per year. Usual length: 50-75 pp.

This official journal of Phi Delta Kappa includes presentations of programs, issues, and ideas of paramount concern to primary and secondary education. Many of the articles, however, deal with important current issues of equal concern to higher education: for example, the entire December 1970 issue was devoted to a discussion of accountability. The 91,000 subscribers are primarily Phi Delta Kappa members engaged in elementary, secondary, and college teaching or administration.

1343 *Review of Educational Research,* American Educational Research Association (1104), 1126 Sixteenth Street, N. W., Washington, D. C. 20036. (202) 223-9485. Frequency: 5 per year. Price: $10 per year. Usual length: 100-150 pp.

The purpose of *Review of Educational Research* is to publish critical, integrative reviews of the research literature rather than reports of original research. Articles identify, summarize, and critically analyze the important studies on topics of current research interest. Each issue contains five to eight such reviews. Although not a journal for light reading, the *Review* does have considerable value as a reference. There are about 12,000 subscribers, most of whom are educational researchers.

1344 *Sociology of Education,* American Sociological Association (1107), 1001 Connecticut Avenue, N. W., Washington, D. C. 20036. (202) 347-7140. Frequency: quarterly. Price: organizations $14 per year; individuals $10 per year. Usual length: 80-110 pp.

This journal provides a forum for studies of education by scholars in all the social sciences from all parts of the world. This approach to analyzing all levels of educational institutions has considerable value, but the appeal of the journal seems limited by its scholarly design and lack of emphasis on the practical application of research findings. Its current circulation is about 3,000.

1345 *Today's Education,* National Education Association (1128), 1201 Sixteenth Street, N. W., Washington, D. C. 20036. Frequency: monthly, except June, July, August. Price: available only to NEA members or to institutions at $7 per year. Usual length: 60-80 pp.

Today's Education is the official journal for one million members of the National Education Association. It presents articles and other regular features designed particularly for its largest group of members—elementary and secondary teachers. Occasional articles focus on higher education or federal policies affecting all levels of education. Journal topics range from thoughtful discussions of major issues to delightful short stories to position statements on federal proposals, written mostly by classroom teachers and NEA staff members. This attractively designed journal is undoubtedly read by more public school teachers than any other professional periodical. In addition to NEA members, its subscribers include over 6,000 college libraries and other institutions.

14.2—*NEWSLETTERS.* In the past decade it seems that everyone with a mimeograph machine has initiated a newsletter. They cover every conceivable area of interest and report all forms of trivia. In general, however, newsletters are especially valuable because they provide current information concerning highly specialized problems, professional groups, and organizations. The fairly extensive group represented in this section is by no means comprehensive, although it does represent most of the areas of special interest included in the taxonomy of this guide. It will be obvious from the annotations that the content, purpose, and possible utility of the newsletters vary a great deal.

1346 *Academe,* American Association of University Professors (1099), One Dupont Circle, Washington, D. C. 20036. (202) 466-8050. Frequency: 5 per academic year. Price: $1 per year. Usual length: 4 pp.

Academe is a readable, informative bulletin dealing with the general business and news of interest to the members of AAUP. It also serves its membership through a regular feature announcing academic vacancies. Circulation is 90,000 —primarily AAUP members.

1347 *ACTivity,* American College Testing Program (1101), P. O. Box 168, Iowa City, Iowa 52240. (319) 351-4470. Frequency: 4-6 per year. Price: free. Usual length: 8 pp.

ACTivity, the official newsletter of the American College Testing Program, provides timely information about the ACT program, activities, and schedules, as well as related educational news on such topics as financial aid, student personnel services, admissions policies, and two-year colleges. It often contains short, newsworthy articles of particular interest to college users of ACT services and to high school counselors. Circulation is 60,000.

1348 *AIR Newsletter,* Wilbur A. Tincher, Secretary, Association for Institutional Research (1109), 102 Martin Hall, Auburn University, Auburn, Alabama 36830. (205) 826-4000, ext. 4763. Frequency: quarterly. Price: free. Usual length: 4-6 pp.

The *AIR Newsletter* is a typical professional periodical presenting association business, reports, and activities. Distributed to AIR members, the circulation is 1,000.

1349 *AVA Member-gram,* American Vocational Association (1108), 1510 H Street, N. W., Washington, D. C. 20005. (202) 737-3722. Frequency: quarterly. Price: included in membership fee. Usual length: 4 pp.

The *Member-gram* of the American Vocational Association is a supplement to the *American Vocational Journal* (1311). It features readable articles on various issues in the rapidly expanding field of vocational education. In addition there are items of current interest to instructors and administrators of vocational programs, notices of available literature, and activities of AVA. It is distributed to the entire membership of AVA; circulation is over 50,000.

1350 *Behavioral Sciences Newsletter for Research Planning,* American Institutes for Research (1157), 710 Chatham Center Office Building, Pittsburgh, Pennsylvania 15219. (412) 281-1100. Frequency: semimonthly. Price: free. Usual length: 8 pp.

Behavioral Sciences Newsletter provides an overview of current behavioral research, focusing on higher education, the disadvantaged, urban education, and labor. It includes brief descriptions of a broad range of research projects from various disciplines plus information on federal, foundation, and institutional research activities. The newsletter is circulated to over 2,500 researchers and research administrators in various fields.

1351 *CAPS Capsule,* ERIC Clearinghouse on Counseling and Personnel Services (1452), 611 Church Street, Ann Arbor, Michigan 48104. (313) 764-9492. Frequency: three per year. Price: free. Usual length: 2-4 pp.

CAPS Capsule has become a major newsletter for counseling and personnel services. It presents current news of research and innovation, stimulating articles and interviews, and reviews of Center activities. An attractive format enhances the subject matter. Recent issues have discussed the future of counseling and guidance, peer counseling, the National Assessment of Educational Progress (1229), and international guidance. Readers are primarily counselors and personnel workers. Circulation is over 13,000.

1352 *Carnegie Quarterly,* Carnegie Corporation of New York (1145), 437 Madison Avenue, New York, New York 10022. (212) 753-3100. Frequency: quarterly. Price: free. Usual length: 8-12 pp.

Carnegie Quarterly is a very readable and attractively designed publication containing interesting reports on a wide variety of projects in education. These reports frequently describe projects supported by the foundation or social problems that have priorities in its current programs. Recent topics related to access to higher education include special minority/disadvantaged programs, social welfare programs, international higher education, new degree structures, and innovations in professional education. In addition, the *Quarterly* presents staff news and reviews of Carnegie publications. It is received by a variety of educators and institutions such as foundations, colleges and universities, and education organizations. Circulation is over 18,400.

1353 *CASC Newsletter,* Council for the Advancement of Small Colleges (1114), One Dupont Circle, N. W., Washington, D. C. 20036. (202) 659-3795. Frequency: bimonthly. Price: free. Usual length: 4 pp.

This is a standard news sheet describing activities and projects of the Council and providing news capsules of general interest. It is distributed primarily to trustees and presidents of member colleges; circulation is 8,000.

1354 *Centergram,* Center for Vocational and Technical Education (1162), Ohio State University, 1900 Kenny Road, Columbus, Ohio 43210. (614) 486-3655. Frequency: monthly. Price: free. Usual length: 4 pp.

Centergram is an in-house newsletter that reviews publications and activities of the Center for Vocational and Technical Education. It is circulated primarily to the vocational/technical education community and generally limited to U.S. Department of Labor administrative personnel and professors and administrators in higher education. Each year the January edition is an open letter regarding what the Center is and does, and the June edition is a description of the ERIC Clearinghouse (1455) operated by the Center. Circulation is 5,500.

1355 *The Chronicle of Higher Education,* 1717 Massachusetts Avenue, N. W., Washington, D. C. 20036. (202) 667-3344. Frequency: weekly, except monthly in summer. Price: $20 per year. Usual length: 8 pp.

The *Chronicle* is easily the best and most widely read news periodical in higher education. Well-edited and attractively designed, this newspaper includes both short news items and in-depth analyses. It also does an excellent job of reporting important new research data and statements of commissions, task forces, and similar groups. Its weekly features include a summary of bills in Congress, "Washington Notes," coming events, job listings, and sentence annotations of recently published books. It currently has over 24,000 subscribers but should be "must" reading for everyone interested in policy issues in higher education.

1356 *The Circular Letter,* National Association of State Universities and Land-Grant Colleges (1121), One Dupont Circle, N. W., Washington, D. C. 20036. (202) 293-7120. Frequency: irregularly, almost weekly. Price: free to members. Usual length: 20-25 pp.

The Circular Letter is a mimeographed review and interpretation of federal legislation and agency activities related to higher education. In addition it includes institutional news and other items of interest. Circulated to 2,000 members of the NASULGC, it is not available for public subscription.

1357 *College and University Bulletin,* American Association for Higher Education (1095), One Dupont Circle, N. W., Washington, D. C. 20036. (202) 293-6440. Frequency: semimonthly. Price: $10 per year. Usual length: 4-8 pp.

College and University Bulletin presents AAHE news, occasional reviews of books, and news articles on topics of current interest in higher education. Articles frequently deal with recent research, federal and state funding and legislation, admissions, finances, campus unrest and reform, plus a variety of other items of interest to AAHE members and other educators. A particularly useful feature is a series of periodic research reports (1395) that summarize current research on selected topics and speculate on implications for future practice. The newsletter is attractive and well edited; it is read primarily by college faculty and administrators. Circulation exceeds 8,000.

1358 *D and R Report,* Conference for Educational Development and Research, 775 Lincoln Tower, 1860 Lincoln Street, Denver, Colorado 80203. (303) 255-3631. Frequency: monthly. Price: free. Usual length: 12-16 pp.

This new publication features concise descriptions of the work being done at nine Research and Development Centers and 14 Regional Educational Laboratories supported largely by the U.S. Office of Education. Each issue is devoted to a particular subject such as early childhood education, vocational education, higher education, urban education, etc. Readers select topics from a list of 18 and receive only those newsletters covering the chosen topics. Circulation is 10,000 — primarily higher education researchers and professors.

1359 *Developing Junior Colleges,* American Association of Junior Colleges (1097), One Dupont Circle, N. W., Washington, D. C. 20036. (202) 293-7050. Frequency: semimonthly. Price: free. Usual length: 4 pp.

Developing Junior Colleges is an outgrowth of AAJC's Program with Developing Institutions. It describes innovation, legislation, and project reports related to developing junior colleges. It presents a simple mimeo format of short review articles, projects, and capsule news items of primary interest to administrators and faculty in junior colleges. Circulation is over 6,000.

1360 *ECS Bulletin,* Education Commission of the States (1178), 1860 Lincoln Street, Suite 300, Denver, Colorado 80203. (303) 255-3631. Frequency: monthly. Price: free. Usual length: 4 pp.

The *ECS Bulletin* is designed to provide educators, legislators, and governors with concise information on educational innovations throughout the states. It combines short news capsules of general interest, reports of ECS activities, and brief articles on a variety of pertinent topics. Circulation exceeds 15,000.

1361 *ECS Legislative Review,* Education Commission of the States (1178), 1860 Lincoln Street, Suite 300, Denver, Colorado 80203. (303) 255-3631. Frequency: weekly, when legislatures are in session; monthly otherwise. Price: free. Usual length: 4 pp.

Legislative Review is the most current newsletter reporting state legislation related to higher education. It provides a concise, rapid review of pending legislation. Primary readers are governors, legislators, and university administrators. Circulation is over 2,000.

1362 *Education Daily,* Capitol Publications, Inc., Suite G-12, 2430 Pennsylvania Avenue, N. W., Washington, D. C. 20037. (202) 659-5641. Frequency: every business day. Price: $175 per year. Usual length: 6 pp.

Education Daily is the only daily publication devoted entirely to reporting news of education. Although it reports a wide range of news and research findings from across the nation, it is especially valuable in publicizing legislation, appropriations, speeches, and hearings pertaining to education at all levels that come out of Congress, U.S.O.E., and other federal agencies. Its design and journalistic style appear more like an average monthly newsletter than the high-priced daily that it is. The *Daily* is intended for education executives.

1363 *Education Recaps,* Educational Testing Service (1115), Princeton, New Jersey 08540. (609) 921-9000. Frequency: 11 per year. Price: $3 per year. Usual length: 12-20 pp.

Education Recaps is one of the best secondary sources of current information on education at all levels. It excerpts reports, articles, and news items that originally appear in about 50 educational journals, newsletters, and releases. *Recaps* includes well-edited, timely items of high readership interest that are presented in a concise, well-designed format. One particular value of *Recaps* is that it often draws material from publications not generally read by most educators. Circulation is 3,500.

1364 *Educational Researcher,* American Educational Research Association (1104), 1126 Sixteenth Street, N. W., Washington, D. C. 20036. (202) 223-9485. Frequency: monthly, except July and August. Price: $5 per year. Usual length: 16-20 pp.

The *Educational Researcher* presents news of federal projects and funding in educational research and general news of new developments and national issues in educational research. It also provides placement information, reviews of new publications, and professional activities of members. The *Researcher* is a very useful and important source of news for research practitioners and administrators of research. Its circulation exceeds 12,000—primarily members of AERA.

1365 *The EPE 15-Minute Report,* Editorial Projects for Education, 1717 Massachusetts Avenue, N. W., Washington, D. C. 20036. (202) 667-3344. Frequency: 20 per year. Price: $12 per year. Usual length: 4 pp.

   The EPE 15-Minute Report is a valuable newsletter for college and university trustees. It is published by the same organization that publishes the *Chronicle of Higher Education* (1355). This report is a readable potpourri of useful information, quotes, and comments on a variety of issues of particular interest to trustees. Circulation is over 3,500.

1366 *ETS Developments,* Educational Testing Service (1115), 1947 Center Street, Berkeley, California 94704. (415) 849-0950. Frequency: quarterly. Price: free. Usual length: 4 pp.

   ETS Developments presents news of research and testing programs at ETS. The news items describe a wide variety of new developments in research on learning, measurement, and education at all levels. The newsletter is attractively designed and well written in nontechnical language. Circulation is 63,000.

1367 *Evaluation Comment,* Center for the Study of Evaluation (1164), 145 Moore Hall, University of California at Los Angeles, Los Angeles, California 90024. (213) 825-4711. Frequency: occasional (about twice a year). Price: free. Usual length: 12-16 pp.

   Evaluation Comment is a useful specialized newsletter. It provides a forum for the discussion of significant ideas and issues in the study of evaluation of educational programs and systems. Like a journal it presents essays on topics related to the field with minimal news of Center activities. Circulation is about 6,000—primarily students in education, research, and administration.

1368 *Financial Aid News,* College Scholarship Service (1211), College Entrance Examination Board, 888 Seventh Avenue, New York, New York 10019. (212) 582-6210. Frequency: several times per year. Price: free. Usual length: 4-8 pp.

   Financial Aid News is one of the few newsletters intended specifically for financial aid administrators. It presents summaries of reports, Washington news, and general information on financing higher education. It also includes announcements of publications, programs, and upcoming activities, many of which are sponsored by the College Scholarship Service. Circulation is 20,000.

1369 *Financing Higher Education,* Southern Regional Education Board (1180), 130 Sixth Street, N. W., Atlanta, Georgia 30313. (404) 875-9211. Frequency: One per year. Price: free. Usual length: 4-6 pp.

   Financing Higher Education is an especially informative and well-edited series of reports dealing with aspects of college costs and who pays them. Each issue contains an illustrated article on a single topic such as federal aid, coordinating boards, student migration, and changing attendance patterns. These studies are sometimes focused on the South but often include data for all states. The newsletter is distributed primarily to college presidents and legislators in the South; circulation is over 1,300.

1370 *Ford Foundation Letter,* Ford Foundation (1148), 320 East 43rd Street, New York, New York 10017. (212) 573-5000. Frequency: 8 per year. Price: free. Usual length: 8 pp.

   The *Ford Foundation Letter* describes programs receiving new grants from the Foundation. Many are related to various aspects of access to higher education. Each edition also features a one-page special report on a selected project of general interest. It is an interesting and well-written newsletter that provides a comprehensive understanding of the Foundation's work. It is distributed to a wide variety of audiences totaling 120,000 readers.

1371 *The Guidance Clinic,* Parker Publishing Co., Inc., Route 59A at Brookhill Drive, West Nyack, New York 10994. (914) 358-8800. Frequency: monthly, except July and August. Price: $36 per year. Usual length: 16 pp.

The Guidance Clinic is a readable, attractively designed newsletter but the price is a distinct disadvantage. It provides articles and essays on a variety of topics including counseling practices, vocational guidance, policies and programs, group counseling, and college counseling. The newsletter is distributed to some 2,000 school guidance counselors.

1372 *The Guidepost,* American Personnel and Guidance Association (1105), 1607 New Hampshire Avenue, N. W., Washington, D. C. 20009. (202) 483-4633. Frequency: monthly, September through May. Price: $10 per year. Usual length: 8 pp.

Previously an attractive news periodical with considerable substantive coverage, *The Guidepost* recently reduced its size and scope. It is now a standard association newsletter presenting business and general news of primary interest to members of APGA. Circulation exceeds 30,000.

1373 *Higher Education and National Affairs,* American Council on Education (1102), One Dupont Circle, Washington, D. C. 20036. (202) 833-4724. Frequency: approximately 40 per year. Price: distributed free in specific quantities to member institutions; individual subscriptions $25 per year. Usual length: 8-12 pp.

Higher Education and National Affairs is one of the most important, comprehensive, and widely read newsletters on higher education. It reports major current events at all levels of government, among educational foundations and associations, and on local campuses. It is probably the best source of information on events in Washington that affect higher education. Individual issues frequently contain reports of research, legislative activity, and major new developments in higher education. Circulation exceeds 38,000, including policymakers in every sector of the higher education community.

1374 *Higher Education in the States,* Education Commission of the States (1178), 1860 Lincoln Street, Suite 822, Denver, Colorado 80203. (303) 255-3631. Frequency: monthly. Price: free (except vol. 1, 10 issues $4). Usual length: 10-20 pp.

This newsletter is an unusually valuable source of information concerning state coordination and governance of higher education. Each issue focuses on a single topic such as major legislative activity in individual states, detailed status reports on items of concern to the states, and periodically updated bibliographies of state and regional agency publications. Continuous pagination through the year, an annual index, and prepunched editions for notebook storage augment the reference value of this document. The principal readers are administrators and professors of higher education. Total circulation is over 5,000.

1375 *IRCD Bulletin,* ERIC Information Retrieval Center on the Disadvantaged (1456), Horace Mann-Lincoln Institute, Teachers College, Columbia University, 525 West 120th Street, New York, New York 10027. (212) 870-4200, ext. 4808. Frequency: 5 per year. Price: free. Usual length: 16-24 pp.

The *IRCD Bulletin* is an important source of information to teachers and administrators concerned with education of the disadvantaged. It usually in-

cludes interpretive articles with selected lists of bibliographic materials in addition to reviews of books and other educational media. Subject areas covered in
recent editions include the effects of disadvantaged environments; the academic,
intellectual, and social performance of disadvantaged youth; programs related
to discrimination, segregation, and integration in education; and materials pertaining to ethnic studies. Circulation is 15,000, which goes to educators at all
levels.

1376 *Junior College Research Review,* American Association of Junior Colleges
(1097), One Dupont Circle, N. W., Washington, D. C. 20036. (202) 293-7050.
Frequency: 10 editions per academic year. Price: $3 per year. Usual length:
4 pp.; occasional expanded editions.

Compiled and edited by ERIC/Junior Colleges (1450), this newsletter reviews
research reports rather than reporting current events. Each edition focuses on
a single topic pertinent to junior colleges. The articles describe recent and current research projects and provide additional references. The reports are readable though compact, and the format is quite attractive. The *Review* is a useful
information source for those interested in junior college education. Circulation
is 3,400.

1377 *Measurement in Education,* National Council on Measurement in Education
(1127), Office of Evaluation Services, Michigan State University, East Lansing,
Michigan 48823. (517) 355-1912. Frequency: 4 per year. Price: $2 per year.
Usual length: 4-12 pp.

Measurement in Education is a series of special reports that are concerned
with the practical implications of measurement and related research and their
application to educational problems of individuals, institutions, and systems.
The emphasis of this series, which was begun in 1969, is upon uses of measurement throughout all levels of education rather than on technical or theoretical
issues. The circulation of about 2,000 goes primarily to NCME members.
Reports include:

1969 Robert L. Thorndike. *Helping teachers use tests.* Vol. 1, No. 1.
1970 Eric F. Gardner. *Interpreting achievement profiles – Uses and warnings.*
Vol. 1, No. 2.
1970 Samuel T. Mayo. *Mastery learning and mastery testing.* Vol. 1, No. 3.
1970 Alden W. Badal and Edwin P. Larsen. *On reporting test results to community groups.* Vol. 1, No. 4.
1970 Frank B. Womer. *National assessment says.* Vol. 2, No. 1.
1971 John C. Flanagan. *The plan system for individualizing education.* Vol. 2,
No. 2.
1971 Richard E. Schutz. *Measurement aspects of performance contracting.*
Vol. 2, No. 3.
1971 Louise Witmer Cureton. *The history of grading practices.* Vol. 2, No. 4.
(407).

1378 *Measurement News,* National Council on Measurement in Education (1127),
Office of Evaluation Services, Michigan State University, East Lansing, Michigan 48823. (517) 355-1912. Frequency: quarterly. Price: $2 per year. Usual
length: 8-12 pp.

Measurement News has a balanced format combining associational items
(conference information, NCME business, and election announcements) and
brief articles on practical aspects of testing. Regular features include "What
the Journals Say about Measurement," "New Measurement Books," and
"What's New from Test Publishers." Practitioners of educational testing will
find this newsletter useful. Most of the readers are members of the National
Council on Measurement in Education. Circulation is 2,700.

1379 *Memo,* American Association of State Colleges and Universities (1098), One Dupont Circle, Washington, D. C. 20036. (202) 293-7070. Frequency: monthly. Usual length: 8-10 pp.

Memo is intended to inform presidents of state colleges and universities about the work of AASCU, activities at other state institutions, and selected current events and issues pertaining to higher education nationally. It is basically an associational newsletter and the news items vary with respect to breadth of interest. Circulation exceeds 1,500.

1380 *NAFSA Newsletter,* National Association for Foreign Student Affairs (1118), 1860 Nineteenth Street, N. W., Washington, D. C. 20009. (202) 462-4811. Frequency: monthly, October through June. Price: $5 per year. Usual length: 10-12 pp.

The *Newsletter* is a typical association bulletin presenting articles, news, and general items of interest to its members. Publications and institutional programs related to foreign student affairs are also reviewed. Circulation is over 2,000, and distribution is primarily to NAFSA members.

1381 *National ACAC Newsletter,* National Association of College Admissions Counselors (1119), 9933 Lawler Avenue, Skokie, Illinois 60076. (312) 676-0500. Frequency: 4-6 per year. Price: institutions $9; individuals $5; fee includes the *National ACAC Journal* (1337). Usual length: 16-28 pp.

The *National ACAC Newsletter* is a well designed and useful associational publication. It presents news and business pertinent to NACAC members and other college admissions counselors. Special features include an employment assistance service, announcements and descriptions of summer workshops in guidance and counseling, and detailed reporting of NACAC conventions. It is circulated to 2,200 members and 1,800 additional individuals and institutions.

1382 *New Human Services Newsletter,* New Careers Development Center, New York University, Room 238, 239 Greene Street, New York, New York 10003. (212) 598-7641. Frequency: quarterly. Price: $5 per year. Usual length: 8-10 pp.

This attractive and well-designed publication is packed with useful information about a variety of paraprofessional occupations and new career opportunities. It reports on federal and state legislation, manpower and labor developments, and new careers in a number of fields in addition to changes in college and university training for subprofessional fields. Anyone interested in the relation of education to work and in vocational/technical education should find this newsletter most helpful. Circulation is about 14,000 and includes a wide range of government and education personnel.

1383 *Newsletter,* American Association of Collegiate Registrars and Admissions Officers (1096), One Dupont Circle, N. W., Washington, D. C. 20036. (202) 293-6230. Frequency: quarterly. Price: free. Usual length: 25-35 pp.

This publication is a quarterly report of Association activities. It includes news items, occasional articles concerning admissions (transfers, record procedures, etc.), and detailed reports of national and regional AACRAO business. It is available only to AACRAO members; circulation is 5,000.

1384 *Newsletter in Higher Education,* Bureau of Indian Affairs, 5301 Central Avenue, N. E., Room 201, Albuquerque, New Mexico 87108. (505) 843-2427. Frequency: bimonthly. Price: free. Usual length: 10-20 pp.

This unique newsletter is a national digest of information pertinent to American Indian higher education. A wide variety of items is presented including higher education opportunities, notable achievements of American Indians, statistical data, legislation, and news of interest from geographic areas of concentrated Indian population. Items are arranged in a simple format and succinctly written. The newsletter provides useful information for anyone concerned with American Indian higher education. Circulation is 3,000, primarily to government agencies, high schools, and community groups.

1385 *NHSC News,* National Home Study Council (1129), 1601 Eighteenth Street, N. W., Washington, D. C. 20009. (202) 234-5100. Frequency: monthly. Price: free. Usual length: 6-8 pp.

NHSC News is a well-designed publication that reports Council business. In addition each edition includes a separate supplement discussing a topic related to the work of NHSC. Recent topics include: NHSC accreditation, research and development in correspondence instruction, home study and the military, attrition and achievement in correspondence study, and home study in the twenty-first century. The *News* is distributed primarily to educational guidance counselors at member schools; circulation is about 1,000.

1386 *NSP Newsletter,* National Education Association (1128), 1201 Sixteenth Street, N. W., Washington, D. C. 20036. (202) 833-4000. Frequency: 6 per year. Price: free. Usual length: 8 pp.

The *NSP Newsletter* is produced by the National Society of Professors, one of three units of the newly formed National Higher Education Association of the National Education Association. It includes articles and reports of current events in higher education of particular interest to professors in four-year colleges and universities. It also reports business news of the National Higher Education Association.

1387 *Occupational Education Bulletin,* American Association of Junior Colleges (1097), One Dupont Circle, N. W., Washington, D. C. 20036. (202) 293-7050. Frequency: monthly. Price: $3 per year. Usual length: 8 pp.

The *Bulletin* is a useful information sheet describing conferences, seminars, new curriculums, research, and publications pertinent to occupational education. It portrays the active scene in semiprofessional and technical-education programs in junior colleges and provides references to further sources of information. The *Bulletin* is circulated to over 3,000 educators and labor personnel.

1388 *Race Relations Reporter* (formerly *Southern Education Report*), Race Relations Information Center (1459), Box 6156, Nashville, Tennessee 37212. (615) 327-1361. Frequency: semimonthly. Price: $10 per year. Usual length: 4-6 pp.

Race Relations Reporter contains information on race relations in a broad spectrum of national life, including politics, sports, entertainment, labor, and all levels of education. Each issue contains brief news items and more extensive news analyses. The items include evaluative commentary reflecting minority concerns and viewpoints. The *Reporter* provides a larger context for understanding race relations in colleges and universities and is a valuable source of current information on minority cultures. It is circulated to 10,000 readers, most of whom are civil rights workers and political leaders. Beginning in 1972 six issues each year will be expanded with a 32-page magazine to provide space for in-depth articles by guest writers and for special summaries of developments on race.

1389 *Regional Action,* Southern Regional Education Board (1180), 130 Sixth Street, N. W., Atlanta, Georgia 30313. (404) 875-9211. Frequency: quarterly. Price: free. Usual length: 8 pp.

Regional Action is intended for educators, government officials, and the general public. It presents articles about developments in Southern higher education, reports on legislation affecting higher education in the region, and news of SREB activities. Articles cover a wide variety of topics including: equal higher education opportunity, financial aid, two-year colleges, planning and coordination, use of resources, adult basic education, nursing programs, campus mental health, and campus unrest. The newsletter has a circulation of almost 9,000.

1390 *Regional Spotlight,* Southern Regional Education Board (1180), 130 Sixth Street, N. W., Atlanta, Georgia 30313. (404) 875-9211. Frequency: monthly, September through May. Price: free. Usual length: 4 pp.

Regional Spotlight is intended for professors and administrators. It provides capsule reports on developments in Southern higher education with special emphasis on innovation. Topics include curriculum development, new administrative programs, research projects, grants received, and other campus news. Each item is clearly headlined for rapid perusal. Circulation exceeds 6,500.

1391 *Report on Education Research,* Capitol Publications, Inc., 2430 Pennsylvania Avenue, Washington, D. C. 20006. (202) 659-5641. Frequency: biweekly. Price: $40 per year. Usual length: 10-12 pp.

The *Report on Education Research* is an independent news service that provides capsule reports on research activities and projects across the nation. It is informative but expensive and focuses primarily on elementary and secondary education projects funded by the federal government.

1392 *Reports on Higher Education,* Western Interstate Commission for Higher Education (1181), P. O. Drawer P, Boulder, Colorado 80302. (303) 449-3333. Frequency: quarterly. Price: free. Usual length: 12 pp.

This newsletter contains information about WICHE programs and articles of general interest on higher education. Much of the content consists of well-written reports of conferences and workshops. *Reports* presents a readable view of the variety of WICHE activities. It is distributed to 21,000 readers, most of whom are higher education administrators, legislators, and government officials.

1393 *The Research Reporter,* Center for Research and Development in Higher Education (1161), 1947 Center Street, University of California, Berkeley, California 94720. (415) 642-0246. Frequency: quarterly. Price: free. Usual length: 8 pp.

The Research Reporter is an unusually well-written and well-edited newsletter that relates research to current major issues in higher education. Each issue focuses on a particular topic and presents two to four articles that frequently tie in the research of the Center. The *Reporter* normally includes one page concerning Center news and publications. Recent topics include graduate education in the 1970s, strategies for relevance, academic reform, campus governance, and campus confrontations. The newsletter is distributed to researchers in higher education, faculty and administrators, and government groups. Circulation is over 10,000.

1394 *Urban Affairs Newsletter,* American Association of State Colleges and Universities (1098), One Dupont Circle, N. W., Washington, D. C. 20036. (202) 659-4275. Frequency: occasionally, about 3 per year. Price: currently free. Usual length: 16-20 pp.

Urban Affairs Newsletter describes programs in urban institutions that are members of AASCU. The programs include community affairs and development activities, inner-city teaching projects, and urban studies curriculums. It has an unattractive format, but the publication is one of the limited sources of information on urban higher education. Circulation is about 850.

14.3—REPORT SERIES. There is a limited but especially important number of report series relating to the access process. These range from highly specialized and sometimes technical research reports to documents intended for broad audiences. The publications of Project TALENT and the Carnegie Commission on Higher Education are not, strictly speaking, report series but are collected and listed here as an aid to the reader because of their special importance.

1395 AAHE RESEARCH REPORTS, American Association for Higher Education (1095), One Dupont Circle, N. W., Washington, D. C. 20036. Frequency: semi-monthly. Price: free with membership in AAHE. Usual length: 4-8 pp.

Research Reports is a new feature prepared by the ERIC Clearinghouse on Higher Education and inserted within AAHE's *College and University Bulletin* (1357). The purpose of these reports, which began in 1970 with funding from the Kellogg Foundation, is to summarize current research on selected topics and to interpret its implications for the future. The reports have been circulated to the *Bulletin*'s 8,000 readers, most of whom are college faculty and administrators.

Reports include:

No. 1. Robert T. Blackburn. *Changes in faculty life styles.* 1970.
No. 2. Marvin W. Peterson. *The organization of departments.* 1970.
No. 3. Jonathan R. Warren. *Current grading practices.* 1970.
No. 4. Virginia Smith. *Financial aid.* 1971.
No. 5. K. Patricia Cross. *The undergraduate woman.* 1971. (1042)
No. 6. Ohmer Milton. *Teaching or learning?* 1971.
No. 7. JB Lon Hefferlin. *Reform and resistance.* 1971.

1396 ACE RESEARCH REPORTS, American Council on Education (1156), One Dupont Circle, N. W., Washington, D. C. 20036. (202) 833-4700. Frequency: 5-7 per year. Price: free, except $3 for "National Norms." Usual length: varies from 15 to 100 pp.

ACE Research Reports, published by the Council's Office of Research, communicate research findings on a variety of questions of general concern in higher education. In addition to the very useful annual report of national norms for entering college freshmen, reports have covered research on black students, student development, attrition, campus unrest, and faculty, plus various technical topics. This series is sent to 500 individuals and organizations and is of special benefit to educational researchers.

Reports published in 1970-71 include:

1970 David E. Drew. *A profile of the Jewish freshman.* Vol. 5, No. 4 (884).
1970 Alan E. Bayer. *College and university faculty: A statistical description.* Vol. 5, No. 5.
1970 Staff. *National norms for entering college freshmen—Fall 1970.* Vol. 5, No. 6.
1970 David E. Drew. *On the allocation of federal funds for science education.* Vol. 5, No. 7.
1971 Alan E. Bayer. *Institutional correlates of faculty support of campus unrest.* Vol. 6, No. 1.
1971 John A. Creager. *Evaluation and selection of academic interns 1967-68.* Vol. 6, No. 2.
1971 John A. Creager. *Goals and achievements of the ACE internship program in academic administration.* Vol. 6, No. 3.

1397 ACT RESEARCH REPORTS, The American College Testing Program (1155), P. O. Box 168, Iowa City, Iowa 52240. (319) 351-4470. Frequency: 6-10 per year. Price: free. Usual length: 10-25 pp.

The ACT Research Reports are technical studies conducted by the ACT Research and Development Division (1155) and other researchers. The series is distributed to 5,000 secondary and postsecondary researchers and counselors, particularly those schools and colleges using ACT services. Past research has included such topics as educational aspirations and goals; financial need; testing;

forecasting college success; college admissions; the flow of high school students to schools, colleges, and jobs; academic accomplishment; and two-year colleges. Recent reports include:

No. 37. Thomas G. Gartland and James F. Carmody. *Practices and outcomes of vocational-technical education in technical and community colleges.* 1970.

No. 38. Melvin R. Novick. *Bayesian considerations in educational information systems.* 1970.

No. 39. George Domino. *Interactive effects of achievement orientation and teaching style on academic achievement.* 1970.

No. 40. Nancy S. Cole and Gary R. Hanson. *An analysis of the structure of vocational interests.* 1971.

No. 41. Eldon J. Brue, Harold B. Engen, and E. James Maxey. *How do community college transfer and occupational students differ?* 1971.

No. 42. Melvin R. Novick, Paul H. Jackson, Dorothy T. Thayer, and Nancy S. Cole. *Applications of Bayesian methods to the prediction of educational performance.* 1971.

1398 CARNEGIE COMMISSION ON HIGHER EDUCATION REPORTS, McGraw-Hill Book Company, 330 West 42nd Street, New York, New York 10036. (212) 971-3333. Frequency: 10-15 per year. Price: see list. Usual length: varies from 30-page pamphlets to 400-page books.

Since its inception in 1967 the Carnegie Commission on Higher Education has sponsored a series of projects on a range of critical issues facing higher education. These are intended to supplement and amplify the reports of the Commission itself. As of this writing 64 research projects have been sponsored, and at least 11 Commission reports are intended. The project reports now available typically rank among the most significant literature currently being produced on a given subject. The widely heralded Commission reports each have numerous recommendations, and some have already made a considerable impact on higher education. A final report that will summarize the Commission's findings and recommendations should be forthcoming in 1973.

Available reports include:

☐ *Project reports*

1. Ronald A. Wolk. *Alternative methods of federal funding for higher education.* 1968. $2.

2. Dale M. Heckman and Warren B. Martin. *Inventory of current research on higher education.* 1968. 1969. $2.75. (1475).

3. Andrew M. Greeley. *From backwater to mainstream: A profile of Catholic higher education.* 1970. $6.95. (764).

4. E. Alden Dunham. *Colleges of the forgotten Americans: A profile of state colleges and regional universities.* 1970. $6.95. (762).

5. Heinz Eulau and Harold Quinley. *State officials and higher education: A survey of the opinions and expectations of policy makers in nine states.* 1970. $6.95.

6. Stephen Spurr. *Academic degree structure: Innovative approaches.* 1970. $6.95. (347).

7. Joe L. Spaeth and Andrew M. Greeley. *Recent alumni and higher education: A survey of college graduates.* 1970. $6.95. (490).

8. Dwight Ladd. *Change in educational policy: Self-studies in selected colleges and universities.* 1970. $6.95. (344).

9. Lewis B. Mayhew. *Graduate and professional education, 1980: A survey of institutional plans.* 1970. $3.95.

10. Oscar Handlin and Mary F. Handlin. *The American college and American culture: Socialization as a function of higher education.* 1970. $4.95. (566).

11. Irwin Sanders and Jennifer Ward. *Bridges to understanding: International programs of American colleges and universities.* 1970. $7.95. (830).

12. Barbara R. Burn. *Higher education in nine countries: A comparative study of colleges and universities abroad.* 1971. $7.95. (813).

13. Rashi Fein and Gerald J. Weber. *Financing medical education: An analysis of alternative policies and mechanisms.* 1971. $6.95.

14. Earl F. Cheit. *The new depression in higher education: A study of financial conditions at 41 colleges and universities.* 1971. $5.95. (151).

15. Leland Medsker and Dale Tillery. *Breaking the access barriers: A profile of two-year colleges.* 1971. $5.95. (752).

16. Eric Ashby. *Any person, any study.* 1971. $4.95.

17. Frank Bowles and Frank DeCosta. *Between two worlds: A profile of Negro higher education.* 1971. $7.95. (770).

18. Alexander Astin. *The invisible colleges.* 1971. $6.95.

19. E. Lee and F. Bowen. *The multi-campus university: A study of academic governance.* 1971. $9.95.

20. Howard Bowen. *Efficiency in liberal education.* 1971. $5.95.

21. Harold Hodgkinson. *Institutions in transition.* 1971. $6.95.

☐ *Commission reports*

1. *Quality and equality: New levels of federal responsibility for higher education.* 1968. $1.95. (150).
   Quality and equality: Revised recommendations—New levels of federal responsibility for higher education. 1970. $1.95. (150).

2. *A chance to learn: An action agenda for equal opportunity in higher education.* 1970. $1.95. (943).

3. *The open-door colleges: Policies for community colleges.* 1970. $1.95. (574).

4. *Higher education and the nation's health: Policies for medical and dental education.* 1970. $2.95.

5. *Less time, more options: Education beyond the high school.* 1970. $1.95. (575).

6. *From isolation to mainstream: Problems of colleges founded for Negroes.* 1971. $1.95. (771).

7. *The capitol and the campus: State responsibility for postsecondary education.* 1971. $2.95. (651).

1399 COLLEGE ENTRANCE EXAMINATION BOARD RESEARCH AND DEVELOPMENT REPORTS, EDUCATIONAL TESTING SERVICE (1167), Princeton, New Jersey 08540. (609) 921-9000. Frequency: usually 5-6 per year. Price: free. Usual length: 15-75 pp.

The College Board Research and Development Reports series publishes research conducted by Educational Testing Service, sometimes in cooperation with college and university personnel. These reports include investigations of such topics as community college students, black students, financial aid awards, student follow-up studies, and various trends in higher education. The reports are distributed to about 1,000 readers, most of whom are researchers.

Recent reports include:

RDR-69-70

No. 1. Christopher C. Modu. *A description of the satisfaction questionnaire for junior colleges in terms of rotated factors.* 1970.

No. 2. John A. Centra. *Black students at predominantly white colleges: A research description.* 1970. (1064).

No. 3. Robert L. Linn, Donald A. Rock, and T. Anne Cleary. *Sequential testing for dichotomous decisions.* 1970.

No. 4. Ronald L. Glaugher and Lewis W. Pike. *Reactions to a very difficult test by an inner-city high school population: A test and item analysis.* 1970.

No. 5. Amiel T. Sharon. *Measurement of college achievement by the College-Level Examination Program.* 1970.

RDR-70-71

No. 1. John A. Centra. *The college environment revisited: Current descriptions and a comparison of three methods of assessment.* 1970.

No. 2. Amiel T. Sharon. *Effectiveness of remediation in junior college.* 1970.

No. 3. Leforne Sequeira. *A study of the CGP financial need indicator.* 1970.

No. 4. Martin R. Katz, Lila Norris, and Gerald Halpern. *The measurement of academic interests.* Part I. *Characteristics of the academic interest measures.* 1970.

No. 5. Lila Norris and Martin R. Katz. *The measurement of academic interests.* Part II. *The predictive validities of academic interest measures.* 1970.

No. 6. George Temp. *Test bias: Validity of the SAT for blacks and whites in thirteen integrated institutions.* 1971. (975).

No. 7. Donald A. Rock, Leonard Baird, and Robert L. Linn. *Interaction between college effects and students' attitudes.* 1971.

No. 8. Dwight H. Horch and Amiel T. Sharon. *Estimating parents' contributions to college costs: The accuracy of three measures of succeeding year family net income.* 1971.

1400 COMPENDIUM SERIES OF CURRENT RESEARCH, PROGRAMS AND PROPOSALS, ERIC Clearinghouse on Higher Education (1453), George Washington University, One Dupont Circle, Suite 630, Washington, D. C. 20036. Frequency: 2-3 per year. Price: free. Usual length: 20-30 pp.

This useful series pulls together information on selected topics of current interest. Each report contains a short essay on the topic and brief annotations of information items. Begun in 1970, the series now includes publications on *Governance, Preparing College Teachers,* and *Recruiting Disadvantaged Students.* Each report includes ongoing or recently completed research projects and programs and, where applicable, lists the beginning and completion dates of each and its source of funding. About 1,000 copies of each issue have been distributed.

Reports include:

No. 1. *Governance.* 1970. Prepared by Carol Shulman. (611).

No. 2. *Preparing college teachers.* 1970. Prepared by Carol Shulman. (319).

No. 3. *Recruiting disadvantaged students.* 1971. Prepared by Carol Shulman. (981).

1401 ETS RESEARCH BULLETINS, Educational Testing Service (1115), Princeton, New Jersey 08540. (609) 921-9000. Frequency: 60-70 per year. Price: free. Usual length: varies from 20-100 pp.

Educational Testing Service conducts a considerable amount of research in many areas related to measurement, evaluation, and learning at all levels of education. Much of the research is reported in this prepublication series, and the majority are also eventually published in professional journals, such as the *Journal of Educational Measurement* (1325), the *American Educational Research Journal* (1306), or more technical periodicals. Although the reports are of high quality, many are quite specialized, and distribution is limited. Some of the recent reports are particularly related to access to college. These include:

1970 Research bulletins

No. RB-70-1 Samuel Messick. *Evaluation of educational programs as research on educational process.*

No. RB-70-2 Andrew G. Bean and John A. Centra. *Multiple college applications.*

No. RB-70-5 Norman E. Freeberg and Franklin R. Evans. *Some biographical correlates of performance for disadvantaged adolescents.*

No. RB-70-7 Rodney T. Hartnett. *A survey of changes in the composition of college and university governing boards during 1968-1969.*

No. RB-70-8 William H. Angoff and Amiel T. Sharon. *A comparison of scores earned on the Test of English as a Foreign Language by native American college students and foreign applicants to U.S. colleges.*

No. RB-70-28 S. M. Zdep. *Educating disadvantaged urban children in suburban schools: An evaluation.*

No. RB-70-38 Amiel T. Sharon. *Measurement of college achievement by the College-Level Examination Program.*

No. RB-70-41 Ronald L. Flaugher. *Testing practices, minority groups, and higher education: A review and discussion of the research.*

No. RB-70-44 John A. Centra. *The college environment revisited: Current descriptions and a comparison of three methods of assessment.*

No. RB-70-50 Amiel T. Sharon. *Effectiveness of remediation in junior college.*

No. RB-70-57 Martin R. Katz, Lila Norris, and Gerald Halpern. *The measurement of academic interests.* Part I. *Characteristics of the academic interest measures.*

No. RB-70-69 John A. Centra and Donald Rock. *College environments and student academic achievement.*

No. RB-70-70 Yehia Badran. *A cost/effectiveness model for educational programs.*

1402 HIGHER EDUCATION SURVEYS REPORTS, College Entrance Examination Board (1112), Box 592, Princeton, New Jersey 08540. (609) 921-9000. Frequency: 4-5 per year. Price: free. Usual length: 15-20 pp.

Higher Education Surveys is a new regional activity of the College Board designed to develop timely information on topics of current interest. Unlike much educational research, these reports are available about one month after questionnaires are mailed to respondents. They typically are distributed to about 7,000 individuals, most of whom are either representatives of College Board member institutions or have a particular interest in topics related to access to college.

Reports include:

No. 1. Warren W. Willingham. *Admission of minority students in Midwestern colleges.* 1970. (1080).

No. 2. Warren W. Willingham. *Professional development of financial aid officers.* 1970. (185).

No. 3. Richard I. Ferrin and Warren W. Willingham. *Practices of Southern institutions in recognizing college-level achievement.* 1970. (308).

No. 4. Richard I. Ferrin. *Developmental programs in Midwestern community colleges.* 1971. (982).

No. 5. Richard I. Ferrin. *Student budgets and aid awarded in Southwestern colleges.* 1971. (188).

1403 NEW DIMENSIONS IN HIGHER EDUCATION, National Laboratory for Higher Education (1172), Mutual Plaza, Durham, North Carolina 27701. (919) 688-8057. Frequency: discontinued. Price: ranges from 15 cents to $6.58. Usual length: varies from 13-128 pp.

This useful series of commissioned papers reports trends and developments throughout higher education. The major emphasis is on curriculum innovations, although individual topics cover a wide range of concerns. Some papers are largely reviews of literature, others emphasize institutional programs, and still others are primarily position papers. The series was discontinued in 1968. Reports 1-14 are available from the U.S. Government Printing Office, and 15-32 are available through ERIC (1449).

The reports are:

No. 1. Winslow R. Hatch and Ann Bennet. *Independent study.* 1960. 25 cents.

No. 2. Winslow R. Hatch and Ann Bennet. *Effectiveness in teaching.* 1960. 20 cents.

No. 3. Winslow R. Hatch. *The experimental college.* 1960. 15 cents.

No. 4. Mervin B. Freedman. *Impact of college.* 1960. 15 cents.

No. 5. E. D. Duryea. *Management of learning.* 1960. 20 cents.

No. 6. Irwin Abrams. *Study abroad.* 1960. 15 cents.

No. 7. Samuel Baskin. *Quest for quality.* 1960. 15 cents.

No. 8. Shirley A. Radcliffe. *Advanced standing.* 1961. 15 cents. (312).

No. 9. Lanora G. Lewis. *The credit system in colleges and universities.* 1961. 20 cents.

No. 10. Charles C. Cole Jr. and Lanora G. Lewis. *Flexibility in the undergraduate curriculum.* 1962. 35 cents.

No. 11. Lanora G. Lewis, J. Ned Bryan, and Robert Poppendieck. *Talent and tomorrow's teachers — The honors approach.* 1963. 35 cents.

No. 12. Winslow R. Hatch. *What standards do we raise?* 1963. 15 cents.

No. 13. Winslow R. Hatch and Alice L. Richards. *Approach to independent study.* 1965. 30 cents. (323).

No. 14. Winslow R. Hatch. *Approach to teaching.* 1966. 20 cents.

No. 15. Joseph Axelrod. *New patterns in undergraduate education: Emerging curriculum models for the American college.* (ED 013 340), 1967. $3.29.

No. 16. Wilbert J. McKeachie. *New developments in teaching.* (ED 013 341), 1967. $6.58.

No. 17. Norman D. Kurland. *Transition from school to college.* (ED 013 378), 1967. $3.29.

No. 18. Mervin B. Freedman. *The student and campus climates of learning.* (ED 013 379), 1967. $3.29.

No. 19. Samuel Baskin, et al. *Innovation in higher education: Developments, research and priorities.* (ED 013 380), 1967. $6.58.

No. 20. Ernest L. Boyer. *Institutional research and the academic program.* (ED 013 381), 1967. $3.29.

No. 21. Lawrence C. Howard. *Interinstitutional cooperation in higher education.* (ED 013 346), 1967. $3.29.

No. 22. Milton J. Horowitz. *Research in professional education.* (ED 013 347), 1967. $3.29.

No. 23. Norman C. Harris. *Developments in technical and vocational education.* (ED 013 098), 1967. $6.58. (720).

No. 24. Robert T. Blackburn. *General education in liberal arts colleges.* (ED 013 348), 1967. $3.29.

No. 25. Sally Cassidy and Alice Haddix. *General education in the complex university.* (ED 026 973), 1967. $6.58.

No. 26. George Bruce Dearing and G. Peter Lederer. *Trends and developments in graduate education.* (ED 026 972), 1967. $3.29.

No. 27. Irwin Abrams and David B. Arnold. *The American college and international education.* (ED 013 349), 1967. $3.29.

No. 28. Edmund W. Gordon. *The higher education of the disadvantaged.* (ED 013 350), 1967. $3.29.

No. 29. Robert T. Jordan, et al. *Impact of the academic library on the educational program.* (ED 013 351), 1967. $3.29.

No. 30. Joseph Katz. *The student activists: Rights, needs and powers of undergraduates.* (ED 013 352), 1967. $3.29.

No. 31. Nevitt Sanford. *Education for individual development.* (ED 013 353), 1967. $3.29.

No. 32. Junius A. Davis. *Applications of the science of measurement to higher education.* (ED 026 971), 1967. $6.58.

1404 NMSC RESEARCH REPORTS, National Merit Scholarship Corporation (1173), 990 Grove Street, Evanston, Illinois 60201. (312) 869-5100. Frequency: 5-8 per year. Price: free. Usual length: 10-20 pp.

This series provides probably the best normative information on talented students available in the country. The research examines the source, identification, and development of intellectual talent. Although the reports are factual and straightforward, they underplay technical jargon in favor of readability and practical utility. Reports are distributed to a selected group of 500. A *Review of Research* is brought out at irregular intervals as part of the series and is distributed to 1,200 people. (The last *Review of Research,* 1970, vol. 6, no. 1, (1031), covered research for a three-year period.)

Recent reports include:

Vol. 6, 1970

No. 2. Fred H. Borgen. *Able black Americans in college: Entry and freshman experiences.* (1062).

No. 3. Donivan J. Watley and Rosalyn Kaplan. *Merit scholars and the fulfillment of promise.*

No. 4. Charles E. Werts and Donivan J. Watley. *Paternal influence on talent development.*

No. 5. Donivan J. Watley and Rosalyn Kaplan. *Progress of merit scholars: Does religious background matter?*

Vol. 7, 1971

No. 1. Donivan J. Watley. *Brain gains and brain drains: The migration of black and nonblack talent.*

No. 2. Fred H. Borgen. *Differential expectations? Predicting grades for black students in five types of colleges.*

No. 3. Donivan J. Watley. *Characteristics and performance of NMSQT participants.*

No. 4. Donivan J. Watley. *Black and nonblack youth: Characteristics and college attendance patterns.*

No. 5. Donivan J. Watley. *Black and nonblack youth: Does marriage hinder college attendance?*

No. 6. Donivan J. Watley. *Black and nonblack youth: Finances and college attendance.*

No. 7. Donivan J. Watley. *Characteristics of academic "brains" in different career fields.*

1405 PROJECT TALENT REPORTS, American Institutes for Research (1157), P. O. Box 1113, Palo Alto, California 94302. (415) 328-3550. Price: varies from $3 to $10. Usual length: varies from 60-600 pp.

The massive amounts of data generated by Project TALENT (1445) have made possible numerous research studies. In addition to the many journal articles, the staff of TALENT has produced a number of major publications. Although individual reports vary in their degree of technicality and their usefulness to different audiences, the series is a source of valuable information from the nation's most comprehensive study of the development of young adults. Typically, 500-1,000 copies of each report have been distributed, with the majority going to secondary school counselors, psychologists, and measurement specialists.

Reports include:

1962 John C. Flanagan, et al. *Design for a study of American youth.* Boston: Houghton Mifflin. $5. (Available from publisher).

1962 John C. Flanagan, John T. Dailey, Marion F. Shaycoft, David B. Orr, and Isadore Goldberg. *Studies of the American high school.* $8.50. (702).

1963 Marion F. Shaycoft, John T. Dailey, David B. Orr, Clinton A. Neyman

Jr., and Stuart E. Sherman. *Studies of a complete age group—Age 15*. $8.50. (893).

1964 John C. Flanagan, et al. *The American high school student*. $10. (885).

1966 John C. Flanagan, et al. *Project TALENT one-year follow-up studies*. $5. (917).

1966 Paul R. Lohnes. *Measuring adolescent personality*. $5.

1967 Marion F. Shaycoft. *The high school years: Growth in cognitive skills*. $5. (892).

1968 E. E. Cureton. *A factor analysis of Project TALENT tests and four other test batteries*. $3.

1968 William W. Cooley and Paul R. Lohnes. *Predicting development of young adults*. $5. (861).

1968 David E. Kapel. *Effects of Negro density on student variables and the post-high-school adjustment of male Negroes*. $3. (707).

1968 W. A. Love Jr. and D. K. Stewart. *Interpreting canonical correlations: Theory and practice*. $3.

1971 John C. Flanagan, Marion F. Shaycoft, James M. Richards Jr., and John G. Claudy. *Five years after high school*. $10; *Appendix II*, $8.

Project TALENT Specimen Set (This includes all tests, inventories, and questionnaires used in the Project TALENT testing, spring 1960.) $3.

1406 PUTTING RESEARCH INTO EDUCATIONAL PRACTICE (PREP), U.S. Office of Education, National Center for Educational Communication, 400 Maryland Avenue, S. W., Washington, D. C. 20202. (202) 963-7782. Frequency: monthly. Price: free. Usual length: 5-25 pp.

Putting Research into Educational Practice (PREP) is a series of interpretive reports and other materials intended to bring research and development findings to bear on practical educational problems. They are produced under U.S. Office of Education contracts in an effort to strengthen educational information services and speed adoption of tested innovations. These monographs are directed primarily to solutions of elementary and secondary educational problems. Findings and applications are presented in a simple format for inexpensive reproduction. In addition to the monographs, PREP kits typically include selected bibliographies and lists of current programs across the country. The kits are sent primarily to state education agencies. States often distribute copies to local communities.

Recent PREP kits include:

No. XVI. *Individualized instruction*. 1970.

No. XVII. *Micro-teaching*. 1970.

No. XVIII. *Reinforcing productive classroom behavior: A teacher guide to behavior modification*. 1971.

No. XIX. *Migrant education*. 1971.

No. XX. *Teacher recruitment and selection*. 1971.

No. XXI. *Teacher evaluation*. 1971.

No. XXII. *A readiness test for disadvantaged pre-school children*. 1971.

No. XXIII. *Educational cooperatives*. 1971.

No. XXIV. *School-community relations and educational change*. 1971.

1407 REPORT SERIES, ERIC Clearinghouse on Higher Education (1453), One Dupont Circle, Suite 630, Washington, D. C. 20036. (202) 296-2597. Frequency: about 10-12 per year. Price: free. Usual length: 10-25 pp.

This series of commissioned reports presents reviews of literature on topics of special current interest to higher education. Begun in 1970, the series is intended to include about 10 reports a year written by knowledgeable authors. Copies are distributed to about 1,000 individuals and organizations throughout higher education.

Reports include:

No. 1. Frank W. Finger. *Professional problems: Preparation for a career in college teaching.* 1970. (320).

No. 2. James Richards. *Assessing student performance in college.* 1970.

No. 3. William T. Trent. *College compensatory programs for disadvantaged students.* 1970. (997).

No. 4. Juan A. Casasco. *Corporate planning models for university management.* 1970. (674).

No. 5. Richard E. Peterson. *The crisis of purpose: Definitions and uses of institutional goals.* 1970. (623).

No. 6. Wilbert J. McKeachie. *Research on college teaching.* 1970. (327).

No. 7. Lewis Paterson. *Consortia in American higher education.* 1970.

No. 8. Amiel T. Sharon. *College credit for off-campus study.* 1971. (803).

No. 9. Jonathan R. Warren. *College grading practices: An overview.* 1971. (425).

1408 SREB RESEARCH MONOGRAPHS, Southern Regional Education Board (1176), 130 Sixth Street, N. W., Atlanta, Georgia 30313. (404) 875-9211. Frequency: 1-2 per year. Price: varies. Usual length: 50-100 pp.

These monographs typically are commissioned essays or research reports on topics of critical interest to higher education both in the South and throughout the nation. The reports on Southern state revenue potential are particularly valuable for those concerned with educational opportunity and tax structures in the region. Many others are highly regarded. Begun in 1960, the reports attempt to provide practical, state-of-the-art information but at the same time recommend possible courses of action.

Reports include:

No. 1. Kenneth E. Quindry and James W. Martin. *Southern states: New revenue potentials.* 1960.

No. 2. John W. Gustad. *The career decisions of college teachers.* 1960.

No. 3. Robert B. Downs. *Strengthening and improving library resources for Southern higher education.* 1962.

No. 4. Kenneth E. Quindry. *Revenue potentials in Southern states.* 1962.

No. 5. W. Starr Miller and Kenneth M. Wilson. *Faculty development procedures in small colleges.* 1963.

No. 6. N. Z. Medalia. *On becoming a college teacher: A review of three variables.* 1963.

No. 7. W. Hugh Stickler and Milton W. Carothers. *The year-round calendar in operation.* 1963.

No. 8. Frederick B. Rowe. *Characteristics of women's college students.* 1964.

No. 9. Kenneth M. Wilson. *Of time and the doctorate: Report of an inquiry into the duration of doctoral study.* 1965.

No. 10. Charles M. Grigg. *Recruitment to graduate study.* 1965.

No. 11. Lewis B. Mayhew. *The collegiate curriculum: An approach to analysis.* 1966.

No. 12. A. J. Brumbaugh. *Establishing new senior colleges.* 1966.

No. 13. Lewis B. Mayhew. *Innovation in collegiate instruction: Strategies for change.* 1968.

No. 14. Lewis B. Mayhew. *Contemporary college students and the curriculum.* 1969. (296).

No. 15. Kenneth E. Quindry. *State and local revenue potential.* 1969.

No. 16. Kenneth E. Quindry. *State and local revenue potential 1969.* 1970. (167).

No. 17. Lewis B. Mayhew. *Changing practices in education for the professions.* 1971.

14.4—*STATISTICAL SERIES*. Much of the baseline demographic and educational statistics bearing upon access to higher education are published in government reports that come out in series or as annual documents. These reports are of fundamental importance to specialists but may seem somewhat obscure to the average professional whose work does not routinely require such information. It is natural that practically all of these statistical reports of major significance are produced by three federal agencies: U.S. Office of Education, the Census Bureau, and the Bureau of Labor Statistics. A key reference for general use is the *Statistical Abstract of the United States* (1419). It includes a wealth of information and references to source documents.

Note: Items 1420 to 1430 are publications of the U.S. Office of Education, listed alphabetically by title.

1409 AMERICAN COUNCIL ON EDUCATION. *A fact book on higher education.* Washington, D. C.: ACE. Quarterly. $35 per year for new subscriptions; $20 per year for renewal subscriptions.

A Fact Book on Higher Education is a series of pamphlets synthesizing statistics on higher education obtained from government and private sources. Data on enrollment, social and economic factors, faculty and students, and earned degrees are presented in convenient charts and tables that review past developments, show projections, and emphasize trends and relationships. Each quarter a 50-page pamphlet devoted to one of the four data categories is issued to replace and update the previous year's charts and tables.

1410 UNITED NATIONS EDUCATIONAL, SCIENTIFIC AND CULTURAL ORGANIZATION. *Unesco statistical yearbook 1969.* Paris: Unesco, 1970, 666 pp. $33; paperback $26.

The *Unesco Statistical Yearbook* is an important source of statistics on the educational, scientific, and cultural life and activities of some 200 countries and territories. The *Yearbook* presents a voluminous amount of worldwide data on public and private educational institutions at all levels. It includes such items as the number of schools, teachers, and students by sex, level, and type of education; students and graduates in higher education by field of study; foreign students in higher education by field of study and country of origin; expenditures on education as related to purpose, national income, level, and type of education; and educational attainment and illiteracy statistics. Also presented are data on area and population, libraries and museums, publications, and other cultural characteristics of national life. A list of other helpful UNESCO statistical publications is included.

1411 U.S. BUREAU OF LABOR STATISTICS. *Handbook of labor statistics 1970.* Washington, D. C.: Government Printing Office, 1970, 400 pp. $3.50.

The annual *Handbook of Labor Statistics* brings together in one volume the major statistical series produced by the Bureau of Labor Statistics and related series from other governmental agencies and foreign countries. It is a particularly valuable basic reference for researchers and planners. In addition to technical notes, the volume includes over 150 tables on the labor force, employment, unemployment, hours, productivity and unit labor costs, compensation, prices and living conditions, foreign labor statistics, and general economic data. See also *Monthly Labor Review* (1336) for current BLS statistics in addition to articles and book reviews.

1412 U.S. BUREAU OF LABOR STATISTICS. *Special Labor Force Reports.* Washington, D. C.: U.S. Department of Labor.

The Bureau of Labor Statistics has published a series of *Special Labor Force Reports* since 1960 on a variety of topics related to employment and unemployment. Articles first appear in the *Monthly Labor Review* (1336) and then come out as reprints, which are available while the supply lasts from the Bureau of Labor Statistics or any of its regional offices. Regularly covered subjects of special interest to educators include educational attainment of workers, employment of high school graduates and dropouts, and characteristics of school-age youth. More than 125 reports have been published through 1971.

1413 U.S. BUREAU OF THE CENSUS. *Census Monograph Series.* Washington, D. C.: Government Printing Office.

The *Census Monograph Series* provides analysis and interpretations of decennial census data and related statistics to illuminate major current problem areas. A series of monographs prepared by various scholars in cooperation with the Bureau of the Census and with the Social Science Research Council followed both the 1950 and 1960 censuses; another series is planned for the 1970 census. Monographs based on the 1960 census are: *Income Distribution in the United States, Education of the American Population, People of Rural America,* and *Changing Characteristics of the Negro Population.* Scheduled for future publication are *The Metropolitan Community* and *People of the United States in the 20th Century.*

1414 U.S. BUREAU OF THE CENSUS. *Census of population: 1960.* Vol. I. *Characteristics of the population.* Washington, D. C.: Government Printing Office, 1963. $236.75.

This series constitutes the major report of the decennial Census of Population. It consists of 58 separate volumes, one for the United States as a whole, one for each of the 50 states, and one each for the District of Columbia and each of the outlying areas. Each part contains four chapters, which are first issued as individual paperbound reports. These chapters present data on: (1) number of inhabitants, (2) general population characteristics, (3) general social and economic characteristics, and (4) detailed characteristics. Statistics are presented for states, counties by urban and rural residence, standard metropolitan statistical areas, urbanized areas, county subdivisions, and places of 1,000 inhabitants or more. Much of this information is also available on tapes (see 1448). See also 1415 for a description of another basic series resulting from the decennial census, *Volume II: Subject Reports.* Final reports from the 1970 census will probably be available by 1972 or 1973.

1415 U.S. BUREAU OF THE CENSUS. *Census of population: 1960.* Vol. II. *Subject reports.* Washington, D. C.: Government Printing Office.

The *Subject Reports* present special analyses of the decennial Census of Population. Each report concentrates on a particular subject. Of special interest to educators are the volumes on (1) school enrollment that presents personal and family characteristics of persons enrolled in school or college and of persons not enrolled; and (2) educational attainment that presents data on years of school completed by age, ethnic origin, occupation, income, and other characteristics. Subjects covered by other reports include national origin and race, fertility, families, marital status, migration, unemployment, occupation, industry, and income. Detailed information is generally provided on a national and regional level; in some reports data for states or standard metropolitan statistical areas are also shown. Subject reports based on the 1970 census are to be issued in 1972. See also 1414 for a description of the primary Census of Population report, *Characteristics of the Population.*

1416 U.S. BUREAU OF THE CENSUS. *Census Tract Reports.* Washington, D. C.: Government Printing Office.

This series includes reports of the decennial population and housing censuses. It contains one report for each standard metropolitan statistical area (SMSA) in the United States and Puerto Rico, showing most of the population and housing data included in the decennial census. Information is listed by individual census tracts. Tables for the 1960 reports contain a variety of information including: (1) general characteristics of the population; (2) age, color, and marital status by sex; (3) labor force characteristics; (4) characteristics of certain minority populations; and (5) occupancy and structural characteristics of housing units. Maps are included. The data are primarily useful to researchers and are widely used in private business for marketing analysis.

1417 U.S. BUREAU OF THE CENSUS. *County and city data book*. A Statistical Abstract Supplement. Washington, D. C.: Government Printing Office, 1967, 673 pp. $5.50.

The *County and City Data Book* is a *Statistical Abstract* (1419) supplement that presents detailed statistical information for all counties, standard metropolitan statistical areas, and cities of 25,000 or more. The tables contain approximately 110 to 150 statistical items for each area represented. These provide data on population, education, employment, income, housing, local governments, and business. Descriptive text, source notes, and state and national maps are included. The data are also available on computer tapes and punchcards for the convenience of researchers and planners.

1418 U.S. BUREAU OF THE CENSUS. *Current Population Reports*. Washington, D. C.: Government Printing Office. $8.50 per year.

A Current Population Survey is conducted monthly by the Bureau of the Census. These surveys are the primary source of census information between decennial censuses. Interviewers talk with a scientifically selected sample of the population to obtain current information on a variety of topics. The *Current Population Reports* based on these surveys are issued in the following series: P-20, Population Characteristics; P-23, Special and Technical Studies; P-25, Population Estimates and Projections; P-26, Federal-State Cooperative Program for Population Estimates; P-27, Farm Population; P-28, Special Censuses; P-60, Consumer Income; and P-65, Consumer Buying Indicators. Information is presented in detailed tables with comment and explanation. The reports periodically present data on the following topics pertinent to the access process: factors related to high school graduation and college attendance, characteristics of American youth, school enrollments, educational attainment, characteristics of students and their colleges, men with college degrees, minority populations, poverty, metropolitan and nonmetropolitan population figures, social and economic conditions, income, and employment.

1419 U.S. BUREAU OF THE CENSUS. *Statistical abstract of the United States 1970*. (90th ed.) Washington, D. C.: Government Printing Office, 1970, 1,018 pp. $5.75.

The *Statistical Abstract of the United States* is the standard summary of statistics on the social, political, and economic character of the United States. It is an especially convenient volume for statistical reference; it also serves as a guide to other statistical publications and sources through its introductory notes to each section, source listings for each table, guide to sources, a section on publications of recent censuses, a guide to state statistical abstracts, and a list of statistical abstract supplements. There are 33 major sections on a wide variety of subjects including education, population, employment, and income. The *Abstract* presents more than 1,300 tables and charts. *The County and City Data Book* (1417) presents similar and more detailed demographic information for individual counties and cities.

1420 Hooper, Mary Evans. *Associate degrees and other formal awards below the baccalaureate, 1968-69.* Washington, D. C.: Government Printing Office, 1969, 118 pp. $1.25.

This publication consists primarily of detailed listings of specific degrees and awards below the baccalaureate level granted by each of 1,135 colleges. These include nearly all the institutions recognized by the United States Office of Education that are known to grant such degrees and awards. In addition, brief summary tables show overall counts of awards granted by institutional control and level, state, and curriculum. The first report on associate degrees covered 1965-66 and 1966-67. Information on bachelor's and higher degrees may be found in *Earned Degrees Conferred* (1422).

1421 Simon, Kenneth A., and Grant, W. Vance. *Digest of educational statistics.* Washington, D. C.: Government Printing Office, 1970, 140 pp. $1.25.

The *Digest of Educational Statistics* is published annually. It provides an abstract of statistical information covering United States education from kindergarten through graduate school. Utilizing materials from both governmental and nongovernmental sources, the *Digest* contains introductory material and 170 tables on a wide variety of subjects, including the number of institutions, enrollments, teachers, graduates, educational attainment, finances, federal educational programs and funds, employment status and job opportunities, educational opportunity, libraries, international education, and research and development. This publication is particularly valuable to researchers, administrators, and policy-makers.

1422 Hooper, Mary Evans, and Chandler, Marjorie O. *Earned degrees conferred, 1968-69.* Part A. *Summary data.* Part B. *Institutional data.* Washington, D. C.: Government Printing Office, 1971, Part A, 38 pp., 50 cents. Part B, 521 pp., $4.75.

This annual two-volume report presents data on degrees earned in more than 1,550 higher education institutions in the United States. Part A contains extensive summary information by level of degree, field of specialization, sex of recipient, state, level of institution, and institutional control. Part B contains a detailed listing of bachelor's, first-professional, master's, and doctor's degrees conferred in each academic field by each institution. It provides an excellent source for finding institutions that offer degree programs in more than 200 major fields.

1423 Barr, Richard H., and Foster, Betty J. *Fall 1968 statistics of public elementary and secondary day schools: Pupils, teachers, instruction rooms, and expenditures.* Washington, D. C.: Government Printing Office, 1970, 33 pp. 45 cents.

This publication is based on an annual survey conducted by the Office of Education in cooperation with state education agencies. It contains tables providing current data on the number of local school districts, high school graduates, teachers, enrollment by grade, pupil-teacher ratio, pupils on curtailed sessions, instruction rooms, estimated total and per-pupil expenditures, and average staff salaries. Data are given for each state and outlying areas and for 14 of the largest U.S. cities.

1424 U.S. Office of Education, National Center for Educational Statistics. *Financial statistics of institutions of higher education: Current funds, revenues and expenditures, 1968-69.* Washington, D. C.: Government Printing Office, 1971, 165 pp. $1.50.

For the years 1965-66 and 1966-67, this publication presented higher education financial data in a series of four reports: (1) *Current Funds, Revenues, and Expenditures*, (2) *Property*, (3) *Student Financial Aid*, and (4) *Federal Funds.*

It was reduced in scope to one volume for the year 1967-68, eliminating data on student financial aid, and presenting a variety of tables on current funds, revenues, physical plant assets, and expenditures listed by region, state, control, level of institution, source, and function. The version for 1968-69 eliminated data on physical plant assets. Data are published about two years after the close of a given school year.

1425 U.S. OFFICE OF EDUCATION, NATIONAL CENTER FOR EDUCATIONAL STATISTICS. *Higher education finances: Selected trend and summary data.* Washington, D. C.: Government Printing Office, 1968, 85 pp. 75 cents.

Higher Education Finances consists of tables presenting summary data on current-fund income and expenditures, plant-fund receipts and expenditures, and investment in plants. Also included are historical summaries and data on research expenditures and special funds such as endowment, student loan, and annuity and living trust. Information is listed by state, control, type of institution, source of funds, and purpose.

1426 WADE, GEORGE H. *Opening fall enrollment in higher education, 1970.* Part A. *Summary data.* Part B. *Institutional data.* Washington, D. C.: Government Printing Office, 1970, Part A, 36 pp.; Part B, 54 pp. $1.25.

Opening Fall Enrollment in Higher Education provides detailed enrollment data on resident and extension students in undergraduate and graduate programs in about 2,500 colleges and universities—all those included in the Office of Education's higher education survey universe. Part A contains summary tables showing recent trends and providing data for both total and first-time enrollments by type of program, level, attendance status, and sex. Part B contains similar data on individual institutions listed alphabetically by state. Published annually since 1946, *Opening Fall Enrollment* is a particularly valuable reference document for educators, researchers, and planners.

1427 SIMON, KENNETH A., AND FULLAM, MARIE G. *Projections of educational statistics to 1978-79.* (1969 ed.) Washington, D. C.: Government Printing Office, 169 pp. $1.50.

Projections of Educational Statistics provides valuable information for planners and educational researchers. It is also a favorite of speech writers. The report covers elementary and secondary schools and higher education institutions in the United States. Individual tables typically cite data for 10 previous years and projections a decade ahead. Information on enrollment, high school graduates, earned degrees by level and field, teacher demand, educational expenditures, and student charges by higher education institutions are presented in 49 tables. Projections assume a continuation of the past 10 years' trends.

1428 WADE, GEORGE H. *Residence and migration of college students: Basic state-to-state matrix tables, fall 1968.* Washington, D. C.: Government Printing Office, 1970, 71 pp. $2.50.

This publication contains the basic data on the residence and migration of students in higher education. Data for the 50 states, for United States Service Schools, and for outlying areas are presented by level of enrollment and by level and control of institution in state-to-state matrix format. These matrixes show how many students migrate from each state to each other state. The data are especially useful for planning purposes. A second report will summarize the data for each state in various analytical relationships. Earlier migration studies were conducted in 1963 by the Office of Education in cooperation with the American Association of Collegiate Registrars and Admissions Officers, in 1958 by AACRAO, and in 1949 by U.S.O.E.

1429 U.S. OFFICE OF EDUCATION. *Statistics of nonpublic elementary and secondary schools, 1965-66.* Washington, D. C.: Government Printing Office, 1968, 50 pp. 45 cents.

This publication provides summary data on the number of nonpublic elementary and secondary schools, enrollments, teachers, student-teacher ratios, curriculums, number of students entering institutions of higher education, libraries, and courses for exceptional children. Information is variously listed by region, state, affiliation, type of facility, and type of student body. The data are generally gathered every few years.

1430 CHANDLER, MARJORIE O., AND HOOPER, MARY EVANS. *Students enrolled for advanced degrees: Institutional data, fall 1969.* Washington, D. C.: Government Printing Office, 1970, 275 pp. $2.25.

The major portion of this publication contains detailed listings of graduate enrollments reported by nearly 900 institutions in more than 200 fields of study. The report provides a useful listing of all schools offering graduate work in a given field and indicates the size of their programs. Other information includes summary data for various levels of degrees listed by control, state, sex of student, and attendance status. A companion report, *Students Enrolled for Advanced Degrees, Fall 1969: Preliminary Report,* provides further summary data and compares 1969 enrollments with those of previous years. The data were gathered in the United States Office of Education's annual survey of students enrolled for advanced degrees.

14.5 — PROCEEDINGS AND YEARBOOKS. There are a few important organizations that each year publish the proceedings of their annual meetings or some reference document of special value. Many have been annotated in appropriate sections. These annual series are collected and listed here simply as a convenient reference.

1431 AMERICAN ASSOCIATION FOR HIGHER EDUCATION, ANNUAL MEETING, One Dupont Circle, N. W., Washington, D. C. 20036. (202) 293-6440.

The proceedings of the annual American Association for Higher Education conference are published in the series *Current Issues in Higher Education,* edited for the past five years by G. Kerry Smith. The papers are selected from among those presented at the conference, typically by scholars, administrators, and political leaders directly involved in the topical issues under discussion.

Topics of the 21st through 25th national conferences were:

1966 *Higher Education reflects — On itself and on larger society.* $5.
1967 *In search of leaders.* $5.
1968 *Stress and campus response.* $7.75.
1969 *Agony and promise.* $7.75.
1970 *The troubled campus.* $7.75.

1432 AMERICAN COUNCIL ON EDUCATION, ANNUAL MEETING, One Dupont Circle, N. W., Washington, D. C. 20036. (202) 833-4700.

The annual meeting of the American Council on Education provides a forum for discussion and debate of various topics of current interest to higher education. This meeting attracts more senior administrators from colleges and universities than any comparable event; it routinely includes addresses by eminent educators. Most of the contributions to the following volumes were prepared for the ACE meeting; they present differing viewpoints and perceptions of the discussion topic. Individual items are annotated as indicated.

1965 Logan Wilson (ed.) *Emerging patterns in American higher education.* (628) $4.

1966 Lawrence E. Dennis and Joseph F. Kauffman (eds.) *The college and the student.* (287) $6.

1967 Calvin B. T. Lee (ed.) *Improving college teaching.* (325) $6.

1968 Charles G. Dobbins and Calvin B. T. Lee (eds.) *Whose goals for American higher education.* $6.

1969 John Caffrey (ed.) *The future academic community: Continuity and change.* (590) $7.

1970 David C. Nichols and Olive Mills (eds.) *The campus and the racial crisis.* (992) $7.

1971 W. Todd Furniss (ed.) *Higher education for everybody? Issues and implications.* (214) $7.

1433 ABSTRACTS FROM ANNUAL MEETING, American Educational Research Association (1104), 1126 Sixteenth Street, N. W., Washington, D. C. 20036. (202) 223-9485.

The American Educational Research Association *Abstracts* includes those papers presented at the annual AERA meeting. In most cases, the abstract was written by the author of the paper. The abstracts are grouped within each volume according to the seven divisions of the AERA (see 1104). Following is a list of editors of the annual volumes:

1968 Henry Hausdorff. *AERA paper abstracts.*

1969 Vincent Crockenberg. *AERA paper abstracts.*

1970 William F. Pilder. *Abstracts/one: 1970 annual meeting paper sessions. Abstracts/two: 1970 annual meeting symposia.*

1971 F. Craig Johnson. *AERA paper and symposia abstracts.*

1434 COLLEGE ADMISSIONS COLLOQUIUMS, College Entrance Examination Board (1112), 888 Seventh Avenue, New York, New York 10017. (212) 582-6210.

From 1954 to 1963 the College Entrance Examination Board published *College Admissions,* a very useful series dealing with various topics and compiled from papers presented at annual colloquiums.

Topics covered at each meeting and the chairmen were:

1954 B. Alden Thresher. *College admissions.*

1955 Frederick C. Copeland. *The great sorting.*

1956 Emery R. Walker Jr. *The interaction of school and college.*

1957 Eugene S. Wilson. *The student from school to college.*

1958 Hollace G. Roberts. *Planning college policy for the critical decade ahead.*

1959 Leslie R. Severinghaus. *The American secondary school.*

1960 John U. Monro. *The search for talent.* (1023).

1961 A. Blair Knapp. *Counseling in school and college.*

1962 Lloid B. Jones. *The changing college preparatory curriculum.*

1963 Katherine E. McBride. *The behavioral sciences and education.*

Individual copies are $3. A complete set of 10 volumes may be ordered for $24. See 242 for additional information.

1435 COLLEGE SCHOLARSHIP COLLOQUIUMS, College Entrance Examination Board (1112), 888 Seventh Avenue, New York, New York 10017. (212) 582-6210.

The College Scholarship Service has sponsored four invitational colloquiums dealing with problems relevant to the financing of higher education. The colloquiums have covered a wide range of topics such as economics of higher education, national student aid programs, identifying talented students, and administering financial aid.

Colloquium topics and their respective directors are:

1962 Byron S. Hollinshead. *Student financial aid and national purpose.* (153) $2.50.

1963 McCrea Hazlett. *Student financial aid and institutional purpose.* (175) $2.
1967 James L. Bowman. *The economics of higher education.* (127) $2.
1970 Alexander G. Sidar Jr. *Financing equal opportunity in higher education.* (183) $1.

14.5
Proceedings
and
Yearbooks

1436 INVITATIONAL CONFERENCE ON TESTING PROBLEMS, Educational Testing Service (1115), Princeton, New Jersey. (609) 921-9000.

The Invitational Conference on Testing Problems has been held annually since 1936, and sponsored by Educational Testing Service since 1948. This well-known conference is of particular interest to those concerned with the applications and social implications of educational measurement. Papers presented at the conferences are published in the *Proceedings,* listed below according to the year the conference was held, the conference chairman, and the central themes of each meeting. Individual copies are available for $2. See 399 for a selection of outstanding papers presented at this conference over an 18-year period.

Conference topics include:

1960 John B. Carroll. *The cooperative research program; Testing in the language arts.*
1961 Paul L. Dressel. *Implications of factor analysis for achievement testing; Use of achievement tests in award of course credit; Extended conceptions of evaluation in higher education.*
1962 Eric F. Gardner. *Creativity; Comparability of scores; Processing educational data.*
1963 Alexander G. Wesman. *Basic concepts, implications, and consequences of measurement; Testing and the medical profession.*
1965 Robert L. Ebel. *Intelligence testing; Teaching and testing values; measurements of educational achievement.*
1966 Julian C. Stanley. *Innovation and evaluation; Natural language and computers in education.*
1967 Benjamin S. Bloom. *Evaluation and research in curriculum development; New approaches to instruction; measurement systems.*
1968 J. Thomas Hastings. *Educational evaluation; The socially disadvantaged.*
1969 Philip H. Dubois. *The nature and measurement of educational achievement; Measuring the performance of systems and programs.*

1437 NATIONAL SOCIETY FOR THE STUDY OF EDUCATION YEARBOOKS, 5835 Kimbark Avenue, Chicago, Illinois 60637.

The National Society for the Study of Education has published the *Yearbook* since 1902. The Board of Directors of NSSE selects the subject to be investigated and appoints committees composed of individuals who represent varying viewpoints on the topic. NSSE then funds, publishes, and distributes the resultant report. Each year two volumes of the *Yearbook* are compiled from articles submitted by both members of the Society's committee and other contributors. The volumes provide comprehensive reviews of topics of general interest to educators.

Recent yearbooks and their respective editors include:

1962 Vol. 61, Part I. Fred T. Tyler. *Individualizing instruction.* $4.50.
   Part II. G. Lester Anderson. *Education for the professions.* $4.50.
1963 Vol. 62, Part I. Harold W. Stevenson. *Child psychology.* $6.50.
   Part II. Warren G. Findley. *The impact and improvement of school testing programs.* $4.50.
1964 Vol. 63, Part I. Ernest R. Hilgard. *Theories of learning and instruction.* $5.50.
   Part II. Daniel E. Griffiths. *Behavioral science and educational administration.* $4.50.

1965 Vol. 64, Part I. Melvin L. Barlow. *Vocational education.* $5. (715).
Part II. W. Reid Hastie. *Art education.* $5.
1966 Vol. 65, Part I. William W. Wattenberg. *Social deviancy among youth.* $5.50.
Part II. John I. Goodlad. *The changing American school.* $5.
1967 Vol. 66, Part I. Paul A. Witty. *The educationally retarded and disadvantaged.* $5.50.
Part II. Phil C. Lange. *Programed instruction.* $5.
1968 Vol. 67, Part I. Robert J. Havighurst. *Metropolitanism: Its challenge to education.* $5.50.
Part II. Helen M. Robinson. *Innovation and change in reading instruction.* $5.50.
1969 Vol. 68, Part I. Harold G. Shane. *The United States and international education.* $5.50.
Part II. Ralph W. Tyler. *Educational evaluation: New roles, new means.* $5.50.
1970 Vol. 69, Part I. Edward G. Begle. *Mathematics education.* $7.
Part II. Albert H. Marckwardt. *Linguistics in school programs.* $5.50.
1971 Vol. 70, Part I. Robert M. McClure. *The curriculum: Retrospect and prospect.* $5.50.

1438 LEGISLATIVE WORK CONFERENCES, Southern Regional Education Board (1176), 130 Sixth Street, N. W., Atlanta, Georgia 30313. (404) 875-9211.

For the last 20 years the Southern Regional Education Board has sponsored a series of annual work conferences for state legislators of the 14 Southern states. The conference goal is to provide a mutually beneficial dialogue between the legislators and educators. The panel discussions and short papers presented at the meeting are available in the annual *Proceedings*.

Recent topics are as follows:

1962 *Coordination and planning.*
1963 *Higher adult education and educational* TV.
1964 *Technical-vocational education and the community college.*
1965 *Quality in higher education.*
1966 *Financing higher education.*
1967 *The organization of higher education.*
1968 *The college campus in 1968.*
1969 *The college campus in 1969: The faculty.*
1970 *New directions in statewide higher education: Planning and coordination* (668).
1971 *Higher education for the future: Reform or more of the same?*

1439 COLLEGE AND UNIVERSITY SELF-STUDY INSTITUTES, Western Interstate Commission for Higher Education (1177), P. O. Drawer P, Boulder, Colorado 80302.

Since 1960 the Western Interstate Commission for Higher Education and the Center for Research and Development in Higher Education (1161) at Berkeley have cosponsored the annual College and University Self-Study Institutes. The purpose of these institutes is to "present significant research findings and informed opinion on broad and fundamental issues in higher education." A list of the editors, topics, and prices of reports containing papers presented at the institutes held from 1962-70 follows. Several of these reports are classic references, but those from 1960-63 are no longer available directly from WICHE.

The institutes considered the following topics:

1962 Terry F. Lunsford (ed.) *The study of campus cultures.*
1963 Terry F. Lunsford (ed.) *The study of academic administration.*
1964 Owen A. Knorr (ed.) *Long-range planning in higher education.* (614). $3.

1965 Owen A. Knorr and W. John Minter (eds.) *Order and freedom on the campus.* (1012). $3.50.

1966 W. John Minter (ed.) *Campus and capitol: Higher education and the state.* (620). $3.50.

1967 W. John Minter (ed.) *The individual and the system: Personalizing higher education.* $3.50.

1968 W. John Minter and Ian M. Thompson (eds.) *Colleges and universities as agents of social change.* $3.50.

1969 W. John Minter and Patricia O. Snyder (eds.) *Value change and power conflict in higher education.* $3.50.

1970 Robert A. Altman and Patricia O. Snyder (eds.) *The minority student on the campus: Expectations and possibilities.* (976). $3.50.

1440 *The World Year Book of Education,* Harcourt Brace Jovanovich, Inc., 757 Third Avenue, New York, New York 10017. (212) 572-5000.

Since 1948 the *World Year Book of Education* has been a joint publication effort of editorial boards in London and New York. Each year a topic is selected and treated comparatively, often on the basis of a particular social science approach. The scope of the international coverage of each topic is exceptionally good. The volumes dated from 1961 through 1966 were edited by George Z. F. Bereday and Joseph A. Lauwerys; those from 1967 through 1970 were edited by Joseph A. Lauwerys and David G. Scanlon. The year books for 1961, 1962, 1964, and 1965 are out of print.

The topics covered from 1961 through 1970 were:

1961 *Concepts of excellence in education.*
1962 *The gifted child.*
1963 *The education and training of teachers.* $12.95.
1964 *Education and international life.*
1965 *The education explosion.*
1966 *Church and state in education.* (810) $12.95.
1967 *Educational planning.* $12.95.
1968 *Education within industry.* (794) $12.95.
1969 *Examinations.* (362) $12.95.
1970 *Education in cities.* (851) $12.95.

SECTION 15: SPECIAL RESOURCES

The sources of information in this section fall into five categories rather different from the periodical publications of section 14. Of course, all of the material up to now has represented an information resource of one sort or another, but the material in this section places emphasis on informational quality rather than substantive character. The first two categories — data sources and information centers — are not publications but rather agencies that deal with prepublished or published materials. The last three categories include secondary references.

15.1 – *DATA SOURCES*. Some important data concerning access to higher education are available only through large national data-generating programs. Much of these data are not published and are of interest primarily to researchers and others writing on the status of the access process. The data include information concerning different groups of students and their characteristics, institutional data, surveys of public attitudes, and demographic data. Some sources are of major national significance like the Census Bureau (1448); others like the American Council on Education Higher Education Data Bank (1441) are minor by comparison but highly relevant to problems of access to higher education.

1441 ACE HIGHER EDUCATION DATA BANK, One Dupont Circle, N. W., Washington, D. C. 20036. (202) 833-4700.

In 1969 the American Council on Education Office of Research established a data bank for the use of researchers and other individuals interested in higher education. The bank includes cross-sectional and longitudinal data pertaining to student characteristics, student development, comparative institutional effects, educational trends, and related research questions. Although costs vary greatly depending upon the nature and complexity of each request, users are advised to expect a minimum cost of $150 to $250. For further details on the nature of the sampling design, the files, the data, the software and hardware capabilities, and the procedures for entering the system, consult the *User's Manual, ACE Higher Education Data Bank*, by Alan E. Bayer, Alexander W. Astin, Robert F. Boruch, and John A. Creager, *ACE Research Report*, 1969, vol. 4, no. 1.

The following *Reports* are also of interest:

John A. Creager. *General purpose sampling in the domain of higher education*, 1968, vol. 3, no. 2.

Robert F. Boruch. *Educational research and the confidentiality of data*, 1969, vol. 4, no. 4.

For an annotation of ACE, see 1102.

1442 AMERICAN COLLEGE TESTING PROGRAM.
COLLEGE ENTRANCE EXAMINATION BOARD.
EDUCATIONAL TESTING SERVICE.

The American College Testing Program, College Entrance Examination Board, and Educational Testing Service are three national organizations directly concerned with access to higher education. They are primary sources of specialized data on access because their operating and research programs generate a great deal of highly relevant information. They do not have systematic programs for supplying information to anyone who requests it, but they do routinely provide a great deal of information to individual institutions. They also make a number of ad hoc arrangements for supplying information to systems and organizations, and each agency does have special means of providing certain types of summary data (see 1155, 1165, and 1167). Inquiries regarding availability of specific information are best directed to the Director of Research of each organization.

1443 NATIONAL CENTER FOR EDUCATIONAL STATISTICS, U. S. Office of Education, 400 Maryland Avenue, S. W., Washington, D. C. 20202. (202) 963-5137.

In 1966 the National Center for Educational Statistics consolidated the various U.S. Office of Education surveys of higher educational information into the Higher Education General Information Survey (HEGIS). By this means annual data are gathered from each higher education institution in the United States on enrollments, finances, degrees earned, faculty, physical facilities, library volume and personnel, adult-education programs, and institutional characteristics as well as projections in selected categories. See section 14.4 for several of the publications that report these data. The catalog, *Recent NCES Publications,* contains a complete listing. In addition, the data are recorded on computer tapes, and written requests for duplicate tapes may be made by contacting the director of NCES. The NCES policy has been, however, to make data available in printed form and to discourage dissemination of raw data.

1444 NATIONAL OPINION RESEARCH CENTER, University of Chicago, 6030 South Ellis Avenue, Chicago, Illinois 60637. (312) 684-5600.

National Opinion Research Center annually conducts a large number of surveys in such areas as health and welfare, occupations and professions, political affairs, education, community affairs, and religion. While summary data are presented in the survey reports, unit data are available for most of the studies and may be secured in either card or tape form at the cost of preparation. Researchers may also take advantage of NORC's Survey Research Service, in which a limited number of questions from several clients are administered to a national sample at a cost below that incurred by one researcher operating independently. The brochure *Survey Research Service* provides general information on this service. The *NORC Newsletter* describes recent studies. For an annotation of *NORC* as a research center see 1174.

1445 PROJECT TALENT DATA BANK, American Institutes for Research (1157), P. O. Box 1113, Palo Alto, California 94302. (415) 328-3550.

Project TALENT is a comprehensive longitudinal study of youth that includes an inventory of abilities, interests, plans, activities, and backgrounds. In 1960 400,000 ninth- through twelfth-grade students throughout the nation were questioned and periodic follow-up data have been or will be gathered at regular intervals throughout a 20-year period. Four types of utilization of Project TALENT data are available to any researcher whose written request has been approved: computer printout, contract research, loan of work tapes, and use of original test materials. For more detailed information on the data bank and suggested research applications, see *National Data Resource for Behavioral, Social, and Educational Research* or *The Project TALENT Data Bank.* Both are available from American Institutes for Research.

1446 ROPER PUBLIC OPINION RESEARCH CENTER, Williams College, P. O. Box 624, Williamstown, Massachusetts 01267. (413) 458-5500.

The Roper Center is organizationally independent from the Roper Organization, Inc. Since 1957 the Center has collected, processed, and made accessible to scholars the basic data from sample surveys conducted by a large number of research agencies throughout the world. Topics surveyed are quite diverse, and many either directly or indirectly intersect with issues of higher educational opportunity. Approximately one-third of the more than 8,000 opinion poll results located at the Center are United States studies; the remaining two-thirds originated in 67 other countries. The Center offers three basic services on a fee basis: search and retrieval, cross-tabulations, and duplication and dissemination of data in either card or tape form. A notebook, *Descriptive Materials,* gives some overall information about the nature of the Center, the content of its data bank, and the types of services available.

1447 U.S. BUREAU OF LABOR STATISTICS, U.S. Department of Labor, Washington, D. C. 20212. (202) 393-2420.

The Bureau of Labor Statistics collects, analyzes, and distributes data in six subject areas: manpower and employment; price and living conditions; wages and industrial relations; productivity, technology, and growth; foreign labor and trade; and occupational safety and health. Much of the data is gathered through monthly surveys, and accounts appear either in one of several periodicals (1336 and 1339) or as bulletins or reports. Copies of published, and under certain circumstances unpublished, data on punch cards or magnetic tape can be made available at cost by writing the Commissioner of the BLS. For more information on Bureau programs and specific data available see *Major Programs 1970 Bureau of Labor Statistics.*

1448 U.S. BUREAU OF THE CENSUS, U.S. Department of Commerce, Washington, D. C. 20233. (202) 735-2000.

The Bureau of the Census collects, tabulates, and publishes a wide variety of statistical data about the nation's people and economy. It conducts quinquennial and decennial censuses, monthly and annual surveys, and other periodic inquiries. The Bureau also responds to requests for searches of the decennial census records and undertakes special censuses for state and local governments. The principal products are printed reports (see 1419, 1417, and 1140), computer tapes, and special tabulations of census data. In recent years, it has developed various materials, such as public use samples of decennial census records, summary tapes, and special tabulations, to assist interested individuals and agencies in their utilization of available data. More detailed information concerning the Bureau's products and services will be found in the *Bureau of the Census Catalog* (1497); *Census Bureau Programs and Publications: Area and Subjects Guide,* which presents information on printed reports; *Guide to Census Bureau Data Files and Special Tabulations,* which covers unpublished data; and the two-part *1970 Census Users' Guide* (1482), which is designed to furnish most of the information data users will need for access to and use of 1970 census data products. Inquiries may be directed to the Director, Bureau of the Census, Washington, D.C. For a further description of the Bureau see 1140.

15.2—INFORMATION CENTERS. As already suggested in the Foreword to this book, the much heralded information explosion has generated an acute need for secondary reference agencies to compile, organize, and summarize information. There are only a few such agencies of special importance with respect to access problems. The ERIC system seems not as effective as it might be, but is nonetheless important and is annotated here in some detail. Up to now most of ERIC's resources have been devoted to bibliographic work as opposed to summarization and interpretation.

1449 EDUCATIONAL RESOURCES INFORMATION CENTER (ERIC), U.S. Office of Education, 400 Maryland Avenue, Washington, D. C. 20202. (202) 963-7624.

ERIC was established in 1965 as a nationwide information network. It consists of a central staff at the United States Office of Education and 20 clearinghouses located throughout the country, each focusing on a specific field of education. The clearinghouses acquire, review, abstract, and index publications related to their specific field. These include books, reports, monographs, journal articles, speeches, and conference proceedings. In addition, each clearinghouse produces information analysis products such as interpretive summaries, state-of-the-art papers, bibliographies, and bulletins and newsletters dealing with topics within their particular scope.

Access to this huge collection of documents is provided by two ERIC reference publications: *Research in Education* (1470) and *Current Index to Journals in Education* (1469) which are published monthly. A third publication, the *Thesaurus of ERIC Descriptors* (1471) is essential for making the most effective use of the ERIC collection. A potential user, however, needs to spend some time poring over these documents before he can begin to understand the rather complex cataloging system. Clearinghouses have limited resources for providing detailed replies to questions on specific topics, so individuals are urged to use the publications cited above. Thus ERIC serves bibliographic and retrieval functions but not as an information center for inquiries.

Documents listed by ERIC may be purchased in hard copy or microfiche form. In addition, each clearinghouse carries microfiche copies of every document included in the total ERIC collection and normally will permit on-site review. Clearinghouses described in the following seven annotations deal with information particularly related to access to higher education.

1450 ERIC CLEARINGHOUSE FOR JUNIOR COLLEGES, Powell Library, Room 96, University of California, Los Angeles, California 90024. (213) 825-3931.

The clearinghouse for two-year colleges processes formal and informal research documents about all aspects of community and junior colleges. Special publications of this center include: *Junior College Research Review* (1376), a four-page monthly review of research reports; a series of monographs that review and interpret research (e.g., 757); a series of topical papers describing models for research or occasional statements on pertinent issues; and a series of books that includes analytical and critical statements on the junior college. These are described in a publication list available from the center.

1451 ERIC CLEARINGHOUSE ON ADULT EDUCATION, 107 Roney Lane, Syracuse, New York 13210. (315) 476-5541 ext. 3493.

ERIC Clearinghouse on Adult Education is responsible for research documents on formal and informal adult and continuing education. It covers programs in all governmental and community organizations, as well as in schools, colleges, and universities. In addition to the basic ERIC services, ERIC/AE produces a varied range of bibliographies, journal articles, literature guides and reviews, and other useful publications. A list of ERIC/AE publications is available upon request from the clearinghouse in Syracuse.

1452 ERIC CLEARINGHOUSE ON COUNSELING AND PERSONNEL SERVICES, 611 Church Street, Ann Arbor, Michigan 48104. (313) 764-9492.

ERIC Clearinghouse on Counseling and Personnel Services focuses on information relevant to personnel work at all levels and in all settings. The clearinghouse will provide special searches for information needed to support institutional research and program development. Special publications and related activities include: *CAPS Capsule* (1351), a newsletter designed to communicate news on research and innovations; *Current Resources Series,* indexes of major information sources in specific subject areas; a monograph series that reviews information on major topics with emphasis on their usefulness for practice; *RICH,* an alphabetical register of personnel workers indexed by activity areas; *Integrated Personnel Services Index, a* semiannual index to relevant literature; and a feature in the *Personnel and Guidance Journal* (1341) called "Reports on Research."

1453 ERIC CLEARINGHOUSE ON HIGHER EDUCATION, The George Washington University, One Dupont Circle, Suite 630, Washington, D. C. 20036. (202) 296-2597.

This center is responsible for documents concerned with undergraduate, graduate, and professional education. In addition to basic ERIC services, the CHE staff and outside consultants analyze and interpret significant research findings and make these available through review papers, monographs, and bibliographies. The center also produces a compendium series (1400), and a report in this series (1407).

1454 ERIC CLEARINGHOUSE ON TESTS, MEASUREMENT, AND EVALUATION, Educational Testing Service (1115), Princeton, New Jersey 08540. (609) 921-9000.

The ERIC Clearinghouse on Tests, Measurement, and Evaluation is one of the newest clearinghouses in the network. It was established in 1970 at Educational Testing Service in cooperation with the Rutgers Graduate School of Education. This clearinghouse is reponsible for documents that: (1) emphasize tests or other measurement devices; (2) concern evaluation procedures and techniques in general; and (3) describe the evaluation materials, procedures, and techniques of specific programs or projects. In addition to indexing and abstracting activities, the center provides on-site reference services and prepares a number of publications—primarily short review papers, summaries, and reviews of literature.

1455 ERIC CLEARINGHOUSE ON VOCATIONAL AND TECHNICAL EDUCATION, The Ohio State University, 1900 Kenny Road, Columbus, Ohio 43210. (614) 486-3655.

This clearinghouse focuses on documents in vocational and technical education (including subprofessional) and the related fields of industrial art education, manpower economics, occupational psychology, and occupational sociology. Specific occupational areas include agriculture, business and office, health occupations, and home economics, in addition to trade and industrial education. Special publications of the Clearinghouse include *Abstracts of Research and Related Materials in Vocational and Technical Education* (ARM), *Abstracts of Instructional Materials in Vocational and Technical Education* (AIM), and a series of information analysis papers.

1456 ERIC INFORMATION RETRIEVAL CENTER ON THE DISADVANTAGED, Horace Mann-Lincoln Institute, Teachers College, Columbia University, 525 West 120th Street, New York, New York 10027. (212) 870-4808.

This center is responsible for research documents concerning youth disadvantaged by their economic, ethnic, or social status. Special publications include: The *ERIC/IRCD Bulletin* (1375) which usually carries an analytic or review article, a related selected bibliography, plus film or book reviews; *The Urban Disadvantaged Series;* and the *Collegiate Compensatory Education Series.* The last two series are published irregularly and consist of annotated bibliographies, reviews, and position papers.

1457 NATIONAL REFERRAL CENTER, Science and Technology Division, Library of Congress, Washington, D. C. 20540. (202) 426-5687.

The National Referral Center provides a single place to which anyone with an interest in the physical, biological, social, and engineering sciences may turn for advice on obtaining information on specific topics. It does not provide technical details in answer to inquiries nor furnish bibliographic assistance; it functions, rather, as an intermediary, directing those with questions to organizations or individuals willing to share their specialized knowledge in the particular field. Referral services are available without charge by telephone, correspondence, or through personal visits. *A Directory of Information Resources in the United States: Social Sciences* ($1.50) and *A Directory of Information Resources in the United States: Federal Government* ($2.75) provide information useful to educators. A brochure, *National Referral Center: Science and Technology Division,* describes the center's scope, services, and publications.

1458 NATIONAL TECHNICAL INFORMATION SERVICE, 5285 Port Royal Road, Springfield, Virginia 22151. (703) 321-8500.

The National Technical Information Service was formerly known as the Clearinghouse for Federal Scientific and Technical Information. It serves as a focal point for the collection and dissemination of unclassified government-sponsored research and development reports and translations of foreign technical literature. It also provides reference and inquiry services to government agencies and the general public through its Information Services Section. Analysts answer subject inquiries in a wide array of scientific and social-scientific fields. The collection presently contains about 600,000 titles available in paper copy or microfiche. Users are supplied with a set of the most relevant titles for review. NTIS issues *Government Reports Announcements* (formerly *U.S. Government Research and Development Reports*), a semimonthly abstract journal providing the widest coverage of technical report literature available to the public. A kit of informational materials is available on request. A document available at $3 per copy is PB-189 300: *The Directory of Federally Supported Information Analysis Centers.*

1459 RACE RELATIONS INFORMATION CENTER, P. O. Box 6156, Nashville, Tennessee 37212. (615) 327-1361.

The Race Relations Information Center is a private, nonprofit organization funded by the Ford Foundation. It gathers and distributes information about race relations and conditions of minority life in the United States. As the successor of the Southern Education Reporting Service, it has continued the SERS library, which contains items about race relations from newspapers and magazines as well as reports of studies and surveys. Microfilm of these holdings has been acquired by about 100 public and university libraries. The center's three main activities are publication of special reports, publication of the semimonthly *Race Relations Reporter* (1388), and responding to questions from the public. While it is especially concerned with the racial problems in education and access to college, its research and staff interests encompass many facets of race relations.

1460 SCHOOL RESEARCH INFORMATION SERVICE, Phi Delta Kappa, Eighth and Union Streets, Bloomington, Indiana 47401. (812) 339-1156.

School Research Information Service was established in 1966 as an agency of Phi Delta Kappa. It stores, retrieves, and disseminates reports of educational research and innovative practices. SRIS relies mostly upon reports within the ERIC system (1449), but it also has several hundred additional documents related primarily to elementary and secondary education. The agency responds to either telephone or written requests and will search the ERIC file for a $2 fee. It also disseminates information on research and innovation through the *SRIS Quarterly.*

1461 SCIENCE INFORMATION EXCHANGE, 300 Madison National Bank Building, 1730 M Street, N. W., Washington, D. C. 20036. (202) 381-5511.

The Science Information Exchange registers more than 100,000 one-page records of research each year, representing projects that are in progress by federal agencies (including the Department of Health, Education, and Welfare) as well as by state, university, private, and commercial organizations. SIE embraces all basic and applied fields of the life, social, physical, and engineering sciences. The Science Information Exchange is prepared to answer both simple, specific questions and broad, complex inquiries and will take requests either by telephone or mail. A brochure entitled *Science Information Exchange* outlines the nature of available information, the costs and types of services provided, and some potential uses of such information.

15.3 — *GENERAL REFERENCES*. This section contains a wide variety of secondary references, bibliographies, and indexes. These are highly selected, and most are quite valuable. In particular the reader should note the ERIC reference documents (1468), the *Encyclopedia of Educational Research* (1466) which includes brief status reports in many topical areas, and Mayhew's *The Literature of Higher Education* (1479) which has become an annual institution.

1462 AMERICAN PSYCHOLOGICAL ASSOCIATION. *Psychological Abstracts.* Washington, D. C.: APA. Institutions $130 per year; individual at private address $30 per year.

Psychological Abstracts is a comprehensive and carefully prepared monthly publication presenting nonevaluative abstracts of literature from around the world in psychology and related behavioral sciences. Each issue contains more than 1,500 entries summarizing articles from over 400 periodicals. Areas covered are experimental, physiological, animal, developmental, social, clinical, educational, and personnel and industrial psychology; personality; methodology and research technology; and general topics. Author and subject indexes are included. This particular abstract series is especially helpful because more research related to access to higher education is published by psychologists than by any other academic discipline.

1463 BURKE, ARVID J., AND BURKE, MARY A. (EDS.) *Documentation in education.* (5th ed.) New York: Teachers College Press, 1967, 413 pp. $7.50.

In addition to showing how to locate information or data, this book provides guidance for detailed bibliographic work in education and serves as an aid in locating resources relevant to either a general problem or a more specific question. It is designed to assist both the experienced and inexperienced researcher in making full use of libraries.

1464 CONFERENCE FOR EDUCATIONAL DEVELOPMENT AND RESEARCH, INFORMATION OFFICE. *Catalog of D & R Projects.* (2nd ed.) Denver, Colo.: Conference for Educational Development and Research, Information Office, 1971, 400 pp. $8.75.

This looseleaf catalog meets a critical need for descriptive information on projects undertaken by the federally funded Regional Educational Laboratories and Research and Development Centers. The catalog organizes projects by fields of investigation such as urban education, adult education, and counseling-guidance. For each field the publication reports the name of each project director and his center or laboratory affiliation; abstracts of each project, including expected outcomes, anticipated audience, and general benefits; and the form in which a completed project's end results are available. The monthly *D & R Report* (1358) contains current news from these centers.

1465 DRESSEL, PAUL L., AND PRATT, SALLY B. *The world of higher education: An annotated guide to the major literature.* San Francisco: Jossey-Bass, 1971, 238 pp. $8.75.

This annotated bibliography was intended to review research important in "understanding and making decisions about higher education problems." The book contains brief descriptions of 700 entries in seven categories: institutional research; governance, administration, and management; students; faculty and staff; curriculum and instruction; research methodology; and related reference material. The entries were selected for their relevance to the interests of college administrators and researchers, and in most cases the selection is justifiable. However, the scope of the book is somewhat less comprehensive than the title suggests.

1466 EBEL, ROBERT L. (ED.) *Encyclopedia of educational research.* (4th ed.) A Project of the American Educational Research Association. New York: Macmillan, 1969, 1,522 pp. $30.

The *Encyclopedia of Educational Research* provides scholars, students, and educational practitioners with a convenient and comprehensive source of research information about many important aspects of education. Its 164 articles summarize research on a wide variety of topics dealing with new interests as well as persistent educational problems. Each article includes an extensive list of references. A number of the articles are annotated in this book; they provide an especially convenient summary and guide to literature on selected topics.

1467 *Education Index.* New York: H. W. Wilson.

Education Index has been a standard abstract reference since 1929. It is a very useful monthly publication providing a cumulative author-subject index to selected educational material in the English language. Although primarily a periodical index, it also includes proceedings, yearbooks, bulletins, monographs, and material printed by the United States Government. Comprehensive subject areas and fields related to all levels of education are indexed. Selection of periodicals is accomplished by subscriber vote based on consideration of subject balance and reference value.

1468 ERIC RESOURCE DOCUMENTS

Educational Resources Information Center (1449) was established in 1965 and represents an attempt to bring reports of all major educational research projects to the attention of those dealing with educational issues. This is accomplished by various useful though limited efforts to summarize literature (see 1450 through 1456), and an abstract system consisting of two periodicals and a "key-word" thesaurus. The fact that ERIC is not yet a total success is partially explained by the size and complexity of the task. Also, it is undoubtedly true that many who could profit most from ERIC have not taken the time necessary to pore over the documents and decipher the system by which reports are identified and retrieved. These documents are described in the three following annotations: 1469, 1470, and 1471.

1469 EDUCATIONAL RESOURCES INFORMATION CENTER. *Current index to journals in education.* New York: CCM Information Corporation, 1970. 12 per year. $9; semiannual and annual cumulative indexes, $40.

CIJE is the companion volume to *Research in Education* (1470). Also published monthly, it lists articles from over 500 journals in education and related areas. Some items have one-sentence abstracts; others have no abstracts at all. All are indexed by subject and by author. A very useful new feature is the Journal Contents Index. This index provides a quick survey of the contents of all journals reviewed by *CIJE*.

1470 EDUCATIONAL RESOURCES INFORMATION CENTER. *Research in education.* Wash., D. C.: Government Printing Office. $21 per year; cumulative annual index, $8.25.

Research in Education is a monthly publication that announces recently completed research and research-related reports in the field of education. Each issue contains about 1,000 listings that have been compiled and reviewed by the 20 ERIC clearinghouses. All items are abstracted and also listed in subject-author and institution indexes. One major shortcoming of RIE is the incomplete coverage of published books and monographs. Although such items comprise some of the most important contributions, they constitute less than five percent of the 1,000 listings.

1471 EDUCATIONAL RESOURCES INFORMATION CENTER. *Thesaurus of ERIC descriptors.* New York: CCM Information Corporation, 1970, 546 pp. $8.95.

Although purported to be a necessary tool for the fullest use of the ERIC collection, the *Thesaurus* is by far the most difficult of the three publications to understand. Its purpose is to provide word-keys (synonyms and related terms) for searchers through the subject indexes of both *Research in Education* (1470) and *Current Index to Journals in Education* (1469), but it seems better suited to assist in a search through computer files at the hands of a trained technician than to a manual search through publications by a busy educator dependent upon the technical instructions provided.

1472 ERIC CLEARINGHOUSE ON HIGHER EDUCATION. *Current documents in higher education: A bibliography.* Washington, D. C.: American Association for Higher Education, 1970, 162 pp. $4 per year.

This bibliography is prepared by ERIC Clearinghouse on Higher Education and published twice a year by the American Association for Higher Education. It is compiled from monthly issues of *Research in Education* (1470). The Fall 1970 edition includes a listing of 1,334 papers and reports on higher education that appeared in the July 1969 through June 1970 issues of *RIE*. Items are listed in 16 categories and a subject index is included. Documents on vocational and technical education, educational facilities, and junior colleges were not included unless specifically related to four-year institutions or specialized curriculums. Abstracts of the documents listed appear in the appropriate issue of *RIE*. Microfiche and photocopies of the complete text are usually available from the ERIC Document Reproduction Service.

1473 FRIESEN, JULIUS (ED.) *America's education press: A classified list of educational publications issued in the United States and Canada.* Syracuse, N. Y.: Educational Press Association of America, 1969, 196 pp. $5.

America's Education Press is a classified guide to periodicals in education. It is based on questionnaire responses from editors of national, state, regional, and local education publications in the United States and Canada. Handbooks, student publications, annual reports, transactions and proceedings, college bulletins, or monograph series are not included. The following information is provided for over 2,000 publications: title, number of issues per year, subscription price, publisher, name and address of the editor, the year founded, and circulation. A title and editor index is included.

1474 GATES, JESSE L., AND ALTMAN, JAMES W. *Handbook of information sources in education and the behavioral sciences.* Wash., D. C.: Bureau of Research, U.S. Office of Education, 1968, 183 pp. (Available from ERIC Document Reproduction Service, No. ED 020 447. $6.58.)

This secondary reference is designed to inform educators and behavioral scientists of services that may assist them in research work. Included are descriptions of guides and directories, multidisciplinary information centers, specialized information centers, data repositories, and abstracting and indexing services. A brief subject index is provided.

1475 HECKMAN, DALE M., AND MARTIN, WARREN B. *Inventory of current research on higher education 1968.* New York: McGraw-Hill, 1968, 198 pp. $2.75.

This inventory of research was sponsored jointly by the Center for Research and Development in Higher Education and the Carnegie Commission on the Future of Higher Education. It catalogs and describes over 1,100 research projects completed in 1966-67 or in progress in 1967-68. Compiled primarily from questionnaire responses of principal researchers, projects are listed under eight subject categories: students, faculty, administrators, structures, functions, governance, graduate and professional education, and economics of higher education. A list of 1,020 "principal researchers" and a useful topical index are provided.

1476 KELLEY, CLARICE Y. *Where it's happening: A selective guide to continuing programs funded by the United States Office of Education.* Garden City, N. Y.: Doubleday, 1968, 58 pp.

This reference booklet covers the Regional Educational Laboratories (1172), Research and Development Centers (1161, 1162, 1164), Educational Policy Research Centers, the Regional Small Project Research Program, Research Coordinating Units for Vocational Education, instructional materials centers for handicapped children and youth, and ERIC (1449). Brief paragraphs describe the type of research and services provided under each category in addition to information needed for contacting individual centers and agencies.

1477 KELSEY, ROGER R. *AAHE bibliography on higher education.* Washington, D. C.: American Association for Higher Education, 1970, 60 pp. $1.

The American Association of Higher Education bibliography is a list of the books about higher education (excluding texts) that publishers exhibit at the annual national meeting of AAHE. The 1970 bibliography includes 1,473 books classified under 16 headings, so the publication does provide a fairly comprehensive list of current books on higher education. The supply of copies is limited.

1478 MANHEIM, THEODORE, DARDARIAN, GLORIA L., AND SATTERTHWAITE, DIANE A. *Sources in educational research: A selected & annotated bibliography.* Detroit, Mich.: Wayne State University Press, 1969, approximately 225 pp. $9.95; individual subject sections $1.25 each.

This work is intended as an introduction to research literature in various fields of education. It cites and annotates those titles "considered to be most useful to the graduate student or advanced undergraduate making his first acquaintance with educational research." The authors have included sections on general educational research literature and nine specific subject areas. The volume is a useful compendium of secondary references.

1479 MAYHEW, LEWIS B. *The literature of higher education 1971.* San Francisco: Jossey-Bass, 1971, 162 pp. $7.75.

Since 1964 Lewis B. Mayhew has prepared *The Literature of Higher Education.* This widely read report provides a concise summary and critical review of most books and monographs related to higher education that are published each year. In addition to the individual reviews, Mayhew provides an excellent overview of issues and problems treated in the literature. *The Literature of Higher Education 1971* reviews more than 150 books published during 1970. Previous editions of the book are available from the American Association for Higher Education for $2.

1480 MEETH, L. RICHARD (ED.) *Selected issues in higher education: An annotated bibliography.* New York: Teachers College Press, Columbia University, 1965, 212 pp. $5.75; paperback $3.50.

This very useful bibliography was developed in connection with higher education courses at Columbia University. It provides a comprehensive review of published literature on higher education from 1955-1965. More than 1,000 books and articles are cited and annotated briefly. Administration receives close attention; problems of the student and the educational process are not well covered, but this reflects the literature of the period.

1481 RENETZKY, ALVIN, AND GREENE, JON S. (EDS.) *Yearbook of higher education.* Los Angeles: Academic Media, 1970, 644 pp. $35.

Although all the information in this volume is also available in several other publications, this document brings it together for handy reference. It consists of three parts: Part I includes essentially the same information reported in *Education Directory* (106); Part II is for the most part a reproduction of the *Digest of Educational Statistics* (1421); Part III is a compilation of material on various programs and agencies that are concerned with higher education. Among the information included in this last part are descriptions of U.S.O.E. assistance programs and listings of the regional educational laboratories, ERIC clearinghouses, state boards of higher education, U.S.O.E. regional offices, accrediting associations, U.S.O.E. offices that administer higher education legislation, and state sources of information on guaranteed student loans. The volume should be of value primarily to educational researchers and students of higher education.

1482 U.S. BUREAU OF THE CENSUS. *1970 Census users' guide.* Washington, D. C.: Government Printing Office, 1970; Part I, 162 pp., $1.25; Part II, 375 pp., $2.75.

This *Guide* is designed to help potential users understand and extract information from the 1970 Census of Population and Housing. Part I includes a brief history of census-taking in the United States, descriptions of 1970 Census data products and services, user education tools needed to work with the data, data delivery facilities and capabilities, and a dictionary of terms and concepts used by the Bureau when generating statistics. Part II is a technical manual describing in detail the range of data that are available from the 1970 Census questionnaires. While Part II is difficult for the layman to understand, questions and comments concerning the *Guide* or any aspects of the decennial census are welcomed by the Data Access and Use Laboratory, Bureau of the Census, Washington, D.C. 20233.

1483 U.S. OFFICE OF EDUCATION. *Directory of educational information centers.* Washington, D. C.: Government Printing Office, 1969, 118 pp. $1.25.

This *Directory* is not intended to be an exhaustive listing of educational information resources; it concentrates on new activities of the following types of organizations: centers funded under Title III of the Elementary and Secondary Education Act of 1965, research and development centers, instructional materials centers for handicapped children and youth, regional educational laboratories, state research coordinating units for vocational and technical education, and state departments of education. Information for the 397 centers listed was gathered by a 1968 questionnaire. The annotations are listed alphabetically by state, and a subject index is provided.

15.4—PUBLICATION CATALOGS. An appropriately selected group of publication catalogs is a very inexpensive and very effective way to maintain contact with important literature. The catalogs included in this section are primarily those of key associations, agencies, and research centers that publish a great deal of quality material relevant to access to higher education. Also included are five commercial publishers whose lists are typically larger and less focused than those of the educational agencies.

1484 AMERICAN ASSOCIATION OF COLLEGIATE REGISTRARS AND ADMISSIONS OFFICERS, One Dupont Circle, N. W., Suite 330, Washington, D. C. 20036.

The American Association of Collegiate Registrars and Admissions Officers currently has over 30 titles in print, including a quarterly journal, informational documents pertaining to admissions procedures, and a series concerning evaluation of foreign-student credentials. Also listed are useful reference publications now out of print but still available in many college libraries and admissions offices.

1485 AMERICAN ASSOCIATION OF JUNIOR COLLEGES, One Dupont Circle, N. W., Washington, D. C. 20036.

In the late 1960s AAJC developed an unusually active and useful publications program. Their list of over 50 low-priced publications centers mainly on the development, programs, problems, and future of junior colleges. Topics cover most subjects common to any type of college but these reports emphasize the special role and characteristics of the two-year institution. All orders of less than $5 must be prepaid.

1486 AMERICAN COLLEGE TESTING PROGRAM, ACT Publication and Information Services, P. O. Box 168, Iowa City, Iowa 52240.

The American College Testing Program's publications list appears in *ACTivity* (1347). It lists current reports, monographs, and publications that provide descriptive information on the use and interpretation of the ACT programs and services. Another pamphlet, *Announcement of the ACT Research Services,* lists publications of research and related projects.

1487 AMERICAN COUNCIL ON EDUCATION, One Dupont Circle, Washington, D. C. 20036.

The American Council on Education is a major source of publications relevant to access to higher education. The books emphasize current problems and goals in higher education such as campus tensions, relevance in teaching, measurement, curriculum, planning and coordination, and computer use. ACE also publishes a variety of directories, periodicals, informational pamphlets, policy statements, and monographs. Approximately 100 publications are available. All orders of less than $5 must be prepaid.

1488 COLLEGE ENTRANCE EXAMINATION BOARD, Publications Order Office, Box 592, Princeton, New Jersey 08540.

The publications of the College Entrance Examination Board are perhaps more directly concerned with problems of access to higher education than those of any other publisher. The current list of publications includes more than 100 books, monographs, pamphlets, periodicals, tests, and visual aids. They are grouped in areas such as guidance, admissions, placement, curriculum, financial aid, research, and international education. Many free publications providing information about College Board programs are distributed widely to schools, colleges, and students.

1489 EDUCATION COMMISSION OF THE STATES, 822 Lincoln Tower, 1860 Lincoln Street, Denver, Colorado 80203.

The Education Commission of the States publishes material dealing primarily with state and federal legislative efforts and the resultant effects upon higher education. Items listed include some 20 studies and papers; a monthly report of bibliographical, legislative, and state program materials in higher education; and a directory of state-level decision-makers in education.

1490 EDUCATIONAL TESTING SERVICE, Princeton, New Jersey 08540. 1947 Center Street, Berkeley, California 94704. 960 Grove Street, Evanston, Illinois 60201.

Educational Testing Service publications fall into three categories: general information about ETS; descriptions of programs and services; and measurement, guidance, and education. Reports in the latter category include practical guides to technical topics, reference publications, and conference proceedings. Many of these publications are based on research projects and reports of many other projects are reported in professional journals. Requests and orders should be addressed to the nearest ETS office, except for special listings.

1491 NATIONAL ASSOCIATION OF COLLEGE ADMISSIONS COUNSELORS, 9933 Lawler Avenue, Skokie, Illinois 60076.

The relatively few materials published by the Association of College Admissions Counselors are all directly related to college admissions. Items listed include the association journal, newsletter, membership directory, maps of colleges, and information concerning the ASK US and Employment Assistance services. Payment must accompany order.

1492 *Catalog of Publications and Audiovisual Materials,* National Education Association, 1201 Sixteenth Street, N. W., Washington, D. C. 20036. Orders of less than $2 must be prepaid.

The NEA has a very large and diversified publications program. The catalog lists over 1,300 books, pamphlets, periodicals, research reports, and audiovisual materials published by NEA and its many specialized publishing units and departments. Most of the publications are prepared by an NEA unit concentrating on a particular area of interest. They cover a wide range of topics in all levels and fields of education, and are directed to a variety of audiences.

1493 ORGANIZATION FOR ECONOMIC CO-OPERATION AND DEVELOPMENT, OECD Publications Center, 1750 Pennsylvania Avenue, N. W., Washington, D. C. 20006.

Although a small fraction of OECD publications are directly concerned with access to higher education, this catalog is a good source of publications dealing with the financial, organizational, philosophical, and international aspects of higher education. OECD is a leading world organization in educational planning as it relates to manpower utilization and economic development. The catalog also tells something about the organization and its programs.

1494 SOUTHERN REGIONAL EDUCATION BOARD, 130 Sixth Street, N. W., Atlanta, Georgia 30313.

The Southern Regional Education Board issues a one-page publications order form listing its published reports, monographs, and a variety of newsletters aimed at news media, educators, government officials, and the general public. Its focus is primarily on current educational issues and problems, particularly relating to the South. These include expansion of educational opportunity, Negro students and colleges, coordination and governance, curriculum, mental health, etc. SREB publishes annually a useful summary of state legislation affecting higher education in the South.

1495 TEACHERS COLLEGE PRESS, Teachers College, Columbia University, 525 West 120th Street, New York, New York 10027.

Teachers College Press is a major publisher in education. Its catalog lists more than 350 books and aids of interest particularly to teachers at all levels and in various fields of education. Although elementary and secondary education are emphasized, guidance and higher education are also represented. Included are numerous titles on liberal education programs as well as other topics, such as admissions, innovation, student freedom, administration, junior colleges, Negro colleges, and specialty schools. A separate listing of additional publications pertaining to educational research is also available. All orders of less than $5 must be prepaid.

1496 *Unesco Publications: Education,* Unesco Publications Center, 650 First Avenue, New York, New York 10016.

This catalog lists nearly 200 publications in English. Materials listed cover various aspects of education, frequently from an international viewpoint. Topics include: curriculum, vocational education, planning, adult education, disadvantaged students, and administration. Other pamphlets list publications in social sciences, science, radio and television, and libraries. A current list of publications is also available, kept up to date by the issue of quarterly supplements.

1497 U.S. BUREAU OF THE CENSUS, U.S. Government Printing Office, Washington, D. C. 20402. $3 per 4 consecutive issues.

This catalog contains annotations on all publications issued by the U.S. Bureau of the Census (1140) as well as the data files (computer tape and punched cards), special tabulations of data (specified by customers and available on a cost basis — see 1448), and other unpublished nonstatistical materials.

1498 *Monthly Catalog, United States Government Publications,* U.S. Government Printing Office, Washington, D. C. 20402. $1 per year, including index.

This catalog, issued by the Superintendent of Documents, provides a monthly listing of the most recent publications put out by nearly 200 government departments, bureaus, commissions, and committees. Each month from 900 to over 2,000 new entries are included as well as previews of publications still in press. Entries are indexed by subject and title; an annual index is included in the December issue.

1499 *Publications of the Office of Education,* U.S. Government Printing Office, Washington, D. C. 20402.

This catalog identifies all Office of Education publications currently available. The annotated list contains approximately 560 titles, including revised editions of surveys that the Office of Education conducts annually. These surveys (see section 14.4 for individual annotations) provide basic national data and projections on finance, enrollment, staff, curriculum, and facilities of public schools, colleges, and universities. Other material includes special reports, program descriptions, books of readings, conference reports, exemplary projects, etc. The 1970 catalog (40 cents) provides convenient order forms.

1500 WESTERN INTERSTATE COMMISSION FOR HIGHER EDUCATION, P. O. Drawer P, Boulder, Colorado 80302.

The Western Interstate Commission for Higher Education general information pamphlet, *This is WICHE,* lists approximately 30 publications in addition to a general description of WICHE and its various programs and research projects. Free publications include the newsletter, *Reports on Higher Education* (1392), and diverse informational pamphlets describing some current programs of interest to students, administrators, and counselors in the western states. A number of recent publications from WICHE's Division of Planning and Management Systems report developmental work on management information systems.

1501 JOSSEY-BASS, INC., 615 Montgomery Street, San Francisco, California 94111.

In the late 1960s, Jossey-Bass became, almost overnight, a major publisher in higher education. Its series on higher education includes books on educational research and specializes in current issues and problems. Topics include innovation and change, academic reform, relevance, activism and protest, high-risk students, and student development. The catalog contains detailed annotations and a listing of contents for current titles. A behavioral science series is also available.

1502 *McGraw-Hill College and University Books, 1971 Catalog: Social Sciences,* McGraw-Hill Book Company, College and University Division, 330 West 42nd Street, New York, New York 10036.

McGraw-Hill has extensive listings in the education section of their textbook catalog. Many of their books are relevant to the processes of access to higher education, administration, guidance, curriculum, etc. McGraw-Hill publishes the books and reports of the Carnegie Commission on Higher Education (see 1398). Their 1971 catalog lists two Carnegie Commission titles. A special catalog is issued by McGraw-Hill's Community College Division.

1503 PRAEGER PUBLISHERS, INC., 111 Fourth Avenue, New York, New York 10003.

Praeger has recently become more active in publishing books relevant to access problems. It publishes approximately 25 books on international, urban, and disadvantaged education.

1504 *Prentice-Hall 1971/Humanities Social Sciences Catalog,* Prentice-Hall, Inc., Englewood Cliffs, New Jersey 07632.

Prentice-Hall, a major textbook publisher, lists a broad range of books relating to education in its current catalog of texts in the humanities and social sciences. Access topics are well represented in areas such as educational philosophy and foundations, instruction, counseling and guidance, and educational research and statistics. Prentice-Hall also publishes a series of paperbacks, each written by a specialist in one particular aspect of education.

1505 *Wiley/Wiley: Interscience Publications Catalog,* John Wiley & Sons, Inc., 605 Third Avenue, New York, New York 10016.

The education section of the *Wiley: Interscience Catalog* lists over 100 titles. Most of them are either textbooks that deal with all levels and fields of education or books that treat more specific areas of instruction, guidance, college environment, etc.

15.5 – BIOGRAPHICAL DIRECTORIES. Certain types of material such as reprints, speeches, or unpublished manuscripts can only be obtained from the author. And, in general, there are numerous occasions when it is useful to have information about individuals working in a professional field. The biographical directories included in this section cover all of the major professions and academic disciplines represented in this guide. There are also included a few very useful specialized directories such as the *State Leaders Directory* (1514) and *Education Directory: Higher Education* (1519), both of which identify administrators in educational agencies and institutions.

1506 AMERICAN ASSOCIATION OF COLLEGIATE REGISTRARS AND ADMISSIONS OFFICERS. Directory issue. *Newsletter,* 1970, vol. 13, no. 2, 213 pp.

The Fall issue of the AACRAO *Newsletter* annually serves as the directory issue. The 1970 issue lists the names and addresses of registrars and admissions officers by state and college at about 1,600 institutions in the United States, 50 outside the U.S., and over 100 affiliate and honorary members. An additional list provides an alphabetical roster of over 5,000 individuals affiliated with AACRAO.

1507 AMERICAN ECONOMIC ASSOCIATION. 1969 handbook of the American Economic Association. *American Economic Review,* 1970, vol. 59, no. 6, 612 pp.

The American Economic Association's *Handbook,* published periodically, contains information compiled from questionnaires mailed to members. The 1969 edition classifies over 12,000 members alphabetically, by fields, by academic affiliation, and geographically. The alphabetical entry provides biographical information such as address, birthdate, academic and employment history, and areas of interest. In addition, the *Handbook* lists tables and summary data obtained from the questionnaire.

1508 AMERICAN EDUCATIONAL RESEARCH ASSOCIATION. *Directory.* Washington, D. C.: AERA, 1969, 206 pp. $3.

The AERA *Directory* is revised and published annually in October. It provides a listing of the names and addresses of over 10,000 AERA members; an additional section serves as a geographical directory. It is probably the most comprehensive single directory for individuals involved in educational research.

1509 AMERICAN PERSONNEL AND GUIDANCE ASSOCIATION. *Directory of members.* Washington, D. C.: APGA, 1968, 193 pp.

This directory lists the names and addresses of over 27,000 members of the APGA. Entries are also classified according to membership in the eight divisions of the organization (American College Personnel Association, Association for Counselor Education and Supervision, National Vocational Guidance Association, Student Personnel Association for Teacher Education, American School

Counselor Association, American Rehabilitation Counseling Association, National Employment Counselor Association, Association for Measurement and Evaluation in Guidance). The *Directory* is revised and published biennially.

1510 AMERICAN PSYCHOLOGICAL ASSOCIATION. *Biographical directory*. Washington, D. C.: APA, 1970, 1,529 pp. $30.

The 1970 edition of the APA *Biographical Directory* provides the addresses, birthdates, educational and employment histories, fields of interest, and information concerning individual membership status in APA for over 30,000 members. The members are also listed both geographically and according to membership in each of the APA's 29 divisions. In 1971 the *Biographical Directory* will be replaced by a membership register.

1511 AMERICAN SOCIOLOGICAL ASSOCIATION. *Directory, constitution, and by-laws*. Washington, D. C.: ASA, 1967, 323 pp. $5.

The American Sociological Association periodically publishes a directory based on information received from a questionnaire mailed to members. The 1967 *Directory* provides information on about 10,000 members, listing in abbreviated form the address, education, special interests, employment, and academic rank of each.

1512 ASSOCIATION FOR INSTITUTIONAL RESEARCH. *Membership directory*. Auburn, Ala.: AIR, 1971, 77 pp.

The 1970-71 edition of this annual membership directory lists the names and addresses of 862 members compiled from the records of the association's secretary. An additional section lists the names of the members by both state and institution or agency. Most members of AIR are affiliated with higher education institutions.

1513 CALKINS, RUSSELL W. (ED.) *Who's who in American college and university administration, 1970-71*. New York: Crowell-Collier, 1970, 681 pp.

In 1968 Crowell-Collier acquired publishing rights to Cook's *Who's Who* series; this is the first volume in the series to appear under new management. Future titles will include *Who's Who in American Education*, which lists educators and officials at all levels, and *Leaders in American Science*. The present volume includes some 11,000 college and university administrators (presidents, deans, librarians, bursars, and others) selected primarily on the basis of inclusion in the United States Office of Education Directory (1519). The biographical listings contain more information and detailed description than most other such listings do. Besides such items as address, educational and employment history, and memberships, the entry includes personal facts in great detail. Biennial revisions are scheduled.

1514 EDUCATION COMMISSION OF THE STATES. *State leaders directory*. Denver, Colo.: ECS, 1971, 112 pp. $2.

This unusual and very useful annual directory lists the names and addresses of state educational personnel for public elementary, secondary, and higher education, and key political leaders concerned with educational matters for each state and territory. Also listed are summary data on various boards and councils in all the states.

1515 JACQUES CATTELL PRESS (ED.) *American men of science: The social and behavioral sciences*. 2 Vols. New York: R. R. Bowker, 1968, 1,793 pp. *Supplement,* 1970, 353 pp. $30 each.

American Men of Science has been published periodically since 1906. The eleventh edition is an eight-volume work—six volumes deal with individuals in the physical and biological sciences, and two include those in the social and behavioral sciences. Supplements are published for both fields. Nearly 40,000 biographical sketches are listed in the two volumes and the 1970 supplement of

The Social and Behavioral Sciences. The entries are based on information received on questionnaires sent to individuals chosen for academic or research achievement or who have attained "a position of substantial responsibility" in a relevant field. Each entry provides address, educational and employment history, area of interest, offices and memberships, and selected publications by the individual.

1516 KLEIN, BERNARD (ED.) *Guide to American educational directories.* (3rd ed.) New York: B. Klein, 1969, 335 pp. $22.50.

This volume offers an excellent well-indexed annotated reference to directories covering a wide range of topics. The annotations cite the number of entries in the directory, the nature of their arrangement, how often the work is published, and details related to ordering the directory. General topic headings of relevance to access to higher education include school administration, adult and evening schools, vocational and technical schools, vocational guidance, junior colleges and universities, correspondence schools, educational associations, research, public schools (by state), ETV, financial aid, and various bibliographies.

1517 NATIONAL COUNCIL ON MEASUREMENT IN EDUCATION. *Membership directory.* East Lansing, Mich.: NCME, 1971, 35 pp.

The NCME *Directory* is issued periodically. Members of NCME are interested in applications of measurement techniques at all levels of education. The 1971 directory lists the names and addresses of 1,847 members; an additional section lists the names of the members by states.

1518 PHI DELTA KAPPA. *National register of educational researchers.* Bloomington, Ind.: Phi Delta Kappa, 1966, 253 pp. $5.

Phi Delta Kappa's *National Register of Educational Researchers* was first published in 1966. Approximately 6,000 researchers in education were identified through published sources and through direct contact with organizations concerned with educational research. These individuals were sent questionnaires that furnished the basic biographical information: name, birthdate, address, present position, educational and employment history, and areas of research. The *Register* also includes summary data about educational and personal history, research areas, and employment data.

1519 U.S. OFFICE OF EDUCATION, NATIONAL CENTER FOR EDUCATIONAL STATISTICS. *Education directory, 1970-71. Higher education.* Wash., D. C.: Government Printing Office, 1971, 515 pp. $3.75.

This annual publication lists 2,500 institutions in the United States that offer at least a two-year program of college-level or occupational studies beyond grade 12. The entries are arranged alphabetically by state and include the following information: address, phone number, and general nature of the institution (accreditation, control, student body, calendar system, types of programs offered, enrollment). A valuable aspect of the *Directory* is the inclusion of names and titles of five to ten top administrators on each campus. Unfortunately, this biographic information is sometimes out of date before the *Directory* is available. (Also annotated in section 1.6.)

Author Index

Boldface numerals in this index refer to item numbers not to page numbers.

A

AACRAO-AID Participant Selection and Placement Study Committee, **808**
Abe, Clifford, **878**
Abrahams, Louise, **649**
Abrams, Irwin, **1403**
Adams, Charles, **107**
Adams, James F., **879**
Adams, Walter, **772, 903**
Advisory Council on Vocational Education, **714**
Agnew, Spiro T., **209**
Aiken, Lewis R. Jr., **397**
Aitken, D. J., **93**
Aker, George F., **804**
Alford, Harold J., **780**
Allen, James E. Jr., **607**
Altbach, Philip G., **1001**
Altman, James W., **1474**
Altman, Robert A., **334, 976**
American Academy of Arts and Sciences, **573**
American Association for Higher Education, **606, 1395, 1431**
American Association of Collegiate Registrars and Admissions Officers, **60, 260, 261, 273, 826, 1484, 1506**
American Association of Junior Colleges, **273, 1485**

American Association of State Colleges and Universities, **582**
American College Testing Program, **173, 880, 1397, 1486**
American Council on Education, **881, 1396, 1409, 1432, 1487**
American Economic Association, **1507**
American Educational Research Association, **398, 1433, 1508**
American Institutes for Research, **1405**
American Legion Educational and Scholarship Program, **193**
American Personnel and Guidance Association, **1, 1509**
American Psychological Association, **349, 398, 1462, 1510**
American Sociological Association, **1511**
Anastasi, Anne, **399, 449, 858**
Anderson, C. Arnold, **505, 927, 932**
Anderson, G. Lester, **1437**
Anderson, James G., **1081**
Anderson, Richard C., **314**
Anderson, Scarvia, **364**
Andre, Thomas, **314**
Angoff, William H., **400, 1401**
Arbolino, Jack N., **781**
Armer, J. Michael, **908**
Arnold, David B., **1403**

447

Arnold, Ruth, **809**
Arnow, Philip, **548**
Ashby, Eric, **1398**
Association for Counselor Education and Supervision, Experimental Designs Committee, **61, 428**
Association for Institutional Research, **1512**
Association of American Colleges, **273**
Astin, Alexander W., **13, 77, 210, 350, 370, 371, 372, 373, 374, 375, 376, 377, 458, 481, 484, 730, 731, 732, 733, 1002, 1020, 1398**
Astin, Helen S., **2, 509, 918**
Axelrod, Joseph, **281, 1403**
Axen, Richard, **1019**

B

Badran, Yehia, **1401**
Baird, Leonard L., **14, 23, 24, 227, 450, 451, 912, 1399**
Baker, George A. III, **647**
Ballotti, Geno A., **763**
Banghart, Frank W., **630**
Barclay, James R., **695**
Barlow, Melvin L., **715**
Barnes, Fred P., **429**
Barr, Richard H., **1423**
Barrios, Ernie, **1082**
Barron, Frank, **1036**
Barron's Educational Series, **78**
Barton, Allen H., **734**
Baskin, Samuel, **335, 1403**
Bayer, Alan E., **472, 494, 509, 890, 918, 928, 1061, 1396**
Bean, Andrew G., **1401**
Bebout, John E., **837**
Becker, Ernst, **146**
Becker, Gary S., **123**
Beezer, Robert H., **896**
Beggs, David W. III, **315**
Begle, Edward G., **282, 1437**
Beilin, Lois A., **291**
Belitsky, A. Harvey, **716**
Bell, Daniel, **283**
Bennet, Ann, **1403**
Benson, Charles S., **124**
Bentley, Joseph C., **41**
Berdahl, Robert O., **650**
Berdie, Ralph F., **3, 4, 735, 913, 914, 915, 916**
Bereday, George Z. F., **810, 1440**
Bereiter, Carl, **536**
Berg, Ivar E., **519, 1044**
Bernard, Jessie, **1040**

Bernstein, Abraham, **838**
Berry, Brewton, **1083**
Birnbaum, Max, **81, 82**
Blackburn, Robert T., **1395, 1403**
Blau, Peter M., **537**
Blaug, Mark, **125**
Blischke, William R., **664**
Blocker, Clyde E., **746**
Bloom, A. Martin, **42**
Bloom, Benjamin S., **284, 295, 401, 452, 859, 977**
Blum, Zahava D., **541**
Blumenfeld, Warren S., **962**
Boggs, John R., **443**
Boocock, Sarane S., **5**
Borgen, Fred H., **1062, 1404**
Boruch, Robert F., **350, 1061**
Bowen, F., **1398**
Bowen, Howard R., **147, 1398**
Bowerman, Charles E., **1070**
Bowler, Adele S., **301**
Bowles, Frank H., **79, 211, 212, 560, 769, 770, 811, 812**
Bowles, Samuel S., **941, 942**
Bowman, Calvert W., **70**
Boyd, Joseph D., **148**
Boyer, Ernest L., **1403**
Boyle, Richard P., **696**
Brandon, George L., **717**
Braskamp, Larry A., **392, 888**
Brazziel, William F., **963**
Brick, Michael, **336**
Bridgman, Donald S., **1021**
Briggs, Leslie J., **316**
Brim, Orville G. Jr., **351**
Brooks, Glenn E., **625**
Broome, Edwin Cornelius, **561**
Brown, Bert, **862**
Brown, Carol A., **1044**
Brown, J. Douglas, **759**
Brown, James W., **331**
Brown, Marsha D., **890**
Brown, Newell, **549**
Brown, Robert L., **520**
Brownell, Richard L., **647**
Brubacher, John S., **562**
Brue, Eldon J., **1397**
Brumbaugh, A. J., **1408**
Bryan, J. Ned, **1403**
Buffie, Edward G., **315**
Burchinal, Lee G., **1084**
Burckel, Christian E., **80**
Burgdorf, Kenneth, **1063**
Burke, Arvid J., **1463**
Burke, Mary A., **1463**
Burkett, J. E., **782**
Burkett, Lowell A., **521**

Burn, Barbara B., 813
Buros, Oscar K., 402
Burt, Cyril, 860
Burt, Samuel M., 718
Butterworth, C. E., 900

C

Caffrey, John, 590, 631
Caldwell, Wallace F., 1003
California Coordinating Council for Higher Education, 672, 689
California Council for Educational Opportunity, 964
California Department of Human Resources Development, 1088
California Legislature, Joint Committee on Higher Education, 673
Calkins, Russell W., 1513
Cameron, Ben F. Jr., 760
Campbell, David P., 15, 62, 228
Campbell, Ernest Q., 948, 1070
Campbell, L. Howard, 240
Campeau, Peggie L., 316
Carbone, Robert F., 186
Carmody, James F., 1397
Carnegie Commission on Higher Education, 149, 150, 574, 575, 651, 771, 943, 1398
Carnegie Corporation of New York, Commission on Educational Television, 783
Carothers, Milton W., 1408
Carter, Thomas P., 1085
Cartter, Allan M., 174, 607
Carver, Ronald P., 965
Casasco, Juan A., 632, 674
Cass, James, 81, 82
Casserly, Patricia L., 302, 311
Cassidy, Sally, 1403
Cavanaugh, William J., 187
Centra, John A., 390, 736, 1064, 1065, 1399, 1401
Chambers, M. M., 126, 652
Chandler, Marjorie O., 293, 1422, 1430
Chauncey, Henry, 352, 403
Cheit, Earl F., 151
Chicago Public Schools, Study Committee on Higher Education, 675
Chickering, Arthur W., 378
Chorafas, Dimitrius N., 814
Christensen, Edward L., 796, 797
Christ-Janer, Arland F., 353
Chronicle Guidance Publications, 194
City University of New York Master Plan, 692
Clark, Burton R., 563, 737, 738, 747
Clark, Harold F., 784, 785, 786
Clark, Kenneth B., 944, 978, 1066, 1067, 1077

Clark, Kenneth E., 16
Clarke, Betty S., 478
Clary, Albert L., 274
Claudy, John G., 1405
Cleary, T. Anne, 966, 967, 1399
Cleaver, Eldridge, 1068
Clifford, Paul I., 358
Coffman, William E., 416
Cohen, Arlene G., 897
Cohen, Elizabeth G., 929
Cohen, Joseph W., 1022
Cole, Charles C. Jr., 898, 1403
Cole, Nancy S., 1397
Coleman, James S., 697, 882, 934, 945, 946, 947, 948
College Entrance Examination Board, 43, 44, 127, 152, 153, 154, 175, 176, 195, 196, 229, 241, 242, 243, 244, 285, 286, 303, 304, 305, 306, 354, 404, 405, 406, 430, 453, 815, 949, 964, 979, 1023, 1399, 1402, 1434, 1435, 1488
College Opportunities, 197
College Placement Council, 550
Columbia University, American Assembly, 576
Commager, Henry Steele, 761
Commission on Human Resources and Advanced Education, 506
Commission to Study Non-Public Higher Education in Illinois, 676
Committee for Economic Development, 839, 840, 841, 842
Committee on Higher Education, 816
Committee on the Student in Higher Education, 379
Community College Planning Center, 843
Comstock, Peggy, 1045
Conant, James B., 607, 698, 844
Conference for Educational Development and Research, Information Office, 1464
Cook, Desmond L., 431
Cooley, William W., 25, 861
Cooper, Alva C., 551
Cooper, Robert L., 1088
Copley, Frank O., 1024
Corson, John J., 608
Council of Graduate Schools, 817
Council of Student Personnel Associations in Higher Education, 262
Counseling Psychologist Editorial Board, 1069
Cowhig, James D., 899, 921
Cox, Lanier, 653
Craig, T., 88, 819
Cramer, M. Richard, 1070
Cramer, Stanley H., 45, 51
Crawford, Norman C. Jr., 177
Crawford, Paul, 46
Creager, John A., 245, 1396
Crites, John O., 17, 538, 556

Crockenberg, Vincent, 1433
Cronbach, Lee J., 307, 355
Croner, Ulrich H. E., 83
Cross, K. Patricia, 439, 748, 883, 1041, 1042
Crossland, Fred E., 246
Cunningham, Donald J., 314
Cureton, E. E., 1405
Cureton, Louise W., 407

D

Dailey, John T., 702, 893
Dalrymple, Willard, 486
Dardarian, Gloria L., 1478
Darley, John G., 677
David, Henry, 495
Davis, Allison, 977
Davis, James A., 18, 26, 380
Davis, Junius A., 230, 408, 439, 1403
Dearing, George Bruce, 1403
DeCosta, Frank A., 770
DeLisle, Frances H., 290
Denison, Edward F., 128, 129
Dennis, Lawrence E., 287
Dent, Albert W., 779
Dentler, Robert A., 845
Deutsch, Martin, 862, 863, 970
Dickey, Frank G., 522
DiGaspari, Vincent M., 203
Dillenbeck, Douglas D., 47, 84
Dinklage, Lillian B., 36
Dobbin, John E., 403
Dobbins, Charles G., 1432
Dodds, Harold W., 609
Doermann, Humphrey, 231
Domino, George, 1397
Donohue, James P., 633
Douvan, Elizabeth, 27
Downs, Robert B., 1408
Draeger, Carolyn, 438
Dreger, Ralph M., 864
Dressel, Carol A., 288
Dressel, Paul L., 288, 289, 290, 297, 409, 410, 411, 1465
Drew, David E., 884, 1396
Dubin, Robert, 317, 318
Duggan, John M., 63, 432
Duncan, Otis Dudley, 537, 539, 543, 930
Dunham, E. Alden, 762
Durr, William K., 1025
Duryea, E. D., 1403

E

East Side Union High School District, 1086
Ebel, Robert L., 356, 412, 699, 1466
Eberly, Donald J., 523
Eckert, Ruth E., 435
Eckland, Bruce K., 473, 474, 865, 931
Education Commission of the States, 634, 719, 1489, 1514
Educational Policies Commission, 577, 578
Educational Records Bureau, 247
Educational Resources Information Center, 1469, 1470, 1471
Educational Testing Service, 413, 414, 635, 1401, 1436, 1490
Egerton, John, 969, 980, 1087
Elam, Stanley, 591, 610
Engen, Harold B., 1397
ERIC Clearinghouse on Higher Education, 319, 611, 981, 1400, 1407, 1472
Erikson, Erik H., 1004
Erlenmeyer-Kimling, L., 866
Eskow, Seymour, 85
Eulau, Heinz, 1398
Eurich, Alvin C., 592, 700
Evans, Franklin R., 1401

F

Fantini, Mario D., 846
Farmer, James, 636
Faust, Gerald W., 314
Federation of Regional Accrediting Commissions of Higher Education, 86
Fein, Rashi, 1398
Feingold, S. Norman, 198
Feldman, Kenneth A., 381, 382
Fenton, Edwin, 701
Ferrin, Richard I., 188, 308, 678, 951, 982
Findikyan, Nurhan, 279, 357
Findley, Warren G., 415, 1437
Fine, Benjamin, 87
Finger, Frank W., 320
Finger, John A., 454
Firestone, Ira J., 351
Fisher, Franklin M., 170
Fishman, Joshua A., 232, 233, 358, 455, 970, 1088
Five College Long Range Planning Committee, 654
Fixter, Deborah A., 1060
Flanagan, John C., 64, 702, 885, 917, 1405
Flaugher, Ronald L., 787, 1401

Subject Index

*Boldface numerals in this index refer to item
numbers not to page numbers.*

Negro-white comparative studies, 862, 973, 974, 1061
  predictive validity in, 965, 966, 967, 974, 975
Discrimination, 952, 957
  in education, 945, 947, 948, 952, 953, 957, 960. *See also*
    Disadvantaged students, selection of
  against women, 1040, 1048
Diversity, institutional
  and admissions policies, 217, 228, 239
  effect of disciplines on, 570
  lack of, 345
  and student development, 377, 575
Dropout studies, section 5.6. *See also* Attrition

E

Economic benefits, educational, 123, 129, 130
  related to costs, 132, 144
Economic growth, national
  contribution of education to, 133, 141, 512
  in OECD countries, 137
  sources of, 128
Economic theory of higher education, section 2.1, 124,
    127, 131, 145. *See also* Finance; Finance policies
  bibliography on, 125
  and earning potential, 130
  and estimated rates of return, 123, 130, 140, 142
  and federal budget allocations, 585
  and human capital investment, 123, 136, 140, 141
  international aspects of, 133, 512, 514, 516
  and national economic growth, 128, 129, 133, 137
  and tax structure, 126, 132, 138, 143
ECS Bulletin, 1360
ECS Legislative Review, 1361
Education Commission of the States, 607, 1178
Education Daily, 1362
Education Index, 1467
Education, philosophical aspects of, section 7.1, 567, 572
Education, public, statistics on, 588
Education Recaps, 1363
Education, sociology of, 704, 932
Education as source of economic growth, 128, 129
  international aspects of, 133, 137
Education, state departments of, 710
Education, value of. *See* Economic benefits; Economic
    theory
Educational goals. *See* Decision-making; Aspiration
Educational and Career Exploration System, 1239
Educational Guidance Information System (EGIS), 1240
Educational objectives, taxonomy of, 284, 295
Educational Opportunity Bank, 156, 170
Educational programs, guides to
  adult education, 804
  college programs for high school students, 301
  continuing education, 805

degree programs at individual colleges. *See* College
    guides
  home study, 799, 805
  military education, 806
  minority/poverty programs, 979
  study abroad, 821, 834
Educational Record, 1320
Educational research, 355, 368
Educational Researcher, 1364
Educational Resources Information Center (ERIC),
    1449, 1468
  Clearinghouse for Junior Colleges, 1450
  Clearinghouse on Adult Education, 1451
  Clearinghouse on Counseling and Personnel Services,
    1452
  Clearinghouse on Higher Education, 1400, 1407, 1453
  Clearinghouse on Tests, Measurement, and Evalua-
    tion, 1454
  Clearinghouse on Vocational and Technical Educa-
    tion, 1455
  Information Retrieval Center on the Disadvantaged,
    1456
Educational statistics. *See* Statistics, educational
Educational Testing Service, 1115, 1167, 1442
Eisenhower Commission, 576
Employment. *See* Occupational distribution
Enrichment programs, 1022, 1024, 1025
Enrollment projections, 263, 264, 267, 272, 440
Entrance tests. *See* Testing
Environmental press theory, 38, 40. *See also* College
    environment
EPE 15-Minute Report, 1365
Equal opportunity. *See also* Admissions, open; Cole-
    man Report; Opportunity programs; Universal
    higher education
  accessibility and, 678, 688
  and admissions policies, 212, 215
  barriers to, 212, 942, 943, 949, 951
  concept of, 947
  and excellence, 565, 593
  federal responsibility in achieving, 960
  finance of, 154, 157, 941, 949
    in California, 169
    in New York, 165
  implementation of, 943, 949, 953
  international aspects of, 621, 828
  policy issues in, 577, 578, 941, 953, 992
  role of community college in achieving, 563, 574, 748
  and segregation, 945, 947, 952, 960
  sociological analyses of, 946, 948, 950, 958, 959
  sociological aspects of, 568, 933
  and statewide planning, 950, 998
  statewide study of, 989
  for women, 1042, 1050
ERIC. *See* Educational Resources Information Center

Human resources. *See* Manpower development; Manpower requirements

I

Illinois Board of Higher Education, 1184
Indecision scale, 23, 31
Independent study, 297, 315, 323
Indian youth, education of, 1083, 1092
Information System for Vocational Decisions, 1242
Information systems, sections 7.5 and 13.3. *See also specific topics,* e.g., Management information systems
Inner city. *See also* Urban education
  community colleges in, 595, 843, 983
  decentralization, 844, 846
  role of high school in, 704
  students, 1076
Innovation, process of, 339, 345, 346
Innovations. *See also subject headings*
  in attendance patterns, 575, 586
  in community colleges, 343
  in curriculum. *See* Curriculum innovation; Curriculum reform
  in degree structures, 347, 575, 604, 762
  in finance methods, federal, 147
  at liberal arts colleges, 334, 335, 336, 337, 348, 379
  in secondary schools, 599, 699
  survey of, 336
  systems analysis of, 341
  in testing, 367
  in urban education, 838, 839, 840, 978
Input-output studies. *See* College environment; Evaluation of college impact
Institute for Social Research, 1168
Institute for the Quantitative Analysis of Social and Economic Policy, 1169
Institute of Higher Education, 1170
Institute of International Education, 1135
Institutional cooperation
  in admissions, 248, 254, 265
  in planning, 654, 663, 667
Institutional effectiveness. *See also* College environment; Evaluation of college impact
  and adaptability, 339
  measurement of, 409, 638
  related to PH.D. productivity, 371
  student achievement and institutional excellence, 375, 390
Institutional research, section 5.4. *See also* Management information systems
  administration of, 444, 446
  bibliography on, 441
  and communication of data, 448

  in community colleges, 443
  functions of, 445
  guidelines for, 439
  science of, 434
  on students, 437, 438
Institutional research, techniques of. *See also* Cost-benefit analysis; Evaluation; Management information systems; Prediction; Testing
  ACT research services as, 437
  for enrollment projections, 440
  evaluation as, 401, 411, 414
  for practitioners, 428, 429, 432, 433, 437, 439
  program evaluation and review as, 431
Institutional Research Program for Higher Education, 1228
Institutional variety. *See* Diversity, institutional
Instruction of talented students
  in higher education, 1022, 1026, 1029
  in secondary school, 1024, 1025, 1030
Instructional method
  and educational objectives, 321, 326
  and evaluation, 401, 408, 410, 411
  and independent study, 297, 315, 323
  individualization of, 324, 578
  innovation in, 329, 338, 593, 600
  and institutional policy, 328
  and learning theory, 329
  and relevance, 281, 296, 300
  research in, 314, 318, 327
  and teacher education, 319, 320, 325
  and teaching tips, 326
Instructional programs, classification of, 293
Instructional technology, 316, 331, 332, 343
  audiovisual, 333
  computer-supported, 341, 342
  history of, 330
  and programmed learning, 322, 331
  and shared costs, 654
  and television, 317, 331
Instructional theory, 284, 295, 314, 316
Integration in higher education
  and academic performance, 1065, 1067
  description of, 976, 1064, 1069, 1071
  extent of, 963, 969, 971, 1061, 1062
  in Florida community colleges, 1075
  and student life, 1064
  student view of, 976
Integration in secondary education
  and academic performance, 942, 948, 950, 954, 955
  extent of, 948, 960
Intelligence, concept of, 867, 872. *See also* Ability and the disadvantaged student, 871, 972
Interests, section 1.2. *See also* Vocational interests
International education, section 8.8, 810, 811, 813, 832. *See also* Access process, studies of; Students, foreign

479

This book was designed by Bert Waggott,

It was composed in Times Roman linofilm by Ruttle, Shaw & Wetherill, Inc., Philadelphia, Pennsylvania,

Printing and binding were done by R. R. Donnelley & Sons Company at their Crawfordsville, Indiana plant.

DATE DUE

GAYLORD   PRINTED IN U.S.A.

OCLC

DEMCO

THE TAXONOMY
for *The Source Book for Higher Education*

I. *Access Processes*

	1. STUDENT GUIDANCE	2. FINANCING EDUCATION	3. ADMISSIONS
THEORY	1.1 Career Development 1.2 Vocational Interest 1.3 The Decision Process	2.1 Economics of Higher Education 2.2 Financing Methods	3.1 National Policy 3.2 Institutional Policy
PRACTICE	1.4 Guidance Procedures 1.5 Research and Technology 1.6 Guides and Directories 1.7 Career Information Sources	2.3 Administration of Financial Aid 2.4 College Costs 2.5 Financial Aid Sources	3.3 Recruitment and Selection 3.4 Administration of Admissions 3.5 Transfer Admissions

III. *The Students*

9. DISTRIBUTION OF TALENT	10. EDUCATIONAL OPPORTUNITY	11. SELECTED STUDENT GROUPS
9.1 The Nature of Ability 9.2 Student Characteristics 9.3 Motives to Attend College 9.4 Who Goes to College? 9.5 Social Mobility	10.1 Discrimination and Equality 10.2 Equity in Selection 10.3 Opportunity Programs	11.1 Student Activists 11.2 Talented Students 11.3 Women Students 11.4 Black Students 11.5 Other Minority/Poverty Students